THE SUPERVISORY CHALLENGE

Principles and Practices

Second Edition

Jane Whitney Gibson, DBA

Nova University

Prentice Hall, Englewood Cliffs, New Jersey 07632

Library of Congress Cataloging-in-Publication Data

Gibson, Jane W.
    The supervisory challenge: principles and practices/Jane W.
  Gibson. —2nd ed.
      p. cm.
    Includes bibliographical references and indexes.
    ISBN 0-02-341792-7 (pbk.)
    1. Supervision of employees. 2. Management. I. Title.
HF5549.12.G53   1995
658.3'02—dc20

Editor: Elizabeth Sugg
Production Supervisor: Tony VenGraitis
Production Manager: Alexandra Odulak
Text Designer: Rebecca Bobb
Cover Designer: Eileen Burke
Cover illustration: Micheal Simpson/FPG International Corporation
Illustrations: Accurate Art Incorporated

© 1995 by Prentice-Hall Inc.
A Simon & Schuster Company
Englewood Cliffs, New Jersey 07632

Previous edition copyright © 1990

Printed in the United States of America

10 9 8 7 6 5 4 3 2 1

ISBN 0-02-341792-7

PRENTICE-HALL INTERNATIONAL (UK) LIMITED, *London*
PRENTICE-HALL OF AUSTRALIA PTY LIMITED, *Sidney*
PRENTICE-HALL CANADA, INC., *Toronto*
PRENTICE-HALL HISPANOAMERICANA, S.A., *Mexico*
PRENTICE-HALL OF INDIA PRIVATE LIMITED, *New Delhi*
PRENTICE-HALL OF JAPAN, INC., *Tokyo*
SIMON & SCHUSTER ASIA PTE. LTD., *Singapore*
EDITORA PRENTICE-HALL DO BRASIL, LTDA., *Rio de Janeiro*

THE SUPERVISORY CHALLENGE

*In memory of Frank Whitney, world's best dad,
and to Raquel Whitney Blackwell, the granddaughter
he always wanted.*

In a world of ambiguity, few things are certain . . .

Preface

In a world of ambiguity, few things are certain. Nowhere is that fact more apparent than in the changing job of the first-line supervisor, which is evolving from the stereotypical autocratic foreman of yesterday to the more facilitative, participative, team leader of today. It is not easy to rise from the ranks and assume supervisory responsibilities. There are no universal theories or easy answers to hand to the new supervisor. This book, however, like the first edition, aims at making the transition easier, by sensitizing new supervisors and future supervisors to the myriad of opportunities and challenges that await them. It offers a comprehensive approach to the principles as well as the practices of supervision while holding to the central belief that, for most supervisors, dealing effectively with people is the most important element of first-line management.

GOALS OF THE SUPERVISORY CHALLENGE

This book is designed to give guidance to the new or aspiring supervisor. It is written with the following overall goals:

- ☐ To offer a comprehensive framework with a human relations focus for students and practitioners to use in understanding the nature and practice of supervision. This inclusive coverage gives the reader the broad background needed to deal with a wide range of supervisory problems.
- ☐ To provide up-to-date coverage on emerging issues of concern to supervisors. These include sexual harassment, organizational ethics, and quality management. This materal assures that the reader is familiar with the new "hot spots" in the field of supervision.
- ☐ To introduce readers to a wide variety of real-world practices through feature stories and actual examples of supervisory behavior. The reader benefits by seeing the actual application of textbook material.
- ☐ To encourage readers to explore their own skill levels and their understanding of supervisory concepts through structured self-assess-

ment exercises, cases, and study-guide material. These features afford the reader the opportunity to bridge the gap between theory and practice immediately.

☐   To acquaint readers with current literature in the field through extensive text references and ten current readings included in their entirety. This literature base gives readers the opportunity to consider what other experts in the field have to say about important issues in supervision.

ORGANIZATION OF THE BOOK

The text is divided into six parts. The first four parts discuss the topics of foundations for effective supervision, dealing with individuals, dealing with groups, and personal strategies for success. Immediately following is a reading section, which highlights a number of important topics through a study of the current literature. Finally, the sixth part is a study guide consisting of true and false, multiple-choice, and matching questions, along with application exercises. This materal provides the student with the chance to review, check his or her understanding of the material, and, of course, to study for exams.

SPECIAL FEATURES

The special features of this book include the text design, the practical up-to-date coverage, pedagogical features and learning aids, a current readings section, a built-in study guide, and instructor resources.

Text Design

The Supervisory Challenge provides a unique three-in-one package which consists of (a) an up-to-date, comprehensive textbook, (b) a readings section, and (c) a detachable study guide.

Practical, Up-to-Date Coverage

The textbook deals with practical issues specifically related to first-line management. The book is written at a level appropriate for college students but will also be very useful to practicing supervisors and training directors. The text focuses on information that students will need to become effective supervisors, from dealing with office politics to negotiating with unions and from managing stress to building an effective team. The text has a number of noteworthy features.

Pedagogical Features/Learning Aids

1.   **Self-Assessment Quizzes** in every chapter help students gauge their prior knowledge of the subject.

2.   **Supervisory Skills** sections provide procedural tips for the aspiring supervisor.

3.   Each chapter begins with an organization chart showing the relationship of chapter topics.

4.   **The Quality Challenge** in each chapter integrates the theme of total quality management introduced in Chapter 2 throughout the text.

5.   End-of-chapter cases help students apply what they have learned to realistic situations.

6.   Key terms are italicized in the text and defined at the end of the chapter.

7.   Review questions reinforce chapter concepts by testing student comprehension.

8.   Chapter objectives and summaries act as "bookends" designed to emphasize ideas and concepts through repetition.

9.   Margin notes highlight important points.

Current Readings Section

The readings section can be considered a "book within a book." It contains ten current and relevant articles such as Barlow and Hane's "A Practical Guide to the Americans with Disabilities Act," Kennedy and Everest's "Put Diversity in Context," and Schilder's "Work Teams Boost Productivity."

Built-in Study Guide

The study guide is a real bonus for both students and teachers. It is organized by chapter and is designed to help students develop mastery of the subject without the expense of buying another book.

Instructor Resources

This book is complemented by an *Instructor's Manual* which contains a complete package of lecture notes, study guide answers, answers to readings discussion questions, and a test bank. Transparency masters complete the *Instructor's Manual*.

NEW FEATURES FOR THE SECOND EDITION

The second edition has been completely updated with the newest literature. The readings are all revised from the first edition, and many new footnotes have been added. Additionally, you will find the following substantial changes:

1.   Chapter 14 in the original edition, "Increasing Productivity," has been replaced with a new chapter entitled "Meeting the Quality Challenge." This new chapter appears as Chapter 2 since it introduces a quality theme which will reappear throughout the book.

2. Each chapter subsequent to Chapter 2 has a box entitled "The Quality Challenge" which reinforces and expands the coverage begun in Chapter 2.

3. A new chapter has been added on the important topic of managing cultural diversity. Chapter 8, entitled "Supervising in the Multicultural Workplace," gives students much needed awareness in this area.

4. Also new for this edition, Chapter 6, "Assuring Equal Opportunity Under the Law," responds to readers' requests for a more detailed discussion of the complicated legal environment within which supervisors work.

5. Coverage on supervising in a union environment has been expanded from half of a chapter in the first edition to a full chapter in this edition.

6. Material on time and stress management, and conducting effective meetings has been made more succinct. The first two subjects have been combined into one chapter and the important topic of meetings has been inserted into the group dynamics chapter.

ACKNOWLEDGMENTS

No author writes a book without a great deal of help. I want to express my gratitude to the many people who have helped create the second edition of *The Supervisory Challenge*. My original editor, Nina McGuffin, was very helpful in getting the project started. Other staff members helped as the manuscript went into production. Tony VenGraitis, Production Supervisor, was never more than a phone call away and worked diligently to keep the book on schedule.

Since writing the first edition, my own supervisory work at Nova Southeastern University has expanded significantly. I am still part of a marvelous management team headed by my dean and friend, Phil DeTurk, who continues to teach me that patience and genuine caring form the best foundation for effective supervision. I still delight in working with my fellow directors, Cleve Clarke, Stuart Horn, Allan Schulman, and Dan Sullivan. And I am still grateful for the continuing support and guidance from my mentor, Richard M. Hodgetts, Professor of Management at Florida International University.

Last, but not least, I want to thank my family for being so generous with my time and for being so self-sufficient so that I could have the pleasure of producing the second edition of *The Supervisory Challenge*.

Jane Whitney Gibson

Brief Contents

Contents

CHAPTER 3
Communicating Effectively   38

PART IV   PERSONAL STRATEGIES FOR SUCCESS

CHAPTER 16
Understanding Organizational Ethics and Politics   326

■ ■ ■ PART I

The overriding objective of Part I is to examine and study the foundations for effective supervision. This involves consideration of a number of important topics including the nature and purpose of the supervisor's job, how to communicate effectively with subordinates and superiors, a fundamental understanding of human behavior, and the making of effective decisions.

Chapter 1 focuses on defining the term *supervision* and discusses the nature of the supervisor's job. In addition to relating ways the supervisor's view of the workers has changed over the last century, attention is directed to the three skills necessary to all supervisors. Consideration is also given to the five functions these first-line managers carry out. Although many people are promoted from the worker to the supervisory level, they do not do well because they are unable to adjust to the demands of the new position. They are managers in name only. They fail to develop the skills so vital to effective supervision and are unable to carry out the functions that are critical to success at this level of the management hierarchy.

Chapter 2 introduces the concept of total quality management (TQM). In the past decade, TQM has revolutionized the way corporate America does business. This chapter presents the key characteristics of successful TQM programs and some of the tools and techniques commonly used in today's businesses. TQM is carried as a theme throughout this text. In each chapter you will find boxes labelled "The Quality Challenge" that build on what you learn in Chapter 2.

Chapter 3 addresses the subject of effective communication. A supervisor's job is to get things done through others. Communication, the process of conveying meanings from sender to receiver, is at the heart of the job. In addition, the nature and importance of both formal and informal communication are examined. Moreover, attention is directed at iden-

Foundations for Effective Supervision

tifying, describing, and discussing how to deal with such communication barriers as semantics, load, and distortion. Consideration is also given to the three major areas of nonverbal communications—kinesics, proxemics, and paralanguage—and the ways in which supervisors can become more effective in these areas.

Chapter 4 deals with understanding employee behavior. There are many things that a supervisor needs to know about human behavior. This chapter gives consideration to providing a behavioral framework through which individual behavior can be understood. The term *personality* is defined and the three general determinants of personality are described. The chapter then goes on to explain the importance of values and perception in understanding employee behavior and to discuss how supervisory style and expectations can affect employee behavior. The last part of the chapter addresses the topic of morale and describes the relationship between satisfaction and productivity.

Chapter 5 discusses problem identification and decision making. The first part of the chapter examines the way in which the decision-making process is carried out. It also explains how this process is modified by such factors as satisficing behavior, subjective rationality, and rationalization. Consideration is also given to identifying the four primary decision-making styles used by supervisors. The last part of the chapter examines group decision-making strategies including the use of brainstorming, the Delphi technique, and nominal grouping.

When you have finished reading all of the material in this part of the book, you will be able to define the term *supervision* and discuss the critical foundations on which effective supervision rests. You will also be aware of the basic challenges that confront those who assume the role of supervisor.

CHAPTER 1

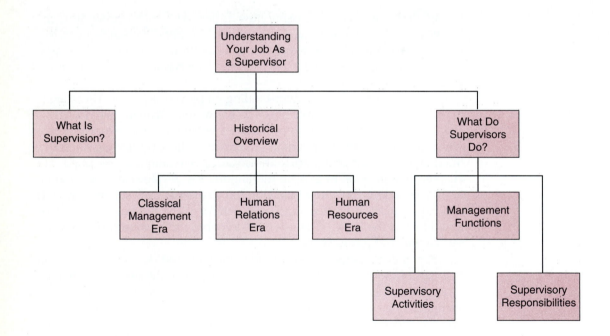

Understanding Your Job as a Supervisor

"No organization can function well if its supervisory force does not function. Supervisors are, so to speak, the ligaments, the tendons and sinews of an organization . . . Without them, no joint can move."*

CHAPTER OBJECTIVES

- ☐ Define the term *supervision* and discuss the nature of the supervisor's job.
- ☐ Relate how managers viewed the workers during the classical management era and how this view changed in the human relations and human resources eras.
- ☐ Describe the three skills all supervisors need.
- ☐ Identify and describe the five functions of supervision.

---

*Peter Drucker, *Management* (New York: Perennial Library, Harper & Row, 1973), 280.

Most managers work their way up the hierarchy, starting from the lower levels. The first of these levels, the supervisor, is the organization's primary link with the workers. Anyone aspiring to higher levels must first do well at this level.

Many new supervisors do not understand the nature and scope of their jobs. Many also have little idea of the skills needed for success at this level and the functions that they must perform. This chapter examines the supervisor's job and provides an overall framework from which to learn about what modern supervisors do.

WHAT IS SUPERVISION?

Here is a definition of supervision.

Supervision refers to first-line management—that is, the first person on the organizational chart who appears above the line workers. Supervisors are known by a variety of names such as foreman, group leader, or head nurse. Whatever the title, the supervisor leads employees in their day-to-day activities of producing the company's goods or services. This daily contact with the workers and primary responsibility for productivity makes the supervisor's job critical to the organization's success.

In recent years the considerable authority once given to the supervisional role has decreased somewhat for several reasons. First, early in this century it was fashionable for bosses to have unquestioned authority. What the supervisor said was the law. With the advent of strong unions and the emergence of participative management approaches, this absolute authority has largely eroded.

Table 1–1 compares the high-tech work environments of today, with their need for participatory techniques, with the more traditional low-tech work environments of yesteryear.

Second, most companies have added layers of middle managers between the first-line supervisor and top management. Now rarely do super-

---

TABLE 1-1

Low Tech	*High Tech*
White male work force	Ethnically diverse male-female work force
Conformity	Multiple life-styles
Blue collar	White collar
Manufacturing	Service sector
Domestic competition	International competition

Source: Philip M. Van Auken, "Control vs Development: Up-to-Date or Out-of-Date as a Supervisor?" *Supervision* (December, 1992): 17. Reprinted by premission of © National Research Bureau, P.O. Box 1, Burlington, Iowa 52601-0001

visors have final say over issues such as hiring and firing. Nevertheless, supervisors are still in a unique position to know what is going on in the organization and to influence those decisions that they do not actually make. To better understand the job of the supervisor today, let's take a brief look at how supervisory management has evolved during this century.

HISTORICAL OVERVIEW

For purposes of our discussion, supervisory management history can be divided into three eras: classical management, human relations, and human resources.

Classical Management Era

Classical management evolved in the early 1900s, when managers were struggling with the problems of the early factory system and trying to find ways to improve efficiency. These individuals fell into two main groups: the scientific managers and the administrative managers.

Scientific management focused on increasing work efficiency.

Scientific management theory taught that all jobs should be studied carefully so that the most efficient way of doing the job could be taught to the workers. The most important scientific manager of the time was Frederick Taylor, who today is known as the Father of Scientific Management. Taylor thought that a human is a rational being and that motivation is achieved through economic reward. Therefore, if a supervisor could teach the worker how to produce more and gain extra money as a result, the worker would be willing to follow orders. The philosophy behind scientific management was a belief that the managers should have a great deal of power and that the workers should do as they are told—for the eventual gain of all involved. This philosophy was based on three important assumptions about workers:[1]

1. Work is inherently distasteful to most people.
2. What workers do is less important than what they earn for doing it.
3. Few workers want or can handle work that requires creativity, self-direction, or self-control.

Under scientific management, supervisors, or foremen as they were likely to be called, were mainly responsible for giving orders and monitoring productivity. Factories were relatively small at the time, so supervisors were not far removed from top management and therefore wielded considerable power.

The other branch of classical theory is administrative management. The most famous administrative manager was Henri Fayol, who today is

---

[1]Raymond E. Miles, *Theories of Management: Implications for Organizational Behavior and Development* (New York: McGraw-Hill Book Co., 1975), 35.

known as the Father of Modern Management. Fayol lived and worked in France as president of a large mining combine. He dedicated himself to setting forth a body of knowledge that could be described as the basis for the field of management, or a framework of principles and rules to use in studying how managers should act. His work culminated with the 1916 publication of *General and Industrial Administration,* which laid out fourteen principles of administration, many of which are still studied today. The following list describes Fayol's principles:

1. *Division of labor.* Increased efficiency will result from specialization of labor.
2. *Authority and responsibility.* Fayol introduced the well-accepted concept that authority and responsibility go hand-in-hand and should be equal.
3. *Discipline.* Fayol believed in respect for the company and obedience to its rules.
4. *Unity of command.* One of the most famous of Fayol's principles, this means that each employee should have one and only one boss.
5. *Unity of management.* All operations having the same objective should come under the authority of one manager.
6. *Subordination of individual interests to the common good.* The good of the company takes precedence over individual needs.
7. *Remuneration of the staff.* Employees should be rewarded fairly for their effort.
8. *Centralization.* Fayol advised that organizations ascertain how much centralized authority was appropriate—that is, how many of the decisions should be made by top management. He recognized centralization as a natural tendency of organizations.
9. *Hierarchy.* The "scalar chain" of command describes the order of rank that runs from the bottom to the top of the organization. Fayol believed formal rank should be respected and employees should use the channels prescribed by the hierarchy. The notable exception is the opportunity to shortcut the long route through the hierarchy when one has the permission of his supervisor.
10. *Order.* From Fayol comes the famous saying, "A place for everything and everything in its place."
11. *Equity.* Equity is a product of friendly justice.
12. *Stability of staff.* Organizations should encourage long-term employment.
13. *Initiative.* This quality is defined as the power to conceive of and execute a plan of action.
14. *Esprit de corps.* Morale is important and depends on harmony and unity among workers.

It was Fayol who also first described the functions of management as: plan, organize, command, coordinate, and control. These functions are discussed later in this chapter.

The supervisor's job was seen as a combination of technical and administrative expertise.

Fayol saw the supervisor's job as a combination of technical and administrative expertise. He noted that as someone achieves higher level management positions the relative importance of technical ability decreases and the importance of administrative expertise increases.

Human Relations Era

By the 1920s, the principles of the classical school, especially of scientific management, were stirring up controversy with workers and theorists alike. The rise of union membership did much to speed the demise of scientific management, which the unions saw as merely trying to get more work out of the employees. Management in the 1920s and 1930s began to realize that people are not purely rational or economically motivated. They began to recognize the importance of social needs and motivators. This significantly different philosophy, which has become known as human relations theory, has three underlying assumptions.

Management began to realize that the workers had social needs.

1.   People want to feel useful and important.
2.   People desire to belong and to be recognized as individuals.
3.   These needs are more important than money in motivating people to work.[2]

The Hawthorne Studies, which took place at the Western Electric Company near Cicero, Illinois, between 1924 and 1932, are widely credited with beginning the human relations era. These studies initially involved efforts to increase productivity by manipulating environmental factors such as illumination. They expanded their focus, however, and made a number of landmark findings, such as the importance of social norms in setting productivity standards as well as the overall importance of group dynamics in the workplace. While scientific managers saw the employee as an economic man, the human relationists began to see the employee as a social man. This shift in viewpoint led to early attempts to make workers happy by paying them more personal attention, instituting suggestion boxes, and listening to their gripes and concerns.

Through the many people involved in the Hawthorne Studies, most notably the Harvard team of Elton Mayo and Fritz Roethlisberger, the nature of the supervisory job was expanded to include interpersonal or human relations skills designed to facilitate "counseling, motivating, leading, and communicating with workers."[3]

Another important person in the human relations period is Chester Barnard, who worked his way up the corporate ladder to become president of the New Jersey Bell Telephone Company. After his retirement he

---

[2]Ibid.

[3]Daniel A. Wren, *The Evolution of Management Thought,* 3rd ed. (New York: John Wiley & Sons, 1987), 247.

wrote the now-classic *Functions of the Executive* to share with his contemporaries what he had learned as a chief executive officer. Although Barnard focused on advice for top executives, many of his teachings are equally appropriate for supervisors. Barnard's *acceptance theory of authority* is particularly relevant to our study of supervision. Barnard said simply that the amount of authority a manager has depends on how much authority the employees recognize. To facilitate the acceptance of authority by workers, Barnard cautioned supervisors that their work assignments (requests) should meet four requirements:

People accept orders if these four conditions exist.

1. The employee must understand the communication.
2. The employee must believe the request or order is not inconsistent with the goals of the organization.
3. The employee must believe the communication is not inconsistent with the goals of the organization.
4. The employee must be mentally and physically able to comply.[4]

Barnard placed primary importance on the role of communication in management. In the classical management era communication was largely regarded as just a necessity to give orders and directives to employees. Barnard recognized the need for upward as well as downward communication and also examined the usefulness of the informal communication system that exists in every organization (see Chapter 3).

Human Resources Era

By the end of World War II, management began shifting from the human relations philosophy. Management theory began to recognize that people were looking for meaningful work and that, if given the chance, people could participate much more fully in a company's decision-making processes. As the human resources philosophy evolved, it developed the following assumptions:

1. Work is not inherently distasteful. People want to contribute to meaningful goals that they have helped establish.
2. Most people can exercise far more creative, responsible self-direction and self-control than their present jobs demand.[5]

The human resources philosophy was a radical departure from previous supervisory styles but much more in keeping with the evolving values of the affluent American society.

A human resources philosophy is based on shared decision making and participative management.

At the heart of the human resources philosophy is a belief in participative management, a management style that relies on group participation

---

[4]Chester Barnard, *Functions of the Executive* (Cambridge, Mass.: Harvard Univ. Press, 1938), 165–166.

[5]Miles, *Theories*, 35.

and shared decision making. This orientation greatly curtails the former authority of supervisors and places them in the role of group leader, coach, and advisor. Many supervisors reared in the traditions of managing according to classical or human relations concepts are still having trouble adjusting to the new values of today's work force, who are more educated, more professional, and more desirous of having a say in things that affect them and their organization.

> "To be up-to-date and globally competitive, firms must cultivate cooperative teamwork, innovativeness and high quality productivity. Supervisors who are more concerned with controlling employees than developing them are simply out of step with today's marketplace realities. Controlled workers are poor team players, uncreative and not very innovative."[6]

Table 1–2 compares the traditional controlling supervisory style, which may have been appropriate during scientific management times, with the developmental, participatory supervisory style that is in demand today. Many of the developmental style characteristics such as empowerment, participative decision making, job enrichment, team building, and listening will be discussed in much greater depth later in this book.

TABLE 1–2
Controlling vs. developmental supervising

Controlling Style	*Developmental Style*
Maximize power over employees	Empower employees to manage their own work
Autocratic, unilateral decision-making	Participative, consultive decision-making
Emphasize rules, procedures, bureaucracy	Emphasize mission, goals, results
Stress efficiency	Stress effectiveness
Job specialization and routinization	Job enrichment and holism
Management of individuals	Management of teams
Directing and ordering	Coaching and mentoring
Talking	Listening
Departmental focus	Corporatewide focus

Source: Philip M. Van Auken, "Control vs. Development: Up-to-Date or Out-of-Date as a Supervisor?" *Supervision* (December, 1992): 18.

[6]VanAuken, *Supervision*, 18.

SELF-ASSESSMENT QUIZ 1–1
Can You Identify the Management Era?

Directions: Carefully read the following statements. If the statement can be attributed to classical management theory, write an "a" at the end of the sentence. If the statement is part of the human relations philosophy, put a "b" at the end of the sentence. If the statement describes a human resources tenet, enter a "c" at the end of the sentence.

1. Money is the number-one motivator of the work force.

2. A happy worker is a productive worker.

3. Most workers want to be treated well.

4. Participative management is an effective leadership style.

5. Downward communication channels are the most important of all.

6. Most workers are a lot more creative than their jobs require.

7. Employees respond well to self-direction and self-control.

8. People want to belong and be members of a team.

9. Many workers are willing to accept responsibility.

10. Workers are basically lazy.

To check your answers, see the answer key at the end of the chapter.

Self-Assessment Quiz 1–1 will help you see whether you can differentiate between the various management philosophies represented by the three management eras.

WHAT DO SUPERVISORS DO?

To understand the supervisor's job, we need to examine the skills required of all managers, the functions that they perform, and their responsibilities to others in the organization.

Supervisory Skills

Supervisors need technical, human, and conceptual skills. The most important of these is technical skills.

Technical skills refer to job-specific knowledge. In a computer department, for example, technical skills include programming, system analysis, debugging, and troubleshooting. Supervisors in such a department need to have these skills at least at the same level or above those of their employees. When employees need help with technical problems, they come to supervisors and expect that they will have the answer.

Human relations skills refer to those abilities needed to deal with people. How do managers motivate and lead people? How do they communicate with employees? How is discipline handled? How are people rewarded? What do managers do with employees who have personal problems or who present problems to other employees? Many managers have

Technical skills refer to job-specific knowledge and skills.

Human relations skills are those needed for dealing with people.

■　■　■　SUPERVISORY SKILLS
The Role of Supervisors

1. Work within the framework of the values and beliefs of the human resources era. The absolute authority of earlier supervisors has eroded. You must learn to lead the workers as a coach and a motivator. If you are a new supervisor, work hard to augment your technical skills with people skills.

2. Understand the philosophical underpinnings of the classical, human relations, and human resources eras. Although most organizations today subscribe to the latter, there are still instances where classical and human relations management styles may be useful. Be able to recognize the differences and understand how these approaches affect subordinates. One group of workers, for example, may be perfectly willing to do repetitive work under a scientific manager who studies the job and teaches them how to do it most efficiently and for the greatest monetary reward. Another group may find this entirely unacceptable and instead seek more job variation and challenge.

3. Examine your own beliefs about people and work in the context of the three management eras. Are you most naturally a classical, human relations, or human resources manager? Are you flexible enough to change when that style does not seem appropriate to your environment?

fine technical skills and are able to handle the actual tasks of the work; however, when faced with managing other people, they find their human relations skills are inadequate.

Conceptual skills are those abilities needed for planning goals, daily activities, workloads, and so on. Is the manager able to analyze a problem, see all its implications, and arrive at an equitable solution? Is the manager able to plan, even when all the variables are not concrete? Can he or she conceptualize goals for next year, the next five years?

Managers at all levels use technical, human relations, and conceptual skills, but the proportion of each varies at each level. Figure 1–1 illustrates the degree of each skill needed at the various levels of management. Note that as one goes higher in the organizational hierarchy, technical skills, (that is, everyday operational skills) become less and less important. Although first-line supervisors use technical skills the most, middle managers use a higher percentage of human relations skills. Top management, on the other hand, is more involved with conceptualizing overall corporate goals and strategy and thus uses conceptual skills more than anyone else.

First-line supervisors do not only use technical skills. They need to use all three types of skills on a daily basis. Opportunities for supervisors to use conceptual skills include planning the weekly work schedule, deciding on production goals, leading goal-setting sessions with individual employees, and preparing the departmental budget for next year. Human relations skills are also used on a daily basis. Examples include motivating employees to reach desired production levels, constructively disciplining

Conceptual skills are those needed for planning.

Supervisors use technical skills more than any others.

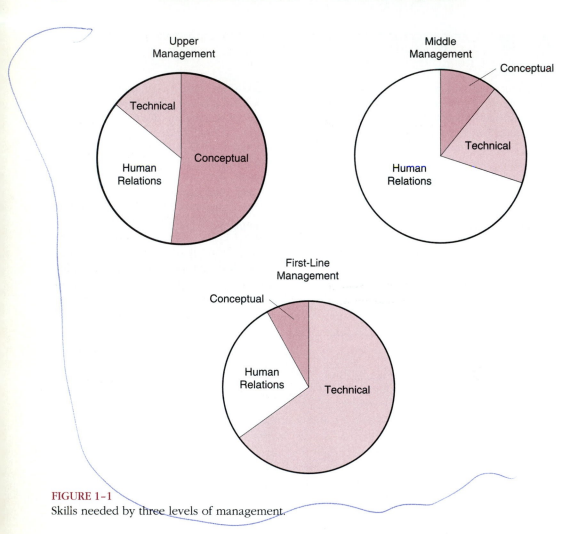

FIGURE 1–1
Skills needed by three levels of management.

employees who do not follow organizational rules, counseling employees who have personal problems, conducting performance appraisals with employees, and introducing new employees into the norms and procedures of the department. Technical skills are perhaps the easiest to identify for the supervisor. Each time supervisors help an employee do the job, train a new employee on work methods, or answer a question regarding equipment or process, they are using technical skills. Supervisors commonly come up "through the ranks"—in other words, they are promoted out of the very group of employees they are now leading. In such cases, supervisors learn their technical skills on the job and possibly outperform others or otherwise distinguish themselves in order to be promoted. Supervisors are often expected to have better technical skills than their employees. Successful supervisors work hard to keep these skills up-to-date so that employees will continue to have respect for, and trust in, their technical knowledge and leadership ability.

Management Functions

Another way to examine what supervisors do is to look at the five functions of management as originally described by Henri Fayol. As mentioned before, these functions are planning, organizing, directing (originally called commanding by Fayol), coordinating, and controlling.

Planning involves deciding on a course of action to achieve some desired goal.

Planning. We have already suggested that supervisors use conceptual skills. *Planning* involves deciding on a course of action to achieve some desired future result. This can be done on a short-term, intermediate, or long-term basis. Long-term organizational planning usually refers to goals that are five or more years in the future. Intermediate planning typically concerns two-to-five-year goals. Short-term planning, often called operational planning, usually looks no further than one or two years into the future. The very nature of the supervisory job mandates that supervisors be mostly concerned with operational planning.

Planning seldom comes easily to the new supervisor. Most incoming supervisors have had little or no planning experience in their previous positions and often receive little on-the-job training in this area. It is assumed that they will know how to plan their manpower needs, budgetary requirements, and performance goals. Many fledgling supervisors get poor performance reviews because they are untrained in planning. Even with careful planning, the future does not always turn out as expected. Yet many competitive organizations bet their existence on the future orientation of their managers, including their first-level supervisors. Careful planning also saves the company money and results in more efficient operations. According to one noted source:

> Supervisors can compare organizational results with plans to determine whether their unit is on schedule and to determine what might be done to improve operations, reduce costs, improve schedules, and improve the quality of the work or services to the customer. Planning also provides the supervisor with the opportunity to analyze operations. It enables the front-line manager to ask questions: "Who is going to do what?" "How much can be accomplished in a given time?" Planning helps supervisors make the most economical use of their people and equipment. Supervisors can, in so doing, economize on labor costs and equipment operations.[7]

---

[7]Lawrence L. Steinmetz and H. Ralph Todd, Jr., *First-Line Management* (Plano, Tex.: Business Publications, 1986), 38.

Organizing. *Organizing* is the process of deciding how to use resources and employees to attain company goals. As part of this process, supervisors are involved in staffing, that is, interviewing and hiring people to fit the department needs. However, the staffing function involves much more than hiring employees. It also involves orienting those employees to company and departmental policies and procedures, providing necessary training and development opportunities, setting work goals and assessing employee performance. (Chapter 7 deals with the entire selecting and training function whereas Chapter 11 talks about conducting effective performance appraisals.)

As another part of the organizing function, supervisors are concerned with deciding how to allocate the work among the employees in the department and how to distribute the money, equipment, and other resources to accomplish these objectives efficiently. Supervisors must remember that efficiency and effectiveness are two different goals. *Efficiency* is involved with using the least costly and time-consuming means to achieve the desired ends. *Effectiveness* is concerned with accomplishing the right goals. Efficiency is "doing things right," whereas effectiveness is "doing the right things." It is entirely possible to be efficient without being effective and vice versa. An example of the former would be instituting budget-saving regulations such as no overtime, which in turn result in unmet production schedules and lost customers. An example of the latter would be meeting productivity quotas for the year but at the same time increasing the staff turnover rate by 50 percent. By carefully organizing the work force and scheduling the work to be done, supervisors strive to be both efficient and effective.

Directing. *Directing* is the supervision of the work force in the accomplishment of its goals. Directing entails leading through example, motivating workers to be loyal and productive, and communicating effectively and continually with employees. The latter is an especially important facet of the supervisory job.

Coordinating. *Coordinating* is the synchronization of individual and group effort for the purpose of attaining efficiency. By its very nature the supervisory job is primarily one of coordination. Supervisors synchronize the work of employees within their department and also coordinate the overall efforts of the department with that of other departments. This coordination of human efforts is often the supervisor's biggest challenge. When one large group of supervisors was asked, "Do you like to supervise?" almost two-thirds answered "no." This negative response was explained by one supervisor who said, "I don't like to supervise because I don't know how."

"Trying to work with demanding deadlines, budgets, and schedules can result in a lot of pressure and frustration. However, most supervisors report

---

Organizing is the process of deciding how to use resources and employees to attain company goals.

Directing is the supervision of the workforce in the accomplishment of its goals.

Coordination is the synchronization of individual and group effort for the purpose of attaining efficiency.

that it is dealing with the ever-present and complex human problems that causes them to question their ability."[8]

The supervisor has a foot in two camps: management and operational employees. Therefore, it may be correct to say that supervisors serve as a bridge between management and the workers who actually produce the goods or services of the company.

Controlling.   The final function of the supervisor is controlling. *Controlling* is the comparison of actual performance with planned performance and the correction of any significant deviations that might have occurred. In order to do this the supervisor must set careful work standards, measure actual work performed, compare results to the standards, and correct any deviations.

Controlling is the comparison of actual performance with planned performance and the correcting of any differences that have occurred.

Supervisory Responsibilities

Supervisors are responsible to many groups in the company.

Supervisors are responsible to many others in the organization. Employees, higher management, peers, and the union all look to supervisors to protect their interests and further their goals. Employees, for example, see supervisors as their representative to upper management. Supervisors who do not represent the concerns and interests of the employees soon lose their support. In one manufacturing department, employees were very concerned about rumors of a 10 percent layoff. When their supervisor refused to question upper management about specifics and counseled the employees instead to be quiet and see what happens, the employees lost confidence in him and took their anxieties to the union shop steward. By not looking after employee interests, the supervisor lost status and respect and was cut off from further discussion on the subject. Supervisors must earn respect from others on a daily basis; it cannot be demanded.

Higher management also believes supervisors represent their interests. To them, supervisors are junior managers who should be most concerned with meeting organizational goals and subsequently advancing into the ranks of middle management.

Supervisors expect their peers to be of one mind with them; after all, they are a group apart from employees (weren't they good enough to be promoted over the other employees?), and they may not quite be sure about the goodwill of upper management. Peers tend to reinforce each other's beliefs that they are the most important group in the company and expect loyalty from each other.

Finally, the union looks to the supervisor as the person most responsible for ensuring equitable treatment and adherence to union contract

[8]D. Kim McKinnon, "Three Steps to Increasing Supervisory Success," *Management Solutions* (January 1987): 12–14.

SUPERVISORY SKILLS
The Supervisory Job

1. Examine your own skill and knowledge base. All supervisors need technical, human relations, and conceptual skills. Where are your weaknesses? Your strengths? Are your human relations skills strong enough to supervise people? Be sure to keep your technical skills honed so that your workers and other managers alike will respect your knowledge of the job.

2. Be aware that previous jobs may not have taught you conceptual skills. Learn how to plan and make it part of your everyday routine. Planning can keep your department competitive and productive

in the intermediate and long-range time periods. It can also facilitate daily operations, such as planning of equitable vacation schedules and planning the assignment of overtime.

3. Be aware of your organizing, directing, coordinating, and controlling roles in the organization and learn the necessary skills to practice these roles effectively.

4. Respond to your responsibilities to various groups in the organization. Peers, employees, upper management, and the union each expect different things from you.

agreements. For this reason, union grievances are most likely to be aimed at the supervisory level. (See Supervisory Skills: The Supervisory Job, above.)

SUMMARY

Supervisors are first-line managers who lead workers in their day-to-day activities. This role has changed greatly over the last century.

During the classical management era the supervisor's major focus was on work efficiency. The individual attempted to organize the work and the people in such a way as to maximize work output. The worker was viewed as an adjunct of the machine.

During the human relations era the supervisor's view of the workers underwent change. Now the workers were viewed as individuals who wanted to belong and to be recognized as important people. The now-famous Hawthorne Studies shed a great deal of light on this area of human relations.

The human resources era represents a major break with the thinking of the past. Today workers are viewed as individuals

who want to contribute to meaningful goals that they have helped establish and to exercise creativity, self-direction, and self-control.

Supervisors rely on three types of skills: technical, human, and conceptual. Technical skills are related to specific job knowledge. Human relations skills refer to those abilities needed to deal with people. Conceptual skills are needed for planning goals, daily activities, and workloads.

Supervisors also perform five functions: planning, organizing, directing, coordinating, and controlling. In performing these functions, they are responsible to a number of well-defined groups within the organization, including peers, employees, higher level management, and the union. Each group expects the supervisor to represent their best interests.

REVIEW QUESTIONS

1. What is meant by the term *supervision?* Put it in your own words.

2. How did classical management supervisors view their subordinates? What assumptions or beliefs did these supervisors have regarding how to manage their people? Explain.

3. During the classical management era some writers set forth principles of administration. What are some examples of these principles? Of what practical value are they to modern supervisors? Explain.

4. How did human relations supervisors view their subordinates? What assumptions or beliefs did these managers have regarding how to supervise their people? Explain.

5. What is the acceptance theory of authority? Of what value is it to the modern supervisor? Explain.

6. How do human resource supervisors view their employees? What assumptions or beliefs do they have regarding how to supervise their people? Explain.

7. Supervisors need to have three types of skills: technical, human, and conceptual. What does this statement mean? In your answer be sure to define and/or describe each of these three skills.

8. What does a supervisor do during the planning process? The organizing process? The directing process? The coordinating process? The controlling process? Be complete in your answer.

9. In what ways is the supervisor responsible to different groups within the organization?

KEY TERMS

Acceptance theory of authority. Theory of authority that holds that the manager's authority is based on the subordinates' acceptance of the manager's orders.

Directing. Supervision of the work force in the accomplishment of its goals.

Conceptual skills. Abilities needed for planning goals, daily activities, workloads, and so on.

Controlling. Comparison of actual performance with planned performance and the correction of any important deviations that have occurred.

Coordinating. Synchronization of individual and group effort for the purpose of attaining efficiency.

Human relations skills. Abilities needed in dealing with people.

Organizing. Process of deciding how to use resources and employees to attain company goal.

Planning. Process of deciding on a course of action to achieve a desired future result.

Technical skills. Job-specific knowledge and proficiency used in accomplishing tasks.

ANSWERS TO SELF-ASSESSMENT
QUIZ 1-1

1. a	3. b	5. a	7. c	9. c
2. b	4. c	6. c	8. b	10. a

CASE 1-1
A Difference in Performance

Paul Carter and Jan Redwing are two new supervisors in Phil Barten's department. Both supervisors have been in their positions for a little over three months.

Phil makes it a point to give each supervisor about ninety days before he reviews their progress and works with them in identifying problem areas and steps they should undertake to correct these areas. One of the things Phil relies on very heavily is feedback from the supervisor's subordinates. This feedback is usually obtained from an evaluation form that the subordinates fill out and submit directly to the supervisor's boss.

A brief review of Paul and Jan's performance shows that Paul's work group is producing 19 percent above standard, whereas Jan's is 26 percent below standard. The performance evaluations have shed some additional light on possible reasons for these work output performances. Here is a brief summary of what the subordinates had to say about Paul and Jan.

Paul
He talks about our assignments and tells us what he wants done, how it should be done, and by when the work must be completed. He is a friendly, warm person, who seems to blend a concern for the work with a concern for us as human beings. We like the way he gives us a chance to use our initiative and creativity.

Jan
She tries very hard to get all the work done on time. She explains what she wants done and by when, and she usually spends most of her time out in the workplace monitoring progress, seeing that everything is on schedule, and working to overcome any problems that crop up. She is great in helping people with work-related problems but seems to have no time or understanding of nonwork-related matters.

1.   In your own words, what type of supervisor is Paul? What assumptions or beliefs does he have about his people? Explain.

2.   In your own words, what type of supervisor is Jan? What assumptions or beliefs does she have about her people? Explain.

3.   Why is Paul's performance record better than Jan's? Be complete in your answer.

CASE 1-2
Chuck's Request

For the last four years Tim Holway has been the office manager in a large sales firm. The office manager's job is to supervise in-house personnel who are providing support help for the salespeople in the field. Most of these employees are clerical and responsible for typing, photocopying, and record keeping.

Tim's salary is not very high, but he receives a commission on all sales. As a result he generally earns more money than anyone in the department except for one or two of the leading salespeople.

Last week Tim decided to take early retirement. To fill the position as quickly as possible, the firm asked if any present employee had an interest in the job. Chuck Strickland has indicated that he would like it. Chuck is the leading salesperson in the area and has been with the company for two years. Explaining his decision to come in from the field, Chuck said, "In order to get ahead with this company, there are only two routes. One is to become a leading salesperson. The other is to get into a management position and work one's way up the hierarchy. I think I would prefer the latter."

In addition to Chuck, two other people have applied for Tim's job. However, Chuck is the leading candidate. Before going ahead and finalizing the promotion, Tim's boss has asked him to talk with Chuck and to be sure that the salesman really wants to give up selling and take an office job. Tim intends to have this meeting with Chuck before the week is over. Right now he is making notes regarding what he should talk to Chuck about.

1. How will Chuck's new job be different from his old one in terms of skills required? In your answer be sure to discuss technical, human, and conceptual skills.

2. How would an understanding of the human resources era be of value to Chuck? Would he not already know all about this? Explain.

3. In what way would the management functions Chuck will be performing—planning, organizing, directing, coordinating, and controlling—be different or new to him? Be complete in your answer.

CHAPTER 2

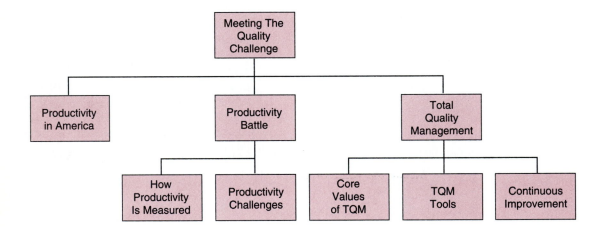

Meeting the Quality Challenge

"The current world competitive situation makes the examination of total quality management a "must" for any enlightened . . . manager."*

CHAPTER OBJECTIVES

☐ Discuss America's current productivity growth rate.

☐ Explain how productivity can be measured and some ways in which it can be increased.

☐ Identify and describe four of the most commonly cited reasons for productivity problems.

☐ Describe what total quality management is all about.

☐ Explain how some of the most popular TQM tools are applied.

☐ Relate the value of continuous improvement in increasing quality.

---

*Warren H. Schmidt and Jerome P. Finnigan, *The Race Without A Finish Line: America's Quest For Total Quality* (San Francisco, Calif.: Jossey-Bass, 1992), 5.

F ew issues today capture the interest of American businesspeople more than the topic of quality. Article after article warns us of the increasing quality of Japanese and European products and the need for America to increase its productivity and quality of goods and services.

This chapter examines the importance of increasing productivity and the role played by quality improvement in this process. It also integrates some of the ways that American firms are increasing their quality to world-class levels and setting the standards for everyone else to follow.

PRODUCTIVITY IN AMERICA

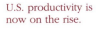

During much of the 1980s the United States had sluggish productivity growth, while other nations such as Japan and Germany were able to achieve much higher annual growth.[1] However, in the early 1990s the United States began to gain steam, while many other nations began to slow down.[2] As seen in Figure 2–1, between 1988 and 1992 U.S. productivity jumped from −1% to 2.7%. What caused this dramatic turnaround? One reason is the spread of total quality management concepts throughout American industry. People are now learning how to do things better *and* faster.

U.S. productivity is now on the rise.

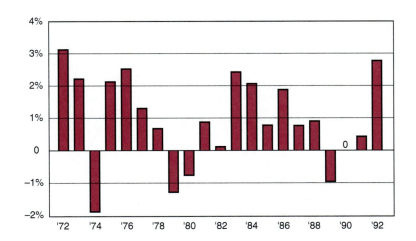

FIGURE 2–1

Measuring productivity.

Source: As reported in "Productivity in U.S. Jumped By 2.7% in 1992," *Wall Street Journal* (February 5, 1993): A2.

---

[1]Richard M. Hodgetts, *Human Relations At Work,* 5th ed. (Forth Worth, Tex.: Dryden Press, 1993), 210–213.

[2]Lucinda Harper, "Productivity in U.S. Jumped By 2.7% in 1992," *Wall Street Journal* (February 5, 1993): A2.

At the same time the Japanese economy began to slow down. The rapid 10% annual productivity increases of the 1970s had fallen into the 6% range during the 1980s and are currently in the 3% range. The same trend is true for Germany, the strongest economic power in Europe, which saw productivity increases drop from 6% in the 1970s to 4% in the 1980s and now down to the 2–3% range.

These data seem to indicate that the productivity challenge for the United States has been answered. In one sense, this is true. America has come from a long way back to prove that it is still the greatest economic power in the world. On the other hand, this is a battle that must be well fought but is never won. The challenge for productivity supremacy will continue during the 1990s, and America's supervisors will play a key role on the battle line.

THE PRODUCTIVITY BATTLE

Productivity is an important quality-related issue because increased quality will bring about increased productivity. This link is clearly seen by looking at how productivity is measured.

How Productivity Is Measured

Productivity is the ratio of outputs to inputs. *Outputs* consist of the value of the goods and services being produced. *Inputs* are the costs of producing these goods and services and include such things as personnel, machinery, materials, and money.

> Productivity is the ratio of outputs to inputs.

In organizations, productivity is most often equated with efficiency of operations. It can be measured with the following ratio:

productivity = total output/total input

Within organizations, there are many measures of productivity—from overall organizational productivity to the productivity of individual departments or workers. Productivity of a typist, for example, may be judged by the number of pages typed in an eight-hour shift. Contrast the productivity rates of Typists 1 and 2:

Typist 1   Productivity = 24 typed pages/8 hours = 3.0
Typist 2   Productivity = 28 typed pages/8 hours = 3.5

Another way of measuring the productivity of the same two typists is to use their salary as the input figure. If Typist 1 earns $5.50 an hour and Typist 2 earns $7.00 an hour, and assuming that they both worked eight hours in producing the output, the following rates would result:

Typist 1   Productivity = 24 typed pages/$44 ($5.50 × 8) = $1.83 per page
Typist 2   Productivity = 28 typed pages/$56 ($7.00 × 8) = $2.00 per page

In this case, Typist 1 is more productive because the output costs the organization less money.

Productivity increase is equally easy to calculate. Suppose the typing supervisor has a long talk with all the typists regarding the necessity of producing more copy in a day, and the following results for Typist 1 are noted:

$$\textit{Typist 1 } \text{Productivity} = \frac{28 \text{ typed pages}}{8 \text{ hours}} = 3.5$$

Typist 1's productivity has increased from 3.0 to 3.5. The percentage of improved productivity can be computed as follows:

$$(3.5 - 3.0)/3.0 = 16\% \text{ productivity increase}$$

Three basic ways can be used to increase productivity. The first, which has just been illustrated, calls for increasing output while keeping input constant.

$$(1) \text{ increased productivity} = \frac{\text{increased output}}{\text{steady inputs}} = \frac{28}{8} = 3.5$$

Another approach is to maintain the current output of 24 pages per day but reduce the hours worked—for example, to 7.5—thus reducing the cost of inputs.

$$(2) \text{ increased productivity} = \frac{\text{steady outputs}}{\text{decreased input}} = \frac{24}{7.5} = 3.2$$

The supervisor's preference, however, would be to increase outputs and decrease inputs at the same time, thus causing an even higher increase in productivity.

$$(3) \text{ increased productivity} = \frac{\text{increased outputs}}{\text{decreased inputs}} = \frac{28}{7.5} = 3.7$$

The preceding discussion illustrates cases of rising productivity. Unfortunately, productivity can also decline. This can happen in any of the following ways:

$$(1) \frac{\text{outputs decrease}}{\text{inputs stable}} \quad (2) \frac{\text{outputs stable}}{\text{inputs increase}} \quad (3) \frac{\text{outputs decrease}}{\text{inputs increase}}$$

In summary, productivity indicates how efficiently a company meets its goals. Increased productivity translates into greater overall profits, a larger market share, increased available capital for research and development, and a more secure job for everyone! With this in mind, where do American firms most commonly find productivity challenges?

Productivity Challenges

There are four important areas where America needs to meet productivity challenges: (a) managerial attitudes and practices; (b) changing values of the work force; (c) government regulations, and (d) growth of the unions.

Some people blame managers for declining productivity.

Managerial Attitudes. Much of the current productivity challenge can be placed squarely on the shoulders of American managers. In many companies, management has not played an active role in either assuming responsibility for this problem or ensuring that the employees are trained and motivated to meet the challenge. Managers have simply delegated the problem down the line, sat back, and watched productivity decline.

Some say Americans have lost the work ethic.

Changing Values of the Work Force. Many people point an accusing finger at the younger, more independent work force of today and say that the American worker has lost the work ethic, which included a commitment to hard work and sacrifice for the good of the company. Today's workers are more likely to be interested in the ways the company can benefit their personal goals. They are more likely to take time off randomly, to look for ways to avoid working hard, and to be indifferent about quality. Employees are no longer satisfied with work being a "one-way street" in favor of the employer.

Many businesses blame government regulation.

Government Regulations. Many companies blame their decreasing productivity on state and federal government agencies, which have forced them to spend large sums of money to meet government regulations. Examples of costly regulations are those involved with the Occupational Safety and Health Act, the reporting regulations of the Employment Retirement Income Security Act (ERISA), and pollution control. Others include the hiring of specialists in such areas as equal employment opportunity compliance and large increases in legal costs.

Others place the blame on unions.

Unions. Many people who take a quick look at the productivity problem place a major share of the blame on American unions, which, they say, are resistant to labor-saving technologies and are always after a bigger piece of pie. The unions, of course, would counter that they are trying to protect employee jobs and ensure them an equitable share of the profit. Given that union membership is declining and many nonunionized industries such as agriculture and retail trade are battling slow productivity growth, it does not seem that unions are primarily to blame.

One of the most effective ways for supervisors to deal with these productivity challenges is through the use of total quality management programs, both as learners and teachers. These programs have been extremely useful in driving up organizational productivity and helping America regain its competitive status. Before studying what total quality management is all about, test your productivity IQ by taking Self-Assessment Quiz 2–1. When considering your answers, note that each "no" or "unsure" answer indicates an area where improvement is needed. Also review Supervisory Skills: Understanding Productivity.

TOTAL QUALITY MANAGEMENT

During the 1980s, a total quality management movement began in America. This movement is particularly important to supervisors, because much of what happens takes place at this level and below.[3] Today an increasing number of businesses are introducing total quality management concepts and using them to increase both quality and productivity.[4]

Total quality management is an organizational strategy.

Total quality management (TQM) is an organizational strategy with accompanying techniques for delivering quality and/or service to customers.

■ ■ ■ ## SELF-ASSESSMENT QUIZ 2–1
Assess Your Productivity IQ

Directions: The following ten questions pinpoint areas where productivity errors are commonly made. Test your productivity IQ by placing a "Y" (yes), an "N" (no), or a "U" (unsure) next to each.

_____ 1. Should managers evaluate their human resource problems as carefully as they evaluate their technical problems?

_____ 2. Should managers first diagnose performance problems before they recommend a solution?

_____ 3. Should managers engage in preventive performance problem solving as well as addressing actual problems?

_____ 4. Should a company's performance appraisal system be based on productivity standards?

_____ 5. Should employee job descriptions focus most heavily on output, standards of performance, and other job-related outcomes?

_____ 6. Should employees receive praise and other forms of positive reinforcement when they do a good job?

_____ 7. Should employees receive consistent and timely feedback on their performance?

_____ 8. Is training designed to improve skills and knowledge really necessary for maximum work efficiency?

_____ 9. Should resources, procedures, equipment, and work flow be both efficient and effective?

_____ 10. Should managers and supervisors be skilled in handling the challenges of their job?

---

[3]Dan Harriger, "Using TQM to Reengineer Human Resources," *HR Focus* (April 1993): 17.

[4]Shari Caudron, "Keys to Starting a TQM Program," *Personnel Journal* (February 1993): 28–35.

SUPERVISORY SKILLS
Understanding Productivity

1. Learn to understand productivity—what it is and the way productivity rates are figured. By keeping records of department—as well as individual—productivity, you can track progress, spot problems, and plan for improvements where needed.

2. Examine the potential areas for productivity problems in your work environment. Are managerial attitudes and practices a problem? In what ways is the nature of your work force contributing to productivity gains or losses? Are unions a part of the "productivity problem"?

3. Once you have diagnosed these problems, you should begin to work on those areas over which you have the most influence. Begin with yourself. How can you better establish an atmosphere conducive to encouraging productivity? Is productivity rewarded in your department either by monetary rewards or by praise and recognition?

4. Be aware that you are in a position to impact on both of the major ways to improve productivity—by better managing human resources and by improving methods and technology. Keep your technical skills honed and current; you must also learn to get the best out of people.

Unlike management fads or quantitative techniques, however, TQM is *not* an addition or supplement to the way management currently runs the enterprise. Rather, it is an organizational strategy that helps define the way the business is managed. This ongoing, continuous process requires management to radically change its operating philosophy, especially at the supervisory level.[5] At the heart of this process is a series of core values that are critical to understanding TQM.

Core Values of TQM

There are 10 core values of TQM.

There is no universal process that is followed lockstep by firms implementing total quality management. However, there are ten core values that are central to the process and, in one way or another, are used to achieve total quality.

Customer-driven quality. Methods, processes, and procedures are designed to meet and exceed customer expectations.

Leadership. Top management fully understands the TQM process (often having been through the same training given to the other personnel) and supports the strategy through both words and deeds.

---

[5]Michael E. Spiess, "Finding Time for TQM Training," *Training & Development Journal* (February 1993): 11–15.

Continual betterment. No matter how high the level of quality, there is an ongoing emphasis on continually "raising the bar" and improving quality still further.

Empowerment. Everyone in the organization is provided TQM training, so they have the necessary tools and techniques for improving quality, and there is a reward and recognition system in place for ensuring continual support for the overall effort. Additionally, workers are empowered to take whatever steps are necessary to get the job done. (For more on empowerment, see Chapter 9.)

Reduced cycle time. In addition to increasing quality, there is a strong effort given to reducing *cycle time,* which is the time needed to deliver the output. Companies follow the cliche, "If it cannot be done better, focus on doing it faster."

Prevention not detection. Quality is designed into the product or service, so errors are prevented from occurring rather than detected and then corrected.

Management by fact. Data-based feedback is used to measure progress and to monitor performance; intuition and gut feeling are put on the back burner.

Long-range outlook. There is a continual monitoring of the external environment to answer the question: What level of quality or service will we need to provide to our customers over the next 12–36 months and how can this goal be attained?

Partnership development. Cooperation is promoted between the organization and its customers and vendors, thus developing a network system that helps drive up quality and hold down costs.

Public responsibility. Corporate citizenship and responsibility are fostered by sharing quality-related information with other organizations that can profit from these ideas and by working to reduce negative impacts on the community by eliminating product waste generation and product defects or recalls.

TQM Tools

There are a wide array of TQM tools that are valuable to both supervisors and workers. The following examines two of the most common and useful tools: data collection and Pareto charts.

Data Collection.   *Data collection* is a tool used to identify, solve, or prevent problems. The information that is collected must meet four criteria:

Data collection must meet four criteria.

1.   Recorded clearly, so that someone looking at the information can easily understand it.

2.   Accurate in terms of reflecting what has actually happened.
3.   Reliable for decision-making purposes.
4.   Helpful in highlighting action to be taken.

There are a number of data collection sheets that are used for gathering and analyzing information. The most common is the check sheet. A *check sheet* is an easy-to-understand form used to answer the question: How often are certain events happening? The major benefit of a check sheet is that it turns opinion into facts. There are four steps involved in constructing this sheet:

There are four steps in creating a check sheet.

1.   Agree on precisely what is to be observed, so that everyone is collecting data on the same event or occurrence.
2.   Decide on the time period during which the data will be collected, such as every morning for two weeks beginning the first Monday of next month.
3.   Design the form so that it is easy to use, ensure that all columns are clearly labeled, and leave enough space to enter the data.
4.   Collect the data consistently and accurately, and make sure that there is sufficient time allowed for getting all of the information.

Figure 2–2 illustrates the most popular type of check sheet used for recording problems or errors. The sheet is laid out so that the specific problems/errors can be identified and their occurrences recorded. This sheet can also be used as a basis for additional analysis. For example, data can be collected for a second week to compare the results. It might turn out that, during the week of January 9–13, some full-time typists were home with the flu and temporary help was being used. Or the department may have been swamped with work, thus driving up the number and types of errors.

Pareto Chart.   A *Pareto chart* is a special form of vertical bar graph that helps to identify which problems are to be solved and in what order. The basic idea behind this analysis is the Pareto principle or *80/20 theory,* which holds that 80 percent of all outcomes can be attributed to 20 percent of all causes. For example, 80 percent of all mistakes are caused by 20 percent of the personnel, or 80 percent of these mistakes can be attributed to 20 percent of all possible causes. Simply put, a small number of problems account for a large percentage of what is going wrong.

Pareto charts typically are based on information from check sheets or similar information-gathering forms. These charts are constructed by following seven basic steps:

1.   Decide on the problem to be examined and how the information will be gathered. For example, identify the major reasons for customer complaints regarding the field service people. Or determine the number of accidents that have occurred on the factory floor over the last twelve months and the major reasons for these accidents.

Problem/Error Check Sheet

Time Period: _January 9-13, 1995_   Date: _1/30/95_

Purpose: _Determine typing mistakes_   Name: _A. Sawyer_

in public relations department   Department: _Public Relations_

Problem/Error	January 9	10	11	12	13	Total	%
Bold Lettering	///	//	////	//	///	14	5%
Centering	//	/	//	/	///	9	4%
Incorrect Page Numbers	/	//	/	/	/	6	2%
Missed Paragraphs	//	//	/	//	/	8	3%
Punctuation	ᴌᴋᴛ ᴌᴋᴛ //	ᴌᴋᴛ ᴌᴋᴛ ᴌᴋᴛ ᴌᴋᴛ ᴌᴋᴛ	ᴌᴋᴛ ᴌᴋᴛ ᴌᴋᴛ ///	ᴌᴋᴛ ᴌᴋᴛ ᴌᴋᴛ ᴌᴋᴛ ᴌᴋᴛ	ᴌᴋᴛ ᴌᴋᴛ ᴌᴋᴛ ///	98	38%
Spacing	ᴌᴋᴛ	////	ᴌᴋᴛ /	ᴌᴋᴛ //	///	25	10%
Spelling	ᴌᴋᴛ ////	ᴌᴋᴛ ᴌᴋᴛ	ᴌᴋᴛ ᴌᴋᴛ ᴌᴋᴛ //	ᴌᴋᴛ ᴌᴋᴛ	ᴌᴋᴛ ////	55	21%
Tables	//	/		/	/	5	2%
Underlining	ᴌᴋᴛ ᴌᴋᴛ //	ᴌᴋᴛ /	ᴌᴋᴛ ///	ᴌᴋᴛ //	ᴌᴋᴛ //	40	15%
					Totals:	260	100%

FIGURE 2-2

There are seven steps in creating a Pareto chart.

2. Determine the unit of measurement. Examples include the number of times something happened, how much it cost, and soon.
3. Select the time period to be studied, for example, all three work shifts for each of the last three weeks.
4. Gather the information. For example, determine how many accidents there have been in the factory over the last twelve months.
5. Compare the frequency and cost of each category relative to all other categories. For example, Defect A occurred 47 times, while Defect B happened 92 times; or Defect A cost $13,375 annually while Defect B cost $21,850 annually.
6. List the categories from left to right on the horizontal axis in their order of decreasing frequency or cost. If there are some categories

with only a few entries, list them as "other." (See Figure 2–3 as an example.)

7. From the tallest bar and moving upward from left to right, draw a line that shows the cumulative frequency of the categories. (An example is provided in Figure 2–4.) This answers the question: How much of the total problem or occurrence is accounted for by each category?

In pulling together the above seven steps, the problem error check sheet in Figure 2–2 can be "Paretoed." The errors reported here in this figure, in order of magnitude, were the following:

Error	Number	Rate of occurrence (%)
punctuation	98	38
spelling	55	21
underlining	40	15
spacing	25	10
bold lettering	14	5
centering	9	4
missed paragraphs	8	3
incorrect page numbers	6	2
tables	5	2

These data can be used to construct a Pareto chart, as seen in Figure 2–4. Notice that the percentage graph runs across the figure from left to right, culminating at 100 percent. A visual analysis of the data shows that punctuation, spelling, and underlining account for 74 percent of all errors.

FIGURE 2-3

A preliminary Pareto chart for customer complaints.

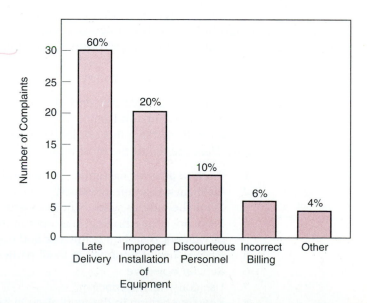

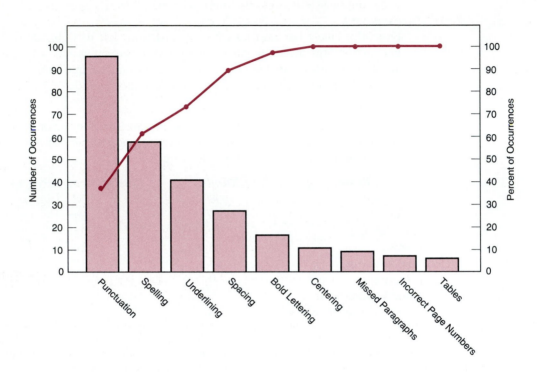

FIGURE 2-4
Typing mistakes in Public Relations.

So, in this order, these are the three problems at which correction efforts would be aimed. The supervisor and work crew can now begin planning a strategy to reduce these errors, beginning with punctuation mistakes.

Continuous Improvement

One of the major TQM concepts is *continuous improvement,* which is typified by supervisors and employees constantly trying to do things better and better. In meeting this challenge, there are a series of commonly used steps. Here are ten of the most useful:

These are useful steps in promoting continuous improvement.

1. Work to achieve maximum quality and maximum efficiency.
2. Maintain minimum inventory.
3. Eliminate tedious work, wherever possible.
4. Maintain a questioning and open-minded attitude for constant improvement based on teamwork and cooperation.
5. Pass on useful information to all parties who can benefit from it.
6. Remain objective.
7. Use constructive criticism.
8. Keep everything in the workplace in order.

9. Keep the workplace clean.

10. Develop procedures for getting things done quickly and correctly, and follow these procedures every time.

Personnel are also taught to ask the right questions in analyzing situations and are empowered to use the answers to help them decide on their course of action.[6] (To learn more about empowerment, see The Quality Challenge: Using Empowerment and Chapter 9 material on ways to motivate employees.) Here is a series of questions used by Zytec, one of America's leading electronic power suppliers:

Who: Who does it? Who is doing it? Who should be doing it? Who else can do it? Who else should do it?

What: What to do? What is being done? What else should be done? What else can be done? What else should be done?

■ ■ ■ **THE QUALITY CHALLENGE**

Using Empowerment

One of the most effective ways to increase quality is to give employees the right to make on-the-spot decisions rather than having to check with the supervisor to get an okay. A good example is provided by customer service, an area that is critical to the success of all businesses. When a customer calls with a problem, the individual wants the person who answers the phone to listen to the problem and to take the necessary action. The customer does not want to be passed from one person to the next. The person who answers the phone must have training in handling customer problems, so that he or she knows the correct steps to take. The supervisor can help in this process by following four basic steps:

1. Let the employees do their jobs without interference from you. If they have a problem or need assistance, let them ask you. Don't interject yourself into the situation.

2. If an employee handles a situation in a matter that you believe was inefficient,

discuss this with the individual, but do so by focusing on the procedures that were used. Do not attach blame or accuse the individual of being inefficient.

3. Encourage employees to take the initiative and use their empowerment to identify and solve problems. When they do something well, let them know. This will encourage them to continue using their initiative.

4. Remember that empowerment often takes away power that used to belong to you and gives it to the employees. Rather than looking on this as a loss of authority, however, you must view it as another step toward increasing the quality of output. There is plenty of other work for you to do. So leave the employees alone to use their power in a way that they believe will best serve the company. Fight the tendency to make decisions in areas that are now outside of your direct domain.

---

[6]Michael Markowich, "Employees Can Be Your Company's Best Customers," *HR Focus* (February 1993): 5.

Where: Where to do it? Where is it done? Where should it be done? Where else can it be done? Where else should it be done?

When: When to do it? When is it done? When should it be done? What other time can it be done? What other time should it be done?

Why: Why does he or she have to do it? Why do it? Why do it there? Why do it then? Why do it that way?

How: How to do it? How is it done? How should it be done? Can this method be used in other areas? Is there any other way to do it?

Integrated into these questions is a consideration of statistical process control tools such as problem error check sheets and Pareto analyses. The objective of these tools is to help the empowered personnel gather and analyze data and then make continuous improvement decisions based on the results.[7] Employees are also taught to evaluate the environment and see if there are some simple steps that can be changed that will result in continuous improvement. For example, is there a better way to organize the work and save time?

■ ■ ■ ## SUPERVISORY SKILLS
Keeping the Emphasis on TQM

There are a number of steps that supervisors need to follow in keeping the work group's emphasis on TQM. Four of the most important are these:

1. Continually look for ways to increase efficiency and effectiveness. One of the biggest productivity challenges is to maintain the work group momentum after achieving early productivity successes. There is a tendency among the personnel to believe that there is nothing else that needs to be done to improve operations. This tendency must be fought by continually directing the workers to look for additional things that can be done to improve operations.

2. If things cannot be done any better, try to do them faster. Look into redesigning the work processes so that extraneous steps can be eliminated and some jobs can be done at the same time rather than one after the other. Where possible, get the personnel to work as a group in redesigning these jobs, so that they have a full understanding of how their jobs must now be carried out. Additionally, by getting them involved in the redesign, they are going to be supportive of the new design because they played a major role in bringing it about.

3. Make TQM an integral part of the supervisory job. Each day, look for ways to improve quality, discuss new ideas with your personnel, and solicit suggestions from them. In this way, supervision of TQM efforts becomes part and parcel of overall supervision.

---

[7]Frank J. Navran, "Empowering Employees To Excel," *Supervisory Management* (August 1992): 4–5.

SUMMARY

Quality and productivity are an ongoing challenge, as organizations attempt to increase both the quantity and quality of their output. In recent years, U.S. productivity has been improving, although this battle will continue to be a supervisory challenge.

Productivity is the ratio of outputs to inputs. There are a number of ways to improve this ratio, including increasing outputs faster than inputs or decreasing inputs faster than outputs. In either event, there are a series of productivity challenges that will affect an organization's ability to do this, including managerial attitudes, the changing values of the work force, government regulations, and unions.

One reason why productivity has increased in recent years is the emergence of the total quality management (TQM) movement. TQM is an organizational strategy with accompanying techniques for delivering quality and/or service to customers. There are a host of TQM core values, including customer-driven quality, leadership, continuous improvement, full participation, reduced cycle time, prevention not detection, management by fact, long-range outlook, partnership development, and public responsibility.

Some of the most popular TQM tools include data collection, check sheets, and Pareto charts. All three are easy to understand and are widely used in industry for identifying problems and developing plans of action for dealing with them. Another key TQM concept is continuous improvement, which is typified by supervisors and employees constantly trying to do things better and better. These TQM tools and concepts will continue to be key weapons in the supervisor's battle to help management increase both productivity and quality.

REVIEW QUESTIONS

1. How is productivity measured? How does productivity increase? How does it decline? Give an example of how each of the latter two changes can come about.

2. If an organization increases its output by 25 percent, will its productivity rise? Why or why not? Explain your answer.

3. In what way are managerial attitudes a challenge to productivity? Defend your answer.

4. Why is it important to realize that TQM is an organizational strategy and not simply a tool? Explain.

5. In what way are the following important core values of TQM: customer-driven quality, continuous improvement, full participation.

6. In what way are the following important core values of TQM: reduced cycle time, prevention not detection, management by fact.

7. How does a check sheet work? When would it be used to help control quality? Give an example.

8. What is a Pareto chart? When would it be used? Of what practical value is such a chart?

9. What is the Pareto principle? Why would supervisors want to be aware of this principle?

10. How do companies go about pursuing continuous improvement? Identify and describe four common steps.

11. Why is empowerment an important TQM idea? Of what practical value is it?

12. What challenge does empowerment present to supervisors? How can they go about dealing with this challenge? Offer two recommendations for action.

KEY TERMS

Check sheet. An easy-to-understand form used to answer the question: How often are certain events happening?

Continuous improvement. A TQM strategy typified by constantly trying to do things better and better.

Cycle time. The time needed to produce the output.

Data collection. A TQM tool used to identify, solve, or prevent problems.

80/20 theory. Often called the Pareto principle, it holds that 80 percent of all outcomes can be attributed to 20 percent of all causes.

Inputs. The costs of producing goods and services, including personnel, machinery, materials, and money.

Outputs. The value of goods and services being produced.

Pareto chart. A special form of vertical bar graph that helps identify which problems are to be solved and in what order.

Productivity. The ratio of outputs to inputs.

Total quality management. An organizational strategy with accompanying techniques for delivering quality and/or service to customers.

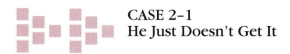

CASE 2–1
He Just Doesn't Get It

Bob Fillworth is a new supervisor at Randell Inc., a small manufacturing firm. Last year, Randell had sales of $9.6 million. This year is likely to see a decline to around $7.5 million. The major reason is that the company's biggest competitors have sharply increased the quality of their output, while Randell has not. In an effort to turn things around and regain lost ground, the firm has introduced a total quality management program. For the past six weeks, a group of consultants has been examining operations, offering preliminary courses in how to get a TQM effort off the ground, and putting together a comprehensive report for top management.

Bob has been to one four-hour training program on TQM tools and techniques. Two major topics were discussed at this meeting: The core values of TQM and the need for continuous improvement. The training consultants tried to explain why an understanding of these ideas is critical to quality improvement. They asked each of the participants to review the materials that were presented and to develop a plan of action that will do one or more of the following: improve customer-driven quality, reduce cycle time, and begin managing based on fact rather than intuition. Another meeting is scheduled for this Wednesday.

Bob has reviewed the materials provided by the consultants, the core values of TQM, and the steps that can often be used to achieve continuous improvement. However, he does not believe that these ideas are anything new. More importantly, he feels that there is very little practical value in what he has learned. "I don't know what type of action plan I'm going to develop," he told a fellow supervisor. "Most of this stuff cannot be used in the workplace. It may make good theory, but it's lousy practice." His friend disagreed with this conclusion. "There's a lot we can learn from what the consultants have told us. I think when you've had more experience, you'll have a better appreciation of what they're talking about. For the moment, however, I intend to work up a dynamite plan that will help increase quality in my department to a new level." As the supervisor walked away, Bob sat at the table slowly shaking his head. "I don't get it," he muttered.

1. In what way are the three core values presented in this case of practical value in improving quality?

2. Why does Bob think that the consultants' ideas are of limited, if any, value?

3. What would you recommend to Bob regarding development of the action plan? Offer him two useful suggestions for action.

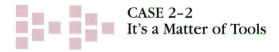

CASE 2-2
It's a Matter of Tools

The Cosmopolitan Insurance Company has been growing rapidly over the last eighteen months. A large percentage of this growth has been the result of new insurance policies the company is offering in the health care area. Cosmopolitan has introduced five new policies that are focused on keeping premiums down and minimizing out-of-pocket expenses by the insured. As a result, a number of major corporations have joined the Cosmopolitan plan, and some of the largest insurance firms in the industry are closely studying these plans so that they can offer competitive policies.

Maria Castenada is a supervisor in the claims department. As the number of policies has increased, so has the number of claims. To meet this growing work burden, Maria has had to double the size of her work group over the last seven months. However, even this is not enough. It has now become necessary to work smarter as well as harder. As a result, Maria and her work group have been given total quality management (TQM) training. They have learned how to use check sheets and Pareto charts. They used them to pinpoint common errors made by claimants in filling out their claim forms, as well as to identify the most common questions of callers regarding how to fill out the forms or regarding what has to accompany a request for payment. While they have not yet had an opportunity to employ this training, Maria's group has planned a meeting for the middle of next week to discuss how they can handle claims more quickly and accurately. For the moment, Maria has asked all of her people to think of the answer to this question: What specific problems can we attack using our TQM training, and what plan of action should we use in applying this training to the resolution of these problems? Maria hopes that she and her work group will be able to cut the time needed to process claims and answer questions by at least 25%, thanks to these new TQM ideas.

1. In what way can a check sheet be of value to Maria's work team? Explain.

2. Could the team take the information in the check sheet and put together a Pareto chart? What would this chart reveal that could be of value to the team in improving work quality?

3. Would reduced cycle time be of any value in improving work quality? Why or why not? Defend your answer.

CHAPTER 3

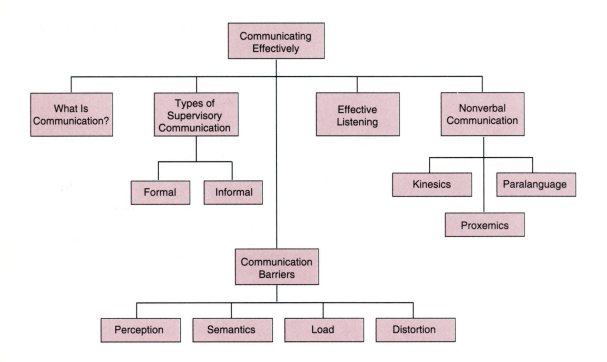

 # Communicating Effectively

"The goal of all good supervisors should be to communicate effectively with everyone regardless of rank or influence in the organization."*

CHAPTER OBJECTIVES

☐ Define the term *communication*.

☐ Describe the nature and importance of downward, upward, horizontal, and diagonal communication.

☐ Understand the value and importance of informal communication.

☐ Identify communication barriers such as semantics, load, and distortion, and discuss how to deal with them.

☐ Explain how to be a more effective listener.

☐ Describe the three major areas of nonverbal communications and explain how supervisors can become more effective in each area.

---

*G. Michael Barton, "Communication: Manage Words Effectively," *Personnel Journal* (January 1990): 32.

E ffective communication is a critical element of supervision. Successful supervisors are always successful communicators. In this chapter, we look at the environment of good supervisory communication, communication barriers, and the importance of listening and nonverbal communication. We begin by exploring what communication is all about.

WHAT IS COMMUNICATION?

Communication is the transfer of *meaning* from sender to receiver. Notice the emphasis on meaning. If meaning does not get through, effective communication has not occurred. The communication process is illustrated in Figure 3–1.

Communication begins when an idea or message to be communicated originates in the sender's mind. This idea must be *encoded,* or put into words, and transmitted to a receiver. Encoding involves the organization of the sender's thoughts into a pattern of words that is accurate and sufficient to express the idea to another party. How the sender chooses to say something is very important to the communication process.

After receiving the message, the receiver must *decode* it by deciding what it means. The opposite of encoding, the decoding process involves

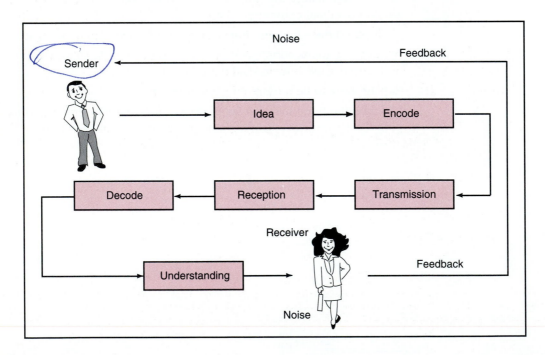

FIGURE 3–1
The communication process in action.

40

hearing a pattern of words and deciphering them to arrive at an *under-standing* of meaning.

Finally, the receiver can become the sender by providing feedback in the form of questions ("Can you tell me more about what you mean?") or statements ("I agree with your comments."). In fact, *feedback* is any look, action, word, or other sign given to the sender that shows that a message has been received and by its nature suggests what meaning was decoded.

Two critical elements often interfere with the communication process. First the coding process is very complex. The way we encode or decode messages is largely based on our past experiences, our attitudes, and values, all of which form our *perception* or interpretation of reality. Perception is a primary stumbling block to effective communication because people's perceptions often are different.

Some components of our perception may be physical traits such as color blindness or a hearing disability that clearly alter our interpretation of reality. The larger part of our perception, however, is composed of psychological qualities such as intelligence, personality traits such as defensiveness or aggressiveness, and our "code of past experience." Psychologists assume that everything we have previously experienced is locked in our minds and has an effect on our behavior. For example, imagine a friend telling you about her wonderful new German shepherd. You automatically remember the dog that bit you when you were a child. The way you distort your face in distaste quickly tells your friend you think she's crazy for buying such a beast! Perception has operated and feedback has occurred.

The second hindrance is *noise*. Noise is anything that interferes with the transfer of meaning. It may be physical noise, such as a loud conversation outside your office door, a fly buzzing, or your friend waving from the hallway. With this general understanding of communication, let's next look at the types of supervisory communication.

TYPES OF SUPERVISORY COMMUNICATION

There are two basic types of supervisory communications: formal and informal. Both are essential to effective supervision.

Formal Communication

Formal communication refers to the routine, organizationally prescribed channels of communication. These channels are reflected in the organization chart. They consist of four categories: downward, upward, horizontal and diagonal.

Downward channels are the most commonly used.

Downward Communication. *Downward communication* channels are the most frequently used. They carry information from an organization's upper levels to its lower levels. This form of communication usually transfers the following five kinds of data.

1.   Specific instructions about what to do and how to do it.
2.   Rationale for a particular job and how it relates to other jobs.
3.   Policies and procedures.
4.   Performance feedback to employees.
5.   Corporate goals and objectives.[1]

To better understand the necessity for multidirectional communication, see "The Quality Challenge: Total Involvement."

Two common ways of transmitting information are oral and written. Oral communications have the advantage of being quick and direct, and the personal delivery system makes employees feel important. However, oral messages can be distorted as they move from one level of the organization to another.

THE QUALITY CHALLENGE
Total Involvement

Quality is not confined to a department or group. It is everyone's job. As a result, communication flows in all directions: up, down, horizontal, and diagonal. A good example is provided by typical group meetings between departments for the purpose of determining how quality can be improved. In the past, many departments have operated almost autonomously of the rest of the organization. The manufacturing people did their job and tried not to be bothered by the problems confronting those in the marketing department; the research and development people worked to isolate themselves from the finance department and other groups that would try to tell them what to do. Today, however, all of this is changing. Supervisors and operating personnel from all departments are sitting down to discuss the overall effects of their actions on each other.

A good example of this is provided by the major American auto firms where cars used to be designed by the engineering people, produced by the manufacturing people, and sold by the marketing force. There was little communication between the three. Now, firms such as Ford Motor and General Motors have formed preproduction groups consisting of people from all major in-house departments, so that they can talk to each other, discuss coordination problems, and plan a course of action that will result in cars moving from the drawing board to the dealer showroom in record time. Also included in these meetings are customers and suppliers who are able to provide important input to the overall process. For example, what do customers want in their new cars? How can outside suppliers play a more useful role in helping the company build a winning car? By answering these questions, the auto manufacturers are finding that they are able to improve the quality of their cars and protect their markets from foreign competition. In the past, each group pretty much kept to itself. Today there is open communication among them and, as a result, auto quality has now reached a new high!

---

[1]Daniel Katz and Robert Kahn, *The Social Psychology of Organizations* (New York: John Wiley & Sons, 1966), 239.

Written communications are more formal and permanent, but their impersonality often causes employees to disregard them. This is especially true if the receiver is confronted with information overload (see discussion of this topic in Chapter 17) or is barraged with countless written documents. Written communications may also be misinterpreted because the reader has no immediate opportunity to ask for clarification or provide immediate feedback.

Effective supervisors find that a combination of oral and written messages tend to work best. First, they communicate orally; then they follow up in writing. Written reinforcement assures the receiver that this is an important topic and also provides a record for future references.

Upward Communication. *Upward communication* channels allow for a two-way information flow from subordinate to supervisor and back. This communication system can greatly assist the supervisor in learning what is going on in the organization. The main benefits of upward communication are:

Upward channels promote a two-way flow of information.

1. Feedback regarding employee attitudes and feelings.
2. Suggestions for improved procedures and techniques as well as for new ideas.
3. Feedback regarding how well the downward communication system is working.
4. Information about work progress and goal attainment.
5. Requests from subordinates for supplies, assistance, and/or support.
6. Surfacing of employee grievances before small problems erupt into major ones.
7. Stronger involvement of employees with the organization and their jobs.
8. Buildup of trust and confidence between all levels of management.[2]

Supervisors who are able to encourage upward communication can learn a lot about the organization. Too often, however, these efforts are sabotaged by problems such as employees who conceal their thoughts because of lack of trust or the belief that management is not interested in their problems; a lack of organizational rewards for employee suggestions and feedback; or a lack of response or accessibility of supervisors. If employees feel that management is too busy to listen to them, they will soon tire of making the effort.

What can supervisors do to encourage upward communication? Research offers the following suggestions:

---

[2]Jane W. Gibson and Richard M. Hodgetts, *Organizational Communication: A Managerial Perspective,* 2nd ed. (New York: HarperCollins, 1991), 220.

Ways to improve upward communication

☐ Get to know employees and make each one feel important.
☐ Pay attention to suggestions from employees and explain why some suggestions cannot be implemented.
☐ Build an atmosphere of trust.
☐ Learn to be a good listener.

Horizontal Communication. *Horizontal or lateral, communication* takes place between people on the same level of the organizational ladder. Much of what occurs in the horizontal channels takes place in the informal system; however, formal horizontal communication does serve a number of important purposes including:

Horizontal communication serves a number of purposes.

1. Coordinates work of interdependent units or departments.
2. Shares information and avoids the time-consuming nature of vertical channels.
3. Facilitates problem solving of all kinds. People are able to share information and learn from each other.
4. Lessens interdepartmental competition and conflict by promoting stronger relationships among people.

There is some evidence that the use of formal, horizontal communication is related to the size of the organization.

> "It is interesting to note that managers in large organizations are significantly more concerned with vertical communication than are managers in small organizations. Managers in the small, entrepreneurial organizations are concerned with internal, horizontal communication. The formal chain of command is more closely adhered to in the bureaucratic organization, whereas horizontal communication is used in the small, entrepreneurial organization."[3]

Diagonal communication links people at different levels.

Diagonal Communication. *Diagonal communication* takes place between people on different levels of the organizational hierarchy. For example, if a lab technologist at University Medical Center wants to speak directly to the head nurse in the pediatric unit, they will use diagonal communication channels. As with horizontal communication, diagonal communication often takes place when people participate in interdepartmental meetings, committees, or task forces. Diagonal paths serve a number of organizational purposes.[4]

1. Serve increased information processing needs of rapidly changing work environments.

---

[3]Larry R. Smeltzer and Gail L. Fann, "Comparison of Managerial Communication Patterns in Small, Entrepreneurial Organizations and Large, Mature Organizations," *Group and Organization Studies* (June 1989): 211.

[4]Donald O. Wilson, "Diagonal Communication Links Within Organizations," *The Journal of Business Communication* (Spring 1992): 129–143.

2. Provide rapid access to needed information for solving complex problems.
3. Facilitate information flow when formal rules are lacking.
4. Deliver clarification on existing policies and procedures.

Like horizontal communication, much diagonal dialogue takes place in the informal communication system.

INFORMAL COMMUNICATION

As important as supervisory communication is, much of the actual communication in organizations occurs in informal channels, often referred to as the grapevine. Many supervisors try to deny its existence or discourage its operation because of the misconceptions about the accuracy of the grapevine. This is wasted effort.

> "Since the grapevine arises from social interactions, it is as fickle, dynamic, and varied as people are. It is the expression of their natural motivation to communicate. It is the exercise of their freedom of speech and is a natural, normal activity."[5]

The good news is that contrary to the common belief that the grapevine carries nothing but rumor and error, studies show that 75 to 95 percent of grapevine information is accurate.[6] The key for supervisors is to work with the informal network, not try to eliminate it.

> "The way to deal with your company's grapevine is to keep a firm grip on it—not to pull it down, but to feel its vibrations. This informal channel is valuable for influencing employee attitudes and perceptions, and it's critical for conveying information to you. By passing information through your organization via the grapevine, you will remain in touch with your employees. You will understand their concerns, and you will have the opportunity to squelch rumors long before you have to sit down and compose a memo."[7]

The informal system has a number of characteristics that clearly distinguish it from the formal system. For instance, an informal system:

Characteristics of the Informal System

☐   Transmits messages fast.
☐   Uses predominantly oral channels.
☐   Handles nonroutine events and news better than the formal system.
☐   Orients itself toward people rather than objects.

---

[5]Jitendra Mishra, "Managing the Grapevine," *Public Personnel Management* (Summer 1990): 214.

[6]Keith Davis, "The Care and Cultivation of the Corporate Grapevine," *Dun's* (July 1973): 44.

[7]Judi Brownell, "Grab Hold of the Grapevine," *The Cornell Hotel and Restaurant Administration Quarterly* (August 1990): 83.

TABLE 3–1

Characteristics of formal and informal communication systems

Variable	Formal Communication	Informal Communication
Speed	Slow	Fast
Nature	Deliberate, planned	Spontaneous
Form	Mostly written	Mostly oral
Focus	Routine events	Nonroutine events
Control	Management	Employees

☐   Falls under the control of the workers, not management.
☐   Motivates employees by keeping them involved and interested.

Table 3–1 compares some of the key characteristics of the formal and informal systems.

A healthy grapevine offers management several advantages. First, it provides a psychological safety valve for employees to let off steam and vent their anxieties and frustrations. Second, the grapevine provides a ready-to-read barometer for supervisors to assess employee satisfaction and motivation. Third, the informal system greatly influences the culture of the organization or the quality of work life for employees and management alike. Healthy grapevines help promote cooperative work teams and establish norms of acceptable behavior. Finally, grapevines help information flow by providing an alternative to overburdened formal channels.

Of course, informal communication also has its drawbacks. First, undeniably there is some degree of error carried in the grapevine. Employees often feed the channel with self-serving information. For example, sales managers may be quick to boast that their group surpassed last month's sales by 10 percent but fail to mention that two new salespeople joined their group a month and a half ago! In addition, information processed by the grapevine lacks the accountability element of the formal system. For example, when someone puts a message into the formal system, all employees know where to take their questions. The originator has obvious responsibility. In the informal system, it is often unclear where the information originated.

COMMUNICATION BARRIERS

Why is it that no matter how hard supervisors try, sometimes they are still misunderstood? This happens because no transfer of *meaning* has occurred or there has been a transfer of incorrect meaning. Four common communication barriers contribute to this problem: perception, semantics,

SUPERVISORY SKILLS
Types of Supervisory Communications

1. Be aware that employees crave information. If they can't get it from you, they will go to less authoritative sources. Make it your business to find out what your employees need to know and make sure they get that information!

2. Understand the relative advantages and disadvantages of oral versus written communications. Use a combination of both if your message is really important.

3. Encourage upward communication. Take the time to ask employees for their input and to listen to them. Give them feedback concerning all results of their input.

4. Do everything that you can to promote a climate of trust. Don't betray the confidence of your employees. Don't hoard information that they need. Be sure that when they hear "news," it is accurate and they're getting it from you.

5. Encourage communication among peers. Set a good example by coordinating efforts with supervisors in other departments. Avoid the trap of the we-they syndrome that often leads to interdepartmental conflict.

6. Tune into the grapevine. It will give you a wealth of information about the concerns of your employees and will allow you to forsee problems as well as opportunities that are developing.

---

load, and distortion. Perception has already been defined as one's interpretation of reality, and it is discussed fully in Chapter 4. We briefly look at the other three here.

Semantics

Semantics is the study of meaning in language.

Semantics, the study of meaning in language, is based on the fact that words are merely symbols for something else, such as a person or a thing. If our words evoke the wrong picture in the mind of the listener, we will not be able to communicate properly. This dilemma can be easily understood if we realize that each of 500 frequently used words has an average of twenty-eight different meanings in the dictionary.[8] But multiple meanings of words are not the only semantical pitfalls. Three other major hazards are contextual meanings, confusion of inferences for facts, and use of emotion-laden words.

Contextual meanings refers to words or statements being interpreted based on their part of speech or use in the sentence. You can *change* the subject. I can ask for *change* from my bank. He can be afraid of *change* in the office. She can bring a *change* of clothes. You can *change* places with me.

---

[8]Philip V. Lewis, *Organizational Communication: The Essence of Effective Management,* 3rd ed. (New York: John Wiley & Sons, 1987), 118.

Confusion of inference for fact represents another significant problem. An inference is an assumption based at least partially on fact. For example, "His report is fifty pages long" is a fact; "his report is long" is an inference. Long compared to what? If this sentence were spoken to ten different supervisors each would probably have a different idea as to the length of the report. How good are you at spotting inference? Take Self-Assessment Quiz 3–1 and then check your answers at the end of the chapter.

Much of the information we process is in the form of inference. The danger lies in mistaking inference for fact or in assuming people can tell one from another. Learn to tell the difference between valid and invalid inferences. For example:

Fact: The boss wants Sam's report done by 9 A.M. tomorrow morning.

Invalid Inference: Sam will finish the report by 9 A.M. tomorrow morning.

Valid Inference: Sam may finish the report by 9 A.M. tomorrow morning.

Emotion-laden words often serve to halt communication. Employees hear a word that makes them angry and they stop listening and concentrate instead on their own reactions. Name-calling is a particularly good example of this syndrome. Telling someone, "You are a real troublemaker" can only make the person feel defensive or angry. Better to say, "When you do _____, it causes a problem for me and I'd like to discuss it." Criticizing the behavior and not the person is an excellent way to defuse the emotional impact of such words. Other emotional words are less obvious than name-calling. Calling an unknown customer "dear," or "honey," for example, may halt any chance of a sale. Effective supervisors try to avoid emotion-laden words of all kinds.

Effective supervisors should also refrain from using vulgarity, crude comments, and obscenities.

■   ■   ■   **SELF-ASSESSMENT QUIZ 3–1**
Fact or Inference?

Directions: For each of the following statements, indicate whether it is a factual statement (F) or an inferential statement (I). Answers are provided at the end of the chapter.

1. John did a fantastic job today.

2. Marion is always late for work.

3. Russell expects a big raise again this year.

4. Linda finished four more circuit boards today than she did yesterday.

5. Sandra sent out 150 bills last week.

6. Charlie complains about everything.

7. Margaret landed a really big account.

8. Webster wants to do only the easy jobs around here.

9. Janet said she felt ill last night.

10. Ruth never takes a lunch break.

"Managers who use vulgarity often feel it adds an extra bit of shock and so-phistication to their interchanges with employees. In most cases, however, it alienates employees and places them on the defensive. Using put downs, snappy replies, and vulgarity destroys the speaker's credibility."[9]

Load

Load refers to both amount and complexity of information.

Communication *load* refers to the amount and the complexity of messages received by an individual. The two types of communication load problems are underload and overload.

Underload occurs when an employee is cut off from the main infor-mation lines of the organization. They are left out of communication be-cause they really don't need the information to do their jobs. Common ex-amples of people who might suffer from underload are route salespeople or customer service representatives. These people are away from the of-fice most of the time and can easily feel left out of or cut off from the main flow of communication. Underload often results in workers feeling apathetic about their jobs and the organization in general.

Overload occurs when an employee is unable to handle all of the in-formation that is being received. Information overload results in inefficient and ineffective information processing, a decrease in the quality of deci-sions, reduced job satisfaction, low productivity, and increased absen-teeism and turnover. In its extreme form, overload can cause employee alienation and even disorientation. For many employees, overload equates with stress and its accompanying symptoms, such as loss of productivity, inability to make decisions, and general irritability.

Distortion

In every organization a good deal of what is communicated becomes dis-torted or changed as it is passed from person to person. This transforma-tion is particularly true for oral communications. Ralph Nichols, a commu-nications expert, found that as information was passed from board of directors to vice presidents to general supervisors (only two levels) 44 per-cent of the message was lost. By the time it got to the workers (the fifth level), 80 percent of the meaning was gone![10]

Reasons for distor-tion

Why does distortion take place? Three of the main reasons are sharp-ening, leveling, and resisting ambiguity. *Sharpening* is the listener's ten-dency to focus on the part of a message that interests him or her and to pass along only that information. In the process only the details that the listener emphasizes are sharpened, and the rest of the message may be

---

[9]G. Michael Barton, "Communication: Manage Words Effectively," *Personnel Journal* (January 1990): 37.

[10]Ralph G. Nichols, "Listening Is Good Business," *Management of Personnel Quarterly* (Win-ter 1962): 4.

lost. *Leveling* is the dropping or discarding of information that is regarded as unnecessary or unimportant. Take the following example. Roger reads a memo on his supervisors's desk. It says there may be a 5 percent reduction in staff over the next six months. But he fails to note the surrounding paragraphs, which portray this event as a remote possibility. He goes back to his desk and calls his friend Barney to say that he read an official notice that there would be an immediate 5 percent layoff and adds that he's sure this is only the beginning! Roger has sharpened the part of the message that caused him the most anxiety and levelled the rest. *Resisting ambiguity* is the habit of taking communicated information and "filling in the blanks" in such a way that the entire message makes sense to us. This process is called *closure*. For example, what do you see here?

Chances are you called the assortment of dots a circle. You filled in the spaces to form a familiar pattern. This is what we do with communication—only we often put the pieces together erroneously and pass them along as if they were fact.

EFFECTIVE LISTENING

Most people are poor listeners.

Communication studies point to an alarming fact: We are a nation of poor listeners. Statistics gathered in the late 1950s still hold true: although we spend about 45 percent of our time listening, we listen with only a 25 percent efficiency rate. That means that after only twenty-four hours, we are able to recall accurately only about one-quarter of everything we have heard.[11] How important is this to the supervisor? According to one communications expert, poor listening could be causing American businesses endless problems.

> "In business, the list of problems caused by poor listening is endless. Because of ineffective listening, letters have to be retyped, appointments have to be rescheduled, orders have to be reprocessed, products have to be remanufactured, and shipments have to be rerouted. Because of poor listening, employees cannot understand and satisfy customers' and clients' desires; and managers cannot understand and satisfy employees' needs. As a result,

---

[11]Ralph G. Nichols, "Listening Is a 10-Part Skill," *Nation's Business* (July 1957): 57.

SUPERVISORY SKILLS
Communication Barriers

1. Be careful in your choice of words. When you are talking to others, be sure to pay attention to the context of your message. Be wary of creating inferences that are disguised as facts. Provide a good example by being precise in your communications. Check for understanding by asking for feedback.

2. Do an audit of your speech habits. Are you a frequent user of emotion-laden words? Be aware of the bias they inject into the communication. Try to eliminate such words, or when you do use them, be aware of their possible effect.

3. Check out your communication load and that of your employees. Are people getting the information they need to do their jobs, or are they being inundated with more than they can handle? Conversely, are some people in your department left out of the communication lines? Are these people unmotivated or apathetic?

4. Understand the effects of sharpening, leveling, and resisting ambiguity. Cut back on the number of levels through which a message must pass. Repeat the important parts of your message, and solicit feedback to see that your message is understood.

---

customers and clients are alienated, and unnecessary employee-employer conflicts disrupt operations and decrease productivity."[12]

Why are people such poor listeners? For one thing, our schools have spent years teaching us how to read and write, but in many cases not even one day teaching us how to listen. For another, we all assume that listening comes naturally and with little effort. Unfortunately, that is not true. Many supervisors have one or more of the following habits characteristic of poor listeners.

Characteristics of poor listeners.

1. Deciding in advance that the subject is uninteresting and therefore not worthy of attention.
2. Focusing on the poor delivery of the speaker rather than on what the individual is saying.
3. Becoming overexcited and anxious to make one's own rebuttal and often missing important points the speaker is making.
4. Focusing on the "bottom line" and missing key ideas.
5. Outlining everything even if it is not being presented in outlinable order.
6. Pretending to pay attention while thinking of something else.
7. Allowing distractions to interfere.
8. Avoiding difficult material and therefore not getting experience at listening and concentrating on difficult subjects.

---

[12]Jack E. Hulbert, "Barriers to Effective Listening," *The Bulletin* (June 1989): 3.

9. Responding emotionally to certain words or phrases.

10. Daydreaming because of the difference between speech speed and thought speed. We can think (therefore listen) much faster than someone can speak to us, so we tune in and out of conversations, gradually losing track of what is being said.[13]

How can you, the supervisor, become a better listener? Some of the most useful tips include the following:

☐ Take active responsibility as a listener; don't put the whole burden on the speaker.

☐ Resist distractions; concentrate on what's being said.

☐ If you're listening to other than a casual conversation, take notes and report to someone else (within one working day) the speaker's intent and the content of the speech.

☐ Identify the speaker's purpose (small talk, emotional unloading, informative report, persuasive address, or entertaining repartee) and adapt to it.

☐ Develop listening skills by identifying speech patterns and themes, rather than isolated facts.

☐ Stay alert if the speaker's delivery is slow; use your thinking time to evaluate, anticipate, and review what the speaker is saying.

☐ Find the areas of interest between you and the speaker. Ask, "What can I learn from this?"

☐ Control your emotions. Don't get upset by trigger words, subjects, or issues.

■   ■   ■   **SUPERVISORY SKILLS**
Effective Listening

1. Examine your listening habits. Do you really listen to your employees? Do they come to you with their concerns? Remember the first rule of listening is to shut your mouth and open your ears! Decide now to invest the time it takes to listen effectively and let your employees know you care. Listening to people makes them feel worthwhile and important to you, and they will probably have some good ideas you may have otherwise missed.

2. When you are too busy to listen, make arrangements to see the person later when the setting is more conducive to your paying full attention. Don't ever pretend to listen, it takes only one occasion of pretense to lose the employees' trust.

3. Help your employees become better listeners. Often just calling people's attention to this problem can help alleviate the problem. Also look into the possibility of a formal listening workshop.

[13]Nichols, 56–60.

Listening can be improved at both the organizational level and the personal level. Dramatic improvement can be made at the organizational level by redesigning office layout so that listening is more natural and comfortable (see Figure 3–2). At the personal level, develop encouraging behaviors such as nodding and eye contact to show the speaker that you are paying attention.[14]

FIGURE 3–2
Communication through the use of office space.

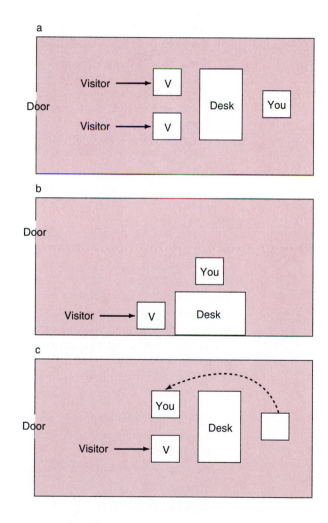

[14]Marilyn Helms and Paula J. Haynes, "Are You Really Listening? The Benefits of Effective Intra-Organizational Listening," *Journal of Managerial Psychology* (June 1992): 17–21.

NONVERBAL COMMUNICATION

In order to be an effective listener, supervisors must be able to read non-verbal cues. This is especially important when verbal messages are restrained, cautious, or misleading. Often verbal messages are completely contradicted by nonverbal context. In this case you will probably believe the nonverbal signals rather than the words. For example, if your boss keeps on writing and never looks up when you are speaking, you are likely to feel that she is not paying attention even if her words assure you that she is paying attention.

A major study that investigated the importance of nonverbal behavior in organizations included these suggestions:

> "Recommendations for improving nonverbal skills included paying more attention to nonverbal cues, especially the facial expressions, engaging in more eye contact, and probing for more information when verbal and nonverbal cues are discrepant. Managers should be aware that most employees feel frustration and distrust when receiving conflicting signals from their supervisors, and should try to modify their behavior by being more honest in communicating their emotions."[15]

Nonverbal communication can be divided into three categories: kinesics, proxemics, and paralanguage.

Kinesics

Kinesics is the study of body language and facial expressions.

Kinesics, the study of body language and facial expression, represents the most common type of nonverbal behavior. Body language can reveal much about what the speaker is trying to communicate (or hold back). *Posture,* for example, can show whether a person is confident, aggressive, timid, tired, friendly, afraid, and so on. *Gestures* help clarify spoken language. These gestures may be in the form of "illustrators," which physically make the same point as the words spoken; "regulators," which pace the conversation; "adaptors," which are habitual, learned behavior patterns; and "emblems," which are gestures having commonly understood meaning in the culture at large. An example of each follows:

> Illustrator: (Point to window) "Look at that bird!"
>
> Regulator: (Patting an employee on the back) "I really want to hear what you think."
>
> Adaptor: (Smoothing down your hair) "I'm ready, let's go."
>
> Emblem: (Waving the hand) "Hello!"[16]

---

[15]Gerald H. Graham, Jeanne Unruh, and Paul Jennings, "The Impact of Nonverbal Communication in Organizations: A Survey of Perceptions," *The Journal of Business Communication* (Winter 1991): 60.

[16]Paul Ekman and Wallace V. Friesen, "Nonverbal Leakage and Clues to Deception," *Psychiatry* 32 (February 1989): 96–97.

In body language, facial expression and eye movements have the most meaning. Ekman and Friesen found that there are six universal facial expressions: anger, happiness, sadness, surprise, fear, and disgust.[17] Even this list is not comprehensive or totally accurate, however, because different cultures teach people to mask their feelings differently. Also, certain feelings are evoked by different incidents in various cultures. This cultural connotation of all body language is important, because a supervisor may have employees from diverse places and ethnic groups.

As for the eyes, they may truly be, as the saying goes, the mirrors of the soul. Eye contact in particular is seen as very influential: If you look at your employees while speaking or listening, they will feel more important and the communication environment will be more open. However, eye contact also has a cultural context. For example, in Hispanic and Oriental cultures, lowered eyes are a sign of respect, and eye contact is, therefore, much less significant.

Table 3–2 shows a variety of common negative nonverbal cues that supervisors should try to avoid. Notice that several of them relate to eye contact.

Proxemics

Proxemics is the study of how we use space.

Proxemics is the study of how we use space and what that use says about us. It is based on the concept that people, like animals, are territorial beings and will protect "their space." At work, people exhibit this territorial behavior in regard to their offices, their possessions, and even their ideas.

In an enclosed office with the traditional desk pattern (see Figure 3–2a, p. 53), communications will be more formal and less open than with the other styles shown in Figure 3–2. Figure 3–2b shows a seating arrangement where the desk is no longer used as a barrier; having open space between supervisor and employees is a sign of equality or openness. If we really want to counsel employees and make them feel at home, we might consider the arrangement in Figure 3–2c, where we come around from behind the desk and sit on the same side as the employee.

It is also interesting to note how people protect personal space. In American culture this space tends to be about 3 feet in radius. If strangers get closer than that, we tend to back off or uncomfortably stand our ground. Even our friends rarely get closer to us than 18 inches. Thus supervisors should be aware of the dynamics of personal space and respect employees' space in order to promote comfortable relationships.

---

[17]Paul Ekman and Wallace V. Friesen, *Unmasking the Face: A Guide to Recognizing Emotions from Facial Clues* (Englewood Cliffs, N.J.: Prentice-Hall, 1975), 22.

TABLE 3-2
Common nonverbal cues

Nonverbal Communication	Signal Received	Reaction from Receiver
• Manager looks away when talking to the employee.	I do not have this person's undivided attention.	Supervisor is too busy to listen to my problem or simply does not care.
• Failure to acknowledge greeting from fellow employee.	This person is unfriendly.	This person is unapproachable.
• Omnious glaring (i.e., the evil eye).	I am angry.	Reciprocal anger, fear or avoidance depending on who is sending the signal in the organization.
• Rolling of the eyes.	I am not being taken seriously.	This person thinks they are smarter or better than I am.
• Deep sighing.	Disgust or displeasure.	My opinions do not count. I must be stupid or boring to this person.
• Heavy breathing (sometimes accompanied by hand waving).	Anger or heavy stress.	Avoid this person at all costs.
• Eye contact not maintained when communicating.	Suspicion and/or uncertainty.	What does this person have to hide?
• Manager crosses arms and leans away.	Apathy and closed mindedness.	This person already has made up their mind; my opinions are not important.
• Manager peers over glasses.	Skepticism or distrust.	He or she does not believe what I am saying.
• Continues to read a report when employee is speaking.	Lack of interest.	My opinions are not important enough to get the supervisor's undivided attention.

Source: G. Michael Barton, "Communication: Manage Words Effectively," *Personnel Journal* (January 1990): 36.

Paralanguage

Paralanguage refers to how we say what we say.

Paralanguage refers to how we say what we say. We convey a lot of meaning by the words we choose to accent and by our tone of voice, loudness or softness, pitch, and rhythm. Consider, for example, all the different ways a supervisor might say, "Sam, I'd like you to be here at 9 A.M."

"Sam, I'd like you to be *here* at 9 A.M." (not at your office)

"Sam, *I'd* like you to be here at 9 A.M." (even though other people might not want you here)

SUPERVISORY SKILLS
Nonverbal Communication

1. Be aware that nonverbal signs often are more important to communication than verbal messages. Watch for conflicting signals. If what your employees say is contradicted by their body language, for example, look further for clarification. Likewise, be careful that your own nonverbal language does not betray your lack of interest or any other emotion that you don't want revealed. Use your nonverbal behavior in a positive way to emphasize points.

2. A knowledge of proxemics can be very helpful. Do not show your power and authority inadvertently by invading the space of your employees. Respect their office or work space the way you would want them to respect yours. Remember that invasion of space tends to put people on the defensive and that listening stops when people get defensive.

3. Watch your tone of voice, loudness, and other paralinguistic cues. Merely switching from your normal voice level to a loud voice can create noise in the communication environment. Employees may concentrate on this strange pattern, not on what you are saying.

4. When interpreting body language or other types of nonverbal behavior, remember to look for clusters of cues, not just isolated ones. For example, crossed arms may not mean resistance but just that the room temperature is too cold.

5. Be aware of the cultural context of nonverbal behavior. For instance, some Latin American and European cultures are more open and less protective of their personal space than North Americans. Be careful that your nonverbal behavior (touch, tone of voice, posture, and so on) does not offend your employees.

"Sam, I'd like *you* to be here at 9 A.M. (don't send your secretary)

"Sam, I'd like you to be here at *9 A.M.*" (not 9:30 like today)

Another example concerns tone of voice. If a supervisor asks an employee to see her the next morning at 8:30 A.M. the tone of voice (friendly, very serious, or angry) will determine the employee's expectations about the upcoming meeting.

Tuning in to the nuances of paralanguage can greatly help supervisors avoid mistakes in interpretation.

SUMMARY

Communication is the transfer of meaning from sender to receiver. The two basic types of communication are formal and informal.

Formal communication takes four forms: downward, upward, horizontal (or lateral), and diagonal. Downward communication is used to carry information from upper to lower levels of the hierarchy. Communication may be in an oral or written mode. Oral is faster; written is more formal and provides a record of what is sent. Upward communication allows for an information flow from subordinate to superior. Supervisors who are able to encourage upward communication can learn a great deal about the organization. Horizontal communication, which takes place between people on the same level of the hierarchy, is particularly useful in coordinating work of interdependent units or departments.

Diagonal communication occurs when people at different levels in different departments communicate.

Informal communication uses the grapevine. In contrast to formal channels, the grapevine is generally faster, and more people-oriented, controlled by the workers, and mainly oral in nature. The grapevine acts positively by providing an outlet for employees' frustrations, but it also has the disadvantage of allowing errors in messages and not furnishing means to accountability.

Communication barriers block the accurate transfer of intended meaning. For instance, the pitfalls of semantics include multiple meanings, contextual meanings, confusion of fact for inference, and emo-

tion-laden words. Another barrier is load which refers to the amount and complexity of messages received by an individual. Both overload and underload of information can occur. A third barrier is distortion which can be caused by sharpening, leveling, and resisting ambiguity.

Most people are poor listeners. They allow themselves to be distracted by certain words or methods of delivery. To be effective one must take an active role and resist all distractions.

Supervisors also need to understand nonverbal communication. The three major categories of nonverbal communication are kinesics, proxemics, and paralanguage. Kinesics is the study of body language and facial expression. Proxemics looks at how people use space and what this use says about them. Paralanguage refers to how people say what they say. All three are important to effective communication.

REVIEW QUESTIONS

1. In your own words, what is meant by the term *communication?*

2. What types of data are communicated with downward communication? How can supervisors improve their downward communication? Explain.

3. What are the main benefits of upward communication? Identify and describe four.

4. How can supervisors encourage upward communication? Explain.

5. Of what benefit is horizontal, or lateral, communication to the organization? Explain.

6. Discuss the purposes that diagonal communications channels serve.

7. How does the informal organization differ from the formal organization?

What are some of the characteristics that distinguish it? Identify four.

8. Are there any advantages of a healthy grapevine? Explain.

9. What is meant by the term *semantics?* In what way are the following terms semantical problems: multiple meanings, contextual meanings, confusion of inference for fact, emotional-laden words.

10. What is meant by the term *load?* In what way is underload a communication barrier? In what way is overload a communication barrier?

11. Three of the main reasons for distortion are *sharpening, leveling,* and *resisting ambiguity.* What does this statement mean? In your answer, be

sure to describe each of the three terms.

12. What are some of the habits of ineffective listeners? Identify five.

13. How can supervisors become better listeners? Offer at least five guidelines for action.

14. What is meant by the term *kinesics?* How can an understanding of this subject be of value to the supervisor in communicating? Explain.

15. How can an understanding of proxemics be of value to a supervisor's communication efforts? In your answer, incorporate a discussion of Figure 3–2.

16. Of what value is an understanding of paralanguage to supervisors? Explain.

KEY TERMS

Communication. Transfer of meaning from a sender to a receiver.

Diagonal communication: Information transferred between people at different organizational levels in different departments.

Downward communication. Information transferred from superiors to subordinates.

Feedback. Any look, action, or word given by the receiver to show that a message has been received and understood.

Grapevine. Common expression to characterize informal communication.

Horizontal or lateral communication. Information transferred to people on the same level of the hierarchy.

Kinesics. Study of body language and facial expression.

Leveling. Dropping or discarding information that is regarded as unnecessary or unimportant.

Load. Amount and complexity of messages received by an individual.

Paralanguage. Major category of nonverbal behavior referring to how people say what they say.

Proxemics. Study of how people use space and what this says about them.

Resisting ambiguity. Habit of taking communicated information and filling in the blanks in such a way as to have the message make sense.

Semantics. Study of meaning in language.

Sharpening. Tendency to focus on the part of the message that interests us and pass along only that part of the message.

Upward communication. Information transferred from subordinates to superiors.

ANSWERS TO SELF-ASSESSMENT QUIZ 3–1

1. Inference. What does "fantastic" mean? What did he actually do? Can it be measured?

2. Inference. Is Marion *always* late? *Often* late? *Occasionally* late? Exactly how often is Marion late?

3. Inference. What is a "big" raise? Even if we know he wants 10 percent, is that "big" if he makes $15,000 a year? $100,000?

4. Fact

5. Fact

6. Inference. Surely, Charlie doesn't complain about *everything*.

7. Inference. How big is "really big"?

8. Inference. Whose definition of "easy"? What is an "easy" job?

9. Fact, if Janet actually said it.

10. Inference. Does Ruth in fact *never* take a lunch break?

CASE 3-1
Gerry's Decision

When Paul Anders arrived at work on Monday morning, he could tell by the look on his secretary's face that it was going to be a busy day. "You have an appointment at 9 A.M. with the plant manager. All of the supervisors are to be there. And the manager wants to talk about next year's budget." Nodding, Paul quickly took his mail from the in-box, walked into his office, and began looking at his "to do" list for the day.

The first, and most important, item on the list was a meeting with the union shop steward. Last month there had been a problem out on the line. One of the workers was involved in a fight and the individual was fired. The union was protesting the firing, claiming that the penalty did not match the offense. At worst, they said, the individual should have been sent home with no pay for three days. Paul's boss told him to meet with the shop steward and work out an arrangement agreement to both sides. Because he would be going to the conference at 9 A.M. and would not be able to attend the meeting with the shop steward, Paul had two alternatives: delay the meeting until tomorrow or have his assistant, Gerry, sit in for him. Paul decided to have his assistant handle the meeting; he instructed his secretary to ask Gerry to come in immediately.

"Gerry," Paul said, "I want you to meet the shop steward over the fight that occurred last month. The steward wants the fellow suspended for three days without pay. We've already fired him so that would mean reinstating him and giving him back pay for all of the other days he has been denied or counting those days toward his vacation time. I want you to negotiate the matter with the steward. Suspension for three days is not a sufficient penalty. We need something a lot stronger in order to show that we won't tolerate fighting. I want you to work it out with the steward. Reinstate the fellow, but do it on our terms. Be flexible but not too flexible. Do you think you can handle it?" Gerry said she could, and with that Paul left for his conference.

Three days later Paul was called to his boss's office. When he arrived, he found the shop steward there. Paul had not thought about the steward since he turned the matter over to Gerry. Paul's boss looked concerned. "The steward tells me that you have agreed to reinstate the worker who was fighting but will not pay the man for any of the days he has been denied. He cannot apply them to his vacation time. The steward tells me that if this is your final decision, he is going to file a formal complaint. Before he does that, I thought the three of us should talk."

The meeting did not last long. Paul agreed to apply all of the days the worker was out toward the man's vacation time, and everyone agreed that the solution was acceptable. On the way out, Paul's boss said, "Your assistant was a lot tougher than she should have been. What instructions did you give her anyway?"

Once back in his office, Paul sent for Gerry. "What did you hear me tell you regarding what to do during your meeting with the shop steward?" he asked. When Gerry was done, Paul could not believe he had said those things to Gerry. "I think we had a communication breakdown," he told his assistant.

1. What did Gerry think Paul had told her? Put it in your own words.

2. What did Paul think he had told Gerry? Put it in your own words.

3. Which of the communication barriers dis-

cussed in this chapter occurred in this case? Explain.

4. How can problems like this be prevented in the future? Explain.

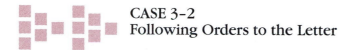

CASE 3-2
Following Orders to the Letter

September is the busiest time of the year at Allworth Manufacturing. Thus, when the production line in section 3 had trouble for the second time in a week, Charlie Bumpers thought he better get it straightened out immediately. As the head supervisor, Charlie is directly in charge of sections 3 and 4.

Charlie called in Pete Peters, the new supervisor in section 3. Their conversation went as follows:

Charlie: Pete, we seem to be having some problems in your section. The line has been down twice in the last five days. This is our busiest time of the year. We can't afford to have reoccurring problems of this type. I want you to drop that inventory control project I have you working on, find out what the problem is out on the line, and get rid of it.

Pete: Okay, I'll get out there, find out what's causing the problem, and get rid of it.

Charlie: Fine.

A fast check of the line revealed that there was a problem with the automatic control unit. Pete checked and found that it would take four hours to pull the unit and install a new one. "If you put in a new one," the maintenance man told him, "you won't have a problem with it for at least eighteen months. It's up to you. I'll do whatever you tell me." Pete told the man to replace the automatic control unit.

By late afternoon the new unit was installed and the line was operating at full speed. However, the next morning, after Charlie had received the previous day's production figures, he called in Pete. "What happened in your section? I thought you were going to fix the problem."

"I did," Pete told him, "The automatic control unit was giving us trouble so I pulled it and put in a new one."

Charlie's voice indicated that he was not happy with this decision. "You pulled the unit in the middle of a workday? Why didn't you wait until the shift was over and have the unit pulled then? You could have done preventive maintenance to get through the rest of the day. You gave up two hours of production time to replace a unit that could have waited for maintenance."

Pete was caught unawares. He thought he had done the right thing. "Look, Charlie," he said, "you told me to get rid of the problem and I did. You didn't say anything about preventive maintenance or not stopping the line."

Charlie realized that the discussion was beginning to get out of hand. "Look, let's stand back and quietly discuss this matter." With that the two men started discussing the matter from the beginning.

1. What did Charlie do wrong? Where did he make a mistake in communicating? Explain.

2. How could the problem have been prevented? In your answer be sure to include the subject of effective listening.

3. What should Charlie and Pete both learn from this experience that will make them more effective supervisors? Explain.

CHAPTER 4

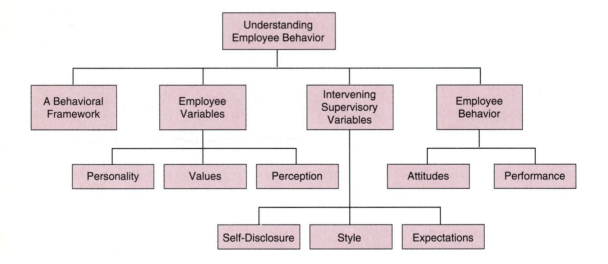

Understanding Employee Behavior

*"Every science begins with individuals."**

CHAPTER OBJECTIVES

☐ Understand a behavioral framework of human behavior.

☐ Define the term *personality* and describe the three general determinants of personality.

☐ Explain the importance of values and perception in understanding employee behavior.

☐ Explain how supervisory style and expectations can affect employee behavior.

☐ Define the term *morale* and describe the relationship between satisfaction and productivity.

*William of Ockham, died ca. 1349.

S upervisors have to deal with many people in the course of their work. Unfortunately, the diversity among people, which makes life so interesting, also can make the supervisor's job much more difficult. Understanding human behavior is a prerequisite to effective supervision. In this chapter we examine the employee variables of personality, values, and perception. Then we look at how supervisory variables interact with the individual attributes and influence employee behavior. Because of their influence, the supervisory qualities are called "intervening" variables in the model. Before looking at each of these, however, let's begin with a behavioral framework that can serve as a guide.

A BEHAVIORAL FRAMEWORK

Any attempt at building a framework or model dealing with human behavior is doomed to be simplistic; nevertheless, there is value in using such a model as a map in the discussion of a very complex subject. Figure 4–1 approaches employee behavior as being determined primarily by two sets of variables: (a) employee variables consisting of personality, values, and perception; and (b) supervisory variables consisting of self-concept, style, and expectations. When examining this framework, keep in mind two things. First, all the individual "employee variables" are also at work in the supervisor. Second, other factors impact on employee behavior. Some of these include the culture of the organization, the technology of the organization, situational qualities such as physical working conditions, and the nature of the work itself. With these limitations in mind, however, Figure 4–1 illustrates quite accurately what this chapter is all about.

EMPLOYEE VARIABLES

Supervisors should understand the individual employee characteristics that Figure 4–1 refers to as employee variables. Whereas each employee is a unique individual, he or she can be better understood by the supervisor who has a knowledge of the concepts of personality, values, and perception.

Personality

Personality is usually viewed as a product of both nature and nurture.

Personality is the complex of unique and measurable characteristics that distinguishes one individual from all others. For purposes of supervisory management, two important areas of personality, personality development and self-concept, warrant study.

Personality Development. How does personality develop? Personality is commonly believed to be a product of both nature and nurture—that is, both heredity and environment play a role. However, not everyone ac-

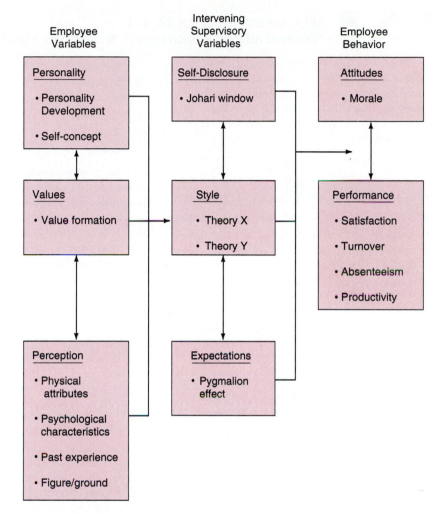

FIGURE 4-1
A behavioral framework.

cepts this explanation. Some sociobiologists, for example, claim that personality is totally dependent on genetic determination. Other groups insist that the individual is a blank slate at birth, subject to the impressions and experiences provided by the environment. What do you believe about personality? Take Self-Assessment Quiz 4–1 and see where you stand on the nature-nurture controversy.

Figure 4–2 depicts the general belief that personality is determined by many factors, which can be grouped in three general classes: genetic, environmental, and situational.

 **SELF-ASSESSMENT QUIZ 4-1**
Nature–Nurture Controversy; Where Do You Stand?

Directions: Listed below are ten factors typically considered to be part of personality. On a scale of 1 to 10, decide whether you think each one is completely or partly determined by heredity or learning. (1 = completely heredity, 10 = completely learning)

1. Intelligence   1 2 3 4 5 6 7 8 9 10

2. Creative Ability   1 2 3 4 5 6 7 8 9 10

3. Temperament   1 2 3 4 5 6 7 8 9 10

4. Wit   1 2 3 4 5 6 7 8 9 10

5. Attitude   1 2 3 4 5 6 7 8 9 10
   toward work

6. Attitude   1 2 3 4 5 6 7 8 9 10
   toward people

7. Values   1 2 3 4 5 6 7 8 9 10

8. Physical   1 2 3 4 5 6 7 8 9 10
   appearance

9. Sociability   1 2 3 4 5 6 7 8 9 10

10. Emotional   1 2 3 4 5 6 7 8 9 10
    makeup

Scoring: A person who believes strictly in the genetic determination of personality will score a 10 on this quiz. Those who believe in sole determination of personality by environment and situation will score a 100. The lower your score, the more you believe heredity is the overriding factor in personality development; the higher the score, the less important you think it is.

FIGURE 4-2
Determinants of personality.

Genetic

Potentialities
Appearance
Left brain–right brain

Environmental

Family
Peers
Experiences
Opportunities

Situational

Economy
Political system
Organization

Genes determine
physical characteris-
tics to a great ex-
tent.

Genetic Determinants. Genes are largely responsible for one's physical build and general appearance. In addition, genes may determine various potentialities in an individual. Perhaps the most controversial issue is the effect genetics has on intelligence. Although several theories have been proposed, little proof is offered and genetic determination remains an area ripe for research.

An interesting area of current study is the field of split-brain research. The work in this field is based on the belief that the right and left hemispheres of the brain each control different abilities and ways of thinking. Table 4–1 separates these characteristics into left- and right-brain functions, according to the latest research. Scientists hasten to add, however, that it is the integrated functioning of both hemispheres of the brain that produce any mental accomplishment.

> "In virtually all activities, there is an interplay between the brain's hemispheres. For example, in reading, the left hemisphere comprehends syntax and grammar, which the right does not. However, the right brain is better at understanding a story's intonation and emotion. The same is true for music and art."[1]

Environment may be
the most important
determinant of per-
sonality.

Environmental Determinants. The environment is often thought to be the most important determinant of personality. As a powerful environmental influence for most people, the family is seen as particularly important in

---

TABLE 4–1

Abilities controlled by left and right hemispheres of the brain

Right Hemisphere	*Left Hemisphere*
Controls left side of body	Controls right side of body
Abstract thinking	Logical thinking
Musical	Mathematical
Emotional	Controlled
Intuitive	Intellectual
Holistic	Analytic
Simultaneous thinking (more than one thing at a time)	Linear thinking
Mystical	Worldliness
Facial recognition	Speech or verbal

---

[1]Larue Allen and John W. Santrock, *Psychology: The Contexts of Behavior* (Madison, Wisconsin: WCB Brown & Benchmark, 1993), 57.

this process. How you are treated by parents and siblings helps determine your earliest development. As the child gets older and enters the school system, peers become an important force in personality development. What is expected by others becomes even more important as the child develops into adolescence.

Experiences and opportunities play a large role in molding a child's personality. What educational background is provided? What knowledge is learned? What different kinds of people have been encountered?

Situational Determinants.   The general environment within which the child is raised also influences the developing personality. A child reared in harsh economic times, for instance, may reflect a more serious, stricter personality than one raised in more secure times. Likewise, children reared in a totalitarian society may be much more guarded in their speech than those brought up in a democratic society.

Self-Concept.   Regardless of how personality develops, a person's self-concept is central to understanding how best to supervise that person. *Self-concept* refers to how people see themselves and how they think others see them. People who are confident and have a healthy self-esteem are generally easier to supervise and need less direct attention. Those who lack confidence and think of themselves as less intelligent or competent, usually require more patience and coaching from the supervisor. Self-concept is also directly related to how open and honest people are about their thoughts and feelings.

Self-concept refers to how a person sees himself or herself.

Values

Values are basic beliefs that determine what is important to us. Values are learned in one's youth and are fairly well set by the age of twenty. What people have experienced and learned to believe as fundamental truths at a very early age is important in framing their approach to life. Thus, people who grew up during the 1930s tend to be more security conscious in comparison to those who were raised during the much more affluent 1950s.

Values are basic beliefs that determine what is important to us.

Teenagers are still learning values; they are at a stage where peer pressure to conform is greatest and respect for adult authority is bound to be questioned. Supervisors dealing with teenagers are cautioned to remember this is a normal stage and should not treat consequent teenage employee behavior with undue harshness. For example, some teenage employees may feel they know how to do everything better than their supervisor. Wise supervisors are tolerant of this attitude and exert some patience in their supervisory style. Figure 4–3 shows the many sources of values.

Personality and values greatly influence the way a person interprets the world. In Chapter 3 the concept of perception was introduced. It is critical to our understanding of employee behavior.

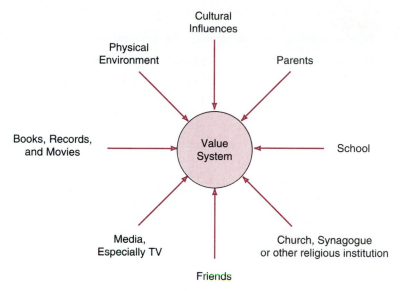

FIGURE 4-3
Sources of value formation.

Perception

Perception is a person's interpretation of reality.

As mentioned in Chapter 3, *perception* is the way a person interprets reality. Individual perception of similar stimuli may vary greatly. One employee thinks his supervisor is a fair, encouraging leader; another employee thinks the same supervisor is demanding and overbearing. Why do people see things so differently? How is perception formed? The key to perception can be summed up in three P's: physical attributes, psychological characteristics, and past experience.

Physical attributes such as size, race, body shape, and appearance influence how people perceive the world and themselves. Other physical characteristics such as handicaps also serve to shape perception. Imagine the different physical and psychological "view" of the world as seen by an employee confined to a wheelchair.

Psychological characteristics also have a very large effect on how we see the world. Values and attitudes are psychological characteristics that everyone possesses. So, too, are the various defense mechanisms we all use to cope with the world around us. Table 4–2 shows several of the more common defense mechanisms. Each has the ability to distort the user's perception.

We code and decode messages and events using the "Code of Past Experience" locked deep within ourselves. We carry in our memories every event and corresponding emotional response that we have experienced. This conglomeration of our past is constantly used in our attempts

TABLE 4-2

Common defense mechanisms seen in organizations

Mechanism	Means of Expression
Aggression	Physical or verbal attempt to cause injury to another. Example: Worker yells at another worker for using his or her tools.
Denial	Refusal to acknowledge a problem exists or to "own" feelings or reactions. Example: Supervisor denies that workers do not like him or her.
Projection	Attribution of our feelings to others. Example: Supervisor not wanting to work overtime reports workers are not willing to work overtime.
Rationalization	Provision of excuses for failure. Example: Sales manager excuses falling group sales by saying nobody has money to buy new cars.
Withdrawal	Physical or psychological removal from the frustrating situation. Example: Frustrated employee calls in sick repeatedly.
Reaction formation	Repression of an impulse and expression of its opposite. Example: Supervisor doesn't like a certain employee but goes out of his or her way to favor that person so as to not show dislike.

to interpret the present and to forecast the future. For example, if our employees have found through hard experience that supervisors do not want any input from them, we will find it difficult to tell them differently. Rather, we will have to use patience and repetitive attempts to change the coding processes of the past.

Looking at Figure 4–4, ask yourself the following questions: How old is the person in the picture? What would you guess her socioeconomic background to be? Her educational background? Would you want to get to know this person? Figure 4–4 is actually a classic picture in the field of perception. Drawn in 1905, it is known as the Old Lady–Young Lady picture because most people clearly "perceive" two different individuals. At first glance, though, their eyes usually capture one figure and they may have trouble seeing the other. If you saw an old lady, look again and try to discover the young lady. If you saw the young lady, now find the old lady.

"Figure-ground" determines the focus and background of perception.

Figure 4–5 illustrates the *figure-ground* concept of perception. Do you see the faces or the vase more clearly? If you see the faces, the black area is the figure for you and the white area is the background. What our perception chooses to focus on greatly affects the way we behave. For ex-

FIGURE 4-4
Old lady–young lady picture.

ample, if you are dealing with an older employee who reminds you physically of your dad, you may have trouble disciplining that person although his work is clearly below par. In that instance, your dad's appearance has become the "figure" and his performance the "ground," which is not a healthy position for a supervisor!

Thus far, we have examined the employee variables of personality, values, and perception. Together they help the supervisor understand and work with individual differences.

INTERVENING SUPERVISORY VARIABLES

As mentioned earlier, supervisors have to consider their own personalities, values, and perceptions as thoroughly as they do those of their employ-

FIGURE 4-5
Faces–vase picture.

■ ■ ■   SUPERVISORY SKILLS
Understanding Employee Variables

1. Remind yourself constantly that people are individuals. Each is different, so although your style and techniques may work with some, you may have to use more creativity and sensitivity in dealing with others. Take into account individual personalities. Get to know your employees and try to understand their backgrounds and values.

2. Be aware that personality and values are not carved in stone. Although they do not generally change without the presence of some significant emotional event, most people can change if this change is shown to be in their best interest and if it is a gradual process.

3. Realize that the concepts discussed in this chapter—personality, values, and perception—are difficult areas for even trained psychologists. Tread carefully when you are dealing with basic beliefs of your employees. Remember the weight of the code of past experience.

---

ees. Additionally, supervisors need to understand the impact of their self-disclosure behavior, supervisory style, and supervisory expectations. All these intervening variables are explored here in the context of what effect they have on employee behavior.

Self-disclosure

> Self-disclosure refers to how much we let others know about ourselves.

Self-disclosure refers to how much we let other people know about how we think and feel. In the work setting it means letting people know what we want done, why we want it done, and how we think they are doing. Generally it refers to the exhibition of open communication behavior. The Johari Window, which can be particularly useful in diagnosing self-disclosure behavior, is a model showing how much people know about themselves as well as how much they reveal to others. Originated by Joseph Luft and Harry Ingham, Figure 4–6 shows the basic configuration of the model.

Notice that there are four quadrants: open, blind, hidden, and unknown. The *open* quadrant refers to information that we know about ourselves and that is known to others either through observation or through self-disclosure of how we think and feel. The *hidden* quadrant contains our secrets—information we know but we are not sharing with others. The *blind* quadrant contains material known to others but unrecognized by ourselves. Finally, the *unknown* area contains that material unknown to ourselves and unknown to others; it might be otherwise called the unconscious mind. Notice that Quadrant 1 is the area where self-disclosure takes place.

Why is self-disclosure behavior so very important? Roger D'Aprix, president of Organizational Communication Services and former manager

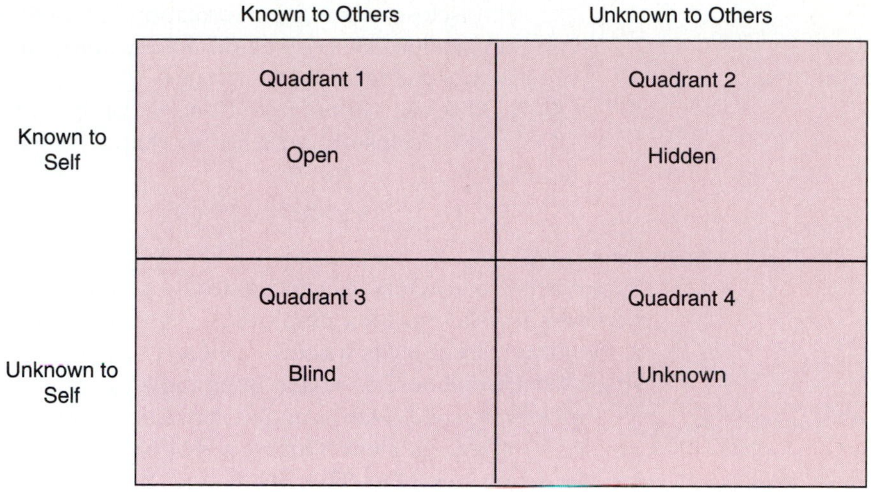

FIGURE 4-6
The Johari Window.

of employee communication for Xerox Corporation, asserts: "The work force wants to know the organization's prospects for success and the issues which jeopardize that success. Further, they want all this expressed in terms that mean something to them. They also want a human presence in the form of a boss to whom they can relate, a boss who knows what's going on and who accepts it as part of his or her job to share information and to be an intermediary to and from the organization."[2]

The message is clear. Effective supervisors must try to expand the size of their open quadrants and shrink the size of the other three. Still, self-disclosure may not be the best prescription in all cases. The following list offers some helpful dos and don'ts in this area.

1. DO self-disclose when the situation under discussion is of mutual concern. DON'T self-disclose when the situation is extraneous to the other person.
2. DO self-disclose when sharing of one's concerns and feelings is reciprocal. DON'T self-disclose beyond some first attempts when the other person is closed-mouthed and obviously unreceptive.
3. DO proceed slowly to engage in self-disclosure behavior with a group that is not used to open communication. DON'T plunge full steam ahead in self-disclosure in an attempt to change the organizational environment quickly.

---

[2]Roger D'Aprix, *Communicating for Productivity* (New York: Harper & Row, 1982): 19.

4.   DO self-disclose when the information is timely and pertinent to the current situation. DON'T self-disclose when your information is stale or irrelevant to the situation at hand.

5.   DO self-disclose within a confronting, problem-solving environment. DON'T self-disclose in an effort to dump your frustrations on others emotionally.[3]

Style

Supervisory style refers to a recognizable pattern of behavior used by supervisors to relate to their employees. Some supervisors, for example, use a friendly, helpful style whereas others use a more formal, authoritative style. What we choose to reveal to employees may be related to our overall supervisory style. Many models have been developed for characterizing styles of management. One very popular model, originated by Douglas McGregor, describes Theories X and Y, which represent two primary ways to supervise employees.[4] Theory X advocates feel that workers are basically lazy and unmotivated and need to be treated in an autocratic manner. Theory Y adherents, on the other hand, believe that people are self-starters, who are capable of much creativity and responsibility. Theory Y supervisors, accordingly, are democratic and participatory in the way they handle their employees. Theories X and Y will be reexamined in more depth in Chapter 10, but they are mentioned here as important intervening variables that often cause positive or negative employee behavior. A point of definition may be in order here. Although a *variable* may be defined as a measurable factor that can be seen or observed in some way, an *intervening variable* is a phenomenon that affects the other variables in an observable way. Thus, in the model used in this chapter, supervisory self-disclosure, style, and expectations are seen as having an important impact on individual employee variables of personality, self-concept, and values.

A recent extension of this theory is called "Theory Z," which refers to an American supervisory style strongly influenced by Japanese management techniques. Theory Z supervisors take a more holistic interest in their employees. This means that supervisors are not only concerned with the nine-to-five performance of their employees but care about their all-around health and happiness as well. Theory Z supervisors are extremely

---

Theory X views the worker as lazy and unmotivated.

Theory Y views the worker as creative and responsible.

Theory Z adapts Japanese management techniques to American organizations.

---

[3]Adapted from Jane Whitney Gibson and Richard M. Hodgetts, "Self-Disclosure: A Neglected Management Skill," *IEEE Professional Communications Society Transactions* (September 1985): 44–45.

[4]Douglas McGregor, *The Human Side of Enterprise* (New York: McGraw-Hill Book Co., 1960).

participatory in their decision making, and generally foster a close family feeling among employees.[5]

Expectations

How we expect people to behave often has a very important effect on how they *do* behave. Exploring this concept, the playwright George Bernard Shaw in 1912 wrote a charming play entitled *Pygmalion,* which tells the story of an English flower girl's transformation into a society lady. In the 1950s the play was adapted into a very successful American musical called *My Fair Lady.* The original Pygmalion, by the way, was a mythical king of Cyprus, who made a female figure of ivory and fell in love with it. Taking pity on him, the Greek god Aphrodite brought the statue to life.

The Pygmalion story line has an important moral for supervisors. If you expect the best from your employees and let them know you think they can do the job, they will not let you down. This idea has become known as the Pygmalion effect. Keep in mind, however, that supervisors who expect poor results often get those results as well.

Research results on the Pygmalion effect have yielded several conclusions:

> "Recent research has confirmed that effective leaders have the ability to create high performance expectations that their employees fulfill. Every manager should understand, therefore, how the Pygmalion effect works."[6]

Finally, before trying to analyze employee behavior, supervisors should take a hard look at other ways in which they may be causing that behavior. Supervisors should ask themselves the following questions. If their answers cause some discomfort, they should try working on their own behavior before they think about employee behavior.

1. Do you criticize your subordinates in private?
2. Do you ask their opinions as if you believe they have something worthwhile to say?
3. Do you avoid playing favorites with your employees?
4. Do you communicate your expectations to subordinates? Are those expectations positive ones?
5. When results are achieved as you desire, do you hasten to praise your subordinates?
6. Do you operate in an atmosphere of trust and openness?

The Pygmalion effect says that supervisors get from employees what they expect from them.

---

[5]William G. Ouchi, *Theory Z* (New York: Avon Books, 1981).

[6]J. Sterling Livingston, "Pygmalion in Management: HBR Classic and Retrospective Commentary," *Harvard Business Review* (September-October 1988): 125.

SUPERVISORY SKILLS
Considering Supervisory Variables

1. Review your behavior using the Johari Window. Are you open and self-disclosing about your thoughts, feelings, expectations, and standards? Do your subordinates have to try to figure you out, often doing it wrong? Or do they know what to expect from you? Be open; be consistent. Otherwise, you will keep your people off balance and their energy will be used in trying to figure you out instead of in doing the job.

2. Be aware that how you act toward your employees has a major influence on the way they will feel about the job and thus on their performance. Always look first to yourself; is your managerial style causing problems? Does it seem to match the needs of the employees and of the job?

3. Remember that expectations play a major role in human behavior. It is up to you to project positive, realistic expectations and to reward people when they have achieved them. When they fall short, use the opportunity to discuss ways of improving performance next time. Positive expectation is one of the most overlooked and cheapest supervisory tools. Use it!

7. Do you create realistic standards against which people are fairly measured?

8. Do you keep your word and avoid trying to make yourself look good at the expense of others?

EMPLOYEE BEHAVIOR

Having gained some insight on differences in individual personality, values, and perception and the ways in which supervisors might influence those variables, let's turn our attention to outcomes: employee behavior. We begin by looking at behavior in terms of attitudes and performance. Of all the ways supervisors have to judge employee behavior, employee attitudes and employee performance are two of the most important.

Attitudes

An attitude is the way someone feels about a person or thing.

An *attitude* is the way someone feels about a given person, event, place, or object. Attitudes, which are far more specific than values, are tied to behavior. For example, an employee may cherish the value of honesty—a very broad, gut-level belief. A related attitude may be a negative attitude about employees who cheat on their expense account. The associated behavior may be that the employee in question openly criticizes the peer who is doing the padding. The nature of the tie between attitudes and behavior has been the subject of debate for many years; some researchers feel that behavior leads to attitudes, whereas others see behavior as a result of attitudes. Consider the employee who begins to arrive late on a regular basis. Is the behavior; tardiness, due to an attitude of disinterest in the job, or is it due to problems at home that lead to the lateness, which in turn leads to an attitude of disinterest in the job? In any event, attitudes and behavior are difficult to understand separately. More importantly, all of the factors discussed in this chapter—personality, perception, self-concept, and intervening supervisory variables—to a large extent determine the attitudes employees have about their work environment.

One employee attitude particularly interesting to the supervisor is loyalty. Supervisors often worry that the employee is more loyal to the peer group than to the supervisor or to the company as a whole. Building loyalty to the organization is thus a primary supervisory responsibility. It takes time and effort to show employees that the best way to support and further their own goals is to work for overall corporate goals. Companies where workers feel a "part of the family" have few loyalty problems.

If employee attitudes are added together, they begin to establish a concept of employee morale. *Morale* can be defined as the way people feel about their jobs. This includes their feelings about the organization, the supervisor, working conditions, and wages and benefits. Fostering and maintaining high employee morale is an important part of the supervisor's job. The causes of low morale are very diverse.

"Problems like duplicating machines that don't work, coffee machines out of filters, and parking lots with pot holes can have as much negative impact on employee performance as low pay, working conditions and promotional opportunities, and repetitive, unchallenging work."[7]

Assessing employee attitudes and morale can best be done by going to the employees directly either through interviews or attitude surveys. Trying to guess what employees think is often a waste of time. If supervisors find that attitudes are negative in relationship to themselves, the job, or the organization, they should take the following steps in order to change those attitudes into more positive ones:

Ways to change attitudes.

1. Identify the improper attitude or behavior.
2. Determine what supports it.
3. Weaken whatever supports it.
4. Offer a substitute for the improper attitude or behavior.[8]

Supervisors must investigate the causes of poor attitudes and morale and work to correct them; attitudes help to determine performance and affect employee turnover, absenteeism, productivity, and satisfaction.

---

[7]R. Bruce McAfee and Myron Glassman, "Job Satisfaction: It's the Little Things That Count." *Management Solutions* (August 1988): 33–37.

[8]W. Richard Plunkett, Supervision: The Direction of People at Work, (6th ed.) (Boston, Mass.: Allyn & Bacon, 1992), 191.

Performance

The essence of effective supervision is to elicit effective performance from the workers. Performance is often measured in terms of productivity, job satisfaction, turnover, and absenteeism.

Turnover and Absenteeism.   When people have negative job attitudes or are dissatisfied with their jobs, they tend to engage in withdrawal behavior. Either they stay home more often, or they quit and look for another job. Many studies have been conducted in this area. At the moment job satisfaction appears to be more closely correlated to turnover than to absenteeism, but more work needs to be done because both absenteeism and turnover are very costly. Encouraging positive attitudes about the organization can help alleviate these personnel problems.

The satisfaction-performance relationship continues to be controversial.

Productivity.   Since the early 1950s, many studies have been conducted in an effort to examine the link between job satisfaction and productivity, which is defined as the ratio of total outputs to total inputs. (Productivity is discussed more fully in Chapter 2.) The results are inconclusive. Some studies have found moderately positive correlations; others have found no relationship; still others have suggested that the relationship is just the reverse—that is, productivity causes job satisfaction. This debatable relationship (or "interrelationship") has become commonly known as the "satisfaction–performance controversy."

■ ■ ■   SUPERVISORY SKILLS
Understanding Employee Behavior

1. Be aware of employee attitudes about the job. Where negatives exist, try to examine the attitude, discover the root cause, and work to remove or weaken that cause. Attitudes can be changed but not without conscious effort to try to deal with their causes.

2. Be a good example. Show positive attitudes about your job and your subordinates. Looking for the good in your people and in the work environment will have a contagious effect as long as you are sincere.

3. Remember that positive attitudes are directly related to performance. If attitudes are not positive, job satisfaction and productivity will decrease, and turnover and absenteeism will rise. If you see a change for the worse in one of these areas, you are also soon likely to see symptoms in one or more of the others. Teach yourself to read warning signs, learn not to treat the symptoms but to look for the underlying causal factors.

Regardless of the direction of this linkage, there is little doubt that performance and satisfaction are in some way linked, just as there is little doubt that the productivity of employees is directly linked to the individual employee variables discussed in this chapter. Remember that employees are complex human beings. Good supervisors know the basic psychological factors at work in people and use that knowledge to make themselves and their employees more effective.

Job Satisfaction. Job satisfaction is probably the most studied work attitude, and many studies use satisfaction interchangeably with employee attitudes. In studies concerning overall levels of job satisfaction across the United States, levels of satisfaction were not found to have changed much

THE QUALITY CHALLENGE
Giving Them Positive Feedback

One of the most important ways to sustain high job satisfaction is to reward the personnel for work well done. This can take a number of different forms. Some of the most common include financial rewards, days off, vacation trips, choice parking spots (typically for a week or a month), pictures placed on the "Employee of the Month" wall, and names added to a plaque of distinguished employees. The latter are often displayed prominently in one area of the building and are typically referred to as walls (or halls) of fame. Whereas every company will have its own recognition system, there are a handful of characteristics that typify all of these efforts:

(1) recognition is always positive and is given to those actions that have resulted in success;

(2) recognition is given openly and tends to be publicized throughout the company or division;

(3) recognition is carefully tailored to the needs of the people, so that everyone is motivated to pursue the reward;

(4) rewards are given soon after they have been earned; and

(5) the relationship between the achievement and the reward is clearly understood by the personnel.

At the Ritz-Carlton hotel chain, widely recognized as one of the highest quality chains in the world, there is a "First Class" card, which is a 3″ × 5″ card that has been specially designed with the company logo and is used for thanking other employees who have done a good job. These cards are completed and sent to the employee by any person in the organization who wants to express his or her appreciation for a job well done. The company also uses a "Lightning Strike," which is a nonmonetary reward from a member of the Executive Committee to an employee who has exhibited outstanding service. Recognition is also given monthly to those who submit the best ideas for improvement. These individuals are recognized on the bulletin board and are given a buffet for two. In addition, there are quarterly receptions for those who generate the most useful ideas. As a result, productivity and job satisfaction at the Ritz continue to be high.

over the last twenty years. Most people who indicate positive attitudes about the job and workplace also report high degrees of job satisfaction. However, if an employee is bored, disinterested, frustrated, or in other ways unhappy about his or her job, the supervisor's responsibility is to try to build more positive attitudes about the job. One way in which the manager can do this is to show a positive attitude in daily activities. Having a positive attitude entails looking for good things to say about employees, showing appreciation for good work, listening to employee concerns, and demonstrating a genuine interest in what employees have to say. "The Quality Challenge: Giving Them Positive Feedback" illustrates how positive feedback can encourage high job satisfaction.

SUMMARY

Supervisors need to understand individual behavior.

Three of the most important influences on employee behavior are personality, values, and perception. Personality is the complex of unique and measurable characteristics that distinguishes one individual from all others. Personality is shaped by genetic, environmental, and situational factors. Values are basic beliefs that determine what is important to an individual. Perception is the way a person views and interprets reality.

Supervisors also need to consider their own personalities. Of greatest importance here are self-disclosure, supervisory style, and supervisory expectations.

Of all the observable signs of employee behavior, employee attitudes and employee performance are two of the most significant. An attitude is the way someone feels about a given person, place, object, or event. Attitudes can affect turnover, absenteeism, and performance.

REVIEW QUESTIONS

1. What is meant by the term *personality?* Put it in your own words.

2. In what way do the following affect personality: genes, the environment, the situation? Explain.

3. How does a left-brain person differ from a right-brain person? Which is more likely to be found in an organizational setting? Explain your reasoning.

4. What is meant by the term *values?* How do values affect the way a person behaves? Give an example.

5. How does *perception* affect a person's behavior? Explain.

6. The Johari Window has four quadrants. What does this statement mean? Of what value is an understanding of the window to the supervisor? Explain.

7. How does a Theory X supervisor act? How does a Theory Y supervisor act? Compare and contrast the two.

8. In what way does the Pygmalion effect play a role in subordinate behavior? Give an example.

9. What is meant by the term *attitude?* Can attitudes be measured? How?

10. Is there any relationship between productivity and performance? Explain.

KEY TERMS

Attitude. How someone feels about a particular person, place, object, or event.

Defense mechanism. Variety of psychological coping techniques that people use to deal with unpleasant or unacceptable situations.

Johari Window. Model of interpersonal relationships that examines what people know and don't know about themselves as well as what people disclose or don't disclose to others.

Morale. Combination of employee attitudes about the job.

Perception. How a person interprets reality.

Personality. Complex of unique and measurable characteristics that distinguishes one individual from all others.

Productivity. Ratio of total output of goods and services to total inputs used in their production.

Pygmalion effect. Cliche suggesting that people often behave as they are expected to behave.

Self-concept. How people see themselves and how they think others see them.

Self-disclosure. How much individuals let others know how they think and feel.

Theory X. Supervisory style premised on the belief that workers are basically lazy and need to be treated in an autocratic manner.

Theory Y. Supervisory style premised on the belief that people are self-starters who are capable of creativity and responsibility.

Theory Z. American supervisory style heavily influenced by the Japanese management techniques of participative management.

Values. Basic beliefs that determine what is important to an individual.

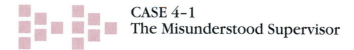

CASE 4–1
The Misunderstood Supervisor

Productivity in the Cheshart Company had once been the highest in the industry. However, for the last year this has not been the case. Output began to drop off rather dramatically about thirteen months ago, just about the time a national union started its effort to organize the workers. The campaign was a bitter one; when the votes were counted, the effort was defeated by a 54 to 46 percent margin.

One of the union's biggest arguments pointed out that the employees were being overworked and underpaid. An attitude survey conducted by the company three months ago reveals that most workers believe this. As a result, the firm believes that this year's union effort may be successful.

Charlie Schering is a supervisor in one of Cheshart's largest departments. Charlie took over the department six months ago and has watched productivity drop dramatically. During this time he has had a chance to talk with his people about their work-related attitudes, and he basically agrees with them. Most are being asked to do a lot more work than the average person in the industry and wage rates are 7 percent under industry average. However, Charlie has been working hard to overcome this problem. Along with a group of other supervisors he has had three meetings with top management and convinced them that they should raise salaries and reevaluate work loads as soon as possible. Management agreed to consider the supervisors' recommendations and to issue a decision within ten days.

Yesterday, as is the custom every ninety days, the workers submitted their written evaluations of their supervisors. Here is a composite of what they had to say about Charlie:

"He follows management's instructions very closely. He works his people very hard and believes that most people could do a lot more work than they really can. He is opposed to any increases in salary and is strongly anti-union. Overall he is a company-person who has little regard for his people. Supervisors like him have created the need for a union in this company."

1.   In terms of the Johari Window, how would you describe Charlie? Be sure to include a consideration of the discrepancy between what Charlie is doing for the workers and the way they perceive him.

2.   Is Charlie a Theory X or Theory Y person? Explain your answer.

3.   What does Charlie need to do in order to improve his relationship with his people? Will this help improve the productivity problem? Explain.

CASE 4–2
I Believe in You

Phyllis Dresser is a new supervisor in her company. She was hired when the firm began expanding its operations six months ago. Phyllis was assigned to Work Group 4, which had been known as one of the toughest in the company. The group almost always had the lowest output, and absenteeism and tardiness always ran 30 to 40 percent above the average of the rest of the firm.

Phyllis looked over the production and employee performance reports before she took the job. During her first week she had a brief meeting with all her employees and told them that she saw herself as someone who was there to help them do a better job. If they had any problems or work-related matters that they wanted to discuss, her door was always open.

Having set the stage, Phyllis began working to carry out her promises. She managed to get half the employees in her group sent to special training programs during her first three months on the job; when they returned, she en-

couraged them to use their new knowledge. Her theme throughout was, "I know you have the ability to do a much better job than you have in the past and I intend to give you that opportunity."

At first, nothing changed. However, slowly but surely, productivity began to rise, and tardiness and absenteeism started falling. At the end of her sixth month as supervisor, the company held its semiannual awards luncheon. A number of people were given plaques and certificates. Five of the people in Phyllis's group were recognized for their outstanding work improvement. On the way out of the luncheon, Phyllis's boss remarked, "If you keep it up, you'll be getting the annual award as outstanding supervisor in the company." Phyllis just smiled.

1.   What has caused the turnaround in Phyllis's department? In your answer be sure to discuss the Pygmalion effect.

2.   How would you describe Phyllis's style: Theory X or Theory Y? Defend your answer.

3.   Why was the supervisor prior to Phyllis unable to achieve what she has achieved? Explain.

4.   Assume the previous supervisor had been a superior one and Work Group 4 had enjoyed a high level of productivity. How might Phyllis's efforts have been received?

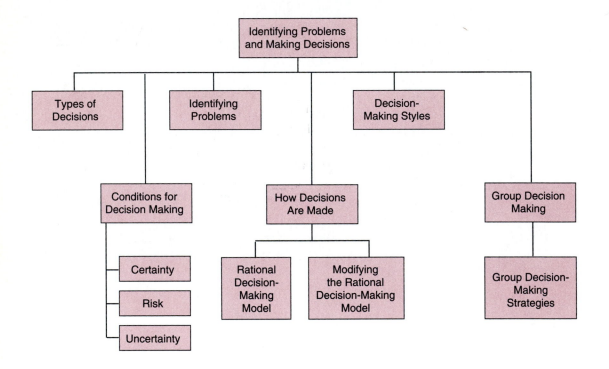

CHAPTER 5

Identifying Problems and Making Decisions

"Perhaps no other attribute so frequently distinguishes the excellent manager from mediocre ones as does the ability to make wise and innovative decisions."*

CHAPTER OBJECTIVES

- ☐ Describe the decision-making process.
- ☐ Explain how the decision-making process is modified by satisficing behavior.
- ☐ Identify the four primary decision-making styles used by supervisors.
- ☐ Examine group decision-making strategies including the use of brainstorming, the Delphi technique, and the nominal grouping technique.
- ☐ Distinguish between programmed and nonprogrammed decisions.
- ☐ Understand decision making under certainty, risk, and uncertainty.

---

*R. Wayne Mondy and Shane R. Premeaux, *Management: Concepts, Practices, and Skills*, 6th ed. (Boston, Mass.: Allyn & Bacon, 1993), 121.

S upervisors spend a great deal of time identifying problems and making decisions. The quality of the results can be enhanced if supervisors anticipate problems and plan decisions for the future. Supervisors who wait for problems to occur and then jump to solutions are not as effective as those who look ahead and begin formulating resolutions. Making effective decisions is an art requiring patience, planning, logic, intuitiveness, and appreciation of the human dynamics involved.

TYPES OF DECISIONS

Supervisors are generally faced with two different types of decisions: routine decisions, such as who to assign to fill out this week's time sheets, and nonroutine decisions, such as how to raise employee morale. Routine decisions, also called *programmed decisions*, rely on the application of rules, procedures, and policies to arrive at a resolution. Other examples of programmed decisions facing supervisors are the following:

There are two types of decisions: programmed and nonprogrammed.

1. Deciding how much vacation time an employee gets and when he or she can schedule that vacation.
2. Deciding what supplies to order.
3. Deciding whether a customer is entitled to a refund when company policy clearly states that all products may be returned for a complete refund within 10 days.

Nonroutine decisions, called *nonprogrammed decisions*, require more creativity and problem-solving skills on the part of the supervisor. Unlike programmed decisions, nonprogrammed decisions have no ready answer. Each situation is unique. Some examples of nonprogrammed decisions facing supervisors include:

1. At what point to recommend the firing of a troublesome employee.
2. How to rotate employees for maximum productivity.
3. What to write in an employee's performance appraisal.

As employees move up the managerial ladder, the proportion of nonprogrammed decisions increases.

Just as it is important to understand the different types of decisions supervisor face, it is also important to understand the conditions under which decisions are made.

CONDITIONS FOR DECISION MAKING

There are three basic conditions under which all decisions are made: certainty, risk, and uncertainty (see Table 5–1).

TABLE 5-1

Conditions for decision making

Certainty	*Risk*	*Certainty*
• Perfect information	• Substantial information	• Limited information
• All alternatives known	• Some alternatives may not be known	• Some alternatives may not be known
• Consequence(s) of each alternative known	• Probability of consequence(s) of each alternative known	• Probability of consequence(s) of each alternative known

Certainty

Under certainty, there is no risk.

Under conditions of certainty, the supervisor has all the verifiable information he or she needs to make a risk-free decision. Depending on which alternative the decision maker chooses, the outcome is certain. He or she has "perfect information." For example, a supervisor who has a budget of $1,000 for overtime on a specific weekend has a choice of scheduling ten $100 per day employees, five $200 a day employees, or some mixture of the two. Knowing their comparable productivity, and the type and amount of work to be done, the supervisor is in a good position to decide who to ask to work overtime.

In reality, very few business or personal decisions are made under conditions of certainty. It is far more common for decisions to be made under risk.

Risk

Most business decisions are made under risk.

Under conditions of risk, the supervisor has substantial, but not perfect, information about the decision situation. The decision maker may not even know all of the possible alternatives available. He or she does know enough, however, to assess a probable outcome to each alternative under consideration before making a decision. For example, when deciding how many units of a certain product to produce in the next month, the supervisor can examine sales records of the previous month and of the comparable period for last year. He can plug in economic factors that impact on sales of the product and get the sales manager's projections of expected sales. Finally, he can consider the costs and profits of making various volumes of this product against making more or less of an alternative product during the same period. Most business decisions are made under conditions of risk.

An important variable that helps determine how successful a supervisor is making decisions under conditions of risk is how risk adverse that supervisor is.

"Every time you make a decision, you are taking a risk. Every decision has a possibility of negative or positive consequences, and there is always the risk that you will be wrong or that someone will disagree with or not like your decision. However, there is always the possibility that the outcome will be positive."[1]

Successful supervisors have to learn how to take calculated risks, remembering that there is usually no perfect solution and that most decisions can be changed or modified in the future. A particularly difficult decision situation occurs under conditions of uncertainty.

Uncertainty

Under uncertainty, nothing is known about outcomes.

Under conditions of uncertainty, the supervisor has very limited information about alternatives and consequences of those alternatives. Not enough is known to even assess probabilities of specific outcomes. Whereas decision making under risk is akin to gambling on an outcome, decision making under uncertainty is a foray into the unknown. Anything can happen. For example, when a supervisor decides to recommend introducing a brand new, unproven software package into her department, she has no historical information to know how the program will work or how it will affect productivity. A smart supervisor might choose to test the new program with just a few employees.

Regardless of the type of decision or the condition under which the decision is made, supervisors must understand the process by which decisions are made and the various decision-making styles that can be employed for both individual and group decision making.

IDENTIFYING PROBLEMS

Problem identification is critical.

The first step in decision making is to comprehend the problem thoroughly. Too often supervisors spot a problem, instantly conclude that they know how to deal with it, and rush into the decision-making process. What they usually end up treating is the symptom, not the cause, of the problem. For example, a supervisor who concludes that "Our problem is a 10 percent increased reject rate" is dealing with a symptom, not a problem. The problem is the cause of the rejects, which could be employee dissatisfaction with the company, equipment breakdown, faulty raw materials, or a host of other items. The supervisor's job is to determine the cause of the problem.

Effective problem analysis includes recognizing a symptom such as a too high reject rate and then investigating cause-and-effect relationships between the symptom and what is behind it.

---

[1]Eleanor Davidson, "Overcoming the Fear of Decision Making," *Supervisory Management* (October 1991): 12.

The causes are the real problem, and the best way to begin to define causes is to ask your employees. Almost always, employees know more about the causes of problems than do their supervisors. Rarely, however, will they volunteer that information, so it is up to the effective supervisor to seek out this information.

> "Your people often know more about a problem than you do—but you can't know that unless you ask them. It's unrealistic to expect workers to volunteer opinions. Some workers underestimate the value of their opinions or knowledge. Others may believe you don't care what they think."[2]

There are other reasons why employees are not more forthcoming about problems in the workplace. Employees may be hesitant to seem critical of an organizational or supervisory decision that has caused a problem. Personal conflict sometimes prevents employees from seeking cooperative solutions. Fear and uncertainty caused by the problem often in themselves keep people from focusing on the causes of the problem. Sometimes, haste to find a solution prevents good problem solving at the front end of the decision-making process.[3]

HOW DECISIONS ARE MADE

Decision making is the process of choosing from among alternatives. To understand the way this process is carried out, we need to examine both the rational decision-making model and the bounded rationality model.

Decision making is the process of choosing from among alternatives.

Rational Decision-Making Model

Whenever we discuss decision making, we imply (if we do not state outright) that the process will be an economically rational one. In other words, we will follow an orderly, sequential process that will result in the best decision. The outline for this sequential process, known as the *rational decision-making model,* shows the steps that a supervisor must take in order to reach a logical decision in an efficient manner (see Figure 5–1). The first two steps, spotting the symptoms and identifying the problem, have already been discussed. Let's now look at each of the other steps.

Develop Decisional Evaluation Criteria.   At the same time they are identifying the problem, supervisors must determine criteria for evaluating the alternative courses of action. Whenever possible, quantitative evaluators should be used. For example, if a supervisor is dealing with a problem

When possible, quantitative evaluators should be used.

---

[2]Joseph T. Straub, "Ask Questions First to Solve the Right Problems," *Supervisory Management* (October 1991): 7.

[3]Roger Fritz, "A Systematic Approach to Problem Solving and Decision Making," *Supervisory Management* (March 1993): 4–5.

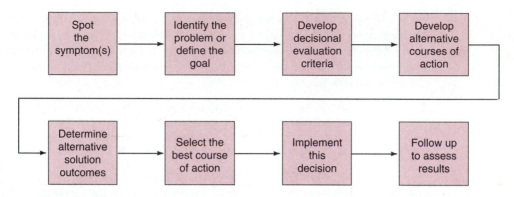

FIGURE 5–1
Rational decision-making model.

employee who comes back late from lunch at least three times a week and then proceeds to loll around and do nothing during the afternoons, a successful solution might involve asking the employee to reduce this behavior to no more than once a month and to restore her productivity to its previous high level. Notice that these criteria are somewhat subjective. It is not always possible to be completely quantitative with criteria; however, it is wise to try. Typical quantitative criteria are cost and time. How much money will the decision require, and how much time will it take to implement or how much time will it save?

Develop Alternative Solutions. After choosing evaluation criteria, supervisors make a list of all the possible solutions under study. Naturally some of these will be long shots or highly improbable paths of action, which the supervisor can in fact ignore. For example, if you're deciding how to increase work productivity in your department, you could choose to fire a large percentage of the work force in order to show the others that the firm means business. But obviously such an act is a foolish alternative unworthy of serious attention. On the other hand, there may be three or four salary bonus programs that have merit. Each should be individually considered in terms of an alternative solution.

Evaluate Alternatives. In this step supervisors analyze all the alternative solutions to determine which one will provide the best results. Sometimes the outcome can be reached mathematically and the supervisor need only compare the various payoffs. For example, if supervisors must decide whether to authorize overtime for clerical staff or hire a temporary clerk to help out during a month-long crunch, and if they have been told to do whichever is cheaper, the supervisor has only to calculate the cost involved and make a decision. Other times the supervisor will subjectively evaluate the outcomes because the outcome cannot be predicted on a mathematical basis alone. For example, a supervisor may conclude that adding two dozen personal computers to the department could save the group a half million dollars in lost time and effort over the next five years. The computers would cost only $50,000, so they will pay for themselves very quickly. On the other hand, because the employees may be very resistant to the idea of using personal computers, the supervisor should realize that the introduction of such a system may lead to worker resistance, especially from those who are afraid that they will be fired or transferred to other jobs. The latter will fight implementation of the system by failing to provide timely information and/or talking their colleagues into joining them in their opposition. As a result, if only in the short run, there may be a loss of efficiency coupled with increased operating costs. This is the stage in the decision-making process to consider any negative effects of the action.

Select the Best Alternative. Once the alternative solution outcomes have been determined, selecting the best one is merely a matter of comparing the net results against the decision criteria. For example, if the objective is profit, the question to be answered is, which of the alternatives offers the greatest profit? If the objective is increased efficiency, the question to be answered is, which of the alternatives offers the greatest increase in work output?

Implementation is often the most difficult step.

Implement the Decision. The next step in the decision-making process is to carry out the decision. This step often proves to be the most difficult for two reasons. First, the personnel who are implementing the decision may not fully understand how to do it. Second, the decision faces the challenge of workability. Despite all objective, rational analysis, will things work the way the supervisor says they will?

Follow Up. After a decision is implemented, follow-up is necessary to evaluate the degree of success in correcting a specific problem or set of problems.

Modifying the Rational Decision-Making Model

The rational model offers some interesting insights into the process of decision making, but it also has a number of important shortcomings. It is difficult to obtain all the information about all the alternatives. Seldom do decision makers identify every alternative associated with any problem. When faced with a production deadline, for example, the supervisor may consider only two alternatives: overtime or the employment of temporary workers.

The supervisor could, of course, go further and investigate job reassignment, administrative duties and so on, but the supervisor would probably not spend the necessary time to gather information about these alternatives. Unless the cost–benefit ratio was very favorable to the efforts involved, the supervisor would simply opt for a solution that was good enough to solve the problem under analysis. The result is less than ideal, but nevertheless provides acceptable decision outcomes.

In reality, the rational approach is often modified by the bounded rationality model, which is characterized by satisficing behavior. *Satisficing behavior* is action that is good enough to meet minimal standards of desired outcomes. This concept was popularized by Herbert Simon, who compared the behavior of highly economic, rational people with those who are "satisficers," as follows: "While economic man maximizes—selects the best alternative from among all those available to him; his cousin, whom we shall call administrative man, satisfices—looks for a course of action that is satisfactory or 'good enough.' Examples of satisficing criteria that are familiar to businessmen are 'share of market,' 'adequate profit,' 'fair price.'"[4]

When people are engaged in making decisions that involve large sums of money or critical payoffs such as the success or failure of a major project, they make every effort to be as rational as possible. However, most supervisory decisions are not highly critical, and so there are copious examples of satisficing behavior. Decisions made in this way are often said to use the *bounded rationality* model. Figure 5–2 shows the steps in this process. Notice that as soon as an acceptable solution is reached, the process stops. There is no attempt to find the optimal solution.

Supervisors make most of their decisions on a satisficing, rather than a purely rational basis, and consequently certain styles of decision making become identified with various supervisors.

Many decisions are simply "good enough."

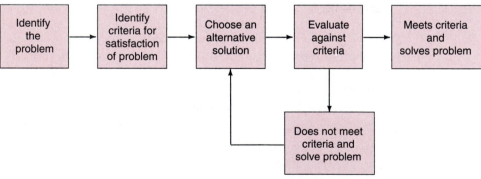

FIGURE 5–2
Bounded rationality: Satisficing decision.

---

[4]Herbert A. Simon, *Administrative Behavior*, 2d ed. (New York: Free Press, 1966), xxv.

SUPERVISORY SKILLS
Effective Problem Solving and Decision Making

1. Know the difference between programmed and nonprogrammed decisions. Invest your time in attending to unique, nonprogrammed decisions and allow rules, policies, and procedures to guide you in resolving programmed decisions.

2. Remember that most decisions are made under conditions of risk. Carefully consider alternatives in light of their probable outcomes.

3. Be sure you are treating causes, not effects. The time spent in problem exploration and identification is perhaps the most valuable time you will spend in making decisions. Ask others in your department for their perspective on the problem; do not rely solely on your own interpretation.

4. Understand that the rational decision-making model is the most logical approach to making decisions if you are convinced that the best solution is necessary. When the situation merits the expense of time and money needed to arrive at an optimal decision, follow the rational decision-making model precisely. However, when there is less at stake, realize that you will not be totally rational in your decision; do not pretend to be. By admitting that you are seeking a satisfactory solution, you leave yourself open for improving your decision later on.

DECISION-MAKING STYLES

Good supervisors are concerned with both decision quality and ease of acceptance.

One way of classifying decision-making styles is shown in Figure 5–3.[5] Notice that there are four quadrants in this figure, each showing various amounts of concern for employee acceptance and concern for the decision's quality.

Quadrant I represents the "Laissez-faire Supervisor." This decision maker either ignores the problem and hopes it goes away, or flips a coin, not really caring which way the decision goes. As lackadaisical as this approach seems, it may be appropriate for some problems where low quality decisions are appropriate and there is no problem with acceptance by employees. An example is deciding what color pens to order.

Quadrant II represents the "I'm the Boss Supervisor." This person makes decisions based on her expertise and legitimate power. The individual shows little concern for what subordinates may think about the decision, but is concerned with a high quality outcome. Again, in certain situations this style is appropriate. Take, for example, a service supervisor who needs to set costs for various types of service calls, or the purchasing supervisor who has to decide to whom to give an order. Employees would probably not even want to participate in this type of decision.

Quadrant III represents the "Nice Guy Supervisor." This person is very worried about acceptance by employees and solicits their input on everything. Low-quality decisions often result, but everyone is relatively

---

[5]Andrew K. Hoh, "Styles of Decision Making," *Supervisory Management* (May 1981): 19–23.

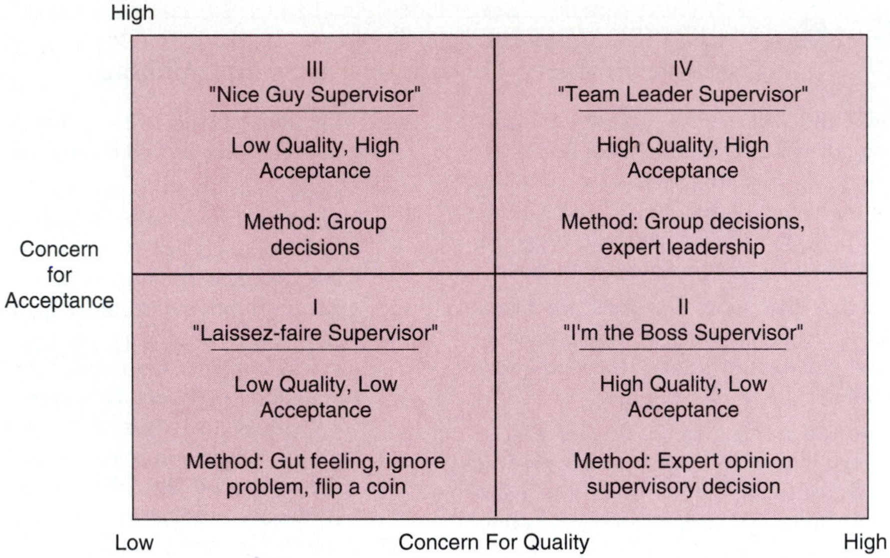

High

III "Nice Guy Supervisor" Low Quality, High Acceptance Method: Group decisions	**IV** "Team Leader Supervisor" High Quality, High Acceptance Method: Group decisions, expert leadership
I "Laissez-faire Supervisor" Low Quality, Low Acceptance Method: Gut feeling, ignore problem, flip a coin	**II** "I'm the Boss Supervisor" High Quality, Low Acceptance Method: Expert opinion supervisory decision

Concern
for
Acceptance

Low   Concern For Quality   High

FIGURE 5–3
Decision-making styles.
Reprinted, by permission of publisher, from *Supervisory Management,* May 1981, © 1981. American Management
Association, New York. All rights reserved.

happy and unthreatened. This may be the most appropriate method for problems concerning employee morale.

Quadrant IV represents the "Team Leader Supervisor," who also uses the method of group decision making but assumes an expert leadership role. Group participation ensures high acceptance, and the supervisor's expertise ensures high quality. Unlike the nice guy supervisor, the team leader supervisor is an active leader in the decision-making process and ultimately holds responsibility for making the decision.

Although many supervisors become typecast in one of these styles, they should try to remain flexible and use the style appropriate for the problem. It is also important to have a good understanding of the pros and cons of group decision making.

GROUP DECISION MAKING

Group decision making has advantages and disadvantages.

Although group decision making offers many benefits, the two most important are: (a) opportunity for widespread expertise to be brought to bear on the problem; and (b) eventual ease of implementation of the solution. Group decision making is also in keeping with the general shift in this country toward participative management; many workers feel better about decisions in which they participate, particularly those that directly affect them.

Unfortunately, a number of pitfalls are associated with group decision making. One major problem is brought about by time and cost considerations. The greater the cost involved, the longer the consideration initially given to the decision. However, people often get tired of long meetings and eventually agree on a solution just to be finished with it. Another major problem, called *groupthink*, occurs when the group camaraderie and cohesiveness are such that people avoid making negative comments or expressing reservations. The following list identifies some symptoms of groupthink.

1. An illusion of invulnerability, or "Nothing bad can happen to us."
2. Rationalization, or "Defending the group's position against all possible misgivings."
3. Unquestioned morality of the group, or "We're the good guys; how can we go wrong?"
4. Stereotyped views of opponents, or "*They* don't have a chance; they're jerks."
5. Pressure against dissenters, or "Don't be a spoilsport."
6. Self-censorship, or "I'm not going to be a wet blanket."
7. An illusion of unanimity, or "Nobody said anything negative so we all agree 100 percent."
8. Self-appointed mindguards, or "Come on, Mary, we know we can count on your support."[6]

How can supervisors maximize the potential of group decision making and avoid some of the problems? The following strategies can help.

Group Decision-Making Strategies

Group leaders play a critical role in effective group decision making.

Effective group decision making is a product of good leadership. The supervisor should identify the problem, select the appropriate group to work on it, and circulate an agenda in advance of the decision-making session. This latter point is very important because the prior notice enables people to give the situation some advance thought and to gather whatever material they need as input for the meeting.

At the meeting the supervisor should keep a low profile and play the role of the facilitator, ensuring that each participant has an opportunity to be heard. If groupthink seems a possibility, supervisors can follow these seven steps[7]:

---

[6]Adapted from Irving L. Janis, "Groupthink" in *Readings and Exercises in Organizational Behavior,* eds. Jane W. Gibson and Richard M. Hodgetts (Orlando, Fla.: Academic Press, 1985), 114–117.

[7]Michael J. Woodruff, "Understanding and Combatting Groupthink," *Supervisory Management* (October 1991): 8.

1. Positively reinforce critical thinking. Sometimes you may need to appoint a "devil's advocate" to critically analyze group ideas.
2. Reserve your opinion on group issues; otherwise, your employees may feel they need to line up behind your ideas.
3. Don't rush decisions on major problems. Give people time to reflect.
4. Air new ideas widely. Invite outside opinion.
5. Don't think silence means consent. Actively seek out the opinions of those who are not forthcoming.
6. Divide the group into smaller groups to critique new ideas; you'll get more participation.
7. Institute a pilot program to test out major new ideas.

Three effective techniques in group decision situations are brainstorming, the Delphi technique, and the nominal group technique. *Brainstorming* is a well-known technique for generating, without evaluation, as many ideas as possible. The approach works by momentum, with group members stimulating each other's creative energy. For example, if a supervisor is trying to solve the problem of low department morale as evidenced by absenteeism and turnover, the group may be asked to name all items that serve to lower morale—that is, all problems they can imagine as having an impact on this problem. This procedure usually generates a long list of items that are written down for all to see. It is important to note that nobody is allowed to comment on anyone's idea at this time—all ideas are good ideas, and the objective is to generate as many of them as possible. "The Quality Challenge: Brainstorming in Action" provides an example.

Brainstorming is a particularly effective way to encourage employees to be more creative. The following list suggests some important steps for increasing creativity.

1. Loosen up emotionally and intellectually. Creative people give free rein to their emotions.
2. Discipline yourself to think creatively. Highly creative people try not to be bound by old ways of looking at problems; they go beyond the familiar.
3. When trying to formulate creativity in a group setting, use approaches like brainstorming. Encourage imagination; discourage criticism.
4. Develop the right climate for creativity by employing a human resources approach to management. People are more creative under conditions of participative management than they are under conditions of autocratic management.[8]

While brainstorming has been very effective in many cases, it does have its limitations.

Brainstorming generates many ideas without evaluation.

---

[8]Jane Whitney Gibson and Richard M. Hodgetts, *Organizational Communication: A Managerial Perspective,* 2nd ed. (New York: HarperCollins, 1991), 164–166.

THE QUALITY CHALLENGE

Brainstorming in Action

Brainstorming is a critical tool in meeting the quality challenge. A good example occurs when employees have identified a recurring problem but are unsure of its cause. In this case, they will form into a brainstorming team and work to identify the cause and then the solutions. This is done by following five basic steps:

1. Identify and define the effect. This is the outcome or problem that is to be examined. Examples include: It takes too long to clean the work area; meetings are unproductive; the machines break down too often; it takes too long to get replacement parts.

2. Determine the causes of the problem. This involves having the participants identify the most likely reasons for the outcome under analysis. In some cases, the group members will have spent time thinking about possible causes, whereas in other cases, they will be approaching the problem for the first time. In either event, it is common to find wide use of brainstorming, with these ideas being written down by one of the participants.

3. Summarize the findings. At this point the participants will identify the major cate-

gories that can be used to pinpoint the causes. Some of the most common groupings include materials, methods, machinery, and people. For example, the major reasons for the problem may be that materials are always received late or the method of feeding the materials into the machine is too slow.

4. Vote for the most likely cause of the problem. Group members now vote for reason(s) they feel are most responsible for bringing about the problem under study. In many cases, this is done by rank ordering them from the most important to least important.

5. Determine a plan of action. Now the group decides the actions that should be taken to resolve the problem. If this approach does not work, then the plan is revised based on the rank ordering and the next most likely cause is addressed. This process continues until the problem is resolved.

If they are still unable to correct the problem, the group will reexamine the situation by turning to another round of brainstorming.

"It doesn't, for example, teach people how to think creatively. Rather, it sets up an environment that encourages creative expression. Also, brainstorming isn't a tool that can be used too frequently. By their very nature, brainstorming sessions should be held only occasionally. Brainstorming should be used to develop creative solutions to resistant problems—and when done right, it can produce a diverse but solid group of workable solutions."[9]

Before proceeding, take Self-Assessment Quiz 5–1 in order to assess your own creativity.

The Delphi technique uses a panel of experts.

The *Delphi technique* has been particularly successful in situations requiring forecasts of future events. Originally created by the Rand Corpo-

---

[9]Andrew E. Schwartz, "Using Brainstorming to Identify Creative Solutions," *Supervisory Management* (October 1991): 4.

■   ■   ■   ## SELF-ASSESSMENT QUIZ 5-1
How Word-Creative Are You?

This quiz calls for word completion. Each example contains three words. These words can all be changed or expanded in meaning by adding one word before or after them. The word that is added is the *same for all three* and either becomes part of the word or helps create a two-word cliché. For example, what word can be added to these three words to alter or expand their meaning:

plane   hot   line

Look at the words again. The answer is *air:* airplane, hot air, airline. Try another:

smith   ball   boot

The answer is *black:* blacksmith, blackball (to reject for membership), and boot black.

Follow this same logic as you complete the following ten groupings. Give yourself only five minutes. When you are finished, join with two of your colleagues. Review all your answers, change any you feel are wrong, and then collectively try to complete any that have you stumped. Do not use a dictionary, but do use freewheeling and imaginative thinking. You have ten minutes to complete this group effort. When the time is up, check your answers with those at the end of the chapter.

_____ 1.	village	light	golf
_____ 2.	up	hard	book
_____ 3.	loose	club	ball
_____ 4.	flash	star	lime
_____ 5.	show	dance	ground
_____ 6.	game	high	fast
_____ 7.	blue	pressure	line
_____ 8.	sky	blood	point
_____ 9.	priest	proof	tide
_____ 10.	door	oven	cheese

ration, the Delphi technique uses a panel of experts who never meet face-to-face to discuss the questions under review. The participants are given a questionnaire, and their answers are summarized and fed back to the members of the group. The participants then answer the questions again, this time using the responses of the first round as additional information. This process continues for four or five rounds, after which some unanimity is usually reached. The Delphi technique avoids the cost, time, and cohesiveness problems of typical group decision making, although it clearly takes longer to reach a decision.

> "Many organizations testify to the success they have had so far with the Delphi technique. McDonnell Douglas Aircraft uses the technique to forecast the future uncertainties of commercial air transportation. Weyerhauser, a building supply company, uses it to predict what will happen in the construction business, and Smith, Kline, and French, a drug manufacturer, uses it to study the uncertainties of medicine."[10]

---

[10]Fred Luthans, *Organizational Behavior,* 6th ed. (New York: McGraw-Hill, Inc., 1992), 509–510.

The *Nominal Group Technique* (NGT) is a mixture of brainstorming and ordinary group processes. It is reputed to be the fastest growing meeting format in use in today's business organizations.[11] As part of NGT, the group meets and goes through four steps:

> NGT is a mixture of brainstorming and ordinary group processes.

1. Individual members answer a specific question by writing their answers without consulting with each other.
2. Each member of the group shares one of her ideas with the rest of the group. This "round-robin" process continues without any discussion of generated ideas. All ideas are written on a blackboard or large sheet of newsprint.
3. When all ideas have been posted, the group engages in an open discussion during which ideas are questioned, clarified, and evaluated.
4. When discussion has been completed, members independently rank items or vote on priorities. The resulting tally of independent votes becomes the group decision.

Like the Delphi technique, NGT avoids group cohesiveness problems, although it maintains the face-to-face element. NGT spurs creativity but does require considerable time to run correctly. Ease of implementation is

■ ■ ■ **SUPERVISORY SKILLS**
Getting the Most From your Group Decisions

1. Weigh carefully the demands of quality and group acceptance when deciding on a style. If acceptance is important, group decision-making styles are most appropriate. Remember, however, that group decision making can be a double-edged sword. Your effectiveness as a leader will be the key as to whether the group merely wastes time or reaches effective, creative decisions that they can support.

2. Remember that most people have creative potential; it is up to you to encourage that potential to unfold. Make use of creative techniques such as brainstorming when involved in group decision making. Not only will it generate more ideas, but it will help avoid groupthink conditions.

3. Group composition is very important. If you want the group to make a bold decision, you have to put people in the group who are willing to take chances. If you are looking for a rather conservative decision that will not make waves, assign people who are unlikely to do anything too dramatic.

4. Remember there are times when supervisors working alone do a better job. Some of these occasions include: (a) when the problem is clearly beyond the scope of most group members; (b) when the decision is too minor to warrant the expenditure of a group's time and effort; and (c) when you need a prompt, sharp, clear decision. In short, do not overuse or overrate group decision making.

---

[11]Ken Blanchard, "Meetings Can Be Effective," *Supervisory Management* (October 1992): 5.

another plus of NGT because final decisions frequently enjoy much group support.

Decision making is a continuing supervisory responsibility. If one problem is solved, another is always waiting in the wings. Some good decisions are never implemented and need further consideration at a later time. Some may be implemented only to find that unforeseen and unwanted consequences have occurred.

SUMMARY

Supervisors are faced with two types of problems: routine, programmed decisions and nonroutine, nonprogrammed decisions. The first type depends on rules, policies, and procedures for solutions, whereas the second requires creative problem solving. All decisions are made under one of three conditions: certainty, risk, and uncertainty.

Effective problem solving requires the supervisor to distinguish between a problem and a symptom. The latter is often the first clue that something is wrong; the former is the reason for this development. Supervisors need to focus their primary attention on the problem.

Decision making is the process of identifying problems and choosing from among alternatives. This process has a series of sequential steps, known as the rational decision-making model. However, when actually carrying out this process, the super-

visor often modifies it by using satisficing behavior, subjective rationality, and rationalization.

Two primary concerns motivate supervisors as they make decisions: the quality of the decision and the ease of acceptance by the subordinates. These two concerns result in four different decision-making styles: the laissez-faire supervisor, the I'm the boss supervisor, the nice guy supervisor, and the team leader supervisor.

Among the benefits of group decision making are the opportunity for widespread expertise and the ease of implementing solutions. However, pitfalls such as groupthink are associated with group decision making. Some of the most effective strategies for group decision making include the use of brainstorming, the Delphi technique, and the Nominal Group Technique.

REVIEW QUESTIONS

1. What is the difference between programmed and nonprogrammed decisions? Give examples of each.

2. Describe the three conditions under which decisions are made.

3. What is a symptom? How does it differ from a problem? Compare and contrast the two.

4. When uncovering the causes of a

problem, supervisors should keep certain things in mind. What are they?

5. In your own words, what is meant by the term *decision making?* Explain.

6. What are the steps in the rational decision-making model? Identify and describe each.

7. Many supervisors are satisficers. What does this statement mean? Explain.

8. What is meant by the term *bounded rationality?* What happens when a supervisor engages in this activity?

9. In what way does rationalization affect decision making? Explain.

10. How does the laissez-faire supervisor differ from the nice-guy supervisor? Compare and contrast the two styles.

11. How does the I'm the boss supervisor differ from the team leader supervisor? Compare and contrast the two styles.

12. In your own words, what is groupthink? How can it be prevented? Explain.

13. How does brainstorming work? How does the Delphi technique work? How does nominal group work? Identify and describe each.

KEY TERMS

Bounded Rationality. Model describing decision making as a process that looks for an acceptable answer to a problem.

Brainstorming. Technique for generating creative ideas from group members; characterized by an open climate that allows anyone to call out suggestions or ideas, piggybacking on the ideas of others, and a general focus on producing as many useful suggestions during the allotted time.

Certainty. Decision making under certainty occurs when one has all of the verifiable information needed to make a risk-free decision.

Decision making. Process of choosing from among alternatives.

Delphi technique. Technique used in group decision making characterized by participants who never meet face-to-face but, instead, provide their input through written questionnaires.

Groupthink. Group decision-making pitfall characterized by the members' feeling that they are right, everyone else is wrong, and their decisions are the best ones.

Nominal group technique. Approach to group decision making that involves a mixture of brainstorming and ordinary group processes in which ideas are first generated and then prioritized in terms of importance.

Risk. Decision making under risk occurs when one knows enough to estimate probable outcomes from decision alternatives.

Rational decision-making model. Model describing decision making as an orderly, sequential process resulting in the best decision.

Satisficing behavior. Action resulting in a decision good enough or acceptable to the decision maker.

Uncertainty. Decision making under uncertainty occurs when one has little or no information about decision alternatives or consequences of those alternatives.

ANSWERS TO SELF-ASSESSMENT QUIZ 5-1

1. Green: Village green, green light, golf green
2. Cover: Cover up, hard cover, book cover
3. Foot: Footloose, clubfoot, football
4. Light: Flashlight, starlight, limelight
5. Floor: Floor show, dance floor, ground floor

6. Ball: Ballgame, high ball, fast ball
7. Blood: Blue blood, blood pressure, blood line
8. Blue: Sky blue, blue book, blue point (a type of oyster)
9. High: High priest, high proof (liquor), high tide
10. Dutch: Dutch door (a door that is divided horizontally so that part of it

can be opened and part of it closed), Dutch oven, Dutch cheese.

How well did you do? Most people get five right when working alone and seven right when working with a group. Remember that creativity can be developed, but you have to work on it!

CASE 5-1
George's Goof

When George Wilson learned that management was computerizing sales information, he did not pay much attention to it. This new information is provided to sales supervisors on a monthly basis. It reports the amount of sales revenue generated in a supervisor's region and gives a general profile of the customer. Each month this profile changes somewhat, because those who made large orders in one month usually do not do so again the next month. The purpose of the computerized data is to help sales supervisors better understand the buying habits and sales trends in their geographic area.

For the last three months George has been receiving these computer printouts. However, he has never bothered to read them. After briefly scanning them, George puts them in the upper drawer of his desk. George feels that the print-outs really do not tell him a whole lot about buying habits. Additionally, because he has been the sales supervisor in his region for eight years, he's convinced he knows more about buying habits and sales trends in the area than anyone else. George also believes the computer printout is too difficult to understand. Seeing the nine columns of numbers, he imagines it would take quite a bit of time to fully understand what information they convey.

Yesterday George received a call from the vice president of sales. "I saw the Sunday edition of the newspaper in your area and noticed that

you didn't advertise a special sale for this coming week. Why not? You know from the computer information we sent you two weeks ago that over 35 percent of the people in your region have indicated that they will be making their buying decision this week. What happened? Did the newspaper lose your ads?" George was aghast. He quickly informed his boss that he would call the newspaper, find out what happened, and get things straightened out at once. Upon hanging up, he got out the latest computer printout. It took ten minutes to decipher everything in it. Sure enough, there was a footnote at the bottom of one of the tables urging George to put together an ad campaign to take advantage of the reports that 38.3 percent of the customers in his region would be making their quarterly purchases during the upcoming week. George immediately called the newspaper and got a one-page ad scheduled for the next day's edition.

1. Why is George overlooking the use of the computer printouts when making decisions? Explain, being sure to include the concept of simplicity in your answer.

2. How would George explain his actions? Include a brief discussion of rationalization in your answer.

3. What lesson should George learn from this oversight? Explain.

CASE 5-2
A Quiet Failure

The McDermott Company, a Midwest manufacturing company, has had great success selling home appliances. The firm's strategy is always the same. First, it invents a household product or modifies one to make it cheaper, smaller, or more efficient. The company then puts together a vigorous advertising campaign and waits for the customer orders to come rushing in. Over the last five years McDermott has developed five new products, and each has sold extremely well.

Two months ago the firm's manufacturing staff revealed their latest product. It is a lightweight, compact, inexpensive vacuum cleaner that is 38 percent more efficient than its closest competitor. Additionally, the machine's noise level has been so greatly reduced that, except for a red light that glows when the machine is in operation, it is sometimes impossible to tell that the machine is on.

The marketing people were delighted with the new product and immediately formed a committee to plan the advertising campaign. The committee has five members—two from marketing, two from production, and one from research and development. The chairperson is a supervisor from the production area. Each day for three weeks the group huddled in a conference room and worked out its plan of attack. On a number of different occasions the vice president of sales asked if she could help out in any way or provide input. "Perhaps we could do a brief market survey to see how well this type of machine will sell," she suggested. The advertising team shrugged off her suggestion. "Thanks," said the chairperson, "but I think we really have everything under control. We don't need any outside input. Our group consists of the best people in the company and I know we're going to come up with a sure-fire sales campaign."

Two weeks later the group revealed their campaign to the executive committee. Some of the committee members objected to the group drawing so much attention to the machine's quiet operation. "Are you sure people want quieter vacuum cleaners?" one member asked. "Why not put greater stress on the portability of the machine?" another suggested. After the meeting the group again convened. All of the suggestions from the executive committee were discarded as useless. "They just don't understand what we're doing," explained the chairperson of the committee. Everyone else agreed.

The ad campaign began last week. Since then there have been countless newspaper stories about, and customer comments on, the machine. In a nutshell everyone loves the efficiency and price of the machine. However, sales are only 41 percent of expectations. The biggest problem seems to be the noise factor. Many potential customers say that they equate noise with power; if the machine is very quiet, they do not believe it is getting the job done. Based on sales results to date, the vice president of sales has ordered an end to the "quiet campaign" and ordered the group to begin developing a new series of ads that stress the machine's power, compactness, and price. "Next time," he told the chairperson of the committee, "spend less time listening to each other and more time listening to the good advice given to you by the executive committee." At their meeting later on, the chairperson of the committee was heard to remark, "How could we have been so wrong?"

1. What happened? Why did the committee make such a big mistake? In your answer include a discussion of groupthink.

2. How could this problem have been prevented? Offer some suggestions.

3. What lessons can be learned from this case? Explain.

▪ ▪ ▪ PART II

S upervisors deal with many people including subordinates, superiors, and other supervisors on a daily basis. Of course, the particular interaction depends on with whom they are interacting and about what. This part focuses on the major types of interactions and how the supervisor should handle them. Although in most cases these are geared toward subordinate dealings, this is not exclusively true.

Chapter 6 sets the stage for this section by presenting the complicated legal framework within which supervisors must work. Special attention is given to all of the significant equal opportunity legislation that has been enacted in the last three decades. Current hot issues such as sexual harassment and the glass ceiling phenomenon are discussed.

Chapter 7 addresses the selection and training of employees. The supervisor assumes a number of important roles in this process, although, especially in large firms, the personnel department helps out. This chapter also explains the purposes of the selection interview and how this interview is carried out. In addition, it discusses the benefits of orientation and who has the responsibility for carrying out this function. In the latter part of the chapter the seven steps in the training process are described and the importance of this function is discussed.

Chapter 8 introduces the student to the role of supervisors in managing a multicultural work force. Demographics show that many more women and minorities will be joining the work force in the near future. With them comes the need for supervisors to value differences and manage a diverse group of workers toward improved productivity.

Chapter 9 examines the topic of motivation. Whether the supervisor is trying to get subordinates to do something or to persuade a superior towards a particular point of view, motivation is important. In this chapter the term *motivation* is explained in terms of need fulfillment and the

Dealing with Individuals

question, "What do employees want from their jobs?" is broached. Motivation is also examined in terms of expectations and some important motivational strategies such as reinforcement, job redesign, and goal setting are examined.

Chapter 10 deals with handling employee problems. These can be quite a headache for the supervisor and every effective first-line manager must learn how to handle them. This chapter describes some of the common discipline problems and reviews four of the personality problems often found in employees. Attention is also directed toward the way in which the discipline process is carried out. The latter part of the chapter explains how employee assistance programs work and discusses substance abuse problems in organizations, specifically alcohol and drug abuse.

Chapter 11 examines the topic of providing effective feedback specifically in terms of telling people how well they are doing and how they can improve. Initial attention in this chapter is devoted to identifying and describing the performance appraisal process. The benefits of an effective appraisal system are discussed, and then the six major types of appraisal used in organizations today are described. Some of the common sources of bias in performance appraisal are also examined. The chapter concludes with a comparison and contrast of the three overall philosophies of performance appraisal interviewing.

When you have finished reading all of the material in this part of the book you will have a solid understanding of the challenges that supervisors face in their efforts to deal with individuals. You will also be aware of some of the most important rules and guidelines that can assist you in your efforts to understand, motivate, and control your personnel.

CHAPTER 6

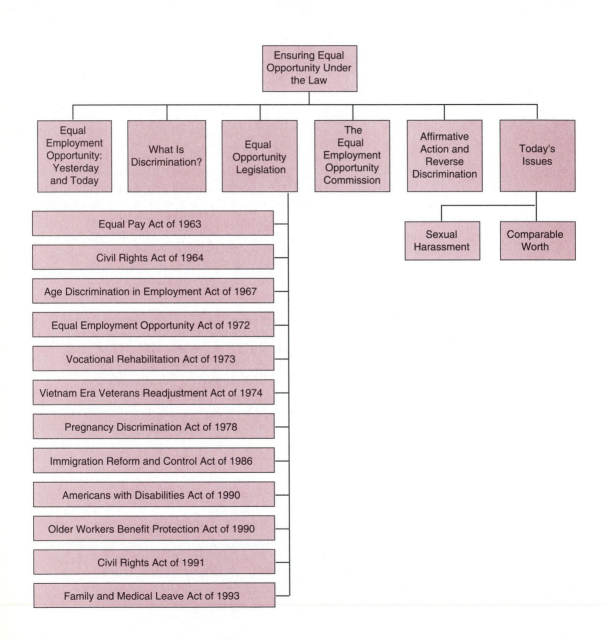

Ensuring Equal Opportunity Under the Law

CHAPTER OBJECTIVES

- ☐ Define discrimination and the related concepts of disparate treatment and adverse impact.

- ☐ Discuss the chronology of important equal opportunity legislation starting with the Equal Pay Act of 1963 and concluding with the Family and Medical Leave Act of 1993.

- ☐ Learn the important aspects of these laws as they relate to the work environment.

- ☐ Investigate the purpose and process of the EEOC.

- ☐ Understand the various types of affirmative action and the complex issue of reverse discrimination.

- ☐ Become sensitive to two important current issues: sexual harassment and comparable worth.

EQUAL EMPLOYMENT OPPORTUNITY— YESTERDAY AND TODAY

Although we often like to think about discrimination and the lack of equal opportunity as problems of the past, they are still very much with us. This chapter looks at discrimination in its many forms and explores a substantial body of equal opportunity legislation that has transformed the way American organizations relate to their employees. It also provides the reader with a legal base with which to study many of the other topics to be covered later in the book. The main agency charged with monitoring the laws, the Equal Employment Opportunity Commission, is described and the issues of affirmative action and reverse discrimination are investigated. Finally, today's hottest issues are introduced: sexual harrassment, the glass ceiling phenomenon, and comparable worth. Before reading further, take Self-Assessment Quiz 6-1 to see what you already know about equal opportunity legislation.

To begin, we ask, what is discrimination?

WHAT IS DISCRIMINATION?

On reading Title VII of the 1964 Civil Rights Act, the most important legislation ensuring equal opportunity, one can infer that discrimination refers to the use of race, color, religion, sex, or national origin as the reason for

---

SELF-ASSESSMENT QUIZ 6-1
What Do You Know About Equal Opportunity Law?

Directions: Answer each of the following questions true or false.

____ 1. To be judged discrimination, actions must be intentional.

____ 2. The first interest in equal rights dates back to 1964.

____ 3. Title VII of the Civil Rights Act of 1964 is still considered the most important equal opportunity legislation.

____ 4. Age can never be a determining factor in employment decisions.

____ 5. The Justice Department is the main federal agency to enforce equal opportunity legislation.

____ 6. It is all right to require that pregnant women go on leave but not until after their sixth month.

____ 7. Organizations are only obliged to hire disabled workers if they can operate within the existing physical constraints of the workplace.

____ 8. Companies are free to have personnel policies that exclude hiring legal as well as illegal aliens.

____ 9. Workers filing discrimination claims may win damages exceeding $1,000,000.

____ 10. Workers may take unpaid leave for childbirth but not for illness of a family member.

Discrimination is treating people differently because of race, color, religion, sex, or national origin.

treating people differently from each other. Thus, it is unlawful to refuse to hire someone because he or she belongs to a minority group or attends a certain church.

Further legislation and court decisions have expanded the meaning of discrimination to include any unequal consequences for people of different race, color, religion, sex, or national origin that are not justified by any business necessity. With this interpretation, employment tests that cannot be proven to be job related are likely to be judged discriminatory in nature.

In addition to the few examples already given, discrimination manifests itself in many ways. It may help to organize these manifestations into three categories: disparate treatment, adverse impact, and present effects of past discrimination.[1]

Disparate treatment is intentional discrimination.

"Disparate treatment" refers to international discrimination against an individual or class of individuals because of race, age, sex, color, religion, or national origin. Examples would include refusing to hire women because it is feared they will get pregnant and leave the organization, and refusing to promote men older than 50 because they might soon retire.

Adverse impact refers to unintentional discrimination.

"Adverse impact" refers to unintentional discrimination, for example, by requiring seemingly harmless qualifications for employment or promotion that in turn serve to disqualify large percentages of some groups. Thus, if an employment test unequally screens out minority employees and if that test cannot be proven absolutely necessary to predict job success, the test is said to have an adverse impact on the minorities in question and to be discriminatory. The Equal Employment Opportunity Commission (EEOC) has developed a "four-fifths rule" to judge adverse impact.

The four-fifths rule measures adverse impact.

The four-fifths rule states that the ratio of minority applicants to minority hires must be at least four-fifths, or 80 percent, that of the ratio of nonminority applicants to nonminority hires. Thus, if out of 20 minority applicants, only five are hired while 15 of 20 nonminority applicants are hired, a charge of adverse impact is highly likely. The four-fifths rule guideline monitors hiring blacks, Native Americans, Asians, Hispanics, women, and men.[2]

Discrimination might also occur through perpetuation of the effects of past discrimination.

> "For example, a policy of hiring persons who are referred by current employees before hiring other applicants may appear to be a nondiscriminatory policy. However, if the work force is white because of discrimination in the past, the use of an employee referral policy in hiring may tend to perpetuate

[1]William P. Anthony, Pamela L. Perrewe, and K. Michele Kacmar, *Strategic Human Resource Management* (Ft. Worth, Tex.: The Dryden Press, 1993), 148.

[2]R. Wayne Mondy and Robert M. Noe III, *Human Resource Management,* 5th ed. (Boston, Mass.: Allyn & Bacon, 1993).

the white work force because new recruits might come primarily from the white community."[3]

To better understand the complicated and sometimes confusing legal requirements surrounding equal opportunity, it is necessary to have a working knowledge of key legislation.

EQUAL OPPORTUNITY LEGISLATION

Beginning with the U.S. Constitution, there has been much concern about equal rights; however, the modern concern with equal opportunity is usually attributed to the Civil Rights Act of 1964. Table 6–1 lists the major acts beginning a year before passage of the Civil Rights Act and continuing up to the early 1990s. Each act will be briefly discussed.

Equal Pay Act of 1963

Equal pay for equal work is the law.

The Equal Pay Act of 1963 forbids discrimination in compensation paid to men and women and based solely on sex. Thus, men and women doing the same or similar jobs must be paid the same. Differences in pay rates

---

TABLE 6–1

Major equal opportunity legislation

Equal Pay Act	1963
Civil Rights Act	1964
Age Discrimination in Employment Act	1967
Equal Employment Opportunity Act	1972
Vocational Rehabilitation Act	1973
Vietnam Era Veterans Readjustment Act	1974
Pregnancy Discrimination Act	1978
Immigration Reform and Control Act	1986
Americans with Disabilities Act	1990
Older Workers Benefit Protection Act	1990
Civil Rights Act	1991
Family and Medical Leave Act	1993

---

[3]Anthony et. al., 149.

are allowed, however, if the differential is based on a factor such as seniority, merit, or quantity or quality of production, that is, any factor other
than sex.

The Civil Rights Act of 1964

*Title VII is the most
significant equal
rights legislation.*

Title VII of this landmark legislation (as amended in later years) passed
under President Lyndon Johnson directly forbids discrimination based on
race, color, religion, sex, or national origin. Title VII covers virtually all
organizations with more than fifteen employees and prohibits any type
of employment action that is based on one of the prohibited areas.
Thus, promotions and training opportunities are covered as well as hiring decisions. The comprehensiveness of this Act has touched just about
every U.S. organization, including government, private employers, and
unions.

Age Discrimination in Employment Act of 1967

*ADEA protects
workers older than
age 40.*

The Age Discrimination in Employment Act (ADEA) forbids discrimination
against employees older than age 40 and covers all companies with twenty employees or more. Government agencies, labor unions, and employment agencies are also covered. ADEA is most often remembered for its
1987 amendment that made mandatory retirement at age 70 illegal; however, it also makes illegal any discrimination in hiring, firing, promotions,
and so on. The Act does allow mandatory retirement for executives whose
pensions exceed $44,000 per year.

*BFOQ's are neces-
sary qualifications to
perform a job.*

ADEA also provides that age may be used as a determining factor in
decision making if it can be proven to be a "bona fide occupational qualification" or "BFOQ." A bona fide occupational qualification is one that can
be proven to be necessary for a person to perform a given job. Pilots, for
example, may be mandatorily retired at age 60 given the reduction in reaction time and related skills after that age. Employers must be very careful, however, that a BFOQ is genuine and not a pretext for laying off older
workers.

Equal Employment Opportunity Act of 1972

*The EEOC was es-
tablished in 1972.*

The Equal Employment Opportunity Act of 1972 was actually an amendment to the Civil Rights Act of 1963. The most important provision of this
legislation created the Equal Employment Opportunity Commission
(EEOC) which administers Title VII and other discrimination legislation.
The EEOC will be discussed more fully later in this chapter.

Vocational Rehabilitation Act of 1973

The Vocational Rehabilitation Act prohibits discrimination against handicapped employees by the federal government or federal contractors. For

purpose of this act, Congress defined "handicapped" in Section 7(7)(B) as any person who:

"(i) has a physical or mental impairment which substantially limits one or more of such person's major life activities.

(ii) has a record of such an impairment, or

(iii) is regarded as having such an impairment."[4]

Unlike Title VII, the Vocational Rehabilitation Act is enforced by the Office of Federal Contract Compliance Programs within the Department of Labor. It is the job of the OFCCP to assure that companies with government contracts of more than $2,500 annually take "affirmative action" to recruit and hire all qualified disabled persons. Further, employers must make "reasonable accommodations" so that the handicapped person may perform adequately and comfortably within the workplace. Both the concept of affirmative action and reasonable accommodations will be expanded later in this chapter. Employers with fifty or more employees and federal contracts of $50,000 or more must file written affirmative action plans with the OFCCP.

The OFCCP monitors affirmative action among government contractors.

Vietnam Era Veterans Readjustment Act of 1974

The Vietnam Era Veterans Readjustment Act of 1974 attempted to protect the rights of returning veterans. The law made it mandatory to provide equal employment opportunities for Vietnam War veterans. Similar to the Vocational Rehabilitation Act, this legislation applies to federal contractors and subcontractors who hold Federal contracts of $10,000 or more. Likewise, employers with fifty or more employees and contracts that exceed $50,000 must file written affirmative action programs regarding the hiring and promoting of Vietnam veterans. The Office of Federal Contract Compliance Programs enforces this act.

Federal contractors must assure equal opportunity to Vietnam veterans.

Pregnancy Discrimination Act of 1978

In 1978, Congress made it illegal to discriminate against a female employee in any way because she is pregnant or may become pregnant. Neither may employees who have had an abortion be treated any differently than everybody else. Nor can women be forced to leave the job temporarily or permanently because they are pregnant. As long as they can perform their job duties, they must be allowed to do so; then they are entitled to the same medical leave benefits as for any other medical condition.

Pregnancy must be treated like any other medical condition.

---

[4]Lloyd L. Byars and Leslie W. Rue, *Human Resource Management* (Burr Ridge, Illinois: Irwin 1994), 31.

Immigration Reform and Control Act of 1986

Throughout the 1980s, there was increasing concern that illegal aliens were being hired, sometimes in the place of American workers, by employers who were ignoring their lack of proper credentials.

> "It is unclear how illegal aliens affect the unemployment rate of domestic workers. Generally, aliens are employed in jobs for which there is little competition with U.S. workers. Nevertheless, illegal aliens may be competing for jobs with unemployed blacks, whose unemployment rates are nearly double the unemployment rates for whites."[5]

It was further suspected that some employers were deliberately recruiting illegal aliens, for example, Mexicans in the Southwest, to work under poor conditions and for below minimum wage. This concern culminated in passage of the Immigration Reform and Control Act. The two major purposes of this bill are to control illegal immigration and to protect U.S. and legal immigrant workers from job loss.

Employers must verify applicant's right to work in this country.

A main requirement of the Act is that employers must verify applicant eligibility to work by a careful check of documents that prove identity and right to work. This has created a lot of paperwork for everyone but has greatly curtailed the deliberate hiring of illegal aliens.

Another requirement of the Act is that employers may not discriminate against U.S. citizens. Neither may they discriminate against any legitimate candidate because of place of national origin. Enforcement of the Act's provisions is quite complicated.

> "The complexity of IRCA enforcement can be attributed to the large number of agencies that may be involved in an IRCA case. Complaints may be handled by the Immigration and Naturalization Service, EEOC, the Special Counsel, the National Labor Relations Board, or the Attorney General. Hearings may be conducted by a variety of personnel."[6]

Employers must be aware that refusing to hire legal aliens out of concern for avoiding to hire illegal aliens is also prohibited under this law. Legal aliens may not be discriminated against because of their country of origin.

Americans with Disabilities Act of 1990

Recently, supervisors have been concentrating on learning the legal requirements involved in hiring the disabled, as defined by the Americans with Disabilities Act (ADA) of 1990 that took effect for companies with

---

[5]James Ledvinka and Vida Gulbinas Scarpello, *Federal Regulation of Personnel and Human Resource Management,* 2nd ed. (Boston, Mass.: PWS-Kent Publishing Co., 1991), 83.

[6]Ibid., 93.

twenty-five employees or more in July 1992. ADA covers many physical and mental conditions, such as epilepsy, hearing or vision impairment, cancer, heart disease, AIDS, and mental retardation. Only a person's ability to do the job is in question.

> ADA calls upon employers to list the essential functions of a position and allows the job interviewer to ask if the applicant can perform those duties. If the applicant can, fine. If the applicant could, but would need some accommodation in the form of workplace changes to do the job, the employer must make those changes if they are 'reasonable.'[7]

In hiring decisions, if the applicant's disability would keep him or her from performing a required job function as stated in the job description and no "reasonable accommodation" would change that fact, it would not be discriminatory to eliminate that person from consideration. On the other hand, people may not be filtered out because of a disability that has no effect on their potential job performance. Table 6–2 summarizes ADA suggestions for making the workplace accessible to the disabled.

The impact of ADA may be most apparent in the hiring process, but it substantially defines legal behavior in all aspects of employment, including firing, promotion, training, and compensation. Beginning in July 1994, ADA extended its provisions to all employers with fifteen or more employees.

ADA requires reasonable accommodation in the workplace.

Older Workers Benefit Protection Act of 1990

In 1989, a controversial Supreme Court decision allowed as legal an Ohio county agency's decision to deny disability benefits to an employee who was laid off at age 61 because its disability plan terminated at age 60.

> "Under the Older Workers Benefit Protection Act, employers may integrate disability and pension pay by paying the retiree the higher of the two; integrate retiree health insurance and severance pay by deducting the former from the latter; and, in cases of plant closings or mass layoffs, integrate pension and severance pay the amount added to the pension."[8]

Under this act, employees also are given a 21-day grace period to consider an early retirement package.

Civil Rights Act of 1991

The Civil Rights Act of 1991 amended the Civil Rights Act of 1964 and was largely a result of controversial Supreme Court decisions of the late 1980s.

---

[7]Marc Hequet, "The Intricacies of Interviewing," *Training* (April 1993):32–33.
[8]Byars and Rue, *Human Resource Management,* 33.

TABLE 6-2

Examples of reasonable accommodation

- Lower drinking fountains and public telephones
- Lower paper towel and paper cup dispensers
- Widen doorways
- Make rest rooms fully accessible
- Install ramps by the doors
- Reserve disabled parking spaces
- Install braille markings on elevator buttons
- Install electric door openers in addition to traditional door handles
- Install flashing alarm lights for the hearing impaired
- Rearrange office furniture
- Lower shelves, books, and materials to be more easily accessible
- Modify phones for the hearing impaired
- Install hand controls in company vehicles

Thus, the 1991 legislation expanded the scope of existing statutes to further protect people against discrimination. Table 6–3 shows the major provisions of the 1991 Civil Rights Act.

Among the more important provisions are the allowance for jury trials by people seeking compensatory damages with possible awards of $50,000 to $300,000.

The Glass Ceiling Commission studies promotions of women and minorities.

As part of the Civil Rights Act of 1991, the Glass Ceiling Act of 1991 was also passed. This legislation established a Glass Ceiling Commission whose purpose was to monitor and study promotional policies of corporations as they related to women and other minorities and top management positions. The idea of a glass ceiling refers to the invisible barrier that seems to keep women and minorities from rising beyond a certain point in the organization.

> It appears that while significant gains have been made by minorities and women in gaining entry to organizations, fewer than five percent of senior management positions are held by women and minorities. Why? Because many times these individuals do not have mentors, lack appropriate networks, or do not have access to executive search firms.[9]

---

[9]David A. DeCenzo and Stephen P. Robbins, *Human Resource Management,* 4th ed. (New York: John Wiley & Sons, 1994), 82.

TABLE 6-3

Major provisions of the 1991 Civil Rights Act

- *Damages and Jury Trials*: Provides for compensatory and punitive damages for victims of intentional discrimination suing under Title VII, the ADA, or federal employment sections of the Rehabilitation Act. The combined amount of compensatory and punitive damages depends upon the size of the employer, with caps ranging from $50,000 to $300,000. Jury trials may be requested by any party seeking compensatory or punitive damages.

- *"Race Norming" of Employment Tests*: Prohibits adjustments in test scores, use of different cutoff scores, or other amendments to employment-related tests based on race, color, religion, sex, or national origin.

- *Expanded Coverage under Section 1981*: Amends interpretation of language in Supreme Court decision in *Patterson* v. *McLean*, regarding the right "to make and enforce contracts." Prior to this decision, Section 1981 was applied to race discrimination in all aspects of the employment contract, that is, hiring, duration of employment, and contract termination. After the *Patterson* decision, Section 1981 applied to hiring only. The Civil Rights Act of 1991 restores the pre-*Patterson* interpretation specifying that the term "make and enforce" contracts includes all benefits, privileges, terms, and conditions of the employment relationship. This is significant since there are no caps on awards for compensatory and punitive damages under Section 1981.

- *Mixed Motive Cases*: Reverses *Price Waterhouse* v. *Tompkins*, in which the Supreme Court held that an employer could avoid liability for discrimination by showing that it would have made the same employment decision in the absence of discrimination. Under the new act, this rule is changed by providing that an illegal employment practice has occurred if discrimination was a motivating factor, even though other factors also motivated the employment decision. In such cases, plaintiffs may recover declaratory and injunctive relief, attorneys fees, and costs.

- *Disparate Impact*: Reverses the Supreme Court decision of *Wards Cove* v. *Antonio*, which stated that plaintiffs injured by disparate impact discrimination had to prove that the challenged practices were not significantly related to legitimate business objectives. Under the 1991 act, an employer must demonstrate that a challenged practice is job-related and consistent with "business necessity" after the plaintiff has shown that the employment practice caused a disparate impact. Once the employer had met its burden, the plaintiff must prove that an alternative practice exists having less of a disparate impact and that the employer refused to adopt it. If the employer can prove that its employment practice does not cause disparate impact, it is not required to show the practice is required by business necessity.

- *Extraterritorial Employment*: Defines "employee" in both Title VII and the ADA to include U.S. citizens employed abroad and provides exemptions for otherwise unlawful employment actions if compliance violates laws of the foreign country where the employee works. Additionally, the 1991 act creates a presumption that violations of Title VII by foreign corporations controlled by an American employer are violations by the American employer itself.

- *Glass Ceiling*: The Glass Ceiling Commission was established to study barriers to advancement of minorities and women in the work force and to recommend means of overcoming those barriers. Also establishes National Award for diversity and excellence in executive management.

Source: Exhibit from *Strategic Human Resource Management* by William P. Anthony, Pamela L. Perrewe, and Michi Kacmar, copyright © 1993 by Harcourt Brace & Company, reproduced by permission of the publisher.

TABLE 6–4

Top ten positions occupied by women: Have you really "come a long way, baby"?

Rank	1990	1940	1890
1	Secretary	Servant	Servant
2	Cashier	Stenographer, secretary	Agricultural laborer
3	Bookkeeper	Teacher	Dressmaker
4	Registered nurse	Clerical worker	Teacher
5	Nursing aide, orderly	Sales worker	Farmer, planter
6	Elementary school teacher	Factory worker (apparel)	Laundress
7	Waitress	Bookkeeper, accountant, cashier	Seamstress
8	Sales worker	Waitress	Cotton-mill operative
9	Child-care worker	Housekeeper	Housekeeper, steward
10	Cook	Nurse	Clerk, cashier

Source: Lloyd L. Byars and Leslie W. Rue, *Human Resource Management*, (Burr Ridge, Ill.: Irwin, © 1994), 33.

Table 6–4 takes a look at the top ten positions held by women in 1890, 1940, and 1990 and questions whether significant progress has really been made.

Family and Medical Leave Act of 1993

On February 5, 1993, President Clinton signed into law the Family and Medical Leave Act of 1993 that had previously been vetoed by President Bush. This legislation covers all companies with fifty or more employees and guarantees that employees may take up to twelve weeks of unpaid leave each year for family matters, including childbirth, adoption, or caring for a sick family member. It also guarantees that the returning employee will have, if not his or her old job, a job of equal status and pay waiting. The Act also requires that the employer maintain the worker on all health care benefits during the unpaid leave.

Executive Orders 11246, 11375, and 11478

In addition to the laws described above, several significant Presidential executive orders have extended the scope of antidiscrimination legislation.

EEO 11246 requires written affirmative action plans.

Executive Order 11246 was issued in 1965 and prohibits Federal contractors and subcontractors from discriminating against employees because of race, sex, color, religion, or national origin. Contractors with business less than $10,000 are not covered by this order. The Office of Federal Contract Compliance Programs (OFCCP) within the Department of Labor monitors the provisions of this law that include the requirement that the contractor or subcontractor include an equal opportunity clause in every subcontract or purchase order. Perhaps even more important, the law requires that contracts that exceed $50,000 have a written affirmative action program.

Executive Order 11375, issued in 1967, extended Executive Order 11246 by prohibiting sex-based discrimination in compensation. Executive Order 11478, issued in 1969, modified some of the previous procedures without changing the spirit of the requirements.

By now, it should be apparent that the field of equal opportunity is replete with legislated provisions. Additionally, many state and local governments have passed additional equal employment laws. It should be noted, however, that in any case where a state or local law is in conflict with a federal law, the legislation most favorable to the group in question prevails.

The next section deals with the Equal Employment Opportunity Commission, the main agency assigned the responsibility of monitoring compliance with antidiscrimination legislation.

THE EQUAL EMPLOYMENT OPPORTUNITY COMMISSION

The main responsibility for enforcing equal opportunity legislation has been given to the Equal Employment Opportunity Commission (EEOC) under the 1972 Equal Employment Opportunity Act. It should be noted, however, that this responsibility is shared with several other Federal agencies, including the Justice Department, the Office of Federal Contract Compliance Programs, the Office of Management and Budget, and the Office of Personnel Management. With this in mind, we will confine our discussion to the operations of the EEOC.

EEOC shares the enforcement role with other federal offices.

■ ■ ■ **SUPERVISORY SKILLS**
Supervising within the Law

1. Be sure you have a working knowledge of the equal opportunity laws. Ignorance not only is not a defense for breeches of law, but it often leads to unwitting mistakes.

2. Take advantage of any training opportunities your company gives you regarding do's and dont's of hiring and working with women and minorities.

3. Remember that you act as a role model for the employees in your department. Do your actions promote equity in treatment of all employees? Do you counsel other employees in the event of insensitive or even illegal activities?

4. In the event of serious infringements such as sexual harassment, be sure to document the incident; never try to bury potentially damaging actions.

The EEOC consists of five members and one general counsel.

The EEOC is based in Washington, D.C., but has offices across the country. The Commission is composed of five members appointed by the President for five-year terms. The President chooses one member to be chairperson and another to be Vice-Chairperson. A general counsel is also appointed by the President for a four-year term, and it is this person who is responsible for conducting litigation. The EEOC monitors employer compliance with the nondiscriminatory practices legislated by Title VII. It hears complaints and investigates where necessary. Figure 6–1 depicts the EEOC process once a complaint has been charged.

The EEOC hears discrimination cases and attempts settlement or pursues an investigation.

Most charges are settled at the first stage by the company and the employee coming to a mutually satisfactory settlement with no admission of guilt. If such a settlement is not possible, the EEOC next begins an investigation either by looking into the complaint with EEOC staff or referring the complaint to the state or local enforcement agency. The company is visited, records are examined, and people are interviewed. With all of the facts gathered, the EEOC decides whether there is a "probable cause" to believe that Title VII has been violated.

While investigating a complaint, the EEOC makes use of the 1978 Uniform Guidelines of Employee Selection Procedures, which were jointly adopted by four federal agencies: the Department of Justice, the EEOC, the Civil Service Commission, and the Department of Labor. These guidelines cover Title VII enforcement as well as Executive Order 11246 and the Equal Pay Act, and they are a common guideline source regarding employment decisions about hiring, firing, transfers, promotions, testing, and other selection practices.

If, at the end of the investigation, no probable cause has been determined, the EEOC ends its participation by informing the complaining party that he or she can file a private suit in federal district court. If, on the other hand, the EEOC finds there is probable cause, it next tries "conciliation," which is a process of negotiation among all parties. Conciliation equates to out-of-court settlement.

If conciliation fails, the EEOC will consider litigation, which is an expensive and time-consuming process that the EEOC usually reserves for important cases with implications beyond the individual case. If the EEOC decides not to pursue the case, the complaining party is issued a right-to-sue notice informing them of their right to take the case to federal court.

The EEOC also issues regulations.

The other major function of the EEOC is to issue regulations regarding employment practices. Basically these regulations interpret Title VII and other antidiscriminatory legislation. Table 6–5 lists some of the more important EEOC regulations that have been handed down in the past.

While the EEOC concentrates on discrimination, i.e., the current workplace practices which unfairly treat some employees differently, affirmative action is another important issue.

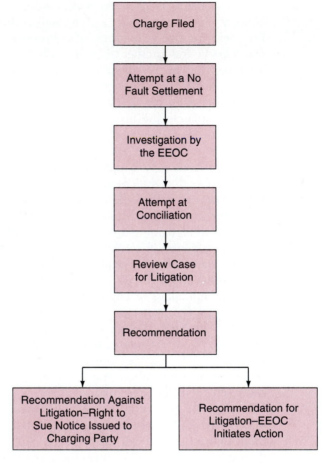

FIGURE 6-1
The EEOC process.
Source: R. Wayne Mondy and Robert M. Noe, III, *Human Resource Management,*
5th ed. (Boston, Mass.: Allyn Bacon, 1993), 89.

AFFIRMATIVE ACTION AND REVERSE DISCRIMINATION

Affirmative action
redresses yesterday's
wrongs.

Unlike antidiscrimination measures that concentrate on today's problems, affirmative action concentrates on redressing past wrongs by requiring employers to hire and promote women and other minorities according to the percentage of qualified women and minorities in the work force.

Roosevelt Thomas, Executive Director of the Americas Institute for Managing Diversity, pointed out there were four reasons for requiring affirmative action plans: (1) white males made up the great majority of workers; (2) U.S. companies were healthy and growing and could ac-

---

TABLE 6–5

EEOC regulations

Sex discrimination guidelines

Questions and answers on pregnancy disability and reproductive hazards

Religious discrimination guidelines

National origin discrimination guidelines

Interpretations of the Age Discrimination in Employment Act

Employee selection guidelines

Questions and answers on employee selection guidelines

Sexual harassment guidelines

Record keeping and reports

Affirmative action guidelines

EEO in the federal government

Equal Pay Act interpretations

Policy statement on maternity benefits

Policy statement on relationship of Title VII to 1986 Immigration Reform and Control Act

Policy statement on reproductive and fetal hazards

Policy statement on religious accommodation under Title VII

Policy guidance on sexual harassment

Source: James Ledvinka and Vida G. Scarpello, *Federal Regulation of Personnel and Human Resource Management*, 2nd ed. (Boston, Mass.: PWS-Kent Publishing Co., 1991), 38.

Affirmative action means different things.

commodate more women and minorities; (3) it was a matter of common decency that past injustices be redressed; and (4) "legal and social coercion were necessary" to end the discriminatory practices of the past.[10]

The exact meaning of affirmative action has always been in question. At least four definitions have emerged over the years.[11]

1. Recruitment of underrepresented groups: seeking applicants from groups that are underrepresented in the employer's work force.
2. Changing management attitudes: trying to eliminate conscious and unconscious prejudices that individual managers and supervisors may have toward groups that are underrepresented in the employer's work force.

---

[10]R. Roosevelt Thomas, Jr., "From Affirmative Action to Affirming Diversity," *Harvard Business Review* (March–April 1990): 107.

[11]James Ledvinka and Vida G. Scarpello, *Federal Regulation of Personnel and Human Resource Management,* 2nd ed. (Boston, Mass.: PWS-Kent Publishing Co., 1991), 166–167.

3. Removing discriminatory obstacles: identifying practices that work to the disadvantage of groups that are underrepresented in the employer's work force and replacing them with practices that do not work to the disadvantage of those groups.
4. Preferential treatment: hiring and staffing preferential for groups that are underrepresented in the employer's work force.

Affirmative action programs generally develop under one of three conditions.[12]

First, as mentioned earlier in the chapter, if a company is a federal contractor or subcontractor with more than $50,000 of government business and employs fifty workers or more, it is required to file with the OFCCP an affirmative action plan assuring goals and quotas for minority workers.

AAPs develop for three reasons.

Second, a federal court may require an affirmative action plan if it has been proven that a company was guilty of past discrimination. A specific action plan called a "consent decree" outlines the affirmative action steps a company must take.

Third, companies may voluntarily decide to establish goals in hiring and promoting women and minorities depending on the extent to which they are currently underrepresented in the organization.

> "The key considerations in an organization's establishment of a legal, voluntary affirmative action program are that it be remedial in purpose, limited in its duration, restricted in its reverse discrimination impact—that is, it does not operate as an absolute ban on nonminorities—and flexible in implementation. When an organization's voluntary AAP has these characteristics, the risk of losing a reverse discrimination suit may be minimized. Nonetheless, there is still some risk of being liable for reverse discrimination."[13]

The issue of reverse discrimination—discrimination against workers because they are not women or minorities—is a hotly debated one. Whereas the courts have mainly favored quotas and goals as the only way to remedy past injustices, some Supreme Court rulings have limited the use of strict quotas. For example, *Firefighters Local Union 1974* v *Stotts* in 1984 found that the courts could not ignore seniority during layoffs in an attempt to lay off no black workers. At the current time, reverse discrimination is still very much of an open issue. There are, however, other open issues in today's workplace. One—the Glass Ceiling Phenomenon—has already been discussed. Two others are sexual harrassment and comparable worth.

---

[12]Randall S. Schuler, *Managing Human Resources,* 4th ed. (St. Paul, Minn.: West Publishing Co., 1992), 38–42.

[13]Ibid., 42.

TODAY'S ISSUES

Perhaps no single issue today is getting more attention than the issue of sexual harassment.

Sexual Harassment

Sexual harassment is unwelcomed sexual behavior.

Sexual harassment can be defined as any unwelcomed behavior of a sexual nature that interferes with a worker's performance in the workplace. The courts have recognized sexual harassment charges since the late 1970s under Title VII, but by 1993, the number of formal sexual harassment charges had reached 10,532 per year, double the number from just five years earlier.[14] It is unknown whether instances of sexual harassment have increased so dramatically or whether people are just stepping forward more readily after the highly publicized sexual harassment charges brought by Anita Hill against Supreme Court Justice Clarence Thomas.

Quid-pro-quo sexual harassment is easy to spot.

Just what constitutes sexual harassment? When does a compliment or a casual comment cease being sociable and start being offensive? Basically, there are two types of sexual harassment. The one that is easiest to spot is quid-pro-quo sexism, where one person promises the other something in return for sexual favors. Thus, if a female boss promises a promotion to a male employee if and only if he will go out with her, this is quid-pro-quo sexual harassment.

The "hostile environment" criteria are harder to prove.

The second type of sexual harassment has to do with creating a "hostile environment" in which the employee is uncomfortable because of sexual innuendo or other offensive behavior. This area is far more difficult to define.

> "A hostile work environment exists where supervisors and/or coworkers create an atmosphere so infused with sexually oriented conduct that an employee's reasonable comfort level or ability to perform is affected severely. To prevail in a hostile work environment claim, the employee need not suffer any economic detriment. However, she or he must establish that the conduct to which she or he was subjected was severe, pervasive, and unwelcome."[15]

How pervasive is sexual harassment? One study showed that 90% of Fortune 500 companies have had sexual harassment complaints and more than one third of these have been sued at least once. The same study estimates that sexual harassment problems cost the average large corporation $6.7 million a year! As people become more willing to speak up about this problem, we can estimate with some assurance that the incidence and cost of this problem will surely rise in the near future.[16]

---

[14]Anne B. Fisher, "Sexual Harassment: What to Do," *Fortune* (August 23, 1993): 84–88.

[15]Jonathan A. Segal, "The Sexlessness of Harassment," *HR Magazine* (August 1991): 71.

[16]Fisher, 85.

SUPERVISORY SKILLS
EEOC and Affirmative Action

1. Know your company's stance on affirmative action. What is the formal policy? Be sure that you understand it and can communicate it effectively to members of your department.

2. Remember that to most employees, the supervisor represents the company. Be a role model for sensitive and appropriate behavior and demand that others act the same.

3. Make training available on difficult issues like sexual harassment. Every employee should know what constitutes a hostile environment, for example.

4. In the event of an EEOC investigation, you will surely be interviewed. Check your facts carefully and be sure to be open and honest in your reporting of those facts.

So how do companies protect themselves and their workers against this peril? First, it is advisable to have a well-publicized sexual harassment policy statement. Put everybody on notice that such behavior will not be tolerated. Second, a supervisory training program is critical in educating first-line managers in what constitutes sexual harassment and how to investigate such claims. Third, an effective decision-making process must be established to handle sexual harassment complaints.[17]

Have a well-known sexual harrassment policy.

What constitutes an effective sexual harassment policy? According to EEOC guidelines, sexual harassment policies should do the following:

- Prohibit sexual and other types of harassment.
- Encourage victims of harassment to come forward with their complaints.
- Promise that filing a complaint will not result in retaliation.
- State that the complaint will be kept as confidential as possible.
- Guarantee that each complaint will be investigated thoroughly and objectively.
- Explain that complaints may be filed with an individual other than the victim's supervisor (who is frequently the harasser).
- Promise that prompt, appropriate remedial and disciplinary action will be taken against anyone in the company who harasses another employee.[18]

Comparable worth is an undecided issue.

An issue related to sexual harassment since it mainly—but not exclusively—impacts on women is the issue of comparable worth.

---

[17]Mark L. Lengnick-Hall, "Checking Out Sexual Harassment Claims," *HR Magazine* (March 1992): 77–81.

[18]Richard M. Hodgetts and K. Galen Kroeck, *Personnel and Human Resource Management,* (Ft. Worth, Tex.: The Dryden Press, 1992), 107.

THE QUALITY CHALLENGE
Promoting Equal Opportunity

Total quality management can be very useful to supervisors in ensuring that their subordinates are provided equal opportunity. In particular, there are three TQM guidelines that are valuable.

1. *Focus on facts.* Many supervisors inadvertently discriminate against their personnel without intending to do so. For example, they will recommend a man for a promotion because they believe this individual is the highest producer in the department when, in fact, there is a woman in the group who generates even more output. Or they will give an average evaluation to a person who speaks with a foreign accent, even though this person has produced more suggestions for productivity improvement than anyone else in the department over the last year. TQM helps supervisors to avoid these mistakes and give credit where it is due by providing them with quantitative data from which to make decisions. For example, before deciding whom to promote or praise, the supervisor will examine production-related records and know with certainty which employee has the lowest number of rejects or produces the greatest number of units. This will not totally eliminate discriminatory decisions, but it will prevent those caused by faulty memory or those that are based on intuition and hunch.

2. *Teach and train everyone.* To increase productivity, TQM provides training to all employees. This is a helpful practice in ensuring equal opportunity because it allows everyone in the work group to improve their skills and increase their performance. So whereas some people may not be as adept at doing their jobs as are others, all receive the requisite training for performing at higher levels. In a manner of speaking, TQM is color- and gender-blind. It offers everyone an opportunity to do a better job. Those who do are then in a position to earn promotions and/or increased salaries.

3. *Continuous improvement.* TQM is an ongoing process. No matter how well the job is done today, employees are taught to look for ways of improving their work procedures. In addition to TQM tools such as flow charting, Pareto analysis, and statistical process control charts, the workers learn how to meet in groups, brainstorm, identify potential solutions to ongoing problems, and generate action plans for implementing these solutions. As a result, there is an ongoing emphasis for continued opportunity, thus encouraging everyone to keep improving their performance. In turn, the supervisor can use these results to ensure that the workers are rewarded accordingly.

These three guidelines provide the supervisor with a closed-loop approach to ensuring equal opportunity for the personnel. By focusing on factual data (guideline 1), giving people the training needed to tap their potential to the fullest (guideline 2), encouraging the workers to constantly strive to improve (guideline 3), and measuring these results objectively (guideline 1), the supervisor can minimize personal bias in evaluation decisions.

Comparable Worth

As we saw in Table 6–4, the traditional jobs held by women have not changed that much in the last 100 years. Typically, these female-dominated jobs—nurses, schoolteachers, and secretaries—were paid less than jobs that were typically held by males, for example, truck drivers, policeman, and management. Gender-based pay systems developed and have persisted to the present day. Although the Equal Pay Act forbids wage discrimination for males and females holding the same job, the issue of comparable wages for men and women holding comparable jobs is an open issue.

> "The point of the comparable worth issue revolves around the economic worth of jobs to employers. If jobs are similar, even though they involve different occupations, why shouldn't they be paid the same? The concern here is one of pay disparities: Women still earn less then men."[19]

Comparable worth advocates want to take the Equal Pay legislation another step and require equal pay for jobs that are similar in terms of required skills, knowledge, and abilities, even though the job functions may be very different.

For general information as to how supervisors can uphold both the letter and spirit of the equal opportunity legislation, see "The Quality Challenge: Promoting Equal Opportunity."

SUMMARY

Discrimination refers to using race, color, religion, sex, or national origin as a reason to treat people differently from one another. Legislation has extended this meaning to include age and disability. Discrimination manifests itself through disparate treatment, adverse impact, or present effects of past discrimination.

There has been much equal opportunity legislation in the past thirty-five years, as shown in Table 6–1. The Civil Rights Act of 1964 was landmark legislation, especially Title VII, which prohibited discrimination in hiring, firing, and all other business decisions. Title VII was amended in 1972 by the Equal Employment Opportunity Act, which established the Equal Employment Oppor-

tunity Commission (EEOC) as the major regulatory agency monitoring equal opportunity. The Civil Rights Act of 1991 established the Glass Ceiling Commission to study the rise of women and minorities in corporate America.

The EEOC was described in terms of its mandate to hear complaints and issue regulations. The complaint process was illustrated in Figure 6–1. Unsettled complaints can result in EEOC litigation or individual suits.

Affirmative action concentrates on redressing yesterday's wrongs by requiring employers to hire women and minorities according to the percentage of qualified female and minority candidates in the work force. The scope of affirmative action can

---

[19]De Cenzo and Robbins, 82.

vary from changing management attitudes to preferential hiring, the latter often leading to the controversial issue of reverse discrimination. Affirmative action programs may be required by the Office of Federal Contract Compliance Programs for federal contractors or by a federal court if a company has been found guilty of past discrimination. Alternately, companies may initiate volunteer affirmative action programs.

A hot issue today is sexual harassment in the workplace. Sexual harassment is defined as unwanted sexual behavior that interferes with a worker's performance or comfort in the workplace. Companies are cautioned to have clear policies and grievance procedures.

Another open issue in American workplaces is comparable worth, the idea that people should be paid similarly for jobs that require similar levels of skills, abilities, and performance. Comparable worth is seen as a systematic way to eliminate old patterns of gender-biased compensation plans.

REVIEW QUESTIONS

1. What is discrimination? Identify and define the three categories of discrimination.

2. Briefly describe the Equal Pay Act of 1963 and the Age Discrimination in Employment Act of 1967.

3. Why is the Civil Rights Act of 1964 considered landmark legislation?

4. According to the Pregnancy Discrimination Act of 1978, how must pregnant women be treated?

5. What was the purpose of the Immigration Reform and Control Act of 1984?

6. What requirements does the Americans with Disabilities Act of 1990 have for American employers?

7. Describe at least four provisions of the Civil Rights Act of 1991.

8. What are the two main responsibilities of the EEOC?

9. Describe the process of an EEOC complaint.

10. What is affirmative action, and how is it related to reverse discrimination?

11. Define sexual harassment. Distinguish between quid-pro-quo sexual harassment and "hostile environment" sexual harassment.

12. Discuss the issue of comparable worth.

KEY TERMS

Adverse impact. Unintentional discrimination in seemingly equitable requirements like employment tests results in disproportional disqualification of certain groups.

Affirmative action. Requirement to hire and promote women and minorities according to the percentage of qualified women and minorities in the work force.

Bona Fide Occupational Qualification (BFOQ). A qualification that can be proven to be necessary for a person to successfully perform a given job.

Comparable worth. The belief that people should be paid comparable pay for dissimilar jobs that require the same level of skills, knowledge, and abilities.

Conciliation. The process of negotiation among the EEOC, the complaintant, and the company being charged to try to reach a settlement.

Disparate treatment. Intentional discrimination against an individual or class of individuals because of race, age, sex, color, religion, or national origin.

Discrimination. **Treating people differently because of race, color, religion, sex, national origin, age, or disability.**

Four-fifths rule. Developed by the EEOC to judge adverse impact, this rule states that the ratio of minority applicants to minority hires must be at least four-fifths, or 80 percent, that of the ratio of nonminority applicants to nonminority hires.

Glass ceiling. The imaginary boundary beyond which women and minorities tend to not be promoted.

Handicapped. As defined by the Vocational Rehabilitation Act of 1973, a handicapped person is anyone who has a physical or mental impairment, has a record of such impairment, or is regarded as having such an impairment.

Hostile environment. A condition of sexual harassment where a person is made to feel uncomfortable in the workplace because of repeated, unwanted sexual behavior, innuendo, or overtures.

Probable cause. A finding of the EEOC of the likelihood of a discriminatory practice by a company that has had a complaint issued against it.

Quid-Pro-Quo sexual harassment. Sexual harassment where direct benefit to the employee has been promised in return for sexual favors.

Reasonable accommodation. Required changes in the workplace to allow disabled employees to work to their full capacity.

Reverse discrimination. Seeming discrimination against white males as a result of affirmative action in favor of women and minorities.

Sexual harassment. Unwanted, uninvited sexual behavior in the workplace.

ANSWERS TO SELF-ASSESSMENT QUIZ 6–1

1. False. Unintentional actions that cause adverse impact are also discriminatory.

2. False. Equal rights were an issue all the way back to the Constitution.

3. True. Much additional legislation merely amended or added to Title VII.

4. False. If age is a bona fide occupational qualification, it may be a legal qualification.

5. False. Although the Justice Department has some authority in this area, the EEOC is the main agency charged with enforcing equal opportunity legislation.

6. False. Pregnancy must be treated like any other medical condition and a pregnant woman cannot be required to go on leave.

7. False. Organizations are required to make "reasonable accommodation" in the workplace to enable disabled workers to perform successfully.

8. False. Although it is against the law to hire illegal aliens, legal aliens may not be discriminated against.

9. False. The Civil Rights Act of 1991 allows claims of up to $300,000.

10. False. The Family and Medical Leave Act of 1993 allows unpaid leave for family illnesses.

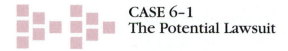

CASE 6-1
The Potential Lawsuit

When Chris Nussman applied for a supervisory position at Graffing, Inc., he filled out a job application, had a 30-minute interview with a member of the Human Resources (HR) Department, and was hired a week later. Chris has been on the job for six months and during this time he has become friends with two other supervisors, Bill Francis and Anne Howe.

Last week Chris and Bill were discussing their annual performance reviews, which are coming up next week. Bill has been with the company for six years and is earning $36,500. Chris was hired for $24,600 and is hoping for a 3 to 5 percent raise. Commenting on this, Bill told him, "Don't worry. You'll get 5 percent because you are one of the lowest paid supervisors. You're even making less than Anne." These comments surprised Chris, but they were later echoed by Anne. "Around here," she told him, "women are paid less than men. It's true from the hourly wage people all the way up the line. I don't like it, but I'm not going to start any trouble. I'm continually ranked in the top 10 percent of all supervisors and my raises are always 3 to 4 percent."

These views are not shared by all of the women at Graffing. Yesterday a group of female hourly workers filed a series of lawsuits charging the company with a violation of the Equal Pay Act. According to the lawsuit, the average male worker is hired for 50 cents an hour more than the average female worker and this wage gap exists at all levels of the hierarchy.

A spokesperson for the group bringing the lawsuit has asked the female supervisors to join in the action. This person has told Anne that the group will be filing a suit demanding equal pay for equal work and, in a separate suit, will be demanding comparable worth for all jobs in the company. The woman also told Anne that their lawyer had managed to get employment data from the firm's HR department. The information reveals that the company's hiring practices discriminate against women, especially at the supervisory level. Although the firm hires only college graduates for these positions, this degree only ensures consideration for entry. It does not guarantee that the person will get the job. In fact, company records reveal that over the last five years, the following supervisory hiring decisions were made:

	Applicants	Hired
Men	324	63
Women	192	9

"We have sufficient data to prove that females are being discriminated against by Graffing," the spokesperson told Anne. "We'd like you to join us in this lawsuit." Anne has promised to give the matter serious thought and get back with the woman before the week is over.

1. If the spokesperson's data are correct, is the company violating the Equal Pay Act?

2. Does the company discriminate against female supervisors in its hiring decisions? Explain.

3. If the company were to lose a comparative worth lawsuit, what would happen to Anne's salary? Defend your answer.

CASE 6–2
The Perplexed Consultant

When Roger Langley was hired by Radford General Hospital, he was told that the hospital wanted an outside consultant to review its operations and to offer recommendations that would help the hospital reduce costs and increase effectiveness. Roger spent most of the first two weeks interviewing personnel, walking around studying people at work, and making notes for his final report. In the process, Roger has found a number of unexpected problems. One of these relates to equal opportunity and the supervisory staff.

During one of his interviews, Roger asked a supervisor about her career goals. The woman told Roger that she was now a unit supervisor and this was as far as she would be going in the hospital. Roger saw this as an opportunity to discuss the possibility of additional training, which would put her in line for a promotion. However, the woman interrupted Roger by noting, "I hear what you're saying, but you apparently don't know how we do things around here. I am 44 years old, and there is an unwritten rule that no one over 40 gets promoted from the supervisory ranks. If you don't make it by this age, you don't make it." Roger found this to be a shocking comment, but when he went to the Human Relations (HR) Department and began looking at their computer records he quickly saw that of the forty-seven people who were promoted from the supervisory ranks over the last three years, the average age was 32 and the oldest person in the group was 38. As a follow-up to this investigation, Roger reviewed the records of four women and three men who appeared to be the most effective supervisors. Each was over 40 years of age and each had excellent performance reviews, but none had been recommended for further promotion.

Roger also found that some of the supervisors were not very effective in their jobs, but they were not demoted or fired. The hospital continued to keep them on staff. In particular,

Roger learned of two incidents that he felt warranted consideration in his report. One was the case of a supervisor who was accused of sexual harassment. When he asked the Associate Administrator about the situation, Roger learned that a young nurse had filed such a charge but withdrew it after talking to the director of HR. The Associate Administrator closed his comments by saying, "We talked to the supervisor and he apologized to the woman. The only problem is that I hear he is still harassing some of the young nurses, but no one has come forward with a complaint so I don't know what to do about it. I guess we'll just have to wait and see what happens."

The other situation Roger learned about involved a supervisor who gained access to the hospital's computerized personnel files to find out how much money everyone was making. In the process he also uncovered confidential information about the medical histories of some of the staff.

Fortunately, the hospital's computer system is programmed to keep track of who gains access to these files (everyone has a log or number), and the supervisor was quickly identified and called in for a meeting with the administrator. The man admitted his action, but said he did not know what he was doing was wrong. Unfortunately, in the interim some of the personnel have learned of the incident, believe that their files may have been viewed by this supervisor, and are threatening legal action against the hospital for not protecting their right to privacy.

Roger believes that when he is finished writing his report, he will have more than enough recommendations for action. In fact, he believes his biggest challenge will be deciding what to keep in the report and what to leave out so that he stays within the thirty-page guideline set for him when he was hired. For the moment, however, he is somewhat perplexed regarding how to handle all of this information.

1. Can the hospital refuse to promote people over 40 years of age? Is this not an organizational privilege?

2. Did the hospital handle the case of sexual harassment correctly? Defend your answer.

3. Did the hospital correctly handle the case of the supervisor who entered the computer files? Explain.

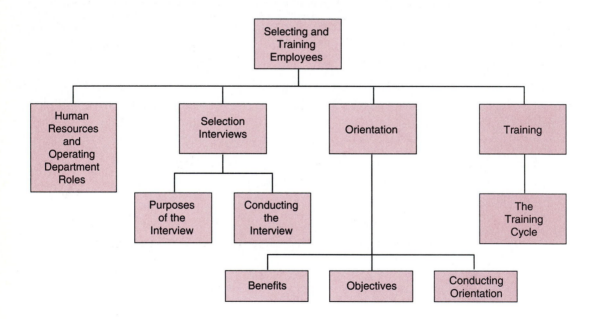

CHAPTER 7

Selecting and Training Employees

*"The long-term success of any organization ultimately depends on having the right people in the right jobs at the right time."**

CHAPTER OBJECTIVES

☐   Define the terms *job description* and *job specification*.

☐   Relate the role of the supervisor in the selection and training of employees.

☐   Describe the purposes of the selection interview.

☐   Explain how the selection interview is carried out.

☐   Discuss the benefits of orientation.

☐   Identify common orientation objectives.

☐   Discuss who has the responsibility for conducting orientation.

☐   Define the term *training* and discuss the seven steps of the training process.

---

*Lloyd L. Byars and Leslie W. Rue, *Human Resource Management,* 3rd ed. (Homewood, Ill.: Irwin, 1991), 112.

How are supervisors involved in selecting and training employees? This chapter looks at the important functions of recruiting, selecting, interviewing, orienting, and training. Before considering these areas, however, we briefly differentiate the role of the supervisor (or the operating department) and the role of the personnel department. Readers should note that in many companies or organizations the term *personnel* has been replaced by *human resources*. In other companies two departments have responsibilities: the personnel department recruits and selects, whereas the human resources department trains and develops. This chapter, however, uses the term *human resources* (HR) when referring to the nonoperating department responsible for any of these functions.

HUMAN RESOURCES AND OPERATING DEPARTMENT ROLES

Recruiting, selecting, orienting, and training are important functions in any organization. In the early years of American industrialization, operating managers performed all of these functions along with their other duties. With the growth of American business, however, and the increasing importance of record keeping and adherence to regulations such as equal opportunity legislation, most of these tasks were assigned to personnel specialists. Today, however, the pendulum is swinging back and more of these decisions are again being assigned to operating departments and supervisors. Although the overview of H.R. versus operating department roles provided here is a typical description, there is considerable variation from company to company. Table 7–1 lists the subfunctions of this process with the department primarily responsible for each.

Operating departments are responsible for alerting the H.R. department to a precise job need and for providing a job description and a job specification. If the job is not a new one, Human Resources will already have conducted a *job analysis* to determine the functions of the position. If the job is a new one, a job analysis needs to be done. In either case, job analysis precedes the writing of a job description or a job specification, and determines the tasks that comprise the job as well as the skills and knowledge necessary to do those tasks. A *job description* is a detailed list of duties and responsibilities attached to the job vacancy. A *job specification* is a listing of qualifications and competencies that the successful applicant will have. Table 7–2 gives a partial example of each.

Once job descriptions and job specifications have been provided to the H.R. department, the latter takes over with the recruitment of candidates. Recruitment may be done by job posting within the organization in a search for internal candidates, as well as external searches through advertisements, employment agencies, and so on. Subsequently, the H.R. department handles the initial screening of respondents including passing out application forms and administering tests.

TABLE 7–1

Where does the responsibility lie?

Function	Responsibility
1. Identification of job need	Operating departments
2. Job description and specification	Operating departments
3. Recruitment of candidates	Human Resources
4. Intial screening of applicants	Human Resources
5. Application forms	Human Resources
6. Testing (if applicable)	Human Resources
7. Selection interviews	Operating departments
8. Background or reference check (if performed)	Human Resources
9. Physical exam (if desired)	Human Resources
10. Selection decision	Operating departments
11. Orientation	H.R. and operating departments
12. Training	Operating departments (supported by H.R.)

TABLE 7–2

Job description and specification

Job Description *Security Guard*	*Job Specification* *Security Guard*
Make hourly rounds of all check points on floors 1 to 5. Make checks of all locked doors on ground floor on an hourly basis. Check the security pass of all people encountered after hours who are not displaying the security badge. Maintain a log of rounds and door checks. Respond to security alarms. Attend monthly security department meetings. Other duties as assigned by director of security.	Prior experience in security field. Competence in a recognized self-defense technique. Competence with a handgun. H. S. Graduate or equivalent.

Supervisors become
directly involved
during the selection
interview.

Supervisors become directly involved in this process at the point of the selection interview. If the supervisor is still interested in the applicant, the file then goes back to H.R. for follow-up work, which generally includes a background or reference check and a physical exam. A selection decision is then made by the operating department.

Once the applicant has been offered a job and has accepted, orientation begins. Orientation is usually a joint operation between the H.R. department and the operating department. Finally, the new employee is ready for ongoing training, which is primarily the responsibility of the operating department, although the H.R. department often provides support through trainers and curriculum development.

SELECTION INTERVIEWS

After job applications have been received, the supervisor is often involved in selection interviews. In most cases the H.R. office will have already screened applicants for minimum qualifications. The interview provides the opportunity to take a much closer look at the candidates. In this process the supervisor can learn a great deal about the candidate(s).

Laws govern the
questions you can
ask applicants.

Interviews have become even more important over the last few years because many previously common employment tests have been ruled illegal or discriminatory. Supervisors must be wary that they do not ask any questions that can be construed as discriminatory. Generally speaking, these are questions having to do with age, marital status, arrest records (unlike conviction records), number and ages of children, and other questions regarding protected categories of race, national origin, sex, and religion. In general, questions with no relevance to the worker's ability to perform the job in question are prohibited. Inattention to the legalities of the selection process can lead to major problems. Detailed information on ensuring equal opportunity under the law is discussed in Chapter 6.

To assess what you currently know about what can and cannot be asked in a selection interview, take Self-Assessment Quiz 7–1.

Before examining the process by which interviews are conducted, let's consider the common purposes of the selection interview.

Purposes of the Selection Interview

A carefully conducted selection interview should accomplish several main purposes:

1.   Allow the supervisor to assess the applicant's skills. One researcher tells us he always looks for five general categories of skills[1]:

---

[1]Thomas F. Casey, "Making the Most of a Selection Interview," *Personnel* (September 1990): 42.

■ ■ ■ **SELF-ASSESSMENT QUIZ 7–1**
Recognizing Legal and Illegal Selection Interview Questions

Directions: For each of the following questions, mark an *L* for legal question or an *I* for illegal question.

_____ 1. How old are you?

_____ 2. Are you planning to get married?

_____ 3. What did you study in school?

_____ 4. How did you learn about this job?

_____ 5. What would be your major strengths in this job?

_____ 6. Are you pregnant?

_____ 7. Have you ever been arrested?

_____ 8. Do you have citizenship or permanent residence in the United States?

_____ 9. Are you willing to relocate?

_____ 10. Who takes care of your children when you go to work?

_____ 11. How did you become disabled?

_____ 12. Do you have any disabilities?

Before proceeding, check your answers at the back of the chapter.

A carefully conducted interview should accomplish these purposes.

   A. Conceptual skills—the ability to think beyond the facts, be creative. . . .

   B. Analytical skills—the ability to organize and interpret information without becoming obsessive about it.

   C. Writing skills—I always request a writing sample and let the hiring manager read it.

   D. Interpersonal skills—how does the candidate interact with you?

   E. Presentation skills—how well could the candidate teach or make presentations?

2. Assist the supervisor in supplementing the data given on the employment application by asking questions that clarify or add details.

3. Allow prospective employees an opportunity to find out more about the job and the company, and to get a feel for the department in which they would be working. Would the applicant fit in well with your organization?

4. Provide the supervisor and the applicant a chance to see if they personally get along with each other.

5. Allow both the supervisors and applicants an opportunity to gather information that will help them predict future successful performance. If success is to be attained, both individuals need to feel that the job is a good match.

Conducting the Interview

Before the interview the supervisor should plan what to say and formulate what to look for. The three most common criteria are appropriate education, relevant experience, and a personality that will facilitate the job.

There are five steps
in the interview
process.

In addition, the supervisor needs a thorough knowledge of both the job vacancy and the applicant's file to date. Studying a person's application in advance helps ensure that the necessary questions will be asked during the interview period.

Once the applicant has arrived, supervisors should carry out five distinct steps (see Figure 7–1).

Step 1 is establishing rapport. Here the interviewer tries to put the applicant at ease by engaging in a short period of small talk, offering the individual some coffee, or discussing general topics such as sports, the weather, local events, and so on.

Step 2 follows with general questioning of the applicant. Open-ended questions such as "How did you learn about this job?" or "Why are you interested in working for our company?" are typically asked. The following list shows areas commonly covered in this phase:

1.   Education and training.
2.   Past experience.
3.   Current and future personal goals.
4.   Expectations about the current job opening.
5.   Knowledge of the company.
6.   Knowledge of the field.
7.   Ability to communicate.
8.   Ability to work with others.
9.   Interest in the job.[2]

Step 3 continues with questioning but this time of a more specific nature. An example would be, "What do you think is the major strength you would bring to this job?" Other examples, are, "What specific skills do you have that would be beneficial to this job?", "What particular experience do you have that relates to this job opening?", and "What part of this job do you think you would like the most (or the least)?" These kinds of questions allow the supervisor to probe into areas of special interests.

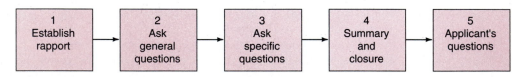

FIGURE 7–1
Steps in the interview process.

[2]Jane Whitney Gibson and Richard M. Hodgetts, *Organizational Communication: A Managerial Perspective,* 2nd ed. (New York: Harper Collins, 1991), 371.

SUPERVISORY SKILLS
The Selection Process

1. Understand the cooperation needed between H.R. and operating departments to successfully accomplish selection objectives. Familiarize yourself with the services H.R. will provide. Identify employment needs and provide adequate job descriptions and job specifications.

2. Organize your thoughts carefully before conducting interviews. What exactly are you trying to learn about the applicants? What questions will you ask?

3. When interviewing, be sure that you do not do all the talking. Pay attention to how applicants express themselves, and be sure they also have an opportunity to ask questions.

4. Be sure you are familiar with the legal aspects of hiring. You cannot just ask any question that comes to your mind without putting your company in risk of a discrimination suit.

Step 4 gives the applicant a chance to ask questions. Remember that an applicant's questions are as important as the supervisor's; it takes two to make an employment decision.

Finally, step 5 provides a summary and closing. At this point the supervisor should be sure to tell the applicant what to expect to happen next. Will a decision be made in the next week? Will others have to be interviewed? Is the applicant still interested in the job?

After interviewing, supervisors choose final candidate(s).

After the interview has been completed, supervisors should immediately write down their evaluation of the applicant. This should be done while the impressions are still fresh in the supervisor's mind. Anyone who has interviewed a series of people knows that even the strongest impressions grow hazy and confused after talking to several people.

After supervisors have finished interviewing, they must narrow the field of candidates to two or three top candidates. This should be done by referring to notes and matching candidates against the job requirements as well as their impressions of how the person will fit into the department. The latter is often difficult, but experienced supervisors often have a gut level feeling for how well an employee will fit in with the rest of the team. Having picked several top candidates, the supervisor may want to ask for a second interview. The second interview is necessary if no one best choice is apparent. If a second interview is held, the supervisor may ask each candidate to speak to one or more other people in the department in order to get a better idea of the nature of the work and to get some additional perceptions on the candidate. The second interview should also be much more specific than the first, focusing on the specific job duties and responsibilities and the candidate's ability and willingness to do each.

Once a final candidate has been chosen, the H.R. department most often takes over again and makes the actual job offer. They complete negotiations with the candidate for salary and fringe benefits and set a starting date.

ORIENTATION

The new employee's first impressions of the company will affect future job satisfaction, motivation, loyalty, and job performance. For this reason, orientation is important and should be conducted in a well-planned, professional manner. Before examining the role of supervisors and H.R. in this process, let's look at the benefits and objectives of orientation.

The new employee's first impressions really count.

Benefits

A number of benefits can be realized from an effective orientation program:

Benefits of effective orientation.

1. Reduction in the anxiety levels of new employees by creating realistic expectations and by removing some of the mystery about the organization.
2. Lessening the amount of time that co-workers or supervisors have to spend helping the new employee.
3. Positive attitudes, high motivation, job satisfaction, and reduced turnover brought about by effective introduction of the worker to the job.
4. Reduced start-up costs because the employee will become productive in a much quicker time than those who are not given proper orientation.

Exactly what should orientation programs expect to accomplish? Effective programs have to be founded on a list of realistic objectives.

Objectives

Orientation programs usually have a number of objectives:

Common objectives of an orientation program.

1. Make the new employee feel like a member of the organizational family as soon as possible.
2. Relieve employee's anxieties so he or she can get a productive start.
3. Inform the new hire of corporate policies and procedures.
4. Create in the new employee a positive attitude about the company.
5. Acquaint the new hire with information on corporate history, philosophy, culture, and values.
6. Inform the new employee what is expected of him in the new job.
7. Accomplish housekeeping chores such as starting payroll and choosing benefits.

Conducting Orientation

Orientation is the most common type of formal training done in American organizations, according to a report by *Training* magazine.[3] It does not follow, however, that the average orientation program is done well.

> "In most organizations, the content and format of orientation programs are determined by historical precedent, fiat and whim. The factors that should shape orientation—the message of the organization and the needs of the new employee—only capriciously influence the information and experiences provided to newcomers."[4]

The H.R. department and the supervisor play important orientation roles.

To provide more effective orientation programs, it is important to know who is responsible and what should be included in orientation. Many experts in the field believe that the responsibility for new employee orientation must be shared by the H.R. department and the immediate supervisor. Who gets to do what can sometimes be a problem. Usually the H.R. department starts the process by developing the orientation objectives and guiding the new employee through the following steps: (a) completion of all personnel forms accompanied by an explanation of what each is for; (b) discussion of the method of compensation increases, reviews, and incentive systems; (c) highlighting of the fringe benefits; and (d) discussion of the duties of the job. At this point H.R. takes the new employee to the appropriate department or has the supervisor come and get the person.

This transfer begins the second phase of the orientation. At this point the supervisor should cover the following areas with the new hire, even though many might have already been discussed at the applicant's interview: (a) functions of the department and how they relate to the overall organization; (b) job duties of the new hire and how these interrelate with the jobs of other department personnel; (c) explanation of specific departmental policies and procedures; (d) tour of the department and an introduction to department personnel; and (e) housekeeping items such as where restrooms and lunchroom are located, where to park, location of emergency exits, and the like. Figure 7–2 is a department orientation checklist designed by the author for use in orienting hourly employees to the university.

After the orientation has been completed, both the supervisor and the H.R. department will have a follow-up. The supervisor will meet with the new employee at the end of the first day and again at the end of the first week to see how things are going. After two weeks, typically, the H.R. department will meet with new employees and review how well they are getting along.

---

[3]Jeff Brechlin and Allison Rossett, "Orienting New Employees," *Training* (April 1991): 45–51.
[4]Ibid., 45.

NAME OF EMPLOYEE _____ JOB TITLE _____

DEPARTMENT _____ STARTING DATE _____

DEPARTMENT ORIENTATION

Items to be discussed by supervisor with new employee. Note: Employee should check off each item as covered.

First Day of Employment

☐ 1. Organization of Department/Center

☐ 2. Department/Center brochures, if applicable

☐ 3. Job description

☐ 4. Hours: starting, lunch, rest periods, dismissal time, hours per week.

☐ 5. Pay: When, where, how paid, overtime, time sheet
(Explain deductions when first check is received)

☐ 6. Holidays and vacations in detail

☐ 7. Rules on:

  ☐ A. Telephone coverage   ☐ C. Absenteeism
  ☐ B. Tardiness   ☐ D. Other

☐ 8. Work station and equipment assignment

☐ 9. Information on location of facilities

  ☐ A. Wash room   ☐ E. Purchasing
  ☐ B. Copier   ☐ F. Comptroller's Office
  ☐ C. Coffee   ☐ G. Other
  ☐ D. Print shop

☐ 10. Introduction to co-workers

During First Two Weeks of Employment

☐ 11. Review first salary check, explanation of deductions.

☐ 12. Employee evaluation process

☐ 13. Invite questions and help on problems

☐ 14. Explain relationship of new employee's work to that of co-workers and that of the unit as a whole.

As indicated by checkmarks, all of the above items have been discussed.

_____
Employee

_____
Supervisor

_____
Date

Upon completion, employee and supervisor are to retain copies and send original to personnel office.

FIGURE 7–2
Orientation checklist.

TRAINING

Organizations conduct training to provide employees with needed skills or knowledge or to improve their current status. Training also seems to have a motivational effect on employees because it shows them that the organization is interested in their development. Motivation is covered more thoroughly in Chapter 8. Although training is often used as a generic term, it is only one of three types of corporate teaching activity—the other two being development and education.

Training means providing the skills and knowledge that employees need to perform their current jobs. *Development* is the furnishing of the skills and knowledge that the employee will likely use on a future job assignment. *Education* is any broad-brush attempt to increase the skills and knowledge of an employee; it is usually not tied to a current or even an anticipated job assignment. Supervisors are most often concerned with training—in particular, the identification of training needs.

Just how important is training as a function in today's organizations? In a 1991 study of the Bureau of Labor Statistics, it was found that "the number of workers who were trained to improve their job skills rose by 13 million from 1983 to 1991."[5] In the same study, questions were asked regarding whether employees needed specific training to get their current jobs and, since being in their current jobs, did they need to take any training to improve their skills. The results speak for themselves:

> "The proportion of workers who said they took training to improve their job skills jumped from 35 percent in 1983 to 41 percent in 1991. Much of the increase was attributable to greater use of formal company programs.
>
> In 1991, 57 percent of all workers reported they needed training to qualify for their jobs, compared with 55 percent in 1983."

When identifying training needs, the manager must be aware of organizational goals, changes occurring in and around the organization that may impact on work processes, external factors such as government regulations that will cause changes in work procedures, and performance gaps between what is expected and what is being achieved.[6] Once training needs have been established, the supervisor follows the steps of the training cycle.

The Training Cycle

The training cycle as portrayed in Figure 7–3 consists of seven steps. Steps 1 and 2 comprise a pretraining phase; steps 3, 4, and 5 are training prepa-

Training provides employees with necessary job-related knowledge and skills.

There are seven important steps in the training cycle.

---

[5]Thomas Amirault, "Training to Qualify for Jobs and Improve Skills, 1991," *Monthly Labor Review* (September 1992): 31.

[6]Dave Georgenson and Edward Del Gazo, "Maximize the Return on Your Training Investment Through Needs Analysis," *Training and Development Journal* (August 1984): 42–47.

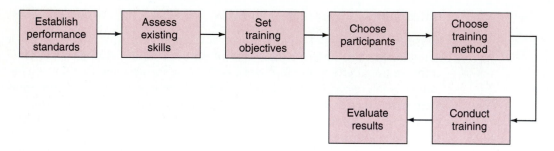

FIGURE 7-3
The training cycle.

ration stages, and steps 6 and 7 are training and evaluation. Let's briefly look at each.

Establishing performance standards is a critical first step. Unless the supervisor has precise guidelines as to what is effective performance, training will be haphazard. Examples of effective performance standards include a reject rate of 1 percent or less, or monthly sales at quota or better.

Assessing existing skills is also a necessary pretraining step. What skills do employees already have? What do they need? Making employees sit through training that is repetitive or too basic for their needs can have a negative effect on their attitudes and performance. Thus the supervisor should have an accurate picture of the current skills and knowledge of the employees.

The third step involves setting training objectives. What is the training expected to accomplish? Table 7–3 provides some good as well as

TABLE 7-3

Training objectives

Good	*Poor*
1. To perform maintenance check on the XJ1 in 3 to 5 minutes.	1. Do better maintenance.
2. To identify the three most common service problems and correct them without calling the service technicians.	2. Understand common service problems.
3. To reduce downtime of the XJ1 from the current 20 percent to 5 percent.	3. Reduce downtime.

some poor examples of training objectives. Effective objectives are specific and measurable. Once objectives have been set, they should be used as a guideline for choosing methods and conducting training and evaluation.

Choosing participants is a touchy issue. Besides asking who needs the training, the supervisor must also consider who wants the training, and who will gain the most from it. Will the whole group or just representatives be trained? Again, the answers will vary greatly depending on what the supervisor is attempting to accomplish. If the supervisor is trying to improve group decision making, for example, the entire group should be included. On the other hand, if the supervisor is attempting to make the operation of a particular piece of equipment more effective, training should include only those who use that equipment, or who are just learning to use it.

The next step requires choosing a training method. Training can occur on the job (OJT) or in classroom settings. The latter includes computer-based training as well as any other formal training that does not take place on the actual job site. Cost is typically a major criterion in deciding whether to employ OJT or classroom training. There are other factors to consider. OJT has one advantage over classroom training because the person learns in an actual work environment and produces results at the same time. Also, because the supervisor typically does the OJT, a close superior-subordinate relationship can evolve. Classroom training, on the other hand, uses a trainer rather than a supervisor and addresses the

■ ■ ■ **SUPERVISORY SKILLS**
Orientation and Training

1. Do not abdicate these important functions to the H.R. office. Understand exactly what your role is in orientation and training.

2. Do not rush through orientation or delegate it to someone else because you are too busy. Getting the employee "off to a good start" is a very important part of your job and ensures that an employee will be a fully functioning member of the team much more quickly. If you properly orient your new employee, the cost of time and effort will pay you back many times in effective performance and longer job tenure.

3. Use foresight in your training program. Don't wait for a performance gap to appear, but rather try to anticipate changing skill needs and potential problems. By training people in advance you can avoid many of these potential problems.

4. Plan training carefully using the seven steps of the training cycle and remember to use motivational techniques to get employees involved.

needs of a group of students at the same time. One expert offered the following guidelines:[7]

1. If you are training a large number of employees, the fixed cost of classroom training is an obvious benefit.
2. When training low numbers of employees on specific, costly equipment, one-on-one OJT seems preferable.
3. When simulated work environments are very costly to produce, use OJT in the actual work environment.
4. When you have extra time to train, go with OJT.

Conducting training is a critical step. Not everyone is able to train adequately, so choosing the trainer is crucial. This person must be able to relate the material to the employees in a way that they will both understand and accept. If a professional trainer is being used, he or she has probably studied effective communication and how people learn. Many of the topics in Chapters 3 and 4 on communication and individual behavior are foundations for effective trainers. If supervisors are doing the training, they may well benefit from a course designed to train trainers. Many large organizations provide these courses at regular intervals; others send their supervisor-trainers to external seminars to learn these skills. (See "The Quality Challenge: Using Training Effectivly.")

One of the most important elements in conducting training is providing a motivational environment for the trainees. One researcher suggests six techniques for motivating employees to learn[8]:

1. Use positive reinforcement, such as verbal praise, positive nonverbal behavior, and smiles.
2. Have trainees set their own personal goals.
3. Design active learning modalities so that employees are involved in the learning process.
4. Minimize stress and anxiety. Be careful not to intimidate trainees or to make fun of them.
5. Be flexible enough to take hints from trainees as to what would make the training more meaningful.
6. Work to eliminate physical barriers to learning such as uncomfortable room temperature as well as psychological barriers such as confusion or anxiety.

---

[7]Stephen L. Mangum, "On-the-Job vs. Classroom Training: Some Deciding Factors," *Training* (February 1985): 71–77.

[8]David Torrence, "Motivating Trainees to Learn," *Training and Development* (March 1993): 55–58.

■   ■   ■   **THE QUALITY CHALLENGE**
Using Training Effectively

Employees need to learn how to improve quality in the workplace, and training in total quality management techniques is critical to quality improvement. However, what tools and techniques will be of most value? In answering this question, most companies begin by giving their supervisory and employee personnel training in a wide variety of tools and techniques. Some of those that have already been described earlier in this book, including the use of check sheets, Pareto analysis, and brainstorming, as well as others that are much more statistical in nature, are carefully explained and discussed. However, this is only the beginning of the training.

Once the participants learn how to use the quality-related tools, they are sent back to the workplace and asked to apply them. For example, workers in a customer service department will spend the next week keeping track of the number and types of complaints and questions that are received from customers. Armed with this information, they will then use this check sheet information to construct a Pareto chart. Then they will brainstorm about the possible reasons for each of the major causes identified by this chart. Next, they will put together a plan of action for dealing with the problem and will then implement their ideas. Finally, they will examine the results to see how well they were able to solve the problem. Regardless of how well they did, they will then take the results back to the next training program, where they will explain what they did and how well things turned out.

If they were able to successfully resolve the problem, this information is reported back to the members of the training group, who then have the opportunity to learn from this experience. If the group was unable to resolve the problem, the trainer and the group at large then discuss what might now be done. In either event, this feedback is useful in helping members of the training group gain experience in applying total quality concepts in the workplace.

"There is no sure-fire way to motivate people. But a good place to start is by cultivating the soil in which their desire to learn can grow. The seeds are involvement, encouragement, and acceptance."[9]

The general topic of motivation will be discussed in Chapter 9.

Finally, the results must be evaluated. How does the supervisor know if the objectives have been met? The following list suggests some general questions to guide the manager through this evaluation stage[10]:

Evaluation of training is the last step.

1. Were the training objectives compatible with organizational goals?
2. Were the trainees sufficiently prepared for the training program?
3. Were the trainees adequately motivated to learn the material in the program?

---

[9]Torrence, 58.

[10]Adapted from Gerald M. Goldhaber, *Organizational Communication,* 5th ed. (Dubuque, Iowa: William C. Brown Co., 1990), 407.

4.   Were the training methods appropriate and administered in a professional way?

5.   Were the training objectives met via the training techniques used?

6.   Did the training results translate into observable on-the-job performance?

SUMMARY

Both the H.R. department and the supervisor are responsible for the selection and training of employees. Human Resources often generates job applicants and provides some initial screening. The supervisor becomes directly involved in the process at the point of the selection interview.

The selection interview provides an opportunity for management to take a close look at the job candidates. When conducting this interview, the supervisor must be careful not to ask questions that can be construed as discriminatory. The steps in the process include: (a) establishing rapport, (b) asking general questions, (c) asking specific questions, (d) answering applicant questions, and (e) providing a summary and closure.

Orientation is an especially important process because it can influence an employee's job satisfaction, motivation, loyalty, and job performance and reduce an employer's start-up costs. Some of the objectives of an orientation program include: informing the individual about company policies and procedures, telling the individual what is expected in the new job, and taking care of housekeeping chores such as payroll start-up, benefits, and so on. Orientation responsibilities are shared between the personnel department and the immediate supervisor.

Training is the providing of the skills and knowledge that employees need to perform their current job. The steps in the training cycle are (a) establish performance standards, (b) assess existing skills, (c) set training objectives, (d) choose participants, (e) choose training method, (f) conduct training, and (g) evaluate results. An important part of effective training is motivating employees to get involved.

REVIEW QUESTIONS

1. How does a job description differ from a job specification? Compare and contrast the two.

2. In the selection and training of employees, what role is played by the H.R. department and what role is played by the operating departments? Use Table 7–1 in your answer.

3. What types of questions are illegal to ask an applicant during the interview process? Identify and discuss three.

4. What are the purposes of the selection interview? Explain.

5. How should the interview process be conducted? Identify and describe the steps involved.

6. What are some of the benefits to be realized from an effective orientation program? Identify and describe three.

7. What are the objectives of an orientation program? Identify and discuss four.

8. Who should conduct the orientation program? Explain your answer.

9. How does training differ from development? How does it differ from education? Explain.

10. How should the training process be carried out? Identify and describe the seven steps involved.

11. How can supervisors provide a motivational environment for trainees?

KEY TERMS

Development. Providing the skills and knowledge that an employee will likely use on a future job assignment.

Education. Any broad-brush attempt to increase the knowledge and skills of an employee.

Job analysis. Study by H.R. to determine the specific functions of a given position.

Job description. Detailed list of duties and responsibilities attached to a job vacancy.

Job specifications. List of the qualifications and competencies that a successful applicant needs to have in order to do the job.

OJT. On-the-job-training that combines learning the task with actually doing it. This type of training is normally conducted by the supervisor.

Training. Providing the skills and knowledge that an employee needs to perform his or her job.

ANSWERS TO SELF-ASSESSMENT QUIZ 7-1

1. Illegal
2. Illegal
3. Legal
4. Legal
5. Legal
6. Illegal
7. Illegal
8. Legal
9. Legal
10. Illegal
11. Illegal
12. Illegal

CASE 7-1
The Inquisitive Interviewer

Janet Wilson was looking through the Sunday papers when she saw the employment ad from Bycomb Insurance. Bycomb, a large local firm, was in the process of hiring additional people. Although the ad did not spell this out, ten were to be salespeople in the field and the other ten would be office personnel.

Janet had been a salesperson for five years. However, when she and her husband decided to start a family, Janet stopped working. Now that her daughter is three years old, Janet feels that this is a good time for her to go back to work. Her mother will take care of the child during the day, and the family will certainly be able to use the additional income.

On Monday Janet went to Bycomb's office and applied for a salesperson's job. The employees she met were quite friendly, and Janet thought the interview went well. However, during her interview she did find herself a bit embarrassed by some of the questions. The three that were most disconcerting were: Who will take care of your daughter when you are at work? Are you pregnant or do you intend to become pregnant during the next two years? Have you ever been arrested?

Yesterday Janet received a phone call from the company indicating that she had been hired. The caller, one of the people in personnel, also told her that he was sorry about some of the questions that were asked during the interview. "We tape all of our interviews so that we can find out if any of our people ask anything that is illegal or improper. In your case a couple of questions should not have been asked, and for that I apologize. However, I want to assure you that we did not consider them in judging your qualifications. You are an excellent candidate, and we look forward to having you join our sales team." Janet thanked the man and told him not to give the matter a second thought.

1. Were any of the questions that upset Janet illegal? Explain your answer.

2. During this interview what kinds of questions should the interviewer have focused on? Identify and describe three of them.

3. What is the purpose of the selection interview? What objectives does it accomplish? Explain.

CASE 7–2
The Entire Focus Is on Productivity

At the Gettlen Corporation the focus is on productivity. The company, a medium-size manufacturer, produces a wide variety of goods under subcontract arrangements with large firms. The products are components that end up being assembled into cars, TVs, and radios by the large firms.

Most of Gettlen's contracts require it to produce the goods within fairly strict tolerances. However, quality is not as important as quantity. If the goods are not delivered on time, the buyer has a right to refuse delivery. More importantly, some buyers, in an effort to ensure sufficient delivery, will contract for 115 percent of the needed output because they know that some firms will not deliver on time and they want to be sure that this does not affect their own production efforts. Aware of this industry practice, Gettlen makes a major effort to replace all workers who leave within five days.

Last week Mary Caughlin, the new head of the personnel department, was conducting an analysis of those production workers who had left the firm within the last ninety days. She discovered three things about all of them. All of them were interviewed and hired on the same day they showed up to apply for the job, there was no orientation program in effect (in fact, there is still no orientation for production workers), and each individual was given only three hours of on-the-job training before being assigned to his or her regular job.

1. Is Gettlen's rapid hiring related in any way to the high turnover? Defend your answer.

2. Is the lack of an orientation program having any effect on the production worker turnover? Explain.

3. Is the lack of training possibly tied to turnover? Defend your answer.

CHAPTER 8

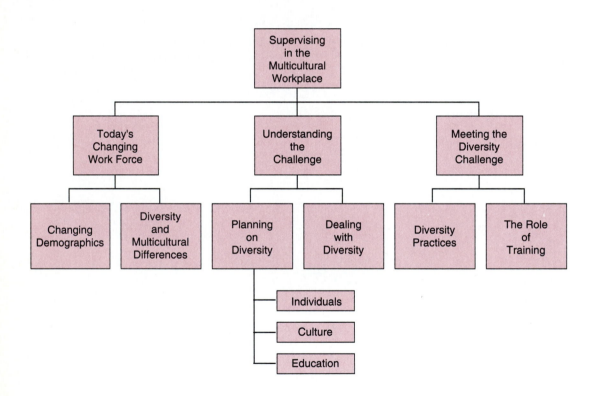

Supervising in the Multicultural Workplace

- Today's Changing Work Force
  - Changing Demographics
  - Diversity and Multicultural Differences
- Understanding the Challenge
  - Planning on Diversity
    - Individuals
    - Culture
    - Education
  - Dealing with Diversity
- Meeting the Diversity Challenge
  - Diversity Practices
  - The Role of Training

Supervising in the Multicultural Workplace

"Although there's been very little change for women and for men of color, the situation looks better than it did five years ago. For one thing, government initiatives are more collaborative and reasonable than in the past. For another, the demographics of the marketplace are starting to catch attention. Companies are realizing they need nontraditional managers to help them succeed with a diverse customer base."*

CHAPTER OBJECTIVES

☐ Study the changing demographics of the work force.

☐ Examine multicultural differences among work force participants.

☐ Discuss some of the ways that supervisors can better understand multicultural differences.

☐ Identify steps that are being taken to meet the diversity challenge.

---

*Ann Morrison, "Diversity," *Training and Development Journal* (April 1993): 39.

America is often referred to as a melting pot, characterized by people from all parts of the world coming to the United States and eventually becoming part of a homogeneous group. In fact, America is less of a melting pot than a "thawing pot" in which people keep many of their initial values and beliefs while adding others that are common to Americans. As a result, the U.S. work force is now heavily multicultural, consisting of a number of different groups from diverse cultures. Today's supervisor must have a basic understanding of how to work with people from a wide variety of cultures. Self-Assessment Quiz 8–1 provides some insights regarding this statement.

■ ■ ■ **SELF-ASSESSMENT QUIZ 8–1**
Multiculturalism in the Work Force

Directions: Answer each of the following questions true or false.

_____ 1. In contrast to previous decades when immigrants to the United States came from Europe, many of today's immigrants are coming from Latin America and Asia.

_____ 2. One reason why communication is a major problem for supervisors is that employees from other cultures often consider it bad manners to ask questions, so they simply tell the boss what they think the person wants to hear.

_____ 3. Research shows that when voicing their opinions, Latin employees are more likely to be candid and direct than are Anglo employees.

_____ 4. Many employees who have come to the United States from other cultures do not volunteer to take the initiative on job assignments because it is considered proper to wait and be assigned such work.

_____ 5. Many researchers believe that one of the first ways to break down multicultural barriers is to provide English training to those who are functionally illiterate or for whom English is a second language.

_____ 6. Some firms have found it productive to change some of their work procedures to accommodate cultural differences, such as offering flexible work hours so these employees can spend more time with their families.

_____ 7. Firms with large multicultural work forces have found that an "English only" policy helps improve communication and reduces misunderstandings.

_____ 8. Whereas many American-born workers like to work on their own, many workers who were raised in foreign countries prefer to work in groups.

_____ 9. Research shows that if supervisors simply try their best to deal with multicultural differences, they are just as effective as their counterparts who have had diversity training.

_____ 10. One of the keys to successful diversity is top management involvement and willingness to both encourage and promote this practice.

Answers can be found at the end of the chapter.

Undeniably, diversity is not anything new to the American workplace, but the approach to diversity is rapidly changing. In the 1970s, a strategy that might have been called vigorous indifference seemed to be the norm. This meant that supervisors and managers worked hard to pretend that differences among employees did not matter—that basically everyone is the same and should be treated the same. This was certainly an improvement over earlier attitudes of intolerance towards differences, although to some degree this intolerance continues to show itself even in today's organizations. Today, vigorous indifference is less likely to be appropriate.

> "By the year 2000, with the pace of change currently occurring throughout the labor force and the marketplace, merely tolerating diversity will no longer be possible if an organization expects to succeed. Instead, a comprehensive approach to valuing and managing employee differences will be required for both individual and organizational success."[1]

TODAY'S CHANGING WORK FORCE

Our society is changing rapidly. The increasingly diverse workplace consists not only of people of different sexes, races, and nationalities, but people of different ages, life-styles, sexual orientations, physical abilities, and religious beliefs. The challenge to supervisors will be to replace the old organizational value of treating everyone the same with the realization that diversity brings new opportunities for everyone.

There are a number of ways of examining the multicultural challenges that face today's supervisor. One way is by looking at the recent changing demographics of the workplace and the ways in which these changes will continue well into the twenty-first century. A second way is to examine some of the multicultural differences that help explain why the work force is becoming increasingly heterogeneous. The following does both of these.

Changing Demographics

One of the most direct ways of examining multiculturalism in the workplace is by analyzing the changing *demographics* or characteristics that can be used to describe the composition of the work force. Table 8–1 provides such data for a thirty-year period. A careful analysis of these data reveal the following:

☐ The percentage of men in the work force has been declining consistently and, by the year 2005, men will account for only 53 percent of the total.

---

[1] Marilyn Loden and Judy B. Rosener, *Workforce America! Managing Employee Diversity as a Vital Resource* (Homewood, Ill.: Business One Irwin, 1991), 11.

TABLE 8-1

The United States labor force: 1975–2005
(16 years of age or older; numbers in thousands)

	1975	1990	Projection 2005
Men	56,271	73,987	89,240
Women	37,377	60,375	78,667
Anglo	82,742	107,177	125,585
Men	50,234	59,298	66,851
Women	32,508	47,879	58,734
Black	9,263	13,493	17,766
Men	5,106	6,708	8,704
Women	4,157	6,785	9,062
Hispanic	NA	9,576	16,790
Men	NA	5,755	9,902
Women	NA	3,821	6,888
Asian	1,643	4,116	7,181
Men	931	2,226	3,783
Women	712	1,890	3,398
Total	93,648	134,362	167,907

Source: U.S. Department of Commerce, 1993.

The demographic composition of the work force is changing.

☐ The percentage of women in the work force has been steadily increasing and, by 2005, women will account for 47 percent of the total.

☐ Anglo workers accounted for 88 percent of the entire work force in 1975, but they will make up only 75 percent of this work group by 2005.

☐ Anglo men accounted for 54 percent of the work force in 1975, but this will drop to 40 percent by 2005.

☐ Although the number of Anglo women in the work force will increase by over 25 million between 1975 and 2005, their overall percentage will remain at 35 percent.

☐ One-quarter of all workers in 2005 will be black, Hispanic, or Asian. Moreover, between 1990 and 2005, the ranks of these employees will swell by almost 15 million.[2]

In addition, the American work force will grow significantly older. By the year 2000, those in the 35–54 age group will constitute 51 percent of the work force, in contrast to 38 percent in 1985. At the same time, the percentage of those in the 16-24 age group will decline by 8 per-

[2]*The World Almanac, 1993* (New York: World Almanac, 1993), 156.

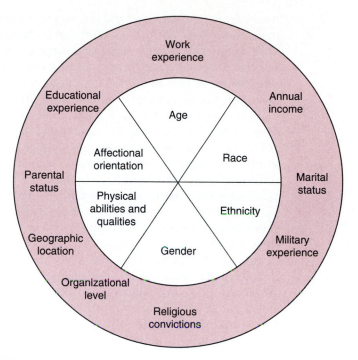

FIGURE 8-1
Primary and secondary dimensions of diversity.
Adapted from Marilyn Loden and Judy B. Rosener, *Workforce America! Managing Employee Diversity as a Vital Resource* (Homewood, Ill.: Business One Irwin, 1991), 20.

cent.[3] These data clearly indicate that the composition of the work force is changing. In 1975, most workers were Anglos and over half of the labor force consisted of white males. In the future, Anglos will continue to make up a large percentage of the work force, but by 2005 Anglo women and blacks, Hispanics, and Asians will collectively account for 60 percent of the work force. These findings help explain why it is important to learn how to supervise in a diverse, multicultural workplace.

Diversity and Multicultural Differences

Diversity has been defined as "those qualities that are different from our own and outside the groups to which we belong, yet present in other individuals and groups."[4] There are a number of variables that characterize diversity. Some researchers have grouped them into two categories: primary and secondary. Primary dimensions of diversity are those human differences that are inborn. As seen in Figure 8–1, examples include age, ethnicity, gender, physical abilities, and race. Secondary dimensions of diversity

There are many differences among multicultural employees.

---

[3]Loden and Rosener, 7.

[4]Ibid., 18.

are those that are acquired and can be modified or discarded. Examples include educational background, income, marital status, religious beliefs, and work experience. When managing diversity, supervisors must keep in mind that there are some differences between people that cannot be changed and others that can. In fashioning a strategy for effectively supervising employees, first-line managers must work within this diversity framework.

As seen in Self-Assessment Quiz 8–1, there are a host of multicultural differences with which supervisors must deal. These differences, to a large extent, can be traced to: (1) the immigration policies of the United States, which now admits millions of people annually from Latin America, Asia, and Europe, and (2) the fact that many Americans have been raised in a multicultural environment. For example, many Cuban families in Miami who arrived in the United States in the early 1960s still speak Spanish as their primary language and cling to their Latin roots. The children are bilingual, celebrate both American and Cuban holidays, and often exchange gifts on both December 25 (Christmas Day) and January 6 (the coming of the Magi). The same analogy holds for Mexican-Americans in the southwest United States, Puerto Ricans in the northeast, and Chinese-Americans in the northwest, to name but three.

Current estimates are that 30 to 40 percent of the annual growth rate of the labor force is accounted for by foreign nationals. Another large percentage comes from blacks and women entering the labor force. (The equal opportunity implications as well as other specific information on groups including disabled workers, women, older workers, and ethnic minorities is discussed in Chapter 6. The challenges diversity presents to supervisors range from communication to motivation to leadership.[5] In terms of communication, for example, some foreign-born employees do not have a full understanding of English. In fact, according to the San Diego-based Cross-Cultural Communication Center, there are more than 140 languages and dialects spoken in the United States and 11 percent of the population speaks a language other than English at home.[6]

In terms of motivation and leadership, supervisors are now finding that the way they manage Anglo men may not be the same approach that is successful in managing other groups of employees. Supervisors can no longer use one generic approach for all workers. In addressing these differences, companies are now helping supervisors deal with this challenge and increase overall work quality by training them to understand multicultural differences and address each situation on its own merits.

---

[5]See, for example, Catherine M. Petrini, "The Language of Diversity," *Training & Development Journal* (April 1993): 35-37.

[6]Charlene Marmer Solomon, "Managing Today's Immigrants," *Personnel Journal* (February 1993): 58.

UNDERSTANDING THE CHALLENGE

The multicultural challenge has a number of aspects with which supervisors must be familiar, including understanding how to communicate effectively with women, blacks, Hispanics and older employees as well as to motivate and lead these employees.[7] In particular, supervisors must learn how to plan and then manage these approaches. The following examines both of these strategies.

Planning For Diversity

Many organizations are now developing plans for managing a diverse work force. In doing so, they are focusing their attention on three areas: individuals, culture, and education.[8]

Individuals.   Multicultural organizations have a wide array of employees who respond differently to similar situations. The challenge for the supervisor is to realize that there are three major differences that need to be examined. One is the ways in which people learn things. Multicultural work groups have different perceptions about instructions, problem-solving tasks, rules, and regulations. Even members of the same group often respond differently to a common problem or issue. A second difference is human relations styles that are preferred modes of relating to other people. Some employees need a great deal of nurturing, affiliation, and cooperation, whereas others prefer to be left alone and respond best to a supervisor who employs a rigid, authoritarian style. A third difference is motivation, as reflected by people's preferences for goals and rewards that influence their behavior. Some people value internal motivators such as praise; others respond best to external motivators such as money. (See Chapter 9 for a complete discussion of motivation.) Some prefer to be directly rewarded for their efforts, as in the case of individuals raised in the United States, where personal effort is encouraged. Others prefer to be rewarded as a member of a group, as in the case of workers raised in the Orient where the culture teaches them to be part of a team and always share credit with the group.

> Culture is the acquired knowledge that people use to interpret experience and to generate social behavior.

Culture.   *Culture* is the acquired knowledge that people use to interpret experience and to generate social behavior. All organizations have a culture, which consists of the shared values and beliefs of the enterprise. *Values* are basic convictions that people have regarding what is right and wrong, good and bad, important and unimportant. One way in which an

---

[7]Wendell Cardell Fitch, "Developing Cultural Literacy," *Leader's Digest* (Summer 1993): 10–11.

[8]James A. Anderson, "Thinking About Diversity," *Training & Development Journal* (April 1993): 59–60.

organization's culture and values is expressed is through the actions and words of the supervisors. These behaviors reinforce the organization's beliefs related to productivity, profit, quality, and other performance-related objectives. They also shape personnel behaviors and norms. However, the culture or values may not be acceptable to or understood by all employees. For example, some of the personnel may not know what is expected of them in terms of performance requirements. Others may find the organization's rules and regulations overly inflexible. To deal effectively with different groups of people, the supervisor must understand their cultural values.

Education.   In promoting productivity, supervisors must know how their own behavior affects their work groups. This often is accomplished by training the supervisors both to accept and to promote diversity. Examples include teaching the managers to: (1) be aware of how their leadership style affects subordinates; (2) learn how to draw from their own cultural contexts and those of others; (3) develop a sense of social ethics and social responsibility; (4) learn how their personal values and ideas affect their view of leadership and diversity; and (5) be willing to accept the challenges associated with managing a multicultural work group.

Dealing with Diversity

Supervisors need to be trained.

Most supervisors, despite their best efforts, have difficulty dealing with diversity. This helps explain why recent industry reports indicate that 40 percent of American companies now offer some form of diversity training.[9] Research reveals that such training is particularly important given the lingering and deep-seated prejudice that exists in many companies.

In dealing with diversity, there are a number of steps that organizations are now taking. One is to make it clear to supervisors that managing diversity is different from affirmative action or valuing differences between people. Table 8–2 provides some key contrasts. The process involves carefully modeled behavior that is pragmatic and strategically driven. Table 8–3 provides further insights on this topic including the long-range, proactive nature of this approach.

Diversity creates a new way of thinking about differences. In particular, the emphasis is given to tapping the creative potential of the diverse work group in enhancing organizational productivity, profitability, and responsiveness to business conditions. Some of the specific steps that are followed in this process include:

1.   Accepting the fact that diversity is a challenge that must be met.

---

[9]Patricia A. Galagan, "Navigating the Differences," *Training & Development Journal,* (April 1993): 30.

TABLE 8–2
Affirmative action and valuing diversity: A contrast

Affirmative Action	*Valuing Diversity*
Initiated through government action	Result of a voluntary decision by the firm
Legally mandated and directed by the government	Productivity-directed by the organization
Quantitative in focus with the emphasis on hiring and promotion goals designed to correct discrimination	Qualitative with the emphasis on valuing the contribution of all employees
Designed to solve problems such as discrimination of minorities	Designed to take advantage of opportunities such as tapping the talents of all personnel
Reactive in nature and designed to correct problems	Proactive in nature and designed to prevent problems

2. Strengthening top management commitment to promoting diversity.
3. Opting for solutions that are best for both the personnel and the organization.
4. Setting goals to be achieved from these diversity efforts and continually reviewing and revising the goals where needed.
5. Maintaining the diversity momentum, thus ensuring that this process does not turn into a short-term fad that is soon abandoned.

"Supervisory Skills: Getting Mentally Prepared" provides additional guidelines that can help supervisors deal with diversity.

MEETING THE DIVERSITY CHALLENGE

There are a number of steps that organizations are now taking to help their supervisors meet the diversity challenge. These fall into two broad areas: diversity practices that successful firms are finding useful, and training programs that are designed to help supervisors more fully understand the nature of diversity and how to achieve it within the organization. The following examines both of these areas.

Diversity Practices

One of the most effective ways of managing a diverse work force is by discovering how other firms have been successful and then emulating their efforts. Some of the corporations that have had the greatest success

TABLE 8-3

Affirmative action, value differences, and managing diversity: A comparative analysis

Affirmative Action	*Valuing Differences*	*Managing Diversity*
Quantitative. Emphasis is on achieving equality of opportunity in the work environment through the changing of organizational demographics. Progress is monitored by statistical reports and analyses.	**Qualitative.** Emphasis is on the appreciation of differences and the creation of an environment in which everyone feels valued and accepted. Progress is monitored by organizational surveys focused on attitudes and perceptions.	**Behavioral.** Emphasis is on building specific skills and creating policies that get the best from every employee. Efforts are monitored by progress toward achieving goals and objectives.
Legally driven. Written plans and statistical goals for specific groups are utilized. Reports are mandated by EEO laws and consent decrees.	**Ethically driven.** Moral and ethical imperatives drive this culture change.	**Strategically driven.** Behaviors and policies are seen as contributing to organizational goals and objectives, such as profit and productivity, and are tied to rewards and results.
Remedial. Specific target groups benefit as past wrongs are remedied. Previously excluded groups have an advantage.	**Idealistic.** Everyone benefits. Everyone feels valued and accepted in an inclusive environment.	**Pragmatic.** The organization benefits: morale, profits, and productivity increase.
Assimilation model. Model assumes that groups brought into system will adapt to existing organizational norms.	**Diversity model.** Model assumes that groups will retain their own characteristics and shape the organization as well as be shaped by it, creating a common set of values.	**Synergy model.** Model assumes that diverse groups will create new ways of working together effectively in a pluralistic environment.
Opens doors. Efforts affect hiring and promotion decisions in the organization.	**Opens attitudes, minds, and the culture.** Efforts affect attitudes of employees.	**Opens the system.** Efforts affect managerial practices and policies.
Resistance. Resistance is due to perceived limits to autonomy in decision making and perceived fears of reverse discrimination.	**Resistance.** Resistance is due to a fear of change, discomfort with differences, and a desire to return to the "good old days."	**Resistance.** Resistance is due to denial of demographic realities, of the need for alternative approaches, and of the benefits of change. It also arises from the difficulty of learning new skills, altering existing systems, and finding the time to work toward synergistic solutions.

Source: Reprinted from *The Training and Development Journal* Copyright April 1993, The American Society for Training and Development. Reprinted with permission. All rights reserved.

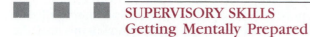

SUPERVISORY SKILLS
Getting Mentally Prepared

One of the major challenges facing supervisors dealing with diversity is mentally preparing themselves for this task. In particular, there are five beliefs that they must accept. These include:

1. Realize that diversity efforts are not attempts to lower hiring barriers or standards of performance. This can be difficult to accept, especially when supervisors see themselves as guardians of traditional, mainstream culture. However, it is critical to the success of any diversity effort.

2. Understand that many diverse people often tap into their cultural heritages to develop ideas, identify and solve problems, and contribute to the achievement of organizational goals. These actions must not be viewed as threats to the organization or the status quo.

3. Be aware that diverse people sometimes openly challenge traditional organization norms that stifle diversity. When this happens, it is important to view these challenges as opportunities to review the norms and determine whether they are roadblocks. It is equally important not to immediately assume that those making the challenge are hostile to the business or its basic values.

4. Keep in mind that some of the behaviors that help dominant group members succeed may not work as well for diverse employees. Thus it is a mistake to believe that there is one set of attitudes and behaviors that is universal to successful personnel. What works well for dominant group members may be unacceptable or unworkable for diverse workers. Additionally, when the latter do try to emulate the majority they may be judged as ineffective, thus supporting their belief that they should not blindly accept the organization's behavioral norms.

5. Realize that organizations that value diversity put their emphasis on changing the corporate culture, not the people who work there. In these enterprises, there is a range of acceptable behavior and supervisory efforts should not attempt to restrict or limit this range.

Source: Adapted from Marilyn Loden and Judy B. Rosener, *Workforce America! Managing Employee Diversity as a Vital Resource* (Homewood, Ill.: Business One Irwin, 1991), 27–35.

in this area include American Express, Colgate-Palmolive, DuPont, Motorola, and Xerox, to name but five.[10]

Research has uncovered a number of diversity practices that are common among these firms.

Management must be personally involved.

One is top management's personal involvement. Firms that successfully promote diversity have executives who not only support this strategy but are actively involved in its implementation. Managers not only talk about the need for diversity, but cajole, demand, and counsel their supervisory personnel to promote diversity at the lowest levels of the structure.

[10]Ann Morrison, "Diversity," *Training & Development Journal* (April 1993): 43.

Minorities must be recruited.

A second practice is the targeting of nonmanagerial recruitment efforts among a wide continuum of personnel. The objective is to hire a diverse work force at the lower levels of the enterprise. In carrying out this goal, the supervisor's job is to help recruit women, blacks, Hispanics, Asians, and other minorities. Once hired, the supervisor's job is then to focus attention on training all employees to be productive members of the work team.

Internal advocacy groups are useful.

A third practice is to use *internal advocacy groups,* which are special-interest groups and networks within the structure that lobby management for changes that will remove barriers to the hiring and promotion. Supervisors play an active role here. They also help the organization by learning about equal employment opportunity (EEO) guidelines and ensuring that these directives are carefully followed. When they discover company rules or regulations that may be in conflict with these EEO standards, they quickly point them out to higher-level management and work to help correct the problem.

Diversity must be incorporated into performance evaluation goals.

A fourth practice is the incorporation of diversity in performance evaluation goals and ratings. In many cases, organizations have biased evaluations that reduce the promotion opportunities of minorities. For example, the performance evaluation may call for judging an individual on the basis of ability to communicate well, but because the person has a foreign accent the evaluation score is negatively affected. By being aware of such biases, supervisors can ensure that their evaluations are valid and accurately reflect the criteria being assessed.

Diversity must be included in promotion recommendations.

A fifth practice is encouraging supervisors to recommend people of color and other minorities for promotion consideration. This practice ensures that these subordinates are not inadvertently overlooked for promotion.

These five practices are often reinforced by upper-level management, which helps the supervisor "stay the course" by implementing action steps for achieving diversity. Some of those used by successful companies include:

These are useful steps in diversity training.

1. Continually focus on diversity problems and as these are identified and solved, look for others. This process of continuous improvement is used throughout the organization, especially at the supervisory level, where the work force is often more diverse than at any other level.

2. Continually collect data on how well the organization is handling its diversity effort and be prepared to take the necessary action. This step is particularly important at the upper levels because supervisors look to higher management for guidance. When the senior managers show that they are interested in promoting diversity, everyone else on the management team gets behind the effort.

3. Implement solutions that are specifically designed to handle problems. Rather than using a generic approach to promoting or imple-

menting diversity, supervisors need to evaluate each situation on its own merits and tailor-design the approach.

4.   Keep a strong focus on results. Many organizations believe that they understand the diversity challenge and are meeting it. However, a close look at one indicator of successful management of diversity shows that minorities are seldom promoted into managerial positions and none of these individuals ever reaches the executive ranks. Effective firms gather quantitative feedback and know, for example, how many minorities they have promoted into supervisory positions. In addition, supervisors are taught how to gather feedback from their work groups so that they know how well they are managing the diversity challenge. These managers have a good understanding of the organizational climate in their work group and are able to accurately assess the results of their efforts.

5.   Keep the momentum. As the organization's diversity program begins to gain steam, management must encourage the supervisors (and other managerial personnel) to expand their efforts. In the beginning, supervisors will plan for the short run, but this time horizon will eventually be expanded to include longer-run diversity plans. There will also be an effort to continually eliminate traditional, nonproductive practices. Finally, the company will work to extend the diversity focus beyond ethnicity and sex and incorporate an increasingly larger number of issues, including the role of older employees in the organization.[11]

The Role of Training

Training is critical to diversity efforts.

Supervising in a multicultural workplace is no easy task. For many first-line managers, it is a challenge for which they are ill prepared. This is why more and more organizations are offering diversity training, especially to these lower-level managers. See "The Quality Challenge: Managing Diversity Effectively" for an inside look on how the chemical group at Monsanto trains its supervisors.

Research reveals that there are a number of guidelines that are useful in providing successful diversity training.[12] While these steps are not totally within the control of the supervisor, they are important to the study of supervision, because without the knowledge and support of the first-line manager, the overall diversity effort will fail.

One of the most important steps is to incorporate training as a part of the broad diversity strategy. This training must cover a wide continuum

---

[11]For more on this, see *Morrison,* 38-43.

[12]Ann Perkins Delatte and Larry Baytos, "Guidelines for Successful Diversity Training," *Training* (January 1993): 55–60.

THE QUALITY CHALLENGE
Managing Diversity Effectively

At the Chemical Group of Monsanto, the management of diversity is a primary area of attention. In achieving its diversity objective, the company has developed a three-part strategy. This plan is designed to raise awareness, to establish accountability as a measure of performance, and to change the processes that support the way people are managed. The program has been particularly helpful in promoting diversity by supervisors. Some of the steps that supervisors now take as a result of feedback on the program include the following:

1. Focus on developing the talents and promotional potential of the personnel. After analyzing turnover data, the company found that minorities and women were twice as likely to leave the organization than were white men. Through lengthy exit interviews, the firm learned that many of these people were leaving because they were not being given challenging work and their jobs were basically dead-end positions.

2. Set aside time for formal discussions with the personnel, using this opportunity to discuss job-related problems, training needs, and career plans. These meetings are called join-ups and their objective is to help jump start the supervisory-subordinate relationship. In most cases, these join-ups involve a minority employee, thus

promoting the firm's diversity effort. Typical sessions last two hours and the supervisor is expected to maintain this formal relationship for eighteen months. Supervisors are trained to handle this facilitative role through a thirteen-day program that immerses them in a host of diversity-related issues. Included in this training are listening skills.

3. Learn to recognize some of the common barriers to promoting diversity. Examples include denial, lack of awareness, a compulsion to help the other party change his or her behavior rather than admitting that both sides may need to change, and an unwillingness to give the diversity effort a chance to succeed because previous efforts by the company have been unsuccessful.

These three guidelines can be difficult to implement. However, Monsanto has found that if supervisors will immerse themselves in the training program and then return to the job determined to make diversity a reality, they will succeed. To a large extent, the success of the effort depends more on the supervisor than on the person the manager is trying to assist.

Source: Patricia A. Galagan, "Trading Places at Monsanto," *Training and Development Journal* (April 1992): 45–49.

---

of concerns, including hiring, retention, and teaching supervisors to carry out these functions effectively, because these activities are critical to the overall productivity and profitability of the enterprise.

A second important step is to conduct a needs analysis of the organization, so that the training group knows the specific types of diversity issues that must be addressed. This knowledge increases the relevancy of the training and ensures that the supervisors learn what they need to know and what they are more likely to use back on the job.

A third important step is to design the program by getting input from a diverse group. Some organizations are unsuccessful because they use the *BOWGSAT method,* which stands for "Bunch of White Guys Sitting Around a Table." Effective training programs must have input from all individuals who can provide insights regarding such diversity dimensions as race, gender, age, and ethnicity. Companies must also consider secondary aspects of diversity such as parental status, organizational level, functional discipline, and educational background. The result is that, although there are white males in the group who provide input, information is also solicited from women, other minorities, young people, old people, upper-level managers, lower-level managers, individuals with master's degrees, and people who did not complete high school. By including such diversity, the company increases the odds that the content of the program will be on target with the needs of its work group as well as that of the enterprise.

A fourth step is to decide on the parameters for the training. In some companies there are no limits regarding what will be covered in diversity training, whereas in other firms some topics or activities are considered to be out of bounds. One group of trainers offered the following explanation:

> A pharmaceutical company for which we developed a workshop let us know that an encounter-group approach that required coworkers to be brutally frank about their negative views of each other was strictly out of bounds. On the other hand, the program manager at another company insisted that her organization had a rough-and-tumble style of interaction, and that managers attending diversity programs would relish an open and confrontational approach. She felt that they would dismiss any programs which, in their minds, were too timid about surfacing the nitty-gritty issues.[13]

A fifth step is to thoroughly test the program before implementing it. Because of the sensitive nature of the issues covered in diversity training, there is a potential for the program to blow up if everything is not handled carefully. This goal is often achieved through the use of a pilot program that is offered to a representative group of diverse participants. Based on the feedback, the program is then modified where necessary (and sometimes retested) and then offered to supervisors throughout the organization.

Sixth, and finally, these diversity training efforts must be viewed by the personnel as part of an ongoing program and not a one-shot program. This is why firms that have developed successful diversity programs blend them into existing programs such as orientation, supervisory skills, coaching, performance evaluation, and management development.

Training is a critical part of every enterprise's diversity efforts, and supervisors play an important role in helping achieve these objectives. To the extent that the organization can get the supervisors involved in both the design and implementation of its diversity strategy, the success of the program is greatly enhanced. "Supervisory Skills: Meeting the Diversity Challenge" offers some additional guidelines.

---

[13]Ibid., 59.

SUPERVISORY SKILLS
Meeting the Diversity Challenge

1. Remember that your positive attitude toward maximizing the many benefits of a diverse workforce is your most important asset in successfully meeting the diversity challenge.

2. Demonstrate to others that you value diversity by keeping it foremost in your mind when you are hiring and promoting. Your determination to first secure and then retain a diverse work force is a critical first step.

3. Use a continuous improvement philosophy towards developing a multicultural work force that not only respects each other but learns to reap the considerable rewards of differing perspectives, strengths, and skills.

4. Advocate training for everyone. Don't wait for problems to arise. Get widespread employee input on what training objectives should be established.

SUMMARY

The workplace of the 1990s is going to be quite different from that of the 1980s because of changing demographics, and these changes will continue well into the twenty-first century. In particular, supervisors are having to manage an increasingly multicultural work force. Some of the specific changes that will take place between now and 2005 include: (1) a continual decline in the percentage of men in the workplace; (2) a reduction in the percentage of Anglo male workers and a leveling off of the percentage of Anglo female workers; and (3) an increase in both the number and percentage of black, Hispanic, and Asian employees. These data help explain why it is important for supervisors to learn how to manage in a multicultural workplace.

Many organizations are now planning for diversity. In doing so, they are focusing their attention on three areas: individuals, culture, and education. In the first area, supervisors must learn that multicultural personnel often have different perceptions about instructions, problem-solving tasks, rules, and regulations. These groups also vary greatly in terms of the amount of nurturing, affiliation, and cooperation they need, and they have widely varying preferences for goals and rewards that influence their behavior. In the area of culture, supervisors must realize that multicultural work groups have a wide variety of values and these values may sometimes need to be modified to bring them into line with those of the organization. In the area of education, supervisors must learn how their own behavior affects their work groups, an objective that is often accomplished by training.

There are a number of steps that organizations are now taking to help their supervisors meet the diversity challenge. These fall into two broad areas: emulating the diversity practices of successful firms, and giving the supervisors training to help them more fully understand the nature of diversity and how to achieve it within the organization. Some of the steps taken by successful organizations include: personal involvement by top management; targeting of nonmanagerial recruitment efforts among a wide continuum of personnel; use of internal advocacy groups; incorporation of diversity in performance evaluation goals and ratings; and the inclusion of diversity in promotion recommendations. In the area of diversity training, common steps include: incorporating training as a part of the broad diversity strategy; conducting a needs analysis; designing the program by getting input from a diverse group; determining the parameters for the training; thoroughly testing the program before implementing it; and making diversity training an ongoing program.

REVIEW QUESTIONS

1. Over the next decade, what is going to happen to the number and percentage of Anglo men and women in the work force? Of what importance is the change to supervisors?

2. Over the next decade, what changes in work force composition will occur among blacks, Hispanics, and Asians? Of what importance is this change to supervisors?

3. In managing for diversity, supervisors are having to focus their attention on individual differences among work group members. What does this statement mean?

4. In managing for diversity, supervisors will have to deal with the issue of multiculturalism. In what way is this an important challenge?

5. In promoting productivity, supervisors must know how their own behavior affects their work groups. What does this statement mean, and what implications does it have for supervisors? Explain.

6. In dealing with diversity, there are a number of steps that organizations are now taking. What are three of these steps? Describe them.

7. Why is it important to diversity efforts that top management be personally involved? Explain your reasoning.

8. Why are firms that are interested in promoting diversity now targeting their recruitment efforts to a wide continuum of personnel?

9. What are internal advocacy groups, and of what value are they in promoting diversity efforts?

10. How do organizations seek to incorporate diversity into performance evaluation goals and ratings? Give an example.

11. There are a number of steps that organizations use to ensure that their diversity efforts stay the course. What are some of these steps? Identify four of them.

12. What are some of the most common steps that are taken by organizations in ensuring that supervisors receive the necessary training in diversity? Identify and discuss four of them.

KEY TERMS

BOWGSAT method. A method of deciding how to design a diversity training program by relying on a "Bunch of White Guys Sitting Around a Table."

Culture. The acquired knowledge that people use to interpret experience and to generate social behavior.

Demographics. Characteristics that can be used to describe the composition of the work force.

Diversity.   Those qualities that are different from one's own and outside the groups to which one belongs, yet present in other individuals and groups.

Internal advocacy groups.   Special-interest groups and networks within the structure that lobby management for changes that will remove barriers to the hiring and promotion of minorities.

Melting pot.   A term used to describe the process by which people from all parts of the world come to the United States and eventually become part of a homogeneous group.

Multicultural.   A term used to describe work groups whose individual members come from diverse cultures.

Thawing pot.   A description of America in which people who immigrate here keep many of their initial values and beliefs while adding others that are common to Americans.

Values.   Basic convictions that people have regarding what is right and wrong, good and bad, important and unimportant.

ANSWERS TO SELF-ASSESSMENT QUIZ 8–1

1. True	3. False	5. True	7. False	9. False
2. True	4. True	6. True	8. True	10. True

CASE 8–1
Getting Things Going

When the Total Protection Insurance Company (TPIC) was founded during the 1950s, the firm's focus was primarily in the area of life insurance. Over the years, however, the company has undergone a number of major management changes, and five years ago it was purchased by a group of private investors who decided to refocus the firm's business. Today TPIC is very active in the health insurance area, and this has proved to be a major boon for the firm. As more and more companies are finding health premiums climbing, TPIC has been developing a series of new product offerings designed to maximize coverage while holding down cost. Small and medium-size firms, in particular, like TPIC's offerings, and the firm has been able to double its annual health care business during each of the last three years. This growth has been accompanied by large personnel increases. Last year the company hired 372 people and has plans to add another 440 next year. The current breakdown of its 2,900 personnel is the following:

Males	1,200
Females	1,700
Anglos	
Male	653
Female	835
Blacks	
Male	318
Female	337
Hispanics	
Male	147
Female	408
Oriental	
Male	82
Female	120
Over 40 years of age	742
Under 40 years of age	2,158

The president of TPIC believes that there will be an increase in the number of women and ethnic minorities in the firm by this time next year, and she believes that in five years women will account for at least 75 percent of the company's total work force. She explained her reasoning at a recent Chamber of Commerce meeting, where she was the guest speaker. "Insurance is a field that requires all employees to put the customer first," she said. "We are a service-driven industry, despite the fact that we would like to believe we are product-driven, as evidenced by the number of new offerings we bring to the market annually. At TPIC we have found that women do a better job of interacting with clients, learning their problems, discussing their needs, and handling their business. And I would expect this to reflect itself in our hirings. At the same time, however, we are recruiting and training people of all colors and creeds. At TPIC we are trying to provide

for all of the insurance needs of our clients, and we intend to have a diverse work force that is capable of meeting this challenge."

1. Based on the data in the case, does TPIC currently have a diverse work force? Defend your answer.

2. Using Figure 8–1 as a point of reference, what are three primary and three secondary dimensions of diversity that will affect the TPIC supervisor's job? Describe each.

3. What can management do to meet this diversity challenge? Offer three recommendations for action.

CASE 8–2
A Changing World

The Clavernett Company, founded in 1988, is a hotel/motel management firm. Clavernett currently operates three hotels in the Midwest, and there are plans to double employment over the next three years.

The head of the company, George Clavernett, had more than twenty years experience with a major hotel chain before deciding to break away and start his own business. Following up an offer to take over the management of a hotel that was having trouble, George brought in his own management team and soon had the enterprise operating profitably. Since then, George has landed two more management contracts.

When George took control of the first hotel, there were 400 people in the organization. Today there are 1,394. The breakdown of the personnel during this period is as follows:

1988		Today	
Males		Males	
Anglo	97	Anglo	244
Non-Anglo	3	Non-Anglo	208
Females		Females	
Anglo	275	Anglo	650
Non-Anglo	25	Non-Anglo	292
Blacks	18	Blacks	222
Hispanics	7	Hispanics	190
Orientals	3	Orientals	88
Total	400		1,394

George is aware of these statistics and believes that this is a good time for introducing diversity training. "Over the next five years we are going to be adding six to ten more hotels to our operation," he explained to one of his vice-presidents. "This will increase our work force to well over 3,000 people, many of whom will be women or ethnic minorities. Moreover, we will need to manage these employees in the most effective way possible. This is why I believe we need to start focusing on diversity training. It is going to be one of the key elements in ensuring our management company continues to perform well." Based on these comments, the vice-president is now drawing up a plan of action for implementing a diversity training program.

1. Has the demographic makeup of George's work force changed very much over the last five years? Be complete in your answer.

2. Is diversity training likely to be of value to the Clavernett company? Why or why not? Defend your reasoning.

3. Where would you recommend the diversity training begin? Which group should be the focal point of the initial effort? Explain your choice.

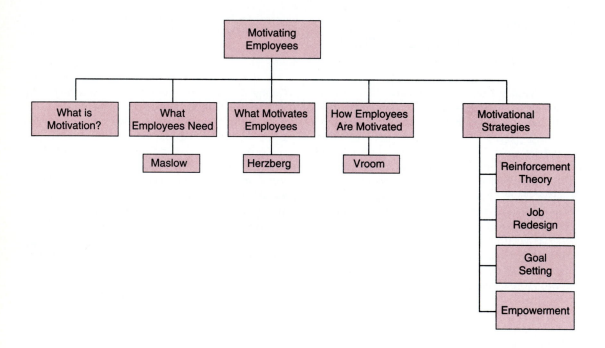

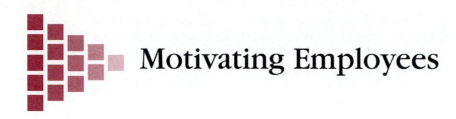

CHAPTER 9

Motivating Employees

*"History is filled with examples of people who accomplished tremendous feats with meager resources. Motivation made their successes possible"**

CHAPTER OBJECTIVES

☐ Explain motivation in terms of need fulfillment.

☐ Describe Maslow's need hierarchy and relate how an organization can satisfy these needs.

☐ Discuss what employees want from their jobs.

☐ Examine motivation in terms of expectations.

☐ Set forth motivational strategies in terms of reinforcement, job re-design, goal setting, and empowerment.

---

*Kenneth M. Dawson and Sheryl N. Dawson, "How to Motivate Your Employees," *HR Magazine* (April 1990): 79.

I f we accept the notion that supervisors spend most of their time trying to organize, coordinate, or control the work of others in order to accomplish organizational goals, then motivating employees is a very large part of the supervisory job. Think for a moment about employee performance. On what is it based? In most cases performance is a combination of ability and motivation.

$$ability + motivation = performance$$

This chapter looks at the first part of this equation. What is motivation? What do employees need? What do they want? How is motivation related to expectations? What motivational strategies can you use?

WHAT IS MOTIVATION?

Motivation comes from the Latin verb *movere,* which means "to move." Thus, *motivation* involves movement of some type—specifically movement related to satisfying a need. The movement may be psychological, as when one changes an attitude, or physiological, as when one works faster. Figure 9–1 illustrates a basic model of motivation. Notice that the process begins with a perceived need in the mind of the individual. This leads to a psychological drive to fulfill the need. The drive turns into action when the individual begins to search for an alternative that will satisfy this need. When an alternative seems promising, the individual chooses it and tries it. At that point the need is either fulfilled and the process stops, or the need still lingers on and the process of searching for solutions continues. Note, however, that even if the need is fulfilled, that fulfillment may wear off at a later time and the whole process begins anew. But what kinds of needs are employees trying to satisfy?

Motivation involves movement of some type.

WHAT EMPLOYEES NEED

Maslow

Like all other human beings, employees have a variety of needs. In the 1950s psychologist Abraham Maslow designed a very famous model for

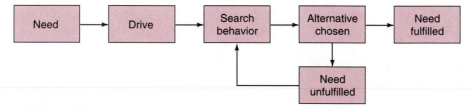

FIGURE 9–1
The motivation process.

174

classifying those needs. The timing of this work is interesting, because during the early 1950s Americans were experiencing unprecedented affluence. Employees were becoming much more independent than their forebearers, and it behooved managers to start worrying about how to motivate employees. Thus it was not by chance that Maslow's theory became so popular.

Maslow's model is often called a *hierarchy of needs*. It consists of five different levels of needs, ranging from very basic physical needs to higher level psychological needs. Figure 9–2 shows the five categories.

According to this model, as we progress up the ladder, each need becomes fulfilled and stops acting as a motivator. When this occurs, the next rung up the ladder becomes the primary motivator. Each group of motivators can be described as follows:

Maslow's hierarchy has five levels.

Maslow's needs list

physical needs—basic needs related to one's physical existence.

safety needs—includes needs such as feeling secure and safe now and in the intermediate future.

social needs—needs to be wanted, loved, and valued.

esteem needs—desire to be respected, honored, and perhaps to stand out from the crowd.

self-actualization needs—desire to fulfill oneself and to become all that one is capable of becoming.

Table 9–1 relates these five levels of needs to the work environment.

How well does Maslow's theory hold up under scrutiny? There are some weak spots. First, it is probably not realistic to assume that every person is motivated by these same factors in precisely this order. Neither may it be realistic to think that a person is predominantly motivated by one set of needs at a time.

FIGURE 9–2
The needs hierarchy.

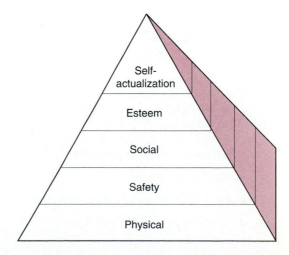

TABLE 9-1
The need hierarchy on the job

Need Category	Employee Needs	How the Organization Can Satisfy These Needs
1. Physical	Food, housing, money to pay bills	Steady salary
2. Safety	Insurance, peace-of-mind, safety in the workplace	Benefits, employee contracts, safety standards, measures
3. Social	Congenial co-workers, friends, participation in activities	Bowling teams, group meetings, picnics, quality circles
4. Esteem	Admiration, prestige, recognition	Company car, deference, fancy office, title
5. Self-actualization	A chance to do something new, exciting, and important; fulfilling work	Autonomy, freedom to be creative

What are the major strengths? Why is it the most famous motivational theory and the one that most practicing supervisors know about? First, it makes us realize that different people are motivated by different things. Moreover, we also must conclude that even the same person is motivated by different things during different stages of life. Understanding employee needs is not enough in itself, however, to explain what employees want from their jobs. We need to delve a bit further into motivation.

■ ■ ■ SELF-ASSESSMENT QUIZ 9-1
Which Job Factors Are Most Important to You?

Directions: Rank the following from "1" (most important) to "10" (least important) according to how important you feel each job factor is to you at the current time.

____ a. Spacious, well-decorated office

____ b. Challenging work

____ c. Friendly and understanding supervisor

____ d. Recognition for a job well done

____ e. Company car and/or private parking space

____ f. Authority to make important decisions

____ g. Co-workers with whom you like to socialize

____ h. Opportunity to learn something new

____ i. Competitively high salary

____ j. Job security

WHAT MOTIVATES EMPLOYEES

Herzberg

In the late 1950s, an American researcher named Frederick Herzberg decided to take a look at motivation from another perspective. He chose 200 engineers and accountants in the greater Pittsburgh area and asked them what made them happy and unhappy about their jobs. Before reading further, take Self-Assessment Quiz 9–1 and find which job factors are most important to you.

Specifically, Herzberg asked the respondents to recall incidents when they felt especially good about their jobs and incidents when they felt especially bad. He found that the incidents they related fell into two distinct categories. Stories chosen to portray positive experiences seemed to have to do with the job content—for example, opportunity for growth, exercise of responsibility, allowance for creativity. On the other hand, stories told to illustrate negative experiences seemed to relate to the work environment and noncontent areas—for example, unpleasant physical surroundings, uncooperative co-workers and supervisors, and salary. Herzberg concluded that there were two sets of factors at work: those related to positive experiences and job content, and those related to negative experiences and job context. He called the first group *motivators* and the second group *hygiene factors*. Table 9–2 shows Herzberg's breakdown, and Table 9–3 shows examples of each in four different occupations.

According to Herzberg, motivation did not take place along a straight line or continuum from dissatisfaction at one extreme to satisfaction at the other. Instead two continua seemed to be represented. First, a lack of hygiene factors could cause dissatisfaction, but their presence would not motivate workers. A lack of motivators would not bring about satisfaction, but their presence would. Figure 9–3 shows this two-dimensional approach to understanding employee motivation.

Herzberg developed a two-factor theory of motivation.

TABLE 9–2

Motivators and hygiene factors

Hygiene Factors	*Motivators*
Company policies	Achievement
Compatible co-workers	Challenging work
Fringe benefits	Opportunity for advancement
Physical surroundings	Opportunity for creativity
Salary	Recognition
Status and security	Responsibility

TABLE 9-3
Occupational examples of hygiene factors and motivators

Profession	Likely Hygiene Factors	Likely Motivators
College professor	Private office Collegial atmosphere Flexible hours Job tenure Salary	Status in community Opportunity to do interesting research Teaching Autonomy Recognition by peers
Route salesperson	Company car Salary and bonus Pleasant co-workers	Autonomy Ability to set own schedule Award ceremonies for outstanding performance
Union organizer	High salary and benefits Travel expenses Union car Support staff for organizing campaign	Responsibility for winning and losing campaign Challenge of organizing new group Excitement of organizing campaign Respect of union for job well done Opportunity to work for something one believes in
Electronic technician	Secure job Competitive edge Clean environment	Opportunity to stay at "cutting edge" of technology Growth opportunities in high tech field Challenging work Respect for one's knowledge

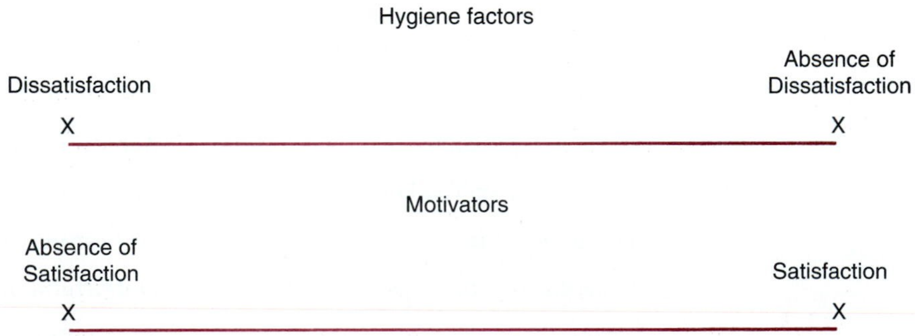

Hygiene factors

Dissatisfaction   Absence of
                                                   Dissatisfaction
X ——— X

Motivators

Absence of
Satisfaction   Satisfaction
X ——— X

FIGURE 9-3
Two-factor theory continua.

Herzberg's theory is comparable to Maslow's.

Herzberg's theory can be directly compared to Maslow's theory. Motivators are similar to Maslow's higher order needs of esteem and self-actualization,whereas hygiene factors can be equated to the lower level needs of physical, safety, and social. Herzberg tells supervisors to pay attention to both of these groups simultaneously. Concentrating on giving your employees better offices, more money, and a happy environment may not produce motivation, but it will keep them from being dissatisfied. Herzberg recommended job redesign techniques, especially job enrichment, to provide the motivators employees need to achieve job satisfaction. We look more closely at job redesign later in this chapter.

The hygiene-motivator theory is not without controversy, however. Subsequent studies have both confirmed and negated Herzberg's findings. Some researchers have questioned the research base and the methodology used by Herzberg.

> "Although Herzberg's two-factor theory became very popular as a textbook explanation of work motivation and was widely accepted by practitioners, it is also true that from an academic perspective the theory oversimplifies the complexities of work motivation. When researchers deviate from the critical incident methodology used by Herzberg, they do not get the two factors. There seem to be job factors that lead to both satisfaction and dissatisfaction. These findings indicate that a strict interpretation of the two-factor theory is not warranted."[1]

Money may or may not be a motivator.

A particularly controversial element of Herzberg's theory is the placement of money or salary as a hygiene factor rather than as a motivator. Many people still feel that money is a motivator not only at lower subsistence levels but also at levels such as esteem, where money might be equated with prestige. The role of money in motivation must be considered by each supervisor. Even within Herzberg's theory, money can be a prime source of discontent when it is not seen to be equitable for that particular job. Even in environments steeped in total quality management principles such as empowerment (discussed later in this chapter), people clearly expect a certain amount of money as an automatic reward for their efforts.

> "These processes cannot be self-sustaining. It comes down to a matter of 'What's in it for me?' We have found that these processes cannot change human nature. Employees want to strive for improvements in quality—but they also want to be compensated accordingly."[2]

Many companies still rely on financial incentives as a basic motivator for their employees. These incentives include: premium pay for overtime or shift work, profit-sharing, employee stock ownership plans, piece rate in-

---

[1]Fred Luthans, *Organizational Behavior,* 6th ed. (New York: McGraw-Hill, Inc., 1992), 160.
[2]Frank A. Papa, "Linkage of Old and New," *Management Review* (January 1993): 63.

centive-pay systems, and bonus plans. Two contemporary financial incentive systems are gain sharing and pay-for-knowledge compensation plans. In the former, the company identifies specific goals and designs pay guidelines to motivate employees to reach or surpass those goals. In the latter, an employee's salary goes up as he or she masters additional skills deemed beneficial to the company.[3]

HOW EMPLOYEES ARE MOTIVATED

Vroom

So far we have looked at what things motivate people. Both Maslow's and Herzberg's theories are considered *content theories*—they focus on what provides motivation to employees. Others have chosen to concentrate on how employees are motivated or precisely what cognitive processes they go through when deciding how hard to strive. The original and still best-known theory in this group of *process theories* is that of Victor Vroom.[4] His approach to motivation is called "expectancy-valence theory." Figure 9–4 portrays the fundamental components of this theory. To work with this model, we need to master the following terms:

Process theory focuses on how employees are motivated.

Key terms in expectancy-valence theory

1. *Employee effort*—exertion the employee decides to put forth in a given endeavor.
2. *First-level outcome*—level of performance achieved as a result of employee effort.
3. *Second-level outcome*—reward the employee will get for achieving a first-level outcome.
4. *Expectancy*—probability from 0 to 1 that a conscious effort will lead to a desired first-level outcome.
5. *Instrumentality*—probability from 0 to 1 that a first-level outcome will lead to a second-level outcome.
6. *Valence*—relative worth or value of a given reward. It is measured from −1 to +1. If a reward has a low valence, employees will not strive nearly as hard to attain it as if it has a high valence.

According to Vroom's theory, employees consciously or semiconsciously decide how much effort to put forth based on their expectancy of achieving a desired level of performance (first-level outcome) and the instrumentality of that performance in earning them the reward most desired. In simple terms motivation depends on the perceived rewards attached to a certain level of productivity.

---

[3]William S. Hubbartt, "Money Talks: How to Use Financial Incentives to Motivate Employees," *Office Systems '91,* (April 1991): 76–80.

[4]Victor H. Vroom, *Work and Motivation* (New York: John Wiley & Sons, 1964).

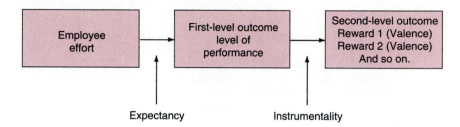

FIGURE 9-4
The expectancy approach to motivation.

Suppose Maryann has an overwhelming desire for promotion (that is, promotion has a high valence). She feels that promotion depends on her achieving the highest sales level in the department. If she expects that her sustained effort can and will succeed in making her the highest-selling person, and that this performance will almost surely guarantee her promotion, she will be very motivated to work hard. On the other hand, if Maryann is very satisfied with the demands and rewards of her current position and does not want a promotion (low valence), she will not be motivated to put forth the needed effort to exceed everyone else's sales figures.

As with other motivational theories, Vroom's theory has both negative and positive aspects:

> On the negative side, Vroom's proposition is not only theoretical but precludes direct application. After all, what manager is really going to try to determine worker motivation via a computation of expectancy and valence? On the positive side, research in the field supports Vroom's basic model, and the model has served as a springboard for additional investigation into the subject of motivation.[5]

MOTIVATIONAL STRATEGIES

We have now examined motivation from several perspectives. Having considered what employees need, what motivates them, and how they're motivated, we can begin to design organizational strategies to provide a motivating job environment. In the rest of this chapter we look at three important strategies: reinforcement theory, job redesign, and goal setting, as well as the newest motivational concept in American organizations, empowerment.

---

[5]Richard M. Hodgetts and Donald F. Kuratko, *Management,* 3rd ed. (San Diego, Calif.: Harcourt Brace Jovanovich, 1991), 420.

SUPERVISORY SKILLS
Understanding Motivation

1. Remember that there are two components to employee performance: ability and motivation. Be sure employees know what to do and how to do it. Assess individual ability by checking training and experience. Discuss the job with the employee; can she explain to you what needs to be done and how to go about accomplishing it? After ensuring that the abilities are indeed present, concentrate on the motivation factor.

2. Understand that motivation is defined differently by different people. We are not all looking for the same things in a job. Re-

gardless of what theory of motivation you subscribe to, the best way to find out what motivates your employees is to ask them!

3. Even if you have asked your employees and feel certain you know what they want, remember that needs change over time; what motivates employees today may not work at all tomorrow. Thus an important supervisory task is to monitor the motivational setting of the job continuously. A slacking off of employee performance may simply mean that the motivational effect of current outcomes is no longer meeting the employee's needs.

Reinforcement Theory

Reinforcement theory is directly related to how learning takes place. Learning refers to any permanent change in behavior that takes place as a result of experience and encouragement. Obviously, learning can spring from many sources, including school, books, teachers, parents, friends, newspapers, and trial and error. In the learning process, support or encouragement, which we'll call *reinforcement* here, plays a key role.

Reinforcement is critical to learning.

Reinforcement theory relies on Thorndike's "law of effect" which can be simply stated as follows:

> "Desirable or reinforcing consequences will increase the strength of a response and increase the strength of a response and increase its probability of being repeated in the future. Undesirable or punishing consequences will decrease the strength of a response and decrease its probability of being repeated in the future."[6]

In organizational settings a great deal of what employees learn is a result of reinforcement. Supervisors, therefore, should know the uses of the four reinforcement strategies: positive reinforcement, negative reinforcement, extinction, and punishment.

Table 9–4 shows the four strategies and the behavioral consequences associated with each. Note that both positive and negative reinforcement strategies strengthen desired behavior, whereas both extinction and punishment weaken undesired behavior. Let's briefly look at these strategies here.

---

[6]Luthans, 215.

TABLE 9–4

Reinforcement strategies and behavioral consequences

Reinforcement Strategy	Behavioral Consequence
Positive	Strengthens desired behavior
Negative	Strengthens desired behavior
Extinction	Weakens undesired behavior
Punishment	Weakens undesired behavior

Positive reinforcement is the creation or use of a pleasant consequence after a specific desirable behavior. Examples would include a pat on the back or verbal praise after successful completion of a task or the offer of increased responsibility. (The latter, by the way, would be a positive reinforcer only to an employee who wants more responsibility.) Positive reinforcement is the most straightforward way of increasing desired behavior and the one most widely recommended for use by supervisors.

Negative reinforcement is the creation or use of an unpleasant consequence after a specific undesirable behavior. To avoid the unpleasant consequence in the future, the object of negative reinforcement starts acting "properly." For instance, if an employee is habitually fifteen minutes late, the supervisor might try the following. As the employee walks in, the supervisor looks up, claps his or her hands, and says, "Now, we can start the day." Chances are the latecomer will be embarrassed and try to be on time the next day in order to avoid the facetious comments. Thus, a desired behavior—being on time—has been reinforced.

Extinction is the deliberate nonreinforcement of an undesirable behavior. This strategy is particularly useful with subordinates who start using some new and annoying habit. For example, suppose an employee starts whistling off key much to the distraction of the supervisor. By calling attention to it, the supervisor runs the risk of elevating its importance and ensuring that it will continue. Sometimes ignoring undesirable behavior is the most effective solution. Of course, if the whistling doesn't disappear by itself, other tactics may be needed.

Punishment is application of a negative consequence to a specific undesirable behavior. Punishment may range from a gentle reprimand to firing someone on the spot. Many experts recommend that supervisors steer away from punishment because it is usually emotionally charged and thus a particularly complex technique for supervisors to use.

There is *little* doubt that the use of punishment tends to cause many undesirable side effects. Neither children nor adults like to be punished. The punished behavior tends to be only temporarily suppressed rather than permanently changed, and the punished person tends to get anxious or 'up-tight' and resentful of the punisher.[7]

In any event, punishment should be used only when all else fails and with the realization that voluntary or involuntary termination of the employee may be the next step.

How can you as a supervisor use this knowledge of reinforcement theory to increase employee performance? With a little careful planning you might follow this three-step process:

Useful principles of reinforcement theory

1. Decide what performance-related behaviors you want to strengthen or weaken. They should be specific measurable behaviors. Always be sure your employees know what you expect of them.
2. Observe the occurrence of these behaviors in the work environment at the present time. How often do they occur? Who engages in them? Is there some apparent pattern to this behavior?
3. Using this observation as a baseline, plan a reinforcement program to meet your goals. Use positive or negative reinforcers to strengthen desirable behavior directly; use extinction or punishment to weaken undesirable behavior, but remember the pitfalls of punishment and use it most sparingly.

Job Redesign

Job redesign concerns strategies having to do with the nature of the work itself. How can we make the work more stimulating and thus more motivational to the employee? Three approaches are commonly used: job rotation, job enlargement, and job enrichment.

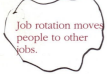

Job rotation moves people to other jobs.

Job rotation teaches employees to do a number of related tasks and allows them to move from one job to another. Instead of doing a single repetitive task all the time, each member in the department rotates at periodic intervals. Theoretically, this approach alleviates boredom. It also enables the department to continue working on a job even when a key person is absent, because now everyone can do all parts of the job. Unfortunately, this latter advantage can be a mixed blessing because many workers believe it's just a way for management to get more work out of them. Nevertheless, when carefully instituted, job rotation can provide added interest to the job.

Job enlargement uses horizontal loading.

Job enlargement involves giving workers more to do by expanding their jobs to encompass more tasks. This expansion entails "horizontal loading" because the new tasks are similar to the original ones. There is no increased authority or responsibility involved for the employee whose job is enlarged. A receptionist, for example, who spends

---

[7]Ibid., 228.

TABLE 9–5
Principles of job enrichment

Principle	Motivators Used
Increased accountability by employee for own work	Responsibility, recognition
Increased authority and job freedom	Responsibility, recognition, opportunity for achievement
Added tasks at increased levels of difficulty	Opportunity for growth and learning
Periodic status reports directly available to employee rather than to supervisor	Recognition
Decreased controls	Responsibility, personal achievement

the day answering the telephone may become bored because of the limited diversity of duties. When a new phone system automatically directs some calls to individual offices, the receptionist may have time to assume other duties such as sorting the mail, typing envelopes, and preparing mass mailings. The receptionist's job has thus become enlarged.

In 1973, a now famous government report entitled "Work in America" was released. It documented that most American workers were dissatisfied with their jobs. It targeted specialization of labor and the limited opportunities for worker autonomy as key reasons for employee discontent. This report did much to popularize the notion that today's workers are looking for more than a decent salary and comfortable working conditions. Management became increasingly aware of the importance of intrinsic motivators such as job autonomy and individual responsibility.[8]

Job enrichment uses vertical loading.

Job enrichment attempts to build these intrinsic motivators into the work. It is built on the motivational theory of Frederick Herzberg. Unlike job enlargement, job enrichment uses "vertical loading" in that the worker is given more authority over both the planning and controlling of the job. When bringing about job enrichment, supervisors can use a number of motivators (see Table 9–5).

Using job enrichment, employees are responsible for the quality of their own work and the timely completion of tasks. The supervisor delegates a good deal of decision-making authority to the individual employee. Let us revisit the receptionist job described earlier. If we were to en-

---

[8]W.E. Upjohn Institute for Employment Research. *Work in America: Report to the Secretary of Health, Education, and Welfare* (Cambridge, Mass.: MIT Press, 1973).

rich that job instead, the receptionist might be in charge of scheduling her own work in order to complete the mass mailing and other duties by a set time. The control over scheduling and the ability to make decisions over how to organize the work day are examples of enrichment rather than enlargement. Most organized attempts to introduce job enrichment have met with at least modest success.

Is job enrichment the answer for everybody? Unfortunately, no. Some employees do not want enriched jobs. They may be quite satisfied with their present level of responsibility. Others may be fearful that they are not prepared to handle increased responsibilities. Still others see their jobs as vehicles to pay the bills and support their leisure-time activities. The latter group see job enrichment as an attempt to get them to work harder. Still, job enrichment can be a valuable motivational tool for many workers.

Goal Setting

Goal setting, the use of specific goals as a way of motivating employees, is not a new technique. Its roots go back to the early 1900s when the "scientific managers" led by Frederick Taylor preached the task concept of doing business, which meant carefully delineating work methods and goals. More recently, goal setting has been translated into management by objectives (MBO), a performance appraisal and control technique discussed in chapter 11.

Latham and Lock did extensive research on how goals affect employee performance. They conducted numerous laboratory experiments and found that "those assigned hard goals performed better than did people assigned moderately difficult or easy goals. Furthermore, individuals who had specific, challenging goals outperformed those who were given such vague goals as to 'do your best'."[9]

Field research among independent loggers pointed out similar results. A total of 1184 logging supervisors were observed to fall into one of the following categories: (1) stays on the job but does not set specific production goals, (2) does not stay on the job but leaves specific production goals, and (3) stays on the job and sets specific production goals. The study concluded that specific goals combined with supervisors who were present on the job had the most significant positive effect on production.[10]

Goal setting uses specific goals to motivate.

---

[9]Gary P. Latham and Edwin A. Locke, "Goal Setting—A Motivational Technique that Works," *Organizational Dynamics* (Autumn 1979): 69–80. As found in James L. Gibson, John M. Ivancevich, and James H. Donnelly, Jr., *Readings in Organizations* (Plano, Tex.: Business Publications, Inc., 1982), 133.

[10]Ibid., 134.

Empowerment

In recent years, organizational scholars and managers alike have conclud-ed that employees can best be motivated when they feel a sense of power and control over their work environment. This phenomenon has come to be called empowerment and was introduced to you in Chapter 2. Al-though most people agree that empowerment is a necessary precondition for total quality management and continuous improvement, it is not al-ways clear how to accomplish this high degree of participation among employees. One consultant tells us that at least four conditions must be met to have an empowered workforce: participation, innovation, access to information, and accountability.[11]

Empowerment depends on four conditions.

Under conditions of participation, employees must be ready, willing, and able to be engaged in the constant improvement central to TQM. This desire seems to be in keeping with the attitude of many employees now gaining power in the workplace.

> "This is exactly what the new breed of employee wants—to be committed to an organization that one can feel proud of, that contributes to society. For tomorrow's employee, being a part of something special that will make a difference is much more important than the rewards sought by yesterday's "me generation."[12]

For empowerment to flourish, organizations need to encourage and re-ward innovation. Without innovation, there can be no constant improve-ment. Likewise, a climate of empowerment requires that information is not hoarded by top management as in traditional organizations, but is readily available to anyone who has use for such information. Finally, the free-dom and responsibility of empowerment must be matched by a feeling of accountability among employees.

Employees should feel clearly accountable in the following areas:

☐ "behaving responsibly toward others
☐ operating with a positive approach
☐ producing desired, agreed-upon results
☐ being responsible for their own credibility and for keeping their word
☐ giving their best."[13]

Empowerment relies on confident, caring supervisors.

The real key to effective empowerment, however, is enlightened su-pervisors who are confident enough in their own abilities to lead with an open, caring respect for employees. This in turn allows those employees a comfortable environment in which to grow.

---

[11]John H. Dobbs, "The Empowerment Environment," *Training and Development* (February 1993): 55–57.

[12]Frank K. Sonnenberg, "A Strategic Approach to Employee Motivation," *The Journal of Business Strategy* (May/June 1991): 41.

[13]Dobbs, 56–57.

SUPERVISORY SKILLS
Using Motivational Strategies

1. Understand the important benefits of reinforcement. Be especially sure to use positive reinforcement as often as merited. Be sure to reinforce desired behavior as quickly as possible. Remember, positive reinforcement costs you nothing and it has many benefits!

2. Be aware that positive reinforcement is especially useful in conjunction with the Pygmalion effect discussed in chapter 4. Expecting good work from your employees and positively reinforcing it when it occurs is a hard combination to beat!

3. Understand the way job redesign works. Whenever possible, try to assign duties and delegate responsibility to make individual jobs more motivational. Be careful, however, that you don't espouse job enrichment and actually deliver job enlargement or job rotation instead. Workers will soon decide that you are merely trying to get them to do more work, not really changing the nature or scope of that work.

4. Use specific goals to motivate your employees. Keep close track of these goals and regularly review them with individual employees. Make sure that employees are aware of how they are progressing with the goals.

5. Most importantly, work to build an empowered work force by nourishing participation, innovation, access to information, and accountability. Lead by example and demonstrate an open, caring attitude of trust and high expectations.

If motivation seems like a complex puzzle, you are catching on!

"As was Don Quixote's quest, motivating employees is an unending challenge. Mandates and occasional pep talks will not energize the work force in the long term. Organizations will succeed in the quest only through a commitment to the techniques that build a corporate culture in which motivation to achieve excellence is constantly reinforced. The future of American business and way of life may depend on companies making this commitment."[14]

SUMMARY

Motivation involves movement of some type, specifically toward satisfying a need. Maslow described needs in terms of a five-part hierarchy: physical, safety, social, esteem, and self-actualization. The hierarchy ranges from basic physical levels to more subtle psychological needs.

In the 1950s, a researcher named Herzberg concluded that two sets of factors play a role in motivation. One set of factors, which Herzberg labeled motivators, gives satisfaction; another set of factors, called hygiene factors, prevents dissatisfaction. Perhaps the most controversial aspect of the

---

[14]Keneth M. Dawson and Sheryl N. Dawson, "How to Motivate Your Employees," *HR Magazine* (April 1990): 80.

theory is the placement of money as a hygiene factor.

Content theories explain what motivates people. Process theories relate how motivation occurs. The best-known process theory is Vroom's expectancy-valence theory.

Motivational strategies are the means by which we seek to motivate employees. Reinforcement theory, for instance, uses learning to modify behavior. Four strategies that rely on learning include positive reinforcement, negative reinforcement, extinction, and punishment. Job redesign focuses on making the work itself more motivational. Three strategies involving job redesign are job rotation, job enlargement, and job enrichment. Goal setting uses specific goals to motivate personnel.

Empowerment relies on conditions of participation, innovation, access to information, and accountability among employees. The supervisor's role is critical in developing a caring, trusting environment.

REVIEW QUESTIONS

1. In your own words, what is meant by the term *motivation?*

2. What are the five needs in Maslow's hierarchy? Draw them in ascending order.

3. In your own words, what needs are contained in each of the five groups: physical, safety, social, esteem, self-actualization?

4. How can an organization satisfy each of the five needs described in the preceding question? Explain.

5. According to Herzberg, what is a motivator? List some examples.

6. According to Herzberg, what is a hygiene factor? List some examples.

7. How does Herzberg's theory tie into Maslow's theory? Explain.

8. Is money a motivator? Name at least three ways that modern organizations use money to motivate employees.

9. How does expectancy theory work in action? Give an example in your answer.

10. How does positive reinforcement work? When is it an effective strategy to use?

11. How does negative reinforcement work? When is it an effective strategy to use?

12. How does extinction work? When is it an effective strategy to use?

13. How does punishment work? Why do many people feel it is an ineffective strategy? Explain.

14. How does job rotation work? Give an example of when it is an effective strategy.

15. How does job enlargement work? Give an example of when it is an effective strategy.

16. How does job enrichment work? Give an example of when it is an effective strategy.

17. How does goal setting work? How effective has it proven to be? Explain.

18. What is empowerment? Name the four conditions that must be present for empowerment to work.

KEY TERMS

Content theories. Motivation theories that focus on *what* motivates people.

Empowerment. A feeling that employees have power and control over their work environment.

Employee effort. Exertion put forth by the employee in a given endeavor.

Esteem needs. Necessities related to the desire to be respected and honored.

Expectancy. Probability that effort will lead to a desired first-level outcome.

Extinction. Reinforcement strategy that deliberately ignores a behavior and through this nonreinforcement brings about a termination of the behavior.

First-level outcome. Level of performance achieved as a result of employee effort.

Goal setting. Use of specific goals as a way of motivating employees.

Hygiene factors. Elements or phenomena that prevent personal dissatisfaction.

Instrumentality. Probability that a first-level outcome will lead to a second-level outcome.

Job enlargement. Expansion of jobs by loading them horizontally.

Job enrichment. Modification of jobs by loading them vertically.

Job rotation. Training of employees so they are able to move from one job to another.

Learning. Any permanent change in behavior that occurs as a result of experience and reinforcement.

Motivation. Movement related to satisfying a need.

Motivators. Factors that cause personal satisfaction.

Negative reinforcement. Unpleasant consequence that results from a specific behavior and that causes the individual to discontinue this behavior.

Physical needs. Most basic necessities related to physical existence.

Positive reinforcement. Pleasant consequence resulting from a specific behavior.

Process theories. Motivation theories that focus on *how* people are motivated.

Punishment. Application of a negative consequence to a specific behavior.

Safety needs. Necessities related to security and protection.

Second-level outcome. Reward achieved for attaining a first-level outcome.

Self-actualization needs. Necessities related to the desire to become all one is capable of becoming.

Social needs. Necessities related to the desire to be wanted, loved, and valued.

Valence. Relative worth or value of a given reward.

ANSWERS TO SELF-ASSESSMENT QUIZ 9–1

Answers b, d, f, and h are considered motivators. Answers a, c, e, g, i, and j are hygiene factors. Note how many of your top five answers were motivators. How many were hygiene factors? Which were most important to you? How would your answers fit within Maslow's theory of need hierarchy?

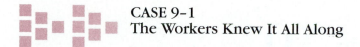

CASE 9-1
The Workers Knew It All Along

The Babson Company recently completed a survey among its supervisors and workers. Supervisors were asked what they felt the workers wanted from their jobs and the company workers were directly asked what they wanted. The employees ranked a list of factors from 1 (most important) to 10 (least important).

After the lists were collected and the totals were compiled, an overall ranking was determined for both the supervisors and the workers. The results are shown at right.

When the final rankings were provided to the supervisors, most admitted that they were surprised. However, the workers were not. As one of them put it, "I could have told you the results before the survey was ever made."

1. In terms of Herzberg's hygiene factors, what do the results show? Explain.

2. In terms of Herzberg's motivators, what do the results show? Explain.

3. What does the company need to do as a result of the findings? Explain.

As Ranked by Supervisors	Factor	As Ranked by Workers
1	Money	5
2	Job security	7
3	Good working conditions	8
4	Good health benefits	9
5	Good pension plan	10
6	Respect	6
7	Chance for advancement	4
8	Interesting work	3
9	Challenging work	2
10	Feeling of being "in" on things	1

CASE 9-2
A Rise in Output

The Joelson Company is a successful manufacturing subcontractor. One of its current jobs is the production and assembly of videocassette recorders.

Each assembly group consists of ten people. Each person performs some of the assembly and then passes the unit to the next person. The average group turns out 100 units a day.

Last month one of the supervisors, Karen Kane, proposed a redesign of the job. She suggested allowing each person to assemble a total unit. After considering the costs involved in restructuring the production facilities to accommodate the change, management decided to give her idea a try. Ten special U-shaped tables were constructed and all of the necessary parts were placed on the table beginning on the right and continuing around to the left. Two weeks ago the assemblers in Karen's group began assembling the total unit. The average worker is now turning out fourteen units a day and Karen believes this total will rise to at least eighteen when the workers become more familiar with all aspects of the assembly.

This week other assembly group members began asking if they, too, could begin assembling units from beginning to end. Management has promised to look into the matter and make a decision very shortly.

1. What type(s) of job redesign did the firm introduce? Describe it (them).

2. Was horizontal loading used? Was vertical loading used? Explain.

3. Why are the workers producing more output than before? Defend your answer.

■ ■ ■ CHAPTER 10

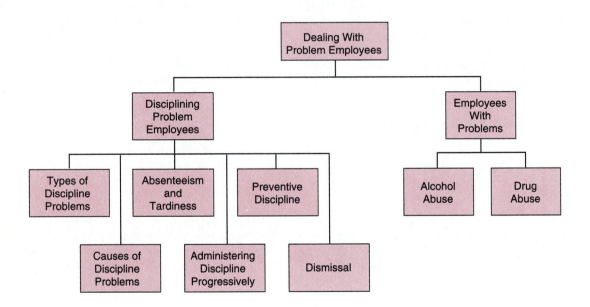

Dealing with Problem Employees

"Confronting problem behavior is a skill—and like other management skills, it can be learned."*

CHAPTER OBJECTIVES

☐   Describe common discipline problems.

☐   Review five common causes of discipline problems.

☐   Relate the way the progressive discipline process works.

☐   Explain the preventive discipline process.

☐   Look at ways to handle absenteeism, tardiness, and dismissal.

☐   Discuss substance abuse problems, specifically alcohol and drug abuse.

☐   Investigate the development of employee assistance programs (EAPS).

☐   Review trends in substance abuse testing.

---

*W. Steven Brown, "The Case of the Incompetent Employee," *Supervisory Management* (November 1992): 1.

Dealing with problem employees and establishing and maintaining an effective discipline system are two of the most difficult tasks facing every supervisor. This chapter considers, first, "problem employees," or those who perform poorly or intentionally break rules and regulations, and, second, "employees with problems," or those whose personal problems such as substance abuse impair their job performance.

DISCIPLINING PROBLEM EMPLOYEES

Discipline refers to corrective action.

Discipline, as the term is used here, refers to any corrective action taken by a supervisor because the employee's behavior has broken organizational rules. Knowing how and when to discipline employees is an essential part of the supervisor's job; unfortunately, it is one duty that is often handled poorly. When rule violations occur, many supervisors look the other way and fail to administer the appropriate penalty. Why does this occur?

Reasons why supervisors fail to discipline effectively.

There are at least three general reasons that supervisors often neglect their duties in administering discipline. First, discipline seems to imply an unpleasant confrontation with the employee. By its very nature, therefore, it is an unpleasant task. Further, supervisors know that discipline discussions often lead to resentment by the employee in question and thus further problems. Second, supervisors often observe that the "rules" are broken randomly around the company and that other infractions have gone "unnoticed" or at least unpunished. This makes it difficult for the supervisor to enforce rules with his or her employees. Third, many supervisors are unsure how to conduct the discipline interview, how to document those discussions, and what to do next. They simply haven't been trained adequately by higher management.

The best way of dealing with discipline situations is a preventive strategy. Next, to discipline problem employees more effectively, the supervisor must be aware of the types and causes of discipline problems, progressive discipline techniques, and the newer strategy of positive discipline. Absenteeism and tardiness are discussed as specific discipline problems, and dismissal guidelines are given.

Types of Discipline Problems

Among the many types of behavior commonly associated with "problem employees" are the following:

1. Employees with a negative and critical attitude, who disagree with everything the supervisor says and generally show their dislike for the boss and the company.

Common forms of discipline problems.

2. Employees who habitually arrive late for work, take longer breaks than authorized, and never return from lunch in time to relieve the next person.

194

3.   Employees who are outright insubordinate by refusing to do what is asked. If the supervisor refuses to allow these people to take off early, they will take off anyway.

4.   Employees who seem to take pleasure in doing as little as possible during working hours. These people produce far less than the norm and do just what is necessary to avoid being fired.

5.   Employees who fail to follow procedures and regulations. For example, these people may "forget" to wear safety goggles on a regular basis because they are not comfortable.

6.   Employees who seemingly come to work only to socialize. Another variation of this theme is the practical joker who is constantly annoying others with pranks and a lack of seriousness.

7.   Employees who seem to argue with everyone about everything. Occasionally this leads to fights in the workplace.

Problem employees cannot be ignored in the hope that their behavior will change. They tend to be nonproductive and disruptive to other employees.

Fortunately for supervisors, these problem employees usually constitute only a small percentage of the supervisor's staff. Understanding the causes of their behaviors can be helpful in handling these employees.

Causes of Discipline Problems

Many disciplinary problems arise as a result of employee frustration. Frustration occurs whenever a person's goals are thwarted by some obstacle. If individuals have a need to feel important and admired, for example, and they encounter a work group that does not accept them as valuable members, their frustration may be expressed as a discipline problem. Frustrated employees engage in a variety of defense mechanisms discussed in Chapter 4. These mechanisms—in particular aggression, denial, and rationalization—can impair job performance.

Here are five categories of discipline causes.

Other discipline problems are due to individual personality problems. Remember that even psychologists have trouble treating people with personality or psychological disorders, so do not feel badly if you have difficulty with these individuals. Chronic complainers, rumor spreaders, habitual arguers, and practical jokers may fit into this category. Likewise, employees who are always angry, hurt, pessimistic, or eccentric are exhibiting troublesome personality characteristics.

A third category of problem behavior originates in employees' personal problems. Family and financial problems are the two most frequent sources of personal problems. A fourth reason for disciplinary problems is poor organizational communications.

In some cases, employees honestly do not understand the essence of the policy or for some reason do not think it relates to them. Either condition indicates a failure of the organization to effectively communicate its policies and procedures. Merely handing a new employee a procedures manual is not enough. The average manual is voluminous, poorly written, confusing, and boring. Few employees consult it unless they have a specific problem. They certainly do not sit down and study it from cover to cover. The lack of effective communication also convinces the employee that regulations and procedures are not all that important; after all, "rules are made to be broken."[1]

A final reason for disciplinary problems concerns employees who do not feel they are an important part of the organization. This belief results in an "us vs. them" frame of mind in which employees delight in taking advantage of the system and in seeing how much they can get away with. Such a complicated problem requires revamping the organizational culture and emphasizing teamwork and responsibility.

Administering Discipline Progressively

Effective discipline requires seven essential steps.

Administering discipline is a progressive process that requires seven essential steps. Figure 10–1 describes this process.

First, either the supervisor must note that a violation has occurred or someone else must report it to the supervisor. At that time the supervisor can choose to ignore the situation or deal with it in a positive manner. Experience shows that the latter is the far more effective method; the former usually leads to bigger problems in the future.

Second, the supervisor should react to the violation quickly. Discipline that takes place long after the event has occurred loses much of its potential benefit. When discipline is delayed, facts become blurred, new priorities emerge, and employees are resentful of rehashed old violations. Reaction to the violation should be directed to the event exactly as it took place. This need for precision leads directly into step three, which is collecting the facts. The supervisor should have a complete picture of what occurred.

The actual meeting with the employee usually takes place during step three. Step four typically occurs at the same time. The supervisor must be sure to listen carefully to the employee's perspective on the violation.

The following guidelines can help to make this disciplinary interview a more useful experience for both supervisor and employee.

Discipline interviews can be productive for everyone involved.

1. Reprimand the employee in private. Unless the responsibility is shared by the group, never discipline an employee in public.
2. Hold your temper: discipline is an emotionally charged situation. Stay in control. Be calm.
3. Confine your remarks to the issue at hand. Don't use the situation to rehash everything the employee has ever done wrong or to remind the employee how much you let him or her get away with.

---

[1]Jane Whitney Gibson and Richard M. Hodgetts, *Organizational Communication: A Managerial Perspective*, 2nd ed. (New York: HarperCollins Publishers, 1991), 381.

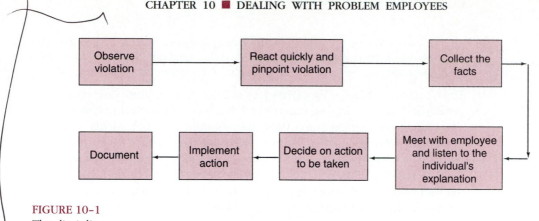

FIGURE 10-1
The disciplinary process.

4.   Be clear about the problem. Be sure the employee is fully aware of those behaviors you want stopped or started.

5.   Focus on the future. How can this problem be avoided from now on?

After meeting with the employee, the supervisor ought to conclude the matter as soon as possible. If there is a clear-cut penalty for this particular violation, the decision is relatively easy. If not, the supervisor has to weigh the alternatives and be sure that the "consequence" is equitable and justifiable. These "consequences" must also be consistent with punishment that has occurred in the past. In either event a decision should be made on what action is to be taken and then communicated quickly to the employee. On most first offenses, employees should receive a warning that a violation has occurred. This approach is in keeping with most companies' policy of progressive discipline, a procedure that notes first offenses but progressively disciplines further infractions with more serious consequences. Some offenses, of course, require a harsh first penalty, even dismissal. Stealing is one example.

Once supervisors have taken the appropriate action, they should be sure to document the case carefully. The single largest mistake that supervisors make in the discipline process is not documenting the facts. Later, should the same violation recur, the supervisor will want to have documentation on exactly what happened in the past. Grievances often result when supervisors try to discharge or seriously discipline an employee for repeated offenses when, in fact, they have no evidence that these previous offenses were ever discussed.

Documentation is very important.

"Most supervisors fail to provide their employees with adequate notice when their expectations are not being met. They ignore problem-employee behavior until they can endure it no more. Then, ultimately, they explode, giving the employee little or no opportunity to correct the perceived deficiencies.

> Having received no notice that his or her job was on the line, the employee perceives the discharge to be unfair. And this apparent unfairness produces the anger that serves as the stimulus for most discrimination claims."[2]

The human resources office can be very helpful in designing a documentation system or in introducing the supervisor to the company's existing system.

When disciplining employees, keep in mind four key words: warning, immediacy, clarity, and consistency. Warning has already been discussed. Immediacy refers to the need to discipline quickly. Clarity emphasizes the need to make perfectly clear to employees exactly what they have done wrong or what is or is not appropriate behavior. Consistency is a very important element in an approach to discipline.

> "The supervisor who enforces the rules some days but not others causes frustration and resentment. . . . Likewise, the supervisor should focus on the act, not the person. Don't be tough or easy on someone simply because you dislike or like the individual. A supervisor who is inconsistent with the disciplinary action may be charged with discrimination by the employee, who may take the issue to court and win."[3]

The way in which supervisors administer discipline has become increasingly important in light of union grievance procedures and government regulations protecting employee rights. Poor handling of disciplinary action can cause serious consequences, such as the following:

☐ Increased grievances that often go to arbitration in unionized organizations.
☐ Increased cases that the company finds hard to defend in arbitration.
☐ Increased turnover resulting in higher recruitment and training costs.
☐ Increased slowdowns, strikes, and other work disruptions.
☐ Increased hostility between employees and supervisors.
☐ Decreased respect for management among the employees.

One way of increasing positive results achieved from the discipline process is by using preventive discipline techniques.

Preventive Discipline

Preventive discipline is a proactive training and development strategy that molds and corrects employee behavior before problems occur. It is also called positive discipline.

Preventive discipline is a proactive strategy.

> "Positive discipline is a performance management system that retains the idea of making progressively serious contacts with an employee when work problems arise, but eliminates the hastiness to use punishment as a means

---

[2]Jonathan A. Segal, "Firing without Fear," *HR Magazine* (June 1992): 125.

[3]Robert N. Lussier, "16 Guidelines for Effective Discipline," *Supervisory Management* (March 1990): 10.

of getting the individual to decide to change behavior and abide by company performance standards. It also provides an administrative system that helps assure organizational justice and consistency in dealing with individuals. Furthermore, the system places a great deal of emphasis on recognizing and reinforcing the good performance delivered by the majority of employees within an organization."[4]

Preventive discipline attempts to foster understanding and acceptance of rules and regulations.

Preventive discipline includes a widely disseminated statement of rules and regulations, efforts to foster understanding and acceptance of those rules and regulations, and a consistent and known set of consequences when these rules and regulations are broken.

Rules, regulations, policies, and procedures are worthwhile only if employees are familiar with them and understand them. The best procedure manuals are worthless if nobody reads them. The supervisor should make sure that each employee knows what is acceptable behavior and should reinforce compliance with rules and regulations in a positive way. As we said in Chapter 9, positive reinforcement is an effective strategy for encouraging desirable behavior. When violations occur, however, they cannot be overlooked. Otherwise employees will soon think that the rules do not matter or, worse yet, that "Joe" can get away with things but they cannot.

Even after the best efforts have been made to build a positive climate for adherence to rules and acceptable standards of performance and behavior, violations will occur and the supervisor must be adequately prepared to administer constructive discipline in a tactful and effective manner. Next we look at two very common discipline problems: absenteeism and tardiness.

Absenteeism and Tardiness

One discipline problem that concerns all supervisors is absenteeism. One recent estimate places the cost of absenteeism to the public and private sector between $20 and $25 billion a year.[5] Work schedules are interrupted, non-absent employees have to pick up the slack, and supervisors' workloads are increased. Absenteeism is a problem for everyone.

Absentee policies should be consistently upheld.

How should supervisors handle absenteeism? First, it is important that there is a well-known attendance policy. This policy should include guidelines explaining how vacation time and other leave can be used to avoid unexcused absence. Effective supervision of absenteeism includes preventive and corrective measures. Preventive measures include rewarding and recognizing good attendance and not just taking it for granted. Corrective measures should follow the same procedures as any other type

---

[4]Chimezie A.B. Osigweh, Yg, and William R. Hutchinson, "Positive Discipline," *Human Resource Management,* Fall 1989, 367.

[5]Johnny Long and Joseph G. Ormsby, "Stamp Out Absenteeism," *Personal Journal* (November 1987): 94-96.

of discipline. What actions supervisors take about absenteeism send strong signals to other employees about what is allowable behavior.

> If absenteeism is allowed to continue unattended for several years, its contagion spreads to others who normally would not take extra time off. In this case, an absence culture prevails, which says that high levels of unexcused absenteeism are normal as well as acceptable.[6]

Likewise, how a supervisor deals with tardiness is noticed by the rest of the staff.

Tardiness cannot be ignored.

> "Tardiness may be a small problem, but supervisors who ignore small problems will not likely have the support of employees in solving larger ones. . . . They may not say anything to their supervisor, but they may speak of it to co-workers, and after awhile the general impression will be that the supervisor is not in control."[7]

Even if the latecomers are among the most productive employees, it is generally bad for morale to allow tardiness to go unnoticed. Failure to enforce one work rule will lead others to expect that you will look the other way when they break other work rules.

Even if you have the best discipline system possible, you will still face times when it will be necessary to dismiss an employee and you will have to deliver the bad news. This is a particularly unpleasant chore for the supervisor.

Dismissal

Dismissal should occur only as a final resort.

In the mid 1840s, the doctrine of "termination at will" was established by a Tennessee court. This basically meant that an employer could terminate an employee at any time for any reason—much the same way an employee could leave a job without notice. In the late 1900s, however, termination at will has largely been replaced by the "just cause" concept, that is, employers can only terminate an employee with a documentable, just cause. Both union contracts and EEO regulations reinforce the need to show cause when terminating an employee. The Civil Rights Act of 1991 further strengthened employee rights by increasing the dollar amounts they can reasonably expect to collect should they win a wrongful firing claim. Surprisingly, most federal civil rights lawsuits are now not in hiring cases, but in wrongful terminations.

> "Most people think civil rights laws are meant to stop discrimination in hiring. But that isn't their practical effect. The vast bulk of antidiscrimination

---

[6]Paul Sandwith, "Absenteeism: You Get What You Accept," *Personnel Journal* (November 1987): 88-92.

[7]Marcia Ann Pulich, "Tardiness—Handling Late Arrivals and Late Lunchers," *Supervisory Management* (February 1991): 9.

SUPERVISORY SKILLS
Discipling Problem Employees

1. Be sure you know your company's discipline policies. If necessary, seek the advice of the personnel office. Do not wait for discipline problems to occur before you find out this information.

2. Do not jump to conclusions when dealing with apparent violations. Carefully collect all the facts, listen to the employee's side of the story, and decide what action is to be taken.

3. Remember to keep the focus of discipline meetings on future behavior. How can future problems be avoided?

4. Be sure to document all aspects of the violation and actions taken. Good record keeping is the key to effective discipline.

5. Should termination of an employee be necessary, get to the point quickly. Don't waste time discussing old problems.

---

enforcement actions and lawsuits allege discrimination not in hiring but in firing."[8]

Termination decisions become even more critical considering that the average wrongful dismissal suit costs an average of $80,000 to defend. Nevertheless, if a serious violation, such as stealing from the company, occurs, you may have to dismiss an employee and do so without a progressive record of actions to back your decision. For those cases where a long history has preceded the decision to terminate, supervisors should have well-documented files on employee behavior and actions leading up to the decision. Documentation should include hard, objective evidence and not subjective or arbitrary data such as hearsay or biased statements.

When dismissal is unavoidable, the following steps are suggested for the termination process:

1. Recheck your facts—both the facts surrounding the case (theft) and the company's termination policy and procedure; be sure that termination is the only logical answer to the situation.

2. Don't try to find a nice way to say "you're fired." There isn't any; come straight to the point. This is not the time to rehash all the old problems.

3. Go over administrative details. When do you expect the person to leave? (Immediate termination is usually recommended.) When will the final paycheck be available? What about insurance coverage and other benefits that the fired employee may keep after termination?

Let's discuss employees who have personal problems that are interfering with their productivity.

---

[8]David Frum, "The Right to Fire," *Forbes* (October 26, 1992): 76.

EMPLOYEES WITH PROBLEMS

Although a variety of physical and psychological problems, such as special needs of the disabled (see Chapter 6) and marital problems, could be found in this category, we limit our attention to an increasingly troublesome problem in industry—substance abuse. Many people are surprised to learn the extent of the problem. Before reading further, take Self-Assessment Quiz 10–1 and see how much you know about this subject.

Were you surprised when you checked the answers to the self-assessment quiz? Let's look at the two specific areas of substance abuse: alcoholism and drugs.

Alcohol Abuse

It is now a well-accepted fact that alcoholism is a disease affecting all types of people. Statistics from the Department of Health and Human Services show that 5 to 10 percent of American workers are alcohol abusers. Figure 10–2 shows the organizational levels of these workers. Many people are surprised to learn that alcohol abuse takes place at all levels of the organization and particularly at the managerial and professional levels.

The cost of alcohol abuse to American industry is staggering: "Alcoholism is an insidious disease that affects more than 10 percent of all American adults. Alcoholism and related diseases take a tremendous toll on the quality of life of both the alcoholic and the alcoholic's family. But apart from the personal cost, alcoholism also exacts a hefty price from organizations employing alcoholics. Alcoholism costs organizations billions

■ ■ ■ **SELF-ASSESSMENT QUIZ 10-1**
What Do You Know About Substance Abuse?

Directions: Answer each of the following questions true or false.

_____ 1. The average drug abuser in the work force is under age twenty-one.

_____ 2. The majority of alcoholics are not steadily employed.

_____ 3. One in every fifty American workers is considered to have a drug or alcohol problem.

_____ 4. There are more alcohol abusers than drug abusers in the work force.

_____ 5. The largest proportion of employed alcoholics are blue-collar workers.

_____ 6. Substance abuse is positively correlated with absenteeism and theft but not with serious accidents.

_____ 7. Substance abuse is thought to account for productivity losses of about $1 billion a year.

Answers are provided at the end of the chapter.

FIGURE 10-2
Organizational level of employed alcoholics per 100 employees.

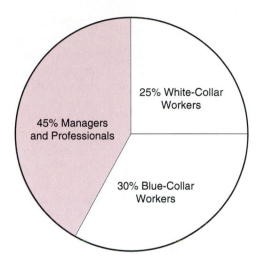

25% White-Collar
Workers

45% Managers
and Professionals

30% Blue-Collar
Workers

Most companies
have a substance
abuse policy.

of dollars each year through absences, accidents, medical costs, and productivity losses."[9]

Due to the magnitude of the problem, most companies have had to
develop a process to deal with alcoholic employees. Many smaller companies simply refer employees to outside services. Others insist that the employee get help or be terminated. Supervisors are key people in this
process because it is usually they who first notice the problem and have
to confront the employee. Signs of alcohol abuse, for example, might include smelling alcohol on an employee's breath when he returns from
lunch, slurred speech, unsteady gait, a sporadic performance level, and increasing lateness or absenteeism. The supervisor should be quite sure of
the problem, however, before approaching the employee. Telling an employee, "It seems that your drinking is affecting your job performance"
may compromise your relationship with an employee whose real problem
may be a reaction to a new medication. Be careful, therefore, not to accuse anyone of an alcohol problem. Unless you are very sure the problem
is alcohol, say instead, "It seems something is affecting your job performance. Let's see if we can figure out what it is and how to rectify it." This
confrontation meeting can be very sensitive. Successful supervisor-em-
ployee conferences on known alcohol abuse contain the following elements. The supervisor:

1.   Documents the effects of the drinking problem on the employee's
     performance. (These may include a deteriorating attitude toward the

[9]Mark R. Edwards and J. Ruth Sproull, "Confronting Alcoholism through Team Evaluation,"
Business Horizons (May/June 1986): 58–83.

job, increased disagreements with co-workers, lowered productivity, and increased absenteeism and lateness.)

2.   Expresses a desire to help.

3.   *Requires* the employee to get help from a rehabilitation program such as Alcoholics Anonymous.

4.   Makes clear to the employee that the consequence of not getting help is termination of employment.[10]

Large companies
have developed
EAPs.

In recent years larger companies have developed internal programs called *employee assistance programs* (EAPs) to handle substance abuse problems as well as a variety of other problems. In some cases these EAPs are run by outside consultants; often they are handled by full-time staff especially trained in this area. Typically, EAPs are open to self-referral or to supervisory referral. They operate on the assumption that substance abuse is a treatable problem and that the employee can be effectively rehabilitated to the benefit of both the individual and the organization. Early indications are that EAPs work!

> "In addition to reducing inappropriate health care utilization and time lost on the job seeking care, an EAP may prevent:
>
> ☐ Reduced productivity.
> ☐ High turnover.
> ☐ Employee theft.
> ☐ Litigation.
> ☐ Lost business."[11]

Perhaps the best known example of the cost benefits of an EAP is found within the McDonnell Douglas Corporation. In 1985, the firm's EAP Director was challenged to prove it could contribute to the bottom line. Services were expanded to serve all 130,000 employees nationwide in a broad area of family and personal services. In a five-year study of employees who used the EAP services compared with employees with similar problems who did not use the EAP, dramatic results were recorded including average individual results as follows: 29% fewer days absent, 42% fewer terminations, and $7,150 less in medical costs. Savings for employees who entered the program in 1989 over the ensuing five years were expected to add up to $6,000,000![12]

---

[10]John M. Ivancevich and William F. Glueck, *Foundations of Personnel* (Plano, Tex.: Business Publications, Inc., 1983), 502.

[11]Peggy Stuart, "Investments in EAPs Pay Off," *Personnel Journal* (February 1993): 44.

[12]"How McDonnell Douglas Cost-justified its EAP," *Personnel Journal* (February 1993): 48.

Drug Abuse

Increasingly, EAPs are expanding to deal with drug abuse among employees. Three to seven percent of employees are suspected of having a drug-related problem. Drug abusers tend to be somewhat younger than alcohol abusers with the average age falling between eighteen and thirty-five. It is a bit less clear how drug abusers can be characterized by level of employment. One study done at a Chicago rehabilitation center found that of 150 cocaine addicts, 70 percent were employed full time. Of those, 34 percent held management-level jobs, 10 percent were professionals, 18 percent were self-employed, and 38 percent were blue-collar employees. Drug abuse is obviously not a problem just of the economically disadvantaged. The national hotline for cocaine abuse found that the typical profile for a female drug abuser was white, age twenty-nine, and earning more than $25,000 per year.[13]

3 to 7 percent of employees have drug-related problems.

Combined with alcohol abuse, drug abuse is thought to cost U.S. industry more than $100 billion. Much of this cost comes from the fact that substance abusers are estimated to work at only 67% of their potential. They are also responsible for the following costs:

> "Substance abusers are absent 2.5 times more days than nonabusers.
> Substance abusers file five times the number of medical claims;
> Substance abusers file five times the number of workers' compensation claims;
> Substance abusers are involved in four to six times the number of off-the-job accidents; and
> Substance abusers are involved in four times the number of accidents that occur on the job."[14]

The corporate philosophy of dealing with drug abusers seems to be somewhat divided. Many simply view it as an illness similar to alcohol abuse and offer help to the troubled employee. Other companies favor a get-tough attitude when dealing with drugs.

> A growing number of major U.S. companies, including such firms as Exxon, Federal Express, Greyhound Lines, Southern California Edison, TWA, IBM, and Lockheed require all job applicants to pass urinalysis tests that screen for drugs.
> The price of being caught can be high . . . on an oil-drilling platform in the gulf of Mexico, a specially trained Labrador retriever, flown in by helicopter from Franklin, La., discovered marijuana in a worker's luggage. The employee was fired on the spot, and shared a ride back to the mainland with the dog and its handler.[15]

---

[13]"Hooked on the Job," *Ft. Lauderdale News* (December 2, 1984): E1.

[14]Laura A. Lyons and Brian H. Kleiner, "Managing the Problem of Substance Abuse without Abusing Employees," *HR Focus* (April 1992): 9.

[15]"Battling Drugs on the Job," *Time* (January 27, 1986): 43.

SUPERVISORY SKILLS
Employees with Problems

1. When you observe employees you suspect of substance abuse, be sure to check your "facts." This is a very sensitive issue, and in the case of drug abuse you are accusing someone of breaking the law (also in the case of alcohol abuse in some industries in some states).

2. Coordinate your approach to these employees with your personnel department and your EAP if available. They will give you valuable advice on how to approach the subject.

3. Be empathetic in dealing with substance abusers, but also be sure they understand that getting help is a prerequisite to keeping their jobs.

4. As with other discipline situations, be sure to document the file carefully.

The issue of drug testing by employers is a hotly debated one. According to Bureau of Labor Statistics estimates, about 67% of large U.S. companies are now doing some type of drug testing. (See "The Quality Challenge: Getting Tough on Quality.")[16] This growing number in organizations is partially due to the passage in 1989 of the Drug-Free Workplace Act, which applies to federal contractors with individual procurement contracts of $25,000 or more and any recipient of a federal grant of any amount. For companies falling under this legislation, drug testing has been an obvious way to ensure compliance. Yet, a great number of companies who are not federal contractors are also choosing to test. The majority of such testing is for preemployment screening. How does drug testing affect employees? What types of signals does it convey about the corporate culture, the lack of trust, and the adversarial relationship between management and employees?

Drug testing is very controversial.

Jack Gordon, editor of *Training* Magazine, suggests that random drug testing, as opposed to drug testing those suspected of some accident or workplace problem, may lead to decreased productivity by employees who feel violated. He refers to the questionable reliability of urine tests as well as the broader legal and ethical questions involved in subjecting employees to personal searches.[17]

In early 1989, the Supreme Court delivered its first rulings on the legality of drug testing. The court upheld the constitutionality of government regulations that require railroad employees involved in accidents to submit to drug tests.[18] Nevertheless, this decision is far removed from

---

[16]Rob Brookler, "Industry Standards in Workplace Drug Testing," *Personnel Journal* (April 1992): 128.

[17]Jack Gordon, "Drug Testing as a Productivity Booster?," *Training* (March 1987): 22-34.

[18]Alain L. Sanders, "A Boost for Drug Testing," *Time* (April 3, 1989): 62.

■ ■ ■ THE QUALITY CHALLENGE
Gettting Tough on Quality

Many firms have now concluded that one of the best ways to achieve high quality is to deal effectively with substance abuse by eliminating the problems or dismissing the employee. Many companies now make it crystal clear that job applicants who test positive for drugs will not be hired. Meanwhile anyone who is hired and eventually tests positive must enroll in a rehabilitation program, and if the individual tests positive in the future, he or she will be fired. Because substance abuse testing is a condition of employment, workers who are dismissed have no legal recourse against the company.

The logic behind this policy is simple. Employees who are substance abusers cost the firm thousands of dollars every year through lost time and inefficient work behavior. With competition increasing and firms having to be more productive than ever, businesses cannot afford to absorb the costs associated with drug abuse problems. As a result, many firms now test employees whose productivity performance indicates that they may be abusers, and the company holds the line on firing those workers who fail to enroll in a rehabilitation program or who later have a relapse and fail the test a second time.

Does this policy really pay off? Research shows that it does. Three of the most common reasons are the following:

1. Once a company is known to drug test job applicants, individuals who are substance abusers will not bother looking for jobs there. This saves the firm the money that would have been invested in reviewing the application and testing the individual.

2. When employees know they can be tested if they show signs of drug use, they are more likely to stay away from all nonprescription drugs. When those who do not abstain are let go, this further reinforces the desire of the remaining workers not to fall into this habit.

3. Firms that test and screen out the low-productivity substance abusers help hold down their costs by removing these employees. In turn, this puts the company in a better competitive, financial position.

Simply stated, many firms are finding that it pays to get tough on quality by being tough on substance abusers.

---

granting companies the legal right to perform random drug testing. While many employees submit quietly to such tests, others quit as a matter of principle; still others take their employers to court.

The California Employment Law Council's "Proposal for Limited Substance Abuse Testing" suggests that testing individuals in these four categories is always legally defensible: job candidates prior to hiring, employees in dangerous jobs, employees who have enrolled in a rehabilitation program, and employees for whom there seems to be evidence that they are under the influence of substance abuse. There are, however, no legal certainties surrounding random drug testing and thus many corporations wisely avoid this type of testing.[19]

---

[19]Lyons and Kleiner, 9.

The following testing guidelines have been offered to employers who decide to use drug tests:[20]

1. Use a reputable laboratory for all tests.
2. Take all urine or blood samples under the supervision of a medical professional.
3. Retest anyone who shows a positive result.
4. Keep all results confidential and at the medical facility.
5. Administer all testing policies and procedures consistently.
6. Monitor the chain of custody of the samples to ensure the validity of test results.

In general, however, most companies seem willing to give drug-using employees a second chance if they agree to rehabilitation. The supervisor, therefore, must have a thorough knowledge of the company policy before dealing with suspected drug abusers.

SUMMARY

Discipline refers to any corrective action taken by a supervisor because the employee's behavior has broken organizational rules. Common types of discipline problems include employees with a negative attitude, insubordinate employees, and workers who socialize too much on the job. These problems may be caused by frustration on the part of employees, individual personality problems, personal problems, poor organizational communication, or failure to include employees in the organization. Discipline should be administered progressively.

The discipline process has seven specific steps. These include: (1) observing the violation; (2) reacting quickly and pinpointing the violation; (3) collecting the facts; (4) meeting with the employee and listening to the individual's explanation; (5) deciding on the type of action to take; (6) implementing

the action; and (7) documenting what has been done.

The best way to discipline is with a positive preventive strategy that corrects behavior before problems start. Preventive discipline includes a statement of rules and regulations and a consistent set of consequences when the rules are broken.

If discipline is poorly handled, the results can be increased grievances, personnel turnovers, slowdowns, and hostility between employees and supervisors. Disciplining should be done in private, and the supervisor should be calm and clear about the problem.

Absenteeism and tardiness are common problems to supervisors. Attendance policies should be established and followed.

If dismissal is necessary, the manager must be certain that termination is the only

---

[20]Ibid, 9.

answer and then come to the point as quickly as possible.

Estimates show that 5 to 10 percent of American workers are alcohol abusers. Supervisors should offer such employees help in a rehabilitation program and make clear that the consequence of not getting help is termination. Increasingly, large companies are offering comprehensive employee assistance programs (EAPs) to their employees. Some companies get tough with drug abuse on the job, but most offer employees a second chance if they agree to get help. Drug testing remains a controversial topic, although many companies are now routinely including drug testing in the hiring process.

REVIEW QUESTIONS

1. In your own words, what is meant by the term *discipline?*

2. Why do many supervisors not take appropriate action when they see a situation that calls for discipline? Explain.

3. What are some of the most common types of discipline problems? Identify and describe three.

4. Many disciplinary problems arise as a result of employee frustration. What does this statement mean? Explain.

5. What are seven steps in the discipline process? Identify and describe each.

6. What are some of the most effective guidelines to effective discipline interviews? Identify and describe four.

7. What are some of the common consequences of poorly handled discipline? Identify and describe four.

8. What is preventive discipline, and how does it work?

9. How should supervisors deal with absenteeism and tardiness?

10. How do the concepts of "Termination at Will" and "just cause" relate to today's dismissal guidelines?

11. How should the supervisor conduct an effective employee conference on alcohol abuse? Explain.

12. How does an employee assistance program work? Explain.

13. Why is drug testing a controversial subject?

KEY TERMS

Discipline. Any corrective action taken by a supervisor because an employee's behavior has broken organizational rules.

Employee assistance program **(EAP).** Programs designed to help employees deal with alcohol and drug abuse problems.

Preventive discipline. Discipline designed to foster understanding and acceptance of rules and regulations and the consequences that will result from a violation of them.

ANSWERS TO SELF-ASSESSMENT QUIZ 10-1

1. False. The average age is between eighteen and thirty-five.

2. False. Sixty percent are regularly employed.

3. False. The number is actually one in ten!

4. True. About 5 to 10 percent of the working population has an alcohol problem, and 3 to 7 percent are drug abusers.

5. False. The largest percentage are managers and professionals.

6. False. Life-threatening accidents as well as public safety are correlated to substance abuse.

7. False. In 1983, the figure was estimated at $60 billion a year.

    Sources: "Hooked on the Job," *Ft. Lauderdale News,* (December 2, 1984): E1; and "Getting Tough on Worker Abuse of Drugs and Alcohol," *U.S. News and World Report* (December 5, 1983): 85.

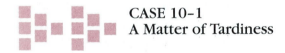

CASE 10-1
A Matter of Tardiness

Jeremy Jesuch is the most productive machinist in his company. Over the last three months the company has had a large number of new orders, and it has been necessary to add a second shift. The supervisor of the department, Carole Mauch, depends very heavily on Jeremy and a small number of other people in the unit who are the high producers.

Yesterday Jeremy arrived late for work. Carole just happened to see him come in as she left her boss's office. People who are late are supposed to report directly to their supervisor and explain their tardiness. Failure to do so means a one-day suspension. Ten minutes later Carole began her usual walk around the plant. Jeremy, who was now at his machine, saw Carole and smiled. Carole then went by the timekeeper's office and looked at the time cards. According to his card, Jeremy arrived five minutes early.

Today Carole had some problem with her car and arrived ten minutes late. As she entered the building, she looked behind her and saw Jeremy driving up. Carole went to her office, hung up her coat, returned a telephone call, and then went out to the work area. As she did, she noticed that two other workers were coming in late. She saw them, but they did not indicate they saw her. They simply turned toward the locker room and entered it.

Five minutes later both men were at their machines. Carole was certain that they had seen her and knew that she was aware of their tardiness. Before saying anything to them, however, she decided to visit the timekeeper's office. Pulling the time cards of all three men, Carole found that Jeremy was clocked in four minutes early whereas the other two men were late.

1. How should Carole handle the tardiness problem with the two men she saw coming in late? Explain.

2. What particular problem does Jeremy's case raise for Carole?

3. What should Carole do about Jeremy's tardiness? Explain.

CASE 10–2
Now What?

Joe Armstrong has been a supervisor for five years and has one of the best records in the firm. One of the major reasons for his success, in Joe's own words, is that he surrounds himself with good people. "I have four assistant supervisors who are the best in the business," he likes to say.

Two months ago one of Joe's assistants, Bill Franklin, had a major personal tragedy. His wife died suddenly. Bill, who is fifty-five, has two children, both of whom are married and live in other parts of the country. Realizing Bill's personal tragedy, Joe and the rest of the assistants have gone out of their way to be helpful. Their concern seems to be helping because Bill's work output is beginning to return to where it was prior to his wife's death. However, something happened yesterday that has Joe worried.

While going through some monthly cost control reports, Joe realized that he needed to talk to Bill about some of the data. He walked down the hall and knocked on Bill's door. Hearing no answer, he thought he'd poke his head in and see if Bill was there. Bill was in his office,

but he did not hear Joe. He had his head on the table, wrapped in his arms, and was quietly crying. On the desk was a small bottle of scotch and a glass that was a third filled. Joe quietly closed the door and returned to his office. About an hour later he saw Bill walk past and he called him into his office. "I'd like to talk to you about some of these data in the monthly cost control report," he said. Bill sat down and the two men went through the report in fifteen minutes. As Bill left, Joe said, "Bill, if there's anything I can do to help you in any way, please don't hesitate to ask." Bill smiled. "You're the first one I'll turn to. I promise." He then left and went back to his office. For the next half hour Joe sat quietly in his office, just staring out the window. "What should I do now?" he pondered.

1. Does Bill have a drinking problem? What do you think?

2. Why did Joe not mention what he had seen to Bill? Explain.

3. What do you recommend that Joe do now? Be complete in your answer.

CHAPTER 11

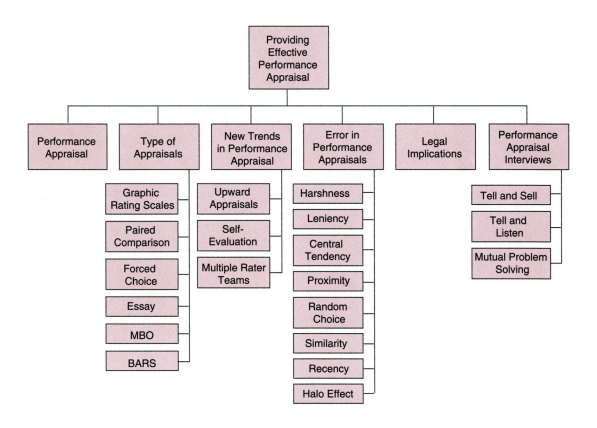

Providing Effective Performance Appraisal

"Performance measurement at work currently rests on the supervisor's shoulders. Consequently, performance information suffers from often justified employee complaints of bias, inflation, unfairness, delinquency, total avoidance, inaccuracy and invalidity."*

CHAPTER OBJECTIVES

☐ Identify and describe the performance appraisal process.

☐ Discuss the benefits offered by an effective performance appraisal system.

☐ Describe the six major types of performance appraisal used in organizations today.

☐ Investigate new trends in performance appraisal.

☐ Discuss some of the common sources of bias in performance appraisal.

☐ Consider legal implications of performance appraisal.

☐ Compare and contrast the three overall philosophies of approaching the performance appraisal interview.

---

*Mark R. Edwards, "Assessment: A Joint Effort Leads to Accurate Appraisals," *Personnel Journal* (June 1990): 122.

Feedback is any recognition of a stimulus.

Benefits of performance appraisal

Feedback is any recognition of a stimulus. In the work setting, feedback can be positive, as in praising an employee for a good job; or negative, such as sending an employee home without pay because of a safety rule violation. This chapter deals with formal supervisory feedback systems, commonly called performance appraisal systems. Performance appraisal skills are a fundamental necessity for all supervisors. This chapter defines performance appraisal and examines the purposes of employee evaluation. It reviews the traditional types of performance appraisal systems in organizations today as well as the new trends in appraisal that promise to revolutionize evaluation systems. Common appraisal errors are discussed, along with the legal implications of the appraisal process. Finally, the chapter examines the actual appraisal interviews that occur between supervisor and employee.

PERFORMANCE APPRAISAL

Performance appraisal is job-related feedback that serves a variety of organizational purposes by providing the following:

- ☐ Unique communication setting promoting open exchanges between supervisor and employee.
- ☐ Historical record of both good and bad employee performance.
- ☐ Formal checkpoint at which time goal attainment can be evaluated, old goals assessed, and new goals formulated.
- ☐ Feedback to subordinates regarding their performance and what they can reasonably expect from the company in the future.
- ☐ Setting for discussing problems not addressed in the normal course of events.
- ☐ Opportunity for management to determine training needs and interests of employees, thus promoting maximum employee development.
- ☐ Basis for current and future decisions regarding salary, promotion, transfers, and terminations.[1]

To be effective, performance appraisal must be systematic. Figure 11–1 shows the four elements of a systematic performance appraisal cycle. First, performance goals must be identified. In a sales department, for example, individual performance goals may be to make quota for each month, to have zero customer complaints, and to have a return rate of not more than 10 percent. These goals must be clearly communicated to employees so they know what is expected of them. In many cases employees will have a hand in actually setting the goals.

---

[1]Jane Whitney Gibson and Richard M. Hodgetts, *Organizational Communication: A Managerial Perspective,* 2nd ed. (New York: HarperCollins Publishers, 1991), 374.

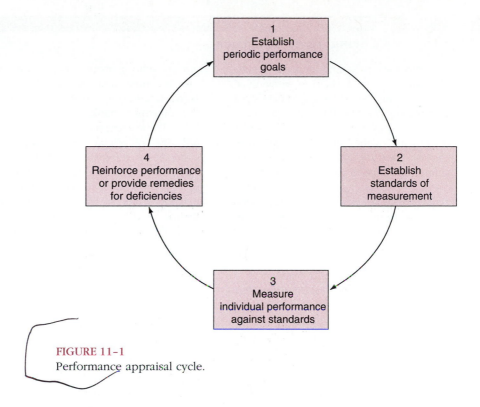

FIGURE 11–1
Performance appraisal cycle.

Next, standards of measurement need to be designed. How will the supervisor know if performance goals have been met? In the case of sales quotas, a numerical figure is attached. Quotas can be measured in dollars or units sold. In the case of customer complaints, the supervisor would need to ensure that all customer complaints, whether by phone, letter, or in person, were recorded and that copies were sent to the supervisor. Returns could be measured in a similar fashion.

Step three is to measure performance against standards. At set intervals the supervisor needs to collect the measurement data and compare it against each employee's goals. How did each salesperson's results measure against quota? Were there any customer complaints about the salesperson's presentation, promises, or delivered service? What was the return rate on the person's sales? This latter question is important because a person who made quota but had 15 percent returns is doing relatively less well than someone who sold 5 percent less than quota but had only 5 percent returns.

Finally, performance appraisal needs to be discussed with the employee. Good performance should be reinforced with recognition, praise, and other rewards when possible. "The Quality Challenge: Giving Them Feedback" provides an example. Substandard performance should be dis-

■ ■ ■ THE QUALITY CHALLENGE

Giving Them Feedback

In many companies personnel receive performance feedback on an annual or semiannual basis. However, firms that are trying to develop a total quality management (TQM) approach to operations are now developing feedback systems that allow anyone in the company to reinforce good behavior. For example, at the Zytec Corporation, winner of the prestigious Baldrige award, if an individual conducts a meeting that is particularly effective, anyone who attended the meeting can send the individual a memo congratulating the person on a job well done. This reinforcement memo (called a Zystroke, which combines the first part of the firm's name with the word that has become synonymous with a pat on the back) is produced in triplicate. One copy is for the person who wrote the memo and the other goes to the individual's immediate boss.

This approach is not unique to Zytec. Most firms with total quality management programs have procedures for allowing personnel to praise each other. For example, the Ritz-Carlton Hotel uses a memo-type system similar to that of Zytec, whereas at AT&T Universal Card Services (UCS), a company team identifies individuals who perform outstanding actions and uses an impromptu meeting at the individual's work station to award the person a plaque with the company's thanks.

These examples all help indicate that the old days of relying on performance appraisal systems to reinforce good behavior are no longer adequate to create and maintain high quality work teams. Today everyone in the organization is getting involved in the process and the feedback can come at any time. Moreover, in some companies, memos and thank you notes are being supplemented by other forms, such as stars that are worn on the collar. For every ten special notes thanking someone for doing a job well, the individual is given a small star, and for every ten small stars, the individual receives a larger star. Over a year's time, an individual can earn two to three large stars, which become part of the person's working garb and are an immediate indication that this individual has been cited by coworkers and supervisors as an excellent performer. In turn, this feedback encourages the personnel to continue their efforts in meeting the quality challenge.

cussed and analyzed, and a plan should be designed to ensure better performance in the future.

TYPES OF APPRAISALS

Although many types of performance appraisal systems are used in organizations today, most can be grouped according to six categories: graphic rating scales, paired comparison, forced choice, essay, MBO, and BARS.

Graphic Rating Scales

Graphic rating scales use degrees of factors to evaluate people.

The most common approach, *graphic rating scales,* uses degrees of factors to evaluate people. The scales allow the interviewer to rate the employee on a series of characteristics such as job knowledge, work quantity, work quality, and reliability. Rating is usually done by assigning a score, such as 1 to 5, for each degree of the characteristic—that is, a 5 for an excellent rating, a 4 for a good rating, and so on. Figure 11–2 provides an example of a graphic rating scale instrument.

	Excellent	Good	Average	Fair	Poor
Job Knowledge					
Work Quantity					
Work Quality					
Reliability					

FIGURE 11–2
Graphic rating scale (partial form).

The graphic rating scale, by its very general format, allows a great deal of subjective appraisal on the part of the supervisor. What is excellent work quality? Supervisors may rate the employee far differently.

In recent years many companies have added descriptive statements to their graphic scales to aid the evaluator in assessing the employee. In Figure 11–2, under the criterion of "job knowledge," the excellent column might also say, "understands the fine nuances of the job; often is asked by others for help." The same criterion under the poor column might say, "lack of job knowledge limits productivity."

Paired Comparison

The paired comparison appraisal compares each of the subordinates to all the others.

The *paired comparison* appraisal compares each of the subordinates to all the others in terms of the criteria being measured. Figure 11–3 uses the four criteria from Figure 11–2 to illustrate a paired comparison. The total scores

Subordinates	Job Knowledge	Work Quantity	Work Quality	Reliability	Total Score
Adams	1	1	3	4	9
Brown	2	5	5	5	17
Cooper	3	3	1	1	8
Davis	4	2	4	2	12
Edwards	5	4	2	3	14

1 = lowest
5 = highest

FIGURE 11–3
Paired comparison.

on the right indicate which individual is the best. Here, it is Brown, whose score of seventeen is the highest. In the case of ties, the manager would choose the most important criterion (perhaps work quality) and use this single ranking to determine which of the two employees ranks higher.

Unlike the graphic rating system, paired comparison is appropriate when evaluating employees as a group. Perhaps management may want to promote one of the group to a supervisory position. According to their graphic rating scales, three employees might be ranked similarly; however, when the paired comparison is used, one will emerge as the highest ranked.

Forced Choice

In the forced choice method the supervisor chooses from a given set of descriptive statements.

In the *forced choice* method the supervisor chooses from a given set of descriptive statements those that are most and least descriptive of a particular employee. This method is particularly appropriate when companies are concerned about the high percentage of above-average ratings being awarded by supervisors. In effect, this method forces supervisors to be more critical. Figure 11–4 shows an example of a forced choice questionnaire where an employee was characterized as always making the customer feel important. Of the four characteristics being appraised, the same employee was judged least likely to misunderstand instructions.

An extension of the forced choice method is the forced distribution method. Here supervisors are instructed to evaluate the group according to some type of predetermined pattern such as a bell-shaped curve. For example, the manager may be told to distribute all appraisals on job quality so that 10 percent are poor, 20 percent fair, 40 percent average, 20 percent good, and 10 percent excellent.

Essay

Essay forms of appraisal may be used either alone or in conjunction with one of the forms already discussed. With essays the supervisor has the op-

Most Characteristic		Least Characteristic
(A)	Always makes the customer feel important	A
B	Often misunderstands instructions	(B)
C	Stays up-to-date on current projects	C
D	Willing to help other employees	D

FIGURE 11–4
Forced choice questionnaire (partial form).

Essay forms of appraisal may be used either alone or with one of the other methods.

portunity to answer open-ended questions regarding the employee's performance. The following questions are typical examples of what might be expected in this type of system: (1) What are the five major strengths of this employee?; (2) How do you compare this employee's performance with that of others doing the same job?; and (3) In which areas does the employee need improvement? Include suggestions as to how this improvement might be achieved.

Management By Objectives (MBO)

MBO involves joint superior-subordinate interaction in the setting of goals.

Management By Objectives (MBO) is a process whereby the supervisor and employee sit down and jointly identify common goals to be accomplished in a given period, define the subordinate's major areas of responsibility in terms of the expected results, and use these measures as a guide for operating the unit and assessing the individual's contribution. The greatest advantages of MBO are (1) that it allows subordinate involvement in the goal-setting process, (2) it offers the opportunity for discussion and clarification of these goals, and (3) it provides a basis for performance evaluation.

To be successful, MBO goals have to be carefully worded so that employees know exactly what is expected of them. They must be specific and measurable; the best goals are often quantifiable. Table 11–1 lists examples of good and poor MBO goals.

Behaviorally Anchored Rating Scales (BARS)

Behaviorally anchored rating scales (BARS) employ scales, usually constructed by behavioral scientists or organizational psychologists, which

---

TABLE 11–1

MBO goals: good and poor examples

Good Examples	Poor Examples
1. Increase sales of product X by 10 percent over last quarter.	1. Sell more product X
2. Reduce customer complaints to service department about product X by more fully explaining its proper use at point of sale.	2. Decrease customer complaints.
3. Increase job knowledge by taking one-week training course on new products given at regional office.	3. Learn more about the job.

---

describe effective and ineffective performance concerning a particular job criterion. Typically, nine statements of appraisal are formulated about each criterion to be evaluated. Therefore, the supervisor may end up rating the individual on five different areas (work quality, work quantity, reliability, and so on) and have nine series of effective-ineffective statements for each. The supervisor then chooses the statement in each area that most adequately identifies the employee's performance. Although it is time consuming to develop and apply, BARS has the advantage that it helps the rater focus on those areas that are most important to the appraisal process. Figure 11–5 gives an example of a behaviorally anchored rating scale for job quality for a college professor. (Note that different BARS scales have to be constructed for each job title.)

> BARS uses scales that describe effective-ineffective behavior.

Which of these techniques is best and why? The answer depends on the size of the organization, purposes of the evaluation, and the time and money available for evaluation. MBO and BARS do have a clear advantage over the other techniques in limiting the subjective nature of appraisals. Table 11–2 compares the methods.

Finally, before proceeding to an examination of new trends in performance appraisal, take Self-Assessment Quiz 11–1 and check your knowledge of the various systems.

NEW TRENDS IN PERFORMANCE APPRAISAL

Several new trends are becoming increasingly popular in American organizations. Each changes the traditional system where supervisors evaluate their direct reports and reinforce the teamwork and participation goals of TQM. These trends are upward appraisals, self-evaluation, and multiple rater teams.

Upward Appraisals

> Employees evaluate supervisors.

Traditionally, employees have no opportunity to evaluate their supervisors. Recently, however, companies like Federal Express and the Southern California Gas Company are giving employees the opportunity to do just that! In some companies, this upward feedback is provided on a one-on-one basis. In others, department employees meet as teams to give feedback to the supervisor; others depend upon anonymous reports. Supervisors are mixed in their reaction to this nontraditional evaluation.

> "Most employees flat out like the idea, but bosses split down the middle. Half of them welcome employee feedback as providing more insights into how they can do their jobs better. The other half have their reservations about this turning of the tables."[2]

---

[2]Robert McGarvey, "But I'm Doing a Great Job!" *USAir Magazine* (May 1993): 64.

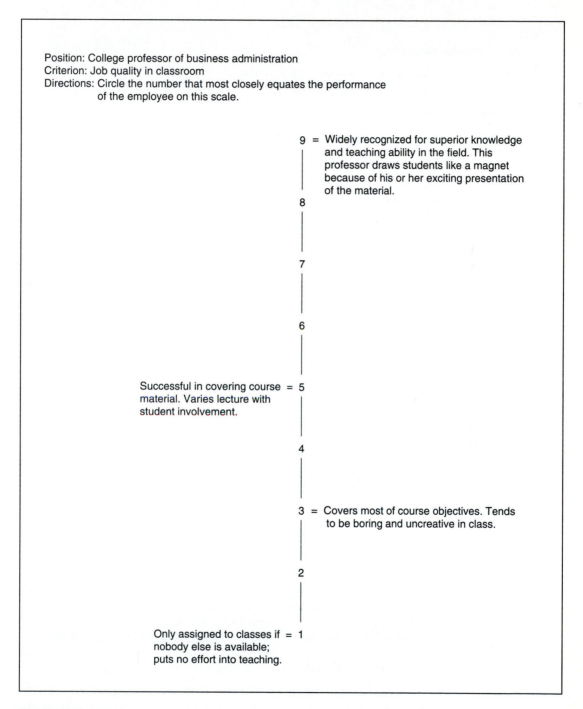

Position: College professor of business administration
Criterion: Job quality in classroom
Directions: Circle the number that most closely equates the performance
         of the employee on this scale.

9 = Widely recognized for superior knowledge
    and teaching ability in the field. This
    professor draws students like a magnet
    because of his or her exciting presentation
    of the material.
8

7

6

Successful in covering course = 5
material. Varies lecture with
student involvement.

4

3 = Covers most of course objectives. Tends
    to be boring and uncreative in class.

2

Only assigned to classes if = 1
nobody else is available;
puts no effort into teaching.

FIGURE 11-5
A behaviorally anchored rating scale.

TABLE 11–2

Comparison of evaluation methods

Performance Appraisal Type	Graphic Rating Scale	Paired Comparison	Forced Choice	Essay	MBO	BARS
Construction time and cost	Low	Low	High	Low	Medium	High
Time required to use	Low	Medium	Medium	High	High	High
Training time for evaluators	Low	Medium	Medium	Low	High	Medium
Usefulness in identifying training and development needs	Low	Low	Medium	Medium	High	High
Usefulness in compensation and promotion decisions	Medium	Medium	Low	Medium	High	High
Ease in comprehension by employees and in employee counselling	High	Medium	Low	Medium	High	Medium
Motivational value to employees	Low	Low*	Low	Medium	High	Medium

*Unless you come out on top

Self-evaluation

Increasingly, written self-evaluations by employees are becoming a formal part of the appraisal process. Employees are usually more aware of their successes and shortcomings than the supervisor. They are often considerably more candid in their comments about themselves.

Employees evaluate themselves.

> "To be meaningful, self-appraisals must be handled consistently throughout the company. The timing and means for self-expression must be formalized, at least within employee levels or business groups, and the data collected should be reviewed with respect by the appraisers. Any disagreements that cannot be resolved should be documented on the formal appraisal form."[3]

Multiple Rater Teams

Employees evaluate each other.

By far the most revolutionary trend in performance appraisal is the increasing use of multiple-rater teams. In most cases, the members of the

---

[3]Charles Lee, "Smoothing Out Appraisal Systems," *HR Magazine* (March 1990): 74.

 **SELF-ASSESSMENT QUIZ 11-1**
Can You Identify the Appraisal Instrument?

Directions: Identify the appraisal instrument best suited to the particular situation described in the following ten questions. Use initials to indicate your response—GRS for graphic rating scales, PC for paired comparison, FC for forced choice, E for essay, MBO for management by objectives, and BARS for behaviorally anchored rating scales.

1. The supervisor needs to use the simplest appraisal instrument possible.

2. Predetermined goals are used as the basis for performance appraisal.

3. Every subordinate is compared to every other.

4. Supervisors answer open-ended questions.

5. The manager wants to appraise the personnel as quickly as possible.

6. Subordinates are involved in the original goal setting.

7. The instrument is job-related but time consuming to construct.

8. Management wants to know which behaviors are most and least descriptive of the person being evaluated.

9. The department needs to rate employees in relationship to other employees in the group.

10. Individual rating scales must be developed for each job title.

Answers are provided at the end of the chapter.

---

evaluation team are peers of the person being evaluated. Further, team data will be analyzed and managed by new computerized systems which continuously monitor performance data.

> "The new model represents a paradigm shift completely different from the hierarchically based, supervisory-driven systems of today. Appraisal systems will be substantially moderated in a fashion similar to the quest for total quality in production. Multiple-rater teams, making continuous measures over a variety of criteria, will provide high-quality information on individuals' performance. This information or data will be analyzed by new tools—intelligent or expert systems combined with multi-rater systems."[4]

The reasons for this dramatic shift in performance evaluation technique is rooted in changes in the workplace itself.[5] Multiple rater assessment is a part of the empowerment process discussed in Chapter 9. It is also in keeping with new, flatter organizational structures where the supervisor's span of control may be as many as sixty or seventy employees. Under such conditions, it becomes a physical impossibility for one person to have enough information to accurately assess each employee.

Another current trend in organizational structure is temporary project management, or work teams, where employees are separated from their

---

[4]Mark R. Edwards, "Accurate Performance Measurement Tools," *HR Magazine* (June 1991): 95.

[5]Mark R. Edwards, "Assessment: A Joint Effort Leads to Accurate Appraisals," *Personnel Journal* (June 1990): 122–128.

■   ■   ■   **SUPERVISORY SKILLS**
Performance Appraisal: Purposes and Types

1.   Be aware that performance appraisals afford supervisors a unique opportunity to counsel employees, gather data to assist in future training and promotion decisions, and improve the individual's and the group's overall effectiveness. Learn the manner in which the appraisal system at your company works.

2.   Understand the various types of appraisal systems. If you feel the format being currently used in your department is not sufficient, perhaps you can suggest a more comprehensive system. Consider the merits of upward appraisals, self-evaluation, and multiple rater teams.

3.   Don't let appraisals wait until you can't put them off any longer. Schedule time the same way you would for any important function.

Multiple rater assessment supports TQM and managing cultural diversity.

traditional supervisor while they work on special projects. Additionally, multiple rater systems are appropriate in light of increased cultural diversity in the workplace.

> "As organizations integrate diverse cultures into their work force, there will be wider recognition of the benefits of multiple-rater performance assessment teams. Multi-rater assessment systems which analyze team data, will reduce evaluation bias and represent each employee fairly and accurately. Studies show compelling evidence that multirater systems yield, for example, higher performance measures for women than do traditional supervisor-only measures."[6]

Keeping these new trends in mind, let us look at the typical errors associated with traditional performance appraisal.

ERROR IN PERFORMANCE APPRAISAL

Performance appraisal systems are only as good as the people who conduct them. In many cases evaluation is clouded with subjective judgment. Having a knowledge of the most common sources of bias can help one become a more effective appraiser. There are at least eight primary sources of bias: harshness error, leniency error, central tendency error, proximity error, random choice error, similarity error, recency error, and the halo effect.

Harshness

The harshness error results in low evaluations.

The *harshness error* occurs when supervisors are extremely hard on their employees. Because they want to be taken seriously, not considered a "soft touch," these supervisors rate all employees more harshly than the

---

[6]Edwards, 95.

employees deserve. These employees, if being rated by someone else, would score higher, no matter what type of appraisal technique was being used. Newly promoted supervisors are often prone to the harshness bias because they want to prove they are equal to the job of being tough on those who were just recently their peers.

Leniency

The *leniency error* is characterized by high performance ratings. Many supervisors are afraid that employees will be resentful or hostile if given poor evaluations, and as a result they tend to be lenient with everyone. These supervisors typically turn in performance evaluations far above normal. Of course, if nobody asks any questions, it also makes it look as if these supervisors have done a good job by fostering such good employees!

The leniency error is characterized by high performance ratings.

Central Tendency

The *central tendency error* occurs when all employees are rated generally around the mean for each criterion. Typically, supervisors score employees on a bell-shaped curve with the majority rated as average on most measures. Very little attempt is made to discriminate between levels of performance by different employees or for performance on different criteria for the same employee. Everyone is seen as "okay."

Central tendency occurs when all employees are rated average.

Proximity

The *proximity error* covers two types of bias. First, items appearing near each other on the questionnaire are often rated similarly, whereas those far apart are not. For example, if item one on a graphic rating scale is job quality and item two is job quantity, they will probably be rated the same or almost the same. If, however, these two criteria were placed on separate pages or had several other criteria separating them, then ratings might be quite different.

Proximity bias applies to closely placed questions.

Moreover, proximity also refers to physical distance between the supervisors' offices and that of their employees. If employees are physically close and there is continual interaction, they will get more favorable reviews than those with whom supervisors have less contact. It is easier to be critical of those we don't have to face on a regular basis.

Proximity to the supervisor also helps one's ratings.

Random Choice

As they are doing performance appraisals, some supervisors become aware that their grades are either too high or too low. They throw in some random praise or criticism to make the appraisal look more balanced. This *random choice* seriously biases the results of the evaluation.

Some evaluation errors occur on a random basis.

Similarity

The similarity error is caused by the perceived similarity between the supervisor and those being appraised.

Each of us is the center of our own universe. It is only human to judge others using ourselves as the primary source of comparison. When supervisors judge positively those whose backgrounds, interests, values, and performance most closely parallel theirs they are guilty of the *similarity error*.

Recency

Most recent performance often influences the evaluation more than any other performance.

Unless supervisors keep records on critical incidents of each employee throughout the year, when the annual appraisal is made, they may be thinking about performance only over the last few weeks. This bias, *recency error*, can work for or against an employee, depending on what has recently occurred. If the manager recently noticed an employee doing something well, the supervisor may give the individual an overall positive performance appraisal, and vice versa.

Halo Effect

The halo effect occurs when the supervisor allows one aspect of performance to dominate all others.

The *halo effect* occurs when the supervisor takes one positive or negative aspect about a person and generalizes this to the person's entire performance. For example, suppose that Tom always comes to work fifteen minutes early and that the supervisor finds this habit most laudable given the fact every other member of Tom's department has to be reminded that they should be at work and ready to start the day at 8:30 A.M. When it is time to evaluate Tom on work quality and quantity, the halo effect of his prompt arrival may positively bias the overall assessment.

Being aware of all of these errors is the first step to effective performance appraisal. Supervisors must also understand the legal implications of the appraisal process.

LEGAL IMPLICATIONS OF PERFORMANCE APPRAISAL

As with other aspects of the supervisory job, such as selection and training (see Chapter 7), the performance appraisal process demands that supervisors be aware of legal obligations. The Civil Rights Act of 1964 established under Title VII (discussed in depth in Chapter 6) that performance appraisal systems were legal as long as they evaluated job-related performance and not personal traits or characteristics. Likewise, Title VII made a number of performance appraisal techniques illegal.

> "Generally, it can be stated that performance appraisal systems may be illegal if the method of appraisal is not job related, performance standards are not derived through careful job analysis, the number of performance observations is inadequate, ratings are based on evaluation of subjective or vague factors, raters are biased, or rating conditions are uncontrolled or unstandardized."[7]

---

[7]Lloyd L. Byars and Leslie W. Rue, *Human Resource Management,* 3rd ed. (Homewood, Il.: Business One Irwin, 1991), 263.

In recent years, case law has shown that companies who take the following steps have a very good chance of being judged within legal boundaries.[8]

1. Conduct a job analysis to decide what behaviors are necessary for successful job performance.
2. Use these behaviors in building a job evaluation instrument. Be sure that your instrument evaluates employees on these behaviors.

Take these steps to avoid legal problems.

3. Train supervisors to apply these performance standards correctly and, especially, uniformly.

    "The uniform application of standards is very important. The vast majority of cases lost by organizations involved evidence that subjective standards were applied unevenly to minority and nonminority employees."[9]

4. Institute a formal appeal procedure and evaluation reviews by higher levels of management.
5. Document evaluations, especially in the case of poor performance. This documentation will be critical in the case of termination and subsequent legal action. (This was previously discussed in Chapter 10.)
6. Provide guidance, counseling, or training to help poor performers improve their work.

PERFORMANCE APPRAISAL INTERVIEWS

The performance appraisal interview is the actual meeting between supervisor and employee during which the employee's performance is discussed. Many of the biases just described are allowed to creep into appraisals because supervisors are insecure about conducting interviews. They just want to get it over, with as little discomfort as possible. Appraisal interviews may be additionally stressful because many companies choose to discuss salary increases and/or promotional opportunities during the same interview. To lessen the employee's concentration on rewards or the absence of rewards, it is often recommended that the performance appraisal interview be a separate meeting from any discussion of remuneration. The advantage of this approach is that supervisors and employees can focus on performance and not rewards. The downside, however, is that this method interferes with the link between pay and performance that many supervisors like to emphasize. Whether or not to treat these two issues—pay and performance—simultaneously is usually not a decision made by first line supervisors, although their opinions can often influence the managers who formulate these policies.

In the following discussion, appraisal interviews are discussed as separate from compensation meetings. One author has suggested that there are

---

[8]Byars, and Rue, 262–263.

[9]Wayne F. Cascio, *Managing Human Resources,* 3rd ed. (New York: McGraw-Hill, Inc., (1991), 274.

three overall philosophies of approaching the performance appraisal interview: tell and sell, tell and listen, and mutual problem solving.[10]

Tell and Sell

Tell and sell is the most traditional method of performance appraisal.

The objectives of this method, which is the most traditional of the three, are to give the employee an evaluation, to get that person to accept the evaluation, and to convince the employee to follow the suggested improvement plan. The approach gives full control to the supervisor and leaves the employee little to say. It is fast and to the point. Unfortunately, however, it often also leaves much unsaid and the employee usually departs feeling some frustration: "Because of the limited motivation and the defensive attitudes that are aroused, the Tell and Sell method is wanting in its effectiveness. A selling situation permits two possibilities: either the product is bought by the person or it is not. . . . Frequently, the subordinate buys the evaluation or says he does in order to get out of the interview situation."[11]

Tell and Listen

The tell and listen approach gets the subordinate more involved in the performance appraisal.

This method also begins with supervisors giving their evaluation to the employee. Then, rather than proceeding to corrective suggestions and terminating the interview, the supervisor encourages the employee to respond, disagree, and/or question. Thus the employee becomes an active part of the evaluation process. This is not a particularly easy method to use because it requires skill in active, nondefensive listening, as discussed in Chapter 3.

Mutual Problem Solving

Mutual problem solving puts the supervisor in the role of helper rather than judge.

The mutual problem-solving approach removes supervisors as judges and makes them helpers. The evaluation is a starting point for discussions as to how and where improvements should be made. These discussions take place between equal partners, although it is clearly the employee who will be expected to do the improving. These interviews are positive in tone and oriented toward the future.

Of the three approaches discussed, the mutual problem-solving approach appears to be most deserving of further study. It has the greatest potential of developing more effective employees, no matter which type of appraisal instrument has been used. The instrument in this method is strictly a starting point for discussion and future plans. The mutual problem-solving approach is the best format to prevent the employee from becoming defensive during the interview.

---

[10]Norman R. F. Maier, *The Appraisal Interview: Objectives, Methods, and Skills* (New York: John Wiley & Sons, 1966), 4–20.

[11]Ibid., 7.

SUPERVISORY SKILLS
Appraisal Bias and Interviews

1. Examine your personal weaknesses in performance appraisals. To which sources of bias are you most susceptible? Do you often exhibit leniency error, harshness error, or halo effect? How do your overall evaluations measure up to those being done by your peers? Be able to assure yourself that your evaluations are absolutely fair and honest.

2. Be sure to keep notes during the year so that your evaluations will not suffer from recency error. Do not trust your memory.

3. Note how you conduct appraisal meetings. Do you get the maximum potential benefit out of these meetings? Are your conversations future-oriented and results-based? Avoid the tell and sell method.

An effective interview depends on supervisory preparation. One expert suggests we follow what he terms the PEOPLE plan. The acronym stands for Preparation, Engagement, Observation and evaluation, Pause, Pledge, and Ensuring results. Preparation consists of the supervisor thinking through what he or she hopes to accomplish. What behaviors do you want to reinforce or change? What is the best way to communicate with this employee? Engagement has to do with logistics (where, when, and opening comments) of the appraisal interview. Observation and evaluation focus on how the employee's behavior affects performance. Pause indicates a period during which the supervisor should sit back and listen. Pledge concerns specific agreements that are reached between supervisor and employee as to what will happen next. What behaviors will change? What are the supervisor's expectations? Finally, ensuring results includes monitoring behavior and following up periodically with the employee. The best performance appraisal interview can be negated by lack of follow-up, which signals the employee that what was discussed didn't really matter.[12]

The question of follow-up is particularly important. Supervisors and employees often have the best of intentions during the performance appraisal interview, but after a few days everything is back to normal.

> "Your job isn't finished with the interview, of course. Continue to coach and train your employee. Observe your employee at problem tasks, and look for improved behavior. If you find improvement, praise your employee promptly. . . . If there is no improvement, find out why and privately coach the correct behavior. Finally, keep communications open until the next appraisal interview."[13]

---

[12]Wally Bock, "How Am I Gonna Tell Him?" *Supervisory Management* (March 1993): 7.

[13]Bob Losyk, "Face to Face: How to Conduct an Employee Appraisal Interview," *Executive* (Winter 1990–91): 91

SUMMARY

Performance appraisal is job-related feedback. There are four steps in this process: (a) establishment of standards; (b) measurement of individual performance against these standards; (c) reinforcement of performance or provision of remedies for deficiencies; (d) and establishment of periodic performance goals.

There are a number of different types of commonly used performance appraisal instruments. Graphic rating scales use degrees of factors to evaluate people. In the paired comparison each subordinate is compared to all of the others in the group in terms of the criteria being measured. According to the forced choice method the supervisor chooses from a given set of descriptive statements those that are most and least descriptive of the employee. The essay form of appraisal provides the opportunity to answer open-ended questions. In management by objectives superior and subordinate jointly define common goals to be accomplished in a given period, define the latter's responsibility in terms of expected results, and use these measures as a guide for operating the unit and assessing the individual's contribution. Behaviorally anchored rating scales describe effective and ineffective performance concerning a particular job criterion and are filled out by the supervisor on each subordinate being evaluated. New trends in performance appraisal include upward appraisals, self-evaluation, and multiple rater teams.

At least eight sources of bias may influence how the supervisor evaluates an employee. The harshness error judges subordinates too severely, whereas the leniency error assigns ratings that are too high. Employees may all be judged to be average when the central tendency error is made. The proximity error refers to similar ratings for criteria that are near each other. Supervisors may throw in random praise or criticism or they may judge employees by their similarity to themselves. Recency error occurs when the most recent performance outweighs the whole performance. Finally the halo effect takes place when one aspect of a person overshadows his or her overall behavior.

Supervisors need to be aware of legal implications of performance appraisal. Most importantly, you must be able to prove that the entire evaluation is job related and that standards are applied uniformly. Formal appeal procedures, documentation, and counselling or training for poor performers are also important.

When conducting the performance appraisal interview, there are three overall philosophies: tell and sell, tell and listen, and mutual problem solving. Where possible, the latter is usually the most preferable. Effective interviewers often follow the people plan: preparation, engagement, observation, pause, pledge, and ensure results.

REVIEW QUESTIONS

1. How does the performance appraisal process work? Explain it in your own words.

2. What are some benefits of the performance appraisal process? Explain.

3. How do the following types of performance appraisals work: graphic rating scales, paired comparisons, and forced choice? Explain each.

4. Describe the following types of per-

formance appraisals: essay, management by objectives, and behaviorally anchored rating scales.

5. What are some of the advantages of using MBO? Be complete in your answer.

6. Many practicing supervisors feel that BARS is a very effective method of performance appraisal. Why is this so? Explain.

7. In your opinion, which type of performance appraisal system is best? Defend your answer.

8. Name and describe three new trends in performance appraisal. How do they support the TQM movement?

9. In what way do the following cause errors in performance appraisal: harshness, leniency, and central tendency? Be complete in your answer.

10. In what way do the following cause errors in performance appraisal: proximity, random choice, similarity, and recency? Be complete in your answer.

11. How does the halo effect work? Give an example in your answer.

12. What legal considerations concern supervisors about performance appraisals?

13. How do the following performance appraisal interviews work: tell and sell, tell and listen, and mutual problem solving? Be sure to describe each in your answer.

14. Why do many people feel that the mutual problem-solving approach to performance appraisal interviews is better than the other approaches? Explain.

KEY TERMS

Behaviorally anchored rating scales. Performance evaluation method that involves developing a series of critical incident behaviors, ranking them on a scale, and then using the scale to evaluate the personnel.

Central tendency error. Performance evaluation error caused by the supervisor giving out average ratings to most of the personnel regardless of their performance.

Feedback. Recognition of a stimulus.

Forced choice Performance appraisal method in which the supervisor is asked to choose from a list of items the ones that are most descriptive of the person being evaluated.

Graphic rating scale. Performance evaluation instrument that uses degrees of factors to evaluate people.

Halo effect. Performance evaluation error caused by the supervisor allowing one positive or negative aspect of an individual's performance to influence the evaluation of that person on all the factors being rated.

Harshness error. Performance evaluation error caused by the supervisor giving out lower ratings than are justified.

Leniency error. Performance evaluation error caused by the supervisor giving out much higher ratings than are justified.

Management by objectives. Process whereby the supervisor and employee jointly identify common goals to be accomplished in a given period, define the subordinate's major areas of responsibility in terms of the expected results, and use these measures as a guide for operating the unit and assessing the individual's contribution.

Paired comparison. Appraisal method in which the rater compares every employee in the work group with every other employee.

Performance appraisal. Job-related feedback.

Proximity error. Performance evaluation error that occurs because items on a questionnaire are located next to each other or because supervisor and employee work close to one another.

Random choice error. Performance appraisal error that occurs because supervisors feel they have been generally rating someone too high or too low so they throw in some random responses.

Recency error. Performance appraisal bias occurring as a result of supervisors looking only at current or recent past performance.

Similarity error. Performance appraisal error in which supervisors judge most positively those workers most like themselves in background and beliefs.

ANSWERS TO SELF-ASSESSMENT QUIZ 11–1

| 1. | GRS | 3. | PC | 5. | GRS | 7. | BARS | 9. | PC |
| 2. | MBO | 4. | E | 6. | MBO | 8. | FC | 10. | BARS |

CASE 11–1
Looking for a Performance Appraisal System

County Hospital is a 500-bed hospital located in a major northeastern state. Until three months ago the hospital was private; however, when the corporation that was running the hospital suffered a financial loss for the fifth straight year, the company decided to close the institution. At this time, the county agreed to take over the hospital.

Upon assuming control of the operation, the county immediately hired a national management consulting firm to examine the operation and make recommendations. The consultants' report was submitted last week. One of the sections deals with performance appraisal. It notes that when the hospital was run by a private corporation, performance appraisal was given little attention. As a result some of the personnel are not performing up to par and others lack the training they should have in order to perform their jobs properly. To rectify the situation, the consultants have recommended that the county

institute a comprehensive management by objectives appraisal system.

In an effort to hear all sides of the issue, the county has asked the administrative staff of the hospital what they think should be done regarding improving the current performance appraisal system. The administrators say that they believe a graphic rating scale or paired comparison method is the best one to use.

The supervisory staff in the hospital disagrees with both the consultants and the administrators. They say that the best system to use is behaviorally anchored rating scales.

The county intends to make a decision on the matter within a couple of weeks. For the moment the chairperson of the committee who is charged with the performance appraisal area investigation wants to brush up on what these various appraisals entail, as well as their strengths and weaknesses.

1. How would an MBO system work at County Hospital?

2. Why do you think the administration preferred a graphic rating scale or paired comparison method?

3. What advantage do behaviorally anchored rating scales have for supervisors? Do you think it would be better than the other proposed methods? If so, why? If not, which one would you recommend and why?

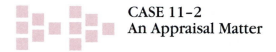

CASE 11–2
An Appraisal Matter

When Josh Louganis was a young man, he attended the local university. Every evening after work he would tuck his books under his arm and walk the fifteen blocks to the university campus. It took Josh six years to complete his undergraduate degree, but he is convinced that this is why he was able to make it all the way up the line to senior supervisor. The plant where Josh works is highly decentralized and the senior supervisor is one of the most important people in the operation. Nineteen supervisors report to Josh. On the organization chart he reports directly to the plant manager, who reports directly to the area executive.

Josh is known as a "tough cookie" when it comes to getting things done. He has been around long enough to know what can and cannot be done; no one pulls the wool over his eyes. Last year a new supervisor told Josh that it was impossible to get delivery of parts in less than three weeks. In truth this supervisor had simply forgotten to reorder and was trying to cover his flanks at the last moment. Josh got on the phone, reordered the parts, and had delivery within one week. When the parts arrived, he took the supervisor down to the shipping dock, showed him the parts, ordered him to supervise their unloading, and then fired him on the spot. "I don't like being lied to," he told the man. "There's no place in the operation for a person like you!"

Despite his reputation, Josh does have one soft spot. He tends to favor individuals who attend night school. As a result it is common to find some of his supervisors wearing ties, tie clasps, or jackets that carry the logo of the local university. Some of them do not actually attend the university, but they do not fool Josh. The company reimburses its supervisors for 50 percent of their educational expenses, and Josh has a friend in the finance department who tells him who is getting reimbursement. On the other hand, all of the supervisors who do attend the local university (there are five of them) have received extremely high evaluations over the years; some of them have been moved to other plants where they have been given senior-level positions. Few of the supervisors who do not attend the local university have received such high performance evaluations.

1. What performance appraisal error is Josh making? Identify and describe the error.

2. In your own words, why is Josh making this mistake? What is the logic behind the error?

3. If you were Josh's boss, what would you do to help prevent this error from occurring in the future? Offer at least two recommendations for action.

PART III

S upervisors often deal with groups. Typically this is their normal work group, but on occasion there are others including unions and interdepartmental committees. The overall objective of this part is to examine the ways in which supervisors carry out this function and to identify some of the guidelines that can be of value to them.

Chapter 12 examines the area of group dynamics. The chapter begins by identifying and describing the differences between formal and informal groups. The ways in which functional groups, project groups, and committees work are also discussed. Attention is also focused on describing how groups are formed. The chapter closes by focusing on how to organize and conduct effective meetings.

Chapter 13 addresses the topic of effective leadership. In addition to defining the term *leadership,* attention is focused on describing the five basic types of power held by supervisors. In addition, Theory X and Theory Y are compared and contrasted. The chapter goes on to describe the three basic types of leadership style—authoritarian, democratic, and laissez-faire—and to identify and describe the five basic leadership styles presented by the Leadership Grid. The latter part of the chapter relates the value of situational leadership theories and discusses how the supervisor can use them. Finally, it offers an explanation of why followership theory is of practical value to the modern supervisor.

Dealing with Groups

Chapter 14 deals with supervising in a union environment. It identifies and describes some of the key labor legislation with which supervisors should be familiar. It also discusses collective bargaining and the role of the labor contract in establishing supervisor-worker relationships. In addition, this chapter compares and contrasts the union shop and the open shop. The latter part of the chapter discusses the role of the shop steward in labor-management relations.

Chapter 15 addresses the maintenance of a safe environment. The emergence of safety and health as work-related factors is described and the importance of the Occupational Safety and Health Act to supervision in the work place is discussed. Moreover, it discusses the types and incidence of job-related safety and health problems and the ways of identifying and developing an effective safety and health program. The chapter closes with a description of the role of the supervisor in safety and health programs.

When you have finished studying all of the material in this section, you will be aware of both the challenges and opportunities that present themselves as the supervisor deals with groups. You will also know some of the most important ways that supervisors can lead the work group and influence its objectives and direction.

■ ■ ■ CHAPTER 12

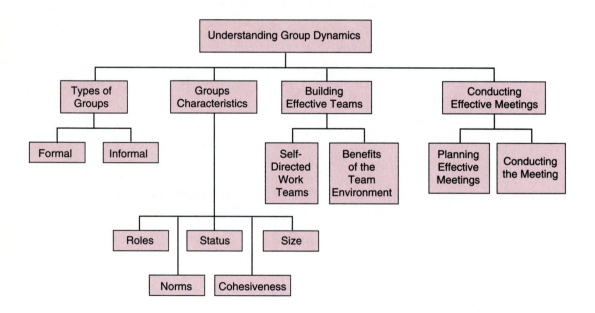

Understanding Group Dynamics

" 'I'd really rather work alone . . .' Forget it, the twenty-first century works in groups."*

CHAPTER OBJECTIVES

- ☐ Identify and describe the differences between formal and informal groups.

- ☐ Explain the way functional groups, project groups, and committees work.

- ☐ Relate the five most important characteristics of groups: roles, norms, status, cohesiveness, and size.

- ☐ Explore the new emphasis on teams, especially self-directed teams.

- ☐ Describe types of meetings including quality circles.

- ☐ Discuss planning and conducting effective meetings.

---

*Gay Lunsden and Donald Lunsden, *Communicating in Groups and Teams* (Belmont, Calif.: Wadsworth Publishing Co., 1993), 3.

S upervisors spend much of their time working with individual employees. But each employee also belongs to one or more groups within the organization, and these groups have a great influence on the behavior of their members. Supervisors, therefore, must understand the roles that groups play in the organization.

A group consists of interdependent, interactive individuals.

Briefly defined, a *group* is a social unit consisting of two or more interdependent, interactive individuals who are striving to attain common goals. *Group dynamics* examines the way in which group members interact in the group setting. Groups whose members must rely on group cooperation in order to achieve their goals are called *teams*. This chapter looks at the types of groups encountered by a supervisor, various characteristics of groups, and ways of working with work groups to build an effective team. It describes the increasing importance of building effective work teams. The chapter concludes with a look at group meetings and how to make them more effective.

TYPES OF GROUPS

Organizational groups can be broadly categorized as either formal or informal.

Formal Groups

Formal groups are created by the organization itself. Three common examples of formal groups are functional groups, project groups, and committees.

Functional groups are created by the organization itself.

Functional groups, sometimes called task groups, are made up of individuals who work together on a regular basis. A clerical pool of typists who form a department or unit is one example of a functional group.

Project groups consist of individuals from different departments and areas who have been brought together to pursue a common goal. After that goal is reached, the group is disbanded. Examples of project groups include those formed for the purpose of specific goal attainment.

Committees, the third type of group, may be either *standing committees,* which exist for an indefinite but usually lengthy period of time, or *ad hoc committees,* which are temporary in nature and come to an end when their purpose is attained.

Informal Groups

Informal groups are created by the employees themselves.

Informal groups, unlike formal groups, are created by the employees themselves. Membership is decided by collective and common interests. Supervisors must realize that a great deal of business is accomplished in the informal group setting. Informal groups include the bowling team or the group that traditionally meets for beer on Friday evenings.

People join groups for many reasons.

People join groups for various reasons. In the case of functional groups, people usually are assigned to them. In other cases people request a specific position because they want to be a part of that particular work team. The three major reasons for joining both formal and informal groups are common goals, frequent contact with other group members, and the perceived personal satisfaction of being a member of a particular group.

GROUP CHARACTERISTICS

To understand how people work together in groups effectively, you ought to know some of the major group characteristics and the effects they have on group interaction. This section examines five of the most important characteristics: roles, norms, status, cohesiveness, and group size. You will recall that group decision making was already discussed as part of chapter 5. Before reading on, however, take Self-Assessment Quiz 12–1 to see how much you already know about group characteristics.

Roles

A role is an expected behavior.

A *role* is an expected behavior. In any group situation, members are concerned with three types of roles: perceived, expected, and enacted. The

---

■ ■ ■ **SELF-ASSESSMENT QUIZ 12–1**
What Do You Know About Group Characteristics?

Directions: Answer each of the following questions true or false.

_____ 1. Roles are always dictated by the formal group.

_____ 2. Group norms help control what, when, where, and how people communicate.

_____ 3. Highly intelligent people tend to be more conforming than people of low intelligence.

_____ 4. Status influences a person's ability to communicate effectively with others.

_____ 5. Managers who spend most of their time talking to and socializing with lower-level employees will increase their status in the organization and improve their communication effectiveness.

_____ 6. Highly cohesive groups tend to work harder than less cohesive groups, regardless of outside supervision.

_____ 7. High cohesion increases verbal interaction among group members.

_____ 8. Highly cohesive groups communicate more with each other and are higher producers than other groups.

_____ 9. Individuals in large groups tend to communicate, on average, more than they do in small groups.

_____10. An ideal size for small group discussion is ten people.

Answers can be found at the end of the chapter.

perceived role is the way individuals believe they *ought* to act. The corollary to the perceived role is the expected role. An *expected role* is the way others expect you to act. Finally, the *enacted role* is the way a person actually does something.

When a person does not know how to interact with the rest of the group, the individual is said to suffer from role ambiguity. *Role ambiguity* occurs whenever a person is uncertain how to act. This often occurs when a job has been inadequately defined and employees are left to develop the role according to their own perceptions. Another common role-related problem is *role conflict*. Here individuals face a situation in which they must assume two roles, but one role is in conflict with the other. A typical example is that of a new supervisor who wants to build esprit de corps among the work group members while also trying to comply with management's directive to keep a tight rein on the personnel.

Norms

Norms are rules of behavior that have group acceptance.

Norms are implied and/or stated rules of behavior that have been accepted by members of a group. Most groups do not have a large number of norms. Usually only those areas or things that are important to the functioning or existence of the group become focal points for normative behavior. For example, the average group does not care where its members attend church, but is usually very much concerned that no member of the group "squeal" to management about the behavior of any other member. Typical company-wide norms include coming to work each day, arriving on time, and observing company holidays.

Norms are extremely important for supervisors to understand because they help control what, when, where, and how people behave. They also are responsible for a large part of the "organizational culture" in a company because they embody many unwritten rules and regulations of expected behavior.

Status

Status is a person's ranking in relation to others.

Status is the relative ranking that one individual in a group has in relation to the others. Status typically carries with it some of the trappings of power. For example, if there are three supervisors of apparently equal rank in the plant, which one has the most status? The answer is easy: The one with the largest office and the nicest furnishings. People assign importance to these physical factors.

Status within informal groups depends on factors such as job competence, experience, and personality. Quite often the person with the most competence will become the spokesperson for the group. Experience is a status factor when people in the group give greater respect and attention to those members who have been around the longest.

Status can also raise a number of problems. *Status incongruency,* for instance, occurs when there is a difference between supposed status and the way the person is treated. For example, if a supervisor begins to speak and the subordinates start looking around the room, talking with one another, or reading, there is obviously a problem. If the supervisor has status based on position, why is everyone treating the individual as if he were unimportant? The answer may be that the employees know this supervisor is on the way out. Or they may feel the manager is so incompetent that it is a waste of time to listen. When status incongruency exists, a supervisor's ability to communicate and persuade can be substantially reduced.

Another status-related problem is status discrepancy. *Status discrepancy* occurs when people do things that are not in accord with their relative ranking in the group. For example, if a union shop steward is seen having lunch with members of management, the union rank and file may ask, "What's he doing talking to those guys? He's supposed to be with us."

Cohesiveness

Cohesiveness is the closeness of group members.

Cohesiveness is the closeness or personal attractiveness that exists between members of a group. When cohesion is high, members are motivated to remain with the group; when it is low, they are motivated to leave the group. Among formal organizations, if there is low cohesiveness, the members will seek promotions, transfers, or reassignments to other groups in the hierarchy or will simply leave the organization and seek employment elsewhere. Within informal organizations low cohesiveness will bring about intragroup conflict and tension.

Cohesion is a vital factor in group performance. Highly cohesive groups tend to work harder regardless of outside supervision. They also tend to produce more work than groups whose cohesion is not as high.

When a group is highly cohesive, morale will be high. However, highly cohesive groups are not always more productive than less cohesive groups. You might recall the "groupthink" concept discussed in Chapter 5, which illustrated how a cohesive group can become isolated and narrow-minded.

To the supervisor, high cohesion results in an increase in both the quality and quantity of group interaction. Members of highly cohesive groups are more cooperative and friendly, and generally behave in ways designed to promote group integration.[1] Members of low-cohesive

---

[1]Marvin E. Shaw and Lilly Mae Shaw, "Some Effects of Sociometric Grouping upon Learning in a Second Grade Classroom," *Journal of Social Psychology* (August 1962): 453–58.

groups are much more independent of each other. They often show little concern for others in the group, do not communicate a great deal with the other members, and, as a result, tend to have lower work output or productivity.

Size

Another important group characteristic is size. Workers tend to be more satisfied in smaller groups (eight or less); as group size increases, there is less satisfaction. The reason for the dissatisfaction can often be traced back to a decline in cohesiveness. Group members find it difficult to interact and share feelings and work assignments with ten people as easily as they can with two people.

Group size affects member satisfaction.

What, then, is the ideal size for effective group dynamics and productivity? This is not an easy question to answer because so many variables can affect the situation. However, many researchers argue that five people is the optimum size for a small discussion group, or one in which there is to be a great deal of interaction. A thorough understanding of group dynamics will help supervisors build effective work teams.

SUPERVISORY SKILLS
Building Effective Teams

1. Be sure to have open communications with the group. Listen carefully to formal or informal group leaders; learn to anticipate problems; be sure that you carefully communicate needed information.

2. Recognize the groups that exist and the importance of their interpersonal relationships. Be careful how you relocate or reassign people; be aware of the resentment caused by interfering with harmonious social relationships.

3. Remember that when role ambiguity or role conflict exists, productivity will decline. Make sure that everyone knows what to do so that communication efforts can be focused toward determining how to get things done (rather than worrying about what is supposed to be done).

4. Pay close attention to the informal group leaders. These people influence the norms to which the other members conform. Your ability to win over the informal group leaders will help ensure that informal group norms are not used against you.

5. Keep in mind that high cohesiveness is important to effective group functioning. However, unless you also are effective in leading your group, this cohesiveness can work against you. A highly cohesive group may agree among the members to do as little work as possible. Remember that open communication, honesty, and a willingness to admit that you are sometimes wrong will go a long way in helping you develop an effective rapport with the group.

6. Give recognition to the group when it is earned. If productivity is up and your manager has complimented you, be sure to pass along the credit to the group that made it possible. You thus become a member of the team and reduce status differences.

BUILDING EFFECTIVE TEAMS

One of the hottest topics in the '90s is teamwork. It appears certain that teams, especially self-directed teams, are a growing force in American business. It is therefore going to be imperative that supervisors know how to create and nurture effective teams. But what is a team? How does it differ from a traditional group? In the words of one expert,

Teams have a group identity and pursue common goals.

> "A *team* is a diverse group of people who share leadership responsibility for creating a group identity in an interconnected effort to achieve a mutually defined goal within the context of other groups and systems."[2]

Perhaps the most important part of this definition is the idea of a group identity. It is this self-image developed by the team that helps them focus their energy and act as a cohesive and motivated group.

Says Marc Bassin, Director of Management and Organizational Development for General Foods,

> "It is precisely the ability of a team to create a cycle of positive dynamics, each impacting and reinforcing the other, that usually enables individual team members to reach higher levels of performance than if they worked individually."[3]

Creating a team organization requires dedication on the part of top management as well as a willingness among supervisors to share some of the traditional power and authority that they have enjoyed. The payoffs are many.

> "In the team organization, managers and employers are committed to their vision. People understand how their own efforts fit into the objectives of their department and the goals of their company. They believe that this vision unites them. They and their bosses and coworkers establish cooperative, congruent goals and rewards so that they can be successful together."[4]

Self-Directed Work Teams

Self-directed teams do whole jobs.

A self-directed work team is simply a team that is jointly responsible for a whole job or discrete section of a job. Such teams become involved in many nontraditional areas concerning their task, such as dealing with vendors and customers, quality control, decision making, and even hiring new members for the team. In recent years, many corporations have instituted self-directed work teams, including General Motors, General Electric, Xerox, and Colgate

---

[2]Gay Lumsden and Donald Lumsden, *Communication in Groups and Teams* (Belmont, Calif: Wadsworth Publishing Co., 1993), 14.

[3]Marc Bassin. "Teamwork at General-Foods: New and Improved," *Personnel Journal* (May 1988): 62–70.

[4]Dean Tjosvold and Mary M. Tjosvold. *Leading the Team Organization* (New York: Lexington Books, 1991), 3.

Palmolive. A recent survey showed that 26 percent of top executives surveyed reported that self-directed teams were already in place in their organizations, whereas more than 50 percent estimated that their organizations would employ self-directed teams within the next five years.

How are organizations that employ self-directed work teams different from traditional organizations? Typically, they have fewer layers of management, and leaders and supervisors act as coaches or facilitators rather than as planners and controllers. Reward systems tend to be skill based rather than seniority based. Information is widely shared among employees rather than hoarded by top management, and employees are cross-trained to learn all aspects of the team job rather than just a narrow span of individual job duties.[5]

Supervisors often find the switch to self-directed work teams a threatening one. Gone is the traditional relationship of boss to subordinates. The supervisor instead must act in the role of coach to encourage productivity, lead group meetings and decision making, and recognize good performance. "The Quality Challenge: A Well-Focused Approach" gives further insight.

Benefits of the Team Environment

Why all of the commotion over self-directed groups? How do they benefit the organization? According to executives whose companies have begun team programs, there are at least seven good reasons for doing so[6]:

There are many organizational benefits to self-directed teams.

1. Improved quality, productivity, and service. Teams seem to support the TQM cornerstone of continuous improvement. This is probably because self-directed teams foster a feeling of employee ownership which in turn leads to improvement in all areas.
2. Greater flexibility. Teams seem to be able to respond faster to changing market conditions and demands than the traditional structure.
3. Reduced operating costs. Empowered teams allow for fewer layers of management and reduced costs.
4. Faster response to technological change. Teams seem to have the communication links necessary to respond quickly to technological change.
5. Better response to new worker values. Today, employees want autonomy, responsibility, and self-initiative that self-directed teams provide.

[5]Richard Wellins and Jill George, "The Key to Self-Directed Teams," *Training and Development Journal* (April 1991): 26–31.

[6]Richard S. Wellins, William C. Byham, and Jeanne M. Wilson, *Empowered Teams* (San Francisco, Calif.: Jossey-Bass Publishers, 1991), 10–13.

THE QUALITY CHALLENGE
A Well-Focused Approach

Team work is critical to total quality efforts. For this reason, more and more companies are teaching their supervisors and lower-line personnel how to work together harmoniously. There are a number of steps in this process:

1. Focus the effort on improving quality. This can take one of two interdependent paths: doing things better and doing things faster. The first thing that teams are taught to do is identify the problem or issue that needs to be resolved.

2. Decide who will do what. This step requires the group to set tasks for all of the members. This can range from having everyone brainstorm the problem to dividing the group into subgroups and having each of these gather specific data related to the problem.

3. Analyze and evaluate without criticism. This steps entails teaching people to evaluate information objectively and work as a team. The personnel must learn how to concentrate their attention on attacking the problem and not each other.

4. Implement the results enthusiastically. Once a problem has been evaluated, the team members must determine what needs to be done and implement this decision. There must be a feeling of teamwork and satisfaction for a job well done.

5. Reward group members for doing a good job. After the work group has successfully solved the problem, the supervisor must learn how to reinforce their behavior by rewarding them through personal praise, laudatory performance reviews, and supportive statements to higher-level management.

In focusing their efforts, most work groups must learn to work as a team. However, the supervisor plays an important role in this process by offering direction and encouragement and, in so doing, becomes an important member of the team.

---

6. Fewer, simpler job classifications. Team membership implies employees who can perform a variety of related job functions. This eliminates the need for so many different job descriptions.

7. Ability to attract and retain the best people. Teams offer the opportunity for participation, challenge, and camaraderie. It is likely that organizations based on worker teams will have the edge in attracting quality employees.

Both traditional organizations and team-based organizations spend a lot of energy on meetings. The next section seeks ways to maximize the payoff of this effort.

CONDUCTING EFFECTIVE MEETINGS

A meeting is a formal gathering of personnel for a predetermined purpose.

A *meeting* is a formal gathering of personnel for a predetermined purpose. Many of the complaints about meetings suggest that employees see them as unnecessary or at least too long or unproductive. Yet their increased use points out the need for supervisors to develop meeting skills.

Like every other management tool that we've studied, meetings have their advantages and disadvantages. The primary advantages of meetings include: enhancing decision making, building esprit de corps, involving people in planning and/or implementing change, sharing responsibility for decisions made and plans activated, and facilitating two-way communication between supervisors and employees. Disadvantages include: spending inordinate amounts of time and money, delaying action on important matters and making poor decisions when group members are more concerned about camaraderie than quality of decisions.

The first rule of conducting effective meetings is: Be sure your meetings have a purpose and that your employees are aware of that purpose. Basically there are three major reasons for calling meetings: disseminating information, problem solving, and facilitating change.

First, as organizations become larger, keeping people up-to-date becomes a growing problem. Meetings are an efficient way of reaching groups of people with news. Speaking to everyone at the same time insures that everyone is hearing the same information.

Second, meetings are often called to solve problems. These meetings may take place at one of three levels: generating ideas, gathering information, or actual decision making.

Idea-generating meetings are designed to look at a problem from many different angles. These meetings are sometimes called *brainstorming*. As mentioned in Chapter 5, the primary purpose here is to come up with as many ideas as possible or as many alternative solutions to a given problem as people can generate.

Information-gathering meetings provide a forum for obtaining more data. At these gatherings the subject of the meeting is put forth and people are then invited to give their ideas and opinions.

Decision-making meetings produce a decision or a program for action. The issue at hand is resolved and will likely not be back on the agenda for some time unless it appears as a discussion item, such as a progress report on implementation of the decision.

The Nominal Group Technique (NGT) and the Delphi Technique are sometimes used in place of or in addition to decision-making meetings. These two techniques were discussed in Chapter 5. The NGT format may actually be used at a decision-making meeting to generate ideas, gather information, and make decisions. Delphi, as you will remember, is used in lieu of a meeting, that is, the participants never actually congregate face-to-face.

In addition to these three types of meetings, American supervisors are often called upon to participate in quality circle meetings. *Quality circles* are groups of workers (usually not more than eight to ten) who, along with their supervisor, meet on company time to discuss ways in which they can be more productive or can improve product quality. Quality circles were started in the United States several decades ago but gained popularity in

Quality circles can help improve productivity.

Japan. In recent years American managers have looked to Japanese management techniques in an effort to spur lagging American productivity. Thus, there has been a renewed interest in quality circles as a management tool. The approach also fits in quite well with the current philosophy of increasing worker participation in organizational decision making.

In addition to increased employee participation, the organization typically profits from quality circles through increased productivity, cost savings, and quality improvement. Supervisors who participate as quality circle leaders also benefit by professional growth. Employees also reap personal and professional growth from participating in quality circles. Although many experts feel that the popularity of quality circles has peaked, it is undeniable that quality circles have had a widespread impact on both the quality movement and the increasing focus on self-directed teams.

Meetings serve to introduce and involve personnel in the change process.

Finally, another major purpose of meetings is to introduce plans for change at an early stage and encourage employees to involve themselves in the process. Experienced supervisors have learned that it is far easier to implement a change when workers are involved in the planning process. People are normally resistant to any kind of change. Organizational behavior experts, however, believe that involving people in the change process is the best way to alleviate many of the negative consequences of this resistance.

Planning Effective Meetings

Once supervisors have decided that a meeting is justified, the next step is planning it. Planning centers around two types of considerations: logistics and meeting content.

Logistics. Logistical considerations of planning meetings tackle the questions of who, when, and where.

Consideration must be given to who is invited to the meeting.

Who you choose to invite to a meeting is critical. Generally speaking, only those who have information about or interest in the subject at hand should be invited.

When the meeting is to be held is also an important consideration.

When you plan to hold the meeting is the next consideration. Analyze the schedules of the participants. When would be most convenient for people to meet? Try to avoid meetings at peak work hours or for late afternoons before a holiday or weekend. The length of time allotted for the meeting is also an important issue. There should be enough time to accomplish the meeting's goals but not so much time that the meeting will drag on and become boring. Meetings lasting longer than 90 minutes often produce diminishing returns.

Where the meeting will be held is another important issue.

Where the meeting occurs is yet another logistical consideration. Try to make the meeting place easily accessible to the participants. Nobody wants to travel across town for a meeting if such a trip can be avoided. Be sure that the meeting room is the appropriate size for the group.

Meeting-room seating arrangements

Conference-table seating arrangements

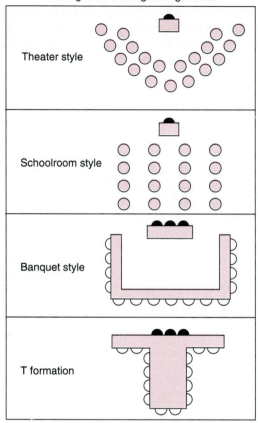

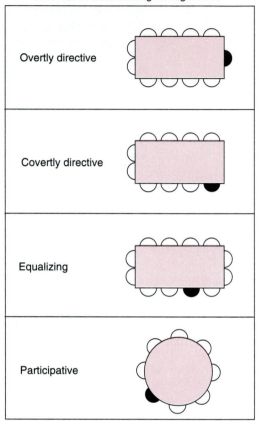

FIGURE 12-1

Management of meetings.

Source: Susan Dellinger and Barbara Deane, *Communicating Effectively: A Complete Guide for Better Managing* (Radnor, Pa.: Chilton Book Co., 1982), 158–159. Reprinted with permission.

Another aspect of logistical planning for a meeting is designing the room's setup. Arrangement of meeting space greatly influences the communication pattern (Figure 12–1).

How does each of these styles influence communication and participation? It is easy to guess that the schoolroom style meeting room leads to more lecture-type presentations such as used in a straight informational meeting, whereas the participative conference table setting would be more appropriate for creative problem solving in which everyone can play a role.

Meeting Content.   Having decided the meeting's purpose and its logistics, the supervisor must decide exactly what will be covered during the meeting. One of the most common errors is lack of direction. Advance planning can prevent this problem. The most effective way is through the use of an *agenda*. An *agenda* is an itemized list of topics to be covered during the meeting.

The agenda provides direction for the meeting.

When preparing agendas, keep in mind the following strategies:

1.   Keep your agenda specific.
2.   Let people know what to expect.
3.   Consider including each item on the agenda.
4.   Include any background reading material with the agenda.
5.   Keep the agenda and the meeting short.
6.   To minimize tension, anticipate conflicts and sandwich them in with conflict-free items.

Agendas should be distributed at least a week in advance.

Agendas should be distributed at least a week in advance, especially if the participants will have to do preparatory work. The advantage of having an agenda is lost if it is received shortly before the meeting and the participants do not have time to read it and think about its contents. Properly used, agendas can set the stage for meetings by establishing clear expectations in the minds of the attending workers.

Conducting the Meeting

Even the best-planned meeting will fall short of expectations unless the supervisor is skilled in conducting it. Five skills seem to be important.

First, putting people at ease is the first task. When meetings are about to begin, supervisors should invite everyone to sit down. They may start by thanking participants for taking the time to attend. They should then clearly state the meeting purpose and refer everyone to the agenda. This introduction helps participants to focus on the task at hand and to begin to think about the subject matter.

Second, ensuring that the agenda remains the guiding force of the meeting is another important skill. As meeting leader, the supervisor must be able to short-circuit conversations that are straying off the agenda. Many meetings result in frustration and discouragement because they have been allowed to stray from the stated purpose. On the other hand, the supervisor must not overstructure the meeting to the point that the participants are not given the opportunity or feel afraid to speak up.

Next, encouraging participation by each employee attending the meeting is a particularly useful skill. It is very easy to assume that everyone agrees with what the supervisor is saying if nobody else says much at all. The manager may be facing deep-seated resistance and never know it. To avoid this unspoken resistance supervisors should ask the participants

SUPERVISORY SKILLS
Planning and Conducting Effective Meetings

1. Be sure to plan the logistics of your meeting carefully. Consider who should be invited and why. What can each person add to the meeting? When should the meeting be held? Where is the most appropriate meeting site? Consider also ways to set up the room so that communication flow will be appropriate to your purpose.

2. Plan the content of the meeting carefully. Write an agenda and be sure to distribute it at least one week in advance. Be sure to include any reading material that em-

ployees should digest in advance of the meeting.

3. When conducting the meeting, be sure to stick to the distributed agenda. Encourage everyone to participate and control unproductive behavior that discourages others from participating.

4. Be sure to follow up your meetings carefully. Let employees know what action has been taken and what they can expect in the future.

for their opinions rather than stating the way they feel about the issue at the beginning of the discussion.

Fourth, avoiding personal agendas and problem behavior requires the supervisor to be very skillful in dealing with people.

"The ability to handle disruptive behavior is the first key skill for successful meetings. Nothing can sandbag a meeting faster than a person who chases tangents or refuses to keep quiet. Confronting the disruptive participant could invite open conflict. Doing nothing could destroy the meeting. Between those extremes lies a middle ground: providing feedback."[7]

For example, if a participant is constantly interrupting other people, the manager might say, "Harry, your interruptions are causing others to lose their train of thought; why don't you jot down your questions and ask them later?" This not only lets Harry know that the supervisor will not tolerate his behavior, but it also suggests an alternate and more productive way to get points across.

Finally, the supervisor must know how to bring a meeting to closure. Three steps should be followed: (1) summarize what has been said and decided on; (2) note what should happen next; and (3) thank everyone for attending.

The final task of conducting an effective meeting is the follow-up. Many supervisors rely on minutes of the meeting (formal notes of what has transpired) or tape recordings so as not to rely solely on memory.

---

[7]Peter M. Tobia and Martin C. Becker, "Making the Most of Meeting Time, *Training and Development Journal* (August 1990): 36.

Nevertheless, all the good suggestions fade away with time and no follow-up occurs. Effective follow-up varies from case to case. Distribution of typed minutes may not be the only necessary step. A memo detailing meeting conclusions and actions may be sent. Or another meeting may be scheduled. Effective supervisors ensure that the actions take place as planned and that employees are kept informed.

SUMMARY

There are two broad categories of groups: formal and informal. Formal groups are created by the organization itself and include functional groups, project groups, and committees. Informal groups are created by the employees themselves.

Five important characteristics of groups are roles, norms, status, cohesiveness, and group size. A role is an expected behavior. A norm is a rule of behavior that has been accepted as legitimate by members of a group. Status is the relative ranking that one individual in a group has in relation to the others. Cohesiveness is the closeness or personal attractiveness that exists between members of a group. Group size is the number of people in a group; this characteristic influences group satisfaction.

One important type of group in organizations is work teams. Teams have a strong group identity and share common goals. Self-directed work teams are a growing phenomenon. These teams get involved in a total job, often interacting with vendors and customers. The team organization changes the job of the supervisor from controller to coach and provides a number of benefits to the company, including improved quality, productivity, and service.

Working with groups and teams requires supervisors to have meeting skills. These skills include knowing how to plan and conduct a meeting. When planning meetings, the supervisors must answer three logistical questions: Who should be invited to the meeting? When should the meeting be held? Where should the meeting take place? Content should be carefully planned and topics circulated in an agenda. To conduct an effective meeting, the supervisor needs to have the skill to do five things: (1) put people at ease; (2) stick to the agenda; (3) encourage participation; (4) avoid personal agendas and problem behaviors from others; and (5) bring closure to the meeting.

REVIEW QUESTIONS

1. In your own words, what is a formal group? What is an informal group?

2. Describe the three types of problem solving meetings.

3. What is a role? What does a supervisor need to know about perceived, expected, and enacted roles? Explain.

4. In what way can role ambiguity and role conflict be problems for the supervisor? Explain.

5. What is meant by the term *norms?* How do norms influence group behavior?

6. What is meant by the term *status?* In what way are status incongrency and status discrepancy problems? What does the supervisor need to know about them? Explain.

7. What effect does group size have on group member satisfaction? Explain.

8. What are self-directed teams, and how do they benefit the organization?

9. How does the traditional supervisor's job differ when self-directed teams are in place?

10. Discuss the three major reasons for calling meetings.

11. How does a quality circle work? Why would a supervisor want to use one of these circles?

12. In what way do meetings help supervisors facilitate change? Be complete in your answer.

13. What are the logistical considerations of planning meetings? Identify and describe them.

14. To conduct effective meetings, the supervisor must have five skills. Identify and describe each.

KEY TERMS

Ad hoc committee. Body of people that has been formed for a particular purpose and that comes to an end when this objective is attained.

Agenda. Itemized list of topics to be covered during a meeting.

Brainstorming. Creative process of generating a large number of alternative solutions to a problem.

Cohesiveness. Closeness or personal attractiveness that exists between members of a group.

Decision-making meeting. Gathering at which decisions are made or programs for action are formulated.

Enacted role. Way in which people actually carry out their roles.

Expected role. Way others expect an individual to act.

Formal group. Social unit created by the organization itself.

Functional group. Social unit made up of individuals who work together on a regular basis.

Group. Social unit consisting of two or more interdependent, interactive individuals striving to attain common goals.

Group dynamics. Study of the way in which group members interact with each other.

Idea-generating meeting. Assembly of people designed to look at a problem from many different angles.

Informal group. Social unit created by the employees themselves.

Information-gathering meeting. Gatherings designed to provide a forum for obtaining more information.

Meeting. Formal gathering of personnel for a predetermined purpose.

Norms. Rules of behavior that have been accepted as legitimate by members of a group.

Perceived role. Way individuals think they ought to act.

Project group. Social unit consisting of individuals from different departments and areas brought together to pursue a common goal.

Quality circle. Group of workers and a supervisor who meet on company time to discuss ways in which they can be more productive or can improve product quality.

Role. Expected behavior.

Role ambiguity. Uncertainty regarding how to act.

Role conflict. Situation confronted by a person who must assume two roles when one is in conflict with the other.

Standing committee. Body of people that exists for an indefinite period of time.

Status. Relative ranking that one individual in a group has in relation to others.

Status discrepancy. Situation that exists when people do things that are not in accord with their relative ranking in the group.

Status incongruency. Condition that exists when there is a difference between supposed status and the way the person is treated.

ANSWERS TO SELF-ASSESSMENT QUIZ 12–1

1. False. Roles sometimes are dictated by the informal group, which brings pressure on the members to conform to these informal roles.

2. True. This is one of the major functions of group norms.

3. False. It is just the opposite; people of low intelligence are more likely to conform.

4. True. People with high status tend to be listened to and believed more readily than those with low status.

5. False. The individual is likely to lose status as a result of such action.

6. False. High cohesion does not mean that the group will work harder, only that the members have strong social ties.

7. True. High cohesion tends to increase all kinds of interaction among the group members.

8. False. The members are likely to communicate more with each other than will members of low cohesive groups, but high cohesion and high productivity are not directly related.

9. False. Just the opposite is true.

10. False. An ideal size is eight or less.

CASE 12–1
Margaret's Point of View

Things have not been going well at the Dandell Corporation. For over eighteen months there has been worker-management conflict. It all came to a head last week when the workers voted to unionize. The vote was overwhelmingly in favor of affiliating with the AFL-CIO. The move was not unexpected by management. When the company's board of directors voted to freeze wages and salaries this year in the hope of bringing the firm into the black for the first time in five years, this decision was more than the workers could stand. Most of the management team was convinced that the unionizing effort would win, and they were right.

Yesterday management called a meeting of its supervisory staff. The purpose of the meeting was to discuss the potential impact of unionization on work output and productivity. Senior-level management believes that this latest development may well result in the worst annual profit picture the firm has ever had. Margaret Sherman, one of the supervisors, does not agree with this projection. During the meeting she explained her reasoning.

"The workers organized for one single reason: economics. The union is going to have only one objective in mind: get across-the-board increases for all of its people. The only way that this can be ensured is if we make a profit. So it will be to the union's benefit to help us increase productivity. Far from finding the workers organized against us, I expect to find my people working harder than ever as members of a highly motivated work team. During the last fiscal quarter my group had the highest productivity of all. I attribute this mostly to high cohesion and morale among the members. This should continue to translate into bottom-line performance."

The manager running the meeting seemed somewhat surprised by these comments. When he regained his composure, he said, "I hope you're right." He then called on another supervisor. The latter said just the opposite of what Margaret did. After the meeting, Margaret gave a lot of thought to her point of view as well as to that of those supervisors who felt the opposite; she is still convinced that the unionizing effort will not cause any problems.

1. What role will group norms play as Margaret works to increase her group's productivity? Explain.

2. In regard to Margaret's statement, is she right or wrong? Defend your answer.

3. If you were advising Margaret on how to be a more effective supervisor, what would you tell her regarding her views on group norms and productivity? Explain.

CASE 12–2
The Unresponsive Group

When her company announced that it was going to computerize production quality information, Jackie Renseller was not sure this was a good idea. However, she was willing to go along with her boss, who encouraged her to "wait and see what type of information the computer people provide us before we say the approach is a bad one." Yesterday, Jackie got the first computer printouts. The data were presented in the form of tables and charts. It took Jackie a while to pore over them and interpret what was there, but once she understood the information, she realized that the printouts were extremely useful. In particular they highlighted areas where problems continually cropped up and identified some of the most common reasons for these problems.

Jackie was so impressed with the information that she decided to call a meeting of her people for the next day. In the interim Jackie prepared photocopies of the computer information. At the start of the meeting she announced the purpose of the get-together and then distributed the printouts to everyone in the group. Jackie then began to discuss the specific problems highlighted in the printout and to ask for suggestions regarding ways they could be handled. To her surprise the personnel did not have much to say. Most of them simply looked at the printouts and seemed to ignore her. A couple of people made some general comments about what might be done, but all in all the meeting was a failure. When the gathering broke up, Jackie decided that in the future she would try to make use of the printouts without a meeting. However, when she shared this decision with her boss, he disagreed. "Meetings are the best way of disseminating this information and deciding what to do as a result. Don't be so quick to give up on them."

1. What did Jackie do wrong in terms of getting everyone ready for the meeting? Explain.

2. Why did Jackie make this mistake? Why did she not spot it as soon as things started going poorly during the meeting?

3. Is Jackie's boss right? Should she call a meeting to discuss the next computer printout? If not, why not? If so, what should she do differently this time? Explain.

CHAPTER 13

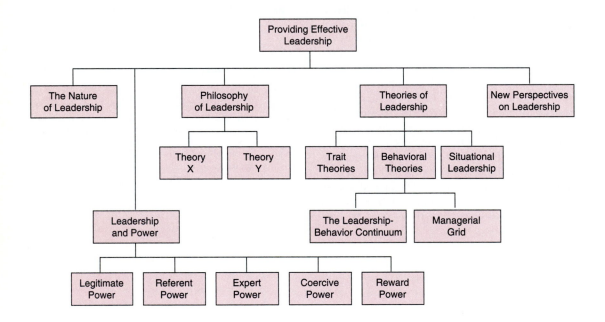

Providing Effective Leadership

"In today's competitive, fast-moving world, leadership cannot be an added premium a company hopes to obtain with every X number of management hires."*

CHAPTER OBJECTIVES

- ☐ Define the term *leadership*.
- ☐ Describe the five basic types of power held by supervisors.
- ☐ Compare and contrast Theory X assumptions with Theory Y assumptions.
- ☐ Examine trait theories of leadership.
- ☐ Identify and describe the five basic leader styles as presented by The Leadership Grid.
- ☐ Relate the value of situational leadership theories and discuss the way the supervisor can use them.
- ☐ Look at new trends in leadership theory with a focus on charismatic leadership.

---

*Leonard R. Sayles, *The Working Leader* (New York: The Free Press, 1993), 82.

Leadership is an influence process.

E very supervisor is a leader. Some have a large number of subordinates; others have a few. Yet all must be able to lead their group or they will fail to fill their role as effective supervisors. We begin our investigation of this critical area by examining the nature of leadership.

THE NATURE OF LEADERSHIP

Leadership has been defined in many different ways. Birnbrauer and Tyson saw it as "getting people to do what you want, when you want, the way you want it done . . . because they want to."[1] Hodgetts called it the "process of influencing people."[2] Certo saw it as "the process of directing the behavior of others toward the accomplishment of some objective."[3] Despite the various definitions, all agree that leadership is an influence process.

In too many instances, leadership has been thought to be synonymous with management. In actuality, some managers are also leaders; many are not. What is the difference between management and leadership? According to Bennis and Nanus,

> "Managers are people who do things right. Leaders are people who do the right things. Managers' activities consist of mastering routines. Leaders' activities consist of using vision and judgment."[4]

Figure 13–1 shows the overlapping roles of leaders and managers. Whereas managers spend their time planning, budgeting, organizing, staffing, and controlling—all activities needed to move the organization forward to accomplish existing goals—leaders spend their time creating new visions, aligning employees with the new vision, and then promoting inspiration and loyalty. Managers deal with the routine; leaders deal with change.[5]

A leader is a person who can gain the willing cooperation of followers in accomplishing organizational goals. Tom Peters, coauthor of *In Search of Excellence* and *A Passion for Excellence,* says that a leader is a "cheerleader, enthusiast, nurturer of champions, hero finder, wanderer, dramatist, coach, and facilitator."[6] Each of these is an important aspect of the leader's job.

---

[1]Herman Birnbrauer and Lynne A. Tyson, "Flexing the Muscles of Technical Leadership," *Training and Development Journal* (September 1984): 48.

[2]Richard M. Hodgetts, *Management: Theory, Process, and Practice,* 5th ed. (San Diego, Calif.: Harcourt Brace Jovanovich Publishers, 1990), 502.

[3]Samuel Certo, *Principles of Modern Management,* 5th ed. (Boston, Mass.: Allyn & Bacon, 1992), 415.

[4]Warren Bennis and Burt Nanus, *Leaders: The Strategies of Taking Charge.* Macmillan Executive Summary, Vol. 1, No. 4, June 1985, 2.

[5]Don Hellriegel, John W. Slocum, Jr. and Richard W. Woodman. *Organizational Behavior,* 6th ed. (St. Paul, Minn.: West Publishing Co., 1992), 384.

[6]Tom Peters and Nancy Austin, *A Passion for Excellence: The Leadership Difference* (New York: Random House, 1985), 265.

FIGURE 13-1

Roles of leaders and managers.

Source: Reprinted by permission from p. 385 of *Organizational Behavior,* 6th ed. by Don Hellriegel, John W. Slocum, Jr., and Richard W. Woodman; Copyright 1992 by West Publishing Co. All rights reserved.

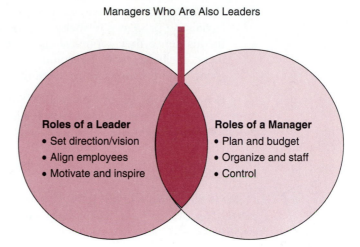

Managers Who Are Also Leaders

Roles of a Leader
- Set direction/vision
- Align employees
- Motivate and inspire

Roles of a Manager
- Plan and budget
- Organize and staff
- Control

1. *Cheerleader.* The leader or supervisor must often adopt the role of cheerleader, whose main task is to encourage the team to victory. The cheerleader loves the team with a passion and shows them a loyalty unsurpassed by anyone. As a cheerleader, the supervisor performs the vital job of building team spirit and camaraderie.

2. *Enthusiast.* As enthusiasts, leaders serve as models by their own enthusiasm for the job, the group goals, and the company.

3. *Nurturer of champions.* Leaders, as opposed to managers, are not afraid of stars in their group. The leader nurtures the innovator of new and unusual ideas, procedures, and products, and does everything possible to give that person the opportunity to explore these ideas.

4. *Hero finder.* The leader looks for heroes who can fire up enthusiasm in the rest of the group. The hero may be a long-standing employee with widely recognized expertise on the job, or the solver of a specific knotty problem of the moment. In either case, the leader pays homage to the hero and encourages others to follow his or her lead.

5. *Wanderer.* Leaders get out among their people and see firsthand what is going on. Good supervisors get to know their employees on a first-name basis. They become one of the team, readily available for employees to discuss ideas and problems.

6. *Dramatist.* The good leader builds up the sense of importance of the team's job. No matter how routine the work may be, effective supervisors let their staff know just where it fits into the goals of the organization.

7. *Coach.* An effective leader, like a coach, is always available to show the team how to do the job a little better. Coaches serve in a training and instructing capacity, and like cheerleaders, they also carefully build team spirit and camaraderie, while getting involved in the job at hand.

8.   *Facilitator.* Effective leaders or supervisors spend much of their time facilitating processes or making things easier for their team members. In this sense they represent the team's interests to upper management, facilitate conflict resolution between employees in the work group, and organize group meetings.

How does one get to be a leader? Supervisors exist because management creates the position. However, leaders need to complement this authority with a power base.

LEADERSHIP AND POWER

Power is the ability to exert influence over other people. All power has a power base. French and Raven suggested five bases: legitimate, referent, expert, coercive, and reward.[7]

Power is the ability to exert influence.

Legitimate Power

Legitimate power comes from the position that a person holds. It goes hand in hand with *authority,* which is the right to command. Legitimate power is vested in the supervisor by higher management, which has delegated at least part of its authority to the supervisor. However, this form of influence is not without its problems. For employees to accept a supervisor's legitimate authority and power, at least four conditions must be present. The employees must:

Legitimate power comes from the organizational position.

1.   understand the orders the supervisor gives to them,
2.   believe that all orders are consistent with the goals of the organization,
3.   believe that the orders are consistent with their own best interests, and
4.   be able to comply with the orders.[8]

Thus, even though employees clearly understand what their supervisor is asking them to do, if they do not find it compatible with the organization's purpose or their own best interests, they will balk at carrying out the order, thus diminishing the supervisor's actual power. Likewise, if employees lack physical or mental ability to perform the task, they will not carry out the order, or at least not to the satisfaction of the supervisor. In addition, a fifth criterion affects employee compliance, that is, the respect

---

[7]John R. P. French, Jr. and Bertram Raven, "The Bases of Social Power," in *Studies in Social Power,* ed. Dorwin Cartwright (Ann Arbor, Mich.: Institute for Social Research, 1959), 154–164.

[8]Chester Barnard, *The Functions of the Executive* (Cambridge, Mass.: Harvard University Press, 1938), 163.

employees have or lack for the supervisor. If supervisors have not earned the respect of colleagues and subordinates, their credibility or integrity will be questioned with a resulting loss of power.

Referent Power

Referent power is based on personality.

Referent power is based on personality and emotion. Supervisors have referent power if they are well-liked by employees and employees want supervisors to feel positively about them. Thus they will carry out the supervisor's directives in order to maintain the positive interpersonal relationship. Holders of referent power are often able to get people to do things without question—things they would never do for someone for whom they had no emotional loyalty. This loyalty can lead to positive or negative results, so the referent power holder must be very conscious of the influence that can be exerted over others and be sure not to abuse that influence.

Expert Power

Expert power is based on knowledge.

Expert power is founded on authority of knowledge. A supervisor holding expert power is recognized as an authority about the work being done. Employees respect the individual because he or she knows how to do the work and how to solve problems; most likely the supervisor often has been with the department for a long time and been promoted up through the ranks. At the same time, expert power may be the least stable power base.

> Of all the types of power, expert power is the one most difficult to retain because one's expertise may be surpassed by someone else's or the knowledge may become irrelevant. Nevertheless, because so many people in modern organizations rely upon knowledge as a source of power, including engineers, accountants, and other staff specialists, expert power continues to be nurtured and cultivated.[9]

Coercive Power

Coercive power is based on fear.

Coercive power, which is based on fear and the use of force, should be considered the least valid organizational power base in modern organizations. Supervisors use it to threaten to demote, terminate, or in other ways punish their employees. Although it may be effective in the short range to get employees to comply with immediate wishes, it is destructive to organizational morale and eventually builds resentment rather than loyalty among the work team.

---

[9]Richard M. Hodgetts and Donald F. Kuratko, *Management,* 3rd ed. (San Diego: Harcourt Brace Jovanovich, 1991), 456.

Reward Power

Reward power is based on the ability to give rewards.

Reward power is based on the ability to give employees things they want. These rewards can take numerous forms including bonuses, overtime opportunities, and/or choice assignments. Supervisors tend to have the most reward power at performance appraisal or merit raise time. Such power often ebbs and flows; therefore, it is usually not a stable power base.

Even if we know what power base(s) supervisors have, we still do not know how they will actually perform as leaders. We must also examine their philosophy of leadership, basic style of leadership, behavior, and the situations within which they function. In addition, we need to consider the often overlooked element of followership—that is, the characteristics of the subordinates.

PHILOSOPHY OF LEADERSHIP

In order to understand styles of leadership, we must examine the underlying philosophies that supervisors hold about people in general. There are two basic ways of perceiving employees. One philosophy assumes that employees are lazy and can be motivated only by money; the other credits them with creativity and an interest in challenging jobs. The former philosophy, *Theory X,* was the norm in the early years of this century. The scientific management theories held dominance. The latter philosophy, *Theory Y,* has become more accepted in recent years with the current emphasis on human resources. The differences between these two philosophies are particularly significant in terms of supervision because the way we perceive people, and our basic assumptions about them, influence our behavior toward them.

Theory X

Theory X assumptions

Theory X supervisors hold four basic assumptions about personnel.

1. People, by their very nature, do not like to work and will avoid it whenever possible.
2. They have virtually no ambition and will shun responsibility whenever they can; supervisors must use close direction to get them to do anything.
3. Security is primary on their list of needs.
4. To get employees to attain organizational objectives the supervisor must employ coercion, control, and threats of punishment.[10]

Supervisors who subscribe to Theory X do not make much use of two-way interaction. They tell their employees what has to be done and then

---

[10]Douglas McGregor, *The Human Side of Enterprise* (New York: McGraw-Hill Book Co., 1960), 33–34.

monitor performance to ensure that things go according to plan. Most of their downward communications are related to work assignments and work progress—that is, "here is what you are to do; here is when I need the work done by; here is how your performance on the job will be evaluated." If any upward communications are encouraged from subordinates, these too are work-related—that is, "here is a problem I am having in getting this work done; can you give more input regarding how to handle this problem; when I am finished with this particular step, what would you like me to do next?" The leader treats the subordinates as if they are unable to think and act on their own. In addition, if an employee makes a mistake, the leader tends to use the situation to punish the guilty employee and let this serve as an example to others. The leader believes that by letting subordinates know that mistakes will not be tolerated, he or she can eliminate their occurrence. The important thing is not to let any failures go unnoticed or unpunished. This logic fits right in with the leader's philosophy. This leader believes the workers have to be monitored closely; the minute they make a mistake, the leader says, "Aha, I told you so. Now I have to lower the boom."

> The use of punishment seems to be a logical method of solving the issue; either the workers do the job or management will get tough. However, the problem rests on the fact that management mistakes causes for effects, the result being a self-fulfilling prophecy. Believing punishment is a necessary tool for effective management, the company introduces it the minute the workers start offering resistance, with mental notes, "See, it's like we said. You have to get tough with these people if you want any performance." Yet it is management's fault that the workers are discontent in the first place.[11]

If Theory X supervisors make any attempt to motivate employees, they usually tie the attempt to money. Bonus plans, piece rate systems, and overtime opportunities are all "motivators" preferred by Theory X supervisors.

Theory Y

Theory Y supervisors also have certain preconceived assumptions about workers, but their concepts are quite different from those of their Theory X counterparts. In essence Theory Y assumptions are the following:

1. Work is as natural to people as resting or playing.
2. External control and threats of punishment are not the only ways to get people to work toward organizational objectives. If they are committed to objectives, personnel will exercise self-direction and self-control.

Theory Y assumptions

3. Commitment to objectives is a result of the rewards associated with their achievement.

---

[11]Hodgetts, *Management: Theory, Process, and Practice,* 473.

4. Under the proper conditions the average human being learns not only to accept but to seek responsibility.

5. The capacity to exercise a relatively high degree of imagination, ingenuity, and creativity in the solution of organizational problems is widely distributed throughout the population.

6. Under conditions of modern industrial life the intellectual potential of the average human being is only partially tapped.[12]

The Theory Y supervisor realizes that employees are important assets, who, if treated properly, will prove to be invaluable to the organization. The way in which the Theory Y leader interacts with the personnel is quite different from that of the Theory X leader. First, major attention is given to opening up two-way communication channels. The leader realizes that it is necessary to both get and give accurate information regarding operations. Second, the Theory Y leader works to create an environment in which management's trust and confidence in the subordinates is evident. Third, the individual strives to develop teamwork. This is done by (1) building effective communications to develop strong intragroup ties, and (2) serving as a linking pin between the group and higher-level management.

When attempting to motivate their employees, Theory Y supervisors look more to internal satisfiers such as recognition, opportunity to develop skills and interests, and increased responsibility. Before examining leadership styles, take Self-Assessment Quiz 13–1 to explore your own personal philosophy of management.

THEORIES OF LEADERSHIP

Many theories of leadership have been formulated to describe who leaders are and how they function. These theories generally can be put into three categories: trait, behavioral, and situational theories. Let's look at each of these groupings in turn, as well as some new perspectives on leadership.

Trait Theories

Trait theories seek common characteristics of successful leaders.

Trait theories search for common characteristics or traits that effective leaders share. More than 100 studies have pursued this goal, but very little conclusive evidence has been found that successful leaders share common traits. Some evidence has been found that at the middle and top levels of management, four traits seem to be shared by the majority of successful leaders: emotional maturity and a wide range of interests, higher than av-

---

[12]McGregor, *The Human Side of Enterprise*, 47–48.

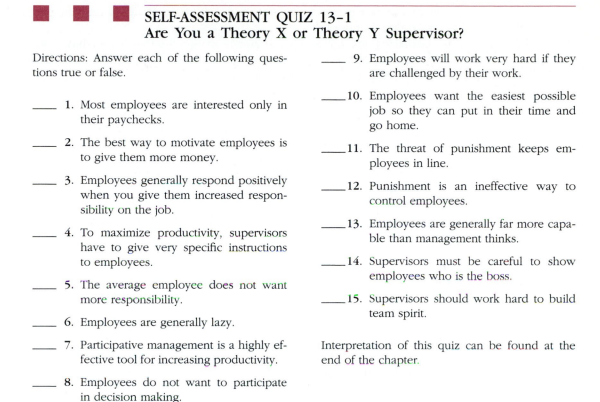

■ ■ ■ **SELF-ASSESSMENT QUIZ 13–1**
Are You a Theory X or Theory Y Supervisor?

Directions: Answer each of the following questions true or false.

_____ 1. Most employees are interested only in their paychecks.

_____ 2. The best way to motivate employees is to give them more money.

_____ 3. Employees generally respond positively when you give them increased responsibility on the job.

_____ 4. To maximize productivity, supervisors have to give very specific instructions to employees.

_____ 5. The average employee does not want more responsibility.

_____ 6. Employees are generally lazy.

_____ 7. Participative management is a highly effective tool for increasing productivity.

_____ 8. Employees do not want to participate in decision making.

_____ 9. Employees will work very hard if they are challenged by their work.

_____10. Employees want the easiest possible job so they can put in their time and go home.

_____11. The threat of punishment keeps employees in line.

_____12. Punishment is an ineffective way to control employees.

_____13. Employees are generally far more capable than management thinks.

_____14. Supervisors must be careful to show employees who is the boss.

_____15. Supervisors should work hard to build team spirit.

Interpretation of this quiz can be found at the end of the chapter.

■ ■ ■ **SUPERVISORY SKILLS**
Some Important Leadership Pointers

1. Remember that as a leader your job is to influence others. You have to assume the responsibility for this activity. This means encouraging, coaching, counseling, facilitating, and nurturing your employees in such a way that they get the work done and, if possible, have a good time doing it.

2. When you use power, always try to use positive power. The best examples are expert and referent power. Try not to use coercive power because it almost always results in hard feelings. Lead by example and influence rather than by force and threat.

3. Keep in mind that most people want to do a good job. Many of them, therefore, will respond better to a Theory Y than a Theory X approach. If you find someone who needs to be prodded or controlled, remember that this employee is more the exception than the rule. By using the right approach with this worker you are likely to change his or her behavior eventually. Don't lose faith in your employees. They will surprise you with their creativity and penchant for hard work.

erage intelligence, inner motivation and achievement drive, and an employee-centered outlook.[13]

Bernard Bass, a leading researcher in the field of leadership, concluded after reviewing many studies that there were some general characteristics that distinguish effective leaders.

> "The leader is characterized by a strong drive for responsibility in task completion, vigor and persistence in pursuit of goals, venturesomeness and originality in problem solving, drive to exercise initiative in social situations, self-confidence and sense of personal identity, willingness to accept the consequences of his or her decision and action, readiness to absorb interpersonal stress, willingness to tolerate frustrations and delay, ability to influence other people's behavior and the capacity to structure social interaction systems to the purpose at hand."[14]

Because of these disparate findings, most management scholars put little emphasis on trait theories and look instead to the more promising behavioral and situational approaches to studying leadership.

Behavioral Theories

Behavioral theories consider the question, how do leaders behave? Two models—the leadership-behavior continuum and Blake and Mouton's managerial grid—are representative of this approach.

The Leadership-Behavior Continuum.   In answer to the question, how do leaders behave?, most leaders can be classified into one of three groups: authoritarian, democratic, and laissez-faire.

Authoritarian leaders are believers in Theory X. They decide what is to be done and the way to do it and then tell their employees. *Democratic leaders* believe in Theory Y and allow their employees to enjoy much autonomy in decision making and implementation. *Laissez-faire leaders* basically withdraw from leadership and allow the group to do what it pleases. They do not want to be involved. This form of leadership is rarely evident at the supervisor level, because the nature of the job necessitates daily involvement with the workers.

Although the two dominant styles are authoritarian and democratic, these should not be seen as two absolute styles but rather as points on the opposite ends of the same continuum (see Figure 13–2). The styles on the far right of the continuum are usually a "pure" democratic participative style, whereas those on the left are associated with a "pure" authoritarian style. Where would you place yourself along this continuum?

There are three basic types of leaders.

---

[13]Don Hellriegel, John W. Slocum, Jr., Richard W. Woodman, *Organizational Behavior,* 6th ed. (St. Paul, Minn.: West Publishing Co., 1992), 390.

[14]Bernard M. Bass, *Bass and Stogill's Handbook of Leadership* (New York: Free Press, 1990), 87.

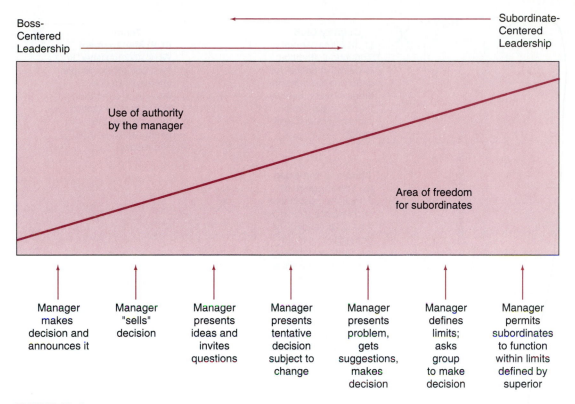

Boss-Centered Leadership

Subordinate-Centered Leadership

Use of authority by the manager

Area of freedom for subordinates

| Manager makes decision and announces it | Manager "sells" decision | Manager presents ideas and invites questions | Manager presents tentative decision subject to change | Manager presents problem, gets suggestions, makes decision | Manager defines limits; asks group to make decision | Manager permits subordinates to function within limits defined by superior |

FIGURE 13-2

Leadership-behavior continuum.

Source: Reprinted by permission of the *Harvard Business Review.* An exhibit from "How to Choose a Leadership Pattern" by Robert Tannenbaum and Warren H. Schmidt (May/June 1973). Copyright © 1973 by the President and Fellows of Harvard College; all rights reserved.

Which style along the continuum is the best style for supervisors? It is popularly believed today that democratic, or subordinate-centered, leadership is more effective than authoritative, or boss-centered, leadership.

The Leadership Grid.   Another popular way of looking at leadership is to assess whether supervisors are oriented toward the task or toward people. *Task-oriented managers* put the goals of the organization first and foremost. They do not engage in personal relationships with their employees and are interested in employee concerns and problems only in as much as such concerns and problems interfere with goal accomplishment. *People-oriented managers* believe that their primary responsibility is for the people who work for them. Only by maintaining good interpersonal relationships, they reason, can the work of the organization be accomplished.

The most popular theory concerning task versus people orientation is the Leadership (formally Managerial) Grid® model, developed by Blake

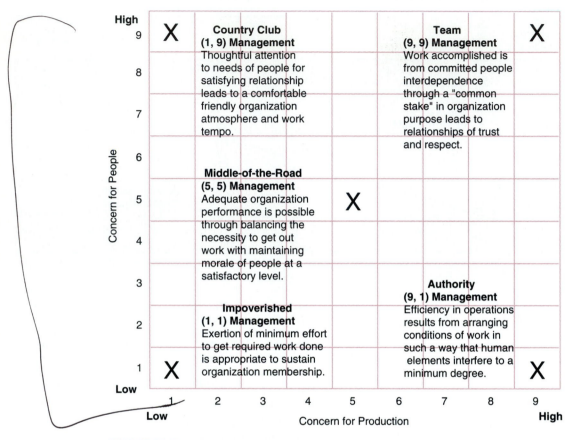

FIGURE 13-3

The Leadership Grid® Figure

Source: The Leadership Grid® Figure from *Leadership Dilemmas—Grid Solutions*, by Robert R. Blake and Anne Adams McCanse (formerly the Managerial Grid Figure by Robert R. Blake and Jane S. Mouton) Houston: Gulf Publishing Company, P. 29. Copyright© 1991, by Scientific Methods, Inc. Reproduced by permission of the owners.

and Mouton (1964), which examines the assumptions driving the behavior of managers. The Grid's nine-point scale is based on varying interaction levels of two basic concerns; concern for people and concern for production. The concern measures from low (1) to high (9). See Figure 13–3.

1. The *1,1 style manager* is often called "impoverished management." This style resembles the laissez-faire style mentioned earlier in the chapter. Such a manager does not show much interest in either people or production and pretty much lets the team do as they wish.

2. The *9,1 manager* is an autocratic Theory X supervisor. This person concentrates on task completion and downplays employee problems, conflicts, and concerns. For example, if conflict arises, the supervisor will quickly stamp it out as being unproductive.

Leadership Grid styles

3. The *1,9 manager* is sometimes called the "country club manager." This supervisor wants interpersonal relations to be smooth and therefore sees the managerial task as providing a harmonious, pleasant work setting. If this person can do this, according to this viewpoint, the work will take care of itself.

4. The *5,5 manager* shows a moderate concern for both people and task. This supervisor may be considered the "compromiser" or the "organization man"—sometimes favoring people concerns and other times task concerns, all in an effort to maintain the status quo. Employees do not know what to expect from this inconsistent behavior, although, on the positive side, such a supervisor is probably striving to be fair and balanced.

5. The *9,9 manager* is the one identified by Blake and Mouton as the most effective style. This supervisor has a high concern for task and a high concern for people. Quality and quantity are stressed through shared decision making, teamwork, and employee involvement. The style here is sometimes called "team management."

Situational Leadership

In addition, there are two more Leadership Grid styles not shown on Figure 13–3. The "9,9 Paternalistic" style promises reward for compliance and punishment for resistance. The "Opportunistic" manager uses any of the styles depending on "What's in it for me?" The manager chooses the style which will give him or her the most benefit. Some observers say that the behavioral theories of leadership are oversimplified and that, in fact, there is no one best way to lead. According to *situational theories,* leadership style should be determined by the situation or the environment surrounding the leader. One of the more popular of such theories is Situational Leadership, as developed by Hersey and Blanchard (see Figure 13–4). Notice that the theory is also based on a two-dimensional approach similar to The Leadership Grid. Once again task behavior (concern for work) is plotted on one axis, and relationship behavior (concern for people) is plotted on the other. The Hersey and Blanchard grid is divided into four basic quadrants, called *S*1, *S*2, *S*3, and *S*4 (the *S* stands for style).

> *Situation theories call for flexible leadership.*

*S*1 is characterized by high task behavior and low relationship. These supervisors are very explicit in their directions to employees but pay little attention to building the relationship between them. In their opinion employees need careful supervision and guidance.

*S*2 represents a leadership style of high task behavior and high relationship behavior. It is closely aligned with 9,9 behavior in the managerial grid. Such a supervisor gives much attention to both the task at hand and the healthy and happy interrelationships among employees and between the employees and the supervisor.

FIGURE 13-4
Situational leadership.

Source: Paul Hersey and Kenneth H. Blanchard, *Management of Organizational Behavior: Utilizing Human Resources,* 5th ed. (Englewood Cliffs, N.J.: Prentice-Hall, 1988), 171.

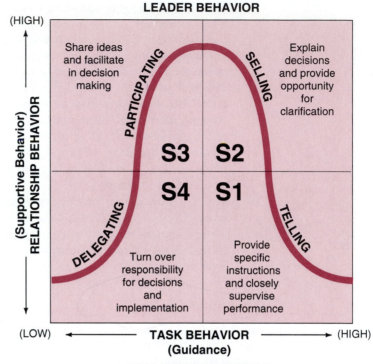

S3 refers to high relationship and low task behavior. Using this type of leadership style, the supervisor puts major emphasis on building sound interpersonal relations and relatively little emphasis on ensuring that the job is done.

S4 refers to low amounts of relationship or task behavior. Unlike Blake and Mouton, who suggested that this type of supervisor is laissez-faire and uninvolved, Hersey and Blanchard saw this supervisor as having delegated authority to capable employees, thus freezing the individual for more important tasks. See "The Quality Challenge: Leading by Delegating Authority" for insight as to how *S4* fits with TQM philosophy.

THE QUALITY CHALLENGE
Leading by Delegating Authority

There are a number of ways that supervisors can lead their groups toward higher quality output. Research shows that one of the most effective approaches is by developing authority. Why? Because most successful groups tend to be heavily empowered to get things done themselves, and they view suggestions or directions from the supervisor to be outside interference. How then do effective supervisors lead their groups? There are two steps that they take.

First, the supervisors remain available to answer questions and offer suggestions when asked. Rather than volunteering information, however, they remain in the background. When they fail to do this, they may even be reprimanded by the work group. For example, in one recent case there was a meeting of a supervisory group for the purpose of identifying a problem in the customer service department and discussing possible solutions. The supervisor of

the group, thinking that he could be helpful, attended the meeting. The worker who was conducting the session began by stating, "Here is the first thing that needs to be done." The individual then turned to the blackboard and wrote, "All supervisors are to leave the room." When the supervisor asked the individual if this statement referred to him, he was told that it did. Once the manager left, the work group began its analysis of the problem.

Second, supervisors play close attention to the results of worker efforts and continually offer praise and encouragement. Simply put, supervisors let their people focus on the work to be done, while they try to improve the work environment in which this work is carried out. In so doing, they reinforce the contingency leadership concepts that have been offered by such authorities as Hersey and Blanchard—lead people based on their level of readiness.

Hersey and Blanchard described the four quadrants as follows:

Telling (S1)—Provide specific instructions and closely supervise performance.
Selling (S2)—Explain decisions and provide opportunity for clarification.
Participating (S3)—Share ideas and facilitate in making decisions.
Delegating (S4)—Turn over responsibility for decisions and implementation.[15]

The *R1* to *R4* on the bottom of Figure 13–4 is a critical dimension of the Hersey and Blanchard model; it is the means to determine the appropriate leadership style. *R,* which stands for "readiness," is composed of a person's (a) ability to do the job, and (b) willingness to do a job. If the readiness level is low, a line drawn up to the grid will show that the S1 leadership style ("telling") is the most appropriate method of supervision. In a similar fashion each maturity level is correlated with a particular management style. This is the essential difference between The Leadership Grid and Hersey and Blanchard's Situational Leadership theory. Although Blake and Mouton feel that the 9,9 style of leadership is always best, Hersey and Blanchard believed there is no one best style because the appropriate

Maturity is an important situational dimension.

---

[15]Paul Hersey and Ken Blanchard, *Management of Organizational Behavior: Utilizing Human Resources,* 5th ed. (Englewood Cliffs, N.J.: Prentice-Hall, 1988), 177–179.

SUPERVISORY SKILLS
Choosing an Effective Style

1. Examine your own leadership style. Are you a task-oriented or people-oriented person? Whatever your answer, do you also have some orientation to the other style—that is, if you are task-oriented, are you also somewhat people-oriented? Your answer will give you some insights to the way in which you attempt to influence your personnel.

2. Identify where you are on The Leadership Grid. Stay with the five styles described in this section. Working with your answer to number one, refine your response by choosing the degree of work and people

orientation that you use. Your final answer may not be right. After all, it is a result of your own self-perception. However, you can get feedback on this perception by talking to your personnel and your boss and modifying your views of your leadership style.

3. Remember that effective leadership is contingency based. The best style will depend on the situation. Sometimes you are best off using a 5,5 style, whereas other times a 9,9 or 9,1 or 1,9 is best. Keep this in mind as you try to match your style to the situation.

---

style depends on the employees. Implicit in this belief is the premise that supervisors are able to move back and forth flexibly from one leadership style to another depending on the readiness of their employees.

New Perspectives on Leadership

This chapter began with a list of leader roles developed by Tom Peters and Nancy Austin. Several of these roles, namely coach and facilitator, have become widely accepted descriptors of effective leadership in a TQM environment. Leaders today spend a large percentage of their time energizing the employees and getting people excited about their job and their goals. With the increasing use of self-directed teams, the traditional directive role of the leader is being replaced by these motivational roles. One current area of study in keeping with the changing nature of leadership is charismatic leadership theory.

Charismatic Leadership Theory. Earlier in this chapter, we discussed French and Raven's model of power bases. *Charismatic leaders* rely heavily on referent power to "fire up the troops." According to one expert, "charismatic leaders are individuals who lead by virtue of their ability to inspire devotion and extraordinary effort from their followers."[16]

To better understand what charismatic leaders do differently than other leaders, see Table 13–1, which lists behavioral components of charismatic as compared to noncharismatic leaders.

---

[16]Richard M. Hodgetts, *Organizational Behavior: Theory and Practice* (New York: Macmillan Publishing Co, 1991), 233.

TABLE 13–1

Behavioral components of charismatic and noncharismatic leaders

	Noncharismatic Leader	*Charismatic Leader*
Relation to Status Quo	Essentially agrees with status quo and strives to maintain it	Essentially opposed to status quo and strives to change it
Future Goal	Goal not too discrepant from status quo	Idealized vision which is highly discrepant from status quo
Likableness	Shared perspective makes him/her likable	Shared perspective and idealized vision makes him/her a likable and honorable hero worthy of identification and imitation
Trustworthiness	Disinterested advocacy in persuasion attempts	Disinterested advocacy by incurring great personal risk and cost
Expertise	Expert in using available means to achieve goals within the framework of the existing order	Expert in using unconventional means to transcend the existing order
Behavior	Conventional, conforming to existing norms	Unconventional or counternormative
Environmental Sensitivity	Low need for environmental sensitivity to maintain status quo	High need for environmental sensitivity for changing the status quo
Articulation	Weak articulation of goals and motivation to lead	Strong articulation of future vision and motivation to lead
Power Base	Position power and personal power (based on reward, expertise, and liking for a friend who is a similar other)	Personal power (based on expertise, respect, and admiration for a unique hero)
Leader-Follower	Egalitarian, consensus seeking, or directive Nudges or orders people to share his/her views	Elitist, entrepreneur, and exemplary Transforms people to share the radical changes advocated

Source: Jay A. Conger and Rabindra N. Kanungo, "Toward a Behavioral Theory of Charismatic Leadership in Organizational Settings," *Academy of Management Review*, (October 1987): 641.

A study by Atwater, Penn, and Rucker showed that charismatic leaders were more dynamic, inspiring, outgoing, sociable, insightful, and enterprising[17] because of their ability to inspire others. Charismatic leaders are also called *transformational* leaders. Transformational leaders motivate employees by engaging in three types of behavior[18]:

1.   Help employees realize the need for change and for revitalizing the organization.
2.   Create a new vision and gain worker commitment to that vision.
3.   Institutionalize the change by creating new technical and political support networks.

SUMMARY

Leadership is the process of influencing people to direct their efforts to the attainment of some particular goal(s). When exercising this influence, the leader often uses power.

Power is the ability to exert influence over people. The five basic types of power are legitimate, referent, expert, coercive, and reward.

To understand styles of leadership, it is necessary to examine the underlying philosophies of supervisors. The two basic philosophies are Theory X and Theory Y. Theory X managers believe that workers are lazy, have no ambition, and want security above all else; to get employees to do things, such managers expect they'll have to use fear, coercion, and threats of punishment. Theory Y managers believe that work is as natural as resting or playing, they see commitment to objectives as a result of the rewards associated with their attainment,

and they think most people are much more creative than their jobs require.

There are three categories of leadership theories: trait, behavioral, and situational. Trait theories seek common characteristics of successful leaders and have been largely inconclusive. The behavioral approach describes how leaders act. Descriptive models representing autocratic, democratic, and laissez-faire leaders are examples. Another behavioral approach is The Leadership Grid with its focus on five basic leadership styles. The situational approach holds that any type of leadership style can be effective depending on the situation. Sometimes supervisors should be task-oriented; sometimes they should be people-oriented; still other times a combination of the two is required.

New perspectives on leadership were discussed, including charismatic leadership theory.

---

[17]Leanne Atwater, Robert Penn, and Linda Rucker. "Personal Qualities of Charismatic Leaders," *Leadership and Organization Development Journal* (Vol. 12, Issue 2, 1991): 9.

[18]Hellriegel, Slocum, and Woodman, 415–416.

REVIEW QUESTIONS

1. In your own words, what is meant by the term *leadership?* Are all managers leaders? Explain.

2. What is meant by the term *power?* Does a leader need power? Explain.

3. Where do the following types of power come from: legitimate, referent, expert, coercive, reward? In your answer be sure to describe each type.

4. How does a Theory X supervisor view subordinates? What assumptions does the individual hold regarding these people? Explain.

5. How does a Theory Y supervisor view subordinates? What assumptions does the individual hold regarding these people? Explain.

6. How do each of the following leaders behave: authoritarian, democratic, laissez-faire? In your answer be sure to describe each.

7. How do each of the following supervisors go about leading their people: 1,1 manager; 9,1 manager; 5,5 manager; 9,9 manager; 1,9 manager?

8. How can the Hersey and Blanchard situational leadership theory help supervisors do a better job? In your answer be sure to describe the theory and provide an example of the manner in which it could be used.

9. What is a charismatic leader? How do charismatic leaders differ from non-charismatic leaders?

KEY TERMS

Authoritarian leader. Theory X advocate whose major interest is in controlling the workers and the workplace.

Authority. Right to command.

Charismatic leader. Dynamic leader who uses referent power to inspire followers.

Coercive power. Power based on fear.

Democratic leader. Theory Y advocate who allows employees a great deal of autonomy in decision making and implementation.

Expert power. Power based on knowledge.

5,5 manager. Individual with a moderate concern for both the people and the work.

Laissez-faire leader. Individual who withdraws from leadership and allows the group to do as it pleases.

Leadership. Process of influencing people.

Legitimate power. Power vested in the organizational position.

9,1 manager. Individual with a high concern for work and low concern for people.

9,9 manager. Individual with a high concern for both the people and the work.

1,1 manager. Individual with a low concern for the people and the work.

1,9 manager. Individual with a high concern for people and low concern for work.

People-oriented manager. Individual who believes that by maintaining good interpersonal relationships he or she also can accomplish organizational work.

Power. Ability to exert influence.

Referent power. Power based on personality and personal liking.

Reward power. Power based on the ability to give employees things they want.

Situational theory. Leadership theory based on the belief that the best leadership style will depend on the situation.

Task-oriented manager. Individual who puts the goals of the organization ahead of everything else.

Theory X. Set of managerial assumptions about employees, including workers are lazy, they have no ambition, they want se-curity above all else, and they do things only when prompted by fear, coercion, and threats of punishment.

Theory Y. Set of managerial assumptions about employees, including work is as natur-al as resting or playing, commitment to objec-tives is a result of the rewards associated with their attainment, and most people are much more creative than their jobs require.

ANSWERS TO SELF-ASSESSMENT QUIZ 13–1

Answers can be interpreted to be support-ive of the Theory X or Theory Y philoso-phies of management. Tally your score and note which philosophy is stronger for you. Does this seem consistent with how you think about leadership?

	Theory X	Theory Y		Theory X	Theory Y
1.	True	False	9.	False	True
2.	True	False	10.	True	False
3.	False	True	11.	True	False
4.	True	False	12.	False	True
5.	True	False	13.	False	True
6.	True	False	14.	True	False
7.	False	True	15.	False	True
8.	True	False			

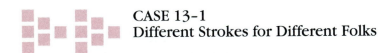

CASE 13–1
Different Strokes for Different Folks

Every year at the Friller Corporation awards are given for outstanding performance. This year two supervisors received $1000 gift certificates for having the highest productivity increases. Janet Baer, who has been a supervisor for six years, achieved an increase of 19 percent. This is particularly commendable because over the last five years, Janet's work group has increased its productivity every year. In fact, since she took over, productivity has risen a total of 113 per-cent. The other supervisor, Karl Madden, is new with the company and in his first year as a su-pervisor. He took over a group that had very poor productivity and managed to get an in-crease of 17.5 percent.

In addition to the awards, management also makes it a practice to interview the workers as a way of determining why these increases oc-curred. "If we find something that the supervisor is doing that others are not," explained the head of production, "we can pass this information along to the others to see if it has any practical value." A summary of the worker comments this year was the following:

Janet Baer
We like the way Janet works closely with us and helps us out if we get into trouble. Also, because she has mastered every job in the unit, she can handle just about every problem. We identify with her and like the way she tries to motivate us with praise and encouragement.

Karl Madden

Karl is a no-nonsense guy. If you don't get the work done, you're out. Our 25 percent turnover this year has really helped our productivity because we've managed to get rid of a lot of deadwood. Karl seems to be more interested in getting the work done than anything else. He probably is not on a personal basis with more than one or two people in the unit. However, you can't fault his performance. He rewards those who do things well and punishes those who do not.

1. In terms of Theory X and Theory Y, how would you describe Janet and Karl? Be complete in your answer.

2. What type of power does Janet use in getting things done? What type does Karl use? Explain.

3. Both use different leadership styles, yet both are effective. How do you account for this? In your answer be sure to address the area of situational leadership.

CASE 13–2
Richie's Style

During its first five years of operation the S. B. Montein Company, an insurance company, recruited sales and office personnel from outside; as openings occurred, at the supervisory level, the company moved people up. Over the last six months, however, the company has been growing so fast that this promotion-from-within policy is proving unworkable. The number of new hires is increasing faster than the company can train and develop new supervisors. For this reason, the company has begun hiring first-line managers from outside.

One of its new supervisors is Richie Wartack. Richie has never worked for an insurance company like Montein. His experience is in the retail business. Richie was a first-line manager for one of the most successful retailers in the region. His ratings were extremely good, and on one of his quarterly performance appraisals his boss wrote, "He keeps close control of operations, knows everything that is going on, and can be relied on to get the work done on time."

Richie started working for Montein three months ago. Since then there has been a 15 percent turnover in his department and the backlog of work has increased from two to eighteen days. Richie's boss was unaware of the situation until earlier this week, when he received a report from a management audit group who had been investigating work procedures in the company for the purpose of recommending more ef-

ficient measures. Before confronting Richie with the report, the boss decided to talk to the head of the personnel department to see if he could get some feedback regarding why so many people are leaving Richie's department. Here is what the head of the department told him:

The people who have transferred out of Richie's department or have left the firm all paint the same picture of him. He is a hard taskmaster. He demands that all employees be on time for work, get their work finished on time, and not goof off. The people who have left the department in the last few weeks tell us that things are getting tougher. I would imagine the reason for this is that Richie is trying to get everyone to work faster to make up the slack for those who are leaving. We have been having trouble hiring for his department, and at the present time he is badly understaffed.

1. Based on your reading of the case, what type of supervisor is Richie? Use The Leadership Grid to describe him.

2. Why is Richie using this style? Why doesn't he opt for a different approach because it must be evident that his current style is not working? Defend your answer.

3. If you were advising Richie, what would you recommend? Be complete in your answer.

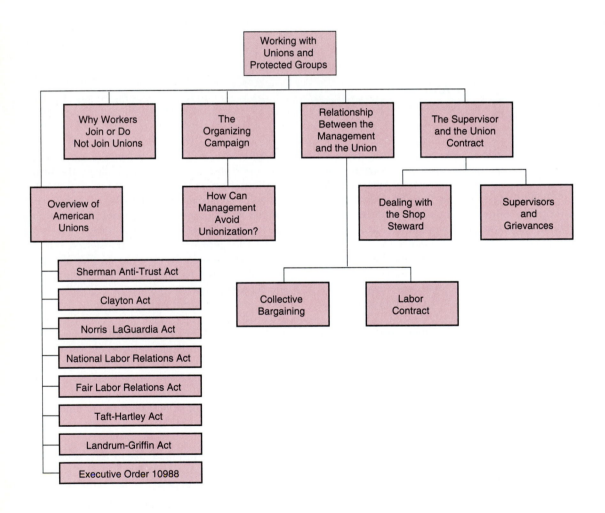

CHAPTER 14

Working with Unions and Protected Groups

- Why Workers Join or Do Not Join Unions
  - Overview of American Unions
    - Sherman Anti-Trust Act
    - Clayton Act
    - Norris LaGuardia Act
    - National Labor Relations Act
    - Fair Labor Relations Act
    - Taft-Hartley Act
    - Landrum-Griffin Act
    - Executive Order 10988
- The Organizing Campaign
  - How Can Management Avoid Unionization?
- Relationship Between the Management and the Union
  - Collective Bargaining
  - Labor Contract
- The Supervisor and the Union Contract
  - Dealing with the Shop Steward
  - Supervisors and Grievances

Working with Unions and Protected Groups

"It is not surprising that the way a member views his/her supervisor has the greatest influence on how that member perceives the relationship in general."*

CHAPTER OBJECTIVES

☐ Explore the history of the labor movement from the late 1800s to today.

☐ Identify and describe some of the key labor legislation with which supervisors should be familiar.

☐ Define the term *collective bargaining* and discuss the role of the labor contract in establishing supervisor-worker relationships.

☐ Examine ways in which management can avoid unionization.

☐ Discuss the role of the shop steward in labor-management relations.

☐ Understand the importance of an effective grievance procedure.

---

*Paul F. Clark, "Determinants of the Quality of Union-Management Relations: An Exploratory Study of Union Member Perceptions," *Journal of Collective Negotiation* (Vol. 18, Issue 2, 1989): 111.

Supervisors face many people problems. One of the most important is dealing with unions, as it requires that the supervisor understand and fulfill sensitive legal responsibilities. Before reading on, however, see how much you currently know about dealing with unions and protected groups by taking Self-Assessment Quiz 14–1.

OVERVIEW OF AMERICAN UNIONS

Modern unions date back to the late 1800s.

Unions have a long history in the United States. In colonial times, they existed as fraternal organizations that provided aid to their members. Today, unions are much more formal; most are affiliated with the AFL–CIO (American Federation of Labor–Congress of Industrial Organizations). As we now know them, unions began to gather strength in the late 1800s with the rapid growth of industrialism. This rising power of unions showed that employees felt they could and should receive more economic benefits from the company than those readily offered to them. The three national labor organizations that emerged in the second half of the nineteenth century were the National Labor Union (NLU), the Knights of Labor, and the AFL.

The National Labor Union was founded in Baltimore in 1966. Their interests focused on reducing the workday, establishment of a federal department of labor, reform of currency and banking laws, and the limitation of immigrants into the country. The latter was a particularly sensitive issue of the day, as union members worried about losing their jobs to immigrants. With the death of their leader, William Sylvis, and the union's un-

■ ■ ■ **SELF-ASSESSMENT QUIZ 14–1**
Working with Unions and Protected Groups

Directions: Answer each of the following questions true or false.

_____ 1. The rights of workers to organize are guaranteed by law.

_____ 2. Companies are free to do everything they can to dissuade employees from joining a union.

_____ 3. Supervisors are rarely involved with union officials.

_____ 4. Union contracts deal almost exclusively with wage and hour issues.

_____ 5. Supervisors can do very little to avoid union grievances.

_____ 6. Equal opportunity legislation covers only hiring practices.

_____ 7. By 1985, blacks and whites were making approximately the same salaries.

_____ 8. Although women are more numerous in the work force, they are still found predominantly in low-paying jobs.

_____ 9. Many companies have affirmative action programs for disabled workers.

_____10. The next generation of protected employees will be seeking upper-level jobs and higher-paid positions.

Answers can be found at the end of the chapter.

fortunate alignment with the Greenback party, the NLU was largely defunct by the mid 1870s.[1]

In 1869, the Knights of Labor was organized in Philadelphia as part labor union and part fraternal lodge. Workers were organized by city and across crafts, and by 1886, the Knights of Labor were able to boast 700,000 members. A schism between moderate leadership who counselled patience and a long-term strategy resisting strikes and an increasingly militant membership, along with their role in the Haymarket Riot in Chicago in 1886 that resulted in eight police and four workers being killed, led to a rapid decline in Knights of Labor membership.[2]

By the time Knights of Labor numbers had fallen to 75,000 in 1893, the American Federation of Labor had already been born. In 1886, Samuel Gompers gathered craft unions together and formed the AFL. Gompers laid a straight-forward strategy focusing on the issues of hours, wages, benefits, and working conditions. These were to be the issues that galvanized and motivated the labor movement for years to come. From the beginning, the AFL was decentralized leaving most authority to the individual craft unions who in turn depended on the AFL to settle disputes among them. Unlike earlier unions, the AFL was almost exclusively made up of skilled workers. It represented its members by negotiating formal contracts of working conditions with employers. These early days of the AFL built the foundation for the labor movement of the twentieth century.

> Gompers and other early leaders, such as Adolph Strasser, cemented the base on which the American trade union movement stood. Their approach accepted the system as it existed and worked within it. They were primarily concerned with improving the lot of the members they represented. This approach is basically retained in the present agency role taken by unions in representation.[3]

In the early 1900s, the concentration on economic benefits continued. You will recall from Chapter 1 that the early scientific management factory system did little to make employees feel important. Money was the main incentive and the piece rate system made many feel they had to work too hard to earn their money. The unions rallied against scientific management ideas and preached strength through numbers.

Nonetheless, it was not until 1935 that an organization for industrial unions as opposed to craft unions was formed. A group of disgruntled AFL members under the leadership of John L. Lewis of the United Mine Workers (UMW) bolted the national convention to form the Committee for Industrial Organization (CIO). The steel workers and auto workers were

The AFL was formed in 1886. [handwritten margin note]

CRAFT UNION [handwritten margin note]

---

[1] John A. Fossum, *Labor Relations: Development, Structure, Process,* 5th ed. (Homewood, Ill.: Business One Irwin, 1992), 27.

[2] David A. DeCenzo and Stephen P. Robbins, *Human Resource Management: Concepts and Practices,* 4th ed. (New York: John Wiley & Sons, Inc., 1994), 579.

[3] Fossum, 30.

early organizing targets of the CIO. By 1937, the CIO group of unions had a membership of 3.7 million, compared to the AFL membership of 300,000.[4] It was not until 1955 that a reunited AFL–CIO under George Meany realized that a merger of these two giants would lead to more power for all of organized labor.[5] The resulting AFL–CIO, headquartered in Washington, D.C., is a federation of national unions that offers a number of benefits[6]:

The AFL and CIO merged in 1955.

1.   Protection from one union raiding another union's membership.
2.   National lobbying efforts.
3.   National strategies to improve the overall image of labor.
4.   Resolution of disputes among members according to procedures and standards of the AFL–CIO.
5.   Political education through the Committee on Political Education.

The AFL–CIO does not engage in collective bargaining; that duty is left to the member national unions.

Union membership in traditional unions is falling.

Union membership grew dramatically during the 1900s, especially during the 1935–1945 decade. However, this growth has leveled off in recent years. By 1992, approximately 16 percent of all workers were unionized. Looking at the private versus public sector, however, statistics show that whereas only 12.1 percent of the private sector is unionized, a full 36.5 percent of the public sector is unionized.[7] Unionization in industrial arenas is declining while white collar unions and government unions are on the rise. Organizations such as hospitals, which were traditionally resistant to unions, are now facing union elections and contractual obligations. In 1990, for example, unions won elections at seventy-one hospitals across the country.[8]

Public sentiment has swung back and forth many times from favor to disfavor regarding unions. This pendulum effect can be seen in the plethora of laws passed to regulate and to police unions. Table 14–1 briefly describes the most influential legislation affecting unions.

The Sherman Anti-Trust Act of 1890

The Sherman Anti-Trust Act forbade restraint of trade.

The purpose of the Sherman Anti-Trust Act, passed in 1890, was to forbid the elimination of trade by monopolistic practices. It was never aimed at unions, but organized labor soon was seen as a trust that limited competition, to be dealt with as any other monopoly, including being the target of court-imposed injunctions. Employers were able to use the Sherman Anti-

---

[4]Fossum, 44.

[5]Fossum, 58.

[6]William P. Anthony, Pamela L. Perrewe, and K. Michele Kacmar, *Strategic Human Resource Management* (Fort Worth, Tex.: Harcourt, Brace, Jovanovich College Publishers, 1993), 596.

[7]DeCenzo and Robbins, 600.

[8]Matthew Goodfellow, "Study Shows Ways to Win, Avoid Union Elections," *Healthcare Financial Management* (September 1991): 48.

TABLE 14–1

Key labor legislation

1890   *Sherman Anti-Trust Act*. Prohibited businesses from restraining trade. An extension to cover unions effectively restricted union growth.

1914   *Clayton Act*. At first thought to be pro-union because it removed unions from Sherman Act. Later interpreted unions as being in "restraint of trade" if engaged in a strike. Allowed yellow-dog contracts (employees agree not to join unions) and injunctions to restrict union growth.

1932   *Norris La Guardia Act*. Outlawed yellow-dog contracts. Gave workers the right to organize and bargain. Did not make bargaining mandatory for management.

1935   *National Labor Relations Act (Wagner Act)*. Management must not interfere with workers' legal right to join unions and must bargain in good faith with elected unions. Created the National Labor Relations Board to administer elections and hear unfair labor practice cases.

1938   *Fair Labor Standards Act*. Established a minimum wage for a major portion of the labor force as well as time and one half pay for hours worked in excess of 40 hours per week.*

1947   *Taft-Hartley Act*. Placed restrictions on unions by declaring the closed shop (company can only hire union workers) illegal and required sixty-day notice before strikes. Federal government given power of injunction over strikes endangering the national interest.

1959   *Landrum-Griffin Act*. Regulated internal affairs of unions by requiring disclosure of bylaws and financial records. Protected individual rights of union members such as rights to vote, attend meetings, and sue the union.

1962   *Executive Order 10988*. Allowed federal employees to join unions, but prohibited strikes (became part of public law under the 1978 Civil Service Reform Act).

*Employees not covered by this act are called "exempt" employees. Most frequently, these are professional, administrative, and executive employees who work at a set salary regardless of the hours on the job. Employees who are covered by the FLSA are called "non-exempts."

Trust Act when unions began organizing campaigns; these unions were seen as being guilty of "restraint of trade."[9]

The Clayton Act of 1914

The Clayton Act was first thought to be pro-union, because it limited the use of injunctions against unions. The courts, however, refused to abide by the spirit of the law and continued to use the Sherman Anti-Trust Act against

[9]DeCenzo and Robbins, 584.

unions, especially if they were engaged in a strike. The Clayton Act also upheld the right of companies to invoke yellow-dog contracts, which required
employees to swear they were not nor would they be union members.

Norris La Guardia Act of 1932

Also called the Anti-Injunction Act, the Norris La Guardia Act reflected the
changed thinking of the American public toward unions that was a natural
outgrowth of the hard times of the Depression. Yellow-dog contracts were
disallowed, and court injunctions against union activities were severely
limited.

National Labor Relations Act of 1935

The National Labor Relations Act, also called the Wagner Act, is considered the most famous piece of pro-labor legislation. This act guaranteed
the workers' right to join unions and to bargain collectively with their own
designated representative. Employers were forbidden to interfere with organizing attempts, to refuse to bargain collectively, or to discriminate in
any way against union members. The National Labor Relations Board
(NLRB) was created to administer the law, to oversee union elections, and
to hear cases of unfair labor practices. The NLRB has in recent years been
somewhat of a political pawn.

The Wagner Act cre-
ated the N.L.R.B.

> ". . . The NLRB has become something of a political tool in that presidents
> have filled board vacancies with individuals of their political persuasion. By
> the start of President Reagan's second term, for example, many unions were
> convinced that the board was turning antiunion. Led by a conservative chair-
> person, it made a number of decisions that unions felt clearly reversed legal
> precedents and favored employers."[10]

Fair Labor Standards Act of 1938

The Fair Labor Standards Act is the most significant law affecting compensation issues. This important legislation regulates minimum wage for all companies involved in interstate commerce as well as overtime pay requirements
and child labor standards. Employees not covered by this act are called exempt and are most frequently professional, administrative, or executive employees who work at a set salary regardless of how many hours a week they
put in on the job. Employees covered by this law are called nonexempt.

Taft-Harley Hartley Act of 1947

By 1947, the pendulum had swung back toward the anti-union advocates,
and Congress passed the Taft-Hartley Act (also called the Labor Management Relations Act) over the veto of President Harry Truman. Taft-Hartley
placed restrictions on unions, including the abolishment of *closed shops,*

---

[10]Richard M. Hodgetts and K. Galen Kroeck, *Personnel and Human Resource Management*
(Ft. Worth, Tex.: The Dryden Press, 1992), 487.

the agreement that all employees must be union members when they are hired. Employees were thus guaranteed the freedom to choose to not join a union as well as the freedom to join a union. The government was again given the right to issue an injunction against a strike that is seen to be dangerous to the national interest. Taft-Hartley also gave the states the right to establish *right-to-work laws*, which prohibit union shop arrangements. Slightly different from the closed shop, the *union shop* requires that all employees join the union within a specified number of days of becoming employed by the company. Figure 14–1 shows the twenty-one right-to-work states, which are primarily located in the South and the West. Compulsory union membership is not allowed in these states.

Taft-Hartley was mainly seen as anti-labor legislation.

Right-to-work laws make it illegal to require employees to join the union.

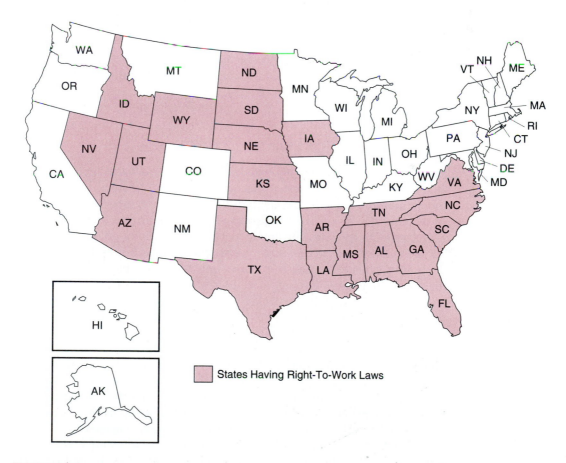

FIGURE 14–1
Right-to-work states.
Source: Figure from Business, 2nd ed. by Fred Luthans and Richard M. Hodgetts, copyright 1992 by the Dryden Press, Reproduced by Permission of the publisher.

Landrum-Griffin Act of 1959

The late 1950s saw Congressional investigations into improper union activities. Teamster President Dave Beck was reputed to have used union funds for his own purposes: more seriously, the Teamsters were felt to be connected with organized crime. Public sentiment began to wonder if all of labor was corrupt. The Landrum-Griffin Act, also called the Labor-Management Reporting and Disclosure Act, spoke to this concern. The Act opened up the internal workings of unions to scrutiny, requiring periodic financial reports. Individual union members rights were protected in the areas of voting, membership, attending meetings, and bringing legal suit against the union.

Executive Order 10988 of 1962

Enacted under President John F. Kennedy, Executive Order 10988 gave federal employees the right to form unions. It allowed collective bargaining on a restricted list of issues, excluding compensation. Strikes were not allowed. This was a landmark executive order and led to others that furthered the rights of government employees. In particular, Executive Order 11491, enacted under President Richard Nixon, further extended collective bargaining rights to federal employees and created the Federal Labor Relations Council to hear grievances about decisions made by agency heads.

Executive order 10988 allowed unions for federal employees.

WHY WORKERS JOIN OR DO NOT JOIN UNIONS

We have seen how union influence has increased and waned in the past 100 years. We have also suggested that white collar professions are becoming more unionized while blue collar industries lose union members. Regardless of whether the supervisor works in the public or private sector, however, they should understand why employees decide to join or not join the union. Table 14–2 lists some of the most important reasons on both sides.

Alert supervisors will see that people still join unions for traditional reasons such as hoping to get more equitable treatment from the company and a larger "share of the pie." Union membership gives many employees a greater feeling of security or a belief that someone (the union) will champion their cause in times of trouble. They believe that in the presence of union membership employee-management relations will be governed by widely accepted and legally binding rules and regulations that their representatives help formulate. Perhaps they believe that, in a representative democracy such as ours, it is only logical that unions have achieved their present importance. In addition to these benefits, some large unions offer their own loan programs, health insurance, and social activities.

Employees join unions for a "bigger piece of the pie."

Employees decline to join unions due to fear or anxiety about losing status or opportunities to advance into management. Other employees do not want to pay dues or become active union members because they realize they will probably still receive most of the same benefits the union has negotiated even without a personal commitment to the unions.

TABLE 14–2

Why workers join or do not join the union

Pros	Cons
Enhancement of job security	Suspicion toward unions
Peer pressure to join	Fear of loss of independence
Improved working conditions	Fear of reprisals
Improved wages	Loss of status
Better benefits	Belief that unions cannot improve anything
Desire to achieve equitable treatment and avoid favoritism	
Chance to attain seniority rights	Dues and other union expenses
	Fear of strikes and lost wages
Fair rules for discipline, promotion, and so on	Desire to move into management
Desire for formal grievance procedure	

Supervisors should realize that the greater the dissatisfaction among employees with conditions in the organization and the treatment they receive, the greater the chance they will opt to join the union. In short, management often creates the very environment that spawns unions; an unhappy worker is union material.

Supervisory behavior has long been associated with employee satisfaction or dissatisfaction and receptivity of employees to union organization efforts. A 1987 study by Scarpello and Vandenberg found the following factors are related to employee satisfaction.

Employee satisfaction increases with supervisors who:

- display technical competence
- set clear work goals
- give clear instructions
- clearly define subordinates' job responsibilities
- back subordinates with other managers
- fairly appraise employee performance
- allow subordinates adequate time to do the job right
- allow subordinates adequate time to learn the job
- inform employees of work changes before they occur
- display consistent behavior toward employees
- help employees get the job done
- give employees credit for their ideas
- listen to and understand employees' work problems
- follow through to get the problems solved
- treat subordinates fairly when they make mistakes

□ show concern for subordinates' career progress
□ congratulate subordinates for doing a good job.[11]

THE ORGANIZING CAMPAIGN

Typically, union efforts begin in one of two ways. Either a group of employees will ask the union to come in, or the union will decide on its own to assess employee interest in joining the union. In either case, the union will hand out handbills, hold meetings, and in other ways encourage employees to sign an *authorization card* requesting a union election. At least 30 percent of the employees must sign these authorization cards before an election can be held.

The actual election is called and conducted by the National Labor Relations Board, who requires that a majority of the employees vote to have this union become their legal bargaining agent.

The NLRB oversees union elections.

> When that majority vote is received, the NLRB certifies the union and recognizes it as the exclusive bargaining unit. Irrespective of whether the individual in the certified bargaining unit voted for or against the union, each worker is covered by the negotiated contract and must abide by its governance.[12]

Merely holding an election, however, is no guarantee that the union will be certified. If the union loses, it must wait at least twelve months before calling another election. Nor is management standing still. Most organizations mount a strong campaign to remain nonunion.

From management's viewpoint, it is safe to assume that the majority of managers do not want to see workers join a union. They feel the union is an unwelcome third party in what should be a two-way relationship.

How Can Management Avoid Unionization?

Unionization often occurs in organizations where employee discontent is not even recognized by management. Sometimes this lack of insight occurs because management feels they are paying a competitive wage and that employees will not be interested in a union. Studies show that wages may not be the central issue for most organizing campaigns. After all, strikes have occurred in companies that pay among the highest rates in their industries, including General Motors, DuPont, and Eastman Kodak.

> . . . Wage rates may be a sufficient reason for employee dissatisfaction, but the real reasons almost always are related to how employees feel about

---

[11]Vida Gulbinas Scarpella and James Ledvinka, *Personnel/Human Resource Management* (Boston: PWS-Kent Publishing Co, 1988), 592.

[12]DeCenzo and Robbins, 611.

management—whether they believe they are being treated fairly, decently, and with respect.[13]

The key to employees feeling respected and fairly treated is an effective communication system. A study done at a Midwestern hospital showed that the majority of employees felt that the hospital administration was indifferent to their needs at best, unfair at worst. A complete revamping of the communication system was undertaken under the direction of a consultant and included supervisory training in effective communications.

> The atmosphere in the hospital began to change. Even supervisors admitted that employee attitudes were better, efficiency noticeably improved in some areas, fewer supplies were wasted, productivity increased, absenteeism declined. Eight months after this project began, a union organizing team passed out handbills, visited employees at home, and held pep rallies at the local motel. They found little interest among employees.[14]

Communication is also very important when an organizing effort has begun. Management is legally allowed to communicate to employees in a nonthreatening way the reasons it feels that unionization is not in the best interests of the employees or of the organization. Deliberate care must be taken, however, to avoid any perception of threat, because employees have the legal right to organize and recognize a union without company interference.

Often, management feels it should take a passive posture in face of unionizing attempts and say nothing; instead, it should present a forceful but equitable argument against union acceptance. Here are some perfectly acceptable reasons to present to employees[15]:

Here are positive management strategies to avoid unionization.

1. Union membership is at an all time low representing only about 16 percent of the work force. This may be because many employees no longer feel unions are necessary.

2. Counter the union's promise to demand higher wages by first assuring that you pay a competitive wage and then advertising that fact. Remind employees that unions cannot guarantee higher wages and that many unionized organizations have actually sustained wage cuts.

3. Counter the union's promise of job security by pointing to the many unionized organizations that have gone through massive layoffs.

4. Point out to employees the intrusive nature of a third party intermediary between management and employees and the loss of individual power to the employee who now has to interact with management through a shop steward.

---

[13]Matthew Goodfellow, "Study Shows Ways to Win, Avoid Union Elections," *Healthcare Financial Management* (September 1991): 52.

[14]Goodfellow, 54.

[15]Paul S. McDonough, "Labor Relations: Maintain a Union-Free Status," *Personnel Journal* (April 1990): 108–114.

5. Discuss the financial obligations of union members to the union. These costs are usually underplayed during organizing attempts but can add up to significant amounts.

6. Inform employees of the negative impact of strikes on them as well as on the organization, and of their obligation to go on strike should the union decide to take that strategy.

> Each situation a company faces requires a specific campaign designed to highlight its particular strengths and weaknesses. Successful campaigns require careful planning and total management commitment. The benefits of remaining free to run a company without the interference of unions, however, make this effort worthwhile.[16]

Employers must be careful, however, to avoid any unfair labor practices during the unionization campaign. Therefore, management should be careful to not:

1. Misrepresent or distort the facts.

2. Intimidate employees or hint at termination or retribution because of union activity.

3. Promise benefits or rewards for not joining the union.

4. Improve wages or working conditions unless such improvements were planned and announced before the organizing campaign.

5. Spy on union activities or make employees feel they are being watched.

6. Interfere with the distribution of union literature or the solicitation of union support by employees.[17]

Management must avoid threat or coercion.

RELATIONSHIP BETWEEN MANAGEMENT AND THE UNION

There is almost an innate conflict between the philosophies of management and union. Management resents the union interfering with the decision-making process, and the union has built its reputation on righting the wrongs of management. Nevertheless, both groups must learn to coexist and to negotiate in good faith with each other. At no time is the conflict between these two factions so evident as during a union-organizing attempt. If that attempt is successful, and the union is legally recognized as the bargaining unit for the workers, management has no choice but to accept the union's presence. Once the union is established, the most common time of conflict is during the collective bargaining process, when a new contract is being hammered out.

---

[16]McDonough, 114.

[17]Randall S. Schuler, *Managing Human Resources,* 4th ed. (St. Paul, Minn.: West Publishing Company, 1993), 448.

Collective Bargaining

Collective bargaining is the process whereby representatives of the elected union and the company negotiate a labor contract. In a broader sense, collective bargaining refers to all management-union interaction regarding the contract. Many forces, such as the state of the overall economy in general and the industry in particular, influence the bargaining process. In recent years, for example, unions at Chrysler and Eastern Airlines agreed to salary cuts to keep the company viable. In the case of Eastern, this viability proved to be short-lived.

To get bargaining under way, the union and management choose representatives to the *negotiating committee*. Neither side has to have the approval of the other for its representatives nor can the two groups refuse to bargain. Typically, the union chooses representatives of the local union and a negotiation specialist from the national union who may be a labor attorney. The company is usually represented by top management, members of the human resources staff, and finance and production managers. Likewise, management may choose to employ a labor attorney to negotiate on their behalf.

Prior to the beginning of negotiations, each side needs to prepare. The union team needs to understand the financial condition of the company and what it can afford to pay, the attitudes of management toward various issues, and the attitudes of employees who they are representing. Management, on the other hand, needs to consider desired changes in contract language, the overall economic package they are ready and/or able to offer, and supportive data to illustrate their points during negotiation.[18]

The Landrum-Griffin Act of 1959 established three categories of bargaining issues: *mandatory issues, permissive issues,* and *prohibited issues.*[19] The negotiating committee must consider the mandatory issues of wages, hours, and conditions of employment. Permissive issues include issues of mutual concern such as product pricing and product design. These issues are not mandatory, but neither are they forbidden topics for the negotiating team. Permissive issues can be further divided into *institutional issues* and *administrative issues*. Institutional issues include security issues, such as rights of the union to strike during the contract, managerial perogatives, and check-off procedures for union dues. Administrative issues are concerned with how employees are treated. Seniority, discipline procedures, safety and health issues, and training are common administrative issues, as is the grievance procedure. Finally, prohibited issues are those concerning illegal activities such as yellow-dog contracts.

Management and union representatives engage in collective bargaining.

Bargaining issues may be mandatory, permissive, or prohibited.

---

[18]Schuler, 553–554.

[19]Schuler, 547–549.

In most instances, the negotiating team is able to come up with an acceptable labor contract, but when negotiations break down completely, a *strike* is possible. A strike is simply an organized refusal by employees to work. Another possible union strategy is to have workers engage in a work *slowdown,* in which everyone is directed to be minimally productive. In extreme cases such as slowdowns and strikes, outside help is often needed to bring the sides together. This can take place through the process of mediation or arbitration. *Mediation* occurs when a neutral third party intervenes to help the two sides come to an agreement. The mediator has no power to make things happen but merely acts as a facilitator to improve communication and conflict resolution. If all else fails, an arbitrator may be appointed to mandate a decision after hearing the best offers of both sides. This is often called *binding arbitration*.

> Binding arbitration requires the decision be accepted by both sides.

The Labor Contract

Contracts vary in length and complexity according to the organization's size. Some documents are only a few pages long, whereas others may run 1,000 pages. In any event, once accepted, the *labor contract* is the legal agreement that both sides are required to uphold until renegotiation. Breach of contract is a serious issue and almost always leads to grievance procedures. Union contracts detail the rights and responsibilities of both union and management. Management rights are listed as activities that are not subject to any union authority. These activities include setting organizational goals, deciding on product mix, and purchasing equipment. The union contract may also refer to management rights by stating that management has the authority to operate the business except in specific cases as defined in the contract.

> The labor contract is the legal agreement that both sides are committed to uphold until renegotiation.

The union rights and responsibilities section of the contract includes details on the union's role in layoffs, terminations, grievances, and so on.

The following list shows typical subjects of a union-management contract.

Membership guidelines
Membership requirements
Grievance procedures
Vacations
Benefits
Pay rates
Holidays
Overtime pay
Benefits of seniority
Work hours
Authorized leave from work
Strike provisions

Timing of contract

Safety and health agreements

Shift differentials

Under membership guidelines the parties agree what type of "shop" the company will be. An *open shop* indicates that workers may individually decide whether to join the union. In a *union shop,* however, all workers must become union members within a predetermined period of time, usually thirty days. In an *agency shop,* employees need not join the union but must pay a "service charge" in lieu of dues. This clause partially answers union objections to "free riders," those employees who do not join or support the union but who reap union negotiated benefits. Remember, ever since the Taft-Hartley Act (1947), closed shops have been against the law. A *closed shop* is one in which only union members can be hired.

In an open shop workers decide whether or not to join the union.

In a union shop all workers must eventually join the union.

In a closed shop only union members can be hired.

THE SUPERVISOR AND THE UNION CONTRACT

The success of daily operations under the union contract is largely the supervisor's responsibility. For this reason, the supervisor must strive to be knowledgeable, equitable, consistent, and thoughtful.

A supervisor must be knowledgeable, equitable, consistent, and thoughtful.

The supervisor must study the contract thoroughly and be knowledgeable about its provisions. Unnecessary conflict can arise, for instance, should the supervisor ask an employee to do something outlawed in the contract. The supervisor should know not only employees' rights, but also management's rights.

Supervisors should be particularly careful to be equitable in their treatment of all employees. Equity issues are of primary concern to the union and a common rallying point in union organization drives. Any actions that may appear to show favoritism should be avoided.

Consistency goes hand in hand with equity. The supervisor should apply all rules with the same degree of stringency to all employees. Effective supervisors let their employees know what to expect from them because their behavior is consistent from one day to the next. Evenhandedness is especially important under the union contract, because inconsistent behavior can lead to time-consuming grievances.

Finally, supervisors should strive to show respect and thoughtfulness toward employees whether they belong to the union or not. Such an attitude can go far in diminishing the gap and reducing the conflict between supervisors and employees. Supervisors are in a particularly uncomfortable position when dealing with employees because in many cases they want to be considered "one of the guys," but on the other hand, they are representatives of management and must maintain a certain distance from employees further down in the hierarchy. In cases where supervisors are also union members, role conflict may occur between supervisors' rights as union members, together with their identification with union "brothers" and "sisters," and their responsibility to look after the best interests of the company. In most companies supervisors and managers are not eligible to belong to the same union as the workers.

Dealing with the Shop Steward

Supervisors should be especially aware of building a good relationship with the *shop steward,* who is the official union representative in a given unit. An employee who has union-related questions or complaints goes first to the shop steward. Like the supervisor, the steward plays a double role in the organization—first as employee and then as a union representative. Supervisors who cultivate a mutual trusting relationship with the shop steward can avoid many unnecessary problems. In situations where the mutual respect does not exist, an "us vs. them" attitude results and, regardless of the issue, the supervisor and shop steward may become entrenched in their opposition. Many grievable issues can be avoided or resolved at a very early stage if supervisors and shop stewards coexist in a cooperative environment. Therefore the best way to build this beneficial relationship is for the supervisor to be open and honest with the steward. The supervisor should be informed of changes, problems, questions, and so on. Both parties should try to avoid a climate of suspicion and conflict. Such a climate is bound to produce a high number of grievances. "The Quality Challenge: Winning Union Acceptance" provides some additional insights regarding how supervisors can work effectively with union personnel.

The shop steward is the official union representative in a given unit.

Supervisors and Grievances

A *grievance* is a formal complaint brought by employees who feel they have been treated improperly under the terms of the labor contract. For instance, employees may complain that they are not getting enough overtime assignments compared with others in the department with less seniority.

A study of union member perceptions about the quality of labor relations in their organizations showed that the way an employee feels about his or her supervisor is the single most important determinant as to how they feel about the labor-management relationship in general.

> When asked to evaluate the quality of the union-management relationship, most union members probably base their answers on the relationship between themselves, their local union representative, and their immediate supervisor.[20]

Even more important to the current discussion, the study showed that the way union members perceive the grievance procedure is the second most

---

[20]Paul F. Clark, "Determinants of the Quality of Union-Management Relations: An Exploratory Study of Union Member Perceptions," *Journal of Collective Negotiations* (Vol. 18, Issue 2, 1989): 111.

THE QUALITY CHALLENGE
Winning Union Acceptance

Introducing quality management concepts into unionized settings can be a difficult chore. Union members and officials are often concerned that these efforts are nothing more than an attempt to cut the number of employees and increase the work load. However, there are some important steps that supervisors can take to deal with this problem and get the unionized personnel to support the quality effort. Five of the most useful are the following:

1. Carefully explain all work changes or new efforts that will be undertaken to increase quality. The focus of the explanation should be directed to answering the most commonly raised questions: How will this affect my job at the company? Will I have to do more work than before? If productivity and quality increase, what will the company do for me?

2. Remember that the workers have a right to be concerned about their jobs. So do not treat their questions as threats or an unwillingness to support these changes. Instead, use them to help you better understand their fears and concerns.

3. Work closely with the group to show them that all changes are designed to protect their jobs, not to eliminate them. In particular, learn about the goods and services being provided by the competition and be prepared to show the employees how the current quality program will help combat this competition and ensure jobs.

4. If mistakes are made in implementing these new quality ideas, treat them as learning experiences from which everyone in the group can profit—"Okay, now we know some of the things not to do, so let's move on from here." This nonthreatening approach helps win the support of the personnel.

5. Work to maintain a team approach, you and the unionized employees focusing your attention on attacking quality problems. This win-win approach minimizes the traditional union-management antagonism and focuses everyone on a common goal.

---

important factor in determining how they feel about labor-management relations as a whole. Thus, if an employee feels the grievance procedure is equitable and effective, he or she is likely to feel positively about labor relations in the company.[21]

How grievances are handled influences the entire labor relations environment.

Grievances typically begin with a meeting between the employee who has brought the complaint, the shop steward, and the supervisor. Most grievances are resolved at this point. If not, the next step is usually a meeting during which higher management and union officials attempt to resolve the situation. If an agreement still cannot be reached, an outside arbitrator may be brought in to make a final binding decision on the matter. Obviously, much time and effort can be spent in grievances; moreover, they serve to heighten the conflict existing between supervisors and employees. Supervisors are therefore cautioned to:

---

[21]Clark, 112.

SUPERVISORY SKILLS
Working with Labor Unions

1. Try to understand why workers in your organization are in favor of unions. If a unionizing campaign has not yet started, consider what management can do to avoid the types of complaints that typically lead to union drives. If your company does have a union, look into its history. Why was it formed? What has it accomplished for the workers? Be careful to stay neutral in your attitude about the union, and do not do anything that might be construed as prejudicial against union members.

2. Be sure to study the contract thoroughly. Do not make uninformed judgments that lead to costly grievances. Effective supervisors maintain an environment where grievances are kept at a minimum.

3. Establish a sound working relationship with the shop steward. Take the first step in ensuring open communications and a candid environment. If you're seen as a supervisor who is honestly trying to administer the union contract in a consistent and fair way, you will experience far fewer grievances, and those that do occur will cause far less damage to working relationships.

---

1. Take every grievance seriously.
2. Work with the union representative.
3. Gather all information available on the grievance.
4. After weighing all the facts, provide an answer to the employee filing the grievance.
5. After the grievance is settled, attempt to move on to other matters.[22]

SUMMARY

Labor unions have a long history in the United States. Three national labor unions emerged in the late 1800s: the National Labor Union, the Knights of Labor, and the AFL. The first organization for industrial unions, the Committee for Industrial Organization (CIO), formed as a splinter group from the AFL in 1935. Nearly 4 million union members united to form the AFL–CIO in 1955. Union membership grew dramatically during the 1900s but has leveled off. Membership among blue collar professions is decreasing, while white collar membership is increasing. The pendulum effect of public opinion regarding unions can be seen in the wide range of legislation that has been enacted since 1890.

The Sherman Anti-Trust Act of 1890 included unions in its prohibition against restraint of trade. The Clayton Act of 1914

---

[22]John M. Ivancevich and William F. Glueck, *Foundations of Personnel* (Plano, Tex.: Business Publications, Inc., 1983), 567.

reversed this provision but allowed yellow-dog contracts and injunctions against unions. The 1932 Norris La Guardia Act gave workers the right to organize and bargain. The National Labor Relations Act of 1935 forbade management from interfering with workers' right to organize and formed the National Labor Relations Board to oversee union elections and hear unfair labor practice cases. The Fair Labor Standards Act of 1938 established a minimum wage, and the Taft-Hartley Act of 1947 declared closed shops illegal and instituted sixty-day cooling off periods before strikes affecting the national interest. The Landrum-Griffin Act of 1959 regulated internal affairs of unions, and Executive Order 10988 allowed federal employees to join unions.

Supervisors should understand the reasons workers join or do not join the union. Employee satisfaction is directly related to how workers feel about their supervisors. Organizing campaigns typically begin with the accumulation of authorization cards. If enough are gathered, elections are held by the NLRB to see whether the union will be certified. While unions are organizing, employers can be involved in positive and legal strategies to avoid ratification of the union, but once the union is elected, collective bargaining is mandatory. The negotiating committee will consider mandatory issues such as wages and hours as well as permissive issues such as seniority and occupational safety and health. Once a contract has been accepted, the supervisor assumes much day-by-day responsibility for making that contract work. Supervisors should strive to develop good relationships with the shop steward and to handle grievances equitably and quickly.

REVIEW QUESTIONS

1. Why did the early Knights of Labor disband, and what new initiatives did the fledgling AFL take?

2. What was the relationship of the early unions to the management movement?

3. What benefits does the AFL–CIO offer to its member unions?

4. Is union growth increasing or decreasing? Explain your answer.

5. What rights did the following guarantee to unions and/or labor: Norris La-Guardia Act, National Labor Relations Act, Landrum-Griffin Act, Executive Order 10988? In each case, be specific in your answer.

6. How does a union organizing campaign work?

7. What is collective bargaining? What happens during this process?

8. How does an open shop differ from a union shop? Which is found in right-to-work states?

9. In what way do the shop steward and supervisor interact? Explain.

10. If there is a grievance, why would the supervisor and shop steward like it solved at their level? Defend your answer.

KEY TERMS

Administrative issues. Administrative issues concern how employees are treated in areas such as seniority, training, and health and safety.

Agency shop. Company in which employees need not join the union but must pay a service charge in lieu of dues.

Authorization card. A card signed by employees stating they are in favor of an election to certify an organizing union as the bargaining agent of their organization.

Binding arbitration. A decision made by a third-party arbitrator regarding the union contract that is legally binding on both management and labor.

Closed shop. Company in which only union members are hired.

Collective bargaining. Process whereby representatives of the union and the company negotiate a labor contract.

Grievance. Formal complaint brought by an employee who feels he or she has been treated improperly under the terms of the labor contract.

Institutional issues. Includes security issues such as rights of the union to strike, managerial perogatives, and check-off procedures for union dues.

Labor contract. Legal agreement governing all labor-management relations that both sides are required to uphold until renegotiation.

Mandatory issues. Include those issues the negotiating committee must discuss, including wages and hours and conditions of employment.

Mediation. Intervention of a neutral third party to attempt to negotiate agreement between management and labor representatives.

Negotiating committee. Management and labor representatives who meet to negotiate a labor contract.

Open shop. Company in which workers are free to join or not join the union.

Permissive issues. Includes those issues that the negotiating committee may discuss but is not under legal obligation to discuss.

Prohibitive issues. Includes issues which the negotiating committee may not discuss because they are forbidden by law.

Right-to-work laws. Laws making it illegal to require employees to join a union.

Shop steward. Official union representative in a given unit.

Slowdown. A deliberate slowing down of work to bring pressure on an employer to yield to union demands.

Strike. Occurs when union members walk off the job and refuse to work to pressure an employer to yield to union demands.

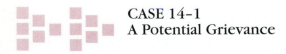

CASE 14–1
A Potential Grievance

Harry Grunding has never been a very effective worker. In fact over the last twelve months he has had the lowest performance evaluations in his unit. Harry is seldom late for work. The main reason for his poor performance is his lack of concentration on the job. Quite often his supervisor, Eunice Jackson, has found it necessary to ask Harry to stop talking to others in the work area or to redo a report that has errors and sloppily made corrections.

In an effort to increase overall unit productivity, the management of this medium-sized appliance manufacturer recently announced that anyone coming in late would be sent home without pay for the day. Eunice does not particularly like the new rule, and she has worked hard to skirt implementing it. For example, last week two of her best friends came in five minutes late. "The bus broke down and we were stuck for thirty-five minutes before another came by," one of them explained. Eunice made no reference to the lateness rule. She simply told them, "You'll have to get going to make up your lost time, so step on it."

Earlier this week Eunice went out to the workplace to talk with one of her people. It was 9:01 A.M. and she wanted the individual to start on a new project as soon as he was finished with the report he was completing. As she began talking to her subordinate, Eunice noticed that Harry had just come in the front door. She excused herself, went over to Harry, and told him that because he was late he would have to go home and forego the day's pay. Harry could not believe his ears. Within ten minutes the shop steward and Harry were both in Eunice's office. The shop steward told her, "It's unfair to send Harry home for being one minute late. Last week two of your employees were five minutes late and you let them get away with it. You can't enforce the rules selectively. It's against the contract. If you don't withdraw your decision, we'll file a grievance." Eunice told both men to wait outside her office and she would be with them in a minute. She wanted to think over the matter.

1. What mistake did Eunice make? Explain.

2. What would you recommend that she do? Why? Defend your answer.

3. What lesson should Eunice learn from this incident? Be complete in your answer.

CASE 14–2
Telling It Like It Is

Turnover in the payroll department at Whett Inc. has been extremely high in recent months. The department needs nine people in order to operate efficiently. Seven of these people have been with the company for over five years. The other two positions, however, have seen people come and go. Specifically, six people have been hired for these two positions and each has left. Two of these new hires were black, one was a woman, one was physically handicapped, and the other two were individuals between the ages of sixty-five and seventy. After reviewing these data, Rob Russell, the department supervisor, wrote the following memo to the head of the personnel department:

Over the last six months a number of people have applied for a job with my department. To keep the union happy, we have hired blacks, women, a handicapped person, and elderly people. In every case these individuals have not worked out. One person wanted more money and, when he did not receive it, he left. Another had a young child in nursery school and was always coming in late and leaving early. A third wanted us to provide a special chair that would enable him to be more comfortable while doing his work. Another was so old he could not remember simple instructions. All of the situations have led to grievances. Given our results with these types of people, I would like to suggest that in the future we be much more careful of whom we hire.

Earlier today Rob received a call from the company attorney's office. They would like him to drop by at 3 P.M. this afternoon so they can discuss this memo. Mentioning it to a fellow supervisor, Rob speculated, "They probably want me to give them more information so they can write these guidelines into the next labor contract."

1.   Think back to Chapter 6. Did Rob's memo violate any laws? Be as complete as possible in your answer.

2.   How would you guess the employees in Rob's department feel about the grievance procedure? Why is the role of the supervisor critical to an effective grievance procedure?

3.   What does the legal department want to talk to Rob about? Explain.

■ ■ ■ CHAPTER 15

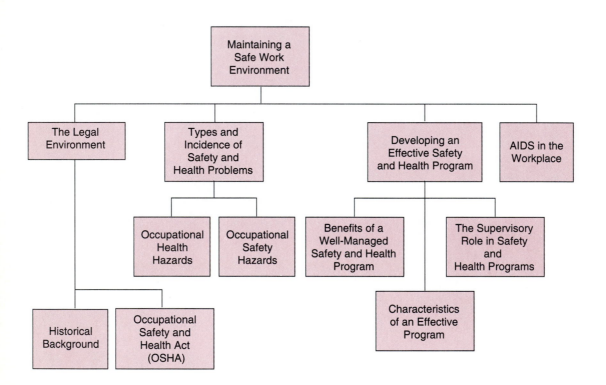

Maintaining a Safe and Healthy Work Environment

"About one American worker in 10,000 dies in an on-the-job accident."*

CHAPTER OBJECTIVES

☐ Describe the emergence of safety and health as work-related factors.

☐ Relate the importance of the Occupational Safety and Health Act to supervision in the workplace.

☐ Discuss the type and incidence of job-related safety and health problems.

☐ Identify ways of developing an effective safety and health program.

☐ Describe the role of the supervisor in safety and health programs.

Most people think American companies are very safe places to work. Consider, however, the following reports:

☐ In 1989, 10,400 workers died from work-related accidents and approximately 1.7 million suffered disabling injuries.[1]

☐ In 1988, the cost of work-related accidents in the private sector alone was more than $93 billion.[2]

☐ A government study showed that between 20 and 38 percent of all cancer in the United States is occupation related.[3]

The cost of occupational health and safety problems in terms of human suffering and organizational productivity is high. This chapter discusses safety in the workplace by first looking at the legal environment of employee safety and health. Next, it examines safety hazards as well as circumstances that commonly surround accidents. Finally, and most importantly, we describe ways to develop effective safety programs. Before you begin to study this chapter, however, take Self-Assessment Quiz 15–1 and see how much you currently know about maintaining a safe environment.

THE LEGAL ENVIRONMENT

The legal aspects of occupational safety and health go back a long way. However, in recent years there have been some significant developments.

Historical Background

Occupational safety and health is not a new issue.

Occupational safety and health are not new issues. The onset of the Industrial Revolution in the early 1800s paired inexperienced men with dangerous machines and chemicals. Workers assumed the risk for their own injury, illness, or death in the workplace. The state labor bureaus of the time reported many grisly accidents. Massachusetts seemed particularly concerned. In 1877, the state passed the first factory inspection law and other states soon followed suit. In 1887, Congress established the Interstate Commerce Commission, at least partly because of the numerous railroad workers hurt or killed in train wrecks.

By the early 1900s, newspapers and magazines began to crystallize public sentiments regarding unsafe working conditions. In 1907, the

---

[1]Randall S. Schuler, *Managing Human Resources,* 4th ed. (St. Paul, Minn.: West Publishing Co., 1992), 485.

[2]Myron I. Peskin and Francis J. McGrath, "Industrial Safety: Who Is Responsible and Who Benefits?" *Business Horizons* (May-June 1992): 68.

[3]W. Edward Stead and Jean Garner Stead, "OSHA's Cancer Prevention Policy: Where Did It Come From and Where Is It Going?" *Personnel Journal* (January 1983): 54.

■ ■ ■ SELF-ASSESSMENT QUIZ 15-1
Occupational Safety and Health

Directions: Answer each of the following questions true or false.

_____ 1. Occupational safety and health are largely matters for the conscience of the individual organization.

_____ 2. It is the sole responsibility of workers to follow safe procedures when doing their jobs.

_____ 3. There is little public interest in workplace safety because establishing safety standards is too costly.

_____ 4. Workers' compensation programs are a product of the increased interest in human resources that took place in the 1960s.

_____ 5. Safety and health issues are one area where state and federal governments have always cooperated.

_____ 6. All work accidents must be recorded.

_____ 7. There is little difference in rates of accidents across industries; it seems all workers are equally prone to accidents.

_____ 8. Safety hazards and health hazards are just different terms for the same thing.

_____ 9. The mining industry has more accidents than any other industry.

_____10. There is no such thing as an accident-prone employee.

_____11. Occupational health statistics are quite accurate because all industries are required to keep careful records.

_____12. Safety manuals are usually adequate in educating employees about safety standards.

Before proceeding, check your answers at the end of the chapter.

deaths of 362 coal miners in West Virginia shocked the country. In 1908, Congress began to get involved by establishing a workers' compensation law for federal employees. In 1910, the U.S. Bureau of Mines was established to foster safety in that industry.

State workers' compensation programs began to spring up shortly thereafter with Wisconsin leading the way in 1911. These early programs, however, were probably limited in value.

> The general level of this type of insurance premium was already so low that there was no real incentive for a company to invest heavily in safety improvements to be eligible for the slightly lower rates offered firms with good safety records. Very few states included compensation for disease, although much was already known about occupational illness. Still, insurance company safety experts helped improve their clients' safety programs and establishment of compensation gave the safety movement a moral boost.[4]

---

[4]Judson MacLaury, "The Job Safety Law of 1970: Its Passage Was Perilous," *Monthly Labor Review* (May 1981): 19.

These state and federal programs were to evolve through the years into the powerful workers compensation laws of today. Workers compensation now provides payments to workers or dependents in the event of occupational injury, illness, or death.

Today, workers compensation costs have become a significant expense to American corporations who pay the entire cost. Individual company cost depends on accident and illness rates at each facility. In 1988, worker compensation programs paid about $30.8 billion to employees with job-related disabilities and survivors of employees killed in job-related accidents.[5]

At about the time workers compensation programs were beginning, state industrial commissions appeared. They were designed to develop and enforce safety regulations. In 1913, Congress formed the Department of Labor, whose mandate included improving working conditions. The Bureau of Labor Statistics started keeping track of accidents in high risk industries such as iron and steel.

Progress in the area of occupational safety and health continued during the war years, but significant legislation did not appear until the 1930s, when the Social Security Act of 1935, the Walsh–Healey Public Contracts Act of 1936, and the Fair Labor Standards Act of 1938 followed in rapid succession. Each was partially concerned with protecting workers from unsafe conditions. Federal occupational safety and health standards, however, were not applied to all industries until 1960, when federal amendments to the Walsh–Healey Act were passed. The decision of the federal government to take a more active role and to supercede state guidelines led to considerable state and industry backlash. The public, however, continued to be alarmed about developments in the area. A centralized health and safety body was definitely needed; the issue was where it would be located.

> Federal occupational safety and health standards were applied to all industries in 1960.

Lyndon Johnson's comprehensive proposal for occupational safety and health in 1968 never came to a vote despite support by unions and consumer groups. Industry was strongly opposed to the proposal, fearing the widespread powers it would give to the Department of Labor. Ironically, unions and business switched sides when considering the Nixon proposal one year later. The critical difference between this and the earlier bill seemed to be that Nixon proposed using a safety and health board, not the Department of Labor, as the controlling body. What eventually passed, however, was a labor-backed, Senate-proposed compromise entitled the Occupational Safety and Health Act of 1970.[6]

---

[5]Wm. J. Nelson, Jr, "Worker Compensation: Coverage, Benefits and Costs, 1988" *Social Security Bulletin,* Volume 54, Issue 3, March 1991, pp 12, 20.

[6]Much of this historical overview is based on a discussion in MacLaury, "The Job Safety Law," 18–24.

Occupational Safety and Health Act (OSHA)

The *Occupational Safety and Health Act of 1970* represented the culmination of decades of concern about workplace safety and health. It established the Occupational Safety and Health Administration (OSHA) within the Department of Labor, where it is administered by an assistant secretary of labor. The act also established the National Institute for Occupational Safety and Health (NIOSH), located within the Department of Health, Education, and Welfare (now the Department of Health and Human Services). NIOSH carries on research regarding occupational safety and health and provides OSHA with necessary information to set standards in the field. NIOSH has concluded, for example, that there are approximately 13,000 potentially dangerous substances in use by industry.[7]

OSHA sets safety standards, conducts inspections, and issues citations.

The purpose of the Occupational Safety and Health Act is to assure workers safe and healthy working conditions. Under the act, OSHA has the right to set standards, conduct inspections, and issue citations and penalties. In the 1970s industry found the setting of these standards to be a major sore point because they felt that OSHA was being extremely picky and unaware of the costs involved in meeting the stipulated standards. For example, firms that were 95 percent pollution free might have to sacrifice 20 percent of net earnings to reach a level of 96 percent. As a result, in 1978 OSHA threw out almost 1,000 safety standards and decided to concentrate on major health hazards. In the early 1980s, OSHA focused on such standards as worker exposure to cotton dust, asbestos, noise, pesticides, lead, and toxic chemicals.[8] Today, OSHA has moved into researching cumulative trauma disorder and problems associated with video display computer terminals and developing training programs for business.[9]

Unannounced inspections by OSHA were another sore spot with industry. In 1978, the Supreme Court decision in *Marshall v. Barlow* mandated that an OSHA inspector must show a search warrant on demand before inspecting a company. The days of unannounced inspection were over, although most companies find it in their best interest to agree to voluntary inspection.

In addition, OSHA requires virtually all employers to keep detailed accident and work-related illness reports. Figure 15–1 portrays OSHA guidelines for deciding what must be reported.

Incidence rates for occupational injuries and illnesses are computed.

These reports are later filed in the form of an annual summary report. Summary reports serve as input for the Bureau of Labor Statistics,

---

[7]Dale S. Beach, *The Management of People at Work* (New York: Macmillan Co., 1985), 523.

[8]"Occupational Safety and Health Administration," *Academic American Encyclopedia* (Danbury, Conn.: Grolier, 1983), 321.

[9]David A. DeCenzo and Stephen P. Robbins, *Human Resource Management,* 4th ed. (New York: John Wiley & Sons, Inc., 1994), 513.

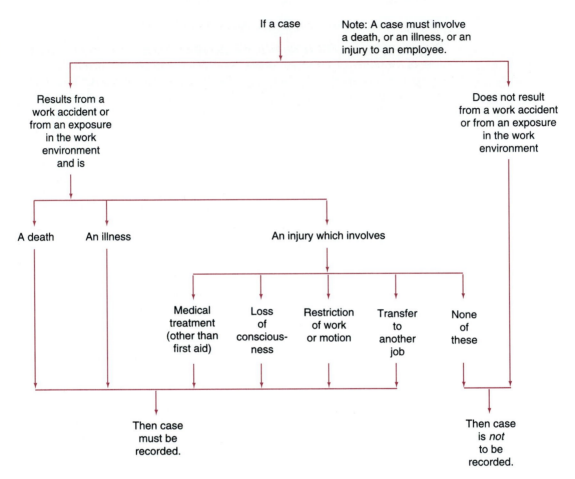

FIGURE 15–1
Recording OSHA cases.

which figures "incident rates" for occupational injury and illness according to industry. Incident rates are computed by the formula:

$$\frac{\text{incident rate}}{\text{per calendar year}} = \frac{\text{number of injuries and illnesses}}{\text{total hours worked by all employees}} \times 200{,}000$$

The 200,000 in the formula represents the base for 100 full-time workers—that is, employees who work forty hours per week, fifty weeks per year. Companies are urged to figure their own incident rates and compare them to industry averages to ascertain how good a job they are doing relative to other firms in the field. But how well has industry done overall? Has there been any improvement? And what types of health hazards concern industry in the 1990s? We address these questions in the next section.

TYPES AND INCIDENCE OF SAFETY AND HEALTH PROBLEMS

Although safety and health hazards are often examined together, they actually entail two types of incidents.

> Safety hazards are those aspects of the work environment that have the potential of immediate and sometimes violent harm to an employee. Examples of injuries are loss of hearing, eyesight, or body parts, cuts, sprains, bruises, broken bones, burns and electric shock.
>
> Health hazards are those aspects of the work environment that slowly and cumulatively (and often irreversibly) lead to deterioration of an employee's health. Examples are cancer, bronchitis, and various psychological disorders. Typical causes include physical and biological hazards, toxic and cancer-causing dusts and chemicals, and stressful working conditions.[10]

As far as occupational safety and health as a whole are concerned, there has been obvious improvement since OSHA came into existence in 1970. It is hard to say, however, whether or not this improvement is largely due to OSHA regulations. The power of OSHA rules and inspections surely contributed to this change but society in general has become more health and safety conscious over the last 25 years. Highly publicized disasters like Three Mile Island, Chernobyl, and Bhopal have raised public awareness of the safety and health dangers in the workplace.

How much improvement has actually occurred? Across industries, the overall incidence of injuries and illness declined from 10.9 percent to 7.9 percent in the fourteen years from 1972 to 1985. There are, however, considerable differences among industries. Table 15–1 shows the incidence rates by industry. Ship building is noticeably higher than those that ranked 2 to 10 percent. OSHA understandably concentrates on high-risk industries, such as ship building and meat packing.

Occupational Health Hazards

Four general occupational health hazards

Occupational health hazards can be classified into four general types.

1. Physical hazards, such as heat, noise, vibration, and radiation.
2. Chemical hazards, such as dusts, toxic fumes, gases, and carcinogens.
3. Biological hazards, such as bacteria, fungi, and insects.
4. Stress hazards, including physical and psychological stressors. (Stress will be presented as a separate subject in chapter 17).[11]

Health hazards vary by industry.

The probability of exposure to health hazards varies greatly by industry. Workplace hazards such as asbestos, benzene, coal dust, lead, cotton dust,

---

[10]John M. Ivancevich and William F. Glueck, *Foundations of Personnel* (Plano, Tex.: Business Publications, 1986), 666.

[11]Dale S. Beach, *The Management of People at Work* (New York: Macmillan Co., 1985), 528.

TABLE 15–1

Industries with the highest injury and illness incident rates in 1988

Rank	Industry	Incident Rate (%)
1.	Ship building & repairing	44.9
2.	Meat packing plants	39.2
3.	Special product sawmills	31.0
4.	Gray iron foundries	30.3
5.	Automotive stampings	30.0
6.	Primary aluminum	29.6
7.	Mobile homes	28.7
8.	Vitreous plumbing fixtures	28.4
9. ⎤ Tie	Structural wood members	28.3
9. ⎦	Truck trailers	28.3
10.	Motor vehicles and car bodies	28.0

Source: Occupational Injuries and Illnesses in the Unites States by Industry, 1988
(Washington, D.C.: U.S. Dept of Labor, Bureau of Labor Statistics, August 1990,
Bulletin 2366):, 2.

radiation, and vinyl chloride are mostly found among miners, chemical and oil refinery workers, textile workers, and a handful of other blue-collar jobs. These substances have been linked to long-term diseases such as emphysema, black lung disease, and cancer. The latter gets considerable attention because it is a leading cause of death in this country and known to be tied, at least partly, to chemicals in the environment.

In the 1980s, local law enforcement officials began prosecuting OSHA violations. In 1983 a dramatic example occurred in Chicago when a worker at Film Recovery Systems Inc. (FRS) died from prolonged exposure to cyanide. The state attorney's office investigated and found illegal immigrant workers spending eight hours a day working with a sodium cyanide solution. The court found FRS's president, plant manager, and plant foremen guilty of murder and sentenced each man to $10,000 fines and 25 years in prison.[12] Since then, maximum OSHA fines have increased from $10,000 to $70,000. Recently, attention has turned to the growing incidence of cumulative trauma disorders (CTDs), or repetitive motion illness. It is now estimated that more than 50 percent of occupational illnesses involve CTDs.

Cumulative trauma disorders account for many occupational illnesses.

---

[12]Paul G. Engel, "Pinstripes to Prison Stripes," *Industry Week* (August 4, 1986): 54–56.

"Once limited to meat packers, poultry workers and plant manufacturing workers, repetitive motion illnesses, commonly known as cumulative trauma disorders (CTDs), have filtered into office settings and retail establishments because these jobs have become "keystroke dependent."[13]

A NIOSH study listed secretaries, typists, telephone operators, and cashiers as those most at risk for developing CTDs. Three factors—force, frequency, and posture—combine and stress the ability of a specific body part to perform normally. Carpal tunnel syndrome is the most common CTD. Tendinitis and slipped discs are also common.

Dangers of passive smoke are leading to workplace restrictions.

Two other health issues currently receiving considerable attention are workplace smoke and the sick building syndrome. In 1986, U.S. Surgeon General Everett Koop urged U.S. companies to become smoke free by the year 2000. In the early 1990s, the Environmental Protection Agency (EPA), charged with protecting public health, urged OSHA to take a hard look at passive smoke in the workplace, as such second-hand smoke had been found to be a Class A carcinogen.[14] Concurrently, about 85 percent of American companies have placed restrictions on smoking in the workplace.[15] Some organizations, including Blue Cross and Blue Shield of Maryland, Merck & Co., and Nova Southeastern University, have completely banned smoking from all facilities. Many more are expected to follow suit.

The health hazards of environmental smoke have been greatly increased because of the profusion of sealed buildings with no access to fresh air. Employees complain of headaches, watery eyes, and respiratory problems.

Smoke, asbestos, and other pollutants can cause "sick buildings."

"Often called 'sick buildings,' office environments containing harmful airborne chemicals, asbestos, or indoor pollution (often caused by smoking) have forced employers to take drastic steps. For many, it has meant the removal of asbestos from their buildings. Because extended exposure to asbestos has been linked to lung cancers, companies are required by various federal agencies like the EPA to remove it altogether, or at least seal it so that it cannot escape into the air."[16]

A response to many of the new health hazards just discussed, *ergonomics* studies the job environment and looks for ways in which changes in equipment can reduce cumulative trauma disorders and other health problems.

---

[13]Michelle Neely Martinez and Joe Lamoglia, "Hands On Answers to Hidden Health Costs," *HR Magazine* (March 1992): 48.

[14]Daniel Gottlieb, "Workplace Regulation Pipeline Is Overflowing," *Purchasing* (March 18, 1993): 61–63.

[15]William P. Anthony, Pamela L. Perrewe, and K. Michele Kacmar, *Strategic Human Resource Management* (Ft. Worth, Tex.: Harcourt, Brace, Jovanovich College Publishers, 1993), 520.

[16]David A. DeCenzo and Stephen P. Robbins, *Human Resource Management,* 4th ed. (New York: John Wiley & Sons, Inc., 1994), 526.

"Another way to alter the work environment and improve safety is to make the job itself more comfortable and less fatiguing. This approach, generally referred to as ergonomics, considers changes in the job environment in conjunction with the physical and physiological capabilities and limitation of the employees."[17]

Occupational Safety Hazards

Among the leading causes of occupational accidents are dangers in the work environment and accident proneness on the part of the employees. Dangers in the work environment include such things as poorly designed or unrepaired machinery and equipment, inadequate lighting and ventilation, lack of protective devices, and extended working hours, which lead to fatigue and carelessness. To combat this classification of accidents workplaces can utilize safety equipment such as safety goggles, hard hats, warning lights and buzzers, safety guards on machinery, and a variety of self-correcting devices. All of these are limited, however, by the willingness of the workers to use them. Workers have many reasons for resisting safety procedures. The hard hat may give one a headache, the steel-toed shoes may hurt the wearer's toes. Others simply don't feel the safety precautions are necessary. They may suffer from the "it can't happen to me" syndrome. No safety measures work in spite of the employees. Only through a cooperative effort between management and employees can these measures reduce accidents.

Supervisors, however, are often unsure how to promote or enforce use of safety procedures or equipment. The first guideline is to observe all safety violations and consistently follow up on them. If the supervisor doesn't take the time to enforce the rules, safety standards will begin to slide. For example, after observing an infraction, the supervisor should try to determine why the employee is not using the required equipment. Understanding the resistance often leads to a more amicable situation.

A supervisor in a public utilities company found that linemen climbing poles to fix electric power lines often tried to avoid putting on their rubber gloves. These gloves were strictly required by the company and OSHA and protected the linemen against possible electric shock or even electrocution. Why would the linemen take such a chance? When the supervisor asked the men, each responded that the gloves were too hot and this limited their manual dexterity. As a result of this finding, a compromise was made. Slightly thinner, more flexible gloves were introduced, and at the same time both the union and supervision firmly required all linemen to wear the gloves. The linemen, in turn, were more willing to comply.

Trying to understand worker resistance is helpful, but OSHA does

---

[17]Randall S. Schuler, *Managing Human Resources,* 4th ed. (St. Paul, Minn.: West Publishing Co., 1992), 498.

SUPERVISORY SKILLS
Safety and Health Hazards

1. First, be familiar with the laws. Then be sure you understand the safety and health hazards of your work environment. Investigate the injury and illness incidence rates at your company. How does your company compare to the rest of the industry?

2. Pay special attention to accident-prone employees in your department. Try to understand the attitudes and behaviors that characterize these people. Work cooperatively with these employees to improve both.

3. Remember that employees are often reluctant to use safety equipment and to follow safety procedures. Create a cooperative effort with employees to follow the safety guidelines. Reward compliance; do not just call attention to those who break the rules.

Some employees are accident prone.

not reward good intentions. The supervisor must make sure safety procedures are understood and obeyed.

Accident proneness among employees is another major cause of industrial accidents. Contrary to popular belief, older workers do not account for more accidents; in fact, studies show that the older workers are involved in significantly fewer accidents than their younger counterparts. Workers under the age of thirty-five accounted for 60 percent of the workplace injuries in 1977, and in 60 percent of those cases, the workers were in the first year of their employment.[18]

A variety of studies have identified several characteristics of the accident-prone employee:

1. Many such employees act too quickly, almost impulsively, before giving thought to the situation they are confronting.
2. Many are not able to concentrate on the task at hand.
3. Many are generally negative in their attitudes about their job, co-workers, and supervisors.[19]

OSHA has identified nine primary causes of industrial accidents[20]:

1. Poor worker training.
2. Inability to do the job.
3. Improper tools and equipment.
4. Poor quality materials.
5. Poor equipment maintenance.

---

[18]Norman Root, "Injuries at Work are Fewer Among Older Employees." *Monthly Labor Review* (March 1981): 31.

[19]John B. Miner and Mary Green Miner, *Personnel and Industrial Relations* (New York: Macmillan Co., 1985), 486.

[20]Myron I Peskin and Francis J. McGrath, "Industrial Safety: Who Is Responsible and Who Benefits?" *Business Horizons* (May-June 1992): 66–68.

6.   Poor working environment.
7.   Incorrect routing of work in progress.
8.   Tight work standards that lead to dangerous shortcuts.
9.   Overly tight production schedules.

Recognizing the accident-prone individual and taking steps to train that person to be more safety conscious is an important part of the supervisor's job.

DEVELOPING AN EFFECTIVE SAFETY AND HEALTH PROGRAM

The first requirement for an effective safety and health program is a strong commitment from top management. Bruce W. Karrh, vice president for safety and environmental affairs for E. I. Du Pont de Nemours and Co. said that the fine reputation Du Pont has in the safety field is due to: "a commitment to safety and health from top management on down through the organization structure."[21] Similarly, Russell DeReamer, former corporate safety manager for IBM stated: "There should be no argument that the same management principles and concepts that are applied to quality, cost, and production, must also be applied to safety."[22]

Benefits of a Well-Managed Safety and Health Program

Some benefits of effective safety and health programs

Management always wants to look at tangible and intangible benefits before deciding the worth of any program. A well-managed safety and health program has a number of each.[23] Tangible benefits, which are the visible, quantifiable benefits that management always looks at first, include the following:

☐   Reduced insurance costs (including workers' compensation and casualty insurance).
☐   Increased worker productivity.
☐   Decreased absenteeism rate.
☐   Decreased turnover.
☐   Reduced costs of litigation.
☐   Reduced number of employee problems such as drug abuse.
☐   Reduced indirect costs such as wages for lost time and cost of training new workers.

---

[21]David S. Thelan, Donna Ledgerwood and Charles F. Walters, "Health and Safety in the Workplace: A New Challenge for Business Schools," *Personnel Administrator* (October 1985): 38.

[22]Ibid.

[23]Herbert G. Hunt III, "Planning for Employee Health and Safety," *Business Horizons* (September-October 1984): 27–28.

Intangible benefits include longer term benefits such as: improved corporate image, increased value of stock, improved employee morale and job satisfaction, improved relations with government regulatory agencies, reduced pain and suffering to injured employees and their families, and increased overall attractiveness of the company as a place for prospective employees to work.

Characteristics of an Effective Program

Once management has realized the benefits of a safety and health program, what strategies can be used to develop an effective one? NIOSH has identified three factors that distinguish successful safety programs: (1) commitment by top management, (2) education and training of *all* employees, and (3) anticipation of likely safety problems and a plan to overcome the problems before disaster strikes.[24] Once the necessary safety guidelines have been structured, it is largely up to the supervisor to enforce them on a daily basis.

Supervisors must enforce safety and health regulations.

Supervisory Role in Safety and Health Programs

The supervisor is the pivotal person in ensuring that safety procedures are followed and in providing training in these procedures to employees. Employees tend to neglect safety procedures unless reminded constantly. After all, it may not be comfortable to wear a helmet or rubber gloves at all times. If these infractions are ignored, however, a general disregard of safety rules will follow. To prevent this, supervisors must first be sure that they are setting a good example by following all of the safety regulations. When an infraction occurs, supervisors should take prompt and consistent corrective action.

Safety training can help ensure a more positive attitude among workers. Such training does not mean just handing employees a book of regulations and warning them to be sure to follow them. Workers need to be made more safety conscious and should participate in specific job safety training, such as ways to safely contain toxic wastes or what equipment to use in construction areas. Training generally occurs when a new worker joins the department, when workers are transferred to new duties, or when new processes are introduced into the work environment. Supervisors should communicate the safety requirements in a face-to-face setting, being sure to explain why the safety precautions are necessary. Statistics presented to show how many electric linemen have been electrocuted as a result of not wearing rubber gloves or a safety belt may help workers appreciate the need for such rules. Safety reminders including posters,

---

[24]Thelan et al., 39.

SUPERVISORY SKILLS
Effective Health and Safety Programs

1. Set a good example by adhering to safety and health regulations. Practice what you preach.

2. Be sure that your employees know the benefits to be gained from your safety and health program.

3. Conduct continuous training in safety and health. Remember that all employees need this training and need to be reminded of the guidelines on a continuous basis.

4. Enforce the regulations firmly and consistently, taking corrective action when necessary. Keep accurate records of all safety and health violations and of all injuries and illnesses.

5. Let your employees know how well the department is doing in safety and health. Share the good news as well as bad news!

newsletter items, and supervisory comments should be a part of the everyday workplace conversations.

One expert on workplace safety training suggested that supervisors hold small group meetings to discuss attitudes, behaviors, and conditions that can improve work safety. He suggested six rules for supervisors and employees alike.

1. "Keep your mind in the present." Avoid distractions that often lead to accidents.

2. "Manage your time and schedule safe work practices into your routine." Avoid saving time by working too fast and without necessary safety precautions.

3. "Change boring routines as often as possible." Supervisors should seek fresh approaches to work so that employee boredom doesn't lead to carelessness and a resultant accident.

4. "Don't take chances." Many workers deal with hazardous equipment or materials every day. Avoid becoming overconfident and taking risks.

5. "Resist peer pressure to be unsafe." Supervisors should create a safety conscious environment where peer pressure will foster safety.

6. "Take personal responsibility." Workers should take responsibility for everyone's safety. A timely warning can save somebody's life.[25]

For further insights in this area, read "The Quality Challenge: Safety and Quality." One further issue is emerging rapidly regarding organizational safety and health—the issue of AIDS in the workplace.

---

[25]Bernard Thompson, "Managing for Safeness," *Management Solutions* (March 1987): 42–43.

THE QUALITY CHALLENGE
Safety and Quality

Safety and quality go hand-in-hand and are particularly important in increasing productivity. A good example is provided by safety problems that result in lost worker time and higher production costs. If these problems can be eliminated, costs decline and output rises. Simply stated, if things are done right the first time, quality will increase. There are five things supervisors can do to ensure increased safety and quality.

1. Make sure that everyone understands the safety rules and abides by them. The value of this guideline is best understood when it is not followed. Mistakes are so costly that it is almost always true that prevention is better than detection. Eliminating safety problems will save more money than carefully monitoring safety hazards to keep accidents to a minimum. Knowledge of safety rules is critical to this process.

2. Remain alert for needed changes in safety rules and procedures. From time to time, it will become obvious that the introduction of new equipment and work processes will outmode some of the old approaches to safety and require new ones. Make note of these and pass them on to your boss or the safety committee that is responsible for acting on them.

3. When people violate safety rules, take the action that is warranted. Be careful to not overlook the matter. Once people believe that you are not serious about enforcing safety regulations, your work group will begin ignoring these directives. This is going to result in increased accidents and could end up jeopardizing your job. So if only to protect your own position, be tough on safety.

4. In determining safety changes that can further reduce problems and drive up productivity, learn to depend on your work group for ideas. They are doing the work and have a better understanding of the dangers that are involved. If they feel that some jobs are more dangerous than initially thought or are reluctant to carry out certain tasks without additional safety equipment, treat their concerns seriously. They may know something you don't.

5. Continually meet with your people to discuss additional steps that can be taken to improve safety. A review of accidents and mistakes can also help in pinpointing problem areas. Remember, as safety increases so does quality and productivity!

AIDS IN THE WORKPLACE

According to then Surgeon General C. Everett Koop, 1.5 to 2 million Americans are currently carrying the HIV virus, which causes the Acquired Immune Deficiency Syndrome (AIDS).[26] No company is exempt. Said Koop, "It is not a matter of 'if' they will have an employee with AIDS, but rather 'when.' "[27] Nothing in recent history has caused so much fear, mis-

---

[26]Bill Patterson, "AIDS in the Workplace: Is Your Company Prepared?" *Training and Development Journal* (February 1989): 39–41.

[27]Vaughn Alliton, "Financial Realities of AIDS in the Workplace," *HR Magazine* (February 1992): 78.

understanding, and shunning of its victims as AIDS. Although the causes and treatments of AIDS are largely unknown, the public is well aware that AIDS is incurable and deadly. However, the public is less aware of the fact that AIDS cannot be contracted through casual contact. Early reactions to AIDS in the workplace resulted in cases of discrimination against persons known to have AIDS or even suspected of having AIDS.

> In one company, an employee with AIDS was fired because of the disease. He won a lawsuit and returned to work. Unfortunately, two-thirds of the other employees stayed home, afraid of catching it. . . . The Vice President of a fast-food chain fired an employee suspected of having AIDS. That company now faces a discrimination suit.[28]

A survey of 2,000 workers showed that about two-thirds of them would be afraid to use the same tools, bathrooms, or lunchrooms as fellow employees with AIDS.[29] Fear seems to be the primary response to contact with AIDS victims.

> "The lesson is simple: prepare supervisors and managers to handle the complex human resources issues created by today's most socially stigmatized, life-threatening illness, before a decision is made that lands your company in court."[30]

In many companies, the legal and ethical realities of the situation now are recognized. These companies now treat AIDS victims as they would anyone else with a serious disease. Although a 1989 survey of more than 300 companies in the San Francisco Bay area showed that only 10 percent had a formal HIV–AIDS policy, this is destined to change, due to antidiscrimination protection afforded by the Americans with Disabilities Act.[31] Companies such as Levi Strauss, Digital Equipment, and CIBA Corning Diagnostics are leading the way by writing and institutionalizing comprehensive AIDS policies that rely on employee education as their cornerstone.[32]

Effective corporate AIDS policies should have at least six components: (1) a formal corporate statement of policy, (2) employee education, (3) hiring and continued employment procedures, (4) benefits and insurance, (5) medical confidentiality, and (6) employee assistance program support.[33]

---

[28]Bill Patterson, "AIDS in the Workplace: Is Your Company Prepared?" *Training and Development Journal* (February 1989) 39.

[29]Patterson, 40.

[30]Eleanor Smith, "Train Supervisors to Be AIDS Savvy" *Personnel* (April 1991): 7.

[31]R. Wayne Mondy and Robert M. Noe, III, *Human Resource Management,* 5th ed. (Boston, Mass.: Allyn & Bacon, 1993), 558.

[32]Stuart Feldman, "Three Successful Programs," *Personnel* (April 1991): 11.

[33]Bill Patterson, "Managing with AIDS in the Workplace," *Management World* (January-February 1989): 44–47.

SUPERVISORY SKILLS
AIDS in the Workplace

1. Supervisors are in a key position to positively influence worker perceptions and attitudes about AIDS in the workplace. The key to supervisory influence is for the supervisor to be well educated about the way AIDS is transmitted. Supervisors may take part in corporate training both as students and as instructors. They can encourage employees to become knowledgeable about this disease and to dispel myths and fears that they may have.

2. If you are supervising a person who has AIDS or is suspected of having it, respect that person's rights, especially the right to medical confidentiality. Encourage him or her to make use of corporate support systems and do whatever you can to help the person stay productive and on-the-job. Remember, the job environment may be the only positive force in the AIDS patient's life.

The corporate policy statement should simply state that the company deals with AIDS as it deals with any other life-threatening disease. The employee education component is extremely important. Here the supervisor plays an important role. The key to employee education is successful communication of the information that AIDS is transmitted only by sexual contact, injection of contaminated blood or use of contaminated needles, or the exchange of bodily fluids such as between an infected mother and her unborn child. Supervisors must themselves be well educated, secure in their knowledge of the subject, and able to reassure worried employees about their safety in the workplace. Most important, corporations need to educate workers about

> . . . the human side of the disease. Facts and figures can tell us what is out there numerically, but we must realize that we are not dealing with numbers, but with people who have feelings and needs. Employers need to cultivate an atmosphere of understanding and compassion, starting with the educational process.[34]

Hiring and continued employment procedures should be the same as for any other employee. AIDS patients should be allowed to remain in the workplace so long as they are able to do the job. Even then, reasonable accommodation must be made to engineer the work environment so that they can continue their employment. Benefits and medical insurance, likewise, should be handled as for any other person. Medical confidentiality is important because the AIDS patient is so likely to be shunned by his or her co-workers. Employee assistance programs are beneficial to both the AIDS patient and his or her co-workers. These programs can provide valuable counseling and stress-relief as well as referral to outside agencies.

---

[34]Patterson, "AIDS in the Workplace: Is Your Company Prepared?", 40.

SUMMARY

Safety and health are major issues in today's workplace. Concern for them can be traced back to the beginning of the Industrial Revolution. However, the last three decades have seen a great deal of legislation related to the area.

The major piece of legislation has been the Occupational Safety and Health Act of 1970, which established the National Institute for Occupational Safety and Health. The act also gave OSHA personnel the right to set standards, conduct inspections, and issue citations and penalties. In recent years, however, OSHA's authority has been legally limited. In particular, unannounced inspections are no longer permitted.

Safety and health hazards vary by industry. Workers face four basic types of hazards: physical, chemical, biological, and stress. These hazards are caused by dangers in the work environment and accident-prone employees. Recent OSHA attention has focused on cumulative trauma disorders, environmental smoke, and sick buildings.

The first requirement for an effective safety and health program is a strong commitment from top management. Other requirements include education and training of all employees and the anticipation of safety problems and planning for them before disaster strikes. The supervisor's role in safety and health programs is to ensure that safety procedures are followed and provide the necessary training to employees.

AIDS is an increasingly common phenomenon in the workplace. Employees meet the threat of contracting AIDS or of working with someone with AIDS with fear and confusion. The supervisor is central to the way the corporation deals with AIDS in the workplace. Most companies already have or will soon develop a corporate policy towards AIDS. Supervisors should be well informed about the way AIDS is transmitted and they should be careful not to discriminate against anyone suspected of having AIDS.

REVIEW QUESTIONS

1. Is occupational safety and health a new issue? Explain.

2. What is the purpose of the Occupational Safety and Health Act of 1970? How does it regulate industry? Explain.

3. How did *Marshall v. Barlow* affect OSHA inspections? Explain.

4. How is an incidence rate computed for accidental injury and illness? Give an example.

5. How does a safety hazard differ from a health hazard? Describe the two.

6. Are the rates of occupational injury and illness relatively the same from industry to industry? Explain.

7. What are the four general types of occupational health hazards? Describe each.

8. What are the two main causes for occupational accidents? Describe each.

9. What are the three requirements for an effective safety and health program? Identify and describe them.

10. Do effective safety and health programs have any bottom-line impact? Explain.

11. What is the supervisor's role in safety and health programs? Be complete in your answer.

12. What should be included in corporate AIDS policies? Why is education critical to dealing with AIDS in the workplace?

KEY TERMS

Cumulative trauma disorders. Illnesses associated with repetitive motion, for example, carpal tunnel syndrome.

Ergonomics. Study of how job environment and improved safety can make jobs more comfortable and less fatiguing.

Health hazards. Those aspects of the work environment that slowly and cumulatively lead to deterioration of an employee's health.

Occupational Safety and Health Act of 1970. Most comprehensive work safety and health act ever enacted, it sets forth safety standards, rules, policies, and enforcement procedures and penalties.

Safety hazards. Those aspects of the work environment that have the potential of immediate, sometimes violent, harm to an employee.

ANSWERS TO SELF-ASSESSMENT QUIZ 15–1

All answers are false.

1. Occupational safety and health is legislated by the federal government through OSHA.

2. It is the responsibility of management to set safety standards and see that they are followed.

3. There is much public interest in this issue.

4. Workers' compensation programs date back to 1911.

5. Politics has certainly entered in the history of safety and health legislation. See opening section of this chapter.

6. Only accidents involving death or certain injuries must be recorded. See Figure 15–1.

7. This is not the case. See statistics present in Table 15–1.

8. Safety hazards have potential to cause immediate harm. Health hazards lead to slow, cumulative health loss. See definitions in key terms section.

9. The construction industry leads with the most accidents.

10. Some employees are indeed accident prone. They tend to act impulsively and do not concentrate on the task at hand.

11. Statistics are probably understated because many illnesses are not readily attributed to occupational hazards.

12. Safety manuals alone are very inadequate. Safety training must be a priority.

CASE 15–1
The "Good News" Is He's Going to Live

Over the last six months there have been ten accidents at the Sharpender plant. The latest one occurred yesterday. Three workers were moving a piece of heavy equipment from one end of the plant to the other. The machine had been placed on four small dollies—one on each corner of the machine. At first, things went quite well. However, when the workers were approximately halfway across the plant, they decided to start moving faster. One got behind the machine and the others took up positions on each side. As they began to move faster, the dolly on the left front corner of the machine slipped out. The worker on the right did not see that this had happened. As a result, when he continued to push, the machine tipped over on its left side. The worker on this side was caught unaware and trapped beneath the heavy machine. It took the other two people, and those who hurried over to help, almost a minute to get the machine off him. An emergency rescue unit rushed the injured worker to the hospital.

Earlier today the senior foreman learned that the hurt employee was out of critical condition and would be all right. "The bad news is: his right leg is broken," the doctor told the foreman, "and he has some broken ribs and a col-

lapsed right lung. The good news is: he's going to live. In the future I suggest that if the workers in your plant want to play around, they do it at home."

The president of the firm and the company attorney have a meeting scheduled with the foreman later today. In the interim, the foreman intends to get all the available accident-related information. In particular the foreman cannot understand how the three workers could have been so foolish as to do what they did. In any event he knows that he is going to have to tell the president what happened, why it happened, and what he intends to do to prevent a recurrence. By the time he meets with them, the foreman intends to have all of these answers sketched out on a note pad.

1.   Does this accident have to be reported under OSHA guidelines? Explain.

2.   Whose fault was the accident? Defend your answer.

3.   If you were the senior foreman, what would you do to help prevent these types of accidents in the future? What would your plan entail? Explain.

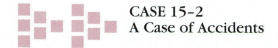

CASE 15–2
A Case of Accidents

The Wilson Trucking firm, which has been in operation for three years, has had a turnover of 85 percent among its drivers. This is mainly due to high insurance rates, and Wilson's consequent strict policy: it fires any driver with less than eighteen months seniority who is involved in two accidents.

At the present time thirty drivers work for Wilson. Here is a breakdown of how long they have been with the firm and how many accidents they have had.

Number of Drivers	Time on the Job	Number of Accidents
7	less than 6 months	5
5	6–12 months	4
6	13–18 months	2
5	19–24 months	1
7	more than 24 months	1

The president of the firm feels that there are still too many accidents and that something has to be done. He has asked the head supervisor to do something about it. The president believes that the problem may be that the firm is hiring too many inexperienced people. "Let's get some people with truck driving experience and quit hiring first-time people," he has urged his staff.

1. Based on the data in the case, what can you conclude about the number of accidents and the personnel who have them? Explain.

2. Is the president right? Could the problem be that there is not sufficient training being given to the drivers? Defend your answer.

3. Are there any other reasons that might be accounting for the problem? What are they? Explain.

PART IV

T he objective of this last part is to examine personal strategies for success. These strategies can take many forms, including effectively managing one's time and stress, dealing with organizational policies and ethics, or developing a career plan.

Chapter 16 examines organizational politics and ethics. In addition to defining the term *ethics,* the chapter sets forth twelve guidelines for checking the ethics of a business decision. The supervisor's role in maintaining ethical standards of behavior in the organization is discussed, as are the five basic reasons that people engage in political behavior in organizations. The chapter closes with an explanation of some of the most common strategies or political tactics used by organizational personnel.

Chapter 17 investigates the topic of stress management. In addition to defining the term *stress,* the nature of stress and some of its most common causes are discussed. The chapter then moves on to discuss some of the possible consequences of stress and describes techniques for managing both personal and organizational stress. Time management is the second important topic in this chapter, with a focus on providing a very practical approach to the topic. This includes describing ways to put together a time log, set up quarterly objectives, draw up weekly plans and schedule daily activities, and become aware of some of the most common time wasters.

Personal Strategies for Success

Chapter 18 is devoted to explaining the ways you can develop career plans and prepare for future challenges. It begins by identifying and describing the six steps in the personal career development process and setting forth and explaining six useful career development strategies. In addition, it discusses ten trends that will face American business during the upcoming decade and notes their effect on the supervisor's job. Next, the chapter examines some of the major ways in which employee characteristics are changing and the impact this will have on the supervisor's job. It also considers some of the predictions concerning worker participation in corporate governance and the way this will affect the supervisor's job. Finally, Chapter 18 relates the impact of the computer on the workplace and the effect of this development on the supervisor's job.

When you have finished studying all of this material, you will know some of the most important personal strategies that supervisors should develop. In particular, you will have gained insights regarding strategy formulation in the areas of organizational politics, stress management, time management, and career planning. You will also have a well-rounded understanding of what it takes to be successful in the supervisory ranks.

CHAPTER 16

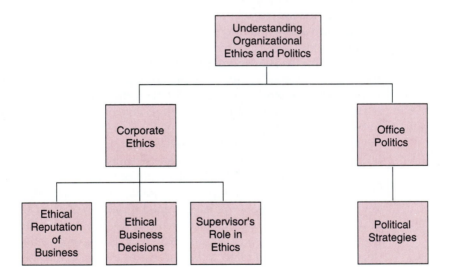

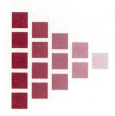

Understanding Organizational Ethics and Politics

*"Practically every week some new ethics scandal hits the headlines, further souring Americans on the business community."**

CHAPTER OBJECTIVES

☐ Define the term *ethics*.

☐ Identify twelve guidelines that can be used to check the ethics of a business decision.

☐ Discuss the supervisor's role in maintaining ethical standards of behavior in the organization.

☐ Describe the five basic reasons why people engage in political behavior in organizations.

☐ Identify and explain some of the most common strategies or political tactics used by organizational personnel.

---

*Philip M. van Auken, "Being an Ethical Supervisor," *Supervisory Management* (October 1992): 3.

rganizational ethics and politics are two of the most important environmental forces in an enterprise. The first helps dictate right and wrong behavior. The second is used by individuals who are attempting to persuade others to their point of view or gain political favor for themselves. Supervisors cannot escape either of these two forces; indeed they must learn to deal with them. Moreover, the two forces are often in conflict. Ethical behavior may restrict the political tactics used by organizational personnel, and those who refuse to be guided by such behavioral codes may be acting unethically. For purposes of simplicity, many businesspeople regard ethics as a guide for handling external relationships, whereas they see office politics as the guide for handling internal relationships. This perspective may be a simplistic way of distinguishing between the domains of the two forces, but it is also a very realistic view. Moreover, ethics often sets the stage for what managers should not do, whereas office politics dictates what they must (or should) do. In any event these are important areas of consideration for anyone studying supervisory management.

CORPORATE ETHICS

Ethics is one of those words that is very hard to define. Everyone knows what it is and yet nobody can precisely explain it. Furthermore, everyone's idea of what constitutes ethical behavior is different. Many people agree that employees should not steal from the company, but at the same time their briefcases are full of pens, pads, and paper clips taken from the office. In the interest of having a common understanding of what ethics is and arriving at our own definition, consider the following definitions from other experts: Steiner and Steiner said, "Ethics is the study of what is good and bad, right and wrong, and just and unjust."[1]

Buchholz observed that "ethics in general is concerned with actions and practices that are directed to improving the welfare of people."[2]

Focusing on "business ethics," as opposed to ethics in general, Sturdivant stated: "Business ethics comprises moral principles and standards that guide behavior in the world of business."[3]

Ethics is doing what is morally right and just when dealing with people. It is interesting to note the attitudes of the general public about the ethics of business. *Business ethics* concerns both the ends and means involved in business decision making.

> Ethics is doing what is morally right and just when dealing with people.

---

[1]George A. Steiner and John F. Steiner, *Business, Government and Society: A Managerial Perspective,* 6th ed. (New York: McGraw-Hill, Inc., 1991), 201.

[2]Rogene A. Buccholz, *Business Environment and Public Policy,* 4th ed. (Englewood Cliffs, N.J.: Prentice-Hall, 1992), 46.

[3]O. C. Ferrell and John Frederick, *Business Ethics* (Boston, Mass.: Houghton Mifflin Co., 1991), 5.

Ethical Reputation of Business

There are two basic camps of thought about business ethics: (1) business should not concern itself with moral issues; and (2) business has a moral obligation to the society it serves.

Some people feel that business should not concern itself with moral issues.

Those who feel that "the business of business is business" warn that business should focus on economic and financial imperatives and not worry about abstract concepts of "right" and "wrong" behavior. According to this view, business may be likened to a game that everyone should play with the sole aim to be a winner. Some of the largest companies today began with some controversial practices in their early days. For instance, John D. Rockefeller, founder of Standard Oil, supposedly "spied on competitors by bribing their employees, gave kickbacks to railroads, blew up a widow's oil refinery when she refused to sell out, and lied to a congressional committee hearing."[4]

Most people feel that businesses should act ethically.

Today more people believe that business is not above moral standards and should seek to act ethically. Surveys have shown, however, that Americans do not think ethical standards in society, especially in business, are high enough. A 1987 survey conducted for *Time* magazine found a low opinion of ethical standards.

> More than 90% of the respondents agreed that morals have fallen because parents fail to take responsibility for their children or to imbue them with decent moral standards; 76% saw lack of ethics in businessmen as contributing to tumbling moral standards; and 74% decried failure by political leaders to set a good example.[5]

Another survey of 1,300 middle managers showed a variety of ethical behaviors.

> "In a nutshell, middle managers' responses to straightforward ethical questions reflect a pure and steadfast virtue usually reserved for Boy Scouts and clerics. When pushed into gray areas where loyalties, goals, and the desire to be honest don't coincide, however, rationalizations for shady behavior begin working their way into decisions."[6]

Many companies have adopted codes of ethics.

With the newspapers full of business scandals such as insider trading and padding of bills by defense contractors, the majority of big businesses have adopted formal codes of ethics. A 1990 report of a survey conducted by the Ethics Resource Center in Washington, D.C., of 2,000 U.S. businesses found that 85 percent of the respondents reported having a written code of ethics

---

[4]Steiner and Steiner, 203.

[5]"Looking to its Roots: At a Time of Moral Disarray, America Seeks to Rebuild a Structure of Values," *Time* (May 25, 1987): 26–29.

[6]David R. Altany, "Torn Between Halo and Horns," *Industry Week* (March 15, 1993): 15.

TABLE 16–1

How business ranks the importance of ethical business issues

Most Serious

1. Drug and alcohol abuse
2. Employee theft
3. Conflicts of interest
4. Quality control
5. Discrimination
6. Misuse of proprietary information
7. Abuse of expense accounts
8. Plant closing and layoffs
9. Misuse of company assets
10. Environmental pollution
11. Misuse of others' sensitive information
12. Methods of gathering competitors' information

Least Serious

Source: Adapted from Robert McCabe, "Wall Street Scandals Spur Ethics Revival, *Sun-Sentinel* (September 22, 1991): 1F.

or written guidelines on ethics.[7] Table 16–1 shows how these same respondents ranked the twelve most important ethical business issues.

Ethical Business Decisions

It is sometimes difficult to make ethical business decisions. Economic needs dominate, individual desires to achieve prevail, and confusion about what is ethical confounds the issue. Before reading on, take Self-Assessment Quiz 16–1 to examine your own attitudes on a number of ethical questions.

One author suggested the following twelve guidelines as a practical way to check the ethics of business decisions.[8]

Here is a checklist to guide the ethics of your business decisions.

1. Have you defined the problem accurately? Do not be emotional; collect the facts.
2. How would you define the problem if you stood on the other side of the fence? This question checks objectivity and enlarges the decision maker's perspective to include other points of view.
3. How did this situation occur in the first place? Examine the problem's history and try to understand all the perspectives involved.

---

[7]Robert McCabe, "Wall Street Scandals Spur Ethics Revival," *Sun-Sentinel* (September 22, 1991): 1F.

[8]Laura L. Nash, "Ethics Without the Sermon," *Harvard Business Review* (November-December 1981): 79–90.

SELF-ASSESSMENT QUIZ 16-1
An Ethics Text

Many situations in day-to-day business are not simple right-or-wrong questions but fall into a gray area. To demonstrate the perplexing array of moral dilemmas faced by twentieth century Americans, here is a "nonscientific" test for slippage . . . Don't expect to score high. That is not the purpose. But give it a try, and see how you stack up.

Put your value system to the test in the following situations:

Scoring Code:
Strongly Agree = SA
Disagree = D
Agree = A
Strongly Disagree = SD

_____ 1. Employees should not be expected to inform on their peers for wrongdoings.

_____ 2. There are times when a manager must overlook contract and safety violations in order to get on with the job.

_____ 3. It is not always possible to keep accurate expense account records; therefore, it is sometimes necessary to give approximate figures.

_____ 4. There are times when it is necessary to withhold embarrassing information from one's superior.

_____ 5. We should do what our managers suggest, though we may have doubts about its being the right thing to do.

_____ 6. It is sometimes necessary to conduct personal business on company time.

_____ 7. Sometimes it is good psychology to set goals somewhat above normal if it will help obtain a greater effort from the sales force.

_____ 8. I would quote a "hopeful" shipping date in order to get the order.

_____ 9. It is proper to use the company WATS line for personal calls as long as it's not in company use.

_____ 10. Management must be goal-oriented; therefore, the end usually justifies the means.

_____ 11. If it takes heavy entertainment and twisting a bit of company policy to win a large contract, I would authorize it.

_____ 12. Exceptions to company policy and procedures are a way of life.

_____ 13. Inventory controls should be designed to report "underages" rather than "overages" in goods received. (The ethical issue here is the same as that faced by someone who receives too much change from a store cashier.)

_____ 14. Occasional use of the company's copier for personal or community activities is acceptable.

_____ 15. Taking home company property (pencils, paper, tape, and so on) for personal use is an accepted fringe benefit.

Score Key: (0) for Strongly Disagree (1) for Disagree (2) for Agree (3) for Strongly Agree If your score is:

0	Prepare for canonization ceremony
1–5	Bishop material
6–10	High ethical values
11–15	Good ethical values
16–25	Average ethical values
26–35	Need moral development
36–44	Slipping fast
45	Leave valuables with warden

Source: "Is Your (Ethical) Slippage Showing?" by Lowell G. Rein, copyright September 1980. Reprinted with the permission of _Personnel Journal,_ Costa Mesa, California. All rights reserved.

4. To whom and to what do you give your loyalties as a person and as a member of the corporation? Conflicts often occur between what you believe to be right and what the corporation seems to demand of you out of loyalty. In other cases, your peers may ask you to go along with something against your personal beliefs.

5. What is your intention in making this decision? If your intentions seem honorable to you, then you are probably on safe ground to proceed. If you cannot answer this question comfortably, you should take a long, hard look at what you are trying to accomplish.

6. How does this intention compare with the likely results? Are the potential outcomes harmful to someone? Does the end justify the means?

7. Whom could your decision or action injure? For example, if you decide to develop a product that when used carelessly could cause serious injury or death, should you assume that all who use the product will exercise due care, or should you decide against its production unless the product can be made with more built-in safety features?

8. Can you engage the affected parties in a discussion of the problem before you make your decision? Try to consider the views of those most likely to be affected by your decisions. For example, if you are deciding how to lay off 10 percent of the work force on a temporary basis, you might want to involve worker representatives in the deliberations on the best ways to accomplish this goal.

9. Are you confident that your position will be as valid over a long period of time as it seems now? Does your decision seem likely to stand the test of time, that is, do the conditions that now make this a necessary decision seem likely to be important in the long run?

10. Could you openly disclose without qualms, your decision or action to your boss, your CEO, the board of directors, your family, or society as a whole? If not, what is there about your decision that you would not want to be made public?

11. What is the symbolic potential of your action if understood? If misunderstood? What will people interpret from your decision to remove a potentially dangerous product from the market? Will your decision symbolize concern for the consumer or guilt?

12. Under what conditions would you allow exceptions to your stand? When is an absolute decision not absolute? Is your belief in truth-in-advertising compromised when your advertising executive mounts a "better than ever" campaign for a product that you know has not substantially changed in twenty years?

What are the benefits of asking these questions? First, the questions would help the individual or the team making the decision to think through ethical considerations normally left to instinct. Values and attitudes would surface, and people would be led to confront the oft-occurring conflicts between personal beliefs and corporate necessity. Second, thinking through these questions would be very beneficial from the organization's standpoint, because it allows analysis of possible consequences and exploration of other alternative decisions that otherwise might not have been considered.

Supervisor's Role in Ethics

As with many other areas, the supervisor plays a key role in establishing an ethical standard of behavior within the department. One expert says that the ethical supervisor:

1. Protects the best interests of others, including customers, employees, and minority members of society.
2. Values employees not only as workers but as people.
3. Tells the truth; doesn't just say what people want to hear.
4. Doesn't play psychological games such as blame-shifting or one-upmanship.
5. Focuses on the mission or ends rather than rules and regulations or means.
6. Is committed to ideals such as honesty, fair play, and quality work.[9]

It is very important that supervisors display high ethical standards. Employees are unlikely to feel compelled to act according to high ethical standards if the supervisor is observed breaking or bending the rules on a routine basis. At the department level many ethical questions are constantly raised. Should personal phone calls be allowed? Is it all right to add a bit here and there to your expense report? Is it routine to call in sick when you do not feel like working? Should you "blow the whistle" on a fellow employee when you observe wrongdoing? In all cases supervisors must be sure that their position on the matter is clear and consistent. Supervisors set the pace, and employees are sure to notice whether they live up to their word. "The Quality Challenge: Ethics Is Profitable" provides some additional insights in this area.

> The supervisor plays a key role in establishing an ethical standard of behavior.

Whistle-Blowing. In most parts of American society children have been taught not to be a "tattle-tale." Many employees feel, therefore, that it is against their very nature to engage in *whistle-blowing,* or to report wrongdoing by their peers. When should organizational whistle-blowing be discouraged? First, supervisors should discourage pettiness and vindictiveness as reasons for one employee to blow the whistle on another.

---

[9]Philip M. van Auken, "Being an Ethical Supervisor," *Supervisory Management* (October 1992): 3.

THE QUALITY CHALLENGE

Ethics Is Profitable

High ethics is important to organizational performance and profitability. In fact, research reveals that successful supervisors tend to have high ethical standards. They do not cut corners; they are honest and forthright in the performance of their duties. Four of the major reasons why high ethical practices are important to supervisors are the following:

1. Workers look at their supervisor as a role model or individual to emulate. If you come in late and leave early, they will try to do the same thing. If there are time clocks, they will think little of having the first person in the work group to arrive clock in all of the rest. So your unethical behavior will result in lost productivity and higher costs for the company.

2. If you find that some of the output is not meeting quality standards and fail to blow the whistle, these items will eventually be returned to the company by the buyer and will have to be replaced. So your failure to do the ethical thing will cost the firm more money in the long run.

3. Poor ethical practices help destroy the reputation of a firm. It may take a while before customers, clients, and others who are doing business with the firm arrive at this conclusion. But when they do, they will take their business elsewhere, and it may be years before these people return, thus costing the firm a great deal of lost revenue.

4. Employees and customers expect managers to act ethically. This is a minimum level of behavior. So to the extent that you do so, you may not make things better for the organization, but you will stop things from getting worse.

Also, observant supervisors can usually spot trouble areas and speak to the wrongdoer before other employees have to face the conflict of deciding whether to complain. If a complaint is lodged, however, the supervisor must investigate the charge and let all involved know the outcome. Supervisors who ignore news of wrongdoing are asking for bigger problems in the future. The employee who made the charge will lose all faith in the supervisor as a fair and just person, and, perhaps more significantly the news will soon circulate that rules are indeed meant to be broken.

The supervisor should investigate all charges made by whistle-blowers.

> Whistle-blowing is also receiving a lot of attention in the executive office. Many companies are now instituting open communication to a top management person in the event that employees have a need to grieve or simply a concern to express. In some companies the manager charged with this responsibility is called an "ombudsman," a word borrowed from the Swedes who used this term for a civil servant who follows up on complaints about government office. One of the reasons so many companies have decided to take this formal approach is because many whistle-blowers are choosing to take their complaints public![10]

---

[10]Michael Brody, "Listen to Your Whistleblower," *Fortune* (November 24, 1986): 77–78.

SUPERVISORY SKILLS
Setting the Example

1. Set the tone for ethical behavior in your department. Employees look to you for an example. If you cut corners and take advantage of the company, employees will feel it is perfectly all right for them to do the same.

2. Let employees know the ethical standards in the department. From their first day on the job employees should know that honesty is valued, quality work is rewarded, and they are expected to act with loyalty and integrity. Reinforce these ideals by re-warding outstanding examples of loyalty and integrity, not just by calling attention to inadequate behavior in these areas.

3. Be sensitive to whistle-blowing and the far-reaching consequences of this behavior. Nothing ruins a department's team spirit as quickly as one employee telling tales on another. However, realize that the employee doing the "telling" may indeed be serving an important function for the organization by uncovering a serious problem that needs to be confronted.

External whistle-blowing is a phenomenon increasingly common to American corporations. Here the consequences are usually much more serious. Consider the experience of Karen Silkwood, as depicted in the movie *Silkwood*. A worker in a nuclear facility in the South, Silkwood went to the press with word of safety hazards in her facility. Some observers feel her untimely, "accidental" death was not a coincidence but a staged retribution for her whistle-blowing. Although most corporate "whistle-blowers" are not afraid of losing their lives, they do stand a very good chance of losing peer respect and perhaps their job. On the other hand, consumer advocates assert that without corporate whistle-blowers or the threat of their existence, American businesses would act far less ethically than they do now. All of this, of course, is a matter of conjecture.

It is fairly obvious that active corporate attention to employee concern is very important.

> In corporations that have not traditionally fostered upward communication, traditional methods may not suffice. A companywide 800 number to an executive with clout can go a long way to encouraging troubled employees to speak up—before they speak out.[11]

OFFICE POLITICS

No discussion of corporate ethics would be complete without considering office politics. Rumors abound about "the only way to get ahead is to play golf with the boss," or "it's not what you know around here but who you know." Simply put, *office politics* involves activities undertaken out of self-

---

[11]Ibid.

interest for personal gain. Typically, political activity is used to increase the power base of the person in question. In this age of respect for education and competence, why is office politics necessary? Apparently, people engage in workplace politics for the following five reasons:.[12]

1. Competition for limited power. There is just so much power in any organization; some is distributed because of one's position in the organization chart; some is awarded because of one's expertise.

2. Lack of concrete goals to judge career progress. If people knew exactly what they had to do to achieve specific career goals in their organizations, political activity would be greatly limited.

3. Personal insecurity. If employees are insecure about their jobs or their performance, they often try to ingratiate themselves to their supervisor in order to protect their jobs. People who know they are valuable to the organization have less need to play political games.

4. Increasing use of participatory management techniques. It is no longer fashionable for supervisors to be authoritarian and completely directive in their leadership behavior. Thus, whereas supervisors could once demand what they wanted, some have now taken to manipulative, political maneuvers to achieve these ends.

5. Avoidance of difficult or unpleasant work. Some employees feel that if they are "in good" with the boss, the boss will not give them the difficult or unpleasant assignments.

The amount of political activity that takes place varies from organization to organization and even among the various departments within the same organization. Production departments are sometimes found to be the least political, whereas marketing departments are often considered the most political. One possible explanation for this finding is rooted in the fact that marketing staffs are typically very competitive and staff members' performance is based on beating others, both within the department and outside the department. Production departments, on the other hand, may have more stable jobs with less competition built into the nature of the work. Cooperative teamwork and coordination of activities are more characteristic of such departments.

Political Strategies

Regardless of where organizational politics occurs, employees are likely to engage in the following strategies or political tactics: (1) trying to please the boss, (2) creating a power base, (3) gaining a competitive edge over one's peers, and (4) discrediting others.

---

[12]Andrew J. DuBrin, *The Practice of Supervision* (Dallas, Tex.: Business Publications, 1980), 110–113.

Pleasing the Boss. The most important quality that is bound to keep your manager happy is loyalty. Such faithfulness does not imply that you always have to agree with the boss, but it does mean showing loyalty in public and going out of your way to try to make him look good to others. Effectively pleasing the boss infers that you must know the individual very well. Try to understand the boss's priorities and look for ways in which you can help advance those goals. The following list offers ten questions that can help you discover what is important to your manager.[13]

1. To whom does your manager report?
2. What are your manager's primary responsibilities?
3. Examine your manager's chief successes. When and where did they take place?
4. Examine any setbacks your manager has had. What is bothering him or her?
5. Does your manager have any internal enemies?
6. How extensive is your manager's authority?
7. What authority has your manager delegated and to whom?
8. What are your manager's major worries or goals?
9. How is your manager evaluated? On what achievements is this person's corporate success based?
10. How does your manager evaluate you?

Trying to please the boss, however, can be overdone. Excess occurs when one becomes known as the manager's "stooge," one who curries favor by ingratiating himself or herself to the boss. If you gain the favor of the latter by this method, you can be assured that you will lose the respect of your peers in time.

Creating a Power Base. All supervisors have some power within the organization, but the amount is likely to vary greatly. As just discussed, some people, employees as well as supervisors, try to gain more power by making their managers happy. Others try to take on more and more responsibility, thereby making themselves of more value to the organization. Still others try to do favors for people, which in turn obligates recipients for future favors. Another aspect of building personal power is called "empire building," which is described as follows: "Gaining and keeping control over human and material resources is the principal motivation behind this tactic [empire building]. Those with large budgets usually feel more safely

---

[13]Adapted from Leslie W. Rue and Lloyd L. Byars, *Supervision: Key Link to Productivity*, 3rd ed. (Homewood, Ill.: Irwin, 1990), 405.

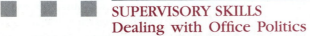

SUPERVISORY SKILLS
Dealing with Office Politics

1. Be aware that office politics is an undeniable part of corporate culture and that ignoring the existence of political tactics and activities only gives greater advantage to the corporate politicians. Many people are political beings, and they've found that the best place to practice politics is in the company, where they spend most of their time.

2. Realize that it is just common sense to practice some aspects of corporate politics, such as knowing the boss well and working to make him or her, as well as yourself, look good. Loyalty is every bit as important in the corporation as it is in any political campaign. Work hard to achieve a reputation as a hard-working, loyal company person, but remember this does not equate to being a "yes man."

3. Watch out for the truly dysfunctional aspects of organizational politics, such as backbiting, and blatant attempts to discredit others. Do not practice these activities, even on an occasional basis, and discourage your employees from engaging in such practices.

---

entrenched in their positions and believe they have more influence over peers and superiors.[14]

Gaining a Competitive Edge. A favorite tactic of those who conscientiously strive to gain a competitive edge over their peers is to hoard information, thinking that if they know more than others they will have a distinct advantage. These people actively gather information on products, events, and other people and file them away for future use. They do not willingly share what they know with others because they believe in the old adage that "knowledge is power."

Unfortunately, other, even worse, tactics are sometimes used to gain a competitive edge. Some employees or supervisors deliberately take the glory for someone else's work to look better to their superiors. Others shift the blame of personal failures by making their shortcoming look like a result of someone else's work.[15]

Discrediting Others. To try to discredit another employee intentionally is perhaps the least ethical tactic of all. It is inherent in some of the strategies in the immediately preceding section. People who deliberately try to discredit others often do so to look better by comparison. They seize every opportunity to say something negative about those they perceive as being in competition with them.

---

[14]Robert Kreitner, *Management*, 5th ed. (Boston, Mass.: Houghton Mifflin Co., 1990), 434.
[15]Rue & Byars, p. 408.

SUMMARY

Ethics is doing what is morally right and just when dealing with people. Some business people feel that companies should not concern themselves with moral issues; most believe they should. In recent years the general public has felt that business ethics is falling.

Although an individual may sometimes find it difficult to make ethical business decisions, they may follow certain guidelines in checking the ethics of a decision. For example, they should accurately define the problem, trace its history and determine who could be injured. These decisions help the manager think through ethical considerations and analyze the decision's possible consequences.

Employees often emulate their boss, so supervisors play a crucial role in establishing an ethical standard of behavior within their department. If the supervisor has high ethical standards, so will the subordinates. To ensure that these standards remain high, supervisors must be sure to give whistle-blowing the attention it deserves. If a subordinate has discovered something illegal or unethical, the supervisor should investigate and, if the charge is true, call it to top management's attention.

Office politics is another major area of consideration for supervisors. People engage in political behavior because there is competition for limited power, a lack of concrete goals by which to judge their career progress, an increasing use of participatory management techniques in the organization, or because they have personal insecurities regarding their job or they want to avoid difficult or unpleasant work.

REVIEW QUESTIONS

1. In your own words, what is meant by the term *ethics?* Explain.

2. Are business ethics higher today than they were ten years ago? Defend your answer.

3. What are some of the guidelines that managers can use as a practical way of checking the ethics of their decisions? Identify and describe five.

4. What are the benefits of asking questions such as those discussed in the preceding question? Identify and describe two benefits.

5. A whistle-blower has just told her supervisor about an unethical practice that she knows is being carried on by other salespeople in the department. What should the supervisor do? Explain.

6. People engage in political behavior for five reasons. What are these reasons?

7. What are some of the most common strategies or political tactics used in organizations today? Identify and discuss three of them.

KEY TERMS

Business ethics. Principles concerned with what is right and wrong in the process of making business decisions.

Ethics. Doing what is morally right and just when dealing with people.

Office politics. Activities undertaken out of self-interest for personal gain.

Whistle-blowing. Act of one employee's reporting another's wrongdoing.

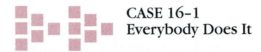

CASE 16–1
Everybody Does It

The Rundstadt Company has a general policy regarding reimbursement of all salespeople. Every individual who returns from a road trip simply files an expense account and is reimbursed within thirty days. The only limitations on reimbursement are that the company will not pay for first-class air travel and that expenses must fall within established limits for food and lodging. For example, for trips to New York City the company will pay up to $150 per day for a room and $75 for food. In Omaha the reimbursement is $80 a day for room and $50 for food.

Susan Wentworth has been a salesperson for a little over a month. During this time she has been assigned to work with Dave DeCamp, an experienced salesperson. Dave has given Susan a wealth of useful information regarding how to sell. However, one bit of advice has concerned Susan. In every city they visited Dave and she received two bills for their hotel stay. One was for the actual amount of the bill; the other was for a figure that was 50 percent higher. They stayed well within the company's limits, so the higher bill could be submitted and would

not be questioned by the accounting people. Dave explained to Susan that all of the salespeople did this. "I give the clerk $10 every time I stay here and he makes me a dummy bill. Since the company would allow me to spend the higher amount anyway, I don't see that anyone is losing by my turning in expenses that are greater than what I've actually put out."

Susan is concerned about saying anything for fear that she will be the one who ends up in trouble. On the other hand, if she does not turn in a bill that is similar to Dave's, the accounting people may question the discrepancy.

1. Is this a case of unethical behavior? Defend your answer.

2. If Susan brought this to her supervisor, what is the first thing the manager should do? Explain.

3. If supervisors have the authority to make whatever decisions they think are right, how would you recommend that the matter be handled? Why? Explain.

CASE 16–2
A Matter of Cutting Back

Things have not been going well at the Rutkin Company. For the last twelve months the firm has been unable to land a major contract. As a result, last week the company announced that it would begin laying off people. The first wave of cutbacks involve 10 percent of the work force, with the biggest cuts coming at the lower levels of the hierarchy.

Jack Lyle is responsible for cutting four supervisors and thirty-six workers from the work force in his division. Yesterday he submitted his proposed cutback plan to his boss. The latter is satisfied with the number of people being laid off but is concerned over the fact that one of the four supervisors has been with the firm for over ten years. "Ted is one of our oldest employees," he told Jack. "Why don't you cut one of your newest supervisors—for example, Jed Ambler?" Jack explained to his boss that the six remaining supervisors are all critical to the productivity of the department. "Sure Ted is one of our oldest employees. But he's also one of our least productive. On the other hand, Jed Ambler, who has been with us only six months, is one of our best. Jed knows how to complete all the monthly cost control reports, is able to use the micro in interacting with the computer and getting the latest production data, and knows how to use this information to control operations in his area. Additionally, I have sent him to the Chamber of Commerce on three occasions, and he does an excellent job of representing us to the general community. Ted has never gone to the Chamber, even though I have asked him to be a luncheon speaker on at least a half dozen occasions. In short, I think we have to cut back on those who are least likely to help us get through this crisis."

Jack's boss listened quietly and then agreed. "I see your point. Fine. I'm approving your cutback plan as proposed. Now let's see if we can't turn things around with this smaller work force."

1. Why was Jack reluctant to lay off Jed? What political strategy did Jed implement that helped ensure his position?

2. What mistake(s) did Ted make? Be as specific as possible.

3. What does this case relate about political strategies and supervisory success? Be complete in your answer.

4. Was it ethical for Jack to lay off Ted who had ten years of service, rather than Jed?

CHAPTER 17

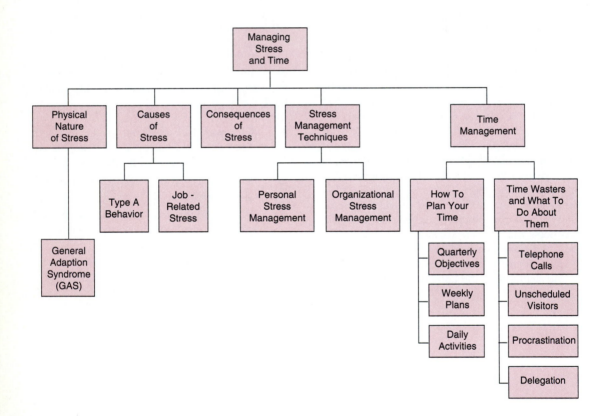

Managing Stress and Time

"The concept of stress is somewhat like the ellusive concept of love; everyone knows what the term means, but no two people would define it the same way."*

CHAPTER OBJECTIVES

- ☐ Define the term *stress*.
- ☐ Discuss the nature of stress.
- ☐ Study the most common causes of stress.
- ☐ Understand the consequences of stress.
- ☐ Describe techniques for managing both personal and organizational stress.
- ☐ Investigate techniques of managing time effectively.
- ☐ Understand how to delegate authority.

---

*Philip L. Rice, *Stress and Health,* 2nd ed. (Pacific Grove, Calif.: Brooks/Cole Publishers, 1992), 3.

S tress occurs at all levels in organizations as a result of many factors including time pressure, personnel conflicts, and sheer quantity of work.

Stress is a topic that seems to concern everyone today. Exactly what is stress? In the words of Hans Selye, considered to be the "Father of Stress Management," *stress* is the "nonspecific response of the body to any demand made upon it." Selye continued by saying that stress is "essentially the rate of wear and tear on the body."[1]

Before continuing with this chapter, find out how much you know about this important topic by taking Self-Assessment Quiz 17–1. Then check your answers at the end of the chapter.

To better understand what stress is, consider Selye's contention that stress can be good or bad depending on one's interpretation of events. Positive stress, which is called "eustress," can be motivational in nature if it is not too intense. Negative stress, which is called "distress," is much more harmful to the human being. This chapter examines stress management and a closely related supervisory issue—time management. We start by debunking a popular misconception that stress is purely a psychological matter. In fact stress is a physical phenomenon caused by a great many different things. To see the consequences of stress, we need to look at its physical nature.

PHYSICAL NATURE OF STRESS

The physical changes that the body undergoes when put under stress are the source of many illnesses. This fact is ironic considering that originally these physical changes evolved to protect early humans against environmental stressors. Walter B. Cannon is credited with first describing what is now commonly known as the "fight or flight syndrome."[2]

When faced with an enemy in the environment, animals and early humans had to muster their strength to do one of two things: run away or stand and fight. Therefore the body's physical reactions during stress help prepare us for fight or flight. Some of the most common physical changes are as follows: increased heart rate, increased respiration rate, increased skin perspiration, increased dilation of the pupils, increased blood pressure, increased muscle strength, decreased gastric functioning, decreased abdominal and surface blood flow, and increased secretion of adrenaline.

Unfortunately, in many circumstances neither fight nor flight is appropriate, and the results can be disastrous. According to conservative es-

> Stress is the nonspecific response of the body to any demand made on it.

---

[1]Hans Selye, *The Stress of Life* (New York: McGraw-Hill Book Co., 1976), 1.

[2]Jonathan C. Smith, *Understanding Stress and Coping* (New York: Macmillan Publishing Co., 1993), 7.

■ ■ ■ SELF-ASSESSMENT QUIZ 17-1
What Do You Know About Stress?

Directions: Answer each of the following questions true or false.

____ 1. Stress is a psychological disorder.

____ 2. Stress is always bad for you.

____ 3. There is no such thing as too little stress.

____ 4. The only way to rid yourself of stress is to avoid those things that cause you stress.

____ 5. Stress has predictable effects on the body.

____ 6. Stress has been a problem for humans since their earliest days.

____ 7. Stress-related diseases are psychosomatic—that is, they have no physical base.

____ 8. The organization can do very little to prevent stress; it depends on the individual personalities of the employees.

____ 9. Very little real correlation exists between stress and physical diseases.

____ 10. The most bothersome problem associated with stress is nervous anxiety.

Check your answers at the end of the chapter.

---

timates in medical textbooks, 50 to 80 percent of all physical diseases are stress-related in origin.

Stress is the principal cause of much cardiovascular disease.

Stress is believed to be a principal cause of much cardiovascular disease, America's number-one killer. It also may be a main contributing factor to the development of cancer, the number-two killer. Additionally, stress can place one at higher risk for diabetes, ulcers, asthma, migraine headaches, skin disorders, epilepsy, and sexual dysfunction. Each of these diseases, and a host of others, is psychosomatic in nature—that is, it is either caused or exacerbated by mental conditions such as stress. Because stress can cause severe physical damage, we examine the stages of stress in the body and the characteristics of the individual highly prone to stress.

General Adaptation Syndrome (GAS)

There are three GAS stages: alarm, resistance, and exhaustion.

Hans Selye theorized that stress goes through three general stages that together constitute the General Adaptation Syndrome (GAS) (see Figure 17–1). Stage one is the alarm stage. At this point the stressor has just been recognized and the body has become mobilized for fight or flight. The body's homeostasis (normal balance) is disrupted and internal organs become ready for action. Stage two, the resistance stage, is the longest stage of the GAS. It begins when the body is persistently exposed to the stressor. The body struggles to resist the alarm reactions and to return to a homeostatic state. Stage three, the exhaustion stage, occurs only if stress continues longer than the body can resist. At this stage organ systems

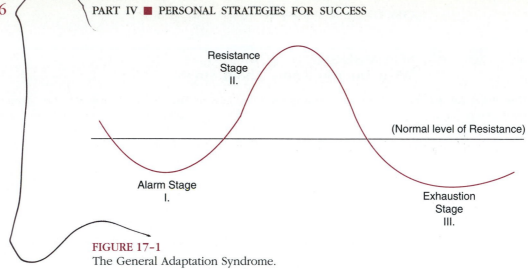

FIGURE 17-1
The General Adaptation Syndrome.

break down. The body can no longer adapt to the stress load placed on it, and the result of the exhaustion stage is a disease of adaptation such as ulcers or cardiovascular disease.[3]

CAUSES OF STRESS

To identify causes of stress, we must look at the nature of stressors. We can divide general causes of stress into at least three categories: environmental, personal, and sudden stressors. *Environmental* stressors include conditions in the environment that cause mental or physical stress. These conditions include noise, pollution, temperature, diet, toxins, and drugs. *Personal* stressors include factors such as family or financial problems as well as amounts of change with which a person has to cope. *Sudden* stressors refer to intense stimuli, such as narrowly averting an automobile accident, or the surge of nervous energy felt when someone startles or scares you.

For purposes of this discussion, let's take a deeper look at two categories of stress that are very apparent in the workplace—Type A behavior and job stress itself.

Type A Behavior

Here is how Type A people behave.

Meyer Friedman and Ray Rosenman, two California cardiologists, gave us the now-famous profile of a high stress individual known as a *Type A person*. This behavior pattern is highly correlated to coronary heart disease and is typified by the following characteristics:

---

[3]Hans Selye, *Stress Without Distress* (New York: Signet Books, 1974), 27.

1. Always moving, walking, and/or eating rapidly.
2. Feeling impatient with anyone who is moving "slowly," or not talking about something of interest to her.
3. Indulging in polyphasic activity—that is, doing two or three things at the same time.
4. Feeling unable to relax or abstain from working.
5. Trying to accomplish more and more things in less and less time.[4]

The list could go on. The Type A person is in a constant race against time, the stereotypical "workaholic." People of this personality type cause stress not only for themselves but also for those around them.

Friedman and Rosenman also described the Type B personality as a low stress individual with varied interests, and a relaxed but active approach to life.

Should everyone strive to be a Type B? Not necessarily. Some Type A's seem to thrive on a hectic pace and actually feel invigorated by the pressures of time urgency. New evidence seems to indicate a difference between coronary-prone Type A's and their healthier cohorts. Those who combine their Type A tendencies with hostility and anger seem to be the most likely to suffer serious health problems.

Job-Related Stress

Another major source of stress for most individuals is their jobs. The quantity and quality of stress vary among occupations. Some jobs are more stress producing than others. For instance, air traffic controllers, who face the daily pressures of protecting the lives of thousands of people, have an occupation that is considered highly stressful. Although this is a dramatic example, every job has potential stressors. Some of the most common are:

1. *Information load.* Whether individuals are overloaded or underloaded, they are likely to experience stress. The underloaded individual is apathetic and bored from being cut off from necessary communication, whereas the overloaded employee feels harried and frantic. In either case absenteeism and turnover increase, and productivity decreases.
2. *Role ambiguity.* Whenever employees are not sure what their job is or the way it relates to other jobs in the organization, role ambiguity occurs. This in turn leads to confusion, lack of focus, and stress.
3. *Role conflict.* Stress occurs when various people seem to be expecting different things from us. Supervisors are particularly susceptible to role conflict because both management and their subordinates

---

[4]Meyer Friedman and Ray H. Rosenman, *Type A Behavior and Your Heart* (New York: Fawcett Crest, 1974), 100–101.

often look to them as their representative. As they try to satisfy everyone's expectations, they often experience considerable personal stress.

4. *Occupational change.* Whenever the work environment changes, stress is inevitable. All change brings some uncertainty with it, and uncertainty interferes with one's mental and physical homeostasis.

5. *Stress carriers.* Employees are often brought into contact with Type A persons, who force stress upon them. The grumpy boss, the forgetful secretary, and the complaining major customer are *stress carriers.*

6. *Physical environment.* Noise, lighting, uncomfortable furniture, and temperature are examples of physical surroundings that can produce stress.

CONSEQUENCES OF STRESS

Stress manifests itself in many ways. Moreover, individuals under stress do not always react the same way: some take up drinking, others turn to drugs, still others become chronically tired or stay home more and more to avoid the stressful situation. The consequences of stress can be divided into five general types: subjective, behavioral, cognitive, psychological, and organizational.[5]

Subjective effects of stress include feelings of anxiety, aggression, frustration, guilt, or shame. Individuals are also apt to feel irritable, moody, tired, tense, nervous, or lonely.

Behavioral effects of stress represent readily visible changes in a person's behavior. Among these effects are such things as increased accidents, use of drugs or alcohol, outlandish or argumentative behavior, laughter out of context, very excitable moods, and/or eating or drinking to excess (or not eating and losing weight rapidly).

Cognitive effects refer to diminished mental ability, and may include such effects as impaired judgment, rash decisions, forgetfulness, and/or hypersensitivity to criticism.

Physiological effects, discussed earlier in the chapter, include the various physical symptoms of stress such as elevated blood pressure and altered blood chemistry.

Organizational effects, readily observable to the supervisor, take the form of absenteeism, diminished productivity, high turnover, poor relations with workers, and/or general job dissatisfaction. Stress wreaks havoc on organizational productivity. Highly stressed employees have more fre-

Five general consequences of behavior

---

[5]Robert E. Callahan, C. Patrick Fleenoe, and Harry R. Knudson, *Understanding Organizational Behavior: A Managerial Viewpoint* (Columbus, Ohio: Merrill, 1986), 446–447.

■ ■ ■ SUPERVISORY SKILLS
Recognizing Stress in the Workplace

1. Be sure you have a good understanding of what stress is and the way it affects the human body. Encourage your employees to face and discuss their stressors.

2. Learn to recognize the physical signs of stress. When your employees exhibit these signs, be aware that they are not functioning with a completely "clear head." Where possible, avoid confrontation until later. Allow problems to simmer down a bit before trying to rectify them.

3. Assess your own stress quotient. If you tend toward Type A behavior, be careful that you are not headed for diseases of adaptation. Set a good example for your employees. Do not try to do more and more in less and less time; if you do, don't

expect the same high stress behavior from others.

4. Do not be a stress carrier! Notice who the stress carriers are in your organization. How can you avoid their dumping stress on you? How can you protect your employees? If one of your employees is a stress carrier, work on modifying this behavior for everyone's betterment. Ignoring stress carriers only makes them worse.

5. Assess your work environment. What physical stressors does it present? Can any of these be avoided or modified? Make modifications where possible, even if employees are not yet complaining. Reducing negative stress in the work environment is a worthy objective for any supervisor!

quent accidents, are often irritable, and are unable to cope with daily situations.

Another organizational consequence that has recently received much interest is corporate liability for employees whose illness is linked to job stress. Some people are suing and winning legal cases where work-related stressors caused burnout. *Burnout* is the work-related equivalent of a nervous breakdown. The burned-out employee has succumbed to long, continuous stress and is no longer able to function at a reasonable level of effectiveness. Increasingly, workers compensation laws are covering injuries resulting from continuing job stress.

"According to the National Institute for Occupational Safety and Health, stress now ranks among the top 10 work-related diseases and represents 11 percent of all workers' compensation claims. . . . All told, U.S. employers reportedly spend $150–200 billion annually on stress."[6]

STRESS MANAGEMENT TECHNIQUES

There are many stressors all around us, and the consequences are far-reaching. What can the individual and the organization as a whole do to manage stress?

---

[6]"Workplace Stress," *HR Magazine* (August 1991): 75–76.

Personal Stress Management

Some personal ways
of handling stress

Choices of personal stress management techniques depend on the individual's personality. (Type A's, for example, are usually too impatient to benefit from meditation.) Four of the most popular techniques, however, are time management, physical exercise, biofeedback, and meditation.

Time management helps one control stress by better organizing time and setting priorities. This important topic in covered at the end of this chapter.

Physical exercise is an appropriate substitute for the fight or flight response of long ago. It provides a physical release for the chemical reactions caused by stress. Exercise not only "burns off" the physical effects of stress but also strengthens the body's organ systems to be better able to withstand stress.

Biofeedback refers to a number of techniques that give concrete feedback to the individual regarding bodily functions such as pulse rate, blood pressure, body temperature, and muscle tension. By being cognizant of these physical phenomena, one can apparently learn to control them, thus willing the body to a more relaxed state.

Meditation encompasses a variety of mental exercises that focus our attention on something other than daily thoughts. Regardless of the type of meditation, it is remarkably useful in lessening one's sensory reactivity and in quieting the stress response. Best of all, when practiced with some regularity, meditation has a carryover effect—that is, it lowers one's normal reactivity even when not actively meditating.

Organizational Stress Management

Some organizational
ways of handling
stress

Currently, at least three different strategies are being widely used: job redesign, environmental reengineering, stress inoculation training, and a variety of wellness programs.

Job redesign strategies start with an effort to determine what is causing job stress and then proceed to change the job so as to relieve this stress. Overload is often found to be a chief contributor. In this case supervisors may follow one of several strategies. Jobs can be redesigned in such a way that less coordination of effort is needed and thus less information processing is required. Alternately, supervisors could identify liaisons who are responsible for coordination efforts, and improve management information systems to provide what is needed at the appropriate time. In other cases jobs may be frustrating because of lack of decision-making authority. Traditional job enrichment approaches work well here because they give workers increased responsibility for decisions in their work area.

Environmental reengineering focuses on changing the physical environment by reducing stressors such as lighting, temperature, noise, vibration, toxins, and so on. Supervisors might adopt one of two strategies for dealing with these stressors. The first concentrates on protecting the workers from the negative consequences of the stressors: workers are required to wear goggles, earplugs, or masks. This strategy is often resisted by the workers and must be firmly enforced by the supervisor. The second strategy focuses on lessening the negative environmental stressors by reducing noise, improving lighting, and lessening the exposure to toxins. This latter choice is far more acceptable as a stress-reducing alternative, but it rests largely on a company's economic analysis of costs and benefits. Astute managers follow this alternative whenever possible instead of waiting for court settlements that force companies into compliance.

Of all corporate stress management efforts, *wellness programs* have been receiving the most attention in recent years. Corporate wellness is part of the current trend to be concerned about the total human being, not just the nine-to-five worker. Programs vary from companies who shuttle employees back and forth to a local health spa during lunch hour to those that invest thousands of dollars to install their own health spa facilities complete with nutritional experts and meditation rooms.

TIME MANAGEMENT

One of the best ways to lower job-related stress is to practice effective time management. Time management involves taking control of external events and personal time.

This chapter is meant to help you understand where your time is going and suggests a three-step approach to more effectively planning your time. It also examines the most common time wasters and offers some practical suggestions as to ways to minimize their effect.

■ ■ ■ SUPERVISORY SKILLS
Managing Stress

1. Be aware of the many consequences of stress. Learn to recognize behavioral and physical signals as well as subjective and cognitive problems such as moodiness or oversensitivity to criticism. When absenteeism, turnover, and productivity problems appear, check the stress level in your department as one possible cause.

2. Watch for stress signs, and if you notice the warning signals mentioned in the chapter, do a thorough examination of the work environment. Know what the stressors are and the ways they are affecting people. Work to eliminate stress in areas under your control. For example, be sure that your employees understand their roles.

3. Explore the possibility of setting up a stress management program for your department. Expose your workers to personal and organizational stress management strategies. Encourage them to examine their own stressors and to try various stress management techniques. Again, lead by example.

The first step to learning time management techniques is to know
where your time is going. At first you may think this is an easy question.
However, studies show that very few people *really* know how their time
is spent on the job. In addition, a great deal of time is spent on unnecessary socializing, low priority busywork, or in other low productivity activities. The trick to starting a time management program is to find out where
your time is going now. The best way to do this is by keeping a *time log,*
or a daily schedule indicating how time is spent. For a period of at least
one week (preferably two), write down all your activities at work on a
half-hour basis.

At the end of the week, sit down and carefully review your time log.
How much time did you spend on major projects with important consequences? How much time went toward counseling or instructing employees? How much time was spent on the phone? Answering letters? In meetings? Socializing? Doing personal chores? Having lunch? How much more
could you have accomplished if you had just a half hour more per day of
productive work?

Now that you have a baseline to work with, we can concentrate on
ways to make better use of your time. The key to time management is
planning. If you follow a three-step approach, you are sure to experience
a dramatic increase in your productive time.

How To Plan Your Time

People offer two common excuses for not planning their time. First, they
feel they lack personal time control. Who is in control of your time? If
your answer is your boss, your subordinates, or anyone else, you must realize that only you can control your time and that you alone are responsible for what you do with it. Of course, you must perform some boss-im-
posed duties and respond to some subordinate-imposed time requests.
However, all in all, you are in control. Components of planned time include quarterly objectives, weekly plans, and daily activities.

Quarterly Objectives.   Planned time must begin with periodic objectives.
Quarterly objectives are a good choice because ninety days is a comfortable time frame for most people. At the beginning of the planning period,
list all major objectives for the next three months. Then, beside each objective indicate the start date, due date, and approximate number of days
or hours for completion. Figure 17–2 shows a sample form filled out for
the first quarter of 1995.

Note that each objective or major project is broken down into its primary components in order to more realistically plan the work that needs
to be done. Also notice that each objective is given a priority according to
A, B, or *C* system. An *A* priority is assigned to something that is very important; a *B* priority is for something that is moderately important; and a

| Quarterly Objectives | | | | |
| For Quarter Beginning: January 1994 | | | | |
Objective	Start	Completion	Time	Priority
1. Prepare marketing plan for new consumer product line A. Analyze market research reports B. Process test market results C. Meet with sales force	1/15	3/15	1 week	A
2. Prepare budget for fiscal 1994 A. Obtain sales forecasts B. Do expense projections	3/1	3/31	3 days	A
3. Institute MBO system in department A. Meet with consultants B. Plan and conduct training	2/1	3/31	2 days	B
4. Investigate hand-held calculators for sales force A. Research available features B. Get competitive bids	1/1	3/31	1–2 days	B
5. Finalize vacation schedule of all employees	1/1	2/1	3 hours	C

FIGURE 17–2
Quarterly objectives.

C priority is for something that is not very important but might be nice to accomplish if there is enough time. Assigning priorities is a critical step in the planning process; without it we often spend time accomplishing our objectives, only to realize later that we have not met the most important objectives. Why does this happen? Often a *C* priority item is easier to do and doesn't take as much time. Thus, we get started on it right away and ignore the all-important *A* priority objectives.

With assigned priorities, you are much more likely to avoid this pitfall, or at least realize what you are doing when you choose to work on *C* priority material. Remember, if something has to be left over at the end of a quarter, it should be a *C* priority time, not an *A* or even a *B*.

The following list provides some examples of ineffective and effective objectives:

Poor: Cut the budget. (Not specific or measurable—no time frame.)

Better: Cut department operating expenses by 5 percent this quarter over last quarter.

Poor: Hire new staff. (Not specific, no time frame.)

Better: Replace Jones and hire new welder by end of February.

Weekly plans help direct work activities.

Weekly Plans.   Once you have a complete list of written quarterly objectives, you are ready to construct a weekly plan. Objectives are of little value without weekly plans of work activities that will help you reach these goals. Once a week make a list of the activities for the next week. Take time to create this list no later than Friday afternoon before you leave the office. If you wait until first thing Monday morning, you are likely to become sidetracked and will be well into the week before you realize you do not have a weekly plan. If Friday afternoon does not work well for you, draw up your weekly plan over the weekend.

After the weekly plan is complete, you are ready to start the new week and begin again to schedule daily activities.

Daily activity schedules are "to do" lists.

Daily Activities.   As with weekly plans, daily activities must not be left until the beginning of the workday. Every night before leaving, determine the daily activity schedule for the next day. Many people write "to do" lists; others schedule work directly on their daily desk calendars. Whichever method you use, keep in mind the following six guidelines:

Useful guidelines in scheduling time

1. Group similar activities together. Try to do all your correspondence at one time of the day or try returning your phone calls at the same time.
2. Schedule your daily activities from your weekly plan. If you don't schedule it, you probably won't do it.
3. Leave some slack time in your schedule. Unexpected demands will always be made on your time.
4. Schedule *A* priority tasks for your peak time of the day. If you are a "morning person," for example, schedule your *A* activities for first thing in the morning.
5. Keep your daily schedule available so you can check off tasks as they are completed and remind yourself of tasks yet to be done.
6. Always schedule some quiet time for yourself. There is nothing wrong with closing your office door and thinking.

Time Wasters And What To Do About Them

What wastes time on the job? If you answer as the typical supervisor, you probably included on your list five key time wasters: meetings (previously discussed in Chapter 12), telephone calls, unscheduled visitors, procrastination, and ineffective delegation.

Telephone Calls.   Almost everyone who is worried about ways to save time mentions the telephone as a primary problem. Some of the most useful tips include: planning your calls in advance, grouping outgoing calls, keeping the length of calls to a minimum, and having your secretary

SUPERVISORY SKILLS
Planning Your Time

1. Remember that only you are responsible for your time. Take charge now.

2. Keep a time log and find out exactly where your time is currently going.

3. Learn to use the three elements of planned time: quarterly objectives, weekly plans, and daily activity schedules.

4. Once you get your own system in place, teach your subordinates ways to plan their time more effectively.

5. Carefully set your priorities and keep your focus on the *A* priorities; don't let *C* priorities take up your time unless you really have nothing else to do.

6. Examine your work patterns. When are your most productive times of the day? Be sure to use that time to your best advantage.

7. Remember that there is enough time to do what is really important.

---

screen calls and reroute them where possible. Try especially hard to be organized on the phone and to work from notes when you are making business calls. This technique will keep you from forgetting something and having to call back. If you do have a secretary, make yourself unavailable for phone calls when you are working on *A* priority tasks or meeting with others. Nothing irks a colleague or employee more than waiting while you accept phone interruptions.

Unscheduled Visitors. Unscheduled visitors are another major time waster. What can be done about people who just drop by? One way to discourage drop-in visitors is to stand up, meet them at the door, and announce that you have only five minutes. If you can help them in that time, fine; if not, suggest that you will have to get back to them later. This procedure encourages the person to get right to the point and discourages idle chitchat that can needlessly use up a lot of time. Another approach is to make the rounds of employee workstations and talk to subordinates there. In this way, when you are ready to leave, all you have to do is walk away. A final tactic is to close the "open door" for a block of time when you are working on *A* priority material.

> "Sure an open-door policy is good. But that shouldn't preclude your blocking time for you to get your work done—say, from 9:00 to 11:00 A.M. each Wednesday and Friday, for instance. People will work around that—just as if you were out. (Top managers keep coming back to 'block time' again and again as the cornerstone to their getting things done.)"[7]

Procrastination. The old adage "Never put off until tomorrow what you can do today" is good advice for the supervisor. Yet human beings do procrastinate, often at the expense of *A* priority items. The primary reason

---

[7]Roy Alexander, "Starving Out the Time Gobblers," *Supervisory Management* (March 1993): 8.

is fear—fear that the job is too complex; fear that something else will go
wrong while we take the time to tackle the new job; fear that we are
going to dislike doing it. The answer is simply to "dive in." Take the first
step; plan and do the first activity. Once you pick up momentum, the task
will seem much easier. Self-imposed deadlines are often helpful.

Delegation.   *Delegation* of authority is the process whereby supervisors
assign duties to subordinates and give them the authority to carry out
these tasks. Delegation creates an obligation on the part of the employee
to complete the task in a satisfactory manner. Successful delegation can
greatly ease the supervisor's time burdens as well as add routine and authority to the subordinate's job. How important is delegation?

Managers who, for one reason or another, fail to delegate wisely
often find themselves overburdened with work and surrounded by under-
developed employees. They become so overrun with daily duties that they
find little time to engage in the most important of all managerial functions—planning and goal setting.

Why are some supervisors so reluctant to delegate? Some of the most
common reasons are:

1.   Lack of confidence in subordinates.
2.   Fear of reprisals from superiors.
3.   Lack of time to train someone else.
4.   Fear of loss of control.
5.   Fear that someone might do the job better.

6.   Liking for the job involved.
7.   Wanting personal credit for the job involved.
8.   Lack of skill in training others to do the job.
9.   Fear that employees will get angry at the delegation.
10. Fear of taking a chance.
11. Lack of patience with learning delegatee.
12. Desire for perfection.
13. Unwillingness to allow mistakes.
14. Desire to maintain status quo.
15. Lack of understanding of what to delegate.

Subordinates are often resistant to delegation for these reasons:

1.   Subordinates prefer for the supervisor to make the decisions rather
     than assume responsibility themselves.
2.   Subordinates are worried about being criticized for making mistakes.
3.   Subordinates lack necessary resources and information to do the job.
4.   Subordinates already feel overworked or without adequate reward.
5.   Subordinates lack self-confidence.[8]

---

[8]Richard M. Hodgetts, *Organizational Behavior: Theory and Practice* (New York: Macmillan
Publishing Co., 1991), 288.

SUPERVISORY SKILLS
Eliminating Time Wasters

1. Do not be a slave to your telephone. Organize your calls; train others to call you at certain times; avoid interrupting meetings to take calls; be prepared before you call back.

2. Shorten the amount of time taken up by unannounced visitors. Be unavailable for idle chitchat; give the person five minutes if there is a legitimate problem, and offer to get back to the person at a later time. Encourage people to get on your schedule if they have lengthy agendas, so you can give them your undivided attention.

3. Take stock of how much time you are spending in meetings. Cut down on it whenever possible.

4. Learn the art of delegation. Start by examining your attitude about delegation. What are you currently doing that someone else should be doing? Analyze your job and pick those routine duties that will free up your time as well as enrich someone else's job. Delegate carefully, making sure delegatees understand their responsibility and authority. Be sure that performance standards and feedback mechanisms are in place.

5. Watch out for unauthorized "time theft" by employees. Set a good example!

If the supervisor has decided to delegate and has appropriate tasks for delegation, how should the supervisor go about instituting the delegation? First, he or she should plan the tasks to be delegated. Who should do each task? How will these new tasks fit with the person's job? What type of training is necessary? What performance standards must be set to ensure that an adequate job will be done? What feedback controls must be set in place so that the supervisor can rest secure that the job will be completed adequately? What degree of authority should be passed along to the delegatee? This last question is not as simple as it sounds. Some supervisors delegate a job but retain all of the authority. They want the employee to report back to them about everything. Others delegate complete authority for the job. In this case, the employees only come back if there is a problem.

Second, the supervisor must make the delegation, being careful to instruct the person adequately and clarify the degree of responsibility and authority that is being transferred. The latter is particularly important. Accountability ultimately rests with the supervisor, but unless the employee is given authority to carry out the new duty, the "monkey" is still on the supervisor's back. Employees are often hesitant and insecure about receiving new responsibilities, thus the way the task is delegated is very important. Hodgetts offered five useful recommendations for avoiding problems during this phase of delegation:

1. Spell out all assignments in terms of the expected results. Let people know exactly what they are to accomplish.

■ ■ ■ THE QUALITY CHALLENGE
Take a Chance

Delegation of work is an area that continues to be a major challenge for today's supervisor. One of the primary reasons is that supervisors hate to give up control. They feel that others cannot do the job as well as they, and they believe that if too much is delegated they will eventually lose their job. After all, if the employees can do the supervisor's work, why does the company need this manager? On the other hand, competitive pressures and the drive to increase productivity and quality are making delegation a major requirement of successful supervision. Here are five steps that can help supervisors delegate authority and meet the quality challenge.

1. Focus on achieving the work group's objectives of increasing quality and reducing time and cost. Do not lost sight of the overall mission.

2. Empower the group personnel to handle much of what needs to be done. Although this means giving up some past supervisory tasks, there are other areas that warrant more attention.

3. Work on becoming indispensible to the group by providing advice, assistance, and general counseling designed to help the members do their individual jobs better and work more harmoniously as a team. This strategy will generate far more productivity than the old supervisory strategy of minimal delegation and close control.

4. In particular, work closely with the team in identifying productivity bottlenecks and problems, and provide the group guidance in resolving these situations. Become more of a coach and less of a boss.

5. Remember that the role of the supervisor during the 1990s will continually change. The technical challenges of tomorrow will be different from those of today. However, the behavioral challenges of creating high performing work groups, developing teamwork, tapping the potential of employees, communicating clearly and concisely, and motivating people to new heights will be the same.

By learning how to delegate authority and focus on managerial behaviors that have long-run value, supervisors can not only meet the quality challenge but also enhance their career opportunities. It's all a matter of being willing to take a chance.

Some helpful ways of delegating effectively

2. Match the person with the job. Determine which subordinates are most qualified, and from this pool choose the one who has the best combination of training and experience.

3. Keep all lines of communication open. If there is a problem, both superior and subordinate can communicate easily with each other.

4. Set up a control procedure for seeing that the job is being done properly, and provide assistance as needed. Be careful, however, not to interfere with work progress or to give the impression of being too control-oriented.

5. Use job performance as a basis for rewards. Those who are willing to assume responsibility and get the job done right should be placed at the head of the list when raises and promotions are given out.[9]

---

[9]Richard M Hodgetts, *Management,* 5th ed. (San Diego, Calif.: Harcourt, Brace Jovanovich Publishers, 1990), 191.

The third step to successful delegation is the follow-up phase. At least during the initial phase the supervisor should be sure to get timely feedback on the progress and completion of the delegated task.

SUMMARY

Stress is the nonspecific response of the body to any demand made on it. Among the many different types of stress, some are personal in nature and others are job-related.

The three main types of stress are Environmental, Personal and Sudden. Environmental Stressors are the physical conditions in the environment such as toxins which cause mental and/or physical stress. Personal Stressors include family or financial problems, and Sudden Stressors are any intense, unexpected stimuli.

The individual most susceptible to the negative effects of stress is the Type A personality. This individual is involved in a chronic struggle to get more and more done in less and less time. The person is often a workaholic.

Job-related stress can take a number of forms: information overload, role ambiguity, role conflict, occupational change, stress carriers, and the physical environment itself. Quality and quantity of stress vary from occupation to occupation.

Stress manifests itself in five general types of consequences: subjective, behavioral, cognitive, psychological, and organizational. Two basic approaches may be taken for dealing with stress: personal stress management techniques and organizational stress management techniques. Examples of personal stress management approaches include time management, physical exercise, biofeedback, and meditation. Examples of organizational stress management techniques include job redesign, environment reengineering, and stress inoculation programs.

Time management is crucial to supervisory effectiveness. To determine how work time currently is being spent, a time log is a valuable tool. The log should be filled out every thirty minutes.

When planning time, the supervisor should focus on three components of time: quarterly objectives, weekly plans, and daily activity schedules. Quarterly objectives are set every ninety days. Weekly plans are then drawn up with goals that are in accord with the quarterly objectives. Daily activity schedules are "to do" lists drawn up the night before to remind the supervisor of what is to be done the next day.

Common time wasters include telephone calls, drop-in visitors, procrastination, and ineffective delegation. Each of these problems was discussed and ways of handling them were offered.

REVIEW QUESTIONS

1. In your own words, what is stress? Is all stress bad? Explain.

2. How do people go about adapting to stress? What are the three stages the body goes through? Briefly explain each.

3. Define and explain the three main types of stressors: Environmental, Personal, and Sudden.

4. How does a Type A person behave? Why is the person likely to have physical problems? Explain.

5. What are some of the most common forms of job-related stress? Identify and describe at least four.

6. What are the five general types of stress consequences? Be complete in your answer.

7. Describe three helpful techniques employees can use for personal stress management.

8. What are some ways that organizations can reduce the stress of their employees? Describe in detail at least three strategies.

9. Quarterly objectives are of little value without weekly plans of activities. Explain.

10. In what way is a daily work schedule a "to do" list? What are some important guidelines in scheduling time? Identify and describe four.

11. How can the supervisor more effectively deal with telephone calls? Offer at least four helpful tips.

12. How can a supervisor deal with unscheduled visitors? Provide at least three recommendations for action.

KEY TERMS

Biofeedback. Techniques that give concrete feedback to an individual regarding bodily functions such as pulse rate, body temperature, and muscle tension.

Burnout. Result of too much organizational stress, whereby employees can no longer perform their job.

Daily activity schedule. "To do" list of work activities for the entire day.

Delegation of authority. Process whereby supervisors assign duties to subordinates and give them the authority to carry out these tasks.

Environmental reengineering. Strategy to change the physical environment in order to reduce stressors such as lighting, temperature, and noise.

Environmental stressors. All physical conditions in the environment that cause mental and/or physical reactions in the body.

Job redesign. Strategy to change the structure of a job to make it more interesting and less stressful for the employee.

Meditation. Mental exercises used to focus attention on something other than daily thoughts.

Pareto's principle. Time management principle that says a small percentage of time accounts for a large percentage of important results.

Personal stressors. Situations that elicit emotional arousal.

Quarterly objectives. Goals set for a ninety-day period.

Role ambiguity. Lack of firm knowledge of the duties and responsibilities of one's job.

Role conflict. Result of opposing expectations that others have of the role holder or the opposing demands made on a person by the various roles he or she plays. An example of the former might be the situation of a supervisor who faces the opposing expectations of upper management and employees. An example of the latter might be the opposing demands on someone who holds the roles of parent and travelling salesperson.

Stress. Nonspecific response of the body to any demand made on it.

Stress carrier. Irritable, demanding person who causes stress to other employees.

Stress inoculation programs. Stress management programs designed to reduce stress in employees' minds.

Sudden stressors. Unexpected, intense stimuli.

Time log. Time calendar used to identify ways daily time is spent.

Type A Person. Person who is in a constant race against time; often a workaholic.

Weekly plans. Plans designed to help managers coordinate all of their activities for the next five-day period.

ANSWERS TO SELF-ASSESSMENT QUIZ 17–1

1. False. Stress is a physical disorder that may or may not stem from psychological problems.

2. False. The absence of all stress is death.

3. False. Too little stress leads to disinterest.

4. False. Some stressors cannot be avoided and stress must therefore be managed.

5. False. Stress has many effects on the body.

6. False. Early humans were protected by the "fight or flight" syndrome.

7. False. Stress-related diseases have physical causes.

8. False. Stress is mediated by individual personalities, but many stressors are found in the work environment.

9. False. Strong evidence links stress and physical disease.

10. False. Nervousness may be uncomfortable, but more serious diseases such as cardiovascular disease and cancer are associated with stress.

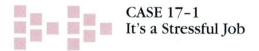

CASE 17–1
It's a Stressful Job

Karl Krenandonk has been with his company for three years. During this time he has been given the highest possible merit pay raise each year. Two months ago Karl's supervisor announced that he was moving to another firm. A few days later Karl was called into the boss's office and offered the job of supervisor. He was delighted at the news and took over the position seven weeks ago. Since then Karl feels he has never worked harder in his life. In fact, he has been working so hard that when he went for his annual physical exam last week, the doctor told him that he was going to have to slow down.

"I know this new job means a lot to you," the doctor said. "However I can see some specific changes in your health and if they continue for much longer, I think you're going to find yourself suffering from mental exhaustion. My suggestion to you is that you either slow down or get yourself another job."

Karl knows the doctor means well, but, on the other hand, Karl feels he cannot slow down. The company is just about to enter its busiest season of the year and, if anything, there will be more work than ever. Karl believes that he can keep on top of everything if he just does not let it make him nervous. "Mental attitude is 90 percent of supervisory success," he told his wife yesterday. "I've got to figure out how to stop stress from getting the better of me. If I can do that, I should have no trouble keeping up with the demands of the job and avoiding a nervous breakdown."

1. In your own words, why is Karl suffering from stress?

2. Is there anything Karl can do to reduce the impact of stress? Specifically, what would you recommend?

3. If your suggestions prove to be insufficient, what would you recommend? Why? Defend your answer.

CASE 17-2
It's All in Her Head

The Palcher Corporation employs an internal management consulting group to help improve efficiency. This group of consultants handles all types of problems—from technical to human. Earlier this week members of the group were in Roberta Foxx's unit. They talked to her personnel for nearly two hours, making notes related to ways they could help the workers do their jobs more efficiently.

Later in the day, one of the consultants came in to see Roberta. The meeting did not last very long, but by the time the consultant left, he apparently had found what he was looking for. Part of the conversation went as follows:

"Roberta, as you know, I'm here to see how I can help you do a better job. One of the things I'd like to get from you is your list of activities for today. Do you have a 'to do' list that I can see?"

"Well I don't have one written out, but I do keep one in my head. I mean, I know what I'm supposed to be doing, and by the end of the day I'll have it done."

"Can you tell me what some of those things are?"

"Well, I'm supposed to have a meeting with some of the finance people later in the day. I

think we're scheduled for about 2:30 P.M.; I don't know off the top of my head. And I want to check on the progress of that shipment from Corning Manufacturing. It was supposed to come in sometime this week. I think it was expected yesterday. In any event I'll know its status by the end of the day. Things like that, you know."

The consultant did not respond to Roberta's last comment. However, he did write some notes on his pad. After talking to Roberta for another ten minutes, he closed the pad. "I think I have enough ideas here to give you some insights regarding ways you can improve your efficiency. Let me write them up and get back with you early next week."

Roberta smiled. "I'll look forward to getting your ideas. I welcome all of the assistance I can get."

1. What did the consultant learn about Roberta's time management planning? Explain.

2. Does Roberta think she has a time management plan? What is her reasoning?

3. If you were the consultant, what advice would you give to Roberta in your report? Be as complete as possible.

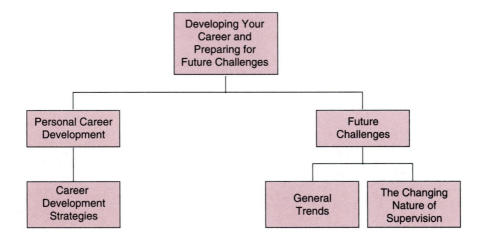

CHAPTER 18

Developing Your Career and Preparing for Future Challenges

"Over the next decades, many forces will alter workstyles and lifestyles, ultimately testing the mettle of us all. But there is no doubt that supervisors are particularly vulnerable."*

CHAPTER OBJECTIVES

☐ Identify and describe the six steps in the personal career development process.

☐ Explain six useful career development strategies.

☐ Discuss ten trends that will face American business during the upcoming decade and note their effect on the supervisor's job.

☐ Explain some of the major ways in which employee characteristics are changing and describe the influence this will have on the supervisor's job.

☐ Discuss some of the predictions that are being made about worker participation in corporate governance and indicate the way in which this will affect the supervisor's job.

☐ Relate the effect of the computer on the workplace and the consequence of this development for the supervisor.

---

*Anne Skagan, "The Incredible Shrinking Organization: What Does It Mean for Middle Managers?" *Supervisory Management* (January 1992): 1.

No study of supervision would be complete without consideration of career planning and future challenges. Every supervisor who hopes to move up the hierarchy needs to formulate a career plan. The usual plan involves both self-assessment and detailed career steps that can be implemented along a time continuum. At the same time supervisors need to be aware of developing trends and the impact of these changes on the nature of their job. This chapter examines both careers and developing trends.

PERSONAL CAREER DEVELOPMENT

Personal career development is becoming increasingly important. Let's look at each of the activities involved in career development (see Figure 18–1).

Career Development Strategies

There are six important career development activities. The following examines each.

Step One: Assess Yourself. Before planning your future career, assess your current performance. Self-Assessment Quiz 18–1 provides a self-audit of your strengths and weaknesses. Be very objective when taking this test.

Pay close attention to those Self-Assessment quiz columns that you have scored 4 or 5. These are areas where you currently exhibit some weakness. Assess each to decide if it is worth the time and effort to improve. You cannot expect to be excellent in all aspects of your job, but you should at least be scoring above average (1 or 2) in each of these critical areas. With this assessment knowledge of yourself, you can begin to examine your current position.

Six activities in personal career management.

Step Two: Assess Your Current Position. Take a realistic look at your current job. What are you learning from this job at the present time? Are your skills growing, or is each day just a repetition of the day before? Will successful performance in this job be likely to lead to future promotions? Are you interacting with other supervisors and managers who can teach you something and help you move along in your career? How happy are you doing what you are doing? How long would you be satisfied staying in this job? In summary, how instrumental can your current job be in helping you progress in your career? Carefully assess the opportunities open to you. Are you taking advantage of training and development? Are you try-

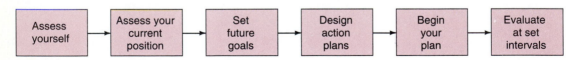

FIGURE 18–1
Personal career development process.

ing to undertake new responsibilities and learn new skills? Even jobs that seem fairly unimportant or boring can be a learning ground. Take advantage of all the opportunities in your environment.

Step Three: Set Future Goals.   After assessing your strengths and weaknesses as well as the opportunities, benefits, and costs of your current position, you are ready to set future goals for yourself. Career development cannot proceed without plans.

Set goals in terms of long range (5–10 years), intermediate range (1–5 years), and short range (up to 1 year). Start with long-range plans. Intermediate and short-range plans should then help you accomplish your long-term goals. For example, if you want to be plant manager in ten years, what steps do you need to take to reach your goal? Within the next five years you will probably have to become production manager, and before that you must be named group leader of the other supervisors. To accomplish these interim steps, you'll want to design action plans.

Step Four: Design Action Plans.   Plans are a good starting point, but they really get off the ground only when you schedule the activities to accomplish your goal. List all the activities needed to reach your first goal—becoming group leader. Include developmental efforts such as returning to school to take group leadership courses and production management courses. Plan to learn as much from others as possible. Suppose Ralph, the current group leader, is retiring next year. Spend time with Ralph and get his insights about the job and the qualifications necessary to be good at it. Seek out new on-the-job experiences that might prepare you for your next goal. Such a step may mean extra work for you with no immediate reward, but consider it an investment in your future. Once you have a comprehensive list of activities, get to work!

Step Five: Begin Your Plan.   Many supervisors become stuck in their current jobs. Even though they have goals formulated and may even have thought of the activities they need to pursue to accomplish their goals, somehow they just never get started. Either they are too busy to worry about tomorrow or they just don't know how to proceed. The key here is get started! Ignore minor setbacks and start implementing your plan.

Step Six: Evaluate At Set Intervals.   At the end of each quarter or six-month period, review your career plans. What have you accomplished? What activities have you started? Where has there been slippage in your plan? Rework your activities as you see new opportunities.

As you work through the preceding six steps of career development, keep in mind the following strategies:

These strategies help implement successful career plans.

1.   *Become known for excellent performance.* Work hard to create a positive image of yourself. Be willing and cooperative in accepting new

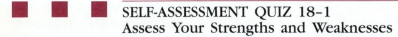

SELF-ASSESSMENT QUIZ 18–1
Assess Your Strengths and Weaknesses

Directions: For each of the following areas, assess your current performance on the job. If you are not working, assess your most recent job performance. If you have never held a job, relate these questions to your schoolwork and how you work with your peers. Be objective in your answers.

		Strength				Weakness
1.	**Communications**					
	I pay attention to what my employees have to say.	1	2	3	4	5
	I regularly keep my employees informed on work matters.	1	2	3	4	5
	I give regular feedback to employees on their performance.	1	2	3	4	5
	My written communications are well-planned and well-written.	1	2	3	4	5
2.	**Motivation**					
	I understand what my employees want and need from their jobs.	1	2	3	4	5
	I give recognition to my workers for a job well done.	1	2	3	4	5
	I create a satisfying climate for my employees.	1	2	3	4	5
3.	**Leadership**					
	My leadership style is appropriate to the group I am supervising.	1	2	3	4	5
	I am successful in getting the work group to strive for organizational objectives.	1	2	3	4	5
4.	**Decision Making**					
	I weigh all the alternatives before making decisions.	1	2	3	4	5
	Whenever possible, I involve my employees in the decision-making process.	1	2	3	4	5
5.	**Planning and Organizing**					
	I am able to plan a course of action and take steps to accomplish goals.	1	2	3	4	5
	I involve my workers in the planning process.	1	2	3	4	5
	I make sure everybody knows the goals and give recognition when goals are met.	1	2	3	4	5

responsibilities. Keep an eye on internal competition and strive to outperform your peers. Try to stand out from the crowd! The following supervisor behaviors have been judged particularly effective[1]:

[1]Adapted from Steven Kerr, Kenneth D. Hill, and Laurie Broedling, "The First-Line Supervisor: Phasing Out or Here to Stay?" *Academy of Management Review* (January 1986): 108. Reprinted with permission.

		Strength			Weakness	
6.	**Self-Management**					
	I am organized and able to set sensible priorities.	1	2	3	4	5
	I am able to work under pressure and manage my stress.	1	2	3	4	5
7.	**Self-Development**					
	I stay current in my field.	1	2	3	4	5
	I am continuing my education in the field.	1	2	3	4	5
	I am gaining new experience in my current job.	1	2	3	4	5
8.	**Development of Subordinates**					
	I help employees develop their career paths.	1	2	3	4	5
	I ensure that each employee has an up-to-date job description.	1	2	3	4	5
	I personally participate in employee orientation.	1	2	3	4	5
	I use performance appraisals to discuss future improvements and opportunities.	1	2	3	4	5
	I make sure that employees get the training they need.	1	2	3	4	5
9.	**Productivity**					
	I involve all employees in quality control and productivity goals.	1	2	3	4	5
	I make sure that employees know how the overall department is progressing in comparison to goals.	1	2	3	4	5
	I set challenging standards and carefully monitor them.	1	2	3	4	5
10.	**Environmental Concerns**					
	I monitor for safety and health problems and try to act with foresight when dealing with them.	1	2	3	4	5
	I am always fair in my treatment of all employees.	1	2	3	4	5
	My employees know they can always come to me with their problems.	1	2	3	4	5

- ☐ Accepts criticism and suggestions.
- ☐ Lets subordinates know what he or she thinks of their work.
- ☐ Displays flexibility.
- ☐ Goes to bat for subordinates and recommends promotions.
- ☐ Emphasizes production, gives direction, plans operations.
- ☐ Follows instructions, company policies, chains of command.
- ☐ Keeps boss informed.

☐ Gives praise verbally to subordinates and in reports to bosses.

☐ Develops subordinates, trains them for better jobs.

☐ Uses rewards and punishment effectively.

☐ Displays competence in human relations.

☐ Creates a climate whereby subordinates feel free to discuss problems with the leader.

☐ Displays technical knowledge of tasks.

☐ Displays consideration and egalitarianism, and uses tact and diplomacy.

☐ Identifies with higher management.

2. *Assign your priorities carefully.* Nothing replaces hard work, but also be sure to concentrate on important tasks. Too often working harder is confused with "working smarter." Everything is not equally important. Put emphasis on doing those things that are visible and considered important by management.

3. *Protect yourself against obsolescence.* Be especially cognizant of the ways your job is changing. Later in this chapter we examine some far-reaching future trends. However, whether considering those distant trends or trends more indigenous to the specific company, be alert to changing job requirements and skills. Failure to keep up with trends can lead to *obsolescence.* Successful supervisors stay ahead of their peers and are never caught by surprise in terms of changing job conditions. Reading in the field, taking courses, and being especially open to new experiences and training are all ways in which you can avoid being outdated. To assess your potential for obsolescence, ask yourself the following questions[2]:

☐ Is my mind free from anxiety over personal matters while I work?

☐ Do I believe in myself and my associates?

☐ Am I open and receptive to advice and suggestions?

☐ Do I look for the pluses before looking for the minuses?

☐ Am I more concerned with the cause of management's actions than with its effect?

☐ Am I curious about the "why" behind actions and events?

☐ Do I read and learn something new each day?

☐ Do I question the old and the routine?

☐ Do I converse regularly with subordinates, peers, and superiors?

☐ Have I a definite program for increasing my knowledge?

☐ Is what I am able to do still needed?

☐ In light of recent trends and developments, will my skills still be required one year from now?

☐ Do I practice my skills regularly?

---

[2]Adapted from W. Richard Plunkett, *Supervision: The Direction of People at Work,* 6th ed. Copyright © 1992 by Allyn & Bacon, Inc. Reprinted with permission.

☐ Do I regularly observe the way others perform their skills?

☐ Have I a concrete program for acquiring new skills?

☐ Do my subordinates, peers, and superiors consider me competent?

☐ Do I consistently look for a better way to do things?

☐ Am I willing to take calculated risks?

☐ Do I keep morally and physically fit?

☐ Have I a specific program for improving my performance?

4. *Keep records of your successes.* Over the years, you will receive letters of commendation, favorable performance appraisals, and other evidence of a job well done. Keep a file of such occurrences. If your company has a newsletter, be sure the newsletter receives news of both your own and your department's outstanding performance. Such efforts are part of image building and of systematically linking your name with success.

5. *Seek broad experience.* Don't be afraid to try something new. And don't complain that additional responsibility is just more work. Take advantage of every situation to learn something new and to illustrate your flexibility and desire to grow. Keep your eyes on long-range opportunity. Mobility and flexibility are extremely important personal characteristics when planning a move up the corporate ladder.

6. *Seek a mentor.* A *mentor* is a person who guides, directs, and/or assists another person. Often a middle- or upper-level manager will take a protégé in the first ranks of management and try to help that person develop his or her career. Mentors can be a tremendous help to the fledgling supervisor. They can provide the special attention that can save you years of bumbling uncertainty in learning the "corporate ropes." Mentoring is not without its demands, however. Most mentors want their protégés to show rapid progress and special promise for the company. On the other hand, if supervisors attach themselves to a mentor who then falls out of favor with the company or leaves, the close association with the person is sure to have an effect on the supervisor. When deciding whether to seek or accept a mentor in a given relationship, therefore, you must be concerned with who that person is and how well respected he or she is within the organization.

7. *Utilize company resources.* Many companies offer career development assistance. Investigate and utilize these resources. "The Quality Challenge: The Supervisor's Career" provides additional steps that can be used in this process.

FUTURE CHALLENGES

To understand the future challenges that are likely to affect supervisors, we need to look at general trends as well as at the changing supervisory environment.

■ ■ ■   THE QUALITY CHALLENGE

The Supervisor's Career

The value of total quality management is not restricted to the worker level. Supervisors can also use TQM tools and techniques to manage their own careers. Here are three useful approaches that can help in this process.

1. *Seek continuous improvement.* One of the TQM guidelines is to encourage the personnel to continually look for ways to reduce errors and problems and to increase output and productivity. This can be a useful guideline for the supervisor as well. For example, by using Pareto analysis the manager can identify the most recurring managerial problems and formulate solutions for them. If the manager finds that a small number of employees are responsible for most of the units being rejected by customers, the individual can work more closely with these employees to help them deal with this problem. If the manager finds that there is not enough time to get everything done during the day, the individual can look for ways of eliminating time wasters. By seeking to continuously improve personal performance, the supervisor can help ensure his or her chances for career advancement.

2. *Teach and train.* Closely linked to the above guideline is the need to teach and train subordinates to improve their own performance. Supervisors are typically rewarded for their ability to generate greater quality output from their people. Working closely with the personnel is critical to this objective. Sometimes this calls for coaching and counseling the subordinates. Other times, it requires sending them for additional TQM training. Still other times, it calls for sitting down with the subordinates and discussing what needs to be done and why. By carefully teaching and training the personnel, the supervisor ensures that these individuals will increase their productivity and, in the process, help increase the probability that the supervisor will be identified by the senior-level staff as an up-and-coming manager.

3. *Quantify results.* TQM encourages everyone to quantify the results of their efforts and to use these data as a basis for future action. For example, workers will use statistical process control charts to determine whether to adjust a process or leave it alone. Supervisors can also use quantitative data, although in a slightly different way. They need to keep track of their accomplishments, for example, work unit output is up 22 percent over last year's level; the quality reject rate is down 17 percent; and the department has reduced overall manufacturing setup time by 14 percent. These data are useful in helping supervisors support their case for promotions and raises. Quite often, higher-level management rewards supervisors most heavily on the basis of measurable performance. TQM encourages the recording and analysis of such outcomes, thus providing an ideal way of both increasing productivity and creating a record of these results for career purposes. As a result, total quality management can be invaluable to the personal career development of supervisors.

General Trends

In recent years, a number of popular books prophesied what stands ahead for American business. Two of the most quoted are Alvin Toffler's *The Third Wave* and Naisbitt and Aburdene's *Reinventing the Corporation*.

Toffler is a futurist whose 1970 *Future Shock* was so popular it has been translated into more than fifty languages. He pins his theories on the observation that the United States is currently moving out of an industrial age characterized by factory production processes and into an information age characterized by large-scale information processing. He predicts not only that the types of jobs available will shift dramatically but also that more and more work will be done in private homes via the computer. Toffler warns that bureaucratic organizational structures cannot keep up with the changing demands of information-loaded businesses today.

> "The knowledge load and, more important, the decision load are being re-distributed. In a continual cycle of learning, unlearning, and relearning, workers need to master new technologies, adapt to new organizational forms and generate new ideas. . . . A company of the future could conceivably have within it a monastery-style unit that writes software . . . a research team organized like an improvisational jazz combo . . . a compartmentalized spy network, with need-to-know rules, operating within the law to scour for merger or acquisition possibilities . . . and a sales force organized as a highly motivated 'tribe' complete with its own war songs and membership rituals."[3]

Naisbitt and Aburdene's book identifies the trends facing American business:

1. Corporations that nurture personal growth will attract the best employees.
2. Managers will have reduced power but will need the skills of coaching and mentoring their employees.
3. Employees will demand ownership in the company.
4. Contractual arrangements whereby temporary employees are hired for specific time periods and purposes will increase.
5. The management hierarchy will weaken and be replaced by networking relationships.
6. The spirit of *intrapreneuring* (creative entrepreneuring carried on within existing organizations) will be increasingly important in giving employees the creative edge.
7. Quality will become the most important corporate output.
8. The scientific approach to management will be replaced by intuition and creative management.
9. Large corporations will strive to capture the creative and personal spirit of small businesses.
10. Large-scale physical facilities will be reduced as people choose to work in other physical locations such as their own homes.[4]

American business faces these trends.

---

[3]Alvin Toffler, "Powershift: Knowledge, Wealth, and Violence at the Edge of the 21st Century," *Newsweek* (October 15, 1990): 88.

[4]John Naisbitt and Patricia Aburdene, *Reinventing the Corporation* (New York: Warner Books, 1985).

The notion of the managerial hierarchy beginning to crumble is supported by Anne Skagen of the American Management Association, who adds,

> "In all sorts of organizations, planners with a bag full of tools are hacking away at the corporate ladder with power in the organization getting pushed down while the middle gradually vanishes. . . . There is no doubt that supervisors are particularly vulnerable."[5]

Skagen goes on to identify five trends:

1. The autocratic "boss" is being replaced by shared leadership. Supervisors, therefore, need exceptional human relations skills including negotiation expertise.
2. The idea of employees being "subordinates" is becoming passé in an increasingly democratic workplace. Employees now are often called associates, partners, or, if you work for Walt Disney World, cast members.
3. New and better communication unhampered by traditional bureaucratic rules and procedures.
4. Greater individuality among employees, greater diversity in terms of culture, age, and life-style "compounds the complexity of the challenge" facing the supervisor.
5. Employee participation throughout the organization with an emphasis on teams.[6]

The challenge to management in general will be to prepare people for new jobs. Some jobs will fade away almost completely, whereas others will cry for qualified people. Human resource analysts need to spot these categories now and plan for the transition. Supervisors need to prepare themselves for the new demands of the team environment that is central to the concept of total quality management.

> "Traditional bosses design and allocate work. Teams do that for themselves. Traditional bosses supervise, monitor, control, and check work as it moves from one task performer to the next. Teams do that themselves. Traditional bosses have little to do in a reengineered environment. Managers have to switch from supervisory roles to acting as facilitators, as enablers, and as people whose jobs are the development of people and their skills so that those people will be able to perform value-adding processes themselves."[7]

Increasingly, companies are going beyond the tenets of TQM and embracing the most popular business concept of the '90s—"reengineering."

---

[5]Skagen, 1.

[6]Ibid, 1–3.

[7]Michael Hammer and James Champy, *Reengineering the Corporation: A Manifesto for Business Revolution* (New York: Harper Business, 1993), 77.

SUPERVISORY SKILLS
Developing Your Career

1. Study the personal career development steps shown in Figure 18–1. Take special care to assess yourself accurately. Set career goals by first consciously taking charge of your career. Don't wait for others to give you that "golden opportunity." Make your own opportunities by planning your development toward goals that are meaningful to you.

2. Build your reputation carefully! Only you can determine what your name will mean in a given organization. Make it synonymous with hard work and good quality. Remember that fast trackers get there by their own hard work and commitment. Unless you are related to the boss, there is no substitute for directed and sustained effort.

3. Be conscientious in your efforts to avoid obsolescence. Keep an eye on the future at all times. Take advantage of opportunities that come your way and ignore temporary inconveniences by keeping in mind your intermediate and long-term career goals.

Reengineering, as defined by Hammer and Champy, the originators of the concept, is defined as follows:

> ". . . The fundamental rethinking and radical redesign of business processes to achieve dramatic improvements in critical contemporary measures of performance, such as cost, quality, service, and speed."[8]

Reengineering goes beyond the continuous process improvement commitment of TQM and suggests that most long-term processes need to be thrown out and redesigned to do the job according to the three major influences of the day: customers who tell suppliers what they want and when, intense competition, and pervasive, persistent change. This will be an important concept to watch during the next few years.

Changing Nature of Supervision

Peter Drucker has been quoted as saying that "no job is going to change more in the next decade than that of the first-line supervisor."[9]

Three of the changes most likely to have consequences for the supervisor are changing employee characteristics, an increase in worker participation, and the effect of computers in the workplace.

Employees are changing.

Changing Employee Characteristics. Figure 18–2 illustrates the many ways in which employees are changing. It should be obvious by now that traditional settings, where the supervisor has relatively great power over

---

[8]Ibid, 32.

[9]Peter Drucker, "Twilight of the First-Line Supervisor?" *The Wall Street Journal* (June 7, 1983): 28.

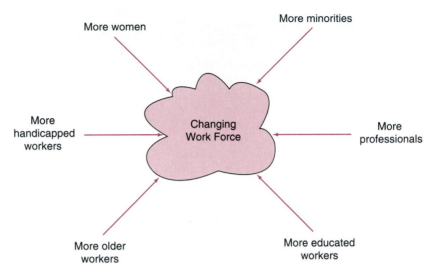

FIGURE 18-2
Changing work force characteristics.

the subordinates, are far less appropriate today given the changing nature of the work force.

Increased Worker Participation.   Dr. Steve Fuller, vice president of Human Resources for General Motors, made the following predictions about worker participation in corporate governance:

Worker participation is becoming more prevalent.

1.   Production employees will sit on boards of directors.
2.   All employees will become salaried, doing away with time clocks.
3.   As in large Japanese firms, employment will be guaranteed for life.
4.   Operating employees will supervise their own work schedules and be asked to approve plant changes.
5.   Supervisors will be elected and evaluated by their subordinates.
6.   For employees not guaranteed lifetime employment, employees will collectively decide who is laid off when times demand such action.
7.   All employees will be eligible for educational and development sabbaticals.
8.   Increased use will be made of employee attitude surveys.
9.   Employee attitudes will partly influence executive bonuses.[10]

Although none of these predictions has come completely true since 1979, there is little doubt that worker participation is on the increase.

---

[10]Leon C. Megginson, Donald C. Mosley, and Paul Pietri, Jr., *Management: Concepts and Application* (New York: Harper and Row, 1986), 640.

The Expanding World of Information Technologies

	• THE TECHNOLOGY AND WHAT IT ENABLES	• PENETRATION/USE
1. IN CURRENT, RELATIVELY COMMON USE		
FAX	Immediate images and text. Faster, clearer, high-resolution, and full-color images with the next generations of machines and the digitalization of the phone network.	About 10 million office fax machines are in use, but the big growth will be in fax cards.[1] Home and home-office fax sales will grow. More than 60 million households should contain a fax by 2000.[2]
CELLULAR TELEPHONY	Communications out of the office, on the road, portable.	7.5 million U.S. subscribers in 1991, and growing.[3]
ELECTRONIC MAIL (e-mail)	Non-real time text communication. Advanced electronic mail, experimental now, will enable users to send and receive graphics, animation, computer programs, and audio recordings.[4]	Use of e-mail in large corporations rose from 67% in 1990 to 98% in 1991.[5] An estimated 11.7 million e-mail users among the work forces of the Fortune 2000 companies should grow to 27 million by 1995.[6]
VOICE MAIL	Storage, retrieval, and forwarding of voice messages, usually from any telephone, anywhere.	
2. LESS WIDESPREAD, BUT RAPIDLY EVOLVING		
LOCAL AND WIDE AREA NETWORKS (LANS AND WANS)	Synergy gained by sharing access at computers and workstations to software, data bases, e-mail, document processing, and so on.	Worldwide revenues for PC LAN products grew at a compound annual rate of 46.3% between 1985 and 1988; 13% growth expected through 1995.[7]
OPTICAL DATA PROCESSING/ STORAGE	Paper reduced or eliminated; documents follow an electronic path, and all communication about them is by computer.	A lifesaver for the insurance industry, which is drowning in paper.
VIDEO-CONFERENCING	Videoconferencing and business TV combine in many applications including purchasing and education.[8]	Costs are decreasing rapidly and use increasing with new telecom technologies.
EXPERT SYSTEMS	Captures knowledge and reasoning. Expert systems screen insurance applications, manage airline gates, schedule workers, and diagnose engine troubles and credit worthiness.[9]	At least 2,000 expert systems are in business use in the U.S., Europe, and Japan.[10]
ELECTRONIC DATA INTERCHANGE (EDI)	Computers talk to each other, transmit data and information, make transactions, report sales, demand inventory, and so on, without human intervention.	As of 1988, about 5,000 companies were using EDI in purchasing. GM uses EDI to communicate with nearly 70% of its 6,000 suppliers and pays about $1 billion a month of its bills electronically.[11]
PICTURE TELEPHONE	Ability to see the person on the other end of the telephone call. Images and graphics will also be possible.	Not yet widespread. AT&T's VideoPhone 2500 has a 3.3 sq. in. screen. More than 10,000 ordered on the first day.[12] Competes with MCI's phone developed by Marconi, at about $750.[13]
THE INTELLIGENT TELEPHONE NETWORK	Emerging developments in telecommunications technology expand services and options, including faster data transmission.	Some services are already available, but not nationwide. Europe, the U.K., for example, is ahead.

The Expanding World of Information Technologies		
	• THE TECHNOLOGY AND WHAT IT ENABLES	• PENETRATION/USE
3. LONGER TERM		
PERSONAL COMMUNICATORS	Locate and contact anyone, anytime, anywhere at one number. Developing out of the intelligent network annd advances in handheld wireless communications devices.	By 1997 as many as 23 million people in the U.S. may be using some form of personal communicator network (PCN).[14] This is an optimistic forecast.
IMAGE MANIPULATION, VIRTUAL REALITY	Real time simulation of any situation, event, or process. Current applications are in architecture, medicine, education, and entertainment.	Experimental. NEC, in Japan, is working on software to enable car designers worldwide to work together on design projects in virtual reality.
ARTIFICIAL INTELLIGENCE	Will replace people and jobs with machines that see, talk, and mimic human judgment.	Experimental today.

1 Lawrence K. Vanston, William J. Kennedy, and Samia El-Badry-Nance. "Forecast for Facsimile." *TE&M*, Sept. 15, 1991. • 2 Judith Waldrop. "Strong Fax Sales Will Challenge Postal Service." *American Demographics*, June 1991; forecast by Technology Futures of Austin, Texas, who also expect that the cost of sending a fax transmission will drop substantially by 1995. • 3 *Statistical Abstract of the United States, 1992*. Table 889, data from the Cellular Telecommunications Industry Association. • 4 Lee Sproull and Sara Kiesler. "Computers, Networks and Work." *Scientific American*, Sept. 1991, pp. 116–123. • 5 Timothy O'Brien. "E-Mail to Be Foundation of New Information Highways." *Network World*, May 25, 1992, pp. 23–24. • 6 Tekla S. Perry. "E-Mail at Work." *IEEE Spectrum*, Oct. 1992, p. 24, reporting a recent study by the Electronic Mail Association, Arlington, Va. • 7 Della Bradshaw. "Cost Is the Determining Factor." *Financial Times*, Sept. 25, 1990. • 8 Peter G. W. Keen. *Shaping the Future*. Harvard Business School Press, 1991, pp. 102–103. • 9 *John Naisbitt's Trend Letter*, Mar. 1, 1990, p. 5. • 10 *John Naisbitt's Trend Letter*, Mar. 1, 1990, p. 5. • 11 John Hillkirk. "Electronic Exchanges Trimming Costs." *USA Today*, Aug. 26, 1988. • 12 *John Naisbitt's Trend Letter*, Oct. 1, 1992, p. 3. •13 Compuserve, Telecom Forum, Dec. 17, 1992. • 14 *John Naisbitt's Trend Letter*, Oct. 1, 1992, p.1.

Source: Joseph F. Coates and Jennifer Jarrett, Editors, *The Future at Work.* Jossey-Bass, Inc., Publishers, May 1993, pp. 4–5.

Effect of Computers in the Workplace.   The trend of increased computerization is undeniable. Figure 18–3 shows the impact of information technology on business for three time frames: current usage common, beginning usage, and future usage. Already large groups of workers have been displaced by computer-operated equipment or robots. This trend will continue, perhaps replacing entire job classifications with machinery. The job classifications replaced, such as assembly workers, are those most likely to work directly under a first-line supervisor. One study noted: "These new technologies will affect everyone's job, but their greatest impact to date has been on workers whose work is labor-intensive, requires relatively little discretion and judgment, and tends to be closely supervised—in short, the kind of work managed by the first-line supervisor."[11]

The other way that computers will affect supervisory work relates to those workers who will be doing their work on computers. On-line activities will allow workers to work physically away from supervisors; some

Computers are displacing workers.

Supervisors will need human relations skills.

---

[11]Kerr, Hill, and Broedling, 111.

 **SUPERVISORY SKILLS**
Meeting Future Challenges

1. Always keep an eye to the future. Use foresight in planning for your needs and those of your employees. Be sure your technical skills are at the cutting edge. Additionally, begin concentrating on your personal skills, which will become more valuable to you as current trends evolve.

2. Examine the changing characteristics of the work force. Be creative in meeting

those changes; supervisors who bemoan the fading of old values and work habits will not be able to capitalize on the opportunities in front of them.

3. Heed Peter Drucker's words that change is inevitable in supervisory jobs. Work with that change instead of resisting it; prepare yourself for the future. Start now!

---

writers, like Alvin Toffler, predicted that many workers will perform their duties in their own home.[12]

As a result of this increased computerization the supervisor will need more human relations skills than ever. The supervisor will be responsible for coordinating the efforts of people who, because of computers, work without the previous amount of interpersonal contact. In sum,

> Tomorrow's first-line supervisors will have to be more technically proficient, as well as more highly skilled in human relations than their predecessors. Also, such individuals probably will expect compensation levels that match these increased skill levels. This will help to position the first line supervisor closer to the ranks of lower level management and further from their subordinates.[13]

SUMMARY

Personal career development consists of six activities: (1) assess yourself; (2) assess your current position; (3) set future goals; (4) design action plans; (5) begin your plan; and (6) evaluate at set intervals.

While working through these six steps of personal career development, supervisors should try to follow strategies: (1) become known for excellent performance; (2) assign your priorities carefully; (3) protect yourself from obsolescence; (4) keep records of

your success; (5) seek broad experience; and (6) seek a mentor.

A number of general trends are going to have an effect on the supervisory environment: the gradual shift from an industrial age to an information age; the demand by employees for ownership in the company; changes in the managerial hierarchy brought about by automated technology; and changing employee characteristics.

---

[12] Alvin Toffler, *The Third Wave* (New York: William Morrow & Co., 1980).

[13] Kerr, Hill, and Broedling, 111.

REVIEW QUESTIONS

1. What is the first step in the personal career development process? Why is this step so important? Explain.

2. What are the other five steps in the personal career development process? Identify and describe each.

3. How can a supervisor work to prevent personal obsolescence? Cite at least five steps the individual can take.

4. What are four strategies that successful supervisors follow in managing their careers?

5. What is a mentor? How useful is a mentor in terms of career progress? Defend your answer.

6. Of the ten trends identified by Naisbitt and Aburdene, which three will have the greatest impact on the supervisory environment? Why? Defend your answer.

7. In what way are employee characteristics changing? How are these changes affecting the nature of the supervisor's job? Explain.

8. In what ways is worker participation in the work force likely to increase? Cite at least five ways. Then discuss the impact of these changes on the supervisor's job.

9. What effect are computers having in the workplace? In what way will these changes influence the supervisor? Explain.

KEY TERMS

Intrapreneuring. Creative entrepreneuring carried on within the organization.

Mentor. Person who guides, directs, and/or assists another person.

Obsolescence. Outmoded knowledge and experience caused by a failure to keep up with changing conditions.

Reengineering. Fundamental rethinking and redesign of business processes to achieve dramatic improvements.

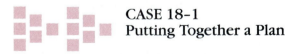

CASE 18–1
Putting Together a Plan

Jim Hanlon is a new supervisor in a large manufacturing firm. Although he has been with the firm for only five months, he was promoted last week to reward his superior performance thus far. This is the fastest promotion ever achieved in the company and Jim is quite pleased with his success. However, he does not want to stop here.

He has his eye on a senior-level management position within the next ten years. Jim has not shared these aspirations with anyone; he believes that it is best to keep these things to oneself so as not to generate any hard feelings or jealousy.

When Jim first began his job five months ago, he set the goal of becoming a supervisor within one year. However, this objective is as far as he had planned. He never expected to be promoted so quickly. Now he feels that he must step back and put together another plan, much more detailed this time, that will help him move up the ladder over the next three years. In particular, he believes that if he proceeds very carefully, he can avoid some of the pitfalls that often accompany a person's fast rise in the ranks. These pitfalls include: (1) not having gained enough experience to do the job well; (2) failing to get a mentor and ending up being blocked from further promotion; and (3) failing to develop specific goals by which to evaluate progress

and redirect one's career so as to prevent winding up in a dead-end job.

1.   What should Jim do in terms of evaluating his personal career development? What steps would you recommend that he take? Describe each.

2.   Are there any career development strategies that Jim should know about? Which ones would you recommend?

3.   Of the strategies identified in the chapter, which one will be of most value to Jim? Why? Defend your answer.

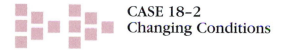

CASE 18–2
Changing Conditions

When Paula Harraden became a supervisor three years ago, she had no idea that the demands of the position would be so great. From what she could remember, her boss never had all of the headaches that currently confront Paula. In particular, two important changes in the company have directly affected her job.

First the company signed a new union contract in the last year. Under the terms of the agreement the workers now have more authority over their own work. For example, instead of having to do a certain amount of work every day, each individual is charged with doing a certain amount of work every week. So if the worker wants to slow up on Monday, Paula can do nothing about it as long as the individual makes up the lost productivity by the end of the week. Additionally, Paula's authority to dismiss or discipline people has been diminished so that it is nearly nonexistent. As a result, most of her time is spent talking to her employees about problems they are encountering and working with them to resolve these situations. When describing the new conditions, Paula has referred to herself as "less of a supervisor of the workers

and more of an equal with them."

Second, over the last six months approximately 5 percent of the total work force has been laid off. Their jobs are now being handled by computers, and the firm has made it clear that over the next year it hopes to cut another 10 percent of the work force. Those employees who remain however are finding that their jobs are becoming more challenging and interesting.

Reflecting on these changes, Paula has been wondering what new changes will take place over the next two years and how these will affect her work environment.

1.   In what ways are the results of the new union contract affecting Paula's work environment? Put it in your own words.

2.   What additional changes is Paula likely to encounter over the next two years? Identify and describe three.

3.   Of the additional changes likely to alter Paula's work environment, which one would you expect to have the greatest impact? Why? Defend your answer.

Readings

The ten readings listed here relate to specific chapters and topics of this book as shown in this table. Each reading is followed by discussion questions. The readings have been chosen because of their practical nature, allowing you to read about applications of the theories and laws that you have studied.

The Benson article, "Quality: If at First You Don't Succeed . . . ," looks at the failed attempts of TQM and proposes some reasons for and solutions to those failures. Advice is also offered as to how to pick an appropriate TQM consultant for your organization.

The article by Barlow and Hane provides a question and answer session dealing with the technicalities of the Americans with Disabilities Act. The complicated concepts of reasonable accommodation, essential job functions, and undue

hardship are explained. Testing and confidentiality rules are also discussed.

The Montebello and Haga article supplements the material in chapter 7 by offering evidence that the best way to keep training budgets intact is to analyze training costs and benefits and present the results in easy-to-understand reports. Tips for picking measurement techniques are offered.

Next, the Kennedy and Everest article, "Put Diversity in Context," casts the spotlight on the impact of culture on organizational communication and understanding. The concept of high-context culture versus low-context culture is described.

Stuart's article, "Fresh Ideas Energize Reward Programs," offers proof that employees are motivated more by recognition than by money. Specific corporate recognition programs are

Author	Reading	Relates to Chapter
Benson	Quality: "If at First You Don't Succeed. . ."	2
Barlow and Hane	"A Practical Guide to the Americans with Disabilities Act"	6
Montebello and Haga	"To Justify Training, Test, Test Again"	7
Kennedy and Everest	"Put Diversity in Context"	8
Stuart	"Fresh Ideas Energize Reward Programs"	9
Schilder	"Work Teams Boost Productivity"	12
Sandbulte	"Lead, Don't Manage"	13
Verespej	"Better Safety Through Empowerment"	15
Maturi	"Stress Can Be Beaten"	17
Stevens	"A Tidal Wave of Technology"	18

identified and many easily transferable examples are presented.

Jana Schilder writes on the timely topic, "Work Teams Boost Productivity." Few topics are as hot today as self-directed work teams and Schilder provides numerous corporate examples of successful implementation of a team environment.

Sandbulte's article, "Lead, Don't Manage," tells of how a utility company CEO changed the corporate culture by delegating authority and responsibility to a wide cross section of employees.

In "Better Safety Through Empowerment", concepts of both Chapter 9 and Chapter 15 (motivation and safety) are combined to look at improved safety in several companies due to employee participation and empowerment. In each example, employee involvement is documented as being the element that turned around the company's safety problem.

Maturi's article, "Stress Can Be Beaten," addresses a major concern in today's corporations—the effects of stress on the health of employees. Maturi describes specific stress-management programs and provides general stress-management tips that anyone can use.

Finally, Stevens writes in "A Tidal Wave of Technology" that new technology will soon change the way we manufacture and sell products. Computers will soon do much of the work currently done by employees.

Together these articles give you the opportunity to read some current literature on topics that you have been studying in class and to learn about specific, practical applications of the material that you are learning.

QUALITY: IF AT FIRST YOU DON'T SUCCEED . . .
By Tracy E. Benson

This report presents a primer to help managers sort through the confusing maze of quality approaches and a shoppers' guide to help in selecting the right consultant.

In ten short years, total quality management (TQM) has become as pervasive a part of business thinking as quarterly financial results. And while it would be difficult to find anyone to disagree with the need to boost the quality of U.S. goods and services, the consensus ends there. In fact, business leaders are as widely divided about how to approach quality as the Democrats and Republicans are about how to reduce the federal deficit. Those on the far left preach the gospel of "Quality as a Philosophy." Focusing on culture as a means to improvement, they advocate spending most, if not all, of a company's budgeted time, energy, and money on vigorous campaigns to end employee apathy. The premise seems to be that real operational improvement can be pursued only once the work force has been collectively convinced of its virtue.

The rightwingers, on the other hand, put their money exclusively on tools and training. Shunning T-shirts, banners, and logos as wasteful corporate jargon, their modus operandi is rooted in two uniquely American tendencies— one toward action and one away from long-term planning. The polarity that prevails between the two camps and its subsequent clamor often serve to undermine the need to get something done. During the last five years, a growing group of moderates has begun to press for the need to integrate the best of both extremes. Delivering tools and training without aligning them with strategic goals is like giving someone "2,317 parts that go into an automobile and then saying 'drive it,'" notes Chuck Holland, president of Knoxville-based QualPro.

Bill Ginnodo, executive director of the Quality & Productivity Management Assn. (QPMA), Schaumburg, Ill., agrees. If you're focusing on activities like problem-solving teams, training, and process improvement without putting them into the context of improving customer satisfaction, improving the quality of the product, and improving market share, "you're missing the point," he says.

Simply adopting quality as a philosophy without the regular use of tools and methods, on the other hand, is equally dangerous. Without a way to apply it practically, the concept remains abstract, and the message on the front lines is that "they don't really mean it."

The key to choosing a path, says Paul T. Hertz, president of the Paul Hertz-Group, Miami, is to know where you want to go. Most companies "make the false assumption that total quality is a generic concept, like everyone's going to Quality World," he says. "There are a lot of levels of quality, and there are a couple of things that will automatically dictate where you wind up. One is the approach that you're going to take, another is the method you're going to use, and another is the implementation that you're going to be using." The critical question that most companies forget to ask is, "Is this going to get us where we want to go?"

LESSONS LEARNED

It's no secret that the path to quality is bumpy. Recent headlines about "failed" programs sent shock waves through organizations and frustrated consultants who declare their efforts have been misunderstood.

Whether quality initiatives have indeed derailed or simply hit a minor speed bump, organizations that are considering how to implement quality and companies that are retooling their existing efforts can learn valuable lessons from those who went before. Following is a list of some of the most common reasons some quality initiatives hit the wall and effective methods for salvaging what may seem like a "failed" attempt.

Inappropriate Motivation

When the impetus to adopt a quality initiative comes from setting a goal to win an award (such as the Malcolm Baldrige National Quality Award) or pressure from a customer to become a certified vendor, companies are most likely to take a "fix-it" approach, says Michael Taggart, executive director of the Unified Technologies Center (UTC), the business-and-industry arm of Cuyahoga Community College, Cleveland. "The biggest challenge is that companies don't want to take the time to really get off to a good start because they're under pressure to get so many people trained or get something launched."

☐   ☐   ☐   THE ANATOMY OF ONE INITIATIVE

Real quality improvement takes hard work, guts, and stamina. Two years of hard work yield several major payoffs for an Indiana paper mill.

One of the most frustrating aspects of a quality manager's job is the management of expectations within the organization. That's because most people have read enough about TQM to know that significant and dramatic changes can take place that will allow the organization to compete more effectively. What interests people most is where we are now (how bad it is) and where we are headed (how good it can get).

Very little time is spent considering what has to be done to get there. That attitude can often undermine the highly disciplined methodology that must be applied in order to get results. Once people know what they're getting into, though, they may be far more helpful and supportive of the entire initiative. Following is a condensed historical snapshot in journal form of two years of a quality-improvement initiative at Kieffer Paper Mills Inc., Brownstown, Ind., taken from the files of QualPro, a Knoxville-based quality-improvement consulting firm.

Absentee owner and Chairman Thomas Phelps attends a conference for top executives, hears a speech on quality, and decides to install a program at the paper mill.

Large banners proclaiming "We will be a quality producer" are hung around the plant, and notices are distributed encouraging employees to do only quality work. There is no perceptible improvement.

Mr. Phelps decides he needs outside help and begins interviewing consultants. After checking references, he chooses QualPro. Basic training in quality principles is delivered by QualPro to managers and union leaders.

Mr. Phelps meets with union leaders and learns that plant workers are aware of quality problems, but have resorted to filing grievances to get management's attention. Union leaders recognize the need for improvement, but voice concerns over management commitment and the ability of workers to handle basic math.

Kieffer announces a $25 million expansion project to produce "engineered" pulp from recycled paper waste. A new twenty-first-century pulp mill with 40 employees will adjoin a nineteenth-century Kieffer paper mill that employs 100. QualPro's quality-improvement methods will be used for the first time in a new start-up.

To establish the need for change, QualPro consultant David Pruett and newly trained project teams begin to document and analyze problems. They find Kieffer is steadily losing old customers and has survived only by developing new niche products and then finding customers to use them. They also learn lost customers are not being tracked.

One team discovers problems such as the lack of a good basis-weight scale, which prompts the shop to "guess" at the weight per square foot of paper they are about to ship. "Guessed" weight results in paper that is 9 percent more costly to the customer than was ordered. This irritates customers, causing them to take their business elsewhere. There is no indication of how long the company has been working with faulty data.

The need for basic education is becoming obvious. Managers learn that two workers who are illiterate are worried. The plant engages a high-school instructor to teach

reading to anyone who is interested. Six employees sign up.

These and other findings gradually convince managers of the need for change. More project teams are formed and assigned specific tasks. Teams use methods learned in training and work with the coordinating consultant until their skills are fully developed.

The need for a measurement system becomes obvious and critical. A major customer returns a shipment complaining the paper is "not stiff enough." Employees develop a unique "stiffness test." The homemade "droop-test" method works, and later a commercial instrument is installed.

A crisis develops at the pulp mill when the dewatering press leaves "crush marks," which cause the sheets to tear, prompting the manager to shut it down. The plant is at a standstill while many solutions are attempted, all unsuccessfully. The pulp mill manager, newly trained in quality-improvement methods, pinpoints the major cause in one hour using a five-factor eight-run DOE (design of experiments—see note). The procedure shows a warped belt on the press is responsible and that higher tension will help. No marks are found after adjustment is made.

The concept of customer satisfaction is gaining ground in the paper mill. A procedure is refined to track rejected shipments by customer, by weight, and by total number of units shipped instead of by total weight alone. Results are closely analyzed and charted, leading to new refinements. Also, a customer profile listing the most important characteristics for each customer is given to the production force.

The consultant notes that operators have become accustomed to control charts and are able to spot trouble sooner. Self-directed, unsupervised six-person work teams in the pulp mill are gaining confidence in their ability to run the process. They learn all jobs in their operation, and test data are made available to all on a computer network.

A major customer of the paper mill is ready to discontinue buying because of paper dirt spots. A work team examines the problem and initiates process changes and improvements. The result: Kieffer is able to guarantee that 98%

of shipped product will meet or exceed specifications. The customer stays and subsequently increases its orders.

One quality team discovers pulp-mill waste can be recycled into paper-production stream. This not only improves the quality of coarser paper, but also eliminates disposal costs of more than $300,000 per year.

Another team finds a way to reuse a $50,000 screen with only $200 in modifications.

The paper mill wins a major order for a national magazine insert requiring stiff and bright heavyweight paper. The plant manager says the plant could not have handled this before DOE demonstrated the need for improved sizing.

Chairman Phelps says the quality-improvement program, which saved more than $1 million, is responsible for the survival of the company during severe price wars during the previous year. Though some problems persist, Mr. Phelps says that overall quality from the pulp mill is so good that customers are finding new products in which to use recycled pulp.

Mr. Phelps announces a 30 percent expansion of the pulp mill, which is running over designed capacity. The mill is running seven days per week because of the elimination of variation in process as well as in product.

Note: Design of Experiments (DOE) is a sophisticated quality-improvement tool that measures the relative impact of several factors in a given process area. The impact of all factors in question is measured simultaneously, eliminating the need to conduct independent and extensive testing on each variable. DOE is generally used to isolate opportunities to refine a process or for process redesign once a set of problems within the process has been stabilized.

No upfront assessment
Because so many companies perceive the quality quest as generic, they often fail to take a studied look at where they are now and compare it with where they want to go. "When that *is* done," says QPMA's Mr. Ginnodo, "the facts are laid out: 'Our customers think our service stinks,' or 'Look at our unit's production costs compared with our competitors' costs.'" That sort of "gap analysis" not only serves to orient the whole initiative, but also demonstrates the need for change to those who will be responsible for carrying it out.

Training as a miracle cure
Although it is a critical component of the overall quality picture, training in and of itself will not produce results. "When the trainer walks away and there's no infrastructure [in the] organization to make quality happen, no plan, no gap analysis, no follow-up, no management support, it's just going to die," says Mr. Ginnodo.

Lack of role definition
It's easy to talk about quality—by now everybody knows the language. But to transform rhetoric into reality, every person within the organization needs to understand specifically what quality means to him or her. "What does the president do differently once total quality is implemented, for example?" asks Dr. Hertz. "Does he or she know that? Do they know how they are going to be acting or thinking differently?" Getting away from abstract conceptual statements, he says, is the only way companies can achieve a permanent transformation of culture.

Failure to address individual management style
Companies often set about improving their working environment by teaching people how to work together on teams. What they usually forget, though, is that the dictatorial management style that exists even in pockets of the organization will obstruct these efforts. "Somebody can be on three teams and have a supervisor who's autocratic, and they're miserable," says Dr. Hertz. "They have to live with that supervisor 90 percent of the time."

Bumping heads with the company's infrastructure
In most cases, companies appoint an individual or department whose sole mission is to coordinate the company's quality-related activities. Unless these individuals work hard to tie elements of the quality initiative directly into things like reward and appraisal systems and career development, "ownership" of the initiative will contin-

ue to reside outside of the various operational areas of the company. Bypassing the organizational structure—not making quality values a part of everyone's job—means that quality will never become integrated into the way people work.

Disconnect between strategic objectives and quality improvement

Quality-improvement projects that are not tied directly into key business needs are apt to send the signal to employees that the whole effort is aimless and ill-conceived. Companies need to identify four to six key quality success measures "that can be understood and addressed by everybody," notes QPMA's Mr. Ginnodo. Without these key measures, such as market share, customer satisfaction, and employee perception of quality, "you really don't have any way of keeping people apprised of your progress and orienting them correctly."

Mismanaging the transition

Organizations often underestimate the pressure of keeping the old system running until the new system is completely installed. "They'll have a batch of bad product, and they know the new system says you really shouldn't send that out," says Dr. Hertz. "But the old system says we have a commitment to the customer—maybe we'll try to slip it by." The result is that managers will "let it slide," but often out of their own frustration will fail to explain the decision to their employees. "For people who go to a training seminar, get turned on by the philosophy, and then come back and see business as usual, they say, 'Quality's dead.' They look at it as a very negative signal."

Giving it up too soon

Because the dramatic improvements tend to come early on, companies whose initiatives seem to slow in the second or third year often make the mistake of seeing their effort as stalled. This is particularly dangerous if there is a perceived setback with a major project or team. Some managers, driven by a self-fulfilling prophecy, will take this opportunity to proclaim,

"I didn't think it was going to work in the first place." That can be tragic, notes UTC's Mr. Taggart, "because if they just tough it out over that one little hump, they may find the breakthrough they need to propel the effort forward."

HOW TO SALVAGE A 'FAILED' ATTEMPT

Whether or not a stalled quality-improvement initiative can be salvaged depends to a large degree on how the managers involved perceive the problem. If the prevailing tendency among management is to say, "I told you so," there's not a lot of leverage to move the effort past the plateau. If, on the other hand, there is a sufficient number of executives (or even one very strong one) who support quality management as a means to increase competitiveness, they can exert enough influence to get the effort back in gear. Either way, there is nothing more dangerous than to allow a quality-improvement initiative to languish in apathy.

Face facts

In the end, it takes unwavering and genuine support from senior managers for a quality-improvement effort to thrive. And even though most executives openly declare their support, many don't take it seriously enough to change the way they behave. When that happens, the power of a quality coordinator to influence change becomes dramatically limited, and his or her ideas will become increasingly ineffective.

To get the effort back on-line, says QPMA's Mr. Ginnodo, the quality manager needs to orchestrate a "sit-down, dragout conversation" amid a cross-functional group representing both management and employees. The idea is to address on a fundamental level everything from progress the company has made to areas of disappointment. Often this sort of open disclosure between people whose expectations have been raised and then dashed will result in a renewed trust and commitment to make it work.

One way to facilitate this dialogue is to conduct an internal survey. By sharing the results with senior managers, says QualPro's Mr. Holland, "we can see if they understand the necessity for having dramatic improvements, if they understand that that's the missing piece of the puzzle they've been working with." When top managers officially sign on, they're ready for action.

Do something

By this time in a typically stalled effort, the company has digested enough rhetoric to sustain another five management fads and has undergone enough training to receive college accreditation. What the company needs now is results. Mr. Holland suggests selecting a few (no more) processes that are key to the customer and working toward improving these dramatically within six months. "In that kind of a situation you can be sure they haven't focused on dramatically improving what's important to the customer. We've got to show them that this stuff works here. We'll be putting the car together for them."

Don't try to move mountains

By and large, quality managers know that to effect lasting change they must tie quality improvement into the company's infrastructure. That can be daunting, though, if what that really means is that systems such as reward and recognition, appraisal, and promotion need to be completely overhauled. Dee Gaeddert, co-author of *Quality On Trial* (West Publishing Co., 1992), suggests that the *existing* systems can, in fact, be used to drive quality improvement into every level of the company.

"You probably have a performance-appraisal system in place, and within that system you may have fifteen factors on which you evaluate any given individual. One of those factors should have to do with how you manage your customer relationships." Avoid using global language like, "Manage your customer relationships more effectively," she asserts, and use this opportunity to get specific. "When you describe what you expect, say, 'I expect you to conduct ten interviews with your customer this year.' Now there's no doubt in my mind what you expect from me. I know how to accomplish that."

Be honest

Nothing engenders trust, loyalty, and commitment among employees more strongly than integrity. Nobody expects the changes that companies and individuals are undergoing to take place overnight. Moreover, employees know that if the transformation is real—that is, if it's more than grist for the corporate public-relations mill—managers and processes will occasionally stumble. The key is to be open. When a manager faces a situation that demands "business as usual," explains Dr. Hertz, "tell your people and your customers why. Tell them, `We know this isn't the right way, we know it's not the way we're going to be doing it, but based on these conditions, we have to do it this way.'|" It boils down to "knowing where you want to go," he says, "knowing that you can't get there overnight, and being open."

PICKING A CONSULTANT

Choosing a consultant to guide your company's quality-improvement initiative is like moving to a new town and selecting a primary-care physician. You want someone who comes highly recommended by those whose opinions you trust, has a depth of background, is up on the latest developments in the field, is an excellent diagnostician, and is either directly affiliated with or in a position to arrange necessary care from the best specialists in the field. Beyond these basic considerations, more subtle issues are likely to affect your search for the right consultant.

For one thing, you need to establish your expectations of the client-consultant relationship from the start. If you want to drive the entire effort yourself—from design to training and through implementation—you'll want to amass a number of firms that specialize in the various components of TQM. If you'd rather rely wholesale on the expertise of one consultant, you'll play a more traditional customer role.

Another alternative is to approach the relationship as a strategic partnership, much the way manufacturing companies are beginning to relate to their suppliers. The Unified Technology Center's (UTC) Michael Taggart says that a situation in which "both parties come to the table with the knowledge of their issues, concerns, and what they want out of it" offers the highest leverage for transformational change.

Beyond offering the best opportunity to blend skills, partnering allows both the client and the consultant to remain true to the objectives. Because of internal pressures to show results, for example, there will undoubtedly come a time when the client company's quality manager will press the consultant to deliver more and deliver it faster.

"Anyone who really has your best interests in mind will be strong enough to look you in the eye and say, 'I know you're anxious to get off the ground, but I strongly encourage that you take the time to do these things.' That's a good test," Mr. Taggart observes, "because later on down the road, you may need to be challenged about what you think you should be doing, and you need to know that you've got a consultant who's willing to be straightforward."

Without establishing a win-win agreement up front, both parties stand to get hurt if the effort fails down the road.

If the client company insists on calling the shots, for example, it may not distinguish that fact later on. "When it doesn't go right," says Mr. Taggart, "they're going to say to the consultant, 'You're the one who did this for us.'"

Successful outcomes are as important to the consultant as they are to the client, says QualPro's Mr. Holland, because "in this business, 'it is by their fruits that you shall know them.'"

Companies often make the mistake of overlooking valuable resources other than traditional consulting companies. Educational institutions, particularly community colleges, offer a wide variety of services to today's industrial companies. "There are over 1,100 community colleges throughout the country," says Mr. Taggart, "most of which have a business-and-industry training component of some sort." Their common mission, he says, is to help companies get competitive advantage through education and training.

The UTC offers northeast Ohio businesses everything from executive-level conferences to training-needs assessment to the development and maintenance of on-site learning centers. And the center partners with the industry arms of other leading community colleges to coordinate and deliver training for clients who operate plants in more than one city.

Whether you select a one-man shop or a larger, more established firm, or choose to tailor a program with your community college, you'll want to be sure the following issues are addressed.

Avoid generic one-size-fits-all treatment

Consulting firms often seek to bolster the credibility of their services by lavishly promoting successes reaped by their secret "formula." Although there is merit in many of these working models (how would TQM have spread without them?), consultants should be open to customizing around a client company's particular business concerns. "All companies do not suffer from the same ills," says QualPro's Mr. Holland. "It's kind of like saying we've got a hospital, and everybody who comes in is going to get penicillin. They've got different ills—you have to provide different treatment."

Upfront assessment

Regardless of the approach, every consulting engagement should begin with some sort of assessment. Like a complete physical exam, it allows the consultant to correctly diagnose the "ills" and then tailor the appropriate treatment. Moreover, it represents an opportunity for the consultant to "get to know the organization," says the UTC's Mr. Taggart, before he or she begins recommending changes.

Look to build internal capability

A good consultant often acts like a therapist. He helps the client get to the root of the problem, guides him toward a long-term practical solution, and then steps out of the way so that the client can solve it. In order to sustain the early improvements that lead to competitive breakthroughs, a company must learn to stand on its own feet, because "at some point, the consultant is going to leave," Mr. Taggart notes.

To avoid falling into the dependency trap, the company should designate a group of people who will ultimately take responsibility for quality improvement throughout the organization. This cross-functional team should be supported through ongoing training and should be fully in place by the time the consultant is ready to cut the company loose. Ideally, these folks should represent most, if not all, of the key operational areas of the company so that their expertise is evenly distributed throughout the company's key processes.

Ensure availability for follow-up
Some consultants are so heavily booked that client companies may find it difficult to get them to move as quickly as they'd like, notes Mr. Taggart. Effective and timely follow-up, though, can often determine whether a project flies or falls. Ask candidates whether they can provide just-in-time training and informal telephone consultations when teams or projects get stuck, he suggests. And find out ahead of time how to make arrangements for these and other types of visits.

Willingness to adjust the plan
Although it is important to trust the consultant's judgment when it comes to things such as as-

sessment and training needs, operational recommendations, and overall timing, flexibility is a must. "You don't want to have someone who feels locked into the direction and may not be as comfortable about changing schedules or priorities," Mr. Taggart says. In the end, you need to know that the sometimes-changing needs of your company drive the plan—as opposed to the plan driving the plan.

DISCUSSION QUESTIONS

1. Describe five of the primary reasons TQM initiatives have failed at many companies.

2. Describe three ways to salvage a TQM program that is failing.

3. What are some basic considerations when choosing a consultant?

4. Discuss at least three of the issues that must be addressed at an early stage with your consultant.

A PRACTICAL GUIDE TO THE AMERICANS WITH DISABILITIES ACT
By Wayne E. Barlow and Edward Z. Hane

Discrimination can be costly. Find out how to comply with the employment provisions of the new Americans with Disabilities Act and limit these costs.

The employment provisions of the Americans with Disabilities Act (ADA) become effective on July 26, 1992, for many employers. This article is intended to provide practical guidance for compliance with ADA from the combined perspectives of the labor attorney and the industrial psychologist. The article addresses the legal requirements of the ADA, and points out the tasks required of employers in order to comply.

It's designed to help employers identify and meet their obligations, and be prepared to defend their actions if challenged.

The ADA bars discrimination against qualified individuals who have disabilities in employment, public services, transportation, public accommodations, telecommunications and other services, in both public and private sectors. It also requires the identification of the essential functions of each job, and a reasonable accommodation to the disabilities of qualified individuals.

The ADA prohibits discrimination against individuals who have disabilities in regard to *all* employment practices, terms, conditions, or privileges of employment. This prohibition covers the entire employment process.

Thus, the principles discussed below should be incorporated into all relevant aspects of an employer's practices regarding individuals who have disabilities.

The following questions and responses will help assess your company's need to comply with ADA, and will provide practical guidance in that effort.

Q: *When are you required to comply?*

A: If you have twenty-five employees or more you must comply by July 26, 1992; if you have 15 to 24 employees you must comply by July 26, 1994.

Q: *What is a disability?*

A: "Disability" is broadly defined in *any* one of three ways:

1. A physical or mental impairment that substantially limits one or more major life activities. (A physical or mental impairment will not constitute a "disability" under this first definition unless the impairment results in a *substantial* limitation of one or more major life activities.)

2. A record of such an impairment

3. Being regarded as having such an impairment. (*Regarded as having a disability* means that an individual whose disability isn't substantially limiting is nevertheless *perceived* as having a substantially limiting impairment; has an impairment that's only substantially limiting because of the attitudes of others toward the impairment; or has no impairment, yet is perceived by the employer or other covered entity as having a substantially limiting impairment.)

A physical or mental impairment is: "[a]ny physiological disorder, or condition, cosmetic disfigurement, or anatomical loss affecting one or more of the following body systems: neurological; musculoskeletal; special sense organs; respiratory (including speech organs); cardiovascular; reproductive; digestive; genitourinary, hemic and lymphatic; skin; and endocrine; or . . . [a]ny mental or psychological disorder, such as mental retardation, organic brain syndrome, emotional

The ADA prohibits discrimination against people who have disabilities. Employment practices, terms, conditions and privileges covered by the ADA include:

☐	Application	☐	Medical
☐	Testing		examinations
☐	Hiring	☐	Compensation
☐	Assignment	☐	Leave
☐	Evaluation	☐	Benefits
☐	Disciplinary	☐	Layoff
	actions	☐	Recall
☐	Training	☐	Termination
☐	Promotion		

or mental illness, and specific learning disabilities." (Substantially limited when viewed in light of the factors noted above, amounts to a significant restriction when compared with the abilities of the average person.)

Q: *Who are "qualified individuals with disabilities"?*

A: "Qualified individuals with disabilities" are individuals who have a disability and meet the skill, experience, education and other job-related requirements of the position held or desired, and who, with or without reasonable accommodation, can perform the essential functions of the position.

EEOC regulations provide a two-step analysis to determine who are "qualified individuals with disabilities."

Step one is satisfied if the individual possesses the prerequisites for the position, i.e., possesses the appropriate educational background, employment experience, skills or licenses.

Step two is satisfied if the individual can perform the *essential* functions of the position with or without reasonable accommodation.

Because the ADA specifically covers "*qualified* individuals with disabilities," a job applicant may be subject to inquiries, tests or other selection devices, provided: 1) The evaluations are job-related; 2) All applicants are subjected to the same evaluations; and 3) An applicant's disability doesn't prevent obtaining an accurate measure of qualifications.

An employer should have the capacity to evaluate applicant qualifications with respect to the position requirements and the essential functions of the position. To carry out such an evaluation accurately and fairly, the employer must identify and document the *position requirements* (skills, experience and education) and *essential functions* of the position.

Q: *When should this be done?*

A: The identification of essential functions should be done before a particular applicant is recruited. If it's done at the time of selection, the process will necessarily be rushed, and the results may not appear to be objective, particularly when the employer's decision is being challenged. The ADA regulations state that written job descriptions constitute relevant evidence to be considered for this purpose *if* they have been prepared *before* advertising or interviewing applicants for the job.

Q: *What steps do you take to determine position requirements and essential functions?*

A: Position requirements and essential functions can be identified by applying job analysis techniques. Job analysis is a systematic inquiry to discover and document job information by interviewing supervisors and incumbents, and observing job performance and work product.

Existing job descriptions may be useful sources of information in this process, but shouldn't be accepted without critical review. An existing job description, probably prepared for another purpose, may not distinguish between essential and marginal job functions. Also, existing job descriptions may not be up-to-date or accurate with respect to current position requirements. If an employer prepares new job descriptions for this purpose, it would be useful to design them also to serve other human resources needs, such as selection, training, performance evaluation and job evaluation.

Whether an employer develops new job information or verifies the information in an existing job description, the following points are critical:

1. Position requirements must be demonstrably job-related. For any skill, education, experience or other requirement identified for a job, an employer must demonstrate that the requirement is related to successful job performance. For this purpose, it may be useful to list the tasks performed in enough detail to make the relationship between position requirements and successful job performance clear. This is similar to the demonstration required by Title VII of the Civil Rights Act to show job-relatedness of selection procedures that have an adverse impact on a protected class.

2. An essential job function is one that's fundamental to successful performance of the job, as opposed to marginal job functions, which may be performed by particular incumbents at particular times, but are incidental to the main purpose of the job. If the performance of a job function is only a matter of convenience, and not necessary, it's a marginal function.

3. The employer must actually require employees to perform the essential job functions. In other words, the functions must exist in reality, as well as on paper.

Q: *What determines an "essential" function?*

A: The functions performed in a position can be observed and recorded during the job analysis. The ADA regulations specify several factors to be considered in determining whether each of these functions is essential. These factors can be evaluated during the job analysis by obtaining answers to the following questions:

1. Does the position exist to perform these functions? If the performance of a particular function is the principal purpose for hiring a person, it would be an essential function.

2. Would the removal of the function fundamentally alter the position? If the purpose of the position can be fulfilled without performing the function, it isn't essential.

3. What's the degree of expertise or skill required to perform the function? The fact that an employee is hired for his or her specialized expertise to perform a particular function is evidence that the function is essential.

4. How much of the employee's time is spent performing the function? The fact that an employee spends a substantial amount of time performing a particular function is evidence that the function is essential.

5. What are the consequences of failure to perform the function? The fact that the consequences of failure are severe is evidence that the function is essential.

6. How many other employees are available among whom the function can be distributed? The smaller the number of employees available for performing a group of functions, the greater the likelihood that any one of them will have to perform a particular function.

Several other types of information that the ADA regulations say may be relevant to the determination of whether a function is essential are: 1) Written job descriptions that are prepared before advertising or interviewing applicants for the job; 2) The terms of a collective bargaining agreement; 3) The work experience of past employees in a job or current employees in a similar job.

Q: *Who should conduct the job analysis to determine position requirements and essential functions?*

A: Whether an employer uses internal staff or a consultant, the determination of position requirements and essential functions should be carried out by persons who are skilled in job analysis techniques and thoroughly familiar with the provisions of the ADA. Many industrial psychologists specialize in these kinds of determination, and employers may find it useful to have the process carried out or monitored and reviewed by a competent industrial psychologist.

Joint actions by employers that have similar jobs, through industry associations or informal groups, can offer an opportunity to minimize costs by sharing efforts.

Q: *How do you accomplish reasonable accommodations and demonstrate that they have been made?*

A: If an applicant is qualified in terms of the position requirements, but unable to perform one of the essential job functions because of a disability, the ADA requires that the employer make a reasonable accommodation, unless it would result in undue hardship. This means that the employer may be required to alter the conditions of a particular job, if this will make it possible for the candidate to perform all essential functions.

However, an employer isn't required to make an accommodation that would cause an "undue hardship" for the employer. Employers should therefore be prepared to evaluate their obligations to make a reasonable accommodation for the disability in question.

An employer is required to accommodate as far as (but not beyond) the point of imposing an undue hardship on the business. "Undue hardship" means "significant difficulty or expense in, or resulting from, the provision of the accommodation." This refers to "any accommodation that would be unduly costly, expensive, substantial, or disruptive, or that would fundamentally alter the nature or operation of the business" (see "Determining undue hardship").

Regulations of the EEOC provide that if an employer asserts that a particular accommodation represents an undue hardship, the employer must nevertheless accommodate if funding is available from another source (see "Finding funding").

According to regulations, "[t]he process of determining reasonable accommodation is an informal, interactive problem-solving technique involving both the employer and the qualified individual with a disability" and may be accomplished by following steps:

1. Analyzing the particular job involved to determine its purpose and essential function

2. Consulting with the individual having a disability to ascertain the precise, job-related limitations imposed by the disability and how those limitations could be overcome with a reasonable accommodation

3. Identifying potential accommodations and assessing the effectiveness each would have in enabling the individual to perform the essential functions of the position

☐ ☐ ☐ DETERMINING UNDUE HARDSHIP

In a case interpreting the Rehabilitation Act of 1973, a federal district court held that the Pennsylvania Department of Public Works had failed to reasonably accommodate three visually impaired employees, when it refused to assume the cost of providing readers to review various documents and fill out various forms. The district court held that the provision for readers was essential to enable the plaintiffs to meet the requirements of the job at a cost of $6,638 per year for each plaintiff. In determining whether such accommodations would impose an undue hardship on the DPW, the court considered several factors including: the overall size of the program and size of its budget; the type of operation and the composition and structure of the work force; and the nature and cost of the accommodations needed. *Nelson v. Thornburgh,* 567 F.Supp. 369 (E.D. Pa. 1983), affirmed, 738 F.2d. 1053 (3rd Cir. 1984), *cert. denied,* U.S. (1/24/85).

☐ ☐ ☐ FINDING FUNDING

The employer must consider whether funds may be obtained or are available from a "state vocational rehabilitation agency, or if Federal, State or local tax deductions or tax credits are available to offset the cost of the accommodation." If so, "only that portion of the cost of the accommodation that could not be recovered—the final net cost to the entity—may be considered in determining undue hardship."

☐ ☐ ☐ TESTING JOB APPLICANTS

The test of permissibility is *not* whether the employer intends to exclude an individual or class of individuals who have disabilities, although the intent of the employer may be relevant to determine whether the employer has complied with the ADA. If a qualification standard, test or other selection criterion results in screening out such individuals on the basis of disability, particular attention must be devoted to it to be certain it's job-related and that the employer can justify its impact under the provisions of ADA.

4.   Considering the preference of the individual to be accommodated and selecting and implementing the accommodation that's most appropriate for both the employee and employer.

The determination of a reasonable accommodation is an individual matter that depends on the exact nature of the disability and the essential function with which the disability interferes. For this reason, reasonable accommodation determinations will be made on a case-by-case basis. Nevertheless, some advance planning may be useful and make the process easier. For example, supervisors and employees can suggest some of the more obvious potential accommodations for a particular function, and these ideas can be documented for future reference. The inquiry about potential accommodations could well be accomplished during a job analysis to identify position requirements and essential functions.

It's important that a written record be kept of accommodations considered and made, and of the reasons that certain accommodations aren't feasible. This information will be crucial if there's any later question about whether the employer made an effort to achieve a reasonable accommodation. Because the issue of undue hardship may be involved, this documentation should include estimates of the cost, effort or difficulty involved for particular accommodations.

Q: *How do you establish qualification standards?*

A: The ADA doesn't prohibit an employer from establishing job-related qualification standards that include education, skills, work experience, and physical and mental standards necessary for job performance, health and safety. Nor does the Act interfere with an employer's right to employ only individuals who can perform jobs effectively and safely, and to hire the best-qualified person for the job.

On the other hand, ADA provides that an employer may not use qualification standards, tests or other selection criteria that have the effect of screening out an individual who has a disability unless the employer shows that the tests or other criteria are job-related for the position in question and consistent with business necessity principles (see "Testing job applicants").

Where an employer administers a test as a condition of employment, it must ensure that the test results accurately reflect the skills, aptitude or other factors that the test purports to measure, "rather than reflecting the impaired sensory, manual or speaking skills of such employee or applicant."

This requirement may make it necessary for an employer to modify the method of administering a test, so that it will give more accurate results for an applicant who has a particular disability. For example, it may be necessary to administer an oral version of a paper-and-pencil test to an applicant who has impaired vision or writing skills. Alternatively, instructions normally given orally may need to be in written form for an applicant with impaired hearing.

Q: *May an employer require a physical examination?*

A: An employer may "make pre-employment inquiries into the ability of an applicant to perform job-related functions." It's unlawful, however, for an employer to conduct a medical examination of an applicant or to make inquiries regarding an applicant's health or disability before making a job offer. Physical agility tests required of applicants are *not* considered medical examinations and employers may require applicants to demonstrate their ability to perform functions of the job (i.e., a work sample test) provided that all applicants are required to do so.

An employer may require a medical examination *after* extending an offer of employment to a job applicant and before the applicant begins his or her employment duties, and may condition an offer of employment on the results of such examination *only* if all entering employees in the same job category are subjected to such an examination regardless of disability.

It should be noted that a test to determine the illegal use of drugs isn't considered a medical examination.

Q: *What confidentiality rules apply?*

A: The regulations strictly define an employer's obligation to maintain the confidentiality of information obtained regarding the medical condition or history of any applicant. Such information "shall be collected and maintained on separate forms and in separate medical files and be treated as a confidential medical record."

Such information may be disclosed only under the following circumstances: 1) to supervisors and managers—only regarding necessary restrictions on the work or duties of the employee and necessary accommodations; 2) to first aid and safety personnel—if the disability might require emergency treatment; and 3) to government officials—investigating compliance with the ADA, on request.

Q: *What do you do to establish that you're accommodating a particular individual, and thus defend against a claim that you haven't reasonably accommodated?*

□   □   □   EMPLOYERS' LEGAL OBLIGATIONS AT A GLANCE

The following points summarize employers' legal obligations under the Americans with Disabilities Act.

1. An employer must not deny a job to a disabled individual because of a disability if the individual is qualified and able to perform the essential functions of the job, with or without reasonable accommodation.

2. If an individual who has a disability is otherwise qualified but unable to perform an essential function without an accommodation, the employer must make a reasonable accommodation unless the accommodation would result in undue hardship.

3. An employer isn't required to lower existing performance standards for a job when considering the qualifications of an individual who has a disability if the standards are job-related and uniformly applied to all employees and candidates for that job.

4. Qualification standards and selection criteria that screen out or tend to screen out an individual on the basis of a disability must be job-related and consistent with business necessity.

5. Any test or other procedure used to evaluate qualifications must reflect the skills and abilities of an individual rather than impaired sensory, manual or speaking skills, unless those are the job-related skills that the test is designed to measure.

With respect to the recruitment and job application process, including pre-employment inquiries, employers:

1. Must provide an equal opportunity for an individual who has a disability to participate in the job application process and to be considered for a job.

2. May not make pre-employment inquiries regarding any disability, but may ask questions about the ability to perform specific job functions and, with certain limitations, may ask an individual who has a disability to describe or demonstrate how he or she could perform these functions.

3. May not require pre-employment medical examinations or medical histories, but may condition a job offer on the results of a post-offer medical examination, if all entering employees in the same job category are required to take such an examination.

4. May use tests for illegal drugs, which are not considered medical examinations under ADA.

A: An employer that follows the steps outlined in this article in a logical and organized way and properly documents the entire process, should be in a position to recreate its accommodation process and thus demonstrate its compliance.

Q: *What kind of documentation is needed to demonstrate compliance with the ADA?*

A: Documentation is a critical part of an employer's efforts and accomplishments regarding compliance with the ADA. It's important to document all facts and events that have a bearing on the placement of individuals who have disabilities. Thorough documentation will enhance communication with all parties involved, make it easier to resolve issues, and provide the basis for a legal defense, if necessary.

Accurate records should be kept of all of the following information and actions:

□ Position requirements and demonstration of their job-relatedness

□ Essential functions

□ Reasonable accommodations considered and implemented

□ Qualification standards, tests, and other evaluations in the placement process

☐ Evidence of job-relatedness of qualification standards

☐ Evaluations of all applicants with regard to qualification standards.

The documentation doesn't need to be a burdensome activity. If an employer follows a systematic record-keeping plan that takes the ADA requirements into account, the documentation can be maintained very efficiently.

Q: *What remedies are available to a plaintiff if an employer is found to be guilty of discrimination based on a disability?*

A: Remedies available for employment discrimination, whether caused by intentional acts or practices which have a discriminatory effect, may include hiring, reinstatement, promotion, back pay, front pay, reasonable accommodation or other actions that will make an individual "whole." Remedies also may include payment of attorney's fees, expert witness fees and court costs.

In addition, compensation and punitive damages also may be available in cases in which *intentional* discrimination is found. In cases concerning reasonable accommodation, compensatory or punitive damages may *not* be awarded to the charging party if the employer can demonstrate "good faith" efforts were made to provide reasonable accommodation. Thus, it's critical that an employer document its good faith efforts to accommodate qualified individuals who have disabilities.

Wayne E. Barlow is a partner in the Los Angeles-based law firm of Barlow & Kobata.
Edward Z. Hane is an industrial psychologist and the director of Personnel Consulting Group in Woodland Hills, California.

DISCUSSION QUESTIONS

1. Define the term *disability* under the ADA.

2. What is an "essential function," and how are essential functions identified?

3. Discuss the concept of providing a reasonable accommodation without undue hardship. What exactly does this mean for the employer?

4. What kind of documentation is required under the ADA?

TO JUSTIFY TRAINING, TEST, TEST AGAIN
By Anthony R. Montebello and Maureen Haga

Despite a $34-million sales bonanza that made a training program at R. R. Donnelley & Sons Company look incredibly good, simple analysis showed that other factors may have deserved the credit. A series of statistical tests provided management with the answers it needed.

Getting budgets approved for training is hard today. Squeezed by unparalleled pressure for cost control and incessant demands for productivity gains, line managers are forced to make tough choices between HR-related programs, such as training, and alternative investments, such as automation. Often, they base their decisions on suppositions about what the different investments will yield.

This is quite a tenuous and uneasy situation for the HRD function and staff. Under increased demand for productivity-related development programs, training budgets are burgeoning faster than the rate of inflation—according to a recent *Training Magazine* survey, they increased in the past year by an average of 7 percent. When tangible dollar delivery expenses, such as travel, lodging and time off the job are factored in, total costs swelled by 20 percent. Ironically, these bloated training budgets are difficult to justify because the payoff of training more often than not is elusive.

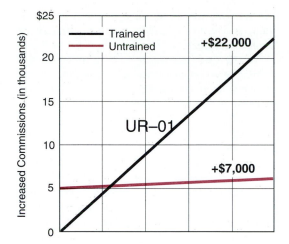

Trained Group Outperforms Control Group

Factors such as gained experience and marketing campaigns contributed to an increase in commissions between two years for a group of sales representatives who received training and a group that didn't. However, commissions for the trained group far exceeded those of the untrained group, indicating that training had an impact.

That's why, more than ever before, HRD professionals must evaluate the impact of training. Says William J. Healy, president of Iselin, New Jersey-based VMI Learning Systems, "Companies are frustrated by investment in training programs that don't feature measurement of results."

These measurements, though necessary, aren't easy. The training department at Chicago-based R. R. Donnelley & Sons, a commercial printing firm, found this out when it tracked and evaluated the results of a training program that took place in May 1990 for senior sales representatives. The training bill added up to more than $125,000, including the costs for instructor certification, seminar delivery and seminar participation. That doesn't count the opportunity cost of keeping the sales representatives away from the office for four and a half days. Senior executives and sales managers understandably wanted to be shown that the investment in both money and time was worth it.

In the end, the trainers proved it was. Along the way, however, they weren't so sure. Initial data suggesting the program had produced an eye-popping $34 million windfall proved to be inconclusive. Further analysis repeatedly showed that what appeared to be impressive numbers actually were insignificant. Only through perseverance did the trainers succeed in their goal. Here's how they did it.

Donnelley determines measures to evaluate training results

The training department teamed up with St. Louis-based Psychological Associates, an international consulting and training firm, to develop a measurement system. The team had to look at three issues in designing the system, which were how to:

☐ Obtain relevant measures of training impact to evaluate its effectiveness.

☐ Design the experiment to balance practical realities with scientific control.

☐ Analyze the results to reach sound conclusions that easily can be communicated to sales supervisors and senior managers.

The first step for the team was to figure out what measures to use in evaluating the results. To do this, it had to consider measurement validity, which refers to whether or not the measurements chosen focus on the right thing. In training evaluation, the right thing is the behavior or result the trainers are attempting to change or influence. For example, if a company develops training to change attitudes toward minorities, observations of service representatives' behavior toward minorities would be more valid than transactions per hour.

Reliability was a related concern for the team. Measures are considered reliable if they consistently measure the variable of interest. A yardstick, for example, is a much more reliable measure of height than subjective judgments of people eyeballing an object. Customer observations of whether a clerk smiled or used a customer's name probably are more reliable than supervisory ratings of customer courtesy or bedside manner. Objective measures, such as sales or production figures, usually are the most reliable.

A third consideration was the timing of the measurement. Often, measures of results aren't possible until several months after training. The longer the time span, the more likely it is that other events, such as a downturn in the business, turnover or additional training, will have an impact on the measure selected. Other considerations in selecting a measure of change have to do with practical considerations, such as cost, availability, accessibility and so on.

The team determined that relevant measures for evaluating the effectiveness of Donnelley's sales training would be behavioral changes and the business results brought about by these changes. The team asked itself, "What is the new behavior that we want to see?" The answer was that it wanted to see if people could close new business as a result of training. Therefore, closure ratios were the measure the team would be using (see Table 1 for other possible measures).

Next step: Developing a measurement system
To help determine what measure to use, the team investigated the four basic testing designs, which are derived from combinations of pre- and post-testing of either one or two test groups.

In the two-group designs, one group is an untrained control (see Table 2 for an explanation of the four designs).

The first evaluation method in which the training team engaged was measuring the results of one trained group. The training session took place in May 1990. Twenty-six sales representatives from nine different product groups attended the four-and-a-half day session. The participants all were senior-level, commission-only workers with a minimum of three years' selling experience at the company.

Before the sessions began, the trainers asked each of the participants to prepare background on a real case. The case needed to involve a prospect whose sale the participant couldn't close. It also had to be a case with which the participant had been working for a while so that a meaningful role-play simulation could be constructed during the training program. In addition, it had to represent significant new business potential that realistically could be pursued soon after the seminar: It had to be challenging but attainable.

During the seminar, participants honed their selling skills by participating in sales simulations that were videotaped and critiqued by a team of peers. They learned about four personality types and how to handle clients who have

---

TABLE 1

Measures of behavioral change and business results.
To evaluate whether its sales training course had any impact, R.R. Donnelley & Sons considered the following measures of behavioral change and business results.

Behavioral Change Measures:	*Business Results Measures:*
• Number of calls	• New business development
• Closure ratio	• Sales volume
• Customer evaluations	• Cost of sale
• Manager evaluations	• Average order size
• Peer evaluations	• Add on sales
• Percent of objections managed	• Commissions
• Product and service mix sold	• Market penetration

TABLE 2

Four common experimental designs.
Following is a list of four commonly used experimental designs, arranged in increasing levels of sophistication. R.R. Donnelley compared the designs for how well each could evaluate whether training alone caused the effect.

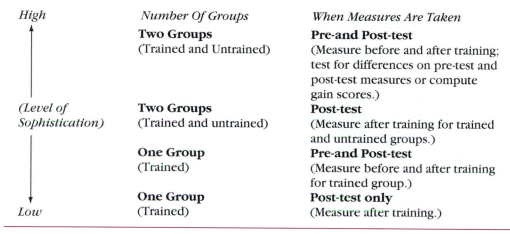

High	Number Of Groups	When Measures Are Taken
	Two Groups (Trained and Untrained)	**Pre-and Post-test** (Measure before and after training; test for differences on pre-test and post-test measures or compute gain scores.)
(Level of Sophistication)	**Two Groups** (Trained and untrained)	**Post-test** (Measure after training for trained and untrained groups.)
	One Group (Trained)	**Pre-and Post-test** (Measure before and after training for trained group.)
Low	**One Group** (Trained)	**Post-test only** (Measure after training.)

---

each one. Before completing the seminar, each participant had to develop a strategic plan for closing the deal in his or her case study. The trainers kept copies of these plans for follow-up purposes.

Using real cases in the training proved beneficial for at least three reasons. First, it increased participant motivation by focusing skills on an important, real-world issue. Second, by encouraging immediate implementation of learned strategies, it minimized the possibility of problems with the transfer of training. Finally, having real sales situations provided the trainers with a quick and dirty means to evaluate training transfer, because follow-up on *hit rate* and total sales generated is straightforward and relatively easy.

Trainers checked on the application of the participants' strategies beginning six months after the training was completed and then every six weeks for a twelve-month period. This time frame paralleled the typical cycle for closing the commercial-printing company's large and complex sales. Most participants needed nine to twelve months to execute their strategies. The results of the follow-up evaluations? Of the

twenty-six participants tracked, fourteen closed their sales within twelve months, accounting for $34,239,000 in new revenue. The average sale was nearly $2.5 million, with a range spanning from $35,000 to $15 million.

To compute the cost-benefit of the training, the team divided the revenue produced by the cost of the training. The resulting ratio, 273:1, shows that for each dollar spent, the company realized a $273 return.

Although the results sound good, there's a problem with them. By measuring only the revenue produced by the trained group after the training, there's nothing with which to compare the results. Did performance behaviors or results improve, get worse or stay the same? It isn't clear.

There is some merit to this testing method, however, as R. R. Donnelley found. It allowed the training team to gauge the level of transfer of training. This is important because if there's no transfer, there are no results. However, this wasn't enough for the company. It needed more evidence, which required a more sophisticated testing design.

By applying the one group, pre- and post-training design method, the team was able to add a baseline for comparative purposes, adding a measure of integrity. It chose commission data of new business for its objective measure. The team members determined that commission data for the year prior to and the year following the training would provide a reliable, valid and relatively short-term measure of performance.

The team found that the trained group increased its commissions by an average of approximately $22,000 from one year to the next. These results are more compelling than those found in the first test, but there's still a problem. This data doesn't provide enough information to rule out other reasons for the increase. For example, any of the following could have affected the commissions data:

☐   Other events, such as price decreases, promotional events, decreases in competition or incentive programs

☐   Natural changes in trainees, such as aging, increased experience, increased knowledge or personality changes

☐   Special or preferential treatment, such as extra attention from a manager, additional follow-up training, special coaching or contacts with other trainees

Without a comparison group, it's impossible to tell whether the increase in commissions was a result of the training or the other factors.

Comparing the after-training commissions data of two groups—one trained and the other untrained—provided some insight. The training team established a control group by searching the sales organization database and randomly selecting people from each of Donnelley's nine product groups represented in the trained group. The people selected for the control group met the same experience criteria as those in the trained group.

The team compared the two groups on pre-test commission means using a t-test statistical analysis (see "How to Measure Results Statistically"). Although the untrained group was earning slightly higher commission on average (approximately $3,000) than the group earmarked for training, the test indicated that the difference wasn't statistically significant. The team concluded that the groups were equivalent before the training.

This determination was important. Unless the two groups are equivalent before training, post-training data can be misleading. For example, the untrained group may be outperforming the trained group before the training. Although the training may improve the performance of the trained group, bringing it up to the level of the control group, the post-test data indicates that the training had no effect, because both groups are performing equally.

On the other hand, the trained group may have already been outperforming the control group before going through the sales training.

☐   ☐   ☐   VITALS

ORGANIZATION
R.R. Donnelley & Sons Company
TYPE OF BUSINESS
Commercial printing firm
HEADQUARTERS
Chicago
EMPLOYEES
33,000

CORPORATE SALES TRAINER
Maureen Haga
YOU SHOULD KNOW
R. R. Donnelley & Sons Company measured the impact of a sales training course and discovered that it yielded a return-on-investment of nearly $13 million.

When the post-test data shows the trained group outperforming the control group, it may erroneously be concluded that the training was responsible. In reality, the training had no effect.

What R. R. Donnelley found by comparing post-training mean commissions was that the trained group had surpassed the control group by more than $12,000. However, the *t*-test analysis indicated that even this difference wasn't statistically significant.

The team had three choices. It could abandon the project, assuming that the training had no effect. It could increase the sample size, assuming that the small sample used didn't allow the *t*-test to detect the differences that actually were there. Or, it could select a more powerful statistical tool. It chose the latter.

The most sophisticated of the tools presented earlier is two-group, pre- and post-training design. This method requires the calculation of gain scores, which are the differences between pre-training and post-training figures. To find the gain scores, the team compared the gain in commissions from the year before the training to the year following the training for each group.

The team determined that the average gain in commission that the untrained control group demonstrated—approximately $7,000—was an effect of history (a marketing campaign) and/or maturation (gained experience). But these factors affected both groups equally. In addition, the team monitored treatment effects to ensure that factors such as special coaching by the sales managers didn't differentially affect the trained group. Moreover, all alternative explanations were ruled out, one by one, to show definitive proof that training caused the increase.

Armed with this evidence, Donnelley's HRD team could claim an average $15,000 gain in commissions attributable to training (the trained group's $22,000 increase minus $7,000 attributed to history and maturation). Now, the *t*-test ratio indicated that the team could be 95% confident that the differences detected were true differences and not simply a result of how the sample was drawn from the population.

Just to be sure of its results, the team performed an Analysis of Covariance (ANCOVA) statistical test, an even more powerful and sophisticated measure. The team used ANCOVA procedures for partialing out or minimizing any pretest differences. The resulting ratio demonstrated that post-test commissions were significantly different when the pre-test differences were controlled.

Unfortunately, it's nearly impossible to explain ANCOVA in any detail to a layman. The team was unable to use this information to make a simple and straightforward presentation to line management.

Demonstrating the impact of training
Although the statistical results were complex, the data that the team acquired provided a means for the team to perform a return-on-investment (ROI) analysis. This provided an effective means of communicating the impact of training.

Here's what the team did: By multiplying the number of participants in the training session (twenty-six) by their average gain in commissions ($22,422), the team calculated the total gain in commissions for the trained group as $582,972. The total gain in commissions for the untrained group from the year before the training to the following year was $191,490, which is the number of sales representatives in the control group (twenty-six) multiplied by their average gain in commissions ($7,365). Subtracting the gain of the control group ($191,490) from the gain of the trained group ($582,972) gave the team the gain in commissions produced by the training, which was $391,482.

This wasn't enough, however. The team needed sales revenue figures to satisfy top management. Commission for the sales representatives were based on an average of 3 percent of total sales. Because the team had determined that the total commission revenue gained as a result of training was $391,482, they were able to figure out that the total revenue produced as a result of training was $13,049,433. Subtracting the costs of training ($125,138) from the total revenue produced gave the team a return-on-investment figure of $12,924,295.

The team communicated these results to sales managers and upper executives through presentations at management meetings, using both statistical results and return-on-investment figures. Response has been favorable.

HOW TO MEASURE RESULTS STATISTICALLY

There are two considerations to keep in mind when selecting statistical procedures: simplicity and power. The most important advice one can offer on the use of statistical procedures is this: Keep it simple. Explaining the results of a complicated statistical test to a layman can be a trying experience.

The other consideration in the choice of statistical procedures is *power,* defined as the sensitivity to detect group differences when in fact they exist. Among other things affecting power is the size of the sample and the choice of the statistical method. Often in evaluation research, the tester must deal with small samples. The *t*-test is most useful for comparing groups when the samples are small—thirty or fewer people. However, if you have fewer than ten or fifteen people per group, the power diminishes to the point that it may be better to abandon the entire evaluation.

To measure the impact of its sales-training course, Chicago-based R. R. Donnelley & Sons used the *t*-test. The *t*-test is used to test whether two means or averages, such as the average productivity measures of the individuals within a trained group and an untrained group, are statistically significantly different.

Computational procedures result in a *t* value and associated probability level (p-value). A probability level of .05 or less indicates that the two means are indifferent. More specifically, it means that the testers can be 95 percent confident that the differences are true differences and not simply a result of how the samples were drawn from the population.

If you hypothesize a direction of the difference between two means (such as, mean A is larger than mean B), then a one-tailed *t*-test is used. This test is more sensitive and powerful for detecting differences than a two-tailed *t*-test. This is because a p-value of .05 (95 percent confidence level) is divided among the two tails of the distribution of scores around the mean. As a result, the mean of the comparison group must fall within either .025 region (above or below the mean) of the distribution rather than a larger .05 area when a one-tailed test is used.

Computational procedures for the *t*-test are available in any introductory statistics text and on commercially available software programs, such as *Microsoft Excel* and *Statistical Package for the Social Sciences*.

The success of the process has opened the door to future tracking of other high-investment training processes. In addition, it has convinced the sales managers of the benefit of training. They now have empirical evidence that allowing their sales representatives to spend some time for analysis and preparation yields higher results in the long-term than just relying on reactive methods.

The demonstrated results of training have had an unexpected benefit as well. Seeing the positive outcome of the training has persuaded other sales representatives to participate in a similar training course. There are now waiting lists for programs that once required a sales job by the trainers to enlist participants.

Through its efforts, R. R. Donnelley & Sons Company discovered that training does indeed pay.

Anthony R. Montebello is vice president of St. Louis-based Psychological Associates.
Maureen Haga is the corporate sales trainer for Chicago-based R. R. Donnelley & Sons Company.

DISCUSSION QUESTIONS

1. Why is it important that human resources departments be able to justify the costs of training?

2. How did the R. R. Donnelley & Sons company track and evaluate the results of a recent training program?

3.   What results did the R. R. Donnelly study produce regarding the value of the training program?

4.   What two considerations should you keep in mind when selecting statistical procedures to measure results?

PUT DIVERSITY IN CONTEXT
By Jim Kennedy and Anna Everest

Your company's success may depend on its ability to compete for tomorrow's multicultural work force. Communication is a key.

He's your new hire. He reminds you a lot of the young men whom you've been hiring for the last twenty years—young, eager, self-assured. You understand each other; you're in tune.

Now put your finger on the backspace key and hold it down . . . for a long time. By the end of this decade only 15 percent of your net new hires will be Anglo-American males. The remaining 85 percent will be females, African-Americans, Hispanics, Asians, and American Indians, according to *Workforce 2000*.

To remain competitive, it will be absolutely necessary for employers not only to embrace diversity, but to seek out all available strategies that will bring them the talent they need in the years to come. One such strategy is to understand our own cultural filters and to accept differences in people, so that each person is treated and valued as a unique individual.

What are the qualities you look for in an employee? If you were asked to list your expectations for the ideal candidate in an interview, what behaviors would your list contain? Most of us would expect the candidate to:

- ☐   Speak clearly.
- ☐   Volunteer information.
- ☐   Ask questions of the interviewer.
- ☐   Be assertive and animated.
- ☐   Maintain good eye contact.
- ☐   Have a personable, yet professional appearance.
- ☐   Verbalize his or her achievements.
- ☐   Seem knowledgeable about our company.
- ☐   Show examples of his or her work.

Just begin to imagine what happens to someone from the dominant Anglo-male culture when these qualities aren't seen in an interview. When the candidate doesn't fulfill these expectations it may become difficult to remain objective or positive.

Edward T. Hall, a cultural anthropologist, has studied cultures around the world and has developed a concept that may be very helpful in communicating with employees from diverse backgrounds. This is the concept of high- and low-context cultures. High-context cultures are more sensitive to the surrounding circumstances or context of an event. This is apparent in communication in which nonverbal cues play a significant role in the interaction.

According to Hall, although no culture exists exclusively at either end of the context scale, some cultures, such as the Asian, Hispanic, and African-American, are high-context; others, such as Northern European, are low-context cultures (see Table 1).

The significance of this model is that most of the new people coming into our work force are high-context, yet most members of management are medium/low-context. In fact, our whole immigration pattern in the U.S. has changed. For

---

TABLE 1

Diversity in context.

Cultures may be placed on a continuum of low- to high-context, based on the relative importance of non-verbal communication. High-context cultures place more value on body language and other cues.

Low	*Medium-low*		*Medium*	*High*
Northern European	Anglo-American Male	Anglo-American Female	Southern European	Asian
				Hispanic
Swiss			Middle Eastern	American Indian
				African-American

---

200 years most of our immigrants came from medium/low-context European countries or Canada. During the last twenty-five years, however, this pattern has changed and, for the rest of the decade, will continue to include more immigrants from high-context cultures.

In high-context cultures, communication is for interaction, not just for information exchange. It's a way to establish and maintain a relationship. In high-context communication, attention is paid to the surrounding circumstances or context of an event, not just the words. The context of a verbal exchange includes the social setting, the use of phrasing, gestures and tone of voice, the person's history, status, and even posture. This makes it a much richer communication, similar to the difference between reading a script versus seeing the play. By contrast, in low-context cultures the words alone tend to carry much of the meaning.

When talking about what's on their minds, high-context people will expect others to pick up what's bothering them and don't feel the need to be specific. The result is, they'll talk around the point, putting all the pieces in place except for the crucial one. Placing it properly is the role of the other person in the conversation. To do this for the listener is an insult and a violation of his or her individuality.

When comparing Japanese communication style to American, one Japanese manager said, "The Japanese probably never will become gabby. We're a homogeneous people and don't have to speak as much as you do here. When we say one word, we understand ten, but here you have to say ten to understand one."

Tone is an important part of communication in other countries. It is high- or low-pitched? It has a big impact on the meaning of Chinese words, because four different tones are used. The word *ma,* which means *mother* also can mean *horse, curse,* or *question,* depending on the tone of voice.

In many Asian cultures, one shows deference to people higher in the social structure by not looking them in the eye. Calling cards in Japan come out immediately and list not only name and title, but also degrees and honors. As one Japanese-American manager explained to us recently, it's considered very bad manners to write anything on a Japanese person's business card—it's like writing across his or her photograph.

Gestures signify another important aspect of communication. In Japan, it's traditional for one to bow, rather than shake hands when meeting someone. One acknowledges others' superior status by bending lower than they do. In many Hispanic cultures it's considered very rude to point with your index finger. Instead, the palm is turned upwards with the fingers held close together when it's necessary to point.

In low-context communication much of these external surrounding factors are screened out. A supervisor communicating with an employee in a low-context communication style would tend to concentrate just on objective facts relating to the employee—perhaps their attendance record or specific performance in meeting job responsibilities.

High-context communication, by contrast, requires far more time, because trust, friend and family relationships, personal needs, and situations also will be considered. In low-context cultures, we seldom take the time in business dealings to build relationships and establish trust. In our culture, if it doesn't work out, we simply break off the relationship and, if we feel seriously aggrieved, we actually may sue the other party.

High-context communication also can sustain or support differences between groups. The coded language of rap music supports keeping outsiders outside and creates a sense of community among those in the know. The music also is used to point out cultural differences. Here are some lyrics from a song titled *Acknowledge Your Own History:* "My forefather was a king; He wore fat gold chains . . . ruby rings, Nobody believes this to be true—Maybe it's because my eyes ain't blue." More than just the words being used must be considered to assess someone from another culture.

People from high-context cultures see themselves primarily as members of a group, often beginning with the family. Children learn to restrain themselves, to overcome their individuality, to maintain harmony in the family. The family is the prototype of all social organizations. Forward-thinking companies already are planning ahead to deal with this. For example, McDonald's has noted that the Hispanic population in this country will grow by 47 percent in the next twenty years. It's now building larger seating areas in many of its new restaurants to accommodate Hispanic families, who place a special value on eating together as a group.

A West Coast company hired a Mexican-American intern from college in Arizona for a summer job. She quit after two days because her father had telephoned and said, "How dare you insult the family by spending the summer away from home." The company couldn't convince her to stay. This same emphasis on family values is seen in the importance Hispanics place on attending funerals for family members—even of distant uncles and cousins. Anglo-American managers often have difficulty understanding this.

A person from a high-context culture values harmony more than individual achievement. Harmony is valued in the family and society and is maintained by saving face, meaning one's dignity, self-respect, and prestige. Asian values that spring from this are ones of modesty and humility about their individual achievements. The welfare and prestige of the group are considered more important than the glory of any one person.

The American values of individualism and self-expression are illustrated in such idiomatic expressions as "The squeaky wheel gets the oil." (The person who makes the loudest noise gets the most attention.) On the other hand, the Chinese and Japanese express their social values in such idiomatic expressions as "Quacking ducks get shot," or "The nail that sticks up gets hammered down." An Asian candidate who's asked why he or she should be promoted may use such words as "It would be my honor to join this department," or "I will be privileged to work with this group," which seem alien to dominant Anglo-American values.

How do these Asian beliefs relate to assertiveness, which is a quality we value for many professional jobs in the U.S.? We tend to attribute this quality to people who use lots of words, gestures, and perhaps a loud, dominant tone of voice. Women, however, often sit with their hands in their laps during an interview. This tends to signal that they are low-key and, perhaps, not assertive. If assertiveness is a quality we really seek in a job candidate, we should look for evidence of actual assertive behavior from the person.

As managers, however, when we look for a quality, such as assertiveness in an employee, we really need to examine whether this characteristic provides the only opportunity to accomplish the objectives of this position. Perhaps such qualities as persistence or attention to detail can help achieve the desired end result. If we can avoid a narrow definition of required qualities, we can be more inclusive of people from other cultures.

General Motors' $40 million advertising campaign of "putting quality back on the road" is the product of an Asian-American woman named Shirley Young, who is vice president of consumer market development. Young has taken command of GM's most crucial marketing effort effectively, yet is described as genteel and diminutive, using such qualities as persistence and tenacity. She isn't at all a fit with the "clubby, male-dominated executive suites in Detroit," according to a June 11, 1990 article in *Business Week*.

Think carefully about the qualities you feel are necessary in all applicants to do any given job. For example, assertiveness may not be the only way to get a job done. Individuals from Asian cultures may achieve more by persistence than by assertiveness or by having a take-charge personality. Persistence and tenacity may be seen on the job in the example of an Asian accountant who wouldn't confront the controller to get a set of figures, but would persist through other channels, until finding what was needed from others at lower levels in the department.

In high-context cultures interpersonal relationships take time to develop and are highly valued. In many cultures, it's considered rude not to establish rapport with another person before getting down to business.

People raised in high-context cultures expect more of others than do the participants in low-context cultures. This principle can relate to relationships inside and outside the family and is based on mutual complimentary obligations. The junior partner owes the senior partner respect and obedience, but receives protection and consideration from the senior partner in return.

The concept of high- and low-context cultures is very useful in differentiating between many different cultures, but it's also useful in bridging the communication gap that exists between men and women. Anglo-American females and culturally diverse people have similar communication characteristics that separate them from Anglo-American males. The simple fact that men communicate for information, and women and culturally diverse people communicate to establish or maintain a relationship, explains some of the difficulty the two groups may have communicating with each other. The communication goals seem almost opposite.

We have found in the research on cultural and gender differences in interviewing we performed in conjunction with San Francisco State University that white females respond in a similar way to persons from culturally different backgrounds on questions about interviewing expectations and behavior. In this study, both Anglo-American females and culturally diverse persons started the interview having less self-confidence than Anglo-American males. It was important for them that the interviewer establish rapport before asking the interview questions.

They didn't talk about their own achievements or emphasize their skills as much as Anglo-American males did. Even such actions as a tour of the office were preferred by women and culturally diverse people as opposed to Anglo-American men. Other similarities between the two groups illustrated a similar focus on the surrounding circumstances versus the bottom line orientation of white males.

"Many frictions arise because males and females grow up in what are essentially different cultures, so talk between men and women is cross-cultural communication," says Deborah Tannen, author of *You Just Don't Understand,* which explores gender communication differences. "White American males engage the world as an individual in a hierarchical social order in which he's either one up or one down. In a white American man's world, conversations are negotiations in which people try to achieve and maintain the upper hand if they can, and protect themselves from others' attempts to put them down and push them around. Life then is a contest, a struggle to preserve independence and avoid failure. Women and culturally diverse people approach the world as a network of connections. In this world, conversations are negotiations for closeness in which people try to seek and give confirmation and support, and to reach consensus."

Women are able to mix talk about business easily with talk about such nonbusiness related activities as family and other interests. Hispanics also frequently mix family and business conversation together, a tendency that can be irritating and confusing to Anglo-American males.

Habitual ways of talking are hard to change. Learning to respect others' ways of talking may be a bit easier. Men should accept that many women regard exchanging details about personal lives as a basic ingredient of closeness, and women should accept that many men don't share this view. Men focus importance on factual information, but women give facts less importance because they're of less use to them. Women and men would both do well to learn strategies more typically used by members of the other group—not to switch over entirely, but to have more strategies at their disposal.

Whether it's communication between men and women or between persons of culturally different backgrounds, what you communicate is limited to what the other person understands. For communication to be effective it must meet the needs of both the message initiator and the recipient.

Consider two aspects of understanding another person: 1) paying attention; and 2) eye contact. Anglo-American males believe in paying attention by looking at the speaker and using verbal fillers or signals such as "uh-huh" or "I see," which signals "I heard you" or "I'm listening." Many other cultures don't use these fillers.

People from India may shake their heads from side to side when paying attention, seemingly disagreeing when in fact, this isn't the case. We may misread body language because we're unfamiliar with it. We assume there will be eye contact in the interview, yet in some cultures it's considered rude to look at someone who's superior to you.

During the Bernard Goetz case in New York, the Anglo-American male judge stopped the proceedings at one point to chastise one of the black teenage boys for showing "disrespect" to him and to the court because, "not once have you looked up at the bench since you have been here in court."

A Hispanic manager spoke of her upbringing in two different cultures. At school in the third grade, the teacher said to her, "Look me in the eye when you speak to me." When she was at home in the evening with her family, her father would say to her, "Don't stare at me." This is a dilemma that many culturally diverse people in the U.S. experience in attempting to be bicultural.

Often, when we meet someone for whom English is a second language, we don't give them credit for the impressive accomplishment of having learned—and being able to communicate in—another language. Instead, we focus more on the mispronunciations or the difficulties the person is having with the language.

Even if a person is fluent in English, it doesn't mean that he or she also is fluent in the American culture. The English language is the worldwide language of business. It isn't bound to any single culture or political system, however. It may be used on a universal basis, but its use by any given individual always is bound to the culture in which it was learned.

Common expressions in English can take on a completely different meaning to someone whose first language isn't English. American English is difficult to understand, partly because we use so many slang expressions, idioms and buzzwords. (Even "buzzword" is American slang.) Our everyday language includes such expressions as "I've had it up to here," "It isn't even in the ballpark," "Let's ramp it up," "My head's in a different space right now," or "I'm getting in touch with myself."

Foreign reporters frequently have difficulty translating the speeches of President Bush, because he's one of the most flagrant users of slang. For instance, in 1989, when Bush was asked what the U.S. action would be in response to the student uprising in Beijing, he responded: "Stay tuned." A Chinese reporter required twenty-two words in Chinese to translate this two-word phrase. The translation came close to this: "Sit close by your radio and listen attentively to what you will hear next. . . ."

The key questions to answer now are, "How are you adapting yourself to the diverse backgrounds of the people with whom you work or the people you interview? Do you treat each individual as if diversity made no difference? Do you value and assess each person as a unique individual? If not you may lose talented workers. This will become a matter of increasing economic survival as companies compete for a rapidly shrinking pool of skilled and talented workers.

If we understand how culture influences the people who work for us, we can respond to them more effectively and do a better job of attracting, hiring and retaining the workers we want. This will be important in a workplace characterized by a smaller number of entry level people and considerably more work force diversity.

It will be an exciting and challenging time for U.S. businesses, as this growing group of diverse workers bring needed characteristics to the workplace, concern for personal relationships, new ways to solve problems, increased flexibility and a greater concern for long-range issues.

Jim Kennedy is president and Ann Everest is vice president of San Rafael California-based Management Team-Consultants Inc., which specializes in interviewing and diversity training.

DISCUSSION QUESTIONS

1. What is the difference between high-context cultures and low-context cultures?

2. How does relationship building vary between high-context and low-context cultures?

3. "Many frictions arise because males and females grow up in what are essentially different cultures, so talk between men and women is cross-cultural communication." Discuss.

4. Why is it important that supervisors understand how culture influences the people who work for them?

FRESH IDEAS ENERGIZE REWARD PROGRAMS
By Peggy Stuart

Employees are motivated more by recognition than by money. Here are corporate strategies ranging from service ribbons to dinner on the Napa Valley Wine Train.

In a troubled economy, companies want to get the best possible performance from each employee—without excessive expenditures. Fortunately, money isn't the only, and not even the best, way to motivate employees to perform.

Results of a survey released last November indicate that recognition for a job well done is the top motivator of employee performance. The interactive telephone survey included more than 200 employee communication managers and was conducted for the Council of Communication Management by New York City-based William M. Mercer Inc.

Recognition was rated 4.9 on a scale of six. Coming in a close second was money.

In their drive to stay competitive, companies increasingly reward and recognize employees as part of their total quality program. These programs provide a range of awards from monetary to nonmonetary and are planned and implemented either in-house or using the help of consultants.

Companies giving monetary awards often base the amount on the actual savings to the company. For example, Dallas-based American Airlines rewards employees for suggestions. The program, called IdeAAs in Action saved the airline $83 million in the first two and a half years.

The maximum award is $37,500, for a suggestion that saves $240,000 or more annually. Awards average $2,000 each. Participation in 1990 was 117 percent more than the previous year. The firm now has approximately sixty people working full-time to analyze employees' suggestions.

One company providing nonmonetary awards is the Washington, D.C.-based Marriott Corp., which honors fifteen to twenty people each year with its J. Willard Marriott Award of Excellence, an engraved medallion bearing the likeness of Mr. Marriott and the words expressing the basic values of the company: dedication; achievement; character; ideals; effort; and perseverance. According to Gerald C. Baumer, vice president, employee communications and creative services, selection is based on remarks made by the nominator and the individual's length of service. They represent a cross-section of Marriott's work force: dishwashers; chefs; housekeepers; merchandise managers; and so on.

The Marriott award is presented at an awards banquet in Washington, D.C., attended by honorees, spouses, nominators and top executives. "We want other employees to look up to these people," Baumer says.

Nonmonetary awards may take the form of *advertising specialties,* useful articles of merchandise that are imprinted with a message or company logo, such as are often given away to a targeted group to promote a product or service. When used as an award for special performance or service to the company, such items can increase the employee's identification with the company.

McDonald's Corp., based in Oak Brook, Illinois, has contracted with Lawrenceville, New Jersey-based Lenox Awards to make available to its owner/operators jewelry bearing the company's well-known golden arches logo. These may be given as awards to employees who provide superior service.

When La Mirada, California-based restaurant chain Denny's Inc. wanted to boost morale and recognize employees and customer service, it created the *Personal Best* recognition program. Each employee was given a ribbon bearing the words, "For you the guest, my personal best" to wear at work. Employees voted each month for the recipient from their job area. Lapel pins were awarded, indicating the number of months the employee had won the award.

□ □ □ REWARD PROGRAMS ON THE INCREASE

Organizations are increasingly using more performance incentives as part of their total quality program. Ninety-four percent of 179 companies recently polled have reward and recognition programs, according to a survey by *Total Quality* and *The Service Edge* newsletters, in cooperation with Maritz Inc. Although most of the programs reward improved service, 30 percent of respondents say they have at least one performance-improvement plan, which the survey defines as programs that measure specific quantitative and qualitative objectives and reward individuals, teams or business units for improvement goals or milestones. The survey also revealed:

□ 64 percent of respondents say their companies measure on an individual level, 25 percent by business unit, 24 percent by functional work groups, 21 percent by department, and 12 percent by specially created teams.

□ 27 percent are paid rewards annually, 24 percent when the event occurs, 22 percent monthly, 17 percent quarterly, and 7 percent weekly.

□ 29 percent named job satisfaction/morale/employee retention as the most valuable by-product of their programs.

—Total Quality Newsletter

John Deere Dubuque Tractor Works in Dubuque, Iowa, doubled employee participation in an employee suggestion program by providing pocket protectors, magnetic calendars and notepads, imprinted with the slogan, "Got an idea? Write it down!" to all participants. Those employees whose suggestions were implemented received the awards in a personal presentation.

Faced with employee morale problems resulting from rapid growth, Ridgeway Development Corp. of Atlanta, Georgia implemented a promotion among its workers by mailing a giant card to their homes each month. The first card contained a mirror and the words, "Face it . . . you make the difference."

Next a small calendar arrived, along with an invitation to participate in the employee suggestion program and a ballot for the Employee of the Month, *Go the Extra Mile* Award. Later mailings included an expandable sponge labeled, "Expand your product knowledge and we'll both grow" and a night light bearing an energy-conservation message. The promotion lasted six months and produced eighty-two Extra Mile nominations. Productivity also increased 25 percent.

Perhaps the most unusual award available is the entertainment package offered by San Francisco-based A Party To Intrigue. This company provides a staff of writers, producers and actors, and scripts customized to interact with participants in a role-playing event, either a murder mystery or a treasure hunt.

One such event was provided to a group of executives during a dinner on the Napa Valley Wine Train. Based on historical data from 1915, the costumes, train cars and the events took participants back to the First International Wine Tasting during the time of The Great War. Another Murder Mystery Weekend took sixty-six employees of Ford Motor Corp. through Chinatown,

Union Square, and the financial district to solve the mystery.

A spectacular method for recognizing and motivating outstanding employees was created for Stamford, Connecticut-based Pitney Bowes by Multi Image Productions Inc. of San Diego, which produces shows incorporating multimedia slide presentations, film, video, music, dancing, and spectacular lighting displays written, staged and produced for individual businesses. The top sales producers of Pitney Bowes were recognized during the production produced and staged in Kona, Hawaii. "Our goal was to give them a type of business theater in which they would feel entertained as well as motivated to reach their goals for next year," says Multi Image Productions President and CEO Fredric W. Ashman.

Budgets for these productions range from $10,000 to $1.5 million, but providing recognition for employees need not be so elaborate. People who feel appreciated by their employers identify with the organization and are more willing to give their best to the job.

Peggy Stuart is assistant editor for Personnel Journal.

DISCUSSION QUESTIONS

1. According to this article, what is the top motivator of employee performance? Do you agree with this finding? Why or why not?

2. Describe the recognition programs of American Airlines and the Marriott Corporation.

3. How are advertising specialties used as awards?

WORK TEAMS BOOST PRODUCTIVITY
By Jana Schilder

Companies that want to remain competitive enlist the support of employees through self-directed work teams.

For many employees, Sunday evenings can be the worst part of the week because Monday morning will arrive soon and with it another work week. But that's not the case for Al Reynolds and Amanda Duntson, employees and co-workers at Northern Telecom's Morrisville, North Carolina, repair facility. Says Reynolds, "I now look forward to coming to work. I don't *have* to go to work. I *get* to go to work." Adds Dunston, "I enjoy what I do. I enjoy the challenge. Every day, I'm learning something new."

These are words that every owner and manager in North America dreams of hearing from each employee on the payroll as the battle to remain competitive in the world, even domestic, marketplace becomes fiercer with each passing day.

Despite these challenges, companies in businesses as diverse as food processing, electrical transformer and office furniture manufacturing, and telecommunications successfully enlist the support of employees, such as Reynolds and Dunston, through self-directed work teams.

Self-directed work teams empower employees to take on more responsibility and make decisions in areas previously reserved for management. Under team direction, employees order materials, schedule and track overtime, calculate productivity, review budgets, and interview prospective new team members. Some advanced teams now even conduct peer performance reviews and provide for employee corrective action.

A recent survey of 476 *Fortune* 1,000 companies published by the American Productivity & Quality Center in Houston indicates that, although only 7 percent of the work force currently is organized in teams, half the companies surveyed indicated they'll rely on them more in the coming years.

"Team direction is one of the best techniques for realizing a payback in quality and customer service. It's the ultimate productivity tool," says Jack Bergman, president of Competitive Concepts, a consulting firm located in Wilmington, North Carolina.

Bergman, who spent thirty-eight years working for General Electric in the U.S., points to a GE plant in Salisbury, North Carolina, that produces lighting panel boards. By using team direction, as well as flexible automation and computerized systems, productivity was increased by 250 percent as compared with other GE plants that produced the same products. Today, more than 20 percent of GE's 120,000 employees work under the team concept.

The concept of self-directed work teams has its roots in several employee involvement strategies, such as sensitivity training, quality circles and "T" groups. But the concept is distinctly different from these strategies because of its relentless focus on improving business results and competitiveness. Productivity gains come from giving teams real authority to act.

"Most quality circles don't give workers responsibility," says Ralph Stayer, CEO of Johnsonville Foods, a sausage manufacturer based in Sheboygan, Wisconsin. "They make things even worse. People in quality circles point out problems; it's someone else's job to fix them."

Other executives have made the same observation, including Rob Burch, vice president of operations for Toronto-based Steelcase Canada, Ltd. "We recognized that our people were underutilized. They weren't being challenged," says Burch, who, as the former director of manufacturing planning, was involved in setting up self-directed work teams at Steelcase's Grand Rapids,

Michigan, facility. "We realized if we wanted to be a successful office furniture manufacturer, our people must be more aware of business issues."

Burch attributes Steelcase's decision to implement self-directed work teams, which have been in place since 1989, to its drive for continuous improvement, as well as customer satisfaction. He estimates that 80–90 percent of the company's nonunion, hourly workers are now in teams. Steelcase's salaried employees now are making the transition.

Schott Transformers, based in Minnesota, is another company changing over to work teams. "By the late 1980s, we knew that our old management structures weren't conducive to growth," says Jim Meyer, director of operations at Schott, a forty-year-old family operation that supplies magnetic components and power systems to the computer and telecommunications industries. "We were an autocratic hierarchy; there was no shared decision making. And by 1989, we weren't meeting customer commitments. We knew we had to change, so we hired consultants to assess the situation. Our new focus became quality and customer satisfaction."

Similar reasons prompted management at Northern Telecom's Morrisville repair facility to implement self-directed work teams. "The *status quo* wasn't going to cut it," says Debra Boggan, former plant manager of the facility and co-founder of Competitive Solutions Inc. in Raleigh, North Carolina. "We understood that being good just put us in the game; to be a leader, we had to adopt a philosophy of continuous improvement."

Boggan, along with Anna VerSteeg, the facility's former operations manager, pioneered the implementation of work teams at Northern Telecom in 1987. The team concept now is being adopted at the company's manufacturing facilities in Creedmoor, North Carolina; Santa Clara, California; as well as in Toronto, Calgary and Montreal.

"In the 1990s, the companies that will succeed are the ones that put innovation and team spirit back into the workplace," says Boggan. "As a plant manager, I felt much more comfortable knowing that 420 people were worried about my business, rather than just my senior management team of fifteen people. Empowering employees—giving them the responsibility for the business—is the key."

According to Harvey Kolodny, a professor at the University of Toronto's Faculty of Management, implementing self-directed work teams is paying off. Results from new facilities that adopt team direction from day one are 30–50 percent better than from traditional management structures. (Results are more difficult to tabulate for redesigned facilities. It's also easier to build teams into a new office or factory than to convert an old one.)

At Northern Telecom's Morrisville facility, business wasn't expected to increase. Telecommunications equipment repair historically had been a money-losing business. Revenue went up 63 percent after implementing self-directed work teams four years ago. Sales also are up by 26 percent and earnings by 46 percent. Productivity per employee increased more than 60 percent, and scrap (materials unusable as a result of manufacturing processes, such as human or machine error, or new product testing) decreased 63 percent. Quality results increased by 50 percent, and the number of quality inspectors dropped 40 percent.

The major difference between self-directed work teams and its predecessors, such as quality circles, is that team direction isn't a program but a profound change in how companies do business. It involves using the collective brainpower of all employees as a competitive strategy, empowering them with the responsibility for all functions of the business.

"Teams alone can't affect change. You must have a change in corporate culture," says Burch. Adds Stayer, "Change starts with individuals. Organizations can't change, but they're made up of individuals. So to get different results, you must change your own behavior first."

A critical aspect on which Northern Telecom, Schott Transformers, Steelcase and Johnsonville Foods management all agree is that self-directed work teams need senior management commitment to succeed. Preferably, work teams should have a champion or champions. More important, team direction is an experiment, and going back is virtually impossible, because it undermines the credibility of the company. Says Stayer, "You don't just hang up a bunch of banners and think you have team direction."

Employees at Johnsonville Foods told Stayer they could produce more sausage faster than he would have ever dared to ask. Since 1986, productivity has risen at least 50 percent. As a result, the company was featured in *Leadership Alliance,* a videotape produced by management guru Tom Peters. This, coincidentally, was the tape that started management at the Morrisville plant thinking about changing over to teams. "That segment of the tape became worn out because it had been viewed so many times," says Boggan.

Boggan and VerSteeg began examining all the barriers that separated management from employees starting with the time clock. "The time clock sent a signal that management didn't trust us," recalls one Morrisville employee. After the clock was removed, employees were told they were responsible for their own breaks, lunches and work hours. There was one caveat: the changes couldn't affect customer service or productivity. (The punch clock was the first thing to go at Schott Transformers, says Meyer.)

"It was as simple as realizing that employees are adults who have responsibilities outside the workplace," says Boggan. "We stopped telling people to check their brains at the front door in the morning and pick them up at five. We started treating people with respect."

Next, Boggan and VerSteeg examined reserved parking spots, the executive dining room and washroom, and dress codes at the Morrisville facility. "It was really hard for some people to take their ties off," says VerSteeg. "The point is, you can wear what you want: a tie or no tie. It's up to the individual. Ties don't make people productive."

Burch agrees with this philosophy. "You don't get involvement and commitment with perks," he says. "The sacred cows have no place in work teams."

One of the biggest changes in implementing self-directed work teams is that it involves the transformation of roles of both managers and employees. "We eliminated the terms *supervisors* and *employees* and replaced them with *coaches* and *players,"* says Diane Pewitt of Northern Telecom's Santa Clara plant, which produces Meridian telephone switching equipment.

Under team direction, managers go from bosses/dictators to coaches/facilitators. Facilitators help guide, direct, and support the team, but they don't control it. This can be a difficult transition for some supervisors to make.

With self-directed work teams, managers gain more support, because everyone becomes responsible for the business. First-line managers, however, may fear losing their jobs, as teams take on traditional managerial responsibility.

"I was a dictator for eight years, but now that style doesn't work any more," says Rick Pederson of the Morrisville facility. "For a time, I was afraid of losing my job. But then I thought that if I could make the transition from supervisor to coach, I would become an asset to the company."

Meyer recalls that the reaction of one manager at Schott Transformers was similar. "Finally, I don't have to make all the decisions around here anymore," the employee told Meyer. Bob Suelflow, another Schott manager, questioned everything about teams, but when he saw employees who weren't dependable suddenly taking responsibility, he realized that team direction was the way to go.

Schott Transformers took all of its 330 employees to lunch in groups. "We were looking for natural leaders. We asked everyone to whom they go for help and how they know they're doing a good job," explains Meyer.

Still, some managers aren't able to make the transition. Statistics at Northern Telecom show that about 25 percent of its first-line supervisors left after team direction was adopted. In hindsight, Burch says Steelcase should have spent more time helping its supervisors understand their new roles. Some supervisors have taken it well, but some won't make it, he says.

Bergman says that one of the key questions then becomes what to do with employees who can't or won't adjust to team direction. "You have to have patience and make every effort to help them, but you also must be firm. Sometimes you have to let people go," he says.

While former managers are learning how to guide work teams, new team members are learning how to cope with new responsibilities. Team members or players must believe that they can have ownership and make real decisions.

"Who knows better what it takes to do the job than the person who does it every day?" asks VerSteeg. "If you let people set the goal and decide how to get there, they'll be challenged to achieve even more than managers ever dreamed."

Generally, the range of reactions to self-directed work teams depends on the quality of the past relationship that the company has had with all its employees, says Harlan R. Jessup, president of TeamWork Management Inc. in Newtown, Connecticut.

"At first, I thought it was a set-up," explains Dunston. "I thought they'd still be watching us, that maybe it was just another way of getting rid of people. But that didn't happen." Adds Rick Pederson, also an employee at Northern Telecom's Morrisville facility, "I like work teams very much because it's like running my own business."

Although most employees welcome the challenge of making decisions that directly affect them, some feel the stress of added responsibility. "You're asking me to take on more responsibilities, to make decisions I thought you were paid to make," says another Morrisville employee, complaining that he used to be able to go home at the end of his shift without worrying.

By all reports, the road to team direction is a rocky one, and it takes about two years to see steady results. "Things won't be neat and tidy. Expect chaos at first. It's also wise to move with caution," says Meyer.

Issues that have been buried for many years come out into the open. For instance, Boggan says that she was shocked the first time a subordinate rattled off a list of her mistakes. But she was willing to listen, as long as the comments produced positive results.

Change is an emotional process and emotions run high when self-directed work teams are being implemented. "It's all right to bring emotions into the workplace. Why leave them at the door? They affect every other decision you make," says Hurt Covington, human resources manager at the Morrisville facility.

Risk-taking also should be encouraged, to continue the learning process. "At Johnsonville Foods, we encourage original mistakes, not boring, repetitive ones," says Stayer.

One of the most important elements in implementing self-directed work teams is training, in such areas as job skills, business knowledge, problem solving, and team dynamics. Training eases the transition from traditional systems to teams, helping everyone to understand change, as well as to deal with their feelings.

Training was a challenge at Schott Transformers, because 90 percent of its work force hadn't been in a classroom since high school. "Some people just wanted to work harder, not smarter," says Meyer.

In the past, traditional training at the Morrisville facility focused on skills training for employees and communication training for managers, as if other employees didn't need to know how to communicate, says Boggan. As a result, everyone at the facility participated in The Working Program, developed by San Jose, California-based Zenger-Miller. The Working Program teaches interpersonal skills, using eighteen two-hour modules. GE used a similar program by Development Dimensions International, based in Pittsburgh.

"It's possible for work teams to fail," says Bergman. He attributes failure to a lack of communication among all involved as well as a lack of senior management support.

Why aren't all companies switching to self-directed work teams? Because it's difficult. "We've been taught ways of responding and change doesn't come easily," says VerSteeg. Meyer adds, "Teams may not work everywhere, but teamwork works everywhere."

Jana Schilder is a consultant based in Toronto.

DISCUSSION QUESTIONS

1. What are self-directed work teams?

2. How do self-directed work teams differ from quality circles?

3. How does the role of the manager change in a team environment?

4. How is training an important element of instituting self-directed teams?

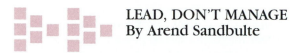

LEAD, DON'T MANAGE
By Arend Sandbulte

Minnesota Power CEO Arend "Sandy" Sandbulte two years ago realized that too much of the utility's decision making was taking place at a higher level than necessary—that company executives were spending too much time pushing papers and signing off on forms that had to wend their way up the corporate chain of command before things could get done. To change that, Minnesota Power began to share more company business information than ever before.

There are many good reasons to develop the right work culture in your organization, but, in the end, you can boil them down to one: It makes good business sense. Employees don't want to feel they are merely robots who put in eight hours a day on the job, collect a paycheck, and then go home. They want to enjoy work. They want to feel they make a contribution. They want to feel respected as people. They want to learn and grow, not stagnate and become bored with their jobs. And if an employee is bored at work, there are probably two reasons.

One, the employee is not taking any initiative to tackle more on-the-job challenges so he or she won't stagnate. Or two, the boss is contributing to frustration and stagnation by not encouraging the employee to tackle those challenges.

That second reason can be sobering. Managers don't like to think that they could be an impediment to fully utilizing their employees' talents and creativity—skills that could be more effectively used to make the organization more successful. But, unfortunately, managers don't spend enough time looking at how employees can help them improve the bottom line. And that's the problem. We need to put a new spin on the word "manager." We need to create a metamorphosis through which managers become "leaders."

That's not to say that management functions won't be important anymore—they always will be. But what will become more important is the ability to lead, because good leaders help shape an organization's culture so that every employee can contribute to success, and feel good about doing so.

What characteristics do good leaders have?

- They know their own strengths and weaknesses.

- They make the path smooth so employees can get their jobs done.

- They are honest and trustworthy and expect the same qualities in their employees.

- They spend less time on day-to-day activities and more time communicating.

- They recognize the value of employees' contributions and let employees know when they've done a good job.

- They serve as models of good leadership that employees can look up to and respect, and they, in turn, respect their employees.

Good leaders also understand that being the boss doesn't mean bossing—it means breaking down barriers to help get a job done in the best way possible; providing employees with the resources, training, and coaching they need; providing them with information so they can see their organization's big picture. It also means stepping aside so employees can analyze business problems and come up with solutions. It means giving employees the authority to make decisions, and letting them take risks and make mistakes with no fear that they will be punished for making them. Not doing so stifles employee creativity and motivation in trying to do the job better.

Some people will argue that leaders are born, not made. Yet, clearly, leadership is a quality that can be developed in every employee. I think the good thing about our efforts is that we are beginning to realize that management doesn't have all the answers—nor should it. Managers don't have to be experts all the time because a tremendous amount of expertise exists already with employees—expertise that you must unleash to solve problems.

Minnesota Power had its supervisory-level people ask several of their co-workers to anonymously rate their leadership capabilities. During the process, they found out that they shone in certain leadership qualities, but that they could improve in other areas. The company then provided the training necessary for people to upgrade their leadership skills.

None of this is easy. Building an organizational culture and developing good leaders is hard work. It means that you must be painfully honest about the effectiveness and rightness of your management style. It takes time, money, patience, and tenacity. What's more, you must truly believe in what you are trying to do, because it means fundamentally changing your attitudes about the workplace and your relationship with co-workers. And you must stay with it when the going gets tough. In fact, it is imperative that workers are convinced that management is changing its leadership style, because, if you approach your corporate-culture efforts as nothing more than a rah-rah program, with management functioning as cheerleaders, your attempt to build better teamwork and employee participation will be doomed.

Employees will be carefully analyzing every move you make as a manager to see if you are really sincere. If there is no substance to back your form, you run the risk of building up employees' expectations and hopes, only to have them become disillusioned when you don't walk your talk.

You have to understand that the process will be uncomfortable at times. When you ask employees to think about how to improve things, to take risks, and to challenge you when they disagree with you, believe me, they will do it. And when they challenge you, it is very tempting to slip back into the "I'm the boss" attitude.

If managers ask, "When can I get back to doing my regular work?" the answer you must give them is that improving our corporate culture *is* their regular work—that it is a never-ending process of improvement, not a quick-fix program with a finite time frame. And that it takes time for good results to develop.

Now maybe I haven't always been successful in my efforts to avoid reverting back to my old management behavior. But I'm determined to develop an awareness, an internal voice that tells me when I should back off and let employees solve a problem. And I'm finding out that often employees can come up with better solutions than I could, since they know their jobs much better than I do.

I now have more time to think about where Minnesota Power should be going in the future, to focus on the external forces that are shaping our business prospects, to map out the road to success, and to provide employees with the resources they need to achieve it.

Remember, developing a new corporate culture for your organization will take years. And the process never ends, because it is a process of continuous improvement. But the benefits are enormous: a vital, growing organization that people are proud to be part of; a work environment that promotes trust, creativity, and job satisfaction; and employees who view supervisors not as tyrants, but as coaches and barrier-busters who provide them with resources so they can get their work done in a better way.

Most important, a participative work culture means that your organization has a better shot at beating the competition. Your workers can help make all of these things happen. And your organization's managers and supervisors can help employees realize their untapped potential by becoming true leaders, not just managers.

Above all, you have to remember this important rule: People have a way of becoming what you encourage them to be, not what you nag them to be.

DISCUSSION QUESTIONS

1. According to the article, why do employees become bored?

2. What characteristics do good leaders have?

3. What changes did the CEO of Minnesota Power make in the corporate culture?

4. What are the benefits of developing a participative work culture?

BETTER SAFETY THROUGH EMPOWERMENT
By Michael A. Verespej

Employee involvement can reduce accidents—and save money.

In 1987 Norfolk Southern Corp. had a fifty-six person corporate safety department and the fourth-best safety record among major U.S. railroads—6.06 reportable injuries per 200,000 manhours worked.

Today, the corporate safety staff numbers just nine—a reduction of 84%.

Yet Norfolk Southern's unionized workers now have the best safety record among U.S. railroads, and the railroad has reduced the number of injuries per 200,000 manhours worked by two thirds, to 2.03. It also has won the industry's E.H. Harriman Gold Medal award for safety for four straight years.

The story is much the same at State Fair Foods. The number of accidents per 200,000 manhours has dropped from 4.93 in fiscal 1990 to 0.36 in fiscal 1992, and the number of lost workdays due to injuries per 200,000 manhours has dropped from 169 in fiscal 1990 to just 2.16 in fiscal 1992.

A third firm, Landstar Transportation, a trucking firm headquartered in Shelton, Conn., has reduced the number of accidents involving its trucks by 41 percent and the average dollar cost per accident by 69 percent from 1989 to 1992.

How are these companies able to work safer with smaller safety staffs?

It's simple.

Just as companies have given the responsibility for manufacturing production back to workers, Norfolk Southern and State Fair gave the responsibility for managing safety back to the employees. And Landstar invested in new technologies and embarked on an extensive safety education program for all employees, not just its drivers.

LANDSTAR

In his first two months as chairman and CEO of Landstar Systems Inc., Jeff Crowe made it clear to employees how deeply he was committed to safety.

He held the first of what is now an annual event, the Landstar safety summit, to emphasize that he wanted the trucking firm to be a safety-first company. Next, he changed the reporting structure so that safety managers report directly to the president's office. And then he warned managers and operations executives that a safety assessment would be a major part of the evaluation of each of Landstar's five trucking operations—one is company-owned, the others are owner-operator companies—at annual review time.

"We had to become a safety-first company," said Mr. Crowe. "I felt that safety was one of the first things I needed to address, because accidents cause injuries and misery to families, and they have a significant impact on operating resources. I cannot underestimate the importance of having 'safety first' as a cornerstone of the culture of the company."

But Mr. Crowe knew that since 85 percent of Landstar's drivers are independent owner-operators, a safety-first culture could become a reality only if, as he explains, "employees see *every* key management person fostering that culture.

"I knew that making safety the responsibility of the safety department wouldn't work and that making safety the responsibility of just the drivers and employees wouldn't work."

Thus, all monthly staff meetings at Landstar now start with a safety review. There is a review of each accident—not to place blame—but to determine how procedures can be changed to prevent that type of accident from occurring again.

Mr. Crowe also increased safety awareness among employees by instituting a President's Safety Award that is now the highest employee recognition award at its annual drivers' convention.

The first visible change in the aftermath of the summit and the decision to put safety first at Landstar came in early 1990 when Landstar added what at the time was a highly reflective—but still experimental—side-stripe tape to its 10,000 trucks to increase their road visibility. That reduced the number of under-ride accidents—in which a car plows into the side of the truck—by 75 percent and reduced the severity of the accidents by 90 percent.

"It was an excellent place to start," says Mr. Crowe, "because it was a clearly identifiable program with clearly identifiable results." In addition, Landstar's $1 million capital investment produced a $4 million savings. "It made believers out of people, demonstrated that a safety program can produce tangible results, and identified us in the market as an innovator and safety leader."

There also are several programs that keep safety on the front burner.

For example, the third Thursday of each month is Safety Thursday, when all workers focus on a particular safety theme. In addition, for its 1,200 nondrivers, Landstar developed a day-and-a-half training program—which is now part of the orientation for new hires—that shows employees that "everyone plays a role and influences safety" and that each accident or insurance loss represents a single act by a single person.

Landstar also asks employees to demonstrate their commitment to safety by displaying a safety certificate in their workplace. There's also a driver education and awareness program to keep drivers safety-conscious. The themes vary monthly and include topics such as back safety, stress management, seatbelt use, driving on ice-slick roads, how to recognize fatigue, and how to maneuver in tight spaces. And last Christmas all drivers got reflective jackets with the company logo on reflective tape.

In addition, a recognition program awards savings bonds of substantial value, cruises, and satin-embroidered jackets to workers with years of accident-free driving. Drivers must be claim- and accident-free, and have no moving violations in the current year, have no vehicle-safety inspection violations in the last three years, have been with the company at least three years, and be among its top 15 percent revenue-producers.

Landstar this year began giving its independent driver-operators the option to add—at cost—convex (eyeball) mirrors for the passenger side. And, in an effort to reduce rear-end and sideswipe collisions, it's offering drivers—again, at cost—an on-board radar system that alerts a driver when he or she is approaching a vehicle in the same lane at a faster speed and suggests a safe braking speed.

"We have positioned safety as the lifeblood of the company, the key to success," says Mr. Crowe. "Safety pays in lower insurance rates and lower losses." And, he says, "if we cut the number of accidents, we are also better citizens in the community."

STATE FAIR

Despite accident rates below the industry average and a strong commitment to safety at the corporate level, workers' compensation costs and injury rates at State Fair Foods Inc.'s burrito- and corn-dog-making plant in Dallas "were still rising," says safety/environmental manager Rick Thompson. So two years ago State Fair President Mike Kenter suggested that Mr. Thompson initiate a grassroots effort to get ideas directly from the plant's 270 employees.

State Fair—a division of Sara Lee Corp.—created worker-safety teams and gave them the authority to correct problems immediately. "Anything they can fix on the spot they do," says Mr. Thompson. At the same time, it got the workers' attention by declaring that top management would begin to rate workers on their safety consciousness.

The teams first attacked the general housekeeping at the plant. "Things were cluttered and stashed right on the floor," says Mr. Thompson. "We found that we had to get rid of piles of junk to open up the plant floor and to make workstations more accessible to in-plant traffic." The teams also began to stress to all employees the

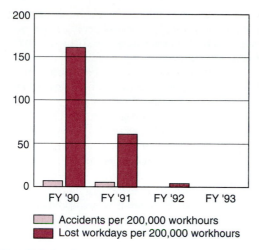

State Fair Foods

necessity of using personal protective equipment—ranging from work gloves to goggles, from ear plugs to insulated gloves for packers of frozen products.

Interestingly, says Mr. Thompson, the committees found the biggest causes of unsafe work conditions were "those little ordinary things" that were overlooked—frayed electrical cords, slippery surfaces, subpar lighting, sharp objects, and nonrounded corners on tables. "It was really a lot of little things," he says. "Slips, trips, and falls have dropped off dramatically."

The second-largest area of improvement by the teams? Ergonomic changes to reduce repetitive-motion injuries. "Whenever possible, we now automate repetitive tasks or jobs where there is continuous lifting," says Mr. Thompson. For example: In the past, employees put corn dogs on trays. Now, thanks to employee ideas and an ergonomics committee that meets regularly to identify high-risk jobs, State Foods uses an automated feeder. It also rotates some 150 workers every two hours to new jobs so they don't spend eight-hour shifts doing hand-grasping, for example.

To date, nearly 70 percent of State Fair's employees have participated in the committees' weekly in-plant audits "combing the floor for a particular hazard," says Mr. Thompson. One week they might look for electrical safety hazards; another, open containers.

And, to keep problems from recurring, accident-investigation teams—which include a floor worker and a supervisor—will study the root cause of an accident—but not to place blame. "They will recreate the incident, take pictures, and interview witnesses," says Mr. Thompson. "We are simply trying to eliminate that type of accident from ever occurring again."

The company also keeps safety in the spotlight through recognition. There are monetary rewards each quarter for employees not involved in accidents, and a trophy case—in the employee break room—for safety awards that the plant wins. And State Foods' president gives pep talks about the company's expectations with regard to safety twice a year at safety cookouts where supervisors grill hamburgers.

As a result, State Fair has now gone two years—and more than one million hours—without a lost-workday accident in an industry that averaged 221 lost workdays per company in 1991. And in 1992 it received Sara Lee Corp.'s President's Safety Trophy, beating out fifty-four other Sara Lee divisions, and the American Meat Institute's highest safety tribute.

NORFOLK SOUTHERN

From 1984 to 1987, Norfolk Southern Corp. cut the number of injuries per 200,000 manhours worked by one-third, making it the fourth-safest railroad in the U.S. But it still wasn't satisfied, because the Japanese steel industry and the U.S. chemical industry, "both inherently riskier," had safety records "100 times better," says Charlie Brenner, assistant vice president, safety and protective services. So, rather than just benchmark chemical-industry safety leader Du Pont—which often goes 75 million to 80 million manhours without an accident—Norfolk Southern *hired* the Wilmington, Del., firm to tell the railroad what it was doing wrong.

"Du Pont told us that our two biggest deficiencies were a lack of responsiveness and that we had made safety a staff—not a line—function," says Mr. Brenner.

As a result, Norfolk Southern reduced its corporate safety staff from twenty to nine, moved the rest of those workers into operating

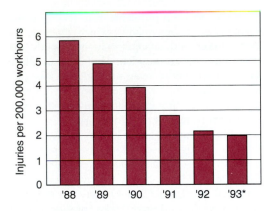

Norfolk Southern

do nothing but conduct a safety audit." Initially, the audits centered on housekeeping issues such as oil slicks. But, over time, the focus has shifted to the work process.

Managers, says Mr. Brenner, must now get back to everyone who turns in a safety suggestion "within thirty days."

There's also recognition for employees who work safely—for example, a key chain for three months of safe work, a mug for nine months of accident-free work, and a jacket for a safe year.

"Recognition is extremely important, but the size of the recognition is unimportant," says Mr. Brenner. "Employees want recognition for reasons of pride. They want to feel that they are part of the team." (Norfolk even names worker designed specialty safety appliances after the employee who designed it.)

To further encourage safety ideas, Norfolk Southern last year began giving five shares of stock to "safety winners"—that is, employees without accidents who also are in a division, in a terminal, or in a working unit that has the lowest incidence of accidents per manhours worked.

"Everyone in that unit who worked safely will get the stock," says Mr. Brenner. "Where there's a tie, both units receive stock, as do all units with no accidents. In 1992 nearly 25 percent—5,900 of the 24,000 eligible Norfolk Southern union employees—received the stock award.

Norfolk also keeps attention on safety through a mandatory ten-minute stretching-exercise program for all employees at the beginning of the day. Also, each morning, "We go over safety rules, either at random or we pick a rule that was ignored in a recent accident," says Mr. Brenner, thus reinforcing that "safety is our first order of business," he says. "We have had a major paradigm shift in the way we think. In the old days we didn't think you could work safely and be productive at the same time. The standard was that you worked until you were rushed and then you just got the job done. Now we have realized that working safely is not only better, but also leads to higher productivity."

divisions, created employee audit and safety teams, and empowered the teams to make any improvements they felt were needed.

Thus, two regional, twelve divisional, and hundreds of local committees now decide safety matters for the railroad. That frees the corporate staff to focus on weekly audits and corporate-wide safety incentives, to set up safety banquets, and to provide statistics required by the federal government and the Association of American Railroads.

"We have employee-led safety committees, weekly auditing for unsafe work practices, shared safety information in newsletters, and continuous use of workers' ideas for improvement of workstations, tools, and equipment," says Mr. Brenner.

For example restraining jacks are now placed underneath freight cars when repair work needs to be done. In the past, only chains were used to hold up the car. And levers used to move cars have been redesigned to waist-high levels so "you don't ever have to bend over at the waist" and push levers around in a semicircle, says Mr. Brenner. "You can now walk in a circle and move hand-to-hand.

"Local safety committees now deal with issues such as the proper speed for forklifts, where to put mirrors on vehicles, and where maintenance needs to be done," says Mr. Brenner. Norfolk also requires each manager or supervisor to go out once a week for an hour "and

In 1992, for example, Norfolk had just 650 reportable injuries, or 2.26 per 200,000 manhours worked, earning its fourth straight E.H. Harriman

Gold Medal award for railroad safety. And by this June, it had reduced injuries per 200,000 manhours to 2.0—its original target for the end of 1995.

Instead of issuing orders, corporate safety employees now analyze data to determine causes of injuries that can be corrected or find trends in information. For example, they found that there is a 75 percent greater probability of a worker getting hurt in the first twelve months when he or she is new to a job, not just new to the railroad. Thus, even veteran workers—shifted to different tasks to fill in for vacationing employees—now receive job-specific training.

And interest in safety has grown and begun to focus on issues such as how to pull locomotives off the track so there is no one underneath the locomotive when that takes place. That's a far cry, says Mr. Brenner, from 1989 when the key concern of workers were things such as "brighter yellow paint on the floor."

DISCUSSION QUESTIONS

1. What did the CEO of Landstar Systems Inc. do to show employees that safety was a priority concern?

2. Describe the safety initiative taken at State Fair Foods Inc.'s plant in Dallas.

3. What steps did Norfolk Southern Corp. take to improve its safety record?

STRESS CAN BE BEATEN
By Richard Maturi

When it's already there, what can companies do to help workers deal with stress?

The hidden effects of stress are costing American firms untold millions of dollars annually in lost productivity, absenteeism, and health-care expenses.

According to an American Management Association survey, 81 percent of respondents report they suffer the ill effects of stress at least once a week. Dr. Peter Hanson, author of *The Joy Of Stress* and *Stress for Success: How to Make Stress on the Job Work for You,* estimates that stress-related illnesses cost U.S. industry more than $150 billion annually.

Adding more ammunition to the study of stress-related illnesses, a 1990 study by Cornell University Medical School, New York, found that job stress can triple the risk of high blood pressure and cause potentially dangerous physical changes to the heart.

Although some forward-thinking companies have already initiated stress-assessment and stress-management programs, most industry executives have unfortunately not adopted them.

Some of the stress-reducing programs in place in some American corporations sound a bit bizarre. For example, executives at H.J. Heinz Co. and Lotus Development Corp. enjoy in-the-office massages. And a hired comedian introduces humor at National Computer Systems, Minneapolis, to relax employees and spur creativity.

A review of early stress-management intervention in worksite situations reveals that most programs target the individual, particularly among the executive and white-collar ranks. New York Telephone, for example, attempted to improve employee health and productivity via a number of individual-level stress-management interventions such as meditation and relaxation techniques.

Today, however, more companies are taking a sophisticated approach to stress management and the whole concept of employee wellness.

Control Data Corp.'s "Staywell" program, which is now marketed to other firms, targets employee health risks. It uses a combination of techniques such as exercise, smoking cessation, hypertension screening and control, weight control, and nutritional counseling, as well as stress management, to create a better health environment for its employees.

Likewise, Johnson & Johnson's "Live for Life" health-promotion program emphasizes stress management as a key component in achieving healthier employees.

Evaluations of both of these innovative programs point toward positive physical, psychological, and behavioral results in terms of lower blood pressure, increased job satisfaction, and decreased substance abuse.

Insurance companies have been in the forefront of stress-management programs. As far back as 1982, Equitable Life Assurance Society of America embarked on its "Emotional Health Program," designed as a comprehensive approach to stress management via prevention and treatment, including referral of employees to an in-house clinical psychologist, physician, and/or counselor.

Northwestern National Life Insurance Co. (NWNL), Minneapolis, offers a free stress booklet to companies interested in evaluating their need for stress-management programs. (To obtain a copy of the booklet, contact Northwestern National Life, Route 6525, P.O. Box 20, Minneapolis, Minn. 55440.)

The booklet contains results of a national survey commissioned by NWNL. According to the survey, seven out of ten workers experience stress often; respondents having multiple stress-related illnesses increased from 13 percent in 1985 to 25 percent in 1991; employees feeling highly stressed jumped to 46 percent in 1991 from 20 percent in 1985; 17 percent of respondents report that stress caused them to miss one or more days of work in 1990; and 35 percent of new employees (those with their employer two years or less) left their previous jobs because of stress.

In addition, the NWNL booklet includes a workplace-stress test constructed by a panel of stress and wellness experts from across the country. The one-of-a-kind stress test is geared to allow employers to quickly measure work-force stress and help identify consequences and solutions.

In addition, twenty-six stress producers and twenty-three stress reducers are ranked by degree of stress created or reduced. For example, three stress points are charged if downsizing or layoffs have occurred in the company in the last year, if workloads vary greatly, or if most work is machine-paced or fast-paced.

Other stress situations include: few opportunities for advancement, new machines or ways of working, high noise or vibration levels, and frequently changing room temperatures in work areas.

On the stress-reducer side, score minus three points for management's taking significant action to reduce stress, employees having current and clear job descriptions, and employees being recognized and rewarded for their contributions. Two-point stress reducers include: employees having access to the technology they need, employer encouraging work and personal support groups, and perks granted fairly based on a person's level in the organization.

Companies can score as well as minus 50, showing no stress, or as poorly as plus 60 points, which represents the highest possible stress level.

Although no stress test is infallible, the NWNL booklet helps to point companies in the right direction by spotlighting possible trouble areas.

"We've had all types of companies request our stress information, from aerospace to sporting-goods firms," says NWNL's Marcia Johnson.

One such company, 3M Co., Minneapolis, currently provides limited stress-management training as part of a prevention emphasis in its employee-assistance program.

"We recognize there are growing demands on employees from both work and home, and we're investigating ways to develop effective buffers to stressful situations," says Dr. Sheryl Niebuhr, clinical supervisor for employee assistance at 3M.

In addition to the stress-management factors 3M is looking into, the company currently provides a variety of other employee-assistance and support-group programs relatively unknown

SOME STRESS-MANAGEMENT TIPS

1. Just do it; don't procrastinate.
2. Plan ahead. Organize your work and set priorities.
3. Reduce the noise level, if possible.
4. Unplug your phone for half an hour and take a break.
5. Work on positive reinforcers and develop a positive attitude about work.
6. Create a pleasant immediate work environment.
7. Set realistic timetables for getting your work done.
8. Allow for inefficiencies and things going wrong.
9. Interact with others. Share your feelings and frustrations.
10. When you leave work, leave the job behind you.
11. Take advantage of the emotional resources available to you.
12. Be flexible and open-minded.
13. Keep a sense of humor.

---

just a few years ago. These deal with widow and child bereavement, arthritis ailments, elder care, and breast cancer. Often, 3M employees receive counseling or support on a one-to-one basis from other employees who have gone through a similar experience and have received special training.

Another place companies can look to for help and information is the National Resource Center on Worksite Health Promotion, Washington, a collaborative effort of the Washington Business Group on Health and the Office of Disease Prevention & Health Promotion of the U.S. Public Health Service. It maintains a computerized database for use in promoting sound health policies and preventing disease on the job.

The U.S. Dept. of Health & Human Services, in its 1988 report, "Proposed National Strategy for the Prevention of Psychological Disorders," lists four distinct categories of action against work-related psychological disorders: job redesign to improve conditions; information dissemination, education, and training; surveillance of psychological disorders and risk factors; and enrichment of psychological health services for employees.

Stress research indicates that neither the amount of work nor the work rate appears to be as critical as the amount of personal control or discretion the employee exercises over these demands.

Evidence also indicates that temporal or transitory work scheduling can have a significant impact on psychological, behavioral, social, and physical well-being. For example, rotating night shifts and permanent night work in particular have been linked to a variety of such disturbances.

"In addition to taking job-redesign considerations into account, it's important to help the employee learn how to recognize and handle stress," emphasizes Dr. Michael McKee, a national expert in biofeedback and stress management in the Psychiatry Dept. of the Cleveland Clinic Foundation.

He says that the first step in stress management lies in being aware of stress in the environment. His own stress-management programs conducted for companies start with a one-hour health-awareness lesson on stress management followed by a six-to-eight-hour stress-management workshop, tailored to the type of workforce.

Dr. McKee cites the three Cs in learning to manage stress: control, challenge, and commitment:

☐ To attain **control,** learn relaxation responses to stress situations in order to make yourself less vulnerable to its ill effects. You can take slow, deep breaths, retire to a quiet place, narrow your field of concentration, or react passively to the stress.

"It's not the problem that is the problem, it's the solution—getting upset—that's the problem. Say to yourself, 'It's not the end of the world, I'll get through this,' " advises Dr. McKee.

☐ Channel your efforts into reinterpreting the stressful situation into a **challenge.** Once it's a challenge, you can learn how to cope with it. Make the smallest change possible that will have a positive impact and then move on to bigger challenges from there.

☐ Make a **commitment** to take care of yourself. Eat well, regularly exercise, take time off for yourself, develop a support system of friends and co-workers, and create a habit of managing stress.

"There's an increasing awareness of the major problems and tremendous cost to American business resulting from stress in the workplace," says Dr. McKee. "Companies and individuals can act to help reduce those stressful situations and learn how to deal with stress effectively."

"It's very important that you realize you can't change people's behavior overnight," warns Mark W. Zalkin, founder of Zalkin Training & Development, Denver. "These are not quick-fix situations; they take time. Stress-management programs plant the seeds, but top management needs to reaffirm its commitment by a constant emphasis on stress management."

DISCUSSION QUESTIONS

1. Identify several places companies can look to for help and information about workplace stress.

2. Identify five stress-management tips provided in the article.

3. Identify and describe the three Cs for learning to manage stress.

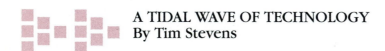

A TIDAL WAVE OF TECHNOLOGY
By Tim Stevens

New technology will sweep us into the twenty-first century, changing forever the way we create, manufacture, and sell products.

Powerful computers, intelligent software, smart manufacturing systems, and multifunction office devices tied to a ubiquitous communications network are but a few of the emerging technologies that will sweep factories and offices around the world into the twenty-first century. We'll be challenged, perhaps enchanted, and likely frustrated at first.

Yet we'll not escape, as the tidal wave of technology gathers force and crashes upon us, changing our lives forever. We'll work more effi-

ciently. Events that used to occur sequentially will occur simultaneously, enabled by information distributed in real time. We'll use less paper in favor of electronic communications and electronic commerce. Manufacturers will maintain ownership of products from cradle to grave, minimizing impact on our environment. Designers/engineers will step *back* to the future, to a time when industrialists wore all hats, when the entrepreneur took his idea to full completion himself. Yet at the same time enterprise-wide computer networks, embedded sensors, and technologies such as machine vision will significantly reduce human intervention in manufacturing processes.

Compact companies with flatter organizations and more highly skilled work forces will create customized, niche-market products for a global marketplace. Long-term cooperative alliances, even with competitors, will spread R&D investment and prototyping costs for higher-risk, potentially high-impact technology. Maturing of the information highway—with everyone connected to everyone and everything—will support short-term conclaves, sharing expertise to exploit brief windows of market opportunity. All of this will be facilitated by new and evolving technology we can take a peak at today.

To start, new products conceived in the mind will be expressed directly on computer and tested there to optimize performance properties. "Ninety-five percent of CAD/CAM systems today are wireframe models, essentially stick figures," says Larry McArthur, CEO of Aries Corp., Lowell, Mass., maker of UNIX-based CAD software tools.

"However, with solids modeling in CAD, you create a shaded image of a real 3D object, which can carry the physical and engineering properties you choose to ascribe to it." Immersed in virtual reality, designers could work parts into desired shape with virtual tools, check assembly of multiple virtual parts, or evaluate the ergonomics of automotive, heavy equipment, aircraft interiors, and controls.

Finite element analysis (FEA) on computer will expose solid models to loads, distortions, or whatever stresses and strains parts will undergo in use. Intelligent software will make inferences about design weaknesses and suggest optimum configurations. "We won't have to go to the real world until we've got it right [on the computer]," says Mr. McArthur.

Although FEA is not new, it will be integrated with solid-modeling design tools in one system and be available on the desktop. "In the future, FEA will be a mainstream engineering tool, not just run on mainframes by experts in white smocks," says Aries spokesman Drexel Ace.

Once a design is optimized, its file will be passed electronically to drive machine tools or any of a number of free-form (mold-less/tool-less) fabrication techniques. Here, parts are actually grown out of vats of liquid resin with UV light beams, or built up from laminates or sintered powders, or sprayed up with a variety of materials in a kind of 3D laser printing.

"Right now we are making parts without tools or fixtures at tolerances of ±0.002 in.," says Dr. Peter Sferro, principal staff engineer in charge of free-form fabrication at Ford Motor Co., Detroit. "In the future, the engineer will be able to make prototype parts or tooling right in his office.

"In the past we had to make large volumes of an item to justify the cost of tooling. Free-form fabrication gives us the technology to win in niche markets, building high-quality parts at small volumes, even one unit. It will completely change the economies of scale.

"The engineer of the future will be more of a generalist, as in the past. No more sketching and handing off to the pattern shop. We want him to work more like Thomas Edison, who conceived and built everything himself. He'll have to have a higher skill level, but at the same time the computer will give him tools he never had before. His office will be more like his garage. Finding ways to stimulate creativity in people to blend with the technology is what will give us the competitive edge."

Out on the production floor, the objectives will be to shorten the time required to produce an item, minimize the stock of raw materials and finished goods in inventory, and reduce the amount of work in process, all while improving quality and minimizing waste. In the future, "discounts will be offered on small orders to reduce inventories and promote just-in-time manufacturing," says Michael Dunham, president of EMS Corp., Milwaukee, maker of manufacturing execution software (MES). This agile-manufacturing approach will need to be flexible, allowing production of different parts on the same line without a lot of switching time between runs.

"Yet the key to just-in-time and agile manufacturing, especially in a continuous process, is being able to understand and measure the properties of products as they are being made," says Larry Kavanagh, director of the advanced-process-control program for the American Iron & Steel Institute.

"In the past, product samples were taken off line for testing by chemical and mechanical means. In the future, properties will be measured on-line in real time with laser beams, ultrasonic testing, or electromagnetic techniques. Then knowledge-based, intelligent software systems will do inference evaluations and adjust production parameters accordingly."

Look for machine vision to replace human eyes in selected inspection and monitoring processes. "In this technology, a camera captures light input—just like taking a picture—but then converts that into a digital stream of data that can be fed into a computer and analyzed or compared to a standard," says Don Lake, marketing manager of EG&G Optoelectronics, which supplies cameras and components.

"At the process level, a lot of functionality will be removed from programmable logic controllers [PLCs] and built directly into the control mechanisms themselves," says Tony Friscia, president of Advanced Manufacturing Research Inc. (AMR), a Boston-based market-analysis and consulting firm. "Control technology will be embedded right in valves, switches, etc., so they will not only open and close, they will have the intelligence to know *when* to do so."

In fact, PLCs—essentially computers that operate devices, but have no screens—may go the way of the dinosaur. "The trend now," says Neal Orr, marketing manager of Taylor Industrial, Edmonton, Alta., "is to control input/output devices directly from a laptop right on the factory floor or even the PC in your office, rather than downloading from computer to PLC. Automatic-identification systems, such as bar-coding, touch memory, and radio-frequency identification, will greatly facilitate movement and tracking of goods throughout a manufacturing facility.

"While bar-coding is approaching saturation in retail applications, only some 30 percent of products in the industrial arena are coded," says George Gilfoil, managing director of CB Consultants, Watertown, Maine, consultants to the automatic-identification industry. "We see that increasing to over 75 percent by the end of the century.

"In the next phase of technology, look for dime-sized buttons that are touched electronically with a probe [touch memory] to replace barcode applications. The buttons will read a tremendous amount of information into a hand-held terminal, including bill of materials [BOM], product details, and hazard warnings. Touch-memory buttons on finished products, such as an appliance, will read out all the service records for the device or provide a wiring schematic, and be updated when service is completed."

Yet for all the advances in process technology and hardware, it will still be information—collected and distributed between man and machine, from machine to machine, and from factory floor to the business/financial minds—that will make the factory of the future a reality.

"Until recently, U.S. manufacturers have been very oriented to and have developed great expertise in the processes themselves, like drilling a hole or welding a joint," says AMR's Mr. Friscia. "However, there hasn't been a good focus on operations, things like capacity utilization, inventory management, and throughput.

"This is where manufacturing execution software will become important. It fits in between and ties together MRP II [manufacturing resource planning] software and direct process control. MES supercharges the planning function, putting all decision-support information in one centralized location. It serves as the foreman by not only tracking information, but by analyzing it, anticipating what will happen, and making changes in advance to maintain high throughput.

"In addition, MES supports customer-oriented business strategies because it allows the customer-service function to provide a real-time update on the progress of any order. The penetration rate of these systems today is less than 5 percent. I believe competitive manufacturing demands will cause this number to rise dramatically in the future."

Moving production closer to the customer turns a traditional salesman into a sales engineer and more, believes Roger Willis, a partner at Andersen Consulting, Chicago.

"We have a client who sells customized equipment. Each shares some standard-design components," he says. "We have developed a knowledge-based [artificial intelligence] software system that allows the equipment to be designed as the customer specifies the things he wants, in the way natural for him.

Inputs to this "configurator system" can be made in a rather random fashion, as the customer thinks of his needs. The software works with some 300 market drivers, listens to the inputs, and designs a unit maximizing the number of standard components that will most closely meet the customer requirements. In minutes it presents a design, a price estimate, and a delivery time. Eventually the system will create a BOM, a complete manufacturing sequence, and initiate orders to suppliers for parts sourced outside for just-in-time manufacture.

"Once an electronic-communication infrastructure exists, it will go off looking for vendors of components that may not currently exist, all because a customer said he wants a certain feature."

Even after a product has been sold, the manufacturer of the future will retain some degree of ownership. "In Germany, for instance, automobile manufacturers will soon have to take back their cars once their life-cycle is complete," says John Mahaffie of Coates & Jarratt, a Washington think tank of futurists. "This will be a bellwether of what will happen in the United States and throughout the world.

"In the future, most hard goods will be designed with the three Rs in mind: reclamation, recycling, or remanufacturing. New designs will be easy to dismantle and use materials that are recyclable and can be easily separated from the waste stream. Coatings and finishes will rejuvenate spent products. At the same time, manufacturers will build things that last longer, with the objective of zero waste in the process.

"When cleanup is required, we may see implementation of nanotechnology, that is, the science of devices smaller than the diameter of a human hair. Masses of tiny nanomachines would literally be thrown into the hopper, acting like enzymes to change the chemistry of materials, or scavenge away impurities."

In the marketplace of the future the name of the game will be communication, with information the currency of the new economy. We'll all be connected worldwide by new satellite networks, wireless communication devices, and a growing information infrastructure, or information highway, which will erase geographic boundaries forever.

It will enable companies and individuals to tap new sources of information, equipment, and services, akin to searching through an international Yellow Pages. It will allow new business alliances to share information, each contributing their expertise to exploit new market opportunities.

"And it will allow a lot more people to work at home," says Mr. Mahaffie. "As more and more work becomes information-oriented, there will be a loosening up of where and when you work. With the information infrastructure in place, the work location will be practically irrelevant."

DISCUSSION QUESTIONS

1. How will the shape of organizations change as we enter the twenty-first century?

2. How will bar-coding likely expand and change?

3. How will technology impact on the production floor?

4. What is MES, and how will it become important?

 Study Guide

Study Guide

To the Student:

This section of your textbook provides you with chapter-by-chapter review questions, exercises, and applications. The true-false and multiple-choice questions will help you study for exams. Each chapter also has a multiple choice test or a crossword puzzle to test your knowledge of key concepts and terms. Application exercises suggest ways in which you can practice what you have learned in the chapter.

To the Instructor:

The student study guide is perforated so that you may assign homework assignments to be completed in the book and handed in. Answers for objective questions and crossword puzzles can be found in your copy of the instructor's manual.

CHAPTER 1:
Understanding Your Job as a Supervisor

True or False: Circle the correct answer.

T	(F)	1.	Supervisors are below first-line managers on the organization chart.
T	(F)	2.	Today's supervisors have the absolute power to hire and fire.
T	(F)	3.	Supervisory authority has not changed much over the years.
T	(F)	4.	Classical management theory started with the Hawthorne studies.
T	F	5.	Frederick Taylor believed that a person is motivated by social incentives.
(T)	F	6.	Henri Fayol was known as an administrative manager who provided principles and functions of management.
T	(F)	7.	Fayol believed that technical skills are unimportant to supervisors.
T	(F)	8.	The Hawthorne studies led people to believe that employees are mainly motivated by money.

T   9. Chester Barnard wrote from the perspective of a practicing supervisor.

T   F   10. People who subscribe to human resource theory believe in participative management.

T   F   11. Scientific managers, more than any other group, believed that employees have much creative potential.

T   12. Only top managers need conceptual skills.

T   F   13. Technical skills are most important to first-line managers.

T   F   14. Motivating people is a human relations skill.

T   F   15. Compared to top managers or supervisors, middle managers are more likely to use human relations skills.

T   F   16. Operational planning is a technical skill.

T   F   17. The five functions of management are planning, organizing, directing, coordinating, and controlling.

T   18. Supervisory planning is mainly long-term in nature.

T   F   19. Effectiveness and efficiency go hand-in-hand.

 T   F   20. Controlling involves comparing actual performance with planned performance.

Multiple Choice: Circle the correct answer.

1. Supervision can best be equated to:
    a. first-line management
    b. middle management
    c. upper management
    d. nonmanagement

2. The earliest of the management eras was the _____ era.
    a. classical
    b. human relations
    c. human resources
    d. administrative

3. The Father of Scientific Management was:
    a. Henri Fayol
    b. Chester Barnard
    c. Frederick Taylor
    d. Elton Mayo

4. Classical managers included scientific managers and:
    a. behavioral managers
    b. administrative managers
    c. human relationists
    d. bureaucrats

5. The author of the famous fourteen principles of administration discussed in chapter 1 was:
    a. Chester Barnard
    b. Henri Fayol
    c. Frederick Taylor
    d. Fritz Roethlisberger

6. The belief in the social needs of workers and the introduction of suggestion boxes and counseling programs were parts of which era?
    a. scientific management
    b. administrative management
    c. human relations
    d. human resources

7. The "acceptance theory of authority" was conceived of by:
   a. Elton Mayo
   b. Abraham Maslow
   c. Douglas McGregor
   d. Chester Barnard

8. Human resource philosophy is quite _____ earlier management theory and reflects today's _____ quite well.
   a. different from, values
   b. similar to, workers
   c. an improvement over, managers
   d. better than, problems

9. The essence of the human resources philosophy is a belief in:
   a. participative management
   b. shared decision making
   c. the creativity of workers
   d. all of the above

10. Disciplining, rewarding, motivating, and leading are examples of _____ skills.
    a. conceptual
    b. human relations
    c. scientific management
    d. technical

11. Operational, intermediate, and long-range are time horizons used in:
    a. planning
    b. organizing
    c. controlling
    d. directing

12. Supervisors use which of the following skills the most?
    a. conceptual
    b. planning
    c. technical
    d. human relations

13. Another word for commanding is:
    a. directing
    b. organizing
    c. staffing
    d. controlling

14. Comparing actual performance to expected performance and correcting any deviations is called:
    a. commanding
    b. controlling
    c. planning
    d. organizing

15. Supervisors are responsible to all of these groups except:
    a. peers
    b. employees
    c. stockholders
    d. employers

Matching: Match the term on the right with the corresponding term on the left.

_____	1. Planning	a.	Acceptance theory of authority
_____	2. Organizing	b.	Father of scientific management
_____	3. Coordinating	c.	Deciding on course of action
_____	4. Controlling	d.	Correcting deviations
_____	5. Directing	e.	Job-specific skills
_____	6. Technical skills	f.	Father of modern management
_____	7. Frederick Taylor	g.	Hawthorne studies
_____	8. Henri Fayol	h.	Abilities for planning
_____	9. Chester Barnard	i.	Supervision of employees
_____	10. Elton Mayo	j.	Synchronization of effort
_____	11. Human relations skills	k.	Deciding how to use resources
_____	12. Conceptual skills	l.	People skills

Applications

1. In small groups, discuss job situations in which classical, human relations, and human resource management styles might be appropriate. Share one scenario for each style with the rest of the class.

2. Students should write a 100-word essay, classifying their management style as classical, human relations, or human resources. Be sure to include why you have chosen a particular school. Share your essays in small groups and then tally the results for the class. How many people felt they were strongest in the classical beliefs? How many were human relationists? Human resource people? Why do you feel people scored as they did?

3. Pick a particular supervisory job with which you are familiar. List the technical, human relations, and conceptual skills that a person in that position will need.

CHAPTER 2:
Meeting the Quality Challenge

True or False: Circle the correct answer

T	**F**	1.	Productivity in the United States is now at an all-time low.
T	F	2.	By the early 1990s, the economies of Japan and Germany were beginning to slow down.
T	F	3.	If outputs remain the same and inputs increase, productivity will decline.
T	**F**	4.	If outputs go up faster than inputs, productivity will decline.
T	F	5.	The cost of producing goods and services is known as input.
T	**F**	6.	Much of the current productivity challenge can be placed squarely on the shoulders of American managers.
T	**F**	7.	The changing values of the work force are resulting in greater support for the work ethic.
T	F	8.	Unions are primarily to blame for the productivity problem in the United States.
T	F	9.	Total quality management is primarily a problem-solving tool.
T	F	10.	One of the core values of TQM is customer-driven quality.
T	F	11.	Continuous improvement is an objective of TQM.
T	F	12.	Increased cycle time will increase productivity.
T	F	13.	Intuition and gut feel are critical elements in the TQM process.
T	F	14.	Data collection is a TQM tool.
T	F	15.	A check sheet is an easy-to-understand, TQM-related form.
T	**F**	16.	A Pareto chart is the same as a check sheet.
T	**F**	17.	The 80/20 theory holds that 80 percent of all causes bring about 20 percent of all results.
T	F	18.	Check sheets can be used in helping to solve Pareto problems.
T	F	19.	Continuous improvement is an important part of TQM.
T	F	20.	One objective of continuous improvement is to maintain minimum inventory.

Multiple Choice: Circle the correct answer.

1. Over the past couple of years, productivity in the United States has:
   a. risen
   b. remained the same
   c. declined a little
   d. declined sharply

2. In recent years, productivity growth in Japan has begun:
   a. to rise sharply
   b. to rise moderately
   c. to level off
   d. to slow down

3. Productivity is measured by the ratio:
   a. output × input
   b. output ÷ input
   c. output − input
   d. output + input

4. _____ is the value of the goods and services being produced.
   a. Productivity
   b. Output
   c. Input
   d. Quality

5. _____ is the cost of producing goods and services.
   a. Productivity
   b. Output
   c. Input
   d. Quality

6. Personnel, machinery, materials, and money are all examples of:
   a. productivity
   b. output
   c. input
   d. quality

7. In which of the following will productivity increase?
   a. outputs decrease and inputs are stable
   b. outputs are stable and inputs increase
   c. outputs decrease and inputs increase
   d. outputs increase faster than inputs

8. In which of the following will productivity decline?
   a. outputs decrease and inputs are stable
   b. outputs increase and inputs decrease
   c. outputs decrease more slowly than inputs
   d. outputs increase faster than inputs

9. All of the following are core values of TQM except:
   a. customer-driven quality
   b. continuous improvement
   c. detection not prevention
   d. full participation

10. All of the following are core values of TQM except:
    a. reduced cycle time
    b. management by intuition
    c. long-range outlook
    d. partnership development

11. The most common form of data collection sheet is the:
    a. Pareto chart
    b. statistical bar chart
    c. cycle time sheet
    d. check sheet

12. The Pareto principle holds that _____ of all outcomes can be attributed to _____ of all causes.
    a. 80 percent; 20 percent
    b. 75 percent; 25 percent
    c. 50 percent; 50 percent
    d. 20 percent; 80 percent

13. Pareto charts typically are based on information from:
    a. statistical bar charts
    b. check sheets
    c. cycle time sheets
    d. scatter point diagrams

14. All of the following help promote continuous improvement except:
    a. maintain an open-minded attitude
    b. eliminate hard work
    c. maintain maximum inventory
    d. use constructive criticism

15. All of the following help promote continuous improvement except:
    a. keep everything in the workplace in order
    b. keep the work place clean
    c. develop effective procedures
    d. remain subjective

Matching: Match the term on the left with the definition on the right.

_____ 1. Cost of producing output

_____ 2. Time needed to deliver the output

_____ 3. Form used to answer the question: How often are certain events happening?

_____ 4. Holds that most results are brought about by a small number of causes.

_____ 5. Outputs/inputs

_____ 6. Constant effort to do things better and better

_____ 7. A vertical bar graph used to decide which problems to solve and in what order

_____ 8. An organizational strategy

_____ 9. Goods and services being produced

_____ 10. Tool for identifying, solving, or preventing problems.

a. Productivity
b. Outputs
c. Inputs
d. Total quality management
e. Cycle time
f. Data collection
g. Check sheet
h. Pareto chart
i. 80/20 theory
j. Continuous improvement

Applications

1. How can productivity be measured in a manufacturing firm? In a hospital? In a university? In each case, give an example. How could one of the ideas you have studied in this chapter be used to increase the productivity in all three of these organizations? Be specific in your answer.

2. Review the core values of TQM. Choose four that are of practical value in increasing productivity and

quality in the company where you work. If you do not work, choose any company you would like and use it as your point of reference. Then write a short description of how each core value can be used.

3. John Andersen's company has a fleet of forty automobiles. Over the past five years, here are the number and types of problems that these cars have encountered:

Problems	Number of occurrences
front end alignment	12
air conditioner broke	7
fuel pump needed to be replaced	5
wheel alignment required	22
battery died	16
transmission problems	8
exhaust system needed work	3
master cylinder leaked	9

Construct a Pareto chart with the above information. Based on your findings, what conclusions can you draw.

4. Review the list of ten continuous improvement ideas provided in the chapter. Rank them from most important to least important, based on your own personal evaluation. Compare your evaluation to that of other members of the class. Based on this comparison, what conclusions can you draw?

CHAPTER 3:
Communicating Effectively

True or False: Circle the correct answer.

T	F	1.	In communication the emphasis is on the transfer of meaning.
T	F	2.	The coding process in communication is very similar from person to person.
T	F	3.	Job instructions are usually carried in the upward communication system.
T	F	4.	Diagonal communications takes place between people at different levels of the organizational hierarchy.
T	F	5.	Written communications are more formal and permanent than oral communications.
T	F	6.	Suggestions from employees travel in the upward communication channels.
T	F	7.	Listening does not take very much time.
T	F	8.	Horizontal communications are the same as lateral communications.
T	F	9.	Over the years the corporate grapevine has earned a good reputation.
T	F	10.	Informal communications are mostly written.
T	F	11.	The formal communication system is best for handling nonroutine events.
T	F	12.	Active grapevines are a sign of organizational trouble.
T	F	13.	Most frequently used words have only one meaning.
T	F	14.	An inference is an assumption based at least partially on fact.
T	F	15.	People stop listening when they hear "emotion-laden" words.
T	F	16.	A large amount of information can be handled if the complexity is relatively low.
T	F	17.	Overload is more often discussed than underload as an organizational problem.
T	F	18.	Leveling refers to focusing on the part of a message that interests us most and passing it along.
T	F	19.	Unfortunately, we listen with only about a 50 percent efficiency rate.
T	F	20.	When verbal and nonverbal signals disagree, we usually believe the verbal message.

Multiple Choice. Circle the correct answer.

1. Anything that interferes with the transfer of meaning is called:
   a. noise
   b. encoding
   c. perception
   d. environment

2. Examples of upward communication include all of the following except:
   a. suggestion boxes
   b. meetings
   c. job instructions
   d. suggestions on ways to do jobs better

3. Which is the most traditional type of organizational communication?
   a. upward
   b. downward
   c. diagonal
   d. horizontal

4. Which seems to be the most effective way of transmitting information downward through the organization?
   a. written
   b. oral
   c. written, followed by oral
   d. oral, followed by written

5. Which is not an example of horizontal communications?
   a. meetings
   b. social events
   c. task groups
   d. memos from the president

6. How much of the information carried in the grapevine is thought to be true?
   a. 10 to 20 percent
   b. 30 to 40 percent
   c. 55 to 75 percent
   d. 75 to 95 percent

7. Which is not a characteristic of the informal communication system?
   a. fast
   b. deliberate, planned
   c. mostly oral
   d. geared toward nonroutine events

8. Emotion-laden words are an example of which type of communication barrier?
   a. semantics
   b. perception
   c. load
   d. distortion

9. Which of the following is not an inferential statement?
   a. His report is too long.
   b. His report is late.
   c. His report is good.
   d. His report is ten pages long.

10. When employees are cut off from the main channels of communication in the organization, they may be suffering from:
    a. overload
    b. perception
    c. underload
    d. resistance to ambiguity

11. Listening is:
    a. easy if you just know how to do it.
    b. something that cannot be learned.
    c. rarely worth all the effort.
    d. important in making employees feel valued.

12. Which of the following is not part of kinesics?
    a. posture
    b. tone of voice
    c. gestures
    d. facial expressions

13. Which part of the body carries the
     most nonverbal meaning?
     a. eyes
     b. face
     c. hands
     d. legs

14. The study of how space is used is
     called:
     a. territoriality
     b. proxemics
     c. paralanguage
     d. kinesics

15. The part of nonverbal behavior that is
     vocal but not verbal is:
     a. kinesics
     b. paralanguage
     c. proxemics
     d. territoriality

Matching: Match the term on the right with the corresponding term on the left.

G 1. Paralanguage
H 2. Semantics
C 3. Kinesics
J 4. Diagonal communications
D 5. Proxemics
E 6. Sharpening
K 7. Leveling
A 8. Lateral communication
F 9. Inference
B 10. Grapevine
I 11. Noise

a. Horizontal communication
b. Informal communications
c. Body language
d. Study of the use of space
e. Adds emphasis to part of message
f. Assumption
g. How people say what they say
h. Study of meaning
i. Interferes with transfer of meaning
j. Involves people at different levels of
    the organization
k. Dropping part of a message

Applications

1. In groups of five, experiment with the
    effects of verbal transmission. The first
    person should write down a statement
    of twenty to thirty words giving some-
    one instructions. Then that same person
    is to whisper it to the second person
    who passes it on to the next person.
    When the fifth person has received the
    message, compare it to the original
    message. Where was the message
    changed? How does the result compare
    to that suggested in the text?

2. Individually, make a list of the typical
    types of "noise" that interfere with a su-
    pervisor listening to an employee. Dis-
    cuss these in small groups and decide
    which are the five most common types.
    What might be done about each one of
    them?

3. How can supervisors know if their em-
    ployees are suffering from communica-
    tion overload? What are some of the
    symptoms? Discuss what supervisors
    might do if they observe these symp-

toms. Should they ever just ignore them?

4. How can a knowledge of proxemics help supervisors in their interpersonal communications with employees? Give three specific examples. In small groups, pick one of the examples previously given and prepare a role play of the situation. Each group in turn should perform their role play for the class, and the entire group should discuss the impact of proxemics in the situation portrayed.

5. Define the characteristics you think a healthy formal communication system should have. Is there any relationship between the health of the formal system and the functioning of the informal system? Discuss.

CHAPTER 4:
Understanding Employee Behavior

True or False: Circle the correct answer.

(T)   F   1.   The behavioral framework used in this chapter presents a complete picture of individual behavior.

(T)   F   2.   Personality consists of a unique set of characteristics.

(T)   F   3.   Most people believe today that personality is almost entirely a matter of heredity.

(T)   F   4.   The right hemisphere of the brain is thought to control the intuitive, creative abilities of a person.

(T)   F   5.   Logical thought, mathematical ability, and verbal skills are thought to be located in the left hemisphere of the brain.

T   (F)   6.   Friends are the earliest conveyors of values.

T   (F)   7.   The economy has little effect on the way personality or values develop.

T   (F)   8.   Self-concept and values are the same thing.

T   (F)   9.   Values have no relationship to time and place.

(T)   F   10. How persons see themselves is called self-concept.

(T)   F   11. The key to coding and decoding messages is the "code of past experience."

(T)   F   12. A defense mechanism employing excuses for failure is called denial.

(T)   F   13. Projection is a defense mechanism whereby persons attribute their feelings to someone else.

(T)   F   14. The Johari Window is useful only in examining employee behavior.

T   (F)   15. The area of the Johari Window that is unknown to others and unknown to self is called the "hidden" area.

(T)   F   16. The Pygmalion effect relies on positive expectations.

T   (F)   17. Supervisory expectations have little or no real effect on employee behavior.

(T)   F   18. Values are basic beliefs.

(T)   F   19. A combination of employee attitudes toward the workplace is called morale.

(T)   F   20. Research concludes that job satisfaction leads to higher performance.

Multiple Choice: Circle the correct answer.

1. Which of the following was not discussed as an employee variable in
   Chapter 4?
   a. perception
   b. expectations
   c. personality
   d. self-concept

2. Which of the following is a determinant of personality?
   a. environment
   b. situation
   c. heredity
   d. all of the above

3. The nature-nurture controversy refers
   to the impact of _____ and _____
   on personality.
   a. heredity and environment
   b. learning and genes
   c. situation and environment
   d. situation and heredity

4. The most controversial trait that is believed by some to be hereditary is:
   a. appearance
   b. creativity
   c. intelligence
   d. motor skills

5. Split-brain research is:
   a. a relatively new study
   b. unproven
   c. in need of more research
   d. all of the above

6. Theory _____ refers to an American
   supervisory style strongly influenced
   by Japanese management techniques.
   a. A
   b. X
   c. Y
   d. Z

7. Which of the following is considered a
   situational variable of personality?
   a. age
   b. family
   c. political system
   d. sex

8. Our most gut-level, basic beliefs are
   called:
   a. values
   b. attitudes
   c. personality traits
   d. regressions

9. Positive self-concept is directly related
   to:
   a. self-confidence
   b. openness in communication
   c. both of the above
   d. none of the above

10. Which of the following is not one of
    the three Ps of perception?
    a. psychological
    b. physical
    c. parental
    d. past experience

11. The defense mechanism whereby a
    person refuses to acknowledge a
    problem exists is called:
    a. withdrawal
    b. denial
    c. rationalization
    d. aggression

12. The focus of our perception is a ques-
    tion of:
    a. values
    b. figure-ground
    c. past experience
    d. all of the above

13. Self-disclosing behavior, in terms of
    the Johari Window, takes place in
    which quadrant?
    ⓐ open
    b. blind
    c. hidden
    d. unknown

14. Research on the Pygmalion effect has
    shown:
    a. Employees try to do what is ex-
       pected of them.

    b. Effective supervisors create high
       expectations.
    c. Supervisory expectations are large-
       ly responsible for productivity.
    ⓓ all of the above

15. Job satisfaction has been most
    successfully correlated to:
    ⓐ productivity
    b. turnover
    c. absenteeism
    d. none of the above

Matching: Match the term on the right with the corresponding term on the left.

G	1.	Theory X
J	2.	Theory Y
H/F	3.	Theory Z
L	4.	Attitude
K	5.	Rationalization
N	6.	Values
M	7.	Withdrawal
A	8.	Projection
B	9.	Morale
E	10.	Self-disclosure
C	11.	Pygmalion effect
D	12.	Blind quadrant
I	13.	Hidden quadrant
	14.	Denial

a. Work-related attitudes
b. Intervening supervisory variable
c. Known to others; unknown to self
d. Known to self; unknown to others
e. Positive expectations
f. Feelings about a specific person or
   place
g. Autocratic management philosophy
h. Japanese management adapted to U.S.
   environment
i. Refusal to acknowledge a problem
j. Democratic management philosophy
k. Basic beliefs
l. Making excuses for failure
m. Attribution of ones feelings to others
n. Physical removal from frustrating situation

Applications

1. Investigate the personality development
   theories of one of the following and relate that theory to employee behavior at
   work. This might be done in small
   groups with a group report to the rest
   of the class. Theorists: Sigmund Freud,
   Erik Erikson, Chris Argyris, Gail Sheehy.

2. In small groups, work on a model of
   values held by various age groups in
   organizations. For example, you might
   divide the work force into three age
   groups; under thirty, thirty to fifty, and
   fifty and older. What different types of
   values would you expect to find in
   each group? Why? What factors caused

these values to form? Present your model to the rest of the class.

3. Draw an approximation of what your overall Johari Window looks like. In small groups, share your findings. Why did you draw it the way you did? What does this tell us about you? Does your group agree with your conclusions? Have you found any implications for improvement?

4. Organize a debate on the performance-satisfaction controversy. One side should take the position that satisfac-

tion leads to performance. The other side should take the position that performance leads to satisfaction. Choose a member to debate the representative of the other team and conduct the debate along guidelines given by your instructor. At least half of the class should act as impartial observers; jot down your own conclusions as the debate progresses. At the conclusion of the debate, see if the class can agree on an answer.

CHAPTER 7:
Selecting and Training Employees

True or False: Circle the correct answer.

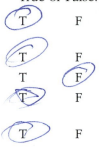

T	F	1. Selection is primarily the function of the human resources (H.R.) department.
T	F	2. Job descriptions detail necessary qualifications of the job applicant.
T	F	3. Actual recruitment of candidates is done by the H.R. department.
T	F	4. Decisions as to whom to hire are made by the operating departments.
T	F	5. Every job applicant attends a selection interview with the operating department.
T	F	6. Questions you can ask at interviews are virtually limitless.
T	F	7. Supervisors often like to assess interpersonal skills at selection interviews.
T	F	8. The most important function of the selection interview is the gathering of information by both the supervisor and the job applicant.
T	F	9. Little planning is needed prior to the selection interview.
T	F	10. The first step of selection interviewing is asking specific questions.
T	F	11. You should wait until you have interviewed all applicants before taking any notes.
T	F	12. Orientation always occurs, one way or another.
T	F	13. Effective orientations are a joint project of H.R. and operating departments.
T	F	14. Orientations can reduce employee anxieties but do not lessen start-up costs.
T	F	15. Both H.R. and supervisors should be involved in orientation follow-up.
T	F	16. Training and development are one and the same thing.
T	F	17. Supervisors are involved more in education than in training.
T	F	18. The first stage in the training cycle is establishing performance standards.
T	F	19. Successful supervisors tackle training needs as they arise.
T	F	20. On-the-job training is always preferable to classroom training.

Multiple Choice: Circle the correct answer.

1. A detailed listing of duties and responsibilities attached to a job vacancy is called a:
   a. job description
   b. job posting
   c. job specification
   d. job analysis

2. Which of the following is primarily a duty of the operating department?
   a. recruitment of candidates
   b. accepting application forms
   c. testing of candidates
   d. selection interviews

3. Which of the following is *not* primarily a duty of the operating department?
   a. training
   b. selection decisions
   c. reference checks
   d. identification of job needs

4. Which of the following is true about selection interviews?
   a. Tests have been eliminated in many companies as part of the selection interview.
   b. Questioning of applicants has become less complicated in the last fifteen years.
   c. Personnel usually does the selection interviews.
   d. All of the above.

5. Which of the following is an illegal question?
   a. Are there any religious holidays you feel obliged to take off?
   b. Are you available to work on weekends?
   c. What do your kids do while you work on weekends?
   d. Have you ever been convicted of a felony?

6. Which of the following is *not* one of the most common criteria for judging job applicants?
   a. appropriate education
   b. appropriate experience
   c. appropriate attitude
   d. appropriate personality

7. Which is the correct progression of selection interview questioning?
   a. General questions, specific questions, applicant's questions
   b. General questions, applicant's questions, specific questions
   c. Applicant's questions, general questions, specific questions
   d. Specific questions, applicant's questions, general questions

8. Which of the following should happen after a selection interview?
   a. Notes should be written down as soon as possible so that impressions will not be forgotten.
   b. The next applicant should be seen as quickly as possible.
   c. You should discuss your thoughts with other people in the department.
   d. Other people should be invited to meet the applicant.

9. Who is primarily responsible for orientation?
   a. human resources
   b. operating departments
   c. training and development
   d. H. R. and operating departments

10. Who is primarily responsible for training?
    a. human resources
    b. operating departments
    c. training and development
    d. H. R. and operating departments

11. Which of the following is a benefit of an effective orientation program?
    a. lower start-up costs
    b. quicker socialization of the new employee
    c. less anxiety on the part of the new employee
    d. all of the above

12. Which is *not* a question recommended for evaluating your orientation program?
    a. Is it quick?
    b. Is it appropriate?
    c. Is it interesting?
    d. Is it flexible?

13. _____ is most often associated with providing skills and knowledge that an employee needs to perform the current job.
    a. Training
    b. Development

    c. Education
    d. Appraisal

14. Before beginning the training cycle, _____ should occur.
    a. formulating objectives
    b. needs assessment
    c. selecting a technique
    d. identifying participants

15. Which of the following is *not* a good training objective?
    a. improve sales performance
    b. lower number of rejects
    c. reduce overtime
    d. all of the above

Matching: Match the term on the right with the corresponding term on the left.

K	1. Job description	a. Responsibility of H.R.
D	2. Job specification	b. Internal hiring procedure
C	3. Education	c. Nonspecific training
E	4. Training	d. Job qualifications
H	5. Development	e. Job specific training
A/I	6. Recruitment	f. One-on-one training
I	7. Selection	g. Prerequisite to selection interview
B	8. Job posting	h. Training for future job
F	9. OJT	i. Responsibility of operating department
G	10. Planning	j. Responsibility of H.R. and operating department
J	11. Orientation	k. Duties and responsibilities of job

Applications

1. Suppose that you are the supervisor in charge of interviewing candidates for a new clerical position in your department. The job description requires typing for four different engineers and transcribing from a dictaphone machine. A word processor will be used for most of the typing. There will also be a small percentage of time spent relieving the switchboard operator. Prepare a list of questions to act as a guide for interviewing the candidates. In small groups take turns role-playing the interviews.

2. You have hired Anne Reese to fill the position. Personnel will be orienting her in terms of benefits and general company policies, but you are in charge of doing department orientation. What areas should you be sure to cover with Anne? How can you get her to be a fully functioning employee in the shortest possible time?

3. Investigate the orientation procedures of at least two local companies. Ask current employees what the process was like or contact the personnel departments for information. Share your findings with the rest of the class.

4. In small groups, share your experiences at selection interviews from the point of view of the applicant and, if possible, the supervisor. How could the interviews have been better conducted?

5. One type of training done in organizations instructs employees in the way to be a good troubleshooter. In small groups, discuss what the supervisor, Joe or Janet Green, should do in each case.

    a. Janet Green is the nursing supervisor at Memorial Hospital. Her paperwork is backlogged, but she gets a call that two of the eight shift nurses have just called in sick. What should she do?

    b. Joe Green hired Ralph Watt to teach a supervision class. On the first night Ralph fails to show up. There are twenty students waiting in the classroom. What should Joe do?

    c. Janet Green is the duty sergeant at the third precinct. Because of an outbreak of flu and scheduled vacations, most officers have been working double shifts for a week. They are exhausted. As the second shift is about to go off duty, the mayor calls and requests a special police escort of ten additional officers in the next hour. How should she staff this order?

CHAPTER 8:
Supervising in the Multicultural Workplace

True or False: Circle the correct answer.

T　　F　　1.　America is a thawing pot for many different cultures.

T　　F　　2.　The U.S. work force is becoming increasingly multicultural.

T　　F　　3.　Research shows that most minority employees have the same values as Anglo male employees.

T　　F　　4.　Research shows that in dealing with multicultural differences, it is not enough for supervisors simply to try their best.

T　　F　　5.　By the year 2005, women will account for approximately 54 percent of the total work force.

T　　F　　6.　By the year 2005, Anglo men will account for approximately 40 percent of the work force.

T　　F　　7.　Approximately one-third of all U.S. workers in 2005 will be black, Hispanic, or Asian.

T　　F　　8.　By the year 2005, there will be fewer Anglo men in the work force than Anglo women.

T　　F　　9.　It is estimated that approximately 26 percent of the U.S. population speaks a language other than English at home.

T　　F　　10.　When communicating with individuals for whom English is a second language, a useful guideline is to try to cover as much information as possible at one time.

T　　F　　11.　Multicultural work groups often have different perceptions about instructions, problem-solving tasks, rules, and regulations.

T　　F　　12.　Research shows that most multicultural workers can all be motivated in the same way.

T　　F　　13.　All organizations have a culture, which consists of the shared values and beliefs of the enterprise.

T　　F　　14.　Today almost 90 percent of American firms offer diversity training to the supervisory personnel.

T　　F　　15.　Research reveals that diversity training is particularly important given the lingering and deep-seated prejudice that exists in many companies.

T　　F　　16.　One of the most helpful steps in managing diversity is to make it clear to the supervisors that this process is virtually the same as affirmative action.

T　　F　　17.　In many cases, organizations have biased performance evaluations that reduce the promotion opportunities of minorities.

T	F	18. Monsanto's use of "join-ups" is designed to help minorities join up for diversity training.
T	F	19. Some of the common barriers to promoting diversity in organizations include denial and lack of awareness of the problem.
T	F	20. One of the most important steps in promoting diversity is to incorporate such training as part of the broad, overall strategy.

Multiple Choice: Circle the correct answer.

1. The percentage of men in the work force has been declining consistently and by the year 2005, men will account for only _____ percent of the total.
   a. 58
   b. 53
   c. 49
   d. 44

2. Anglo workers accounted for _____ percent of the total work force in 1975 but will make up only _____ percent of this work group by 2005.
   a. 95; 64
   b. 91; 79
   c. 88; 75
   d. 80; 40

3. Anglo men accounted for _____ percent of the work force in 1975, but this will drop to _____ percent by 2005.
   a. 58; 50
   b. 56; 46
   c. 54; 40
   d. 50; 33

4. Current estimates are that _____ percent of the annual growth rate of the labor force is accounted for by foreign nationals.
   a. 30–40
   b. 25–35
   c. 20–30
   d. 15–25

5. When determining how well the communication has been understood, supervisors should do all of the following except:
   a. look for nonverbal signs that indicate confusion or embarrassment on the part of the listener.
   b. be alert to a qualified yes to the question: Do you understand?
   c. have the listener repeat what has been said and check these comments for accuracy.
   d. stay alert for appropriate laughter and efforts by the employee to focus on the subject at hand.

6. In dealing with people who are currently learning English, all of the following are useful guidelines for supervisors except:
   a. invite the individual to verbally share his or her ideas.
   b. try to limit the amount of time the individual takes to communicate.
   c. listen to what the person is saying before assuming that you do not understand.
   d. carefully observe the individual's body language.

7. _____ is the acquired knowledge that people use to interpret experience and to generate social behavior.
   a. Conviction
   b. Diversity
   c. Culture
   d. Value

8. _____ are basic convictions that people have regarding what is right and wrong, good and bad, important and unimportant.
   a. Morals
   b. Values
   c. Ethics
   d. Cultures

9. In promoting diversity, which of the following is least likely to be of value to a supervisor?
   a. Be aware of how your leadership style affects higher level management.
   b. Develop a sense of social ethics and social responsibility.
   c. Learn how your personal values and ideas affect your view of leadership and diversity.
   d. Be willing to accept the challenges associated with managing a multicultural work group.

10. Which of the following steps are useful in tapping the creative potential of the diverse work group in enhancing organizational productivity, profitability, and responsiveness to business conditions?
    a. identifying diversity problems in the organization
    b. strengthening top management commitment to promoting diversity
    c. opting for solutions that fit a balanced strategy that is best for both the personnel and the organization
    d. all of the above

11. All of the following are renowned for having developed diversity programs except:
    a. American Express
    b. Colgate-Palmolive
    c. U.S. Steel
    d. Xerox

12. All of the following are common diversity practices except:
    a. personal involvement on the part of top management
    b. the targeting of nonmanagerial recruitment efforts among a wide continuum of personnel
    c. the use of BOWGSAT
    d. the incorporation of diversity in performance evaluation goals and ratings

13. A(n) _____ is a special-interest group and network within the structure that lobbies management for changes that will remove barriers to the hiring and promotion of minorities.
    a. diversity focus group
    b. minority maximization group
    c. BOWGSAT
    d. internal advocacy group

14. All of the following help the supervisor "stay the course" by implementing action steps for achieving diversity except:
    a. Solve diversity problems, and move on to other matters.
    b. Continually collect data on how well the diversity effort is going, and be prepared to take the necessary action.
    c. Implement solutions that are designed to specially handle any problems.
    d. Keep a strong focus on results.

15. The BOWGSAT is:
    a. a widely recommended method for ensuring diversity in organizations
    b. more widely used in industrial firms than in service organizations
    c. not recommended for promoting diversity in organizations
    d. gaining increasing favor in recent years

Matching: Match the term on the left with the definition on the right.

_____ 1. A description of America in which people who immigrate here keep many of their initial values and beliefs while adding others that are common to Americans

_____ 2. The acquired knowledge that people use to interpret experience and to generate social behavior

_____ 3. Basic convictions that people have regarding what is right and wrong, good and bad, important and unimportant

_____ 4. Special-interest groups and networks within the structure that lobby management for changes that will remove barriers to the hiring and promotion of minorities and people of color

_____ 5. A term used to describe the process by which people from all parts of the world come to the United States and eventually become part of a homogeneous group

_____ 6. A term used to describe work groups whose individual members come from diverse cultures

_____ 7. Characteristics that can be used to describe the composition of the work force

_____ 8. A method of deciding how to design a diversity training program by relying on a "Bunch of White Guys Sitting Around a Table"

_____ 9. Those qualities that are different from one's own and outside the groups to which one belongs, yet present in other individuals and groups

a. Demographics

b. Culture

c. Multicultural

d. BOWGSAT method

e. Thawing pot

f. Melting pot

g. Internal advocacy groups

h. Values

i. Diversity

Applications

1. How will the overall demographic makeup of the work force change over the next fifty years? Use the data in this chapter to extrapolate your answer. Based on your information, what overall conclusions can you make? Discuss two of them.

2. How can supervisors today more effectively promote diversity in the work group? What practical steps can they take? Why would this be of value to the organization? Be complete in your answer.

3. What will supervisors in the year 2005 need to know about diversity in the work force? Why? Defend your answer.

4. What is the linkage between productivity and effective diversity programs? In your answer, be sure to explain the logic of this relationship.

CHAPTER 9:
Motivating Employees

True or False: Circle the correct answer.

T   F   1.   Performance is considered to be the sum of effort plus motivation.

T   F   2.   Need fulfillment is a temporary process; many satisfied needs become active needs again.

T   F   3.   Maslow's hierarchy of needs consists of five levels.

T   F   4.   Granting an employee autonomy is a primary way organizations can satisfy the esteem need.

T   F   5.   Security needs are the most basic of all.

T   F   6.   Maslow's theory has been largely replicated and confirmed by other researchers.

T   F   7.   Herzberg saw motivation as one continuum with hygiene factors on one end and motivators on the other.

T   F   8.   Fringe benefits, recognition, and responsibility are hygiene factors.

T   F   9.   Herzberg's methodology and research base have been questioned by other researchers.

T   F   10.   Everyone agrees that money is a basic motivator.

T   F   11.   Vroom's expectancy-valence theory of motivation is considered a content theory.

T   F   12.   Expectancy is the probability that a first-level outcome will lead to a desired reward.

T   F   13.   The amount of value a given reward has for an individual is called instrumentality.

T   F   14.   Learning is a temporary change in behavior based on experience.

T   F   15.   Punishment is the most effective reinforcement technique.

T   F   16.   Both positive and negative reinforcement strengthen desired behavior.

T   F   17.   Herzberg's motivation theory led to job enrichment.

T   F   18.   Job enlargement provides vertical loading of a job.

T   F   19.   Employee productivity generally increases if the employee is given concrete goals.

T   F   20.   The four conditions necessary to have an empowered workforce are participation, accountability, information ownership, and centralized authority.

Multiple Choice: Circle the correct answer.

1. Which of the following is *not* true about Maslow's theory?
   a. It consists of five different levels of needs.
   b. It reflected the need in the early 1950s to motivate people.
   c. It does not hold up well under close scrutiny.
   d. Usually three or more levels are motivators at a given time.

2. Status and reputation are motivators at which of Maslow's levels?
   a. self-actualization
   b. esteem
   c. social
   d. security

3. Herzberg's two factor theory considers _____ factors to cause dissatisfaction and _____ to cause satisfaction.
   a. hygiene, motivators
   b. motivators, hygiene
   c. motivators, dissatisfiers
   d. none of the above

4. Hygiene factors seem to relate to:
   a. job context
   b. environmental concerns
   c. physical surroundings
   d. all of the above

5. Which of the following is *not* a motivator according to Herzberg?
   a. creativity
   b. advancement
   c. salary
   d. recognition

6. Which of the following does not consider money a motivator?
   a. Maslow
   b. Herzberg
   c. Vroom
   d. none of the above

7. The intervening variable between first-level outcome and second-level outcome is called:
   a. instrumentality
   b. performance
   c. valence
   d. expectancy

8. The strength a given reward has for a given employee is called:
   a. instrumentality
   b. performance
   c. valence
   d. expectancy

9. Effective reinforcement takes place:
   a. immediately after a behavior
   b. randomly
   c. at a given time each week
   d. any of the above

10. The best and safest method of reinforcement for supervisors to use is:
    a. positive reinforcement
    b. negative reinforcement
    c. punishment
    d. extinction

11. Ignoring a specific behavior in the hope that it will go away is called:
    a. positive reinforcement
    b. negative reinforcement
    c. punishment
    d. extinction

12. The first step in applying reinforcement theory is:
    a. Observe how and when desired behaviors occur.
    b. Identify behaviors you want to strengthen or weaken.
    c. Start using positive reinforcement whenever an employee does something good.
    d. none of the above

13. The job redesign technique that asks employees to learn a series of related jobs is called:
    a. job enlargement
    b. job enrichment
    c. job rotation
    d. job engineering

14. Studies about goal setting show that which of the following is the *most* effective in increasing production?
    a. supervisory presence, loose goals
    b. supervisory absence, loose goals
    c. supervisory presence, concrete goals
    d. supervisory absence, concrete goals

15. Which of the following is *not* a characteristic of empowerment?
    a. access to information
    b. centralized authority
    c. participation
    d. innovation

Matching: Match the term on the right with the corresponding term on the left.

_E_ 1. First-level outcome
_F_ 2. Empowerment
_I_ 3. Job rotation
_A_ 4. Hygiene factors
_J_ 5. Job enrichment
_B_ 6. Job enlargement
_D_ 7. Valence
_H_ 8. Negative reinforcer
_C_ 9. Extinction
_G_ 10. Learning

a. Prevent dissatisfaction
b. Horizontal loading
c. Preference for an outcome
d. Strengthens desired behavior
e. Level of performance achieved
f. Employee power and control over the workplace
g. Permanent change in behavior
h. Weakens undesired behavior
i. Cross-training of employees
j. Vertical loading

Applications

1. In class, tabulate everyone's answers for Self-Assessment Quiz 9–1. Analyze the results. How do you think the results would differ for:
   a. A freshman, undergraduate class in supervision.
   b. A master's level course given to first-line supervisors.
   c. A doctoral level course given to upper management.

2. This chapter has provided several answers to the question, "Is money a motivator?" In small groups, come up with an answer to this question. Try to formulate a model to explain your answer. Present your models to the class.

3. Write a 200-word essay evaluating your motivational needs at the current time using either Maslow's hierarchy of needs or Herzberg's two-factor theory.

4. Interview two to three practicing supervisors about ways they motivate their employees. How do their answers fit in with the theories and strategies described in this chapter?

CHAPTER 10:
Dealing with Problem Employees

True or False: Circle the correct answer.

T	(F)	1.	Most supervisors have been trained in effective discipline techniques.
(T)	F	2.	Most supervisors find it unpleasant to have to discipline subordinates.
(T)	F	3.	One reason supervisors often fail to discipline employees is that they have let previous violations go unnoted.
T	(F)	4.	Many discipline problems occur because employees do not feel they are an important part of the organization.
(T)	F	5.	Frustration is a common cause of discipline problems.
(T)	F	6.	Individual personality problems are often root causes of discipline problems.
T	(F)	7.	Supervisors should be equipped to deal with individual personality problems.
(T)	F	8.	The "just cause" concept has largely been replaced by a "termination at will" policy.
(T)	F	9.	It is always better to document the file when disciplining an employee than to be less formal about the process.
(T)	F	10.	Preventive discipline attempts to mold employee behavior before problems occur.
(T)	F	11.	The first step in the disciplinary process is to note that a violation has occurred.
(T)	F	12.	When discussing violations with employees, decide in advance what action should be taken so that you can clearly tell them the consequences of the violation.
(T)	F	13.	Most organizational violations merit a warning stage for a first occurrence.
T	(F)	14.	Effective discipline takes place after a cooling off period has transpired.
T	(F)	15.	Disciplining employees in public is a good idea because it warns others that violations of rules will not be tolerated.
(T)	F	16.	Two people committing the same violation should always receive exactly the same penalty.
(T)	F	17.	If you have to dismiss someone, come straight to the point; don't rehash old problems.
T	(F)	18.	Most large American companies refer their substance abusers to outside agencies.

T   F   19.   Substance abuse takes place at all levels in the organization.

T   F   20.   The majority of large U.S. companies are now doing some type of drug testing.

Multiple Choice: Circle the correct answer.

1.   Which of the following is not a common reason for poor discipline by supervisors?
     a.   It is hard to discipline their friends.
     b.   They don't know when violations occur.
     c.   They are unsure how to approach the discipline situation.
     d.   Discipline is an unpleasant task.

2.   Which of the following is not a typical behavior pattern of a "problem employee?"
     a.   habitual tardiness
     b.   outright insubordination
     c.   independent attitude
     d.   excess socializing

3.   Which of the following is a common cause for discipline problems?
     a.   frustration on the part of employees
     b.   personality problems
     c.   employees who do not feel important to the organization
     d.   all of the above

4.   Which of the following is an important guideline to handling absenteeism?
     a.   There should be a well-known absenteeism policy.
     b.   Policies should be consistently upheld.
     c.   Recognize and reward good attendance.
     d.   all of the above

5.   Most federal civil rights lawsuits are in the area of _____.
     a.   hiring
     b.   discipline

     c.   terminations
     d.   promotions

6.   The best way of dealing with discipline situations is:
     a.   prevention
     b.   counseling
     c.   confrontation
     d.   termination

7.   Poorly handled discipline can lead to:
     a.   increased grievances
     b.   increased productivity
     c.   increased respect for management
     d.   decreased turnover

8.   During a meeting with an employee regarding a violation, which of the following should *not* take place:
     a.   Tell the employee about previous violations you have noticed but ignored.
     b.   Concentrate on future behavior.
     c.   Discipline the employee in private.
     d.   Listen carefully to the employee's version of the event.

9.   Which is *not* a key guideline when deciding on the consequence for the violation that has occurred?
     a.   consistency
     b.   severity
     c.   equity
     d.   justification

10. The single biggest mistake that supervisors make in the discipline process is:
     a.   failure to document the facts
     b.   failure to coordinate with the personnel office

c. failure to be familiar with discipline procedures

d. failure to address the violation in a timely fashion

11. Which of the following is *not* one of the four key words to be used when disciplining employees:
    a. warning
    b. immediacy
    c. clarity
    d. relativity

12. When terminating employees, which of the following is *not* a guideline?
    a. Be sure there is no alternative.
    b. Do it quickly; don't try to soften the blow.
    c. Go over administrative details such as benefits and final checks.
    d. none of the above

13. Which of the following is true about drug abuse in industry?
    a. The average drug abuser is over thirty-five years old.
    b. Drug abusers are found at all levels in the organization.

14. Which of the following is *not* true about alcohol abuse in industry?
    a. The average alcohol abuser is between thirty-five and fifty-five years old.
    b. Alcohol abusers are found mainly at lower levels of the organization.
    c. Small companies generally refer alcohol abusers to outside agencies for mandatory rehabilitation.
    d. none of the above

15. Which of the following is a guideline to supervisor's handling of alcohol abuse incidents:
    a. Suggest the employee get help.
    b. Express a willingness to help.
    c. Document the effects of the drinking on the employee's performance.
    d. none of the above

c. Substance abusers are absent ten times more than nonabusers.

d. all of the above

Matching: Match the term on the right with the corresponding term on the left.

H	1.	Discipline
J	2.	Step 1 of discipline process
I	3.	Preventive discipline
A	4.	Result of poor discipline
B	5.	Absenteeism
G	6.	Termination at will
F	7.	Just cause
C	8.	EAPs
D	9.	Substance abuse
E	10.	Drug testing

a. Increased grievances
b. Costs $20-$25 billion annually
c. Handle substance abuse problems
d. Costs more than $100 billion annually
e. Very controversial issue
f. Provable reason(s) for termination
g. Termination at whim of management
h. Corrective action
i. Positive discipline
j. Observe a violation

Applications

1. Investigate the employee assistance program of a local firm. If possible, get copies of their literature on their EAP. Share your findings with other members of the class.

2. In small groups, develop two scenarios to role play for the entire class. The first scenario should be an example of ways a supervisor deals with a discipline problem poorly. The second scenario should be an improved version of the first.

3. In small groups, design a one-day training program for supervisors to better equip them to handle discipline cases on the job. Outline your day's activities. Share these designs with the rest of the class.

4. In addition to the employee problems discussed in this chapter, others such as marital problems or psychological problems cause problems on the job. In small groups, choose one such problem to focus on. Define the problem. What are the likely symptoms of this problem? How is it likely to impact on the job? How should the supervisor deal with this problem?

CHAPTER 11:
Providing Effective Performance Appraisal

True or False: Circle the correct answer.

T **F** 1. Effective job-related feedback always occurs spontaneously.

 T F 2. The first step in the performance appraisal cycle is to establish performance goals.

 T F 3. Performance appraisals can provide supervisors with information regarding training needs.

T **F** 4. The essay type of performance appraisal is the most common technique in use today.

 T F 5. Paired comparison performance appraisals compare each employee to every other employee in the group.

T **F** 6. Forced choice instruments make the supervisor decide if each employee is good or bad.

T **F** 7. Loosely formulated goals are best when using MBO as a performance appraisal technique.

T **F** 8. BARS instruments are usually designed by the supervisor.

 T F 9. Once established, BARS instruments can be used for any position in the company.

T **F** 10. The fastest performance appraisal technique is the graphic rating scale.

 T F 11. Multiple rater assessments facilitate teamwork and empowerment.

T  **F** 12. When supervisors rate all employees as well above average, they may be showing the central tendency error.

 T F 13. Legally, performance appraisals can evaluate job-related and non job-related behavior.

T **F** 14. Items appearing close to one another on the performance appraisal instrument are more likely to be rated similarly.

 T F 15. A bell-shaped curve would be a graphic representation of the leniency error.

T **F** 16. Halo effects are always positive.

T **F** 17. We tend to evaluate those who look and act like ourselves more harshly than those who do not.

T F 18. Forgetting past events in favor of recent events is called the recency error.

T **F** 19. The most effective philosophy of the performance appraisal interview is tell and sell.

T **F** 20. The fastest performance interview is tell and listen.

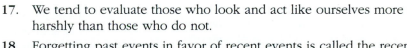

Multiple Choice: Circle the correct answer.

1. With which type of performance appraisal does the appraisal instrument provide a basis for planning and control?
    a. MBO
    b. graphic rating scale
    c. BARS
    d. paired comparison

2. Which is *not* one of the new trends in performance appraisal?
    a. multiple raters
    b. downward appraisal
    c. upward appraisal
    d. self-evaluation

3. _____ is any verbal or nonverbal recognition of a stimulus.
    a. Performance appraisal
    b. Feedback
    c. Forced choice
    d. Positive reinforcement

4. If managers want to use the most popular performance appraisal method, they will choose:
    a. MBO
    b. BARS
    c. paired comparison
    d. graphic rating scale

5. Which of the following is appropriate when you want to evaluate employees as a group?
    a. MBO
    b. forced choice
    c. paired comparison
    d. BARS

6. When supervisors are instructed to evaluate their employees according to some type of predetermined pattern such as a bell-shaped curve, they are using which technique?
    a. essay
    b. forced choice

    c. forced distribution
    d. paired comparison

7. The performance appraisal system that is a cooperative effort between supervisor and employee is
    a. paired comparison
    b. MBO
    c. BARS
    d. essay

8. Effective MBO goals must be:
    a. measurable
    b. specific
    c. quantifiable
    d. all of the above

9. The hardest, most expensive, and most time-consuming system is
    a. MBO
    b. BARS
    c. essay
    d. forced choice

10. Which of the following is the *least* subjective?
    a. graphic rating scales
    b. essay
    c. paired comparison
    d. BARS

11. Supervisors who want to be seen as "tough" often show the _____ bias on performance appraisals.
    a. leniency
    b. harshness
    c. recency
    d. halo

12. Proximity error refers to:
    a. physical distance between supervisor and employee
    b. physical distance between items on the instrument
    c. amount of interaction between supervisor and employee
    d. all of the above

13. If you dislike the way employees dress and this dislike negatively biases you against them on all aspects of their performance, you are displaying a

    _____.

    (a) negative halo effect
    b. positive halo effect
    c. similarity error
    d. random choice error

14. Which is a legal requirement for performance appraisals?
    (a.) job-related criteria
    b. once-a-year administration

c. graphic rating format
d. subordinate evaluation of superiors

15. The performance interview style that places the supervisor in the role of a counselor or helper is:
    a. tell and listen
    (b.) mutual problem solving
    c. tell and sell
    d. confrontation

Matching: Match the term on the right with the corresponding term on the left.

G	1.	Halo effect
I	2.	Leniency error
C	3.	Tell and listen
B	4.	Multiple rater appraisal
F	5.	Mutual problem solving
J	6.	Performance appraisal
A	7.	Paired comparison
D	8.	Job quality
H	9.	BARS
E	10.	Tell and sell

a. New trend in performance appraisal
b. Group performance evaluation
c. Uses active listening skills
d. Rating criterion
e. Fastest interview technique
f. Supervisor acts as a helper
g. Generalizing on one characteristic
h. Job-related behavior scales
i. Overly generous evaluations
j. Job-related feedback

Applications

1. Suppose you have been asked to prepare a BARS instrument to evaluate the performance of fast food servers in the local hamburger chain. What criteria would you evaluate? Pick two and prepare nine-point BARS scales for each.

2. Investigate two local companies—one large and one small—and find out how they do performance appraisals. If possible, collect copies of the instruments they use. Describe them to the class.

3. Suppose you are Rick Knowles's supervisor and it is time for his performance appraisal interview. Rick has scored high on everything with the exception of his attendance and punctuality. Role-play the interview with Rick. First use the tell and sell method; next try the tell and listen method; finally use the problem-solving method. Compare your results in terms of anticipated future consequences, end-of-interview feelings by both you and Rick, and time consumed by the meeting.

CHAPTER 12:
Understanding Group Dynamics

True or False: Circle the correct answer.

T F   1. A team is a group whose members must rely on cooperation to achieve its goals.

T **F**   2. Informal groups have very little power in organizations.

T **F**   3. Project groups are made up of individuals who work together on a regular basis.

T **F**   4. How persons believe they should act is called the "enacted role."

T F   5. "Role ambiguity" occurs when a person is uncertain how to act.

T **F**   6. "Roles" are rules of behavior that have been accepted as legitimate by members of a group.

T F   7. "Status" refers to the relative ranking that one person has in relation to others.

T F   8. High cohesion is an attraction for group membership.

T **F**   9. Highly cohesive groups are always more productive than less cohesive groups.

T F   10. People tend to feel more personal satisfaction with small groups.

T **F**   11. Self-directed work teams are a thing of the past in American businesses.

T F   12. In a team environment, the role of the supervisor changes from that of the traditional boss to one of coach and facilitator.

T **F**   13. Self-directed groups improve morale but have been found to be negatively correlated to productivity and quality.

T F   14. Team organizations require fewer layers of management than traditional organizations.

T **F**   15. The only appropriate purpose of meetings is to solve problems.

T **F**   16. Time and cost are two advantages of meetings.

T **F**   17. Agendas should be distributed about a day in advance of the meeting.

T **F**   18. When conducting meetings, the supervisor should use the agenda as a loose guideline but not be governed by it.

T F   19. Long meetings are usually very productive.

T **F**   20. Follow-up after the meeting is an important supervisory responsibility.

Multiple Choice: Circle the correct answer.

1. Which of the following is not an example of a formal group?
   a. task group
   b. project group
   c. committee
   d. voluntary group

2. The least permanent type of formal group is:
   a. task group
   b. project group
   c. committee
   d. voluntary group

3. Which is *not* a main reason for joining a group?
   a. nearness
   b. privacy
   c. productivity
   d. personal satisfaction

4. The way others expect you to act is called the:
   a. anticipated role
   b. expected role
   c. perceived role
   d. enacted role

5. Rules of behavior accepted as legitimate by members of a group are called:
   a. roles
   b. norms
   c. group dynamics
   d. informal dynamics

6. When there is a difference between supposed status and the way the person is treated, _____ exists.
   a. status incongruency
   b. status discrepancy
   c. perceived status
   d. status conflict

7. The closeness or personal attractiveness that exists between members of a group is called:
   a. status
   b. cohesiveness
   c. nearness
   d. group dynamics

8. As groups grow larger, which of the following is *not* likely to occur?
   a. Subgroups will form.
   b. Member satisfaction will increase.
   c. Cohesiveness will decrease.
   d. Member morale will decrease.

9. The first rule of effective meetings is:
   a. Invite the right people.
   b. Decide on the meeting's purpose.
   c. Circulate an agenda.
   d. Keep the meeting short.

10. Which of the following is a problem-solving meeting?
    a. brainstorming sessions
    b. idea-generating meetings
    c. gathering of information
    d. all of the above

11. Agenda items should be _____.
    a. short
    b. clear
    c. specific
    d. all of the above

12. Supervisors should start meetings by _____.
    a. putting people at ease.
    b. getting straight to the point.
    c. laying down the rules of the meeting.
    d. finding out if everyone is prepared.

13. The supervisor should encourage participation by:
    a. refraining from giving an opinion.
    b. asking people for their opinion.
    c. listening carefully.
    d. doing all of the above.

14. Employees who exhibit dysfunctional behaviors at meetings should be:
    a. barred from future meetings.
    b. soundly reprimanded.
    c. apprised of the consequences of their behavior.
    d. ignored.

15. When meetings are over, effective supervisors:
    a. thank everyone for attending.
    b. ensure that everyone knows what was decided.
    c. follow up where necessary.
    d. all of the above.

Matching: Match the term on the right with the corresponding term on the left.

J	1. Ad hoc committee	a. Expected behavior
I	2. Brainstorming	b. Relative ranking of group members
H	3. Functional group	c. Acting in conflict with one's status
G	4. Role conflict	d. Created by employees themselves
F	5. Standing committee	e. Standards of behavior
C	6. Status discrepancy	f. Group that exists for indefinite period of time
E	7. Norms	g. Conflict between two simultaneous roles
B	8. Status	h. Task group
A	9. Role	i. Generates creative alternatives
D	10. Informal group	j. Group that exists temporarily for a specific purpose

Applications

1. List all the groups you currently belong to and indicate whether they are formal or informal.

Group	Formal	Informal
_____	_____	_____
_____	_____	_____
_____	_____	_____
_____	_____	_____
_____	_____	_____
_____	_____	_____
_____	_____	_____
_____	_____	_____
_____	_____	_____
_____	_____	_____
_____	_____	_____

2. Next analyze each group you belong to in terms of the group characteristics described in Chapter 12. Describe each group's norms, status, cohesiveness, and size.

3. Still using the list of groups identified in question 1, describe your role(s) in each group. What is your perceived role? Is there any role ambiguity or role conflict apparent to you?

4. In small groups of three to six students, make lists of group norms observed in your supervision class. For example, there is probably a norm for meeting times. How many norms can you agree to? Share your list with other groups in the class.

5. The plant manager has asked you to call a meeting with your department to discuss the current number of product rejects. Company policy holds that rejects should not exceed 1 percent of output, but your department has been running at well over 3 percent for the last six months. Plan your meeting. What is its purpose? Prepare an agenda.

CHAPTER 13:
Providing Effective Leadership

True or False: Circle the correct answer.

T	F	1.	The leader as a cheerleader builds team spirit and loyalty.
T	F	2.	The smart leader never nurtures other people to be champions.
T	F	3.	All leadership depends on a power base.
T	F	4.	Reward power is the power someone has to force employees to follow directions.
T	F	5.	Legitimate power is the type of power most closely associated with authority.
T	F	6.	Personal charisma is most closely linked to expert power.
T	F	7.	No leader has more than one type of power base.
T	F	8.	Theory X and Theory Y are two opposite leadership philosophies.
T	F	9.	The use of punishment is more closely associated with Theory Y than with Theory X.
T	F	10.	Theory X motivation is usually related to money.
T	F	11.	Theory Y motivation is usually related to such goals as responsibility, recognition, and growth opportunities.
T	F	12.	Many definite leadership traits have been identified.
T	F	13.	The democratic leader basically follows the tenets of Theory Y.
T	F	14.	Laissez-faire leadership means "let's do it my way."
T	F	15.	Participative leadership is usually positively correlated with employee satisfaction.
T	F	16.	Laissez-faire management is most closely related with the 9,9 style on The Leadership Grid.
T	F	17.	Two-dimensional leadership theories generally look at task-related behavior and people-related behavior.
T	F	18.	Situational leadership takes into account the readiness level of employees.
T	F	19.	Situational leadership prescribes a one best leadership style.
T	F	20.	Charismatic leaders rely on coercive power.

Multiple Choice: Circle the correct answer.

1. According to Tom Peters, leaders are all but which of the following:
   a. enthusiastic cheerleaders
   b. nurturers of champions and heroes
   c. autocratic taskmasters
   d. organizational wanderers

2. The ability to exert influence over other people is called:
   a. power
   b. management
   c. leadership
   d. authority

3. The right to command is called:
   a. power
   b. authority
   c. leadership
   d. management

4. Power based on personality and personal liking is:
   a. coercive power
   b. referent power
   c. expert power
   d. legitimate power

5. Power based on your authority of knowledge is:
   a. coercive power
   b. referent power
   c. expert power
   d. legitimate power

6. Power based on fear and the use of force is:
   a. coercive power
   b. referent power
   c. expert power
   d. legitimate power

7. The person most closely associated with Theory X and Y is:
   a. Chester Barnard
   b. Tom Peters
   c. Douglas McGregor
   d. John French and Bertram Raven

8. Theory X supervisors believe which of the following:
   a. Employees have much potential for creativity.
   b. Employees do not want any authority or responsibility.
   c. Employees are committed to organizational objectives.
   d. Employees are capable of exercising self-control and self-direction.

9. Leadership models that attempt to find common characteristics among successful leaders are called:
   a. trait theories
   b. behavioral theories
   c. situational theories
   d. transformational theories

10. The most popular behavioral leadership theory is called:
    a. leadership continuum
    b. Situational Leadership
    c. trait theory
    d. Leadership Grid

11. The ideal leadership style according to Blake and Mouton is:
    a. 1,1
    b. 5,5
    c. 1,9
    d. 9,9

12. The Leadership Grid style often called "impoverished management" is:
    a. 1,1
    b. 5,5
    c. 1,9
    d. 9,9

13. The Leadership Behavior Continuum describes _____ vs _____ leadership.
    a. Theory X; Theory Y
    b. traditional; nontraditional
    c. democratic; autocratic
    d. old; new

14. The situational leadership style characterized by high task behavior and low relationship behavior is called:
    a.   S1, telling
    b.   S2, selling
    c.   S3, participating
    d.   S4, delegating

15. Which of the following does *not* describe the charismatic leader?
    a.   concern for vision
    b.   ability to motivate followers
    c.   personal enthusiasm
    d.   focused on planning

Matching: Match the term on the right with the corresponding term on the left.

_N_ 1.   Leadership Grid   a.   Participative
_D_ 2.   Country club management b.   Hersey and Blanchard
_L_ 3.   S4   c.   1,1 leadership
_J_ 4.   Autocratic   d.   1,9 leadership
_C_ 5.   Laissez-faire   e.   McGregor
_B_ 6.   Situational leadership   f.   "Telling" leadership
___ 7.   Democratic   g.   9,9
___ 8.   Theory X and Y   h.   Above average IQ
___ 9.   Employee readiness   i.   Cheerleading
_G_ 10. "Best" grid style   j.   9,1 leadership
_M_ 11. Compromise style   k.   Situational factor
___ 12. Follower style   l.   "Delegating" leadership
___ 13. Leadership trait   m.   5,5 leadership
_F_ 14. S1   n.   Blake and Mouton
_I_ 15. Coaching   o.   Game Player

Applications

1. Prepare a role play using situational leadership as your base. Have a supervisor give instructions to three different people on ways to do the same job. Have each employee represent a different readiness level. Present your skit. Reflect on the ease or difficulty encountered when switching leadership styles.

2. Interview two or three business people who have read *A Passion for Excellence*. What were their attitudes about the book? What are your reactions to the way Peters and Austin describe leadership qualities?

3. In small groups, consider the appropriate leadership style for supervisors of the following groups:
    a.   Loggers
    b.   Executive secretaries
    c.   Professors
    d.   Data processing programmers
    e.   Cooks
    f.   Machinists
    g.   Department store clerks

CHAPTER 14:
Working with Unions and Protected Groups

True or False: Circle the correct answer.

T   (F)   1.   Labor unions are strictly a twentieth-century phenomenon.

T   F   2.   Union membership continues to grow at a steady rate.

T   F   3.   The National Labor Relations Act ensured workers the right to organize and created the National Labor Relations Board to administer elections.

T   F   4.   Union contracts outline the rights and responsibilities of both management and the workers.

T   (F)   5.   The collective bargaining process is completely controlled by internal circumstances.

T   F   6.   Open shop contracts indicate that workers have the choice to join the union or not.

T   F   7.   Yellow-dog contracts are against the law.

T   (F)   8.   Right-to-work laws refer to legislation guaranteeing workers the right to organize.

T   (F)   9.   The supervisor has little to do with the union on a daily basis.

T   (F)   10.   Supervisors should maintain a formal distance from the shop steward.

T   F   11.   Most grievances are solved at the supervisory level.

T   F   12.   The Taft-Hartley Act gave states the right to establish "right-to-work" laws.

T   (F)   13.   Federal employees are not allowed to join unions.

T   (F)   14.   At least 60 percent of employees must sign authorization cards before a union election can be held.

T   F   15.   Wages are the central issue for all organizing campaigns.

T   F   16.   Management is allowed to encourage employees in a nonthreatening way to not join the union.

T   F   17.   One positive management strategy to avoid unionization is to discuss the financial obligations of union members to the union.

T   F   18.   During collective bargaining, the negotiating committee must discuss "prohibited issues."

T   (F)   19.   Administrative issues of the collective bargaining process include security issues, rights to strike, and managerial prerogatives.

T   (F)   20.   In a "union shop" employees need not join the union but must pay a service charge in lieu of dues.

Multiple Choice: Circle the correct answer.

1. The major impetus for large-scale growth of labor unions was:
    a. World War I
    b. industrialism
    c. the Civil War
    d. assembly lines

2. Internal affairs of unions were regulated under the:
    a. Sherman Anti-Trust Act
    b. Norris LaGuardia Act
    c. Taft–Hartley Act
    d. Landrum–Griffin Act

3. The earliest legislation that seriously influenced the ability of unions to grow was:
    a. Sherman Anti-Trust Act
    b. Norris LaGuardia Act
    c. Taft–Hartley Act
    d. Landrum–Griffin Act

4. Which of the following is *not* a main reason workers decide to join unions?
    a. peer pressure
    b. fear of strikes and lost wages
    c. job security
    d. to improve working conditions

5. When is union-management conflict most evident?
    a. during the organization campaign
    b. during collective bargaining
    c. during grievance procedures
    d. while choosing union representatives

6. Negotiating the contract is done through a process called:
    a. arbitration
    b. contract resolution
    c. collective bargaining
    d. brainstorming

7. Under a union contract that stipulates that all workers must join the union after employment, a _____ exists.
    a. yellow-dog contract
    b. closed shop
    c. open shop
    d. union shop

8. Which is a common component of a union contract?
    a. overtime pay
    b. seniority rights
    c. safety and health agreements
    d. all of the above

9. Once the contract has been agreed on, the _____ has the key daily responsibility for making it work.
    a. supervisor
    b. shop steward
    c. management
    d. union

10. Which of the following is *not* legal for a company to do when trying to avoid unionization?
    a. Promise benefits or rewards for not joining the union.
    b. Remind employees that unions cannot guarantee higher wages.
    c. Discuss the financial obligations of union members to the union.
    d. Inform employees of the negative economic impact of strikes.

11. Seniority, discipline procedures, and safety and health issues are common _____ issues.
    a. mandatory
    b. institutional
    c. administrative
    d. nonbinding

12. A process whereby a third party imposes a decision after hearing the sides of both management and the union is called:
    a. mediation
    b. binding arbitration
    c. collective bargaining
    d. negotiation

13. In an _____ shop, employees need not join the union but must pay a "service charge" in lieu of dues.
    a. open
    b. closed
    c. union
    d. agency

14. Which of the following should a supervisor *not* do regarding a grievance?
    a. Try to avoid the grievance by ignoring it to see if it will go away.
    b. Work with the shop steward.
    c. Gather as much information as possible on the grievance.
    d. Take every grievance seriously.

15. Which of the following is *not* a benefit that the AFL–CIO offers its member unions:
    a. national lobbying
    b. collective bargaining
    c. political education
    d. protection from membership raiding

Matching: Match the term on the right with the term on the left.

___C___ 1. Shop steward
___D___ 2. Collective bargaining
___B___ 3. Arbitration
___G___ 4. Yellow-dog contract
___E___ 5. National Labor Relations Board
___A___ 6. Landrum Griffin
___J___ 7. Mandatory issues
___F___ 8. Mediation
___H___ 9. Taft–Hartley Act
___I___ 10. Executive Order 10988

a. Established by National Labor Relations Act
b. Outside decision
c. Union representative
d. Negotiation
e. Regulated internal union affairs
f. Neutral third party
g. Unlawful
h. Abolished closed shops
i. Allowed federal unions
j. Wages, hours, and conditions of employment

Applications

1. Study the key labor laws portrayed in Table 14–1. Reflect on the pro- or anti-union attitude of each and try to understand the way each law fits in with the social, political, and economic trends of the times. How can you explain the apparent changes in public sentiment toward unions?

2. Based on what you have read and what you know about unions today, what do you predict the rest of the century will bring in terms of union membership? Explain your answer.

3. Write a case study about a recent, interesting strike. Examine the events that led up to the strike. Where did negotiations seem to break down? What could have been done by management to avoid the strike?

4. In small groups, suppose either that you are: (a) to design a training program for supervisors to educate them in ways to deal with the new union, or (b) to design a seminar to teach supervisors ways to avoid discrimination in the workplace. What topics would you cover? How would you conduct the training? How could you tell if you accomplished your goals? Be complete in your answers.

CHAPTER 15:
Maintaining a Safe and Healthy Environment

True or False: Circle the correct answer.

T   F   1. Occupational safety and health hazards have become a problem only in the last fifty years.

T   F   2. Workers compensation programs are run by the individual states.

T   F   3. Significant safety legislation began with the passage of the Taft–Hartley Act.

T   F   4. The National Institute for Occupational Safety and Health (NIOSH) is an agency of the Department of Labor, which collects statistics on occupational accidents.

T   F   5. NIOSH warns that there are approximately 500 dangerous substances in the workplace.

T   F   6. The purpose of the Occupational Safety and Health Act was to coordinate the efforts of the individual states.

T   F   7. OSHA inspectors are allowed by law to make unannounced inspections at any time.

T   F   8. Companies are required by law to keep records of all accidents involving deaths or injuries requiring transfer, medical treatment, or restriction of work activities.

T   F   9. Companies are required to calculate annual incidence rates of occupational injury and illness according to a given formula.

T   F   10. Safety hazards may be defined as those things that slowly and cumulatively lead to a deterioration of an employee's health.

T   F   11. There has been little or no improvement in overall occupational safety and health since the passage of the Occupational Safety and Health Act.

T   F   12. White-collar occupations are usually free of safety and health hazards.

T   F   13. The construction industry has the highest industry incidence rate.

T   F   14. Health hazards include physical and chemical hazards but not biological hazards.

T   F   15. Occupational health statistics are most likely inflated by workers who want to blame everything on the workplace.

T   F   16. The two main reasons for accidents in the workplace are dangers in the work environment and accident proneness by employees.

T   F   17. Supervisors have little day-to-day responsibility for safety; safety programs are the responsibility of personnel or middle management.

T   F   18. The best time to train employees in safety techniques is when they are observed breaking the rules.

T   F   19. As long as supervisors are committed to safety, it really does not matter about upper management's attitudes.

T   F   20. Reduced insurance costs are an intangible benefit of effective health and safety programs.

Multiple Choice: Circle the correct answer.

1. Which of the following is *not* true about the Occupational Safety and Health Act of 1970?
    a. established the Occupational Safety and Health Administration (OSHA) within the Department of Labor
    b. represented a culmination of years of concern about worker health and safety
    c. removed the workers' compensation program from state control
    d. required employers to keep detailed accident records

2. OSHA is administered by the:
    a. Assistant Secretary of Labor
    b. President
    c. Assistant Secretary of Health and Human Services
    d. State Department

3. One of the earliest government agencies established to protect workers was:
    a. Fair Labor Standards Bureau
    b. U.S. Bureau of Mines
    c. Department of Health, Education, and Welfare
    d. OSHA

4. Which of the following is *not* true about the National Institute for Occupational Safety and Health (NIOSH)?
    a. It is housed in the Department of Health and Human Services.
    b. It was established by the Occupational Safety and Health Act of 1970.

    c. It provides OSHA with needed research upon which to base OSHA standards.
    d. none of the above

5. NIOSH has concluded there are approximately _____ dangerous substances in use by industry.
    a. 100
    b. 500
    c. 1,300
    d. 13,000

6. Which of the following is *not* considered a common injury resulting from a safety hazard?
    a. cancer
    b. loss of eyesight
    c. broken bones
    d. burns

7. OSHA estimated that more than 50 percent of workplace illnesses are caused by:
    a. cumulative trauma disorders
    b. environmental smoke
    c. sick buildings
    d. environmental toxins

8. Which of the following is *not* a major category of health hazards?
    a. physical
    b. stress
    c. chemical
    d. none of the above

9. Which of the following is *not* a primary reason why occupational injury statistics are probably understated?
   a. Most occupational diseases do not show up for a long time.
   b. Workers do not know that their diseases originated in the workplace.
   c. Companies don't keep records of workers' illnesses.
   d. none of the above

10. Which of the following characterizes the accident-prone employee?
    a. usually tries too hard to get the job done fast
    b. concentrates on the task at hand to the exclusion of all outside interference
    c. gets bored easily and doesn't pay attention to what he or she is doing
    d. has positive attitude about the job

11. The first requirement for an effective safety and health program is:
    a. top management commitment
    b. interest by the employees
    c. careful training of the employees
    d. a supervisor who sets a good example

12. Which of the following is *not* a tangible benefit of a good occupational safety and health program?
    a. reduced insurance costs
    b. increased productivity
    c. improved corporate image
    d. decreased turnover

13. Which of the following is a characteristic of effective safety and health programs?
    a. top management commitment
    b. training of all workers
    c. anticipation of safety problems and forward-looking plans
    d. all of the above

14. Which of the following pieces of advice should a supervisor follow?
    a. Be sure to reprimand any safety violation, but don't reward safe behavior; they're only doing their job.
    b. Set a good example by carefully following all of the safety procedures.
    c. Let employees learn safety from the safety manual.
    d. Don't make a big deal out of safety; it's only common sense.

15. Who should be trained in safety procedures?
    a. new employees
    b. young employees
    c. all employees
    d. accident-prone employees

Matching: Match the term on the right with the corresponding term on the left.

_____ 1.   NIOSH

_____ 2.   OSHA

_____ 3.   Cumulative trauma disorders

_____ 4.   Health hazards

_____ 5.   Safety hazards

_____ 6.   Workers compensation

_____ 7.   Toxic chemicals

_____ 8.   Marshall vs. Barlow

_____ 9.   Heat, noise, radiation

_____10.   First significant occupational safety & health legislation

a.   Administered by state

b.   Administered by Department of Labor

c.   Administered by Health and Human Services

d.   Social Security Act

e.   OSHA focus in the '80s

f.   OSHA focus in the '90s

g.   Dangerous aspects of work environment

h.   Leads to slow and cumulative deterioration in employee health

i.   Physical hazards

j.   Ended on-demand inspections

Applications

1. Contact the human resources department of a major firm in your area, and ask who is in charge of their safety training program. Contact that person and ask for an interview regarding the types of training and communication they do with employees to increase their safety consciousness. Report back to the class.

2. Go to the library and do some reading on accident-proneness. Write a profile of the accident-prone employee. What characterizes these individuals? How can supervisors encourage them to improve their safety records?

3. Investigate the report-keeping mandated by OSHA regulations. You can do this by library research and/or interviewing local human resource professionals who work in this area.

4. Investigate the workers compensation laws in your state. Write a summary of what these laws cover.

CHAPTER 16:
Understanding Organizational Ethics and Politics

True or False: Circle the correct answer.

T	F	1.	The reputation of business in terms of ethics is generally very good.
T	F	2.	Ethics refers to a precise set of rules that guide our everyday living.
T	F	3.	Everyone agrees that business should be concerned with ethical questions and moral values.
T	F	4.	The majority of big businesses have a formal code of ethics.
T	F	5.	Conflicts often occur between what a person believes to be right and what a corporation demands from that person.
T	F	6.	Supervisors play little role in establishing ethical standards of behavior.
T	F	7.	Ethics is not something one should have to tell employees about; it should come naturally.
T	F	8.	Whistle-blowing almost always involves exposing corporate secrets to external parties.
T	F	9.	Supervisors should basically ignore whistle-blowing.
T	F	10.	Whistle-blowing is always bad.
T	F	11.	Relatively few people are involved in office politics.
T	F	12.	Politics is typically used to increase the power base of the individual.
T	F	13.	Politics often occurs because of the presence of concrete goals and career paths.
T	F	14.	Insecure employees tend to engage in office politics to a greater extent than secure employees.
T	F	15.	Supervisors often use political measures to get employees to arrive at decisions the managers want.
T	F	16.	Marketing departments have been found to be the least political department in organizations.
T	F	17.	One common political strategy is trying to please the boss.
T	F	18.	All supervisors have relatively the same amount of organizational power.
T	F	19.	Information hoarding is a favorite tactic of those trying to gain a competitive edge on their peers.
T	F	20.	The worst political tactic is trying to make one's boss look good.

Multiple Choice: Circle the correct answer.

1. Ethics can best be described as:
    a. hard and fast rules of behavior.
    b. moral principles about right and wrong.
    c. personal attitudes about business.
    d. corporate codes of conduct.

2. Business ethics concerns:
    a. just behavior toward the external public.
    b. morally correct behavior toward employees.
    c. the ends and means involved in business decisions.
    d. all of the above

3. Those who feel that the "business of business is business" believe all but which of the following?
    a. Business should focus on economic and financial considerations.
    b. Business has one goal—to make profit.
    c. Business should worry about abstract concepts of right and wrong.
    d. Business should play to be a "winner."

4. According to a 1990 survey of 2,000 U.S. businesses, which is the most serious ethical business issue?
    a. Drug and alcohol abuse
    b. Discrimination
    c. Pollution
    d. Theft

5. Which of the following questions is not suggested in the chapter as a guideline to making ethical business decisions?
    a. What is your intention on making this decision?
    b. What happens if you get caught?

    c. Have you defined the problem accurately?
    d. Whom could your decision injure?

6. Which of the following most accurately describes the supervisor's role in ethics?
    a. The supervisor sets the ethical standards for the department.
    b. Supervisors should reflect the ethical standards of their superiors.
    c. Supervisors have little role in corporate ethics: that is a role for top management.
    d. Supervisors should mandate that employees behave ethically even if they, themselves, do not.

7. According to advice given in the chapter, whistle-blowers should follow all but which of the following guidelines?
    a. Focus on the charge itself.
    b. Go directly to the media.
    c. Anticipate personal consequences.
    d. Know when to give up.

8. Which is not one of the most common reasons for political behavior in organizations?
    a. competition for limited power
    b. personal insecurity
    c. concrete paths to career progress
    d. avoidance of difficult work

9. According to research, which is the correct order of amount of political activity found in departments (from highest to lowest)?
    a. marketing, production, personnel
    b. production, personnel, marketing
    c. marketing, personnel, production
    d. personnel, production, marketing

10. The most used tactic to gain a compet-
    itive edge over one's peers is:
    a. hoarding information
    b. telling tales
    c. working harder than anyone else
    d. getting more education

11. Gaining and keeping control over
    human and material resources is the
    principal motivation behind:
    a. gaining a competitive edge
    b. personal power
    c. empire building
    d. supporting the boss

12. The least ethical political tactic of all
    is:
    a. information sharing
    b. power building
    c. empire building
    d. discrediting others

13. Loyalty to the corporation and to one's
    manager is:

    a. a good political strategy for any-
       one's career
    b. a poor political strategy for one's
       career
    c. only good for upper-level man-
       agers
    d. a waste of time

14. It is important for supervisors to real-
    ize that:
    a. people are political beings
    b. politics is always dysfunctional in
       the organization
    c. political maneuvering is more im-
       portant than doing good work
    d. office politics should be elimin-
       ated

15. Office politics is:
    a. to be avoided at all costs
    b. an undeniable part of the corpo-
       rate culture
    c. the best opportunity to get ahead
    d. a disgraceful part of corporate life

Matching: Match the term on the right with the most appropriate term on the left.

_____ 1. Ethics
_____ 2. Business ethics
_____ 3. Code of ethics
_____ 4. Whistle-blowing
_____ 5. Personal insecurity
_____ 6. Amount of political activity
_____ 7. Marketing department
_____ 8. Empire building
_____ 9. Hoarding information
_____ 10. Discrediting others

a. Caterpillar Corporation
b. Varies from company to company
c. Increases political activity
d. Most dysfunctional political activity
e. Moral standards
f. Code of right and wrong in business
g. Expanding one's power base
h. Striving for a competitive edge
i. Most political department

Applications

1. Using library resources and/or personal phone calls to corporate headquarters, locate the code of ethics of a major corporation. Bring it in to share with the class. What does this document tell you about the corporation?

2. Do your own survey regarding people's perceptions of ethical standards in business. Ask twenty people in the general public as well as twenty businesspeople if they think ethical standards in business are on the rise, declining, or about the same. Compare your findings with those cited in Chapter 16.

3. In small groups, discuss what types of ethical dilemmas your university might face. To what ethical principles should it subscribe? Explain.

CHAPTER 17:
Managing Stress and Time

True or False: Circle the correct answer.

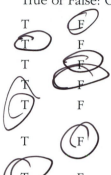

T   F   1. Stress affects everyone in the same physical ways.

T   F   2. "Eustress" is less harmful to a person than "distress."

T   F   3. Stress is usually "all in the mind."

T   F   4. The ideal goal is to eliminate stress from your life.

T   F   5. The "fight or flight" response is an evolutionary response pattern that is still appropriate for modern life.

T   F   6. Walter Cannon is generally referred to as the Father of Stress Management.

T   F   7. The General Adaptation Syndrome (GAS) consists of three stages.

T   F   8. Diseases of adaptation occur when someone reaches the exhaustion stage of the GAS.

T   F   9. Job stress is a sudden stressor.

T   F   10. The Type A personality is characterized by hurried activity, workaholism, and impatience.

T   F   11. There are two types of stress consequences: behavioral and physiological.

T   F   12. Efforts to rectify physical stressors such as noise and lighting are called environmental reengineering.

T   F   13. Wellness programs pay bonuses to employees who do not take their sick days.

T   F   14. Most people know where their work hours are going.

T   F   15. The key to time management is planning.

T   F   16. Writing down priorities is helpful but not necessary.

T   F   17. Plans are no good unless you schedule activities to advance those plans.

T   F   18. Taking phone calls as they come in will save you time in the long run.

T   F   19. Supervisors who do routine or technical tasks are probably not delegating properly.

T   F   20. Once you delegate a job, you are no longer accountable for it.

Multiple Choice: Circle the correct answer.

1. Stress is:
   a. the nonspecific response of the body to any demand
   b. always bad
   c. a psychological condition
   d. to be avoided at all costs

2. Stress is directly related to which of the following?
   a. cardiovascular disease
   b. cancer
   c. asthma
   d. all of the above

3. Which of the following is *not* a cognitive stressor?
   a. overcrowding
   b. job stress
   c. loneliness
   d. noise

4. Which of the following is *not* a physical stressor?
   a. drugs
   b. diet
   c. sudden explosion
   d. climate

5. Which of the following is a Type A *least* likely to do?
   a. engage in hobbies
   b. take work home
   c. accept more and more responsibility
   d. constantly watch the clock

6. Which of the following is a subjective effect of stress?
   a. mental blocks
   b. drug abuse
   c. heart attacks
   d. feelings of anxiety

7. Absenteeism, decreased productivity, and increased turnover are _____ effects of stress.
   a. behavioral
   b. cognitive

 organizational
   d. physical

8. Which of the following is *not* primarily a personal stress management technique?
   a. time management
   b. physical exercise
   c. job redesign
   d. biofeedback

9. The stress management technique that teaches employees to regulate bodily functions is called:
   a. time management
   b. biofeedback
   c. environmental reengineering
   d. stress inocculation

10. The first step for starting a time management program is:
    a. sign up for a course
    b. keep a time log
    c. make periodic plans of objectives
    d. plan weekly schedules

11. Which of the following is *not* a guideline for scheduling time?
    a. Group related activities together.
    b. Avoid quiet time; don't waste time daydreaming.
    c. Leave some slack time in your schedule.
    d. Keep your daily schedule visible.

12. Which of the following is a commonly cited time waster?
    a. meetings
    b. phone calls
    c. overcontrol
    d. all of the above

13. Which of the following will help you control your telephone time?
   a. Establish periods for taking your calls.
   b. Return calls as you receive them.
   c. Take calls immediately whenever possible.
   d. Be spontaneous on the phone.

14. The primary reason for procrastination is:
   a. lack of time
   b. boredom

   c. fear
   d. disinterest

15. Problems can be avoided during delegation by:
   a. avoiding delegation
   b. only delegating tasks employees want to do
   c. planning the delegation carefully
   d. avoiding feedback in the early stages

Matching: Match the term on the right with the corresponding term on the left.

_J_	1.	When to do daily schedules
_E_	2.	Key to effective time management
_C_	3.	Hans Selye
_A_	4.	When to do weekly plans
_H_	5.	Walter Cannon
_B_	6.	First step of time management
_D_	7.	Shame, anxiety, aggression
_E_	8.	Assigning duties to subordinates
_K_	9.	Noise, pollution, temperature
_L_	10.	Information load, job ambiguity
_F_	11.	Excess use of drugs or alcohol
_G_	12.	Hostility, aggression, hurriedness

a. Friday afternoon
b. Time log
c. Father of time management
d. Subjective stress effects
e. Delegation
f. Behavioral stress effects
g. Type A characteristics
h. Fight or flight syndrome
i. Planning
j. Last thing daily
k. Environmental stressors
l. Job stress

Applications

1. Using Figure 17–2, keep a time log for at least two work (or school) days. Analyze how your time is spent.

2. In small groups, role-play a supervisor delegating a task to an employee. Take turns playing the supervisor and employee. The rest of the group should critique the supervisor's performance. How could this person have done a better job? Did the employee feel comfortable with the delegated task?

3. Call a large local company and ask about its stress management efforts. Ask them to send you any literature they may have. Prepare a brief case study on this company and what it is doing in stress management.

4. Read one of the following classics in the field of management and write a three- to five-page critique of the book.
   a. Hans Selye, *The Stress of Life,* (New York: McGraw-Hill Book Co., 1976).
   b. Hans Selye, *Stress Without Distress,* (New York: Signet Books, 1974).
   c. Meyer Friedman and Ray H. Rosenman, *Type A Behavior and Your Heart* (New York: Fawcett Crest, 1974).

5. In small groups, discuss job stress. What causes it? Are there any intervening variables such as employee personality? What effects does job stress have? Prepare a simple model showing the relationship of stressors, intervening variables, and effects.

CHAPTER 18:
Developing Your Career and Preparing for Future Challenges

True or False: Circle the correct answer.

T   F   1. Most supervisors have a good understanding of their strengths and weaknesses.

T   F   2. When planning your career, start by formulating short-term goals.

T   F   3. Supervisors should ignore their current jobs and instead concentrate on assessing future opportunities.

T   F   4. Once supervisors have made career plans, they should forget about them and concentrate on the present.

T   F   5. Successful supervisors sit back and wait for upper management to give them a break.

T   F   6. Plans without activities to forward those plans are worthless.

T   F   7. Supervisors should concentrate on being busy all the time, regardless of what they are accomplishing.

T   F   8. Successful supervisors watch out for signs of obsolescence at every point of their career.

T   F   9. Technical knowledge of the task is not an important skill for the supervisor.

T   F   10. Supervisors who display flexibility and who can accept criticism and suggestions are usually judged to be effective.

T   F   11. Identification with one's subordinates rather than with upper management is a correlate of improved subordinate performance.

T   F   12. Successful supervisors concentrate on one job at a time and strive not to spread themselves too thin by taking advantage of every new experience that comes along.

T   F   13. Acquiring a mentor is a sure way to advance in the company.

T   F   14. Mobility and flexibility are extremely important personal characteristics when planning a move up the corporate ladder.

T   F   15. Supervisory work is not expected to change much in the next twenty-five years.

T   F   16. Toffler's *The Third Wave* suggests that the American economy is still firmly entrenched in the industrial age.

T   F   17. In the future, managers are expected to have more personal power.

T   F   18. Although technology is changing rapidly, employee characteristics are expected to remain about the same.

T   F   19. Computers will have little impact on the jobs of supervisors.

T   F   20. Future supervisors are likely to need less human relations skills because they will be interfacing with computers.

Multiple Choice: Circle the correct answer.

1. The first step for successful personal career development is to:
   a. assess your current position
   b. assess yourself
   c. assess your company
   d. plan your future goals

2. The final step in the personal career development process is to:
   a. begin your plan
   b. evaluate at set intervals
   c. assess your current position
   d. design action plans

3. Which of the following is true about self-assessment?
   a. It should lead to action to correct all weaknesses.
   b. It should be followed by assessing your current job.
   c. It is not necessary for most supervisors.
   d. all of the above

4. Which of the following is true about setting career goals?
   a. Set short-range goals only.
   b. Start by setting long-range goals.
   c. Setting goals is a waste of time; you never know what fate will hand you.
   d. all of the above

5. Which of the following are methods of avoiding obsolescence?
   a. taking courses
   b. reading in your field
   c. taking advantage of new experiences
   d. all of the above

6. Which of the following is *not* associated with effective supervision?
   a. keeping the boss informed
   b. giving feedback to subordinates

   c. identifying with subordinates
   d. using rewards and punishment effectively

7. Which of the following skills is *not* effective in avoiding obsolescence?
   a. practicing skills regularly
   b. consistently looking for a better way to do things
   c. having a definite program for increasing your knowledge
   d. none of the above

8. Which of the following is true about mentors?
   a. They can be a big help to a new supervisor.
   b. Mentors rarely press you to show fast progress.
   c. Close association with mentors who leave the company is never a negative.
   d. Mentors are of little help in learning about the organizational hierarchy.

9. According to Skagen, which of the following is not a trend?
   a. Autocratic methods of leadership are becoming more entrenched
   b. New and better communications
   c. Greater diversity among employees
   d. Increased employee participation

10. Which of the following is *not* one of the trends identified by Naisbitt and Aburdene?
   a. Employees will demand ownership in companies.
   b. Organizational hierarchies will strengthen.
   c. Entrepreneuring will continue to be a key organizational concept.
   d. Physical facilities will be reduced in size.

11. Which of the following job categories is most likely to shrink by the year 2000?
    a. software designers
    b. teleconferencing experts
    c. factory workers
    d. service workers

12. Peter Drucker believes that no job is going to change more in the next decade than that of the _____.
    a. factory worker
    b. supervisor
    c. middle manager
    d. computer programmer

13. Regarding worker participation, which of the following is *not* a prediction made by G. M. Vice President Steve Fuller?
    a. All employees will go on the time clock.
    b. Production workers will sit on boards of directors.
    c. Supervisors will be elected by their subordinates.
    d. Employee attitude surveys will become more important.

14. Which of the following is *not* likely to be a changing characteristic of the work force?
    a. less educated
    b. more minorities
    c. more women
    d. more older workers

15. Which of the following is *not* a likely consequence of increased computerization of the work force?
    a. more use of robots
    b. more workers in the factory setting
    c. less interpersonal contact
    d. displacement of some categories of workers

Matching: Match the term on the right with the corresponding term on the left.

_____ 1. Reengineering

_____ 2. Intrapreneuring

_____ 3. Mentor

_____ 4. Obsolescence

_____ 5. Naisbitt and Aburdene

_____ 6. Toffler

_____ 7. Excellence performance

_____ 8. Supervisory trend

_____ 9. Work force characteristic

_____ 10. Assess yourself

a. *Powershift* and *Future Shock*

b. *Reinventing the Corporation*

c. Person who guides another person

d. Strategy for career development

e. Reduced power

f. Out-of-date skills and knowledge

g. Creative entrepreneuring within the organization

h. More professionals

i. Fundamental redesign

j. Step one of career planning

Applications

1. Carefully work through the six steps of the personal career development process. Write a self-assessment paper showing your analysis of each step. Your final step, evaluation, will be merely a short projection of when and how you intend to evaluate your progress. End your analysis with conclusions about what you have learned from this process.

2. In small groups, use Self-Assessment Quiz 18–1 as a model and design a questionnaire to be used in assessing one's current job. After you have agreed on an instrument, use it to assess your current job or a job you have held recently.

3. Using the personal obsolescence questions in the text, carefully analyze your potential for becoming obsolete. Prepare a written summary of this analysis and end with a personal plan to avoid obsolescence.

4. In the library find two or three articles on mentoring. What is the current feeling on the value of mentors? What do you think? Share your findings with others in the class.

Name Index

Unruh, Jeanne, 54

Van Auken, Philip M., 6, 11, 327, 333

Vanston, Lawrence K., 378

Vroom, Victor H., 180, 181

Waldrop, Judith, 378
Walters, Charles F., 314
Wellins, Richard S., 244
William of Ockham, 63
Wilson, Jeanne M., 244

Wilson, Donald O., 44
Woodman, Richard W., 258, 259, 266, 272
Woodruff, Michael J., 95
Wren, Daniel A., 9

Subject Index